ROUTLEDGE HANDBOOK OF LAW AND SOCIETY IN LATIN AMERICA

An understanding of law and its efficacy in Latin America demands concepts distinct from the hegemonic notions of "rule of law," which have dominated debates on law, politics, and society, and that recognize the diversity of situations and contexts characterizing the region.

The *Routledge Handbook of Law and Society in Latin America* presents cutting-edge analysis of the central theoretical and applied areas of enquiry in socio-legal studies in the region by leading figures in the study of law and society from Latin America, North America, and Europe. Contributors argue that scholarship about Latin America has made vital contributions to longstanding and emerging theoretical and methodological debates on the relationship between law and society.

Key topics examined include:

- The gap between law on the books and law in action
- The implications of legal pluralism and legal globalization
- The legacies of experiences of transitional justice
- Emerging forms of socio-legal and political mobilization
- Debates concerning the relationship between the legal and the illegal.

The *Routledge Handbook of Law and Society in Latin America* sets out new research agendas for cross-disciplinary socio-legal studies and will be of interest to those studying law, sociology of law, comparative Latin American politics, legal anthropology, and development studies.

Rachel Sieder is a senior research professor at the Center for Research and Graduate Studies in Social Anthropology (CIESAS) in Mexico City. She is also an associate senior researcher at the Chr. Michelsen Institute in Bergen, Norway. Her research interests include human rights, indigenous rights, social movements, indigenous law, legal anthropology, the state and violence. Her books include: edited *Demanding Justice and Security: Indigenous Women and Legal Pluralities in Latin America* (2017); edited with John-Andrew McNeish, *Gender Justice and Legal Pluralities: Latin American and African Perspectives* (2012); and edited with Javier Couso and Alexandra Huneeus, *Cultures of Legality: Judicialization and Political Activism in Latin America* (2010). She has an MA in Latin American Studies and a PhD in Politics from the University of London.

Karina Ansolabehere is a full-time researcher at the Institute of Legal Research of the National Autonomous University of Mexico, and part-time researcher at FLACSO-Mexico (Facultad Latinoamericana de Ciencias Sociales, sede México). She is a sociologist from the University of Buenos Aires, has a Masters in Economic Sociology from the University of General San Martin, and a PhD in Research in Social Sciences with specialization in Political Sciences from FLACSO-Mexico. Her topics of interest are judicial politics, human rights, judicialization of human rights, legal cultures, and political theory, with special focus on Latin America. She has taught courses on sociology of law, judicial politics, human rights, and political theory. She is a member of the National Researchers System of Mexico. Ansalobehere has a degree in sociology from the University of Buenos Aires, Argentina, and a PhD in Social Sciences with specialization in Political Sciences from FLACSO-Mexico.

Tatiana Alfonso is an assistant professor at the Autonomous Technological Institute of Mexico (ITAM) Law School in Mexico City since 2017. Her research interests include human rights, sociology of law, sociology of race and ethnicity, sociology of development, and methodologies for legal research. In her work, she explores the relation between law and social inequalities with a focus on how legal and political institutions may have distributive effects between unequal actors in society. In pursuing those interests, she has carried out research on racial discrimination and human rights, social movements and legal change, and property rights of indigenous peoples and Afrodescendant communities in Latin America. She is a psychologist and a lawyer from Universidad de Los Andes (Bogotá, Colombia) and holds a Masters and a PhD in Sociology from the University of Wisconsin-Madison.

ROUTLEDGE HANDBOOK OF LAW AND SOCIETY IN LATIN AMERICA

Edited by Rachel Sieder, Karina Ansolabehere, and Tatiana Alfonso

Routledge
Taylor & Francis Group
New York London

First published 2019
by Routledge
605 Third Avenue, New York, NY 10017
2 Park Square, Milton Park, Abingdon, Oxon, OX14 4RN

First issued in paperback 2021

Routledge is an imprint of the Taylor & Francis Group, an informa business

Copyright © 2019 Taylor & Francis

Publisher's Note
The publisher has gone to great lengths to ensure the quality of this reprint but
points out that some imperfections in the original copies may be apparent.

Library of Congress Cataloging-in-Publication Data
Names: Sieder, Rachel, editor. | Ansolabehere, Karina, editor. |
Alfonso Sierra, Tatiana, editor.
Title: Routledge handbook of law and society in Latin America /
edited by Rachel Sieder, Karina Ansolabehere, Tatiana Alfonso.
Description: Abingdon, Oxon ; New York, NY : Routledge, 2019. |
Includes bibliographical references and index.
Identifiers: LCCN 2019003250 (print) | LCCN 2019005191 (ebook) |
ISBN 9781315645193 (Master) | ISBN 9781317291282 (Adobe) |
ISBN 9781317291275 (ePub) | ISBN 9781317291268 (Mobi) |
ISBN 9781138184459 (hardback) | ISBN 9781315645193 (e-book)
Subjects: LCSH: Law–Social aspects–Latin America.
Classification: LCC KG99 (ebook) | LCC KG99 .R68 2019 (print) |
DDC 340/.115098–dc23
LC record available at https://lccn.loc.gov/2019003250

ISBN 13: 978–1–03–209246–1 (pbk)
ISBN 13: 978–1–138–18445–9 (hbk)

Typeset in Bembo
by Wearset Ltd, Boldon, Tyne and Wear

CONTENTS

FIGURES

TABLES

CONTRIBUTORS

Tatiana Alfonso is an assistant professor at the Autonomous Technological Institute of Mexico (ITAM) Law School in Mexico City since 2017. Her research interests include human rights, sociology of law, sociology of race and ethnicity, sociology of development, and methodologies for legal research. In her work, she explores the relation between law and social inequalities with a focus on how legal and political institutions may have distributive effects between unequal actors in society. In pursuing those interests, she has carried out research on racial discrimination and human rights, social movements and legal change, and property rights of indigenous peoples and Afrodescendant communities in Latin America. She is a psychologist and a lawyer from Universidad de Los Andes (Bogotá, Colombia) and holds a Masters and a PhD in Sociology from the University of Wisconsin-Madison.

Karina Ansolabehere is a full-time researcher at the Institute of Legal Research of the National Autonomous University of Mexico, and a part-time researcher at FLACSO-Mexico (Facultad Latinoamericana de Ciencias Sociales, sede México). She is a sociologist from the University of Buenos Aires, has a Masters in Economic Sociology from the University of General San Martin, and a PhD degree in Research in Social Sciences with specialization in Political Sciences from FLACSO-Mexico. Her topics of interest are judicial politics, human rights, judicialization of human rights, legal cultures, and political theory, with special focus on Latin America. She has taught courses on sociology of law, judicial politics, human rights, and political theory. She is a member of the National Researchers System of Mexico. Ansalobehere has a degree in sociology from the University of Buenos Aires, Argentina, and a PhD in Social Sciences with specialization in Political Sciences from FLACSO-Mexico.

Leticia Barrera is a sociolegal researcher from CONICET (Argentina's National Research Council) at Instituto de Altos Estudios Sociales (IDAES), Universidad Nacional de San Martín, and an adjunct professor of Legal Theory at the Law School of Universidad de Buenos Aires, Argentina. Her research interest focuses on the production and circulation of knowledge among legal experts within bureaucratic institutions, inside and outside state structures. She has authored many works on this subject, including articles, book chapters, and the book *La Corte Suprema en Escena*, an ethnography of the Argentine Supreme Court of Justice. She is currently working on a new project about the Ministerio Público Fiscal of Argentina, the office in charge of public prosecution at federal level.

Lucía Dammert is an associate professor at Universidad de Santiago de Chile. In the past 20 years she has worked with national and local governments, research organizations, and international cooperation agencies in issues of urban violence in Latin America. She has an extensive list of publications in international journals. Among her most recent books published in English include: *Maras* (2011) edited with Thomas Bruneau and *Fear of Crime in Latin America* (2012, Routledge). She has been appointed as member of the Advisory Board on Disarmament Issues of the General Secretary of the United Nations (2017–2020). She is also a global fellow of the Woodrow Wilson Center for Scholars in Washington, DC.

Pedro Fortes is a Visiting Professor at the Doctoral Programme of the National Law School (PPGD/UFRJ), a research associate at the Centre for Socio-Legal Studies at the University of Oxford, and a public prosecutor at the Attorney General's Office of Rio de Janeiro. He holds a DPhil (Oxford), a JSM (Stanford), a LLM (Harvard), a MBE (Coppe/UFRJ), a BA (Puc-Rio), and a LLB (UFRJ). Currently a co-chair of CRN Law and Development (LSA), WG Law and Development (RCSL), and the stream Exploring Legal Borderlands (SLSA), his research interests include law and development, law and technology, consumer law, and civil procedure. Key publications include Pedro Fortes, Larissa Boratti, Andrés Palacios and Tom Gerald Daly (eds.), *Law and Policy in Latin America: Transforming Courts, Institutions, and Rights*, (2017); Pedro Fortes, "How Legal Indicators Influence a Justice System and Judicial Behavior: The Brazilian National Council of Justice and 'Justice in Numbers'" in *The Journal of Legal Pluralism and Unofficial Law* (2015). Forthcoming publications include: "The Transformation of Brazilian Legal Profession" (with Maria Bonelli) in Abel, Schultz, Sommerlad and Hammerslev, *Lawyers in 21st Century Societies* (2019); and "Brazil: Dramas of Televisual Justice" (with Germano Schwartz) in Robson and Schulz, *Ethnicity, Gender and Diversity: Law and Justice on TV*, (2019).

Janice Gallagher is an assistant professor of Political Science at Rutgers University-Newark. Her research focuses on state-civil society relations, specifically how informal institutions, relationships, and mobilization shape judicial, and human rights outcomes. She was previously a postdoctoral fellow at the Watson Institute at Brown University, and holds a PhD in Government from Cornell University. Her book manuscript (in process) is entitled: *Bootstrap Justice: Activists, Advocates, and the Search for Mexico's Disappeared*. She is also co-PI on a project led by Dr Lisa Hilbink, entitled: "Equal Rights and Unequal Remedies: Understanding Citizen Perceptions of and Engagement with the Judicial System." Her research has appeared in Comparative Political Studies and other venues, and she is also a publicly engaged scholar with publications based on her research in popular venues such as the Huffington Post and openglobaldemocracy.net.

Mauricio García-Villegas has a PhD in Political Science from the Catholic University of Louvain (Belgium) and is a doctor honoris causa from the Escuela Normal Superior de Cachan (France). He is a professor at the Institute of Political Studies and International Relations (IEPRI) of the National University of Colombia, as well as a researcher at Dejusticia and a columnist for the Colombian newspaper *El Espectador*. He is an affiliated professor at the Institute for Legal Studies of the University of Wisconsin (USA) and the Institute of Political Studies of the University of Grenoble (France). Among his most recent publications are: *Normas de Papel* (Bogotá, 2009); *La Eficacia Simbólica del Derecho* (Bogotá, 2014); *El Derecho al Estado* (with J.R. Espinosa, Bogotá 2013), *Les Pouvoirs du Droit* (Paris, 2015) and El Orden de la Libertad (2017).

Roberto Gargarella is a lawyer and sociologist from the Universidad de Buenos Aires (UBA, 1983–1985); Doctor in Law (UBA, 1991). Master in Law (University of Chicago, 1992); Doctor in Law (University of Chicago, 1993). Postdoctoral studies at Balliol College (Oxford, 1995). Professor of Constitutional Theory and Political Philosophy, UBA and Universidad Torcuato Di Tella. Gargarella has been a professor and a researcher at the Universities of Bergen and Oslo (Norway), Pompeu Fabra (Spain), and Columbia and New School (USA). Has also been a visiting scholar at the University of Harvard. He received a John Simon Guggenheim grant (1999) and also a Harry Frank Guggenheim grant (2002). He has published numerous books and articles, including, *The Legal Foundations of Inequality (2010), Latin American Constitutionalism (2013)*, and also *"La Justicia Frente al Gobierno"; "Las Teorías de la Justicia Después de Rawls"; "Los Fundamentos Legales de la Desigualdad"* y *"El Derecho a Protestar: El Primer Derecho."*

Camila Gianella holds a PhD in Psychology from the University of Bergen. She holds an MSc from Charité – Universitätsmedizin Berlin and a degree in Psychology from the Pontificia Universidad Católica del Perú, where she is currently a professor at the Faculty of Psychology. She is also a researcher at the Chr. Michelsen Institute (CMI) and global fellow at the Centre for Law and Social Transformation, Bergen, Norway, where she is part of a series of projects, including, "Elevating Water Rights to Human Rights: Has it Strengthened Marginalized Peoples' Claim for Water?," "Abortion Rights Lawfare in Latin America, Operationalizing a Rights-Based Approach to Health Service Delivery," and "Political Determinants of Sexual and Reproductive Health: Criminalisation Health Impacts and Game Changers and Litigating the Right to Health."

Manuel A. Gómez is Professor of Law and Associate Dean of International and Graduate Studies at Florida International University College of Law in Miami, United States of America. He holds a JSD and a JSM from Stanford University School of Law, and a specialization in procedural law and a law degree (cum laude) from the Universidad Católica Andrés Bello (Venezuela). Professor Gómez is the author, editor, or co-editor of numerous publications in the field of dispute resolution and governance and the globalization of the legal profession. In general, Professor Gómez's research scholarship pays special attention to the impact of culture and social norms, and economic and political forces in the genesis and operation of the law with a predominant geographical interest on Latin America.

Juan F. González-Bertomeu is an assistant professor at ITAM in Mexico City, where he teaches courses on legal theory and philosophy, constitutional theory, and the economic analysis of law. His research topics revolve around constitutional theory, rights, and the empirical study of legal and judicial institutions. He received an LLB at Universidad Nacional de La Plata, Argentina, and obtained an LLM, and a JSD degree from New York University.

Martha Gutiérrez is professor of law and human rights at the Universidad Jorge Tadeo Lozano (Bogotá). She has a PhD in Political Science and a MA in Latin American Studies from the University of Salamanca. Her research interests lie in comparative politics in Latin America with focus on the judiciary branch, human rights, and transitional justice. Some of her works have been published in *América Latina Hoy*, the *Journal of Political Science* (RCP), and in the books: *Transitional Justice in Latin America: The Uneven Road from Impunity Towards Accountability* (Routledge, 2016); *Human Rights and Conflict Resolution: Bridging the Theoretical and Practical Divide* (Routledge, 2017); and *The Inter-American Human Rights System: Impact Beyond Compliance* (2018).

Linn Hammergren is a former World Bank senior public management specialist, who now works as an independent consultant on justice reform issues. She has a PhD in Political Science from the University of Wisconsin-Madison. Best known for her work on Latin America, she has broadened her focus to include Eastern Europe, Southeast Asia, Africa, and the Pacific. In recent years, she has done assessments for and evaluations of donor projects, emphasizing performance evaluation, the organization and use of institutional statistics, and identification of practices, and procedures impeding service improvement. Prior to joining the World Bank, she worked as an internal consultant for the United States Agency for International Development (USAID), designing, and managing justice projects in Peru, El Salvador, and Costa Rica, as well as overseeing a regional USAID program run by ILANUD (Latin American Institute for the Prevention of Crime and the Treatment of Offenders). She has published three books and numerous chapters, monographs, and articles on justice reforms in Latin America and other regions.

Tanya Katerí Hernández is the Archibald R. Murray Professor of Law at Fordham University School of Law. She received her AB from Brown University, and her JD from Yale Law School. She was previously a Law and Public Policy Affairs fellow at Princeton University and faculty fellow at the Institute for Research on Women at Rutgers University. Professor Hernández is a fellow of the American Bar Foundation, the American Law Institute, and the Academia Puertorriqueña de Jurisprudencia y Legislación. Her scholarly interest is in the study of comparative race relations and anti-discrimination law. Her books include, *Racial Subordination in Latin America: The Role of the State, Customary Law and the New Civil Rights Response* (including Spanish and Portuguese translation editions), and *Multiracials and Civil Rights: Mixed-Race Stories of Discrimination.*

Lisa Hilbink has a PhD from the University of California, San Diego, and is an associate professor of Political Science at the University of Minnesota, Twin Cities. Her research and teaching center is on the judicial role in democracy and democratization, with a particular focus on Latin America and Iberia. She is the author of the award winning book: *Judges Beyond Politics in Democracy and Dictatorship: Lessons from Chile* (2007), an expanded version of which was published in Spanish by FLACSO-Mexico in 2014. She is also co-editor (with Ofelia Ferrán) of *Legacies of Violence in Contemporary Spain* (Routledge 2016), and is finishing a book on Judges for Democracy associations in Spain and Latin America. Her newest research project, with Dr Janice Gallagher, examines the origins of public perceptions of judicial institutions and their consequences for access to justice in the Americas.

Alexandra Huneeus is a professor of Law and Legal Studies at the University of Wisconsin, Madison. She received her PhD, JD, and BA from the University of California, Berkeley, and was a postdoctorate at Stanford University's Center on Development, Democracy, and the Rule of Law. Her scholarship focuses on human rights law, with emphasis on Latin America. Her work stands at the intersection of law, political science, and sociology, and has been published in the *American Journal of International Law, Harvard International Law Journal, Law and Social Inquiry, Yale Journal of International Law, Leiden International Law Journal*, and by Cambridge University Press. In 2017, Professor Huneeus was named to serve a ten-year term as foreign expert jurist in the Colombian Special Jurisdiction for Peace (JEP), a court created as part of the Colombian peace process.

Isabel Cristina Jaramillo Sierra is a professor in the Law Faculty at the Universidad de Los Andes, Bogotá. Professor Jaramillo Sierra holds a lawyer degree from Universidad de Los Andes (Cum Laude, 1997) and an SJD from Harvard Law School. Her academic work has centered on the question of feminist legal reform: how is it imagined and pursued; how may we think about what is gained and lost in reform. Her books on the reform of abortion law (with Tatiana Alfonso, *Mujeres, Cortes y Medios*, Bogotá, Universidad de Los Andes, 2008) and the influence of family law in producing families, poverty, and exclusion (*Derecho y Familia en Colombia. Historias de Raza, Sexo y Propiedad, 1580–1990*, Bogotá, Universidad de Los Andes, 2013) are recognized as critical contributions to the field in Latin America. She has also been consultant to the Colombian Government on issues of sexual and reproductive rights, and institutional reform for the transition. In 2015 and 2017 she acted as ad hoc judge to the Colombian Constitutional Court and the State Council. She was nominated in 2017 to the Colombian Constitutional Court by President Juan Manuel Santos.

Sergio Latorre is an assistant professor in the School of Law, Political Science and International Relations at the Universidad del Norte in Colombia. He holds an JSD and an LLM from Cornell University. His research interests focus on knowledge practices and legal technologies of property and land ownership in rural Colombia. Through an ethnographic lens, he looks at state and non-state bureaucratic practices that materialize the relationship between the public and private domains in post-conflict institutional settings. These research topics connect to broader scholarly and public debates on land, environmental regulation, transitional justice, and peace in Latin America.

Julieta Lemaitre is judge at the Justice Chambers of the Colombian Special Jurisdiction for Peace, created in 2018 to implement the transitional justice component of the peace agreements. Before her appointment, she taught at the Law School in Universidad de Los Andes, where she has been a full professor since 2007. She has a law degree from Universidad de Los Andes (1995), a Masters in Gender and Religious Studies from New York University (1998) and a doctoral degree in law (SJD) from Harvard University (2007), specializing in law and social theory. In the academic year 2014–2015 she was Robina Human Rights visiting scholar at Yale Law School and PRIO global fellow 2014–2017. She works on law and social movements, law and violence, violence against women, and sexual and reproductive rights. She has published articles on these issues in the *Harvard Human Rights Journal*, the *International Journal of Constitutional Law*, the *Law and Society Review*, *Social & Legal Studies* and *Feminist Legal Studies*, as well as many book chapters in edited volumes. Her books include, *El Derecho como Conjuro* (2009) and *La Paz en Cuestión* (2011), and edited *La Quintíada* (2013) and *Derechos Enterrados* (2011).

Fiona Macaulay is a senior lecturer in the Division of Peace Studies and International Development at the University of Bradford, England. Previously she worked at Amnesty International, the Institute of Latin American Studies at the University of London, and the University of Oxford's Centre for Brazilian Studies. Her areas of research are gender relations, politics, human rights, and the criminal justice system, especially the prison system, in Brazil and Latin America more generally. Her focus is on institutional reform dynamics – the opportunities for, and resistance to, policy reform within justice institutions, and how civil society exerts influence on these institutions. She is currently researching the entry of police and military officers into politics in Brazil, and has worked with the Brazilian police on combating gender-based violence, with the Brazilian Forum on Public Security.

Alejandro Madrazo Lajous studied law at the Faculty of Law of the National Autonomous University of Mexico (UNAM) and at ITAM, graduating with honors from the latter. Subsequently, he obtained a master's degree and a doctorate, both in Law, from Yale University,

USA. He is a research professor at the Center for Research and Teaching of Economics (CIDE). Madrazo Lajous has published in peer-reviewed journals in Mexico and abroad about the teaching of law, the history of legal thought, freedom of expression, electoral justice, sexual and reproductive rights, tobacco control, and drug regulation. He has also directed several key cases of public interest litigation before Mexico's Supreme Court on issues related to freedom of expression, abortion rights, and same-sex marriage. He is the coordinator and founder of the Drug Policy Program at CIDE.

Elena Martínez Barahona has a PhD in Political Science from the European University Institute (Florence). She is currently professor of Political Science and a research member at the Institute of Latin American Studies at the University of Salamanca. Her research interests lie in comparative politics in Latin America with a focus on the judiciary, transitional justice, and security issues. She is the author of *Seeking the Political Role of the Third Governmental Branch: A Comparative Approach to High Courts in Central America* (VDM, 2009). Elena Martínez Barahona was born in Spain, and her work on political institutions has involved field research in Central America, Brazil, Dominican Republic, Mexico, and Venezuela. She has been a visiting professor in several European and Latin American Universities, and has been involved in policy research and consultancy projects for both national governments and international organizations.

Fernanda Emy Matsuda is a full-time professor at the Federal University of São Paulo (UNIFESP). She received her MA (2010) and a PhD in Sociology (2016) from University of São Paulo. She worked as a researcher at the Center of Studies on Crime and Punishment of Getulio Vargas Foundation Law School in São Paulo, at the ILANUD and at the Center for the Study of Violence from the University of São Paulo (NEV-USP). She worked as consultant at Conectas Human Rights, at the Center of Studies on Citizen Security from the University of Chile and at the National Penitentiary Department from Ministry of Justice. Much of her work has been on improving the understanding and the performance of criminal and juvenile justice systems, mainly through the application of sentencing studies and qualitative methods. Her current interests of research are gender violence, feminist movements, institutional violence, and responsibility of the state.

Rodrigo Meneses Reyes is a professor and dean of the Department of Legal Studies at CIDE in Mexico City. He also teaches deviance and social control in the faculty of political sciences of the National Autonomous University of Mexico (UNAM-FCPyS). His main areas of expertise are urban regulation, informality, and the criminal justice system in Latin America. His current research projects include studies on the history of crime and violence in Mexico City, the role of public lawyers in sentencing decisions and judicial processes in Latin America, and the regulation of informality in urban Latin America.

Verónica Michel is an associate professor of Political Science at John Jay College-CUNY, in New York City. Originally from Mexico City, she obtained a BA in International Relations from the Universidad Nacional Autónoma de México and a PhD in Political Science from the University of Minnesota. Her research interests include human rights and victim rights, rule of law, comparative and international criminal justice, cause lawyering, and legal mobilization, with a regional focus on Latin America. Dr Michel has published in peer-reviewed journals such as *International Studies Quarterly*, *Law and Society Review*, and the *Journal of Human Rights*. Her first book, *Prosecutorial Accountability and Victims' Rights in Latin America*, was published in 2018.

Catalina Pérez Correa is a professor and researcher at CIDE in Mexico City. She received her LLM and JSD from the Stanford University Law School. She has been a visiting fellow at the Schell Center for International Human Rights at the Yale University Law School and at Georgetown Law School. Her research focuses on the study of legal procedures and practices – particularly the functioning of the criminal justice system – from an interdisciplinary perspective. She has conducted several surveys in Mexican prisons to study prison conditions, due process rights, inmates and their families, and prison guards. She also studies gender in the criminal justice system and drug policy in Latin America.

Francisca Pou Giménez is a professor of Law at ITAM in Mexico City, where she teaches Constitutional Law and Comparative Constitutional Law. She holds degrees from Pompeu Fabra University (LLB) and the Yale Law School (MA and PhD). Before joining ITAM, she clerked for Justice Cossío in the Mexican Supreme Court. Her work focuses on judicial review, the relations between institutional design and performance in the judiciary, Latin American constitutionalism, modalities of constitutional change, and fundamental rights. In this last domain, she addresses comparative normative discussions, mechanisms of rights protection, and the relations between internal and external sources of rights.

Julio Ríos–Figueroa is an associate professor of Political Science at CIDE in Mexico City. He received his PhD in Politics from New York University. He is author of the book *Constitutional Courts as Mediators: Armed Conflict, Civil-Military Relations, and the Rule of Law in Latin America* as well as co-editor with Gretchen Helmke of the volume *Courts in Latin America*. Professor Ríos-Figueroa has been a Hauser research scholar at the New York University School of Law, a visiting professor at the Juan March Institute in Madrid, and O'Gorman fellow at Columbia University. He is the current editor of *Política y Gobierno* and was 2017–2018 Andrew W. Mellon fellow at Stanford's Center for Advanced Study in the Behavioral Sciences.

Carlos Rivera Lugo is presently an independent researcher and scholar, member of the Working Group on Critical Legal Thought of the Latin American Council of Social Studies and of the Editorial Board of the Latin American Journal *Crítica Jurídica*. He is also currently professor of the Master's Program in Human Rights of the Autonomous University of San Luis Potosi, Mexico. He was founding dean and professor of the Eugenio Maria de Hostos School of Law in Puerto Rico. His main research interests are in Marxist and other critical thought regarding law and the state, including the normative plurality, and increasing autonomy of the material sources of governance and social regulation in Latin America, particularly with regard to what recently has been referred to as "the common." He has published several books, including: *Not One More Life for the Law! Reflections on the Present Crisis of the Legal Form* (2014) and *Juridical Communism* (2013), co-authored with Oscar Correas Vazquez.

Marta Rodriguez de Assis Machado holds an MA (2004) and PhD (2007) in Philosophy and Theory of Law at University of São Paulo and since 2007 is a full-time professor at the Getulio Vargas Foundation Law School in São Paulo and co-director of the Center of Studies on Crime and Punishment in the same institution. She is also a senior researcher at the Brazilian Center of Analysis and Planning (CEBRAP); global fellow at the Centre on Law and Social Transformation (CMI/ University of Bergen); and one of the senior researchers at the Maria Sibylla Merian International Center for Latin America Conviviality in Unequal Societies. Her research is located in the interdisciplinary field of law, political science, and legal sociology, and focuses on the relations between social movements and law.

Laura Saldivia Menajovsky is an Argentine lawyer. She holds an MA and PhD in law from Yale Law School. She is a constitutional law professor at University of Palermo and University of Buenos Aires. She has taught constitutional law, human rights, discrimination, and sexuality and the law at National University of General Sarmiento and National University of La Matanza (Buenos Aires, Argentina). She is a former human rights senior legal advisor at the National Secretariat of Human Rights, Argentina. She was also in charge of Research Programs at the Institute of Public Policy on Human Rights of MERCOSUR. Her fields of research include law and sexuality, laicism, globalization, equality, and non-discrimination. Among her most recent publications is her book *Subordinaciones Invertidas: Sobre el Derecho a la Identidad de Género*.

Rachel Sieder is a senior research professor at the Center for Research and Graduate Studies in Social Anthropology (CIESAS) in Mexico City. She is also an associate senior researcher at the Chr. Michelsen Institute in Bergen, Norway. Her research interests include human rights, indigenous rights, social movements, indigenous law, legal anthropology, the state and violence. Her books include: edited *Demanding Justice and Security: Indigenous Women and Legal Pluralities in Latin America* (2017); edited with John-Andrew McNeish, *Gender Justice and Legal Pluralities: Latin American and African Perspectives*, Routledge-Cavendish (2012); and edited with Javier Couso and Alex Huneeus, *Cultures of Legality: Judicialization and Political Activism in Latin America*, (2010). She has an MA in Latin American Studies and a PhD in Politics from the University of London.

Fredrik Uggla holds the chair of Latin American Studies at Stockholm University, Sweden. A political scientist, Uggla's research interests have centered on the politics of democratization and institutional reform in Latin America, and on different forms of political participation and influence. His research has been published in journals such as *Comparative Political Studies*, *Journal of Latin American Studies*, *Latin American Politics and Society* and *Comparative Politics*. In parallel to his academic career, Uggla has worked for the Swedish International Development Cooperation Agency with postings at Swedish embassies in Latin America and in the Middle East and North Africa, and has had frequent assignments as an expert on themes related to support for democracy, human rights, and civil society.

Ana Luiza Villela de Viana Bandeira holds an MA (2018) in Social Anthropology and is a lawyer, graduated from the Getulio Vargas Foundation Law School in São Paulo (2014). Currently she is the coordinator of the Innocence Project Brasil, an international organization dedicated to exonerating wrongfully convicted detainees. Her research background is concentrated in the field of the criminal judicial system, in gender intersections, and police violence. She has worked as a researcher in juvenile detention centers in São Paulo, with the aim of understanding the different meanings of sexuality in youth detention; she has also researched the concept of victims of police violence, based on ethnographic research.

Bruce M. Wilson has a PhD at Washington University and is a professor of Political Science at the University of Central Florida, Orlando, and an associate senior researcher at the Chr. Michelsen Institute, Bergen, Norway. His research on comparative judicial politics focuses on marginalized groups' use of courts in Latin America. His peer-reviewed research has appeared in *Comparative Political Studies*, *Journal of Latin American Studies*, *Health and Human Rights*, *Comparative Politics*, *Latin American Politics and Society*, among other journals. His books are, *Costa Rica: Politics, Economics, and Democracy* (1998) and as co-author, *Courts and Political Power in Latin America and Africa* (2010). He is currently project director for "Elevating Water Rights to Human Rights" a major research grant funded by the Norwegian Research Council (2017–2021).

ACKNOWLEDGMENTS

This volume is the outcome of nearly three years of work, which would not have been possible without the support of many people and institutions. First we want to thank Natalja Mortensen at Routledge for her unflagging support and faith in the editorial team. Second, our thanks to each and every one of our authors who enthusiastically signed up for the project of a Handbook of Law and Society in Latin America, trusted in our editorial skills and were patient with deadlines, responding graciously to comments, and suggestions for revisions.

The annual conferences of the Law and Society Association (LSA) provided wonderful formal and informal settings to discuss the chapters and findings presented in this volume. We owe a special debt of thanks to the LSA for the support extended through the International Research Collaborative on the future of law and society in Latin America, which facilitated the attendance of different authors at panels, helping to cement the identity of a volume that has involved numerous scholars working in different countries and continents. The LSA conference held in Mexico City in 2017 came at a particularly fortuitous time for the Handbook, an undertaking, which – together with the conference itself – has energized scholarly networks and forged new initiatives in the study of law and society in the region.

We owe a particular debt of thanks to Andrea Pozas-Loyo, Alexandra Huneeus, Lisa Hilbink, Janice Gallagher and María Paula Saffon for their participation in a seminar we held at the Instituto de Investigaciones Jurídicas at Mexico's National Autonomous University (UNAM) to discuss a draft version of our introductory essay, where they generously shared insightful comments and suggestions, which helped us enrich our depiction of the complex relationships between law and society in Latin America. This kind of enthusiastic scholarly collaboration is precisely what has made the Handbook such fun to edit. We also recognize the important space for intellectual exchange extended by the Bergen Exchanges on Law and Social Transformation in 2017. In Bergen we were able to receive feedback from law and society scholars from four continents, something which immeasurably helped us to refine the specificities of the field in Latin America. A special thanks also to Monserrat Rangel González and Mercedes Pisoni for their careful support with the chapter bibliographies and the index, respectively.

Rachel Sieder
Karina Ansolabehere
Tatiana Alfonso

1

LAW AND SOCIETY IN LATIN AMERICA

An Introduction

Rachel Sieder, Karina Ansolabehere, and Tatiana Alfonso

In common with other regional traditions of law and society studies, law and society research in Latin America is concerned with the relationship between law – understood broadly as norms, institutions, and practices – and long-run patterns of development, political environment, institutional forms, and cultural specificities. However, as we argue in this introduction, even when it is impossible to characterize such a diverse region, the distinctive contours of socio-legal research in Latin America have been particularly shaped over time by key political and historical junctures, and by the changing nature of the socio-legal academy.[1] Unsurprisingly, law and society scholarship in the late twentieth century was marked by shifts in the region's political history: from the initial optimism about legal transplants during the period of the Alliance for Progress, and the subsequent law and development movement, through the pessimism of the years of dictatorship when authoritarian legal orders were consolidated, to the role that human rights and new constitutional orders have played in numerous states following transitions from authoritarian rule and civil war. More recently, scholarship has focused on issues such as the justiciability of the rights of indigenous and Afrodescendant peoples, the relationship between law and legal institutions, and social change, or the judicialization of governmental corruption that has led to highly charged confrontations between executives, legislatures, and the judiciary in many countries of the region.

Latin America's socio-legal academy has also developed during recent decades. It is smaller and less institutionalized than its United States and European counterparts, and its members tend to be more directly involved in attempts within their countries (and increasingly across the region as a whole) to secure progressive social change through law. It is also an academy characterized by a high degree of methodological heterogeneity and rich cross-disciplinary dialogs, straddling law, legal philosophy, sociology, political science, history, anthropology, and cultural studies. Compared to the USA and Europe, less large-scale quantitative comparative research is undertaken, a result both of funding limitations and the relative lack of established expertise in cross-regional quantitative legal analysis.[2] Although the division between Marxist and liberal approaches has marked the history of Latin American law and society scholarship, it is also the case that rather than developing around specific theoretical and methodological trends or departures (as in the United States and European socio-legal academy), empirically informed socio-legal scholarship has tended to be led by a focus on specific issues and problems: for example, gender discrimination, or police violence, to name just two topics that have generated a wealth of research in recent years. Multidisciplinary approaches including historical, jurisprudential, ethnographic, and institutional analyses are increasingly a standard feature of such scholarship. This volume aims to map the emerging contours of law and society research in Latin America and contends that an understanding of how law has been studied in the region can contribute to understandings of law more broadly.

Law and society is a field with shifting boundaries. For that reason, any attempt to define its limits and shape is a controversial and complicated enterprise. In the United States and Europe, we can identify historical trajectories of the field's development with reference to certain organizations, universities, and research centers such as, for example, the Law and Society Association in the United States,[3] the University of Wisconsin, Oñati in the Basque country,[4] the Center for Social Studies (CES) in Coimbra, or human rights programs at the Institute of Latin American Studies in London, or at the Chr. Michelsen Institute in Norway. By contrast, within Latin America itself the field has not been as closely linked to the development of particular organizations, although – as we signal in this introduction – a diversity of institutions in different countries has played a key role in its formation at distinct moments in time.[5]

We use here two criteria to identify the law and society field in Latin America. The first is a pragmatic one: Latin America as both a site of interest and a place of production for law and society studies. Second, despite the field's diffuse contours in a region where no one association or publication exists that articulates academic production, we define it according to a common denominator, namely the shared interest in *law in action*. Rather than specific methodological or theoretical perspectives, this is what primarily defines law and society studies in the region. Widely different contributions all share a concern to understand how law functions in practice: how it is represented and imagined by different groups, the distinct ways in which law is used and invoked, and the effects it produces. As a consequence of this point of departure, and in contrast to earlier attempts to survey the field of socio-legal studies in the region (see the important contribution of García-Villegas and Rodríguez-Garavito 2003), we do not attempt to characterize law or law and society in the region. The diversity of the legal, social, and political trajectories of 17 countries makes this an impossible task and ultimately, we would argue, one of limited analytical purchase, given that many features of law – understood as a social construction – in Latin America are in fact now common to law everywhere. Although one of our points of departure is the profound gap between law in action and law on the books throughout the region, the idea that social life is or can ever be ordered by legal norms is on the wane in most socio-legal scholarship. In addition, the blurring of the lines between the legal and the illegal is a global phenomenon, not just one restricted to the Global South (Comaroff and Comaroff 2006, 2016). Latin America has long been characterized as a region which simultaneously fetishizes the law, affording it great symbolic power, while at the same time offering a panorama of weak rule of law or even "lawlessness." Yet these characteristics – even were they found to hold uniformly throughout the region – now appear generic to socio-legal realities in most of the world.

Given the aforementioned diversity our review is necessarily partial. What we aim to do in this introduction, therefore, is to map tendencies. The tendencies we identify are not causal factors as such, but rather the product of a specific shared historical context defined by the superposition of new constitutional realities, legal pluralism, spiraling violence, and the rise in the importance of human rights narratives, together with the consolidation of an increasingly professionalized and internationally connected socio-legal academy within Latin America and beyond. This translates into an agenda in which classic concerns about the symbolic efficacy of the law combine with a focus on legal institutions and the convergences between legality and illegality in a region of acute and enduring socioeconomic, racial, and gender inequalities.

What historical processes of state formation explain persistent violations of human rights and extremely high levels of violence? What is the role of law and legal institutions in either perpetuating or transforming these patterns? Can new constitutional rights be enforced, altering entrenched historical patterns of socioeconomic and racial inequalities? These questions have been central to the recent expansion of socio-legal scholarship on Latin America, which is shaped by the tension between the imperfection and indeterminacy of law and legal institutions on the one hand, and the increased recourse to those institutions by a range of actors, on the other.

In the following section, we trace the main thematic foci and perspectives of key junctures in the development of law and society scholarship in the region. As we will show, the field has become more complex and rich in recent years, and is now characterized by a diversity of themes and a critical mass of studies on specific issues.

Key moments in the study of law in action in Latin American law and society scholarship

Although it is far from easy to identify all studies of law in action in Latin America, there is a consensus in the literature that the law and development movement, linked to the Alliance for Progress in the 1960s, constituted the starting point for growing interest in the link between law and social change in the region (García-Villegas and Rodríguez-Garavito 2003). From then to the present we can identify certain long-run shifts in perspectives. First, earlier thinking about law in action as "noncompliance" or the lack of observance of legal norms susceptible to transformation by means of "appropriate" reforms has given way to an understanding of law in action as a complex process wherein the gap between law in action and law on the books is a constitutive feature of law itself (and therefore, to a recognition that the "benevolent" effects of judicial reforms are contingent on a multitude of legal, political, and social processes). Second, there has been a movement away from approaches that conceived of the state as a unified, homogenous actor, toward a broad understanding of the state as a fragmented space containing multiple legalities and powers. Third, whereas in the 1960s law and its production was understood as predominantly state-centered, it has increasingly come to be understood as an increasingly international and subnational phenomenon involving different dynamics between formal state structures, international bodies, and a range of political and social actors, and disputing processes occurring at different scales. In addition, we can observe a densification of the academy as the number of studies carried out by scholars based in Latin America and those outside the region has increased, together with the links between them. Thematically, the field of study itself has also become broader: law in general, the legal professional, and legal reform are no longer at the center of analysis and more specific agendas have multiplied. One example would be the different studies concerned with legal mobilization around a range of issues, or another the broadening of research on judicial actors and institutions. In what follows we present a brief overview of key junctures and topics.

The origins of concern with law in action in Latin America can be traced back to the 1960s with the rise of the law and development movement (Trubek and Santos 2006). Defined by attempts to modernize countries deemed "underdeveloped," this movement understood law as a privileged tool for the transformation of the traditional into the modern, with legal transplants, and the reform of the legal profession at its core. The state (conceived of as a unitary entity) would thus, be afforded the tools required to achieve economic development and political modernization. Binary dichotomies – tradition/modernity; compliance/noncompliance with rules and laws – defined the analytical framework of the movement, whose central aim was to establish the legal foundations of the developmentalist state, for example, through measures such as agrarian reforms. Critical studies that questioned the assumed relationship between legal reforms, the legal profession, and their influence on development were developed largely outside Latin America, specifically within the North American academy by David Trubek and Marc Galanter (1974), founders of the law and society movement in the USA.

Another important moment in the thematic evolution of law in action perspectives in Latin America was connected to the emergence of authoritarian developmentalist regimes. Guillermo O'Donnell's influential publications, *Modernization and Authoritarianism* (1972) and *The Bureaucratic Authoritarian State* (1982), questioned the relationship between democracy and development assumed by modernization theory (which was the paradigm underpinning the law and development movement), and focused on the forms of state domination generated by political projects to restrict popular political participation in favor of business interests. These studies posited that such tendencies were constitutive of modern socio-political and economic dynamics in South America, especially in Argentina and Brazil. However, the legal dimensions of authoritarian rule were not as central to regional theories of the state as was the case, for example, in Asia (Ginsburg 2003). In this context, studies concerning law and society were organized around two issues or axes: on the one hand, the (non)-functioning of legal institutions and the judiciary, and on the other, the start of the Marxist tradition of critical legal studies in Latin America, which questioned the power of law to transform society, emphasizing instead its nature as a mechanism of domination.

The first group of studies concentrated on analyzing deficiencies in terms of judicial independence and functioning in the region, using United States measures of judicial independence and constitutional control as the standards for comparison. These descriptive and comparative studies were carried out by United States academics, such as Carl Schwarz (1973), Joel Verner (1984) and David Clark (1975), and were notable for their lack of historical contextualization of the relationship between judicial and political power in Latin America. The second group of studies was developed by Latin American Marxist lawyers, who aimed to challenge hegemonic legal perspectives and promote alternative uses of law. Under the banner of critical legal studies (*Crítica Jurídica*), these perspectives were promoted by Mexican, Brazilian, and Argentine scholars, including Oscar Correas (an Argentine who developed his academic career in Mexico) and Carlos Cárcova, also from Argentina. Although their studies were largely theoretical and philosophical as opposed to empirical, the importance of this growing movement questioning the progressive nature of law cannot be overstated. For example, these critical perspectives contributed to the concept of "alternative law" that underpinned the founding of ILSA, the Latin American Institute for Alternative Law and Society (*Instituto Latinoamericano para una Sociedad y un Derecho Alternativo*) in Colombia in 1978. ILSA's collaborative action research with popular and social movements – which continues to the present day – focused on supporting counter-hegemonic forms of law "from below." These groups of legal scholars were largely comprised of university professors who trained future generations committed to these critical perspectives. They also created spaces for intellectual exchange and diffusion, such as the Marxist journal *Crítica Jurídica*, published by the National Autonomous University of Mexico (UNAM) and publications such as *El Otro Derecho* or *Beyond Law* in the case of ILSA. This current of research built a trenchant critique of state law, and also prioritized alternative ways of understanding and conceiving of law. In this sense, its concern with issues of noncompliance was channeled into alternative practices and forms of social regulation or law.

The third moment in the historical trajectory of law and society studies in the region was that of the transitions to democratic rule in the Southern Cone and Central America. With these transformations, the concern for the rule of law and the relationship between democracy and development, together with the challenges of how to respond to the massive violations of human rights committed under the previous regimes, raised new expectations and questions about the role that law and legal institutions could play in the new democracies. The transitions to democracy also brought a new impulse to legal reforms to strengthen the rule of law, which was understood in two registers: first, legal security for investment, and second, equality before the law and the seeking of justice for human rights violations committed by the authoritarian governments. Legal scholars and public intellectuals such as Carlos Nino in Argentina played a central role in developing a progressive legal agenda in the context of transition, inspiring a generation of law and society scholars across the region. Dating from this period, international human rights regimes came to play an increasingly important role as local actors invoked international instruments in order to pressure for domestic change (Keck and Sikkink 2001). At the same time, the agenda for judicial reform was supported by multilateral agencies, led by the World Bank, to the point that it is possible to talk of a second wave of the law and development movement concerned with cementing the transition to open market economies through the "rule of law" (Dezalay and Garth 2002). A similar set of legal transplants was promoted across the region at this time, including judicial councils for the selection of judges, and judicial training schools to professionalize practitioners (Carothers 2001). Simultaneously, the first prosecutions against perpetrators of human rights occurred, including the emblematic trial of the former leaders of the military junta in Argentina, together with the first attempts to democratically overturn amnesty laws that prevented the prosecution of those responsible for gross violations of human rights, as in the case of Uruguay in 1989. In subsequent years, processes of transitional justice for gross violations of human rights under authoritarian rule that occurred following the transitions in both the Southern Cone and Central America became a key field of comparative study, increasing scholarly interest in Latin America's legal institutions and socio-legal mobilizations. Such was the significance of the regional experience that it is estimated that more than half of all human rights trials carried out in the world have taken place in Latin America (Payne et al. 2015). Subsequently the global law and society field of transitional justice studies increased exponentially, and within this the leading role played by studies of Latin America, many carried out by regionally-based scholars, has been indisputable. The principle questions guiding this research have to do with discovering the most adequate combination of transitional justice mechanisms to achieve legal convictions for past human rights violations, truth, and reparations for victims, and with the relationship between processes of transitional justice, democracy, and human rights (see chapter by Martínez and Gutiérrez in this volume; Skaar, García-Godos, and Collins 2016). This ongoing area of research is marked by a particularly fluid exchange between scholars based in the region and their counterparts in the USA and Europe, and also by a high degree of movement between academia, nongovernmental organizations (NGOs), and different think tanks. In the following section, we identify a fourth moment in the field, one that shapes the different agendas presented in this volume.

Contemporary Trends in Law and Society Scholarship in Latin America

The fourth moment we identify for the field of Latin American law and society studies is anchored in the critique of neoliberal governance and development, which gathered force at the end of the 1990s, and is marked by the (productive) tension between more studies concerned with the optimal functioning of legal institutions, and those focused on the ways in which systemic socioeconomic and racial inequalities in the region relate to socio-legal phenomena.

Rising expectations about law and legal institutions were enshrined in the first wave of constitutional reforms, which both expanded the canon of rights and increased the autonomy and power of legal institutions (see the chapters by Gargarella, Pou, González-Bertomeu, Uggla, and Michel in this volume). The so-called new constitutionalism in Latin America commenced with the Brazilian constitutional reform of 1988 and in subsequent years spread across the region. Most of the new charters sought to install legal orders reflective of the socio-political projects advanced within the transitions, incorporating broad bills of rights and in many cases also revising the structure of the state (Negretto 2013). In terms of new recognitions, special mention should be made of the incorporation of indigenous peoples' rights in response to the demands of the continental-wide indigenous movement, which began to develop in the 1980s. The most far-reaching transformations in this sense occurred in Ecuador and Bolivia, with the approval of so-called pluri-national constitutions in 2008 and 2009, respectively. These constitutions ostensibly aimed to recognize the specificities and claims of indigenous people – and to a lesser extent in the case of Ecuador, Afrodescendants, thereby incorporating different perspectives on politics, law and society within the legal orders of those nation-states (Santos 2005; Yrigoyen 2011).The region-wide wave of multicultural and pluri-national constitutional engineering implied the formal recognition of legal pluralism and spheres of autonomy for indigenous governance, representing a radical break with monist republican traditions. Scholar-activist networks such as the Latin American network of legal anthropology (*Red Latinoamericana de Antropología Jurídica*, RELAJU) played a fundamental role in circulating regional scholarship on multicultural constitutionalism and innovative jurisprudence on indigenous rights between countries in the region (Chenaut, Gómez, Ortiz, and Sierra 2011), and United States and European scholars also developed important comparative studies on these topics (Van Cott 2000, 2008; Sieder 2002; Schilling-Vacaflor and Kuppe 2012; Yashar 2005).

Many of the new constitutions incorporated international human rights law into the constitutional block, opening up unprecedented opportunities for judicial innovation and encouraging closer relations between domestic and international courts. This has been referred to as the double movement of constitutionalization of international law and the internationalization of constitutional law. In addition, these constitutional reforms strengthened – at least in the books – the power of constitutional courts, generating new opportunity structures for their institutional development and the assumption by high courts throughout the region of new roles in the resolution of political and social conflicts (Helmke and Ríos-Figueroa 2011). Yet while shifts to more democratic models of state organization pointed to renewed expectations in the law, they also revealed the immense difficulties of building state security forces and legal systems respectful of human rights, together with challenges for democratic governance posed by the massive increase in social and criminal violence. Although the mass disappearances, killings, and massacres committed by the military-authoritarian regimes receded, in contexts of persistent institutional weakness, widespread poverty and acute socioeconomic and racial inequality the shift to elected government and the promise of liberal, rights-protecting constitutions failed to guarantee the fundamental human rights of most citizens. Authoritarian, arbitrary, and extrajudicial practices on the part of state agents persisted. Consistently high levels of social violence affect large sectors of the population: roughly a third of all recorded global homicides occur in Latin America and some of the worst homicide rates in the world are registered among poor, non-white urban youth in the region's cities, such as San Salvador, Rio de Janeiro, or Caracas. Prevailing social attitudes reinforce messages that certain sectors are beyond the protection of the law. Deep-rooted race and class discrimination plays a central role in weakening social ties, solidarity, and a sense of moral obligation of the rich and powerful toward the poor and excluded (Vilhena Vieira 2011; Méndez, O'Donnell, and Pinheiro 1999). At the same time, these sectors are often viewed by elites as dangerous populations to be contained and so are disproportionately penalized by criminal law – indeed the penal system functions largely to protect elites from the poor. While this is not a purely Latin American phenomenon and has been amply docu-mented in the USA by law and society scholarship, excessive use of force, and unlawful killings by police forces, combined with high levels of social violence extending to vigilantism and so-called "social cleansing," underscore a central concern for regional law and society scholarship (Brinks 2006; Snodgrass Godoy 2006). In the years following the transitions and the issuing of the new constitutions, much law in action scholarship in Latin America has focused on violence, the relations between legality and illegality and issues of accountability on the part of the military and security forces, and state actors more generally. Critical race studies, while central to scholar-ship on institutional violence in the USA, is only starting to make inroads to law and society analyses in Latin America, but is a growing area of research.

The new constitutions were studied as processes of institutional reform, and also as doctrinal shifts that posed complex legal dilemmas for the judiciary (Negretto 2013). The different pro-cesses of constitutional transformation and their influence on emergent legal doctrine led legal scholars to shift from their traditional focus on civil (and criminal) law, to a renewed concern with the study of constitutional law (Couso 2010). For example, the question of how to incorp-orate the criteria of the Inter-American Court of Human Rights into domestic adjudication, and how international norms are appropriated and vernacularized by judicial actors, dominated studies of "constitutionalism in action" (see chapter by Pou in this volume). The annual SELA or Seminar in Latin America on Constitutional and Political Theory run by Yale Law School since the mid-1990s has proved to be a particularly important North–South hub for regional law and society scholarship on the new constitutionalism.[6] Interest was reflected in a greater number of studies of comparative constitutionalism, not just within Latin America but also between countries of the Global South (Bonilla 2013). This, in turn, implied transformation in the socio-legal communities and a widening of conversations and interactions, bringing new perspectives to the analysis of constitutional change in the region, evidenced by the circulation of concerns with progressive constitutionalism or activist courts in favor of social rights (Yamin and Gloppen 2011; Langford, Rodríguez-Garavito, and Rossi 2017).

A focus on the reform and design of legal institutions, as well as their functioning and polit-ical and social consequences, was one of the principle ways in which the new socio-political dynamics in Latin America were translated into law and society research agendas. In the early 1990s, much scholarship was markedly normative and instrumentalist in character, in effect engaging in the ideological construction of the state; the "state effect" described so incisively by Timothy Mitchell (1991). Scholars invoked abstract notions such as the "rule of law" and the Weberian dictum of state monopoly over the means of coercion, invariably contrasting ideal-ized forms of law in the North with their absence in the South (Rodríguez-Garavito 2011, 13). Following an initial wave of studies signaling the links between law, democracy, and inter-national rule of law promotion, with a particular focus on judicial reform (Domingo and Sieder 2001; Dakolias 1996; Pásara 2007), research more identified with the methods of North Amer-ican political science developed causally driven empirical analyses of existing state institutions. Focusing on institutional design and judicial behavior (and drawing on United States studies of judicial behavior), these works strengthened the field of comparative judicial politics (Ansolabe-here 2007; Hilbink 2007; Helmke 2005, Finkel 2008; Domingo 2000; Ríos-Figueroa and Staton 2012; Kapizewski 2012). The legacy of these pioneering studies, examining the relation-ship between justice and politics in contexts of authoritarianism and emergent democracies, continued with new research concerned with the factors explaining the different roles assumed by judicial institutions, and their capacity to generate social transformation by (re)distributing power and resources (Gloppen et al. 2010; Gauri and Brinks 2010). The judiciary was conceived as an arena for social justice and accountability claims, particularly with regard to international human rights standards and norms (see the chapter by Ansolabehere in this volume). The dimensions of international politics, the diffusion of legal ideas, and relations between legal institutions, civil society, and social movements promoting certain issues and causes came to constitute central issues in the field of study. These were generally approached from perspectives of legal mobilization, or of constitutional change understood as processes of legal mobilization (see the chapters by Saldivia, Wilson and Gianella, and Machado et al. in this volume). Topics which have generated a rich body of comparative and single case studies across the region in this register include movements in favor of sexual and reproductive rights, and health rights (Albarracín 2011; Bergallo and Michel 2016; Yamin and Gloppen 2011). Scholarship has circulated through congresses of USA scholarly networks regularly attended by Latin American academics, including the Latin American Studies Association (LASA) and the American Political Science Association (APSA).[7] In addition to interest in the functioning of courts, research on legal institutions, their reform and the challenges facing them also experienced an increase (Halliday 2013), especially on state prosecution bodies (see chapter by Michel in this volume); the police (see chapter by Dammert in this volume); prisons (see chapter by Macaulay in this volume) and the national human rights institutions created in the 1990s, which constituted a key case of legal diffusion and innovation (see chapter by Uggla in this volume). As well as political science and sociology, legal anthropology has also provided critical ethnographic analyzes of penal institutions, judicial bureaucracies, and processes of legal reform – for example, the work of Argentine, and Brazilian scholars such as Sofía Tiscornia, María Victoria Pita, María José Sarrabayrouse, Josefina Martínez, and Roberto Kant do Lima (Tiscornia 2004; Tiscornia, Kant de Lima, and Eilbaum 2009).This reflects the shift within law and society scholarship toward more decentered understandings of the state, with a focus on the micro-politics, subjectivities, and material practices that underpin the making of the law (see chapter by Barrera and Latorre this volume).[8] As more constructivist perspectives have gained ground vis-à-vis normative approaches in Latin American law and society scholarship, concern with legal pluralism has extended beyond the initial focus on indigenous peoples. Earlier approaches championing legal pluralism as emancipatory have been superseded by work that analyzes the fragmented nature of state power –for example, exploring the role of paramilitary and parastatal elements in contemporary state formations. More generally, ethnographic and anthropological approaches to the study of law and justice in Latin America are gaining ground (Brunnegger and Faulk 2016).

Yet despite tendencies toward decentering the state and growing sociological and legal anthropological concerns with processes of state formation and transmutation, the axis of civil society/state (or social movements/state) remains fundamental to the field of law and society in Latin America, perhaps to a much greater extent than in other regional traditions of law and society scholarship. The analysis of legal institutions signaled above has been accompanied by a huge increase in research on processes of legal mobilization by different social movements, in turn linked to a broader literature analyzing the role of different civil society groups in securing greater rights guarantees and state accountability (Mainwairing and Welna 2003; Peruzzotti and Smulovitz 2006; Isunza and Olvera 2010). In Latin America, social movements have framed their demands in the language of rights and have used legal change and strategic litigation as central tools in their efforts to secure socioeconomic, political, and cultural transformations. Law and society scholars have analyzed the nature and effects of these strategies, often with reference to an international law and society literature focused on the processes, practices, and subjectivities through which the transnationalization of human rights occurs (Keck and Sikkink 1998; Risse, Ropp, and Sikkink 1999; Merry 2005; Merry and Goodale 2007; on Colombia see Santos and García-Villegas 2001; on Mexico see Hernández 2016). Social movement theory has shaped regional law and society scholarship, with a theoretical and methodological emphasis on concepts and tools such as framing, discourse analysis, network analysis, and both single case and causal multi-case comparative studies (see Lemaitre and Sandvik 2015 for an insightful critique of the application of social movement theory to violent contexts). Of particular concern has been the analysis of emancipatory or counter-hegemonic processes of socio-legal mobilization, what Boaventura de Sousa Santos and César Rodríguez-Garavito in a signal volume (2005) called "legal globalization from below."

Compared to the early 1990s, socio-legal mobilization linked to issues of governance and social justice now occupies a more prominent role in regional law and society research agendas. Many scholars are themselves public intellectuals, key figures in national debates and reform processes promoting liberal, "emancipatory," and rights-based understandings of law. While most law training throughout the region remains highly formalistic, a number of key nodes exist that encourage human rights litigation and law in action perspectives – for example, the Universidad de Los Andes in Bogotá, or the ITAM in Mexico (see chapters by Fortes and Gómez in this volume). Prominent NGOs and civil society organizations engaged in strategic litigation and applied socio-legal research – such as DeJusticia in Colombia, CELS (Centro de Estudios Legales y Sociales) in Argentina, Fundar in Mexico, or the Instituto de Defensa Legal in Peru – have further shaped the field. Indeed the co-production of knowledge and the fluidity of relations between academia, civil society, and (increasingly) national and regional legal institutions are distinguishing features of law and society scholarship in Latin America. To provide just one example of this kind of interface: the Guatemalan Instituto de Estudios Comparados en Ciencias Penales (ICCPG) was established by former students of Argentine legal scholar and human rights activist Alberto Binder at the start of the 1990s. The ICCPG developed applied empirical socio-legal research in Guatemala and has played a key role in advancing human rights-based reform of the criminal justice system in that country. Former ICCPG director Claudia Paz y Paz Bailey spearheaded the national fight against impunity during her time as head of the Guatemalan public prosecution services and subsequently as part of the interdisciplinary group of experts appointed by the Inter-American Commission on Human Rights to investigate the forced disappearance of 43 students in Ayotzinapa, Mexico. Similar examples of such fluidity and cross-regional exchange can be found in the law and society field in many countries throughout the region. Internships at the Inter-American Commission and Inter-American Court, together with the work of organizations such as CEJIL (Center for Justice and International Law) (which engages in strategic litigation within the Inter-American System) and key United States-based organizations – for example, the Center for Reproductive Rights in New York – have played a vital role in consolidating transregional epistemic law and society communities characterized by increasingly international practitioner perspectives on law.

Last, but not least, all these changes in the role of law, and in the relationships between politics and law, combined with the diversification of the academy interested in understanding law in action, implies a revision of theoretical approximations. The incorporation of longer historical perspectives, reflections about the frontiers between the legal and the illegal, the focus on the constitutive tension between law, civilization, and barbarism in Latin America, law and race studies, law and gender, international relations, and legal compliance are all important in re-theorizing approaches to the study of law and society in the region and beyond, and are the focus of the first section of this Handbook. We underline the need to question persistent dichotomies in the study of law, such as compliance/noncompliance, legal/illegal or state/non-state. Critical interrogation of these often taken for granted binaries, in the light of developments in Latin America and in dialog with scholarship from other regions of the world holds out the promise of new critical agendas for law and society scholarship.

Organization of the Handbook

The chapters that follow are divided into four parts: Part I Law, Politics, and Society; Part II New Constitutional Models and Institutional Design; Part III Law and Social Movements; and Part IV Emergent Topics. Together the chapters provide an overview of longstanding concerns and recent innovations in law and society scholarship from Latin America. They also evidence its rich interdisciplinary tradition, drawing on legal philosophy, comparative politics, sociological approaches, and – increasingly – the turn toward more ethnographic and micro-level approaches to analyzing the constitution of law that have long been in evidence in United States and European law and society research. At the same time, many of the issues that regional law and society scholarship has analyzed, including the indeterminacy of the law and the line between the legal and illegal, or the social and political dimensions of efficacy and compliance, are increasingly of concern to law and society scholarship more broadly. As law and society as a field becomes more global in nature, North–South dichotomies – which were always informed by an enduring parochialism in northern scholarship – are ever harder to sustain.

The chapters in Part I of this Handbook, "Law, Politics, and Society," address a number of key cross-cutting theoretical and conceptual debates, which have featured prominently in Latin American law and society research. These include: the nature of the state and the relationship between state formation, law and legal change; the role that culture plays in compliance or noncompliance; the dynamics between law and the deep-rooted and intersecting inequalities of race, gender and class, together with the persistently high levels of social violence that characterize the region; and legal pluralism and the relationship between legality and illegality. In his contribution, Argentine legal theorist Roberto Gargarella reflects on the specificities of constitutional development in Latin America over the *longue durée*, underlining what the regional experience has to offer to political and constitutional theory more generally. He identifies five distinct phases of Latin American constitutionalism since the foundation of the republics, reflecting on the shifting dynamics between law, politics, and different institutional, and normative configurations. He concludes that despite comparatively broad bills of rights, and a long-standing tradition of social rights constitutionalism, the power structures of the state in Latin America's constitutions (what Gargarella calls the "engine room") remain highly concentrated. Gargarella's analysis thus, tempers more presentist analyses of "neo-constitutionalism" that overestimate the transformative power of law. In their chapter on law and the state in Latin America, political scientists Lisa Hilbink and Janice Gallagher review recent trends in the literature and assess their implications for future research. They identify two broad approaches to the problem of weak states and weak rule of law in the region: on the one hand, those that focus on institutional barriers such as lack of judicial independence or access, and lack of state embeddedness in society; and on the other, those that emphasize the role different actors external to the judiciary play in shaping the state and law. These two approaches, although closely related, and complementary to our current understanding of the law and the state, have reached high levels of specialization on their own and to some extent, a certain level of independence from each other.[9] In fact, as Hilbink and Gallagher's review signals and González-Bertomeu's chapter shows, analysis of institutional features tend to focus on how courts work and to theorize explanatory factors that are internal to them. Conversely, and as Wilson and Gianella in this volume show for the case of social movements, scholars that analyze processes of judicialization tend to pay more attention to the role of actors outside of the courts. Among the recent trends highlighted by Hilbink and Gallagher are a shift from a sole focus on apex courts toward studying lower courts; a growth in studies comparing subnational units, institutions, and issues; and analyzes of citizens' attitudes to the law and their experience of the state more broadly.

Their chapter points to the increasing complexity of comparative research on law and the state in Latin America, and its richness.

In her chapter Rachel Sieder discusses the concept and practice of legal pluralism, a central concern of law and society scholarship, and places the regional literature on legal pluralism (which has tended to focus largely on indigenous peoples and the struggles to formally recognize their autonomy rights) in dialog with the extensive research on legality, illegality, and violence in Latin America. She reviews key contributions and conceptual approaches to legal pluralism in the regional scholarship, and offers a typology of different types of illegality. Emphasizing the contributions that constructivist, anthropological approaches to law have made to regional scholarship, Sieder points to the complex interplay between different legal, quasi-legal, and illegal regimes – or what she terms "fragmented sovereignties" – in securing order and "plural constellations of governance" in Latin America. Mauricio García-Villegas considers the historical roots of the regional "culture of noncompliance" with the law, referencing a wide range of allusions to noncompliance in Spanish and Portuguese literary tropes and historical works. As he emphasizes, interest in noncompliance is relatively marginal to United States and European law and society research, yet it is a central – although still understudied – aspect of social and political life in Latin America. García-Villegas identifies three approaches in the literature: noncompliance as rational choice; as political resistance to authority (drawing on both *iusnaturalis* and Marxist traditions); and as response by both the powerful and the powerless to contextual specificities. He points to a normalized "practice of exception" in Latin America and underscores the relevance of its analysis for understanding the apparent expansion of noncompliance, violence, and illegality in the contemporary world. In her chapter Julieta Lemaitre signals the long-running tension between civilization and barbarism in Latin America, with law historically constituted on the side of elite civilizing forces and barbarism representing those who live in regions "without God or law" i.e., beyond state legality. Opposing the simplistic idea that what these regions and sectors lack is the presence of the state or the arrival of the law, Lemaitre argues that violence is a central problem of law in Latin America that neither liberal nor Marxist or post-Marxist perspectives have adequately theorized. Calling for theories of law grounded in the realities of the region, she also advocates a social constructivist approach to exploring the regulation of social order in zones "without law," with an emphasis on uncovering what is seen as legitimate and what is normalized. In their chapter Leticia Barrera and Sergio de la Torre consider the technical and material dimensions of bureaucratic and legal knowledge, and the ways in which ethnographic, anthropological approaches have in recent years explored the processes by which the state is instantiated in Latin America. They argue that technical aspects of the law (including doctrines, regulations, case files, and protocols, together with legal routines and procedures) structure forms of expertise, governance, and knowledge relations, thus constituting law's "inner life." Drawing on examples from their own work (on the field of judicial practice in Argentina and disputes over land tenure in Colombia) they argue for a focus on state bureaucracy and its legal technologies as an object of enquiry on its own terms. In other words, rather than taking the gap between law on the books and law in action as a point of departure, Barrera and la Torre maintain that fine-grained analysis of the material aspects of law making within institutions provides a different way of knowing about how law works and is experienced as different "knowledge practices" by a range of actors.

Isabel Jaramillo reviews the development of feminist legal theory in Latin America and considers its contributions to the transnational field of law and gender studies. Providing an account of the different ways in which Latin American feminist legal scholars have confronted tensions between transnational and local feminist organizing and scholarship, and between sexual inequality and other forms of oppression, she identifies three broad approaches, which she terms

11

solidaristic, radical, and political feminism. Jaramillo analyzes the different actors and constituencies, issues, conceptual premises, doctrinal innovations, and scholarly production that have marked these three currents. She concludes that feminist scholarship from the region is particularly characterized by contributions that emphasize multiple subordinations and the intersectionality of race, class, ethnic, and gender inequalities. Tanya Hernández examines dynamics between race and law in Latin America, mapping recurrent research themes in the socio-legal literature on race, which has mainly focused on Afrodescendant populations, and the ways in which states throughout the region have addressed ideas of race and racial discrimination. She explores three sets of socio-legal debates: the limits of multicultural constitutional reform for full political participation; the limits of the regional emphasis on criminal law to address discrimination; and the challenges to recent attempts to deploy United States style affirmative action policies. Highlighting the traditional separation between indigenous/ethnicity and Afrodescendant/race, Hernández ends by insisting on the need to name the racial nature of structural violence in order to elucidate the nature of state formation and power in Latin America, something which is gaining more traction not just in regional law and society scholarship but in the social sciences overall.

The final two contributions of this section consider the relationship between law and development in the region. From a liberal perspective, Pedro Fortes reviews the checkered history of the law and development movement in Latin America, describing its different phases, conceptual framings, and key actors. He revisits the project of legal development through the transformation of legal education and professional lawyering, concluding that centers of excellence in legal education were indeed established in Latin America and that the current challenge is how to extend innovative approaches and the empirical study of law beyond these nodes. He concludes by insisting on the needs for capabilities or human needs-based definitions of development, advocating an empirically, and incrementally-based approach. By contrast, Carlos Rivera Lugo reviews Marxist perspectives on the relationship between law and the economy, emphasizing the importance of what he refers to as a "dissenting, decolonizing and creative endeavor" in Latin America that has attempted to develop Marxist thought beyond its European origins. Rivera Lugo considers the relationship between law – understood as a tool for domination and the reproduction of capital – and the current stage of globalized neoliberal political economy as reflected in Latin American contexts. He warns against perspectives that overemphasize the relative autonomy of the law and underlines the need to analyze law and economy in tandem. He also points to the generative potential for Marxist thought of current dialogs between different historical experiences of the communal, and those of indigenous peoples in Latin America, something which holds out the promise of a break with Eurocentric framings of the region's historical development, pointing to the radical potential of its autochthonous legal expressions.

Part II, "New Constitutional Models and Institutional Design," signals the growth in the region of studies of law in action focused on legal institutions, an area that was of marginal interest to law and society studies even two decades ago. This section of the Handbook focuses on research into ombudsmen, police, judicial institutions, constitutional courts, and the Inter-American System of Human Rights. While the content of the chapters necessarily differs, they share a series of concerns: independence-accountability; power-efficacy; improvement of criminal justice versus abuses of criminal justice; the diffusion of human rights; and transformations of the legal profession. Interest in the independence and accountability of the judiciary, ombudsmen, and police focuses on the possibilities of judicial institutions controlling political power. This continues to be a central topic in the study of legal institutions in Latin America. These general concerns are underpinned by a shared regional history of political instability, authoritarianism, and super-presidentialism, which in turn has generated conceptual debates about what independence is and how it can be measured, and about accountability functions more broadly. However, at the same time as scholars focused on institutional and extra-institutional determinants of institutional behavior, they have also analyzed the performance of these institutions.

In accordance with neo-institutionalist perspectives in political science, these studies share a certain baseline assumption that institutional performance depends not only on rules but also on interests, power relations, and the perspectives of the different actors involved. Studies of judicial institutions, judicial behavior, and ideational studies underline such concerns. In this sense, they share perspectives, which emphasize the dynamic, and contingent nature of judicial independence, accountability, power, and efficacy. Nonetheless, it is important to underline the fact that reflections on power and efficacy also imply the study of undesired or unanticipated consequences. Multiple problems are generated by awarding power to institutions that operate as authoritarian enclaves or which are driven by bureaucratic inertia and corruption. Studies of institutions that form part of the criminal justice system – police, prosecutors' offices, and prisons – best express this tension between improvement and abuse. In all these cases, in addition to an interest in institutional reforms and their possibilities, research has also traced processes and identified practices that violate human rights or which operate as mechanisms to criminalize groups considered as dangerous because of their social class, race, or because of links that exist between state security institutions and criminal organizations.

As well as these shared concerns, we can identify two overarching issues in this section of the Handbook. One is the diffusion of ideas, tools, and institutions of human rights, which foregrounds the diffusion of doctrinal and legal institutions, the relation between domestic and international courts, the role of the Inter-American System, the new demands on the judiciary that assumes a fundamental role in social change and human rights accountability, and the tensions, and conflicts that this implies. The other overarching issue is that of the legal profession. Research on legal institutions signals that legal professionals are key actors (although by no means the only ones): these include lawyers, judges, public prosecutors, and defenders. The relationship between the legal profession and legal institutions is marked by a double movement or tension: legal professionals are the main implementers of reforms, which at the same time impact their professional exercise.

The analysis of legal institutions in Latin America set out in this section enables the reader to identify different research perspectives. Some are more concerned with causal explanations and frameworks; others with more descriptive or ethnographic approximations. Critical perspectives exist alongside constructivist and positivist approximations. The chapters in Part II therefore, signal a diversity of theoretical and methodological perspectives, as well as research interests (as signaled in the first section of this introduction). A brief description of the chapters serves to illustrate the diversity of themes, concerns and perspectives.

Juan González-Bertomeu's chapter on judicial politics in Latin America reviews the main themes in this field, which is in turn one of the signal innovations in studies of law in action in the region. González-Bertomeu identifies five central issues: independence; power; judicial conduct; legal culture and ideas; and judicial activism and compliance with sentences. His contribution sets out a multiplicity of competing perspectives on the analysis of judicial politics, without trying to integrate them into a single approach. The chapter by Francisca Pou also focuses on high courts, but from a different vantage point. Analyzing the regional characteristics of constitutional justice, Pou emphasizes what she considers to be the main Latin American innovations in constitutional law, such as hybrid judicial review models that overcome the dichotomy between United States and European models. She also underlines efforts by high courts in the region to develop communications policies to facilitate links with the wider public, and the importance of relations between high courts and other tribunals in the circulation of legal ideas. Verónica Michel's chapter reviews research approaches to a new subject of study in the region; public prosecutor's offices. As well as signaling the most relevant research, she indicates the three underlying areas of enquiry that inform it: judicial politics (particularly with reference to theories of judicial independence, power, and accountability); studies on the functioning of criminal justice systems, focusing particularly on abuses and the repressive use of criminal law; and finally, research examining legal responsibility for human rights violations and the importance of prosecutorial bodies in these processes. For his part, Fredrik Uggla in his contribution on human rights ombudsman's offices revisits the relationship between independence and efficacy, tracing the spread, and evolution of these institutions throughout Latin America since the 1990s. Uggla underlines the importance of interactions between ombudsman's offices and other institutions, and signals what comparative experience indicates about positive results. In her chapter on the police, Lucía Dammert indicates the research deficit on police institutions in the region, proceeding to review reform processes, actors' behavior, and overall tendencies, such as the trend toward militarization of the police. Fiona Macaulay analyzes prison systems, pointing to what she calls "prisoner capture," a process involving extensive reliance on pretrial detention, the hyper-penalization of petty crimes that increases the prison population, and self-government of carceral institutions by organized groups of prisoners. For Macaulay the overall context of rollback of social welfare provision and the absence of policies for social integration explains the region's overreliance on criminal law. Karina Ansolabehere's chapter focuses on the ways in which domestic judicial powers function as arenas for human rights. She signals three different research agendas that have marked the field in Latin America in recent years: the reception of international human rights law; legal responsibility for human rights violations; and social justice. In her chapter, she observes that these different research strands examining the relationship between the judiciary and human rights in the region are not always in dialog. Considering future prospects for the Inter-American Human Rights System, Alexandra Huneeus underlines the importance of geostrategic analysis of human rights regimes in a global context marked by the advance of anti-globalization discourses, the decline of United States hegemony and the rise of authoritarian populisms. She revisits the body of legal and sociolegal scholarship on the Inter-American System and human rights in the region to examine how it can be reframed in order to inform new questions posed by the changing world order. Finally, Manuel Gómez considers changes in research agendas on legal professionals in Latin America. He underlines the importance of the legal profession, especially the role of lawyers in processes of judicial reform. One of the central distinguishing features of Gómez's chapter is precisely the relative paucity of research in this area, which in turn signals new possibilities for future agendas.

Part III of the Handbook turns the spotlight on the relationship between "Law and Social Movements" in Latin America. To some extent, this section is the counterpart of the preceding section focusing on institutions and constitutions, and signals the two principal ways in which the relationship between law and society has been problematized in recent years: on the one hand, a focus on institutions and, on the other, a concern with questions of equality and the transformative potential of law and legal institutions. One good example of the complementary relation between the emphasis on institutions on the one hand and the role of social actors in shaping them, on the other, is the dialog between the scholarship on judicial politics and judicialization of politics, respectively. The first field – as mentioned above and explained by González-Bertomeu – builds on the idea that institutional features, internal politics, and level of embeddedness of the institutions may explain institutional performance and outcomes.

Scholarship that focuses on social movements as agents of the process of judicialization of politics – as illustrated in Wilson and Gianella's chapter in this section – explains the processes through which social grievances and claims are transformed into legal claims, target specific institutions, and ultimately also play a role in shaping institutional responses. The empirical puzzle of how institutions work is composed by the two counterparts and even though the two camps share many theoretical debates, each strand of research is now producing its own set of scholarship.[10] The common denominator of this section lies in the ways in which law has been used to advance a range of social justice causes, and in the analysis of the types of judicial, political, and social responses such efforts have generated. In synthesis, this section focuses on the ways in which civil society actors have used law to pursue social change. Understandings of the judicialization of politics as broad processes, which include more than resort to judicial review mechanisms, underpin these preoccupations. What are the factors which lead to the judicialization of politics? Why do some causes find more success in the courts than others? What processes of legal and political diffusion occur to facilitate judicialization? These are some of the questions considered in this Part III of the Handbook. The different chapters are united by an interest in the ways in which the activation of legal mechanisms and discourses generates transformative processes. Although they recognize more sanguine or indeed pessimistic perspectives on these issues (Rosenberg 2008), in general authors recognize the difficulty of determining generic answers and underline the importance of understanding specific contexts and processes. Perhaps for this reason, in-depth single country, or issue case studies have increasingly been complemented by more comparative analyses, which seek to uncover the causal factors underlying successful cases of transformative judicialization. The chapters in this section are informed by diverse concerns and issues, including the factors contributing to judicialization, transitional justice, social movements, and framing processes, the circulation of legal knowledge and democratic constitutionalism. This diversity of approaches illustrates the multiple entry points to analysis of law and social movements in Latin America, although by no means do we cover all the social movements in the region that have made recourse to legal mobilization – for example, indigenous movements, and environmental movements are two important cases not covered in detail in this section.

In their chapter, Bruce Wilson and Camila Gianella revise the evolution of the literature on the judicialization of politics in Latin America. They identify different moments in this process, including an initial concern with questions of accountability and a subsequent turn to the use of the judicial arena as a means to advance different social causes. Their review underlines some of the causes that have had most echo in Latin American processes of judicialization, including rights to health, social, economic and cultural rights, and LGBTI (lesbian, gay, bisexual, transgender, and intersex) rights. Laura Saldivia's chapter analyzes processes of legal change linked to rights to sexual diversity, an area that has witnessed significant advances in some countries in the region. Saldivia anchors her analysis in the case of Argentina, the first country in the world to pass legislation to recognize rights to sexual identity, and analyzes the ways in which this legal advance was diffused from a peripheral country to the core of global rights agendas, as well as the ways in which the movement in favor of rights to sexual diversity contributed to generating new constitutional interpretations. In their chapter Marta Machado de Assis, Ana Luiza Villela de Viana Bandeira, and Fernanda Matsuda consider the advances and obstacles encountered by women's movements with respect to rights to legal abortion. On the basis of a case study of Brazil, they contrast the struggle against domestic violence with the agenda on reproductive rights. They explore the reasons underlying the different advances in both movements' struggles, pointing to the key role played by framing in legal mobilization and the ways these are tied to different moral and discursive disputes over women's rights. Lastly, Elena Martínez Barahona and Martha Liliana Gutiérrez consider the importance of transitional justice studies in Latin America, signaling recent advances in the field and future research agendas.

Part IV of the Handbook focuses on what we have termed "Emergent Topics," including corruption, impunity, and drug trafficking, military jurisdiction, and land conflicts, all central contemporary challenges for Latin America's legal and political systems and societies. As we have underlined in this introduction, scholarship concerned with the inefficacy of the law and high levels of violence and impunity has long characterized law and society studies in Latin America. The changing dynamics between legality and illegality remains a central analytical concern, together with the ways in which beliefs and behaviors related to the law change over time through the interplay between different forms of agency, structural features, and contests over power. Yet as we have signaled in this introduction, the coincidence between hyper-legality and growing judicialization, and the massive growth in criminal activities is not just a Latin American but rather a global phenomenon (Comaroff and Comaroff 2006, 2016). The contributions in this section offer new perspectives on the relationship between corruption, organized crime, legal reform, and enforcement in Latin America, which in turn suggest important lines of enquiry for analyzing the socio-legal dimensions of current regional and global reconfigurations of politics and economics.

In the first chapter of the section, Rodrigo Meneses approaches the persistent and still novel issue of urban regulation and the theorization of Latin American cities as specific sites of socio-legal research. Meneses reviews the existent research on urban regulation to show the indeterminate nature of urban property regimes in the region. He illustrates this argument by reviewing the scholarship on street regulation and the social and construction of public space through constant and iterative processes of interaction between authorities and the population. The chapter by Tatiana Alfonso Sierra maps the contribution of Latin American socio-legal research to the understanding of a classical legal institution: property. She argues that law and society research in the region has approached the institution from different perspectives and theoretical frames, creating a fragmented landscape, and parallel conversations. Her chapter reviews this literature, identifying five key theoretical contributions as well as the ways in which a common interest on law in action around property has evolved into different subfields. The first, on law and development, has established a solid conversation with policy makers and development agencies with a new emphasis on alternative forms of property and not only on private individual property. The second line of research in the region explained the rapid urbanization processes of Latin American cities with the formality/informality binary and has evolved to conversations with urban studies and planning tools, dealing with property as one possible set of relations for organizing the city. The third contribution is a more anthropological approach based on the idea of the plurality of legal forms and the fourth set of questions deals with ideas of property rights in a globalized age. Finally, the chapter presents a fifth line of research in which the study and defense of territorial rights of ethnic groups in Latin America is starting to get closer to debates about property. The author calls for an integrated analysis of property – and legal institutions in general – as a multifaceted institution that allows us to understand how law mediates between social and economic processes, social outcomes, and power struggles in society. In her chapter, Linn Hammergren reviews both existing scholarship and multiple journalistic and official sources on corruption and organized crime in the region, setting out what we know to date about regional trends. She provides an extensive overview of relevant research and its limitations, drawing on scholarship and data from four countries – Brazil, Colombia, Guatemala, and Mexico – and identifying shared and country-specific patterns. Hammergren ends her chapter with a call for more theory building and causally inferred research exploring the impacts of contemporary configurations of corruption and organized crime on the prospects for legality and justice in the region. In his chapter, Julio Ríos-Figueroa analyzes the "new militarism," which has seen a renewed prominence of the military in Latin America's internal security affairs, including the fight against organized crime, terrorism, and even mass protests deemed a threat to national security. He reviews three areas where this new militarism is in conflict with rule of law and democracy: the clash between constitutions and the military's mission statements; the scope and nature of military justice, and; the dynamics between national courts and the regional human rights system with respect to judicial oversight and the appropriate limits on military power. Ríos-Figueroa emphasizes the need for more socio-legal analyses of the new militarism, arguing it is one of the key features shaping the future of the region's fragile democracies. Alejandro Madrazo and Catalina Pérez Correa also underline the need for more socio-legal analyses of the so-called "war on drugs" in Latin America, which – as they point out – offer possibilities for the study of criminal law in action. They argue that the (United States-led) emphasis on treating narcotics as a criminal and public security issue, rather than a health and public safety issue, has been disastrous for the regional prospects for democratic rule of law. Madrazo and Pérez Correa trace the ways in which the increasingly punitive enforcement of drug laws has led to the militarization of public security, hyper-penalization of drug-related crimes, the criminalization of consumers, the frequent violation of due process rights and an increase in corruption, torture, and use of lethal force by state authorities. They conclude with a call for more ethnographic analyzes of processes of criminalization in order to reveal the consequences of drug policies, and for more attention to the impacts of drug policies and the new militarism on Latin America's constitutional orders and law in action.

Concluding Thoughts

This Handbook attempts to provide a broad panorama of law and society research in Latin America, signaling regional concerns, setting out research trajectories and findings, and underlining the contributions of law and society research in Latin America to wider debates in law and society. Probably the most signal feature of contemporary law and society scholarship in the region is its questioning of key dichotomies that have characterized dominant narratives on law and society: compliance/noncompliance; legality/illegality, and; law on the books/law in action. We have identified two main cleavages: first, more theoretically versus more methodologically driven studies of Latin America's legal institutions and practices, and; second, the persistence of more normative as opposed to more constructivist approaches to law. These cleavages continue to structure the field in what we consider to be productive tensions.

Nonetheless, a number of areas not addressed here are necessary to enrich future law and society scholarship in Latin America. First, there is a need for more long-run historical analyses and debate with historians of law and society in Latin America. Historians of the region's colonial and republican periods have documented and analyzed the central role that law, litigation, and contestations over justice played in structuring relations between governments and populations in previous periods and over the *longue durée* (see for example, Salvatore and Aguirre 1990; Cutter 1995; Carey 2013). Analysts of the contemporary period need to consider the historical role of courts in political struggles in Latin America, as well as the legal history of particular claims and engagements. The long-run traditions of resort to the courts for routine individual and collective claims highlighted by historians, contrasts with the current emphasis of socio-legal analysts on constitutional rights litigation, support structures for strategic judicialization, and far-reaching legal and political transformations. This contrast between what Rodrigo Uprimny referred to as "protagonistic" versus "routine" justice (2016) – i.e., constitutional jurisprudential developments versus citizens' everyday encounters with ordinary justice – requires greater reflection by law and society scholars in order to generate more regionally grounded theory. Second, inevitably a number of important topics have not been included here, including law and migration, and commercial law and legal globalization from above, to name just two. Reflection on these issues is vital for the future development of the field. Third, the contributions in this Handbook point to the unevenness of production of socio-legal scholarship and statistical data across the region. While some countries figure prominently in the literature (this varies according to topic), others are notably absent. Greater attention to the outliers and to least similar cases in the future can only enrich our understandings of the dynamics between law and society across the region. In conclusion, we hope that this Handbook stimulates a broader set of conversations about law and society in Latin America and points to the contributions scholarship from and about the region can make to global law and society studies.

Notes

1 A third contributory factor, which we do not explore in any detail here, is the changing public role of lawyers throughout the region.
2 The varying quality and availability of official statistics across the region is another significant factor, as is the uneven access to decisions of the high courts in the 17 countries.
3 In the USA, the definition of the field has been paired with the emergence, changes, and fractures of the Law and Society Association and law and society programs in universities.
4 The Oñati International Institute for the Sociology of Law has been a center of production of world-wide socio-legal research as its founders – the Basque country, the Socio Legal Research Committee and the International Sociological Association – aimed in 1989. The Oñati institute has fulfilled this mission through academic conferences, publishing venues, and a varied offer of academic programs. As has been shown by Ibarra (2018), an analysis of the production of Oñati reveals some of the main features and topics of socio-legal research in and about Latin America and how the field can be mapped through the academic production of alumni and scholars around Oñati.
5 These northern-based centers and associations have been important hubs for the development of law and society studies in Latin America, enabling North–South and South–South interaction and exchange. English has dominated as a language of publication, although Spanish and Portuguese are also important for the transnational circulation of knowledge.
6 SELA's sponsoring institutions include: the University of Palermo and the University of Buenos Aires (Argentina); the Getulio Vargas Foundation (Brazil); the Adolfo Ibañez University, the University of Chile, and the Diego Portales University (Chile); the University of Los Andes (Colombia); the Autonomous Technological Institute of Mexico (ITAM) and the Center for Economic Research and Teaching (CIDE) (Mexico), and UNAM; the Paraguayan Institute for Constitutional Law; the Pontifical University of Peru (PUCP) and the Peruvian University for Applied Science; the University of Puerto Rico and the Pompeu Fabra University in Barcelona. For a history of SELA see https://law.yale.edu/centers-workshops/yale-law-school-latin-american-legal-studies/sela/history-sela Consulted November 20, 2017.
7 By the 1990s a critical mass of regionally-based law and society scholars had been trained in the USA (and to a much lesser extent in Europe), a trend which continues. In addition, national government-funded research councils in Argentina, Mexico, and Brazil have for many years promoted "internationalization" of nationally produced research, favoring publications in English by academics working in those countries.
8 In contrast to law and society studies in the USA and Europe, litigant-centered approaches have only recently gained ground within the field in Latin America, although there is a long regional tradition of legal anthropological studies on indigenous justice systems and litigants' disputing strategies within them – see for example, Nader (1990), Collier (1973), and Sierra (2004).
9 This volume includes one chapter on each of these trends that Hilbink and Gallagher signal; the first, by González-Bertomeu in Part II, reviews research on the main topics examined by scholars of judicial politics; the second, by Wilson and Gianella, analyzes the external side of judiciary-society relations, that is the role of social movements in advancing social causes.
10 That is the reason why this volume includes two different chapters that review recent developments and future agendas of each of the research strands. See González-Bertomeu on judicial politics in Part II and Wilson and Gianella on the process of judicialization of politics in this section.

References

Albarracín, Mauricio. 2011. "Corte constitucional y movimientos sociales: el reconocimiento judicial de los derechos de las parejas del mismo sexo en Colombia." *Revista Sur*, Vol. 8 (14): 7–33.

Ansolabehere, Karina. 2007. *La Política Desde la Justicia: Cortes Supremas, Gobierno y Democracia en Argentina y México*. Mexico: FLACSO.

Bergallo, Paola and Agustina Ramón Michel. 2016. "Abortion." In Juan González-Bertomeu and Roberto Gargarella (eds.), *The Latin American Casebook: Courts, Constitutions and Rights*. London and New York: Routledge: 36–59.

Bonilla, Daniel. 2013. *Constitutionalism of the Global South*. New York: Oxford University Press.

Brinks, Daniel. 2006. *The Judicial Response to Police Killings in Latin America. Inequality and the Rule of Law*. New York: Cambridge University Press.

Brunnegger, Sandra and Karen Faulk (eds). 2016. *A Sense of Justice. Legal Knowledge and Lived Experience in Latin America*. Stanford, CA: Stanford Universtiy Press.

Carey, David. 2013. *I Ask for Justice. Maya Women, Dictators and Crime in Guatemala, 1898–1944*. Austin, TX: University of Texas Press.

Carothers, Thomas. 2001. "The many agendas of rule-of-law reform in Latin America." In Rachel Sieder and Pilar Domingo (eds.), *Rule of Law in Latin America: The International Promotion of Judicial Reform*. London: Institute of Latin American Studies: 4–16.

Chenaut, Victoria, Magdalena Gómez, Héctor Ortiz, and María Teresa Sierra. 2011. *Justicia y Diversidad en América Latina. Pueblos Indígenas ante la Globalización*. Mexico: CIESAS/FLACSO Ecuador.

Clark, David. 1975. "Judicial protection of the constitution in Latin America." *Hastings Constitutional Law Quarterly*, Vol. 2: 405–42.

Collier, Jane. 1973. *Law and Social Change in Zinacantán*. Stanford, CA: Stanford University Press.

Comaroff, Jean and John Comaroff. 2006. "Law and disorder in the postcolony: an introduction." In Jean and John Comaroff (eds.), *Law and Disorder in the Postcolony*. Chicago, IL: University of Chicago Press.

Comaroff, Jean and John Comaroff. 2016. *The Truth about Crime: Sovereignty, Knowledge, Social Order*. Chicago, IL: University of Chicago Press.

Couso, Javier, Alexandra Huneeus, and Rachel Sieder (eds.). 2010. *Cultures of Legality. Judicialization and Political Activism in Latin America*. New York: Cambridge University Press.

Cutter, Charles. 1995. *The Legal Culture of Northern New Spain, 1700–1810*. Santa Fe: University of New Mexico Press.

Dakolias, Maria. 1996. *The Judicial Sector in Latin America and the Caribbean: Elements of Reform*. Washington, DC: World Bank.

Dezalay, Yves and Bryant Garth. 2002. *The Internationalization of Palace Wars. Lawyers, Economists and the Contest to Transform Latin American States*. Chicago, IL: Chicago University Press.

Domingo, Pilar. 2000. "The independence of the supreme court in Mexico." *Journal of Latin American Studies*, Vol. 32 (3): 705–35.

Domingo, Pilar and Rachel Sieder (eds.). 2001. *Rule of Law in Latin America: The International Promotion of Judicial Reform*. London: Institute of Latin American Studies.

Finkel, Jodi. 2008. *Judicial Reform as Political Insurance. Argentina, Peru and Mexico in the 1990s*. Notre Dame, IN: University of Notre Dame Press.

García-Villegas, Mauricio. 2002. *Normas de Papel: La Cultura de Incumplimiento de las Reglas*. Bogotá, DeJusticia/Siglo del Hombre Editores.

García-Villegas, Mauricio and César A. Rodríguez-Garavito (eds.). 2003. *Derecho y Sociedad en América Latina: Un Debate Sobre los Estudios Jurídicos Críticos*. Bogotá: ILSA/Universidad Nacional de Colombia.

Gauri, Varun and Dan Brinks (eds). 2010. *Courting Social Justice: Judicial Enforcement of Social and Economic Rights in the Developing World*. Cambridge and New York: Cambridge University Press.

Ginsburg, Tom. 2003. *Judicial Review in New Democracies: Constitutional Courts in Asian Cases*. New York: Cambridge University Press.

Gloppen, Siri, Bruce Wilson, Roberto Gargarella, Elin Skaar, and Morten Kinander. 2010. *Courts and Power in Latin America and Africa*. New York: Palgrave Macmillan.

Halliday, Terence. 2013. "Why the legal complex is integral to theories of consequential courts." In Diana Kapiszewski, Gordon Silverstin, and Robert A Kagan, (eds.), *Consequential Courts: Judicial Roles in Global Perspective*. New York: Cambridge University Press: 337–48.

Helmke, Gretchen. 2005. *Courts under Constraints: Judges, Generals, and Presidents in Argentina*. New York: Cambridge University Press.

Helmke, Gretchen and Julio Ríos-Figueroa (eds). 2011. *Courts in Latin America*. Cambridge and New York: Cambridge University Press.

Hernández, Aida Rosalva. 2016. *Multiple InJustices: Indigenous Women, Law, and Political Struggle in Latin America*. Tucson, AZ: Arizona University Press.

Hilbink, Lisa. 2007. *Judges Beyond Politics in Democracy and Dictatorship: Lessons from Chile*. Cambridge and New York: Cambridge University Press.

Ibarra Rojas, Lucero. 2018. "América Latina y la mirada socio-jurídica del Instituto Internacional de Sociología Jurídica de Oñati (IISJ)". *Oñati Socio-legal Series* [online], forthcoming. Available from: http://ssrn.com/abstract=3124993 Consulted December 10, 2018.

Isunza Vera, Ernesto and Alberto Olvera (eds.). 2010. *Democratización, Rendición de Cuentas y Sociedad Civil: Participación Ciudadana y Control Social*. Mexico City: CIESAS.

Kapiszewski, Diana. 2012. *High Courts and Economic Governance in Argentina and Brazil*. New York: Cambridge University Press.

Keck, Margaret and Kathyrn Sikkink. 1998. *Activists Beyond Borders: Advocacy Networks in International Politics*. Ithaca, New York: Cornell University Press.

Langford, Malcolm, César Rodríguez-Garavito, and Julieta Rossi (eds.). 2017. *Social Rights Judgements and the Politics of Compliance. Making it Stick*. Cambridge and New York: Cambridge University Press.

Lemaitre, Julieta. 2011. "¿Constitución o barbarie? Como repensar el derecho en las zonas 'sin ley.'" En *El Derecho en América Latina*, ed. César Rodríguez-Garavito: 47–68.

Lemaitre, Julieta and Kristin Sandvik. 2015. "Shifting frames, vanishing resources, and dangerous political opportunities: legal mobilization among displaced women in Colombia." *Law & Society Review*, Vol. 49 (1): 5–38.

Mainwairing, Scott and Christopher Welna (eds.). 2003. *Democratic Accountability in Latin America*. Oxford: Oxford University Press.

Méndez, O'Donnell, Pinheiro (eds.). *The (Un)Rule of Law & the Underprivileged in Latin America*. South Bend, IN: University of Notre Dame Press.

Merrill, Calvin and Kelsey Mayo. 2015. "Charting the 'classics' in law and society. The development of the field over the past half-century." In Austin Sarat and Patricia Ewick (eds.), *The Handbook of Law and Society*. Malden MA and Oxford: Wiley Blackwell: 18–36.

Merry, Sally Engle. 2006. *Human Rights and Gender Violence: Translating International Law into Local Justice*. Chicago, IL: University of Chicago Press.

Merry, Sally and Mark Goodale (eds.). 2007. *The Practice of Human Rights: Tracking Law between the Global and the Local*. Cambridge and New York: Cambridge University Press.

Mitchell, Timothy. 1991. "Society, economy and the state effect." In George Steinmetz (ed.) *State/Culture: State Formation after the Cultural Turn*. Ithaca, Cornell University Press: 76–97.

Nader, Laura. 1990. *Harmony Ideology*. Stanford, CA: Stanford University Press.

Negretto, Gabriel. 2013. *Making Constitutions: Presidents, Parties, and Institutional Choice in Latin America*. Cambridge and New York: Cambridge University Press.

Pásara, Luis (ed.). 2007. *Los Actores de la Justicia Latinoamericana*. Salamanca: Ediciones Universidad de Salamanca.

Payne, Leigh A., Francesca Lessa, and Gabriel Pereira. 2015. "Overcoming barriers to justice in the age of human rights accountability." *Human Rights Quarterly,* Vol. 37 (3): 728–54.

Peruzzotti, Enrique and Catalina Smulovitz (eds). 2006. *Enforcing the Rule of Law. Social Accountability in the New Latin American Democracies*. Pittsburgh, PA: University of Pittsburgh Press.

Ríos-Figueroa, Julio and Jeffrey Staton, J. 2012. "An evaluation of cross-national measures of judicial independence." *The Journal of Law, Economics, and Organization*, Vol. 30 (1):104–37.

Risse-Kappen, Thomas, Stephen Ropp, and Kathryn Sikkink. 1999. *The Power of Human Rights: International Norms and Domestic Change*. New York: Cambridge University Press.

Rodríguez-Garavito, César (ed.). 2011a. *El Derecho en América Latina. Un Mapa para el Pensamiento Jurídico del Siglo XXI*, Buenos Aires: Siglo XXI editores.

Rodríguez-Garavito, César. 2011b. "Global governance, indigenous peoples, and the right to prior consultation in social minefields." *Indiana Journal of Global Legal Studies*, Vol. 18 (1): 263–305.

Rosenberg, Gerald N. 2008. *The Hollow Hope: Can Courts Bring About Social Change?* Chicago, IL: University of Chicago Press.

Salvatore, Ricardo and Carlos Aguirre (eds.). 2001. *Crime and Punishment in Latin America: Law and Society Since Late Colonial Times*. Durham, NC: Duke University Press.

Santos, Boaventura. 1995. *Towards a New Commonsense: Law, Science and Politics in the Paradigmatic Transition*. New York: Routledge.

Santos, Boaventura and Mauricio García-Villegas (eds.). 2001. *El Caleidoscopio de las Justicias en Colombia*. Bogotá: Ediciones Uniandes/Siglo del Hombre.

Santos, Boaventura and Rodríguez-Garavito, César (eds.). 2005. *Law and Globalization from Below: Towards a Cosmopolitan Legality*. Cambridge and New York: Cambridge University Press.

Schilling-Vacaflor, Almut and René Kuppe. 2012. "Plurinational constitutionalism: a new era of indigenous-state relations?" In Detlef Nolte and Almut Schilling-Vacaflor (eds), *New Constitutionalism in Latin America – Promises and Practices*. Burlington, VT: Ashgate: 347–70.

Schwarz, Carl. 1973. "Judges under the shadow: judicial independence in the United States and Mexico." *California Western International Law Journal*, Vol. 3: 260–332.

Sieder, Rachel (ed.). 2002. *Multiculturalism in Latin America: Indigenous Rights, Diversity and Democracy*. New York: Palgrave Macmillan.

Sierra, María Teresa (ed.). 2004. *Haciendo Justicia: Interlegalidad, Derecho y Género en Regiones Indígenas*. Mexico City: CIESAS/ Porrúa.

Skaar, Elin, Jemima García-Godos, and Cath Collins. 2016. *Transitional Justice in Latin America: The Uneven Road from Impunity to Accountability*. New York: Routledge.

Snodgrass Godoy, Angelica. 2006. *Popular Injustice: Violence, Community, and Law in Latin America*. Stanford, CA: Stanford University Press.

Tiscornia, Sofía (ed.). 2004. *Burocracias y Violencia. Estudios de Antropología Jurídica*. Buenos Aires: Antropofagia.

Tiscornia, Sofía, Roberto Kant de Lima, and Lucía Eibaum (eds). 2009. *Burocracias Penales, Administración Institucional de Conflictos y Ciudadanía. Experiencia Comparada entre Brasil y Argentina*. Buenos Aires: Antropofagia.

Trubek, David M, and Alvaro Santos. 2006. *The New Law and Economic Development: A Critical Appraisal*. Cambridge and New York: Cambridge University Press.

Uprimny, Rodrigo. 2016. "Justicia rutinaria y protagónica: una caracterización de la justicia colombiana." In Mauricio García-Villegas and María Adelaida Ceballos Bedoya (eds), *Democracia, Justicia y Sociedad: Diez Años de Investigación en DeJusticia*. Bogotá: DeJusticia: 181–91.

Van Cott, Donna Lee. 2000. *The Friendly Liquidation of the Past: The Politics of Diversity in Latin America*. Pittsburgh, PA: Pittsburgh University Press.

Van Cott, Donna Lee. 2008. *Radical Democracy in the Andes*. Cambridge: Cambridge University Press.

Verner, Joel. 1984. "The independence of supreme courts in Latin America: a review of the literature." *Journal of Latin American Studies*, Vol. 16 (2): 463–506.

Vilhena Vieira, Oscar. 2011. "Desigualdad estructural y estado de derecho." In *El Derecho en América Latina*, ed. César Rodríguez-Garavito: 27–46.

Wolkmer, Antonio Carlos. 2015. *Pluralismo Jurídico, Fundamentos de Uma Nova Cultura no Direito*. 4th edition. São Paulo: Saraiva.

Yamin, Alicia Ely and Siri Gloppen (eds). 2011. *Litigating Health Rights. Can Courts Bring More Justice to Health?* Harvard, MA: Harvard University Press.

Yashar, Deborah. 2005. *Contesting Citizenship in Latin America: The Rise of Indigenous Movements*. New York: Cambridge University Press.

Yrigoyen, Raquel. 2011. "El horizonte del constitucionalismo pluralista: del multiculturalismo a la descolonización." En *El Derecho en América Latina*, ed. César Rodríguez-Garavito: 139–59.

PART I

Law, Politics, and Society

2

LATIN AMERICA'S CONTRIBUTION TO CONSTITUTIONALISM

Roberto Gargarella

Introduction

Latin American constitutionalism has faced challenges and problems that have not appeared in other contexts, which makes it fertile ground for reflections on contemporary constitutional and political theory. The particularities of this history include the emergence of egalitarian constitutions in inegalitarian societies; substantial discussions about constitutional transplants and the value of "importing" foreign legal instruments; a longstanding exercise of socioeconomic rights (which is only just initiating in other areas of the world); issues of multiculturalism and indigenous rights; substantial experience with "unbalanced" versions of the system of "checks and balances" (due to the presence of so-called hyper-presidentialist regimes); and the succession of numerous and frequent constitutional changes, among several others.

Despite such richness and its potential for socio-legal studies, Latin America's constitutional history – comprising over two centuries – has not been the object of systematic academic and public attention, at least until recently. In what follows, I examine five distinguishing aspects of the region's constitutional tradition, which – I argue – correspond to five different "constitutional waves" that emerged in the region, in its 200 years of existence:

1   A first period of *constitutional experimentalism*, which emerged during the post-independence period
2   A second, *foundational period*, which took place in the mid-nineteenth century (particularly between 1850 and 1890), when the basic structure of the organization of powers was established
3   A third period of *social constitutionalism*, which was inaugurated by the Mexican 1917 Constitution and when the basic structure of the organization of rights was established
4   A fourth, *post-dictatorial period*, which emerged after the massive violation of human rights committed by Latin American governments during the late twentieth century; and finally
5   A fifth, *multicultural period*, which was consolidated at the beginning of the twenty-first century, expressed in constitutions that were for the first time opened to the needs and interests of marginalized groups, particularly those of aboriginal, or indigenous collectivities.

The chapter thus presents a periodization of Latin America's constitutional history and highlights how the political circumstances and needs of each period framed specific legal demands, generating in turn distinct institutional features. Focusing on several countries, I discuss key contributions of leading legal scholars in each of these historical periods and show that, despite regional trends in the contributions to constitutionalism, there were also significant differences between countries. Despite such differences and the specific contributions discernible for each period, I argue that Latin American constitutional history shows two major continuities: first, a power structure that is politically concentrated and territorially centralized, and; second, a generous and extensive declaration of rights that combine individual and social rights.

Experimental Constitutionalism (1810–1850)

In chapter 2 of his most influential work, *Bases and Starting Points for the Political Organization of the Argentine Republic* (1852), Argentina's principal legal and political theorist Juan Bautista Alberdi defined the first constitutions of the region in the following terms:

> What are, of what consists, the obstacles contained in the first Constitutions? All of the Constitutions that came out of South America during the war of independence were the complete expression of the prevailing need of the times. This need was ending the political power that Europe had exercised over the continent, starting with the conquest and continuing with colonialism: and as a means to ensure its complete extinction, this need meant going as far as denying Europe any type of superiority whatsoever in these countries. Independence and external freedom were the vital interests that preoccupied the legislators at the time.
>
> *(Alberdi 1981, 26)[1]*

This original, initial period of constitutionalism was fundamentally aimed at the consolidation of independence, which explains the abundance of institutional features meant to concentrate power as a means of ensuring order and stability. It was, without doubt, the time of greatest experimentation in the region's constitutional history, and although with a wide variation among institutions, all aimed to recapture power and achieve order. Those attempts included atypical and short-lived attempts such as that of "Moral Power," which Simon Bolivar presented at the Congress of Angostura in 1819 (later invoked by the 1999 Venezuelan Constitution); the "Moderating Power" approach à la Benjamin Constant attempted in Brazil in 1824, in Nicaragua in 1826, in Mexico in 1836, and implicit in the Moral Code and the "Visiting Senators" (moral guardians) put forward in 1823 by Juan Egaña in Chile. We also see forays that are decidedly corporatist, for example, Senates composed of clergy, military officers, large landowners, and industrialists, such as the proposals of Lucas Alaman in Mexico (1834), those incorporated into the 1919 Argentine Constitution; monarchist experiments such as those launched early on by Manuel Belgrano in Argentina, or carried out by Agustín Iturbide in Mexico in 1821 (Mexico would briefly experiment with this again in 1863); the "three-headed" executive system studied at an early stage in Venezuela and Peru; and ultra-federalist attempts evident in, for example, the 1863 Colombian Constitution.

In sum, this period was characterized by constitutional proposals that were more ambitious, imaginative, and varied than what would come later.

The Foundational Period and the Consolidation of (Hyper-)Presidentialism (1851–1917)

In the mid-nineteenth century a crucial political movement took place in Latin America, arising from the gradual but resolute rapprochement of liberal and conservative forces that, until then, had waged bloody battles against each other in most of the countries of the region.[2] In some, such as Argentina, Brazil, or Mexico, the coming together of these two sides occurred through direct negotiation of the constitution, with the two opposing forces together, sitting at the same table. In others, such as Chile, the pact acquired "deferred" aspects when the "hard" constitutional conservatism embodied in the 1833 Constitution began to "thaw," giving way to gradual liberalization. In Colombia, the opposite occurred: the "hard" constitutional liberalism imposed by successive constitutions in 1853, 1858, and 1863 began to lose strength, opening the way for increasing conservatism that was consolidated in the 1866 Constitution (Gargarella 2010, 2013).

This period is especially important because it was when the structure to organize power, territorial organization, and rights recognition was established in the most significant of the region's constitutional orders; structures that endure to the present. Once the liberal-conservative pact was consolidated, much of the initial experimentation ended: decidedly corporatist attempts at constitutional engineering were dropped; monarchist experiments tailed off too; "three-headed" executives disappeared; and institutions such as the "Moral Power," "Moderating Power," and "Visiting Senators" vanished from the constitutional map.

From the mid-nineteenth century onwards constitutional proposals became more defined and less open to structural experimentation; margins of experimentation subsequently became much narrower. Regardless of the specific institutional arrangement in each country, all of them emerged from the tension and negotiation between liberals and conservatives, which defined the period. The liberal-conservative pact thus determined the general structure of constitutional power; stabilized through a system of "checks and balances" this ultimately "unbalanced" relations in favor of the Executive.

Something similar can be seen in the area of territorial organization with the tension between centralism and federalism. Moreover, with regards to rights, the main question was how to integrate the demands of liberals and conservatives, historically opposed because of the religious factor. The formulas for integration chosen at the time were diverse, and in most cases left much to be desired. They ranged from maintaining silence on the matter, the option favored by the Mexican constituent assembly in 1857 – which omitted the demands of both groups – to double invocation and direct superposition of the demands of both sides, for which the Argentines constituents inclined in 1853 (establishing religious tolerance in Art. 14 and special status for the Catholic Church in Art. 2).

Both liberals and conservatives feared anarchy and unbridled majoritarianism above all else, so it was not difficult for the two sides to agree on the need for constitutional provisions to curb the (increasingly) menacing power of the majority. The constitution was thus based on a strong principle of "mistrust" of majoritarian power – a coincidence that is without doubt very forceful in explaining the motives and nature of the legal arrangements made in this period, manifest in the counter-majoritarian organization of power that concentrated authority in the Executive and cemented elitist measures of selection for both senate and judiciary.

A similar dynamic reemerged in the area of rights: liberals and conservatives agreed on the need to limit political rights, at least for the time being, in the aim of preserving other rights – particularly those related to property, contracts, and free trade – which they saw as threatened by the expansion of majority rule. In his work *The Economic and Renter System*, Alberdi demanded freedoms that were "unlimited and very abundant for our people," among which he included "civil liberties" such as the "*economic freedoms to acquire, sell, work, navigate, trade, transport and exercise any industry*" (Alberdi 1920, 64–5). Similar demands were echoed by the liberal José María Samper of Colombia, especially at the time of the 1886 Constitution, Samper 1861, 1893, or by Andrés Bello of Chile. Bello, primarily engaged in drafting the Civil Code, justified his position arguing that:

people are less apprehensive for the preservation of their political freedom than their civil rights.... Rarely is a man so devoid of egoism that he prefers the exercise of any political rights conceded by the fundamental code of the State to the preservation and maintenance of their interests and existence, or that he would feel more injured when arbitrarily deprived of, for example, the right of suffrage, than when he is violently stripped of his property.

(Jaksic 2001, 212)

The second thing to highlight is the curious formula for organizing power chosen by the architects of the liberal-conservative pact: this involved a partial overlap between the demands of liberals – a system of *checks and balances* following the American style – and those of conservatives – a system organized around the Executive. The chosen scheme involved "opening" a deep "wound," in a model that held balance itself as its organizing principle.[3] By disrupting the balance at the outset, tilting the organization of power in favor of the Executive (proposed by Alberdi, who argued in favor of combining the American and the Chilean models), the rationale of the system of checks and balances that gave the system its meaning and appeal was, from the first moment, directly jeopardized. Many of the persistent problems affecting the health of Latin American institutions are related to that normatively dubious initial decision so difficult to justify. Despite its shortcomings, the general structure contained lessons that subsequent constitutional theorists would systematically disregard: namely that the concern for certain fundamental rights (say, to private property or contracts) does not necessary imply the inclusion of long list of rights in the constitution. Rather, it demands certain guarantees regarding the organization of power – in this case, restrictions on the political capacities of the majority who threaten those rights.

In sum, this peculiar model of (unbalanced) checks and balances, which wanted to combine the Spanish monarchical/conservative constitutional model with the United States liberal model, represents Latin America's principle contribution to constitutionalism.

The Era of Social Constitutionalism (1917–1950)

Between 1850 and 1890 Latin American constitutionalism was defined not only by what was explicitly included in the magna cartas, but also by what was left out. The exclusion or relegation of the "social question" is central to any analysis of the first period of Latin American constitutionalism. Colonial and postcolonial political inequalities produced what Argentine historian Tulio Halperin Dongi defined as a dominant model of "progressive authoritarianism" – a "blend of political rigor and economic activism" (1980, XXXI). This "progressive authoritarianism" reflected the increasing levels of coercion and political repression that began to characterize the region in the late nineteenth century. These tensions exploded early in the following century, forcing the ruling elite to provide immediate answers to the demands it had hitherto postponed. The responses, which would became more explicit and emphatic with the *1930 crisis*, took different and very significant forms, ranging from the passage from "Regulatory State" to "Welfare State" in some countries, to the adoption of more open political systems in others (the examples of Juan Domingo Perón's government in Argentina and Getulio Vargas' government in Brazil stand as the main illustrations of the development of a strong welfare state in Latin America). At the constitutional level, the overwhelming response was the emergence of *social constitutionalism*, entailing the introduction of comprehensive lists of social, political, cultural, and economic rights in the constitution.

The earliest and most significant illustration of social constitutionalism was Mexico, where the crisis reached dramatic levels, first expressed in a successful revolutionary movement, and, soon after, in a very pertinent constitutional reform that resulted in the 1917 Constitution. This 1917 Constitution was exceptionally long, robust in its declaration of rights, and strongly committed to social rights, which was at the time a complete novelty. In fact, the Mexican Constitution was a global pioneer of *social constitutionalism*. This accompanied the enactment of the Constitution of the Republic of Weimar, in 1919; the creation of the International Labor Organization (ILO) (ILO 1919); and the development of the Welfare State and the Keynesian economic model. Among many other clauses, the Mexican Constitution included Art. 27, which declared that the ownership of lands and waters within the boundaries of national territory were "vested originally in the Nation"; and Art. 123, which incorporated wide protections for workers and recognized the role of trade unions; regulated labor relations reaching very detailed issues, which in a way covered most of the topics that later came to distinguish modern Labor Law, such as working hours; child labor; the rights of pregnant women; the minimum wage; the right to vacation; the right to equal wages; health and safety conditions; labor accidents; the right to strike and lockout; arbitrations; dismissals without cause; social security; and the right to association. The 1917 Mexican Constitution decisively changed the history of Latin American constitutionalism. Since its adoption, most countries in the region gradually began to change their basic constitutional structure. Following Mexico's early example, most began to include a long list of social rights in their constitutions: Bolivia modified its constitution to this effect in 1938; Cuba in 1940; Uruguay in 1942; Ecuador and Guatemala in 1945; and Costa Rica in 1949.

Among the new expressions of Latin American social constitutionalism, the examples of Argentina and Brazil became particularly influential. At the same time, both these cases properly illustrate the peculiar character of this new constitutional wave, which combined generous social clauses with remnants of the old model, of ahighly-concentrated organization of power. In Argentina, political leader Juan Domingo Perón became the main proponent of these new changes toward social constitutionalism. Perón had been one of the key figures during the government of General Farrell, who had come to power in 1943, through a military coup. Perón became the Secretary of Labor of Dictator General Farrell, a position from where he strengthened his contacts with the trade unions, and promoted numerous labor laws, which favored the interests of the working class and the labor movement. Later Perón was elected to the presidency. During his mandate, distinguished by its concentration of powers and authoritarianism, Perón insisted on the importance of guaranteeing that the "economically disadvantaged" were "protected from the egoism, prepotency and exploitation of the economically strong" (Sampay 1975, 478; Perón 2008). Those social commitments were assumed in the 1949 constitution, which was enormously influential in the region, despite its short life.

In Brazil, President Getulio Vargas led the drive toward social constitutionalism. During his years in government, Vargas promoted the enactment of two constitutions. The first in 1934 – the more innovative of the two because it represented a significant rupture concerning the traditional Brazilian political-constitutional structure (Bercovici 2009). The second, sanctioned in 1937, accompanied the creation of the *Estado Novo* and contributed to strengthening the powers of the Executive. Again, as in the case of Argentina, social constitutionalism came hand in hand with the creation of a strong presidentialist and authoritarian regime.

The new socially oriented constitutions in Latin America became an expression of the social change that had taken place in the region during the first half of the twentieth century, namely the incorporation of the working class as a decisive political and economic actor. The correspondent constitutional innovation was the incorporation of generous, detailed, and robust lists of social rights.

From Anti-Presidentialism to Human Rights (1980–2000)

During the 1970s, numerous Latin American countries lost their democratic character and fell under the rule of dictatorial governments. Democracy would prevail again only after a decade or more.[4] The long decade of dictatorial rule had two important constitutional consequences: the first has to do with a constitutional discussion around *hyper-presidentialism* and the extent of Executive powers. The second has to do with *international human rights law* and, particularly, the importance acquired by human right treaties in political environments.

The first discussion emerged at the end of the authoritarian wave and concerned hyper-presidentialist systems. For the first time during those years, many legal and political science scholars seemed to agree on a basic point, namely that there was a causal relation between hyper-presidentialism and the pattern of political instability that had characterized the region's public life during the entire century. For the first time, activists and scholars from different countries and positions agreed in their critique of a central aspect of the dominant organization of power (Nino 1987; Linz and Stepan 1978; Linz and Valenzuela 1994). According to Carlos Nino, for example, "the diagnosis of the time was that a crucial, although not the only factor, explaining the fragility of [the institutional system] was a presidential system that had grown excessively" (Nino 1992b, 38). For Nino, as for many others, it was clear that in a hyper-presidentialist regime, the president concentrated too much power, too many responsibilities and too may expectations in his/her own figure, during a fixed term. Consequently, any sudden change in the people's attitudes toward the president or his/her popularity, as well as any significant crisis, tended to put the entire political system under stress. Any political or economic crisis thus, became transformed into a systemic crisis. Still worse, given the lack of "escape valves" in the system, the removal of the president tended to appear as the only way out of the crisis. Given these assumptions, the parliamentary alternative appeared to pose an alternative distribution of political power and different "escape valves" (Ackerman 2000; Linz and Valenzuela 1994). Unfortunately, these theoretical reflections that gained so much attention within academic circles were promptly abandoned.[5]

While this constitutional discussion focused on the organic part of the constitution, the second was directed toward the dogmatic part, or the declarations of rights. After the human rights atrocities committed by the military regimes, Latin American politicians and legal scholars began, for the first time, to seriously pay attention to the introduction of human rights reforms in their respective legal systems.[6] For a variety of reasons, those reforms had been delayed or dismissed for decades: for many, discussions about human rights were a waste of time because they were merely superstructural issues. Yet given the cruelties imposed by the military regimes most people began to recognize the importance of establishing legal barriers against torture or mass killings (see, for example, the constitutional reforms in Chile of 1980 or Brazil of 1988).

Such initiatives expressed the reconciliation of certain parts of the left with the discourse of rights in particular, and with constitutional law in general. Moreover, many constitutions granted human rights a new legal status, which produced an interesting effect among conservative sectors of the judiciary. For the first time many conservative judges began to take arguments based on the value of human rights, seriously.

During these years of transition to democracy, several countries began to initiate the investigation, prosecution, and punishment of those responsible for gross violations of human rights committed by dictatorial governments (Sikkink 2012; Acuña and Smulovitz 1996). Argentina, Brazil, Bolivia, Colombia, Costa Rica, Chile, and El Salvador were among the many countries that followed that route, attempting to ensure more protections for the rights most negatively affected by the recent authoritarian governments. In addition, many Latin American countries decided to incorporate international law into their domestic systems, mainly by granting special status to such norms. In some of them, such as Argentina and Bolivia, human rights treaties were explicitly awarded the status of constitutional laws. In others, such as Costa Rica or El Salvador, treaties were awarded supra-legal status (Rossi and Filippini 2010). Some constitutions, like those of Peru or Colombia, included interpretive clauses in their texts, incorporating specific references to international law. Others, like Brazil's 1988 Constitution, refer to the existence of non-enumerated rights, among which are those related to principles and treaties to which Brazil is party. Guatemala's 1985 Constitution makes reference to international human rights law by establishing guidelines for the country's foreign policy, while Chile's constitution assigns special duties in the area of human rights for all state agencies (for more on these and other alternatives of incorporation, see Dulitzky 1998).

Multicultural Rights/Indigenous Rights. Constitutionalism in the Twenty-First Century

The most recent phase of development in Latin American constitutionalism occurred in the late twentieth century. Reforms included texts of distinct character, but here I focus my attention principally on Venezuela (1999), Ecuador (2008), and Bolivia (2009). Although these constitutions did not involve the introduction of substantive changes in relation to the documents that preceded them, they significantly expanded the existing lists of rights. This was accomplished, above all, by the incorporation of concern for the rights of the most disadvantaged sectors of society namely, sexual minorities, ethnic minorities, and particularly indigenous communities.[7] If the first wave of constitutional reforms in the twentieth century was distinguished by its emphasis on the "social question," this latest wave of reforms was characterized by its emphasis on the "indigenous question." For the first time, Latin American constitutionalism addressed an issue that had been largely invisible since the founding of the postcolonial republics.[8] A crucial step in the direction of constitutionalizing indigenous rights occurred in 1987 in Nicaragua, following the conflict that confronted the Sandinista government with indigenous Miskitos.[9] The Nicaraguan Constitution was modified in order to include numerous references to the rights of the indigenous peoples – including their right to maintain, exploit, and enjoy the fruits of their communal properties. The Guatemalan Constitution of 1985 dedicated Section III of its text to indigenous communities, and made reference to respect for indigenous' language, habits, and traditions (Art. 66). It also included protections of their lands and agrarian cooperatives (Arts. 67 and 68); and references to their right not to be discriminated against (Art. 69). The 1988 Constitution of Brazil also showed some openness toward the "indigenous question," in particular including special protections reserved for indigenous groups in Chapter VIII of the text. These pioneer cases were then followed by the *Convenio 169* enacted by the ILO. The advent of this covenant, which became the principle international instrument in support of demands by indigenous groups, substantially changed legal discussion on the subject. The agreement included clauses granting respect for the culture, way of life and institutions of indigenous peoples. It also referred to the right to prior consultation of indigenous peoples, in the case of any legal or administrative measure that might affect them.

After the enactment of the *Convenio 169*, a new wave of constitutions emerged, which addressed the indigenous question. The new documents included complete lists of indigenous rights and adopted favorable stances toward legal pluralism. Among these new constitutions were those of Colombia, 1991; Paraguay, 1992; Argentina and Bolivia, 1994; Ecuador 1996 (and 1998); Mexico 1992 and 2001, and Venezuela, 1999. These documents defined the State as multicultural or pluricultural (as in the cases of Colombia, Peru, Bolivia, and Ecuador);

guaranteed the right to cultural diversity (Colombia and Peru); and/or proclaimed the equality of cultures (Colombia and Venezuela). In this way, these new constitutions challenged the inherited monocultural model that had predominated in the region since the nineteenth century (Yrigoyen Fajardo 2011, 132).

This new wave of constitutions was followed by significant social struggles for the implementation of the new rights, and in 2007 the Assembly of the United Nations enacted the universal Declaration on the Rights of Indigenous Peoples, which became a crucial and foundational event in international law. The Declaration gave a detailed account of the individual and collective rights of indigenous peoples, and established basic, minimum standards that all the States promised to respect. It also made reference to the rights related to issues such as cultural identity, education, employment, and language. It also guaranteed indigenous peoples' right to be different, and also referred to their right to economic, social, and cultural development. The United Nations (UN) document was then followed by a new set of constitutions, which codified additional advances; those of Ecuador 2008 and Bolivia 2009.[10] Both of these charters incorporated numerous articles trying to address the problems affecting indigenous communities in their respective countries. Both countries declared themselves "pluri-national States" (Art. 1 of their respective constitutions); recognized indigenous peoples' rights to use their own language (Bolivia's Constitution, in its Art. 5, considered the language of ethnic minorities to be official languages); made reference to the existence of collective rights, which included the right of indigenous peoples to "maintain the possession of lands of ancestral territories" (Ecuador's Constitution, Art. 51); and opened their legal systems to indigenous communities' rights to develop jurisdictional functions, according to their traditions (Ecuador's Constitution, Art. 171), among others. Most notably, both constitutions made reference to the indigenous principle of "good living," *buen vivir,* or *sumak kawsay* (Bolivia, Art. 8, Ecuador, Arts. 275–279), an interpretative principle aimed at defining a new and more respectful relationship between human beings and nature, and at constituting an alternative to dominant, consumerist, and profit-oriented Western culture.

This overemphasis on the incorporation of new rights that has characterized Latin American constitutionalism over the last decades, however, does not mark the dawning of a "new kind" of Latin American constitutionalism. Conversely, the so-called "new constitutionalism" simply reinforces certain features *already very much present* in the constitutional framework of Latin America.[11] After the last waves of reforms, in fact, we find that: (i) the organic part of the new constitutions is still characterized by a power structure politically concentrated and territorially centralized and, at the same time; (ii) the dogmatic part of the new constitutions is still characterized by its generous and extensive declaration of rights, which combine individual and social rights of various kinds. In sum, in the same way that it is important to highlight the interesting contribution of recent Latin American constitutional thought, particularly with respect to indigenous rights, it is important to underline that, in the end, the two main features that began to characterize Latin American constitutionalism in the early twentieth century have remained as vigorous as ever.

Conclusions

In the preceding pages, I identified several important issues that help us identify the distinctive features of the regional constitutionalism. A relatively short-lived initial period of "experimentation" was followed by a liberal-conservative consensus reached in the mid-nineteenth century, a pact that clearly manifested itself in the constitutional organization of power. Ever since, a particular institutional structure has been maintained in Latin America in which power is territorially concentrated and inclined toward the Executive branch. This scheme seems to be based above all on a general distrust of the general population – the meeting point facilitating the liberal-conservative pact – which has resulted in political systems that, with certain exceptions, generally discourage citizen participation as well as the various forms of popular control and decision-making. At the same time, the liberal-conservative model has created difficulties for legislatures to function independently of the Executive and judicial branches that are regularly threatened by the enormous capacity of the ruling party (usually expressed in the Executive) to intervene in its affairs.

The other fundamental constitutional change signaled here took shape a century later, particularly in the mid-twentieth century, when some of the demands associated with the "social question" that the leaders of the liberal-conservative pact had decided to postpone were integrated into the existing structure. Significant changes were made to the declarations of rights typical of the nineteenth century: today, the old lists of "classical liberal rights" have been appended to include broad commitments to social, economic, and cultural rights.

The importance of what has changed this century does not, however, match the importance of what has not changed: the old-fashioned power structures that enshrine concentrated power as well as the highly-restricted access to popular participation in politics. It is within this framework that the "new" regional constitutionalism was produced. Once again, what stands out most of all are the continuities. After the introduction of the latest reforms, Latin American constitutions have not substantially changed their traditional, basic structure: they still have highly centralized organization of powers, like the ones that were established during the "foundational period" and they still exhibit long and strong declarations of rights, like the ones that were introduced during the period of "social constitutionalism." In other words, the "engine room" of most Latin American constitutions – this is to say their organization of powers – remained basically untouched after more than 200 years of constitutionalism and the introduction of significant novelties at the level of rights.[12] More specifically, the "new" concerns expressed by Latin American constitutions in the twentieth century, regarding social rights, human rights, multicultural rights, participation, and democracy, have not permeated the "old" distribution and organization of power. As a consequence, those scholars and activists interested in the promotion of substantive constitutional changes in Latin American constitutions would be advised to concentrate their energies in promoting changes at the level of the "engine room" of those constitutions. How could and should the organizations of powers be modified in order to make them consistent with present, shared concerns related to human rights and democracy?

Yet despite the criticisms that we can formulate against regional constitutionalism, it also seems clear that it has developed in a rich and fruitful fashion. Despite the more than 200 constitutional reforms produced over the course of 200 years, the picture is not one of "constitutional chaos" – where each new constitution sought to establish a totally new paradigm – but rather of a set of constitutions that have moved creatively and with innovative proposals within channels that ultimately can be traced back to the original constitutional projects at the beginning of the region's history of constitutionalism.

Notes

1 These early responses, Alberdi recognized, had been adequate in formulating that *against which* the constitutions should be conceived: "All the ills of America were thus comprised of and defined by its dependence on a conquering government belonging to Europe: by consequence all remedy for their ills were seen in removing the influence of Europe" (ibid.).

2 The question surrounding the reasons for the liberal-conservative pact – its process of progressive con-fluence or *fusion* – after decades of armed conflict must still be answered with precision. Some might say that the change was due to the threatening (albeit fleeting) presence of radicalized groups (above all in Colombia, Peru, and Chile) following the 1848 "red revolutions" in Europe. Others might point, however, to the concern for self-subsistence and awareness of the costs that continued hostility imposed on both sides. For the time being, I will leave the question open in order to concentrate directly on the examination of how the pact translated into the constitutional domain yet adding, in any case, that the pact gradually spread across the region between 1850 and the close of the century.

3 It is possible to raise many objections to the scheme for the organization of power proposed at the time by James Madison, yet regardless the objections, his scheme purported to follow the distinctive virtue of balance between powers based on the attribution of relatively equal power to each of the distinct branches of government.

4 In Argentina, General Jorge Rafael Videla led a military government that remained in power from 1976 to 1983. Brazil suffered a military coup in 1964, and the new dictatorial government endured until 1985. In Chile, General Augusto Pinochet carried out a military coup against the socialist govern-ment of Salvador Allende, and ruled the country between 1973 and 1984. In Bolivia, General Hugo Banzer led a military government between 1971 and 1978. Uruguay also had military and civic-military governments during the period, at least between 1973 and 1984. General Alfredo Stroessner governed Paraguay under military rule for 35 years, between 1954 and 1989. In Nicaragua, Anastasio Somoza and his successors ruled the country until their overthrow in 1979. In Peru, albeit with a more «social» orientation, Dictator General Juan Velasco Alvarado governed the country between 1968 and 1975.

5 The movement against the hyper-presidentialist system began to lose force after the 1980s: numerous academics challenged the alleged link between hyper-presidentialism and democratic instability (Cheibub and Limongi 2002; Eaton 2000; Linz and Valenzuela 1994; Nino 1987, 1992; Przeworski et al. 2000; Samuel and Eaton 2002; Shugart and Carey 1992; Shugart and Mainwaring 1997). The other, probably more significant element explaining the gradual fading of the anti-presidentialist drive had to do with the harsh economic crisis that followed a period of "structural" (or neoliberal) "adjustments" during the 1990s. In effect, the crisis that dominated the region during those years did not end with the classical military coups of the previous decades, even though it still provoked a profound institutional crisis involving massive social mobilization and collective distress. Paradoxically, however, many people read this in an opposite fashion, considering that Latin Americans had finally learned to deal with pro-found crisis through democratic politics as opposed to military intervention. At the same time, many began to demand a strengthening of presidential authority, in the face of the "authority vacuum" or "political chaos" that seemed to affect so many countries in the region in the wake of the crisis. Although democratic politics had failed to address the social crisis, ultimately developments served to vindicate strong presidential authority.

6 The extended character of the violations of human rights was related to many factors, but the existence of the so-called National Security Doctrine was particularly important. This emerged during the time of the Cold War, on the initiative of the US, which trained many of the region's future military strong men in the School of the Americas. The Doctrine called on the armed forces to focus their work on national security to prevent the growth and expansion of leftist ideologies. This in turn contributed to new military governments using the coercive powers of the State against their own population in the name of a war against communism.

7 The tendency across the region has been to expand constitutional protections of rights. According to a recent study by Gargarella, Filippini and Cavana (2011), current Latin American constitution's guaran-tee, among other rights, the protection of gender equality (Argentina Art. 37; Bolivia Arts. 11, 15, 26; Colombia Art. 40; Costa Rica Art. 95; Ecuador Art. 65; Nicaragua Art. 48; Paraguay Art. 48; Domini-can Republic Art. 39; and Venezuela Art. 88); affirm the existence of a pluri- or multicultural State or national identity (Bolivia, Colombia, Ecuador, and Paraguay, Art. 1 in all cases; Mexico Art. 2; Nica-ragua Art. 5; Peru Art. 2 inc. Art. 19; Venezuela Art. 6); give protection to the environment (Argentina Art. 41; Bolivia Art. 33; Brazil Art. 22; Chile Art. 19 inc. Art. 8; Colombia Art. 79; Costa Rica Art. 50; Ecuador Art. 14; El Salvador Art. 117; Guatemala Art. 97; Honduras Art. 143; Mexico Art. 4; Nicara-gua Art. 60; Panama Art. 118; Paraguay Art. 7; Peru Art. 2; Dominican Republic Art. 66; Uruguay Art. 47; and Venezuela Art. 117); Culture (Argentina Art. 75 inc. Art. 22; Bolivia Arts. 21, 30; Brazil Art. 23; Chile Art. 19 inc. Art. 10; Colombia Art. 70; Costa Rica Art. 77 y sigs.; Ecuador Art. 21; El Salvador Art. 53; Guatemala Art. 57; Honduras Art. 151; Mexico Art. 4; Nicaragua Art. 58; Panama

Art. 80; Paraguay Art. 73; Peru Art. 2; Dominican Republic Art. 64; and Venezuela Art. 101); establish health rights (Argentina Art. 75 inc Art. 22; Bolivia Art. 18; Brazil Art. 6; Chile Art. 19 inc. Art. 10; Colombia Art. 49; Costa Rica Art. 46; Ecuador Art. 32; El Salvador Art. 1; Guatemala Art. 93; Honduras Art. 145; Mexico Art. 4; Nicaragua Art. 59; Panama Art. 109; Paraguay Art. 68; Peru Art. 7; Dominican Republic Art. 61; and Venezuela Art. 83); education rights (Argentina Art. 75 inc. Art. 22; Bolivia Art. 17; Brazil Art. 6; Chile Art. 19 inc. Art. 9; Colombia Art. 67; Costa Rica Art. 77 y sigs.; Ecuador Art. 27; El Salvador Art. 53; Guatemala Art. 71; Honduras Art. 153; Mexico Art. 3; Nicaragua Art. 58; Panama Art. 91; Paraguay Art. 73; Peru Art. 13; Dominican Republic Art. 63; Uruguay Arts. 70, 71; and Venezuela Art. 102); the right to food (Argentina Art. 75 inc. Art. 22; Bolivia Art. 16; Brazil Art. 6; Colombia Art. 44; Costa Rica Art. 82; Ecuador Art. 13; Guatemala Art. 99; Honduras Art. 123; Mexico Art. 4; Nicaragua Art. 63; Panama Art. 56; Paraguay Art. 57; Dominican Republic Art. 54; Uruguay Art. 46; and Venezuela Art. 305); and housing rights (Argentina Art. 75 inc. Art. 22; Bolivia Art. 19; Brazil Art. 6; Colombia Art. 51; Costa Rica Art. 65; Ecuador Art. 30; El Salvador Art. 119; Guatemala Art. 118; Honduras Art. 178; Mexico Art. 4; Nicaragua Art. 64; Panama Art. 117; Paraguay Art. 100; Dominican Republic Art. 59; Uruguay Art. 45; and Venezuela Art. 82); etc.

8 According to researcher Raquel Yrigoyen Fajardo, Constitutional Law has historically offered three main responses to the "indigenous question," namely: (i) "assimilation or attempts to convert *Indians* in *citizens* … so as to prevent their violent uprising"; (ii) "civilization and Christianization … of those deemed 'savage,' so as to favor the broadening of the agricultural frontiers"; and (iii) "offensive or defensive wars against the Indian nations … in order to annex their territories to the State" (Yrigoyen Fajardo 2011, 126).

9 However, there was a first movement in that direction in the Guatemalan Constitution of 1985, which made reference to the rights that peoples and communities had to their cultural identity.

10 Among other relevant constitutional provisions – provisions that had their predecessors in Convention 169 of the ILO 1989 – some of the following can be cited: (i) the Constitutions of Argentina (Art. 75.17), Bolivia (Arts. 30–6 y 394 III); Ecuador (Art. 57.4), Nicaragua (Art. 5), Panama (Art. 123), Paraguay (Art. 64), Peru (Arts. 88 y 89) and Venezuela (Art. 119), similar to the Constitution of Bolivia (Arts. 30.6 y 394, III), recognized the right of indigenous peoples to the property of the land that they had traditionally inhabited. Those of Bolivia (Arts. 30.17 y 171.1), Brazil (Art. 231.2), Mexico (Art. 2. A. VI), and Nicaragua (Arts. 89 y 180), consecrated the rights of use and enjoyment of natural resources to indigenous peoples; (ii) those of Argentina (Art. 75.17), Bolivia (Arts. 30.16 y 402), Colombia (Art. 330), and Ecuador (Art. 57.6), affirmed their right to participate in the exploitation of specific natural resources; (iii) finally, and maybe most interestingly for the purposes of our discussion, some constitutions established the right of consultation regarding natural resources for the indigenous peoples. In the case of Bolivia, for non-renewable natural resources (Art. 30.15), in Brazil, for hydraulic and mining resources (Art. 231.3), in Ecuador, for natural, non-renewable resources (Art. 57.7), and in Venezuela, for all the existing natural resources in native habitats (Art. 120) (Aguilar et al. 2010).

11 For alternative views, arguing that the wave of recent reforms radically changed the landscape of Latin American constitutionalism see, for instance, Pisarello 2010 and 2011; Pastor and Dalmau 2009 and 2011. Discussing these views see, for instance, Couso 2013.

12 I explore this issue in Gargarella (2013).

References

Ackerman, B. (2000), "The New Separation of Powers," 113 *Harvard L. Rev.*, 634–42.

Acuña, C. and Smulovitz, C. (1996), "Adjusting the Armed Forces to Democracy. Successes, Failures and Ambiguities in the Southern Cone," in E. Jelin and E. Herschberg, *Constructing Democracy. Human Rights, Citizenship and Society in Latin America*, Boulder, Colorado.

Aguilar, G., LaFosse, S., Rojas, H., and Steward, R. (2010), "Análisis Comparado del Reconocimiento Constitucional de los Pueblos Indígenas en América Latina," *SSRC, Conflict Prevention and Peace Forum*.

Alberdi, J.B. (1981), *Bases y puntos de partida para la organización política de la República Argentina*, Plus Ultra: Buenos Aires.

Alegre, M. (2009), "Democracy without Presidents," Available at: www.law.yale.edu/documents/pdf/Democracy_without_Presidents.pdf. Accessed November 17, 2017.

Cheibub, J. and Limongi, F. (2002), "Modes of Government Formation and the Survival of Democratic Regimes: Presidentialism and Parliamentarism Reconsidered" *Annual Review of Political Science*, 5: 151–79.

Couso, J. (2013), "Las democracias radicales y el nuevo constitucionalismo latinoamericano," paper presented at the Seminario Latinoamericano *SELA*, organized by Yale University. Available at: www.law.yale.edu/system/files/documents/pdf/sela/SELA13_Couso_CV_Sp_20130420.pdf. Accessed November 17, 2017.

Dulitzky, A. (1998), "La aplicación de los tratados sobre derechos humanos por los tribunales locales: un estudio comparado," en M. Abregú & C. Courtis, comp., *La aplicación de los tratados internacionales sobre derechos humanos por los tribunales locales*, Buenos Aires: Del Puerto-PNUD.

Eaton, K. (2000), "Parliamentarism versus Presidentialism in the Policy Arena," *Comparative Politics*, 355–76.

Gargarella, R., Filippini, L., and Cavana, A. (2011), *Recientes reformas constitucionales en América, Latina,* Reporte UNDP.

Gargarella, R. (2010), *The Legal Foundations of Inequality*, Cambridge: Cambridge University Press.

Gargarella, R. (2013), *Latin American Constitutionalism, 1810–2010*, Oxford: Oxford University Press.

Halperin Donghi, T. (1980), *Design and Construction of a Nation*, Caracas: Biblioteca Ayacucho.

Jaksic, A., (2001), *Andrés Bello. La pasión por el orden*, Santiago de Chile: Editorial Universitaria.

Linz, J. and Stepan, A. (1978), *The Breakdown of Democratic Regimes*, Baltimore: The Johns Hopkins University Press.

Linz, J. and Valenzuela, A. (1994), *The Failure of Presidential Democracy*, Baltimore: The Johns Hopkins University Press.

Nino, C. (1987), ed., *Presidentialism vs. Parliamentarism*, Buenos Aires: Council for the Consolidation of Democracy.

Nino, C. (1992), "Qué reforma constitucional?," *Propuesta y control*, vol. 21, 37–59.

Pisarello, G. (2010), "El nuevo constitucionalismo latinoamericano y la constitución venezolana de 1999: balance de una década," Available at: www.sinpermiso.info/articulos/ficheros/venezuela.pdf. Accessed November 17, 2017.

Pisarello, G. (2011), *Un largo termidor. Historia y crítica del constitucionalismo antidemocrático*, Quito: Corte Constitucional del Ecuador.

Przeworski, A., Alvarez, M., et al. (2000), *Democracy and Development*, Cambridge, Cambridge University Press.

Rossi, J. and Filippini, L. (2010), en P. Arcidiácono et al., *Derechos sociales: justicia, política y economía en América Latina*, Bogotá: Siglo del Hombre-Universidad de Los Andes.

Samuels, D. and Eaton, K. (2002), *"Presidentialism And, Or, and Versus Parliamentarism: The State of the Literature and an Agenda for Future Research,"* Paper presented at the Conference on Consequences of Political Institutions in Democracy, Duke University, April.

Samper, J.M. (1861), *Ensayo sobre las revoluciones políticas y la condición social de las repúblicas colombianas*, Paris: Imprenta de E. Thunot.

Samper, J. (1893), *Los partidos en Colombia*, Bogotá: Imprenta Echeverría Hermanos.

Shugart, M. and Carey, J. (1992), *Presidents and assemblies, constitutional design and electoral dynamics*, Cambridge, Cambridge University Press.

Shugart, M. and Mainwaring, S. (1997), "Presidentialism and Democracy in Latin America: Rethinking the Tems of the Debate," in M. Shugart and S. Mainwaring, eds., *Presidentialism and Democracy in Latin America*, Cambridge: Cambridge University Press.

Sikkink, K. (2012), *The Justice Cascade. How Human Rights Prosecutions are Changing World Politics*, New York: Norton & Company.

Viciano Pastor, R. and Martínez Dalmau, R. (2009), "Los procesos constituyentes latinoamericanos y el nuevo paradigma constitucional," manuscrito no publicado, Universidad de Valencia.

Viciano Pastor, R. and Martínez Dalmau, R. (2011), "El nuevo constitucionalismo latinoamericano: Fundamentos para una construcción doctrinal," *Revista General de Derecho Público Comparado*, 9, 1–24.

Yrigoyen Fajardo, R. (2011), "El horizonte del constitucionalismo pluralista: del multiculturalismo a la descolonización," en C. Garavito comp., *El Derecho en América Latina. Un mapa para el pensamiento jurídico del Siglo XXI*, Buenos Aires: Siglo XXI.

3

STATE AND LAW IN LATIN AMERICA

A Critical Assessment

Lisa Hilbink and Janice Gallagher[1]

Introduction

In Latin America, generally speaking, both the state and the law have historically been quite weak. Although lawyers played an integral role in state-building efforts in the region (Dezalay and Garth 2002; Mirow 2004; Pérez-Perdomo 2006), state development was often stunted (Centeno 2002), and the reach and capacity of the state, including its legality, remain extremely uneven across geographic and social divides (O'Donnell 1993; García-Villegas and Espinosa 2013). Moreover, the construction of an *Estado de Derecho*, in which state actors and ordinary citizens alike are held to previously established and public legal rules and limits, and in which the law is a vehicle through which rights can be realized,[2] has proven a stubborn challenge (O'Donnell 2010).[3]

The problems of weak states and weak law became a central focus for analysts starting in the 1990s, as many countries in the region emerged from an era of brutal authoritarianism. Human rights advocates and democratic reformers, those seeking to promote neoliberal economic development, and those concerned with rising rates of violent crime all sought to make law matter in ways that it had not in the past (Carothers 2001; Rodríguez-Garavito 2011). Although motivated by different substantive concerns, a wide variety of scholars and practitioners converged around the shared goal of understanding and responding to the "un-rule of law" in Latin America (Méndez, O'Donnell, and Pinheiro 1999).

Writing in 2001, Domingo and Sieder noted that rule of law promoters working in Latin America had "increasingly adopted the language of 'state reform,'" reflecting "a necessary re-evaluation of the role of the state in terms of its relationship to society" (2001, 149, 151). Convinced that courts, as the primary state institutions charged with holding leaders and citizens within legal bounds, were the key to "good governance" (both political and economic), practitioners pinned their hopes on, and invested hundreds of millions of dollars in, the strengthening of judicial institutions. In the decade and a half since, socio-legal work on the state and law in Latin America has proliferated. We now have a much better understanding of the sources of, barriers to, and limits of judicial effectiveness, as well as of a variety of alternatives to state-based rule of law. What have we learned, what trends are evident in the literature, and what are the implications for future research?

This chapter addresses these questions through an overview of key works in the socio-legal literature on the weak state/weak law problem in Latin America. We organize the literature into two categories: (1) works centered on the institutional sources of and barriers to legal effectiveness, including works that emphasize the embeddedness of state institutions in social and economic contexts; and (2) works that consider how actors outside the state – social movements, civil society, revolutionary movements, transnational networks – have moved the needle in terms of state responsiveness to legal claims, or, at times, have circumvented, or substituted for state legal institutions and processes. This review is by no means exhaustive – it skews toward more recent works and those originally published in English – but it provides a schematization of books, chapters, and articles, that, broadly conceived, speak to the ways in which state respect for and fulfillment of law are enhanced, impaired, enabled, or challenged in contemporary Latin America.

Institutional Sources of and Barriers to Legal Effectiveness

Institutional Design

Perhaps the most persistent strand of law and society research dealing with the weak state/weak law problem in Latin America has centered around how to best design and reform judicial institutions – especially courts – so that they are independent, efficient, accessible, and, thereby, more effective.[4] Historically, material and symbolic state power in Latin America has been concentrated in a powerful executive. Even in places with substantial records of democratic contestation and participation, where government leaders have faced regular moments of electoral or "vertical" accountability, few countries had robust systems of checks and balances, or "horizontal accountability" (O'Donnell 1999). Institutions of horizontal accountability – courts being the most obvious – are charged with ensuring that the law is being respected before, during, and after election cycles, by rulers and ruled alike, and with providing redress and sanction when it is not (O'Donnell 1999, 39). But to carry out these functions both effectively and legitimately, the officials who populate the courts and other institutions of horizontal accountability must be separate and independent from those who issue the laws or enforce orders (Shapiro 1981; Domingo 1999; Brinks 2005); the institutions must be accessible, physically and culturally, to all citizens (Garro 1999); and they must be sufficiently staffed and resourced to process legal claims in a timely and meaningful manner (Buscaglia and Ulen 1997; Pásara 2014).

This institutionalist logic has both driven and been reinforced by a number of studies arguing that formal institutional features, whether previously established or introduced by reforms, correlate with or directly cause greater accountability rulings, rights protection by courts, or other desired legal outcomes. Notable works have identified the formal independence of prosecutorial bodies and/or courts as crucial to the willingness and ability of actors therein to hold state officials to account for legal abuses, past or present (Skaar 2011; Ríos-Figueroa 2012). Building on the premise that public prosecutors and/or investigating judges often face disincentives to pursue cases against other state actors, Michel and Sikkink (2013) emphasize the facilitating role that the *figura de querellante*, or mechanism of private prosecution, has played in permitting the investigation and trial of state agents for human rights violations in those Latin American countries where it is present, arguing that its absence explains the dearth of trials where it is not.[5] Scholars of Costa Rica and Colombia have attributed dramatic shifts toward political accountability and/or judicial rights protection to the creation of new constitutional courts/chambers, as well as to specific standing and procedure rules (around the *amparo* and the *tutela*, respectively) that have made citizen access to these courts much easier (Cepeda-Espinosa 2005; Faúndez 2005; Wilson 2005, 2011; Wilson and Rodríguez Cordero 2006).[6] Couso and Hilbink (2011) argue that the incipient activism apparent in both the Constitutional Tribunal and (lower) ordinary courts in Chile after 2005 can be explained, in part, by institutional reforms. And comparing the role of constitutional courts across time in Colombia, Peru, and Mexico, Ríos-Figueroa (2016) theorizes that it is key institutional conditions (independence, access, and expansive judicial review powers) that render such tribunals effective or ineffective in mediating conflicts between civilian and military authorities around internal security issues.

Formal institutions do seem to matter, then, but as recent literature on judicial reform suggests, changes to the formal organizational rules, along with investments in infrastructure, frequently do not translate to improvement in judicial performance (Hammergren 2007, 306; Pásara 2014).[7] Socio-legal scholars, particularly in political science, have thus sought to provide explanations for when and why judicial reforms succeed or fail, as well as to offer theories on the origins of judicial behavior that point to factors beyond formal institutional rules and structures.

Sources of and Barriers to Institutional Reform

A number of works build on the premise that strengthening judicial independence and effectiveness is not, on its face, in the interest of political leaders, who might prefer to minimize any potential checks on their power. Only when faced with political competition will politicians have an interest in building up the judiciary (e.g., Chávez 2004; Beer 2006). Finkel (2008) distinguishes between legislation and implementation of judicial reforms, and argues that, in Argentina, Peru, and Mexico, leaders incentivized by international financial institutions passed judicial reform *legislation* but tended to delay *implementation*. Not until these leaders anticipated they would be electorally defeated did they implement – believing that judicial reforms would constrain the power of their successors and provide a form of "insurance" against their rivals' political agenda.[8]

Other scholars challenge the notion that reforms for more independent and effective courts are always or only a strategic response to changing levels of political competition, emphasizing the importance of contextual factors, ideas, and processes of political persuasion to the timing and content of judicial strengthening reforms (e.g., Hilbink 2009; Nunes 2010a). Ingram (2016) offers perhaps the most thorough test to date of competing arguments regarding the origins of judicial reform, offering a multi-method analysis of subnational reform in Mexico and Brazil. He finds that it is shared programmatic commitments on the part of political and judicial leaders that drive court-enhancing reforms, and, in particular, that actors with left-liberal convictions are most likely to advance and support robust reforms. Absent such ideational motivations, he shows, electoral incentives are insufficient to produce reform.

Explanations for Judicial Behavior

Even successful institutional reforms may not lead to behavioral or "positive" independence on the part of judges, however. Although few would argue that formal guarantees of judicial independence, such as long and secure tenure or stable salaries and budgets, are irrelevant, studies find a weak, even negative, correlation between *de jure* (on the books) and de facto (in action) independence (Brinks 2005; Ríos-Figueroa and Staton 2012). Scholars have thus sought to provide alternative explanations regarding the conditions that constrain or enable judicial assertiveness in defense of legal norms and principles. In so doing, some have drawn on the United States judicial behavior literature, whose main axis of debate is around attitudinalism – which holds that judges decide cases sincerely, based on their personal policy preferences (Segal and Spaeth 2002) – and the "separation of powers" (SOP) approach, which posits that judicial decisions will reflect judges' strategic calculations about how actors in the other branches can and will respond (Epstein and Knight 1997).[9]

Given the record of political subordination of the judiciary in many Latin American countries, numerous analysts have built on the SOP approach to proffer strategic explanations for positive judicial independence. Helmke (2005), for example, argues that the informal institution of insecure tenure in Argentina produced "strategic defection" on the part of high court judges, as sitting supreme court judges anticipated a change in government or regime and sought to demonstrate independence from the faltering incumbents so as to have a better chance of retaining their seats in the subsequent administration. In a similar vein, Iaryczower, Spiller, and Tommasi (2002) and Ríos-Figueroa (2007) have argued for the importance of the distribution of elite power – especially divided government – for establishing the conditions in which judges will be willing and able to assert whatever legal authority they are given.

Some authors have called attention to internal institutional dynamics, separate from, or in conjunction with the broader political context. Their work illuminates how judicial assertiveness is encouraged or discouraged through organizational structures and cultures and reproduced over time. Based on a longitudinal analysis across regimes in Chile, Hilbink (2007) demonstrates that the institutional structure and ideology of the judiciary, grounded in the ideal of judicial apoliticism, provided understandings and incentives that rendered judges unequipped and disinclined to assert themselves in defense of rights and rule of law principles under both democracy and dictatorship. Ansolabehere (2007), contrasting high court behavior in Argentina and Mexico, argues that justices' preferences are constituted, and their decision-making patterns reinforced, by their relationships vis-à-vis both the elected branches and the lower courts. Kapiszewski (2012), comparing the behavior of high courts in Argentina and Brazil, finds that "court characters," constituted by a set of specific informal institutional features (stability, perceived legitimacy, professionalism, and cohesion), account for both patterns of judicial decision-making and responses of elected leaders to judicial decisions.

Other authors have offered accounts highlighting the agency of judges themselves in increasing their effectiveness in holding the other branches accountable. With empirical support from Mexico, for example, Staton (2010) contends that, in a democratic setting where a free press is operative and the public has means to hold politicians accountable for defiance of judicial authority, judges have opportunities to communicate their decisions strategically to the public and thereby enhance their power vis-à-vis the other branches of government. In other words, judges may be able to actively build greater authority by leveraging public pressure for politicians to comply with legal standards imposed in judicial decisions. Landau (2015) argues that the Colombian Constitutional Court has been able to create "audiences" in civil society, especially among the middle class and through the mechanism of the *tutela*, that insulate or protect the constitutional court from political retaliation. Ingram (2016) highlights the role of judges in transmitting ideas about and lobbying for reforms to strengthen judicial independence in Mexican and Brazilian states.

Finally, and relatedly, as institutionalized patterns of judicial behavior have begun to change in the region, some have contended that a key explanatory factor is a shift in judges' understandings of and convictions about the judicial role in the political system, which color their perceptions of the strategic context itself (Landau 2005; Nunes 2010b; Couso and Hilbink 2011; Hilbink 2012; Ingram 2016). These authors all point to the transformative impact of judicial training abroad, whether in Spain, Germany, or the United States, and/or to changes within Latin American law school and judicial academy curricula to emphasize neo–constitutionalism (Couso 2007, 2010).

The Embeddedness of Law and Courts

Regardless of their differences, all of the works discussed to this point center their analysis on state institutions and actors – specifically, courts and judges. Given that "people do not encounter legal rules; they encounter interpretations of legal rules"[10] by state officials (whether judges or those answerable to judges), this makes sense. But not all institutional analysts presume that meaningful variation and change occur within courts and judicial systems. Indeed, some studies illuminate how institutional dynamics reflect and reproduce existing power relations and behavioral patterns, in societies where the historical distribution of wealth and resources is highly unequal.

For example, in his 2008 book analyzing judicial responsiveness to police killings in Argentina, Brazil, and Uruguay, Brinks finds an inverse relationship between the rate of homicides committed by police and the percentage of such killings that end in conviction. Through a comparative analysis of how police killings are processed in five cities, he argues that the social context of profound inequality and social exclusion, and the political dynamics this creates, are what ultimately perpetuate both high levels of police killings and low judicial responsiveness thereto. Bergman (2009) offers a parallel argument on the relevance of institutions in garnering citizen compliance with tax law. He finds that the institutional effectiveness of national tax enforcement agencies is heavily affected by the dominant social equilibrium, of "compliance" (in Chile) and "noncompliance" (in Argentina). These equilibria, rooted in longstanding patterns of state-societal relations, necessarily limit prospects for change.

Another group of scholars has focused on how judicial reforms have at times exacerbated racism and inequality, and have failed to improve access to justice. Brinks and Botero (2014) find that even in contexts in which historically marginalized groups are incorporated and recognized via new legal rules, these rules are easily ignored because of the absence of the "lateral supports" necessary for implementation – ancillary rules, state agencies, and civil society organization. Gallagher (2015) shows that cases of lethal violence in Chihuahua, Mexico and "false positives" cases in Colombia progress more slowly through the new, oral justice systems than comparable cases in the older, written system. Vieira, writing in Rodríguez-Garavito (2014), argues that in contexts of vast inequality, efforts to promote legal impartiality are undermined by the mechanisms through which the poor are demonized and made invisible, and immunity is maintained for those with the most economic resources. Escalante (2015) analyzes the ongoing criminalization of indigenous people and practices in the Mexican justice system despite legal reforms. Sieder (2014) argues that, regardless of constitutions that guarantee indigenous autonomy and rights, when movements for indigenous rights clash with the resource extraction model backed by the logic of global economic growth, there is not the necessary international pressure to obligate the state to honor these rights. In sum, changing the rules does not change the underlying power asymmetries.

Societal Mobilization for Greater Legal Responsiveness

Civil Society: Promoting Accountability and Setting Agendas

The institutionalist scholarship surveyed above focuses largely on the choices, actions, and interactions of judges, politicians, and other elite actors. Another branch of the literature puts non-state actors front and center, considering them, alternatively, as advocates of judicial accountability, as co-producers of the knowledge, frameworks, and incentives that meaningfully impact judicial performance, or as political entrepreneurs that work to create alternatives to failing state judicial systems.

Many Latin American scholars have explicitly built on the social movement and legal mobilization literature that emerged in the United States in the wake of the civil rights movement to assess the impact of strategic litigation (Rodríguez-Garavito 2010; Ansolabehere 2016) and of cause lawyers (Meili 2001). Many legal mobilization scholars working in Latin America and other areas of the Global South have focused on the innovative ways that social movements are using law as part of counter-hegemonic projects that challenge neoliberalism, especially in the realm of social, economic, and cultural rights (Sousa Santos and Rodríguez-Garavito 2005; Rajagopal 2006; Hernández, Sieder, and Sierra 2013). Rodríguez-Garavito (2009, 2014) explores the ways in which social movement and civil society pressure activate constitutions and high courts in the region, contributing to both material changes in public policies and symbolic changes in how the public defines and perceives the urgency and nature of rights violations. Lemaitre and Sandvik (2015) challenge the classic political opportunity structure framework (McAdam, McCarthy, and Zald 1996), arguing that people and social movements in violent contexts confront constantly shifting frames, resources, and political opportunities. Drawing from a case study of internally displaced women in Colombia, they show how the rapidly shifting legal landscape results from the state's need to pass new laws to reassure citizens of their ability to respond to violence, and how this in turn creates challenges for the movement.

Another group of scholars has explicitly built on O'Donnell's concepts of accountability in order to understand the legal effects of the new webs of social movements, nongovernmental organizations (NGOs) and media that sprouted after the last wave of Latin American democratization. Peruzzotti and Smulovitz (2006) develop a social accountability approach, which considers media, movements, and associations as non-electoral forms of vertical accountability. Within their edited volume, Fuentes argues that the lack of social movement mobilization is a key part of explaining why police violence is met with legal impunity in Chile, while Behrend focuses on the importance of ideologically distinct newspaper unions in pushing forward the investigation into the murder of an Argentine journalist. While Brinks (2008) delineates the way in which inequality and exclusion preclude effective investigations and prosecutions of police killings in many cases, he also shows that normative and informational failures can be mitigated by institutional features that provide judicial actors the incentives and tools necessary to conduct a thorough investigation and trial. When the normative environment is sufficiently open – that is, where judges analyze and respond to the information in the case files rather than automatically acquitting any accused police officer – Brinks finds that NGO intervention in cases via the mechanism of private prosecution and/or popular demonstrations significantly improve conviction rates. Focusing on Mexico and Colombia, Gallagher (2017) further explores the role of civil society in activating and improving the quality of investigations into lethal violence. She argues that civil society actors perform separate but synergistic roles in promoting accountability: activists impose a political cost to impunity, while advocates are able to channel activist pressure into concrete judicial advances by facilitating the exchange of investigative information between family members of victims and state investigators.

Several works argue that, besides changing political incentives and intervening directly in legal processes, non-state actors shift the way that judicial officials think about law. Couso, Huneeus, and Sieder (2010) examine how indigenous movements, human rights organizations, and members of civil society shape legal cultures, attributing the increased judicialization of politics in Latin America in part to changes in ideas and beliefs about law traceable to non-state actors. González Ocantos (2016), argues that in transitional justice processes, NGOs serve as key conduits of international legal standards, transmitting ideas about the content and authority of international laws through interactions, conversations, and trainings with judges, who are then equipped to overturn amnesty laws and statutes of limitations on human rights violations. Dancy and Michel (2016) argue that when victims and human rights lawyers serve as private prosecutors, they generate "prosecutorial momentum," which inspires more claims-making against state agents who abuse human rights, which in turn emboldens state actors to get behind human rights prosecutions.

Transnational Pressure for Judicial Accountability

While many of the preceding accounts include international actors, their primary focus is on domestic actors and processes. Human rights scholars coming from the field of international relations, however, have honed in on the role of transnational and intergovernmental actors in shaping the human rights behavior of states in both their domestic and international arenas. The boomerang and spiral models (Keck and Sikkink 1998; Risse-Kappen, Ropp, and Sikkink 1999) theorize how local human rights activists, frustrated by the lack of responsiveness by their own governments, exert pressure through foreign governments and intergovernmental institutions like the United Nations and the Organization of American States. Brysk (2000) focuses on the processes through which indigenous social movements work together, mobilizing resources across borders, to encourage the recognition of indigenous rights in international law. Anaya (2009) traces the ways in which international pressure translates into foreign and domestic human rights policy in Mexico, and subsequently (2011) sets out to explain the high levels of transnational pressure around the systematic killing and disappearances of women in Ciudad Juárez. He finds that reliably documented cases of grave bodily harm, dense advocacy networks, and issue resonance with international norms will activate the most robust international pressure. Though the effectiveness of these Transnational Advocacy Networks (TANs) has been widely debated by international relations scholars, several human rights scholars have responded by analyzing large cross-national datasets to show that TAN pressure results in changes in state behavior (Simmons 2009; Kim and Sikkink 2010).

Competing with and Challenging State Legal Institutions and Processes

The social movements and civil society organizations discussed to this point seek to improve the performance of judicial institutions and strengthen state capacity. Another set of social movements has sought to circumvent and/or undermine formal legal systems, often constructing informal and autonomous alternatives to state law and courts. O'Donnell (1993) noted that in the "brown areas" of state absence, social movements often construct alternative, autonomous systems of justice. Van Cott (2006) framed the discussion of informal justice institutions along the degree to which they substitute (or complement) the state's formal justice system, and whether they compete with (or accommodate) it.

Indigenous movements, many of which mobilized as a response to the neoliberal policies of the 1980s and 1990s, have long resisted state-led efforts to impose standard national justice systems (Yashar 2005). In many Latin American countries, these struggles have resulted in legal recognition and autonomy (Cleary 2000). Indigenous movements in Panama and Nicaragua, for example, won substantial autonomy following United States-backed armed movements (Van Cott 1994), and in Mexico, the *usos y costumbres* law in Oaxaca (Eisenstadt 2007) established zones in which indigenous forms of legality are officially sanctioned. Constitutional rights for indigenous people were pioneered in Colombia (1991) and Bolivia (1994–1996), and soon diffused throughout the region. These rights have included the recognition of customary law and collective property rights (Van Cott 2001). What effect has this official recognition and sanctioning of indigenous autonomy had on the state, and specifically on courts? Sieder (1999; 2002) highlights the difficulties of overlapping sovereignties and jurisdictions between the state and indigenous communities, as well as the problems that arise between worldviews and legal systems that differ in who they regard as the primary rights-holder: the individual versus the group.

In many cases, local institutions providing justice are both challenging the state and substituting for it. Faúndez (2005) sees Peruvian community justice institutions challenging the state by defiantly adjudicating crimes outside of their limited jurisdiction using unorthodox punishments like lashings. These same institutions, however, have lobbied to be recognized by the state and are effectively substituting for a Spanish-only justice system that excludes and is widely mistrusted by many citizens of rural communities. Godoy (2006), analyzing community lynchings in Guatemala, asks where the line is between informal, indigenous justice, on the one hand, and vigilante justice, on the other. She finds that community-based justice works best with its own members, when shame is an effective sanction. Krupa (2009) warns that the codification of indigenous autonomy in Ecuadorian law leads to the false dichotomy of state law and all alternative forms of justice. This leads many to mistakenly assume that extra-legal punishments like lynchings represent indigenous forms of justice, vilifying, and delegitimizing them.

While all efforts at self-rule challenge the state's role as the sole entity with the authority to govern its claimed territories, there are a number of case studies of efforts to roll back, dismantle, and confront the state's legal authority, often using violent means. Armed insurgencies challenge not only the state's monopoly on the use of force, but also its role as the primary provider of legality – and many explicitly articulate alternative legal projects. The Zapatistas in Mexico, for example, work with local Autonomous Municipal Councils to implement customary law (Mattiace 2003; Eisenstadt 2006). In Colombia, communities refusing to collaborate with any armed actors in the midst of the conflict have declared their autonomy, implementing their own systems of justice – and have suffered massive attacks from state, paramilitary, and guerrilla forces as a result (Mouly, Idler, and Garrido 2015; Kaplan 2017). Interestingly, Ernst (2013), studying one of Mexico's largest criminal organizations, finds that instead of an all-out attack on the state, the criminal organization strives for legitimacy, constructing governance-like codes of behavior, including a quasi-judicial system with a formalized punishment process. Their goal is to ensure their own survival – which includes co-opting state officials and winning over local populations. All of these non-state actors seek to provide some form of local justice to address the claims and grievances of the local population – claims and grievances that have been, at best, ignored, and, at worst, provoked by the state.

Conclusions

Socio-legal scholarship in the Americas has long been bifurcated along North/South lines, a split that derives not only from cultural and linguistic differences, but also from a sense that the main challenges on the two sides of the Rio Grande are distinct. In Anglo America, the implicit assumption is that state and legal institutions, however imperfect, enjoy relatively high levels of independence and legitimacy, whereas in Latin America, they are frequently absent, co-opted, corrupt, or perverted. However, recent political developments in the United States (as well as Europe) are beginning to lay bare the problematic nature of this assumption, rendering the extensive scholarship on the state and law in Latin America of increasing relevance to law and society scholars in the Global North.

As this chapter has shown, engaged scholars in Latin America have devoted their research energies to exploring the potentials and pitfalls of legal and institutional reform to address the region's dire shortcomings in regimes of legality. Taken as a whole, the works signal three shifts in how we might better understand, explain, and redress these shortcomings: they have begun to look down

– away from high courts to low; they have shifted the gaze out – away from national units and toward subnational and cross-sector or comparisons; and they have started to examine how average citizens perceive and respond to the state and law. We close by elaborating on these three directions, and articulate their implications, and suggestions for future scholarship.

First, whereas earlier institutionalist work tended to focus on the politics of high courts, recent scholarship has increasingly sought to understand the local courts and other legal institutions with which most citizens interact (e.g., Brinks 2008; Ingram 2016). Although the picture at the top is by no means perfect, many scholars now underscore the "new legal order" that reigns in many Latin American countries, where apex courts are "more efficient, more effective, and far more consequential" than they have ever been (Brinks 2012, 61). At the same time, crime, violence, corruption, and impunity are the lived reality for vast swaths of the population in many countries, who often feel abandoned by the judicial system (Davis 2010; Malone 2010; Imbusch, Misse, and Carrión 2011). As researchers seek to explain why and how legal norms and institutions matter – or do not – in the lives of everyday citizens, they should continue to look more closely at the incentives, practices, and outcomes of local-level legal processes and at how citizens gain effective recourse and remedies for arbitrary, corrupt rules, and rights violations.

Second and relatedly, analysts are moving away from country and regime-level analyses, and toward studies that examine, often comparatively, how the state and law function across subnational units, social categories, or case issues. Brinks and Botero (2014) remind us that while most conceptions, measures, and causal explanations of the rule of law are still formulated at the national level, we have long known that a state's presence and capacity across its territory varies drastically (O'Donnell 1993). To be sure, although "in some contexts and for some people, the law effectively guides social interactions and [serves as] a source of both rights and responsibilities," the "new rule of law regime is poorly distributed" both geographically and socially (Brinks and Botero 2014, 216). This disparity is highlighted by the crisis of violence in the region – which continues to devastate some provinces, cities, and rural areas, while leaving others virtually unscathed (Koonings and Kruijt 2007). These uneven experiences with law and the state demand a shift in predominant units of analysis, research design, and themes.

Third, as scholarship moves away from national level institutional accounts of the state and law, socio-legal scholars are taking more seriously the ways in which citizen perceptions of state legitimacy and capacity are formed, transmitted, reproduced, or changed, and how these perceptions inform and infuse behavior around legal norms and institutions (e.g., Bergman 2009; Hilbink and Heimark 2015; Gallagher 2017). These dynamics are reflected in the reformulation of key concepts, including the rule of law itself, away from technical, juridical understandings toward a more behavioral emphasis that considers how citizens interact with each other as well as the concrete ways citizens experience the state (Bergman 2009, 2012). This shift is fostered by the interdisciplinary of the socio-legal field, which embraces a diversity of methodological approaches. Traditional barriers between fields of inquiry can and should break down as researchers attempt to understand more profoundly the overlapping systems of state legality and control that structure relationships, experiences, and perceptions.

Notes

1 The authors thank Matthew Ingram, Mariano Sánchez Talanquer, Whitney Taylor, and the editors of this Handbook for their helpful comments and suggestions during the preparation of this chapter.
2 The term "Estado de Derecho," literally "state of law," is the Spanish equivalent of the "rule of law," which can be defined in "thin" (procedural) or "thick" (substantive, usually democratic rights-based) terms. In Latin America, the "thick" version is often signaled by the addition of the adjective(s) "democrático" or "social y democrático" to the phrase rule of law ("Estado de Derecho").

3 The three countries that are often held out as exceptions to this assessment, at least at the national level, are Uruguay, Costa Rica, and Chile (see O'Donnell 2010, 148).

4 See Kapiszewski and Taylor (2008) for an earlier, in-depth review of the scholarship on judicial politics in Latin America. A related literature, reviewed in the Kapiszewski and Taylor but not taken up here, examines if and how constitutional reforms or rewrites alter political practice, including more equal rights protection in the region. See Francisca Pou's chapter in this Handbook.

5 On the role of private prosecution in increasing judicial responsiveness to police killings in contemporary Latin America, see Brinks 2008.

6 Gargarella (2013, 187–90) notes that in both the Costa Rican and Colombian cases, it was rather modest changes to legal standing and procedure that produced notable, if perhaps unintended, changes to the "engine room of the constitution," – that is, to the relationship between citizens and institutions.

7 Indeed, Pásara goes so far as to title his 2014 book-length overview of judicial reforms in the region, *Una Reforma Imposible* (An Impossible Reform).

8 Ginsburg (2003) is usually credited with the idea of empowered courts as political insurance, though Finkel came up with the term independently for her 2001 PhD dissertation.

9 The United States judicial behavior literature is, of course, not limited to these two perspectives, but for the purposes of this chapter, we limit ourselves to referencing these two major theoretical approaches.

10 O'Donnell (2010, 108, fn. 37), citing Houtzager (2001).

References

Anaya, Alejandro. 2009. "Transnational and Domestic Processes in the Definition of Human Rights Policies in Mexico." *Human Rights Quarterly* 31(1): 35–58.

Anaya, Alejandro. 2011. "Explaining High Levels of Transnational Pressure over Mexico: The Case of the Disappearances and Killings of Women in Ciudad Juárez." *The International Journal of Human Rights* 15(3): 339–58.

Ansolabehere, Karina. 2007. *La Política desde la Justicia: Cortes Supremas, Gobierno y Democracia en Argentina y México*. México City: FLACSO México.

Ansolabehere, Karina. 2016. "One Norm, Two Models: Legal Enforcements of Human Rights in Mexico and the United States." *Mexican Law Review 8(*2): 93–129.

Beer, Caroline. 2006. "Judicial Performance and the Rule of Law in the Mexican States." *Latin American Politics and Society* 48(3): 33–61.

Bergman, Marcelo. 2009. *Tax Evasion and the Rule of Law in Latin America: The Political Culture of Cheating and Compliance in Argentina and Chile*. University Park: Pennsylvania State Press.

Bergman, Marcelo. 2012. "The Rule, the Law, and the Rule of Law: Improving Measurement and Content Validity." *Justice System Journal* 33(2): 174–93.

Brinks, Daniel. 2005. "Judicial Reform and Independence in Brazil and Argentina: The Beginning of a New Millennium?" *Texas International Law Journal* 40: 595–622.

Brinks, Daniel. 2008. *The Judicial Response to Police Killings in Latin America*. New York: Cambridge University Press.

Brinks, Daniel. 2012. "A Tale of Two Cities: The Judiciary and the Rule of Law in Latin America." In *Handbook of Latin American Politics*, edited by Peter Kingstone and Deborah Yashar, 61–75. New York: Routledge.

Brinks, Daniel and Sandra Botero. 2014. "Inequality and the Rule of Law: Ineffective Rights in Latin American Democracies" In *Reflections on Uneven Democracies: The Legacy of Guillermo O'Donnell*, edited by Daniel Brinks, Marcelo Leiras, and Scott Mainwaring, 214–39. Baltimore: Johns Hopkins University Press.

Brysk Alison. 2000. *From Tribal Village to Global Village: Indian Rights and International Relations in Latin America*. Palo Alto, CA: Stanford University Press.

Buscaglia, Edgardo and Thomas Ulen. 1997. "A Quantitative Assessment of the Efficiency of the Judicial Sector in Latin America." *International Review of Law and Economics* 17(2): 275–91.

Carothers, Thomas. 2001. "The Many Agendas of Rule of Law Reform in Latin America." In *Rule of Law in Latin America: The International Promotion of Judicial Reform*, edited by Pilar Domingo and Rachel Sieder, 4–15. London: ILAS.

Centeno, Miguel Ángel. 2002. *Blood and Debt: War and the Nation-State in Latin America*. University Park: Pennsylvania State Press.

Cepeda-Espinosa, Manuel. 2005. "The Judicialization of Politics in Colombia: The Old and the New." In *The Judicialization of Politics in Latin America*, edited by Rachel Sieder, Line Schjolden, and Alan Angell, 67–103. New York: Palgrave Macmillan US.

Chávez, Rebeca. 2004. *The Rule of Law in Nascent Democracies: Judicial Politics in Argentina*. Stanford: Stanford University Press.

Cleary, Matthew. 2000. "Democracy and Indigenous Rebellion in Latin America." *Comparative Political Studies 33*(9):1123–53

Couso, Javier. 2007. "The Seduction of Judicially Triggered Social Transformation: The Impact of the Warren Court in Latin America." In *Earl Warren and the Warren Court*, edited by Harry N. Scheiber, 237–64. Lanham, MD: Lexington Books.

Couso, Javier. 2010. "The Transformation of Constitutional Discourse and the Judicialization of Politics in Latin America." In *Cultures of Legality: Judicialization and Political Activism in Latin America*, edited by Javier Couso, Alexandra Huneeus and Rachel Sieder, 141–60. New York: Cambridge University Press.

Couso, Javier and Lisa Hilbink. 2011. "From Quietism to Incipient Activism." In *Courts in Latin America*, edited by Gretchen Helmke and Julio Ríos-figueroa, 99–127. New York: Cambridge University Press.

Couso, Javier, Alexandra Huneeus, and Rachel Sieder. 2010. *Cultures of Legality: Judicialization and Political Activism in Latin America*. New York: Cambridge University Press.

Dancy, Geoff and Verónica Michel. 2016. "Human Rights Enforcement from Below: Private Actors and Prosecutorial Momentum in Latin America and Europe." *International Studies Quarterly 60*(1), 173–88.

Davis, Diane. 2010. "The Political and Economic Origins of Violence and Insecurity in Contemporary Latin America: Past Trajectories and Future Prospects." In *Violent Democracies in Latin America*, edited by Enrique Desmond Arias and Daniel Goldstein, 35–62. Durham: Duke University Press.

Dezalay, Yves and Bryant Garth. 2002. *The Internationalization of Palace Wars: Lawyers, Economists, and the Contest to Transform Latin America*. Chicago: University of Chicago Press.

Domingo, Pilar. 1999. "Judicial Independence and Judicial Reform in Latin America." In *The Self-Restraining State*, edited by Pilar Domingo, Andreas Schedler, Larry Diamond, and Marc Plattner, 151–76. Boulder: Lynne Riener.

Domingo, Pilar and Rachel Sieder, eds. 2001. *Rule of Law in Latin America: The International Promotion of Judicial Reform*. London: ILAS.

Eisenstadt Todd. 2006. "Indigenous Attitudes and Ethnic Identity Construction in Mexico." *Mexican Studies 22*(1): 107–29.

Eisenstadt Todd. 2007. "Usos y Costumbres and Postelectoral Conflicts in Oaxaca, Mexico, 1995–2004: An Empirical and Normative Assessment." *Latin American Research Review 42*(1): 52–77.

Epstein, Lee and Jack Knight. 1997. *The Choices Justices Make*. Washington, DC: Congressional Quarterly Press.

Ernst, Falko. 2013. "Beyond the Licit–Illicit Divide: Approaching the Realities of Organized Crime-state-Interactions in Michoacán, Mexico." Available at https://ecpr.eu/Filestore/PaperProposal/07f705e2-d51c-469c-900c-84818363d0e6.pdf. Accessed July 10, 2018.

Escalante, Yuri. 2015. *El Racismo Judicial en México: Análisis de Sentencias y Representación de la Diversidad*. México: Juan Pablos.

Faúndez, Julio. 2005. "Community Justice Institutions and Judicialization: Lessons from Rural Peru." In *The Judicialization of Politics in Latin America*, edited by Rachel Sieder, Line Schjolden, and Alan Angell, 187–209. New York: Palgrave Macmillan US.

Finkel, Jodi. 2008. *Judicial Reform as Political Insurance*. Notre Dame: University of Notre Dame.

Gallagher, Janice. 2015. "Tipping The Scales Of Justice: The Role Of Organized Citizen Action In Strengthening The Rule Of Law." PhD diss., Cornell University.

Gallagher Janice. 2017. "The Last Mile Problem: Activists, Advocates, and the Struggle for Justice in Domestic Courts." *Comparative Political Studies 50*(12): 1666–98.

García-Villegas, Mauricio and José Rafael Espinosa. 2013. *El Derecho al Estado: Los Efectos Legales del Apartheid Institucional en Colombia*. Bogotá: Dejusticia.

Gargarella, Roberto. 2013. *Latin American Constitutionalism, 1810–2010: The Engine Room of the Constitution*. New York: Oxford University Press.

Garro, Alejandro Miguel. 1999. "Access to Justice for the Poor in Latin America." In *The (Un)Rule of Law and the Underprivileged in Latin America*, edited by Juan Méndez, Guillermo O'Donnell, and Paulo Pinheiro, 278–301. Notre Dame: University of Notre Dame Press.

Ginsburg, Tom. 2003. *Judicial Review in New Democracies: Constitutional Courts in Asian Cases*. New York: Cambridge University Press.

Godoy, Angelina. 2006. *Popular Injustice: Violence, Community, and Law in Latin America*. Stanford: Stanford University Press.

González Ocantos, Ezequiel. 2016. *Shifting Legal Visions: Judicial Change and Human Rights Trials in Latin America*. New York: Cambridge University Press.

Hammergren, Linn. 2007. *Envisioning Reform: Conceptual and Practical Obstacles to Improving Judicial Performance in Latin America*. University Park: Pennsylvania State Press.

Helmke, Gretchen. 2005. *Courts under Constraints: Judges, Generals, and Presidents in Argentina*. New York: Cambridge University Press.

Hernández, Rosalva, Rachel Sieder and María Teresa Sierra (eds.). 2013. *Justicias Indígenas y Estado: Violencias Contemporáneas*. Mexico: FLACSO-Mexico/CIESAS.

Hilbink, Lisa. 2007. *Judges Beyond Politics in Democracy and Dictatorship: Lessons from Chile*. New York: Cambridge University Press.

Hilbink Lisa. 2009. "The Constituted Nature of Constituents' Interests: Historical and Ideational Factors in Judicial Empowerment." *Political Research Quarterly 62*(4): 781–97.

Hilbink Lisa. 2012. "The Origins of Positive Judicial Independence." *World Politics 64*(4): 587–621.

Hilbink, Lisa and Katrina Heimark. 2015. "Public Perception, Judicial Legitimacy, and the Rule of Law: Disaggregating Opinion, Disentangling Concepts." Paper presented at the Annual Meeting of the American Political Science Association, San Francisco, CA, September 26.

Houtzager, Peter. 2001. "'We Make the Law and the Law Makes Us': Some Ideas on a Law and Development Research Agenda." In *Making Law Matter, Rules, Rights and Security in the Lives of the Poor*, edited by Richard Crook and Peter Houtzager, 8–18. Norwich: IDS Bulletin 32(1).

Iaryczower, Matías, Pablo Spiller, and Mariano Tommasi. 2002. "Judicial Decision-Making in Unstable Environments: Argentina 1935–1998." *American Journal of Political Science 46*(4): 699–716.

Imbusch, Peter, Michel Misse, and Fernando Carrión. 2011. "Violence Research in Latin America and the Caribbean: A Literature Review." *International Journal of Conflict and Violence 5*(1): 87–154.

Ingram, Matthew. 2016. *Crafting Courts in New Democracies: The Politics of Subnational Judicial Reform in Brazil and Mexico*. New York: Cambridge University Press.

Kapiszewski, Diana. 2012. *High Courts and Economic Governance in Argentina and Brazil*. Cambridge: Cambridge University Press.

Kapiszewski, Diana and Matthew Taylor. 2008. "Doing Courts Justice? Studying Judicial Politics in Latin America." *Perspectives on Politics 6*(4): 741–67.

Kaplan, Oliver. 2017. *Resisting War: How Civilians Protect Themselves*. Cambridge: Cambridge University Press.

Keck, Margaret and Kathryn Sikkink. 1998. *Activists Beyond Borders: Advocacy Networks in International Politics*. Ithaca: Cornell University Press.

Kim, Hunjoon and Kathryn Sikkink. 2010. "Explaining the Deterrence Effect of Human Rights Prosecutions for Transitional Countries." *International Studies Quarterly 54*(4): 939–63.

Koonings, Kees and Dirk Kruijt. 2007. *Fractured Cities: Social Exclusion, Urban Violence and Contested Spaces in Latin America*. London: Zed Books.

Krupa, Christopher. 2009. "Histories in Red: Ways of Seeing Lynching in Ecuador." *American Ethnologist 36*(1): 20–39.

Landau, David. 2005. "The Two Discourses in Colombian Constitutional Jurisprudence: A New Approach to Modeling Judicial Behavior in Latin America." *George Washington International Law Review 37*: 687–741.

Landau, David. 2015. "Beyond Judicial Independence: The Construction of Judicial Power on the Colombian Constitutional Court." PhD diss., Harvard University.

Lemaitre, Julieta and Kristin Sandvik. 2015. "Shifting Frames, Vanishing Resources, and Dangerous Political Opportunities: Legal Mobilization among Displaced Women in Colombia." *Law & Society Review 49*(1): 5–38.

Malone, Mary Fran. 2010. "The Verdict Is In: The Impact of Crime on Public Trust in Central American Justice Systems." *Journal of Politics in Latin America 2*(3): 99–128.

Mattiace, Shannan. 2003. *To See with Two Eyes: Peasant Activism and Indian Autonomy in Chiapas, Mexico*. Albuquerque: University of New Mexico Press.

McAdam, Doug, John McCarthy, and Mayer Zald. 1996. *Comparative Perspectives on Social Movements: Political Opportunities, Mobilizing Structures, and Cultural Framings*. New York: Cambridge University Press.

Meili, Stephen. 2001. "Latin American Cause-Lawyering Networks." In *Cause Lawyering and the State in a Global Era*, edited by Austin Sarat and Stuart Scheingold, 307–33. New York: Oxford University Press.

Méndez, Juan, Guillermo O'Donnell, and Paulo Pinheiro. 1999. *The (Un)Rule of Law and the Underprivileged in Latin America*. Notre Dame: University of Notre Dame Press.

Michel, Verónica and Kathryn Sikkink. 2013. "Human Rights Prosecutions and the Participation Rights of Victims in Latin America." *Law & Society Review* 47(4): 873–907.

Mirow, Matthew. 2004. *Latin American Law: A History of Private Law and Institutions in Spanish America*. Austin: University of Texas Press.

Mouly, Cécile, Annette Idler, and Belén Garrido. 2015. "Zones of Peace in Colombia's Borderland." *International Journal of Peace Studies* 20(1): 51–63.

Nunes, Rodrigo. 2010a. "Politics without Insurance: Democratic Competition and Judicial Reform in Brazil." *Comparative Politics* 42(3): 313–31.

Nunes Rodrigo. 2010b. "Ideational Origins of Progressive Judicial Activism: The Colombian Constitutional Court and the Right to Health." *Latin American Politics and Society* 52(3): 67–97.

O'Donnell, Guillermo. 1993. "On the State, Democratization and Some Conceptual Problems: A Latin American View with Glances at Some Postcommunist Countries." *World Development* 21(1): 355–69.

O'Donnell, Guillermo. 1999. "Horizontal Accountability in New Democracies." In *The Self-Restraining State: Power and Accountability in New Democracies*, edited by Andreas Schedler, Larry Diamond, and Marc F. Plattner, 29–51. Boulder: Lynne Reiner.

O'Donnell, Guillermo. 2010. *Democracy, Agency, and the State: Theory with Comparative Intent*. New York: Oxford University Press.

Pásara, Luis. 2014. *Una Reforma Imposible: La Justicia Latinoamericana en el Banquillo*. Lima: Fondo Editorial, Pontificia Universidad Católica del Perú.

Pérez-Perdomo, Rogelio. 2006. *Latin American Lawyers: A Historical Introduction*. Stanford: Stanford University Press.

Peruzzotti, Enrique and Catalina Smulovitz (eds.). 2006. *Enforcing the Rule of Law: Social Accountability in the New Latin American Democracies*. Pittsburgh: University of Pittsburgh Press.

Rajagopal, Balakrishnan. 2006. "Counter-Hegemonic International Law: Rethinking Human Rights and Development as a Third World Strategy." *Third World Quarterly* 27(5): 767–83.

Ríos-Figueroa, Julio. 2007. "Fragmentation of Power and the Emergence of an Effective Judiciary in Mexico, 1994–2002." *Latin American Politics and Society* 49(1): 31–57.

Ríos-Figueroa, Julio. 2012. "Justice System Institutions and Corruption Control: Evidence from Latin America." *Justice System Journal* 33(2): 195–214.

Ríos-Figueroa, Julio. 2016. *Constitutional Courts as Mediators: Armed Conflict, Civil-military Relations, and the Rule of Law in Latin America*. New York: Cambridge University Press.

Ríos-Figueroa, Julio and Jeffrey Staton. 2012. "An Evaluation of Cross-National Measures of Judicial Independence." *The Journal of Law, Economics, and Organization* 30(1): 104–37.

Risse-Kappen, Thomas, Stephen Ropp, and Kathryn Sikkink. 1999. *The Power of Human Rights: International Norms and Domestic Change*. New York: Cambridge University Press.

Rodríguez-Gavarito, César. 2009. *La Globalización del Estado de Derecho: El Neoconstitucionalismo, el Neoliberalismo y la Transformación Institucional en América Latina*. Bogotá: Universidad de Los Andes.

Rodríguez-Gavarito César. 2010. "Beyond the Courtroom: The Impact of Judicial Activism on Socioeconomic Rights in Latin America." *Texas Law Review* 89: 1669–98.

Rodríguez-Gavarito, César. 2011. "Global Governance, Indigenous Peoples, and the Right to Prior Consultation in Social Minefields." *Indiana Journal of Global Legal Studies* 18(1): 263–305.

Rodríguez-Gavarito, César. 2014. *Law and Society in Latin America: A New Map*. Oxon: Routledge.

Segal, Jeffrey and Harold Spaeth. 2002. *The Supreme Court and the Attitudinal Model Revisited*. New York: Cambridge University Press.

Shapiro, Martin. 1981. *Courts: A Comparative and Political Analysis*. Chicago: University of Chicago Press.

Sieder, Rachel. 1999. "Rethinking Democratization and Citizenship: Legal Pluralism and Institutional Reform in Guatemala." *Citizenship Studies* 3(1): 103–18.

Sieder, Rachel. 2002. "Recognizing Indigenous Law and Politics of State Formation in Mesoamerica." In *Multiculturalism in Latin America: Indigenous Rights, Diversity and Democracy*, edited by Rachel Sieder, 184–207. London: Palgrave/Macmillan.

Sieder, Rachel. 2014. "Indigenous Peoples' Rights and the Law in Latin America." In *Law and Society in Latin America: A New Map*, edited by César Rodriguez Gavarito, 1–19. Oxon: Routledge.

Simmons, Beth. 2009. *Mobilizing for Human Rights: International Law in Domestic Politics*. New York: Cambridge University Press.

Skaar, Elin. 2011. *Judicial Independence and Human Rights in Latin America: Violations, Politics, and Prosecution*. New York: Palgrave and Macmillan.

Sousa Santos de, Boaventura and César Rodríguez-Garavito (Eds.). 2005. *Law and Globalization from Below: Towards a Cosmopolitan Legality*. New York: Cambridge University Press.

Staton, Jeffrey. 2010. *Judicial Power and Strategic Communication in Mexico*. New York: Cambridge University Press.

Van Cott, Donna Lee. 1994. *Indigenous Peoples and Democracy in Latin America*. New York: St. Martin's Press.

Van Cott, Donna Lee. 2001. "Explaining Ethnic Autonomy Regimes in Latin America." *Studies in Comparative International Development 35*(4): 30–58.

Van Cott, Donna Lee. 2006. "Dispensing Justice at the Margins of Formality: The Informal Rule of Law in Latin America." In *Informal Institutions and Democracy: Lessons from Latin America*, edited by Gretchen Helmke and Steven Levitsky, 249–73. Baltimore: Johns Hopkins University Press.

Wilson, Bruce. 2005. "Changing Dynamics: The Political Impact of Costa Rica's Constitutional Court." In *The Judicialization of Politics in Latin America*, edited by Rachel Sieder, Line Schjolden, and Alan Angell, 47–65. New York: Palgrave.

Wilson, Bruce. 2011. "Enforcing Rights and Exercising an Accountability Function." In *Courts in Latin America*, edited by Gretchen Helmke and Julio Ríos-figueroa, 55–80. New York: Cambridge University Press.

4

LEGAL PLURALISM AND FRAGMENTED SOVEREIGNTIES

Legality and Illegality in Latin America

Rachel Sieder

Legal pluralism – the existence of multiple legal systems or normative orders within the social field – has long been a central concern of law and society studies. In Latin America, contemporary debates and anthropological-legal perspectives on the phenomenon of legal pluralism have focused principally on the legal norms, practices, and authorities of indigenous people – their *derecho propio* – and latterly on the challenges of recognizing indigenous jurisdictions, rights, and ways of life within dominant legal orders following the regional turn to "multicultural constitutionalism" (Van Cott 2000) and the codification of indigenous peoples collective rights in international and regional human rights law. Although shifting dynamics between legality, illegality, and violence are widely understood to negatively affect indigenous people, these have not tended to be a central subject of enquiry for studies of legal pluralism in the region. My aim in this chapter is to encourage greater dialog between the regional literature on legal pluralism and analyzes of the role played by various non-state forms of law or para-legalities in securing order in contemporary Latin America. Although they consider different processes, making reference to distinct empirical and conceptual problems, I argue that the study of legal pluralism in the region has much to gain from engaging with contemporary anthropological debates on sovereignty and i/llegality in order to consider not just the relationship between subaltern legal orders and state and supranational legalities, but more broadly the changing nature of what Franz and Keebet von Benda-Beckmann and Julia Eckert refer to as "plural constellations of governance" (2009b, 3). What role do non-state forms of law or paralegal orders play in securing different forms of rule in Latin America? I argue below that one productive way to think about the multifaceted and dialectical relationship between the legal and the illegal in Latin America's plural legal orders – and the claims of subaltern groups for recognition of their forms of law or *derecho propio* – is with reference to the concept of overlapping, fragmented sovereignties. In what follows, the first section of this chapter signals the limited recognition legal pluralism and subaltern legalities that occurred with the constitutional transformations of the 1980s and 1990s and then briefly reviews the Latin American literature on legal pluralism and its key conceptual debates. A second section addresses the dynamic interplay between law and illegality in the constitution of the region's plural constellations of governance. I suggest a heuristic distinction between different types of illegality, pointing to the conceptual, and empirical issues these signal. A third section advances the concept of fragmented sovereignties as a means of reconceptualizing legal pluralities. This recognizes subaltern struggles and the roles that law plays in these, at the same time as situating them within broader transformations in configurations of governance and rule that point to the ever greater blurring of the legal and the illegal, where criminalization and suppression of subaltern claims for citizenship underlines the gap between the promises of multicultural constitutionalism and the experiences of indigenous peoples across the region.

Legal Pluralism and Subaltern Legalities in Latin America

Legally Plural States: From De Facto to De Jure

In contrast to other colonial and postcolonial contexts, where referents such as kinship or war were the principal organizing categories of politics, in Latin America claims to legitimacy, calls to action, and political pacts to establish or refound the nation-state have typically been staked in the language of the law (Salvatore, Aguirre, and Joseph 2001). Dominant narratives conceive of law and the legitimacy it confers in largely formal terms, generally centered within a unitary state and flowing downwards to society. In large swathes of Asia and Africa officially sanctioned legal pluralism involving distinct legal jurisdictions and codes for different racial, ethnic, or religious groups was a central part of the colonial and postcolonial state compact. In Latin America, Spanish colonial rule was similarly characterized by hierarchical and racialized legal pluralism (the *Leyes de Indias*). However, following independence in the nineteenth century the new nations by and large modeled themselves on the legal systems of the USA and continental Europe, subjecting native peoples to Liberal laws, which rejected recognition of cultural difference and promoted assimilation in theory at the same time as they reproduced exclusionary racial hierarchies in practice. These racialized hierarchies were central to the forced labor and enslavement that underpinned the plantation and *hacienda* systems, forms of coercive control effected through both law and lawlessness that revealed the limited purchase of liberal legal universality. The effect of this transformation of state law, its remaking as the antithesis of formal legal pluralism, was to marginalize and criminalize indigenous systems of justice and governance. Yet despite the absence of *de jure* legal pluralism, in many countries a de facto form of indirect rule came to characterize relations between states and indigenous peoples in the twentieth century, as the norms, authorities, and practices of native communites became intertwined and superimposed on figures of agrarian law (for example, the *ejido* in Mexico after the 1930s, or the *comunidades campesinas* and *comunidades nativas* in Peru after the 1969 agrarian reform of the Velasco Alvarado government).

The continental mobilization of indigenous peoples' social movements that occurred in the final decades of the twentieth century can be understood in one sense as part of a long tradition of subaltern groups invoking rights and citizenship. Yet as well as demanding the benefits and protections of citizenship historically denied to them in practice, these movements also called for recognition of indigenous peoples' collective rights to self-determination and difference. Framing their claims in the transnational language of human rights, activists, and advocates argued that a degree of autonomy for the norms, authorities, and practices that comprised indigenous systems of governance be guaranteed as an integral part of respect for subaltern indigenous identities, cultures, and ways of life. These demands went beyond appeals for de facto legal pluralism to be recognized *de jure*, constituting instead part of broader moves to refound national constitutions and issue new laws that would supposedly counter the systematic racist exclusion and violence suffered by the continent's native peoples. The evolution of international human rights law provided support for such claims: specific rights for indigenous peoples were recognized through International Labor Organization Convention 169 on Indigenous and Tribal Peoples (ILO C.169), approved in 1989, the first international treaty, which committed states to recognize their rights to exercise their own forms of law. Ratified by a majority of Latin American states throughout the 1990s, ILO C.169 had a major influence on the region's constitutional reform processes during the subsequent decade (Van Cott 2000; Yrigoyen 2011). In 2007, the approval of the United Nations (UN) Declaration on the Rights of Indigenous Peoples by the UN General Assembly set out a stronger formulation for recognition of indigenous self-governance, establishing rights to self-determination within the sovereignty of existing nation-states – something the first UN Special Rapporteur on Indigenous Peoples, Mexican sociologist Rodolfo Stavenhagen, had referred to many years previously as "internal self-determination" (Stavenhagen 2002). The emergent jurisprudence of the Inter-American Court of Human Rights since the mid-2000s also reaffirmed the centrality of indigenous peoples' specific forms of law and governance in safeguarding rights to territory and consultation to ensure free, prior and informed consent (FPIC) about development projects or other government initiatives that stood to affect their ways of life (CEJIL 2014).

Legal recognition of semiautonomous spheres for indigenous justice was a marked feature of constitutional reforms in the Andean region. Colombia was the first country to approve a new constitution recognizing legal pluralism in 1991, followed by Peru (1993), Bolivia (1994), Ecuador (1998), and Venezuela (1999). The most recent constitutions of Ecuador (2008) and Bolivia (2009) went further than previous formulations, declaring that henceforth these states would be based on principles of ethnic pluralism and "plurinationalism." In the Andes these new constitutional regimes specified indigenous jurisdictions and mechanisms or general principles for coordination between ordinary and indigenous law; in Colombia – and to a much lesser extent in Ecuador – special regimes were extended to some Afrodescendant populations. Even in countries where constitutional recognition of legal pluralism was much weaker, such as Mexico or Guatemala, indigenous movements revitalized their own forms of law as part of broader processes of ethnogenesis and judicialized demands that their goverments uphold the commitments set out in ILO C.169 and the UN Declaration to recognize their jurisdictional autonomy. Yet by the 2000s, the onslaught of extractivist forms of economic activity focused on indigenous territories and the multiple and renewed forms of violence this entailed led many analysts to ask whether the formal recognition of legal pluralism in late twentieth century Latin America was not in fact a facet of contemporary forms of capitalist accumulation premised on continuities of racialized colonial frames.

Studies of Legal Pluralism and Indigenous Law

In 1990, Rodolfo Stavenhagen and Diego Iturralde published *Entre la Ley y la Costumbre*, an influential collection of essays underlining the continuing existence of indigenous peoples' legal systems and emerging international legal principles demanding their recognition. Earlier accounts of the forms of governance and dispute resolution in indigenous communities had long been a mainstay of anthropological studies in the region (research often supported by official indigenist institutes). To the extent that these studies theorized legal pluralism, they tended to follow mid-twentieth century anthropological conceptions emphasizing the existence of multiple legal orders within the boundaries of the nation-state.[1] Interdisciplinary studies of legal pluralism multiplied from the 1990s onwards as activist scholars – primarily lawyers and anthropologists – engaged with the challenges of coordinating state law and indigenous legal orders under the aegis of the new constitutional orders. A significant hub for this research was the activist-scholar network, the *Red Latinoamericana de Antropología Jurídica* (RELAJU), which since 2000 held biannual conferences throughout the region. Ethnographic studies continued to focus on documenting justice practices within indigenous communities (see for example, García 2002;

Orellana 2004) and also provided accounts of the legal hybrids generated by justice sector reforms, which recognized a greater role for indigenous laypeople and "culturally specific" forms of mediation, for example, Adriana Terven's work on the juzgado indígena in Cuetzalán in the Mexican state of Puebla (Terven 2009) or Orlando Aragón's research on the officialization of indigenous justice in Michoacán (Aragón 2016). Research published by legal scholars tended to compare constitutional provisions and emerging jurisprudence on issues of coordination across different countries (Yrigoyen 2010, 2011; Condor 2009, 2010; Sousa and Grijalva 2012; Sousa and Exeni 2012). Some studies explicitly combined applied anthropological and legal analysis, such as that by Colombian anthropologist Esther Sánchez Botero (2010), which considered test cases before that country's constitutional court where the author herself had provided special anthropological testimony.

While most publications had a strong normative bent in favor of greater autonomy for indigenous law they also drew on a range of theories of legal pluralism in order to analyze how different legal orders interact. Rather than engaging theoretical debates on legal pluralism per se, the primary concern of these studies was to document and legitimate indigenous justice practices.[2] Multicultural reforms – formulated in a strictly legal register – invariably presented state law and indigenous law as separate, bounded entities, posing the central policy challenge as one of coordination between systems. Yet anthropological and sociological analysis of legal pluralism had long adopted constructivist perspectives and pointed to the porous boundaries between different forms of law as social practice and their mutually constitutive natures. Sally Falk Moore's classic formula of the "semiautonomous sphere" (1973) was often cited as a point of departure.[3] Other analysts explicitly deployed Bourdieu's concept of the legal field to analyze power relations in the constitution of subaltern justice practices, for example, Juan Carlos' Martínez's research on justice practices in the Mixe region of Oaxaca, Mexico (Martínez 2004). Boaventura de Sousa Santos's formulation of *interlegality*, which explicitly aimed to move beyond the traditional legal anthropological conceptualization of different legal orders as separate entities, proved highly influential among Latin American analysts of legal pluralism, pointing as it does to the counter-hegemonic potentials of subaltern forms of law, and the imbrication of the "local" and the transnational.[4] The emphasis Santos' concept of interlegality placed on the dynamism of relations between different legal orders and norms and their heterogenous nature lent itself to empirical studies, which were concerned with the ways in which regimes of multicultural recognition and international human rights were affecting systems of indigenous or community justice. For example, the volume edited by María Teresa Sierra in 2004 explicitly used Santos's analytical framing to explore the uses of law and dynamics between hybrid justice practices and gender relations in different indigenous regions of Mexico, emphasizing the cultural logics and strategies deployed by litigants in context (Sierra 2004). Indeed studies of gender and law concerned with changes in indigenous community law have been a significant area of empirical and interpretative contribution from Latin America. While documenting the exclusion of women from community governance systems and their lack of access to justice, research in Mesoamerican and the Andean regions has also explored how elements such as multicultural justice reforms, legal innovations to address gender discrimination, the influence of human rights nongovernmental organizations (NGOs), and the organization of indigenous women themselves is contributing to transformations of gender ideologies and justice practices within indigenous communities (Barrera 2016; Calla and Paulson 2008; Chenaut 2014; Franco and González 2009; Hernández 2016; Lang and Kucia 2009; Nostas and Sanabría 2009; Sieder and Sierra 2010; Sieder 2017; Sieder and Barrera 2017). These studies emphasize the inherently dynamic nature of subaltern forms of law; by documenting how different actors understand justice and the measures they take to try and secure it, they reveal how indigenous women and their allies are challenging and reframing custom in order to favor women's participation and more appropriate forms of remedy for the specific problems they face. Deploying intersectional perspectives, which explicitly reject separation of the axes of race, class, gender, and other forms of discrimination, such research suggests that group auto-nomy rights for indigenous peoples can be combined with greater gender justice for indigenous women. In this way it counters more abstract philosophical debates – and empirical findings from other regions of the world – which maintain that autonomy for indigenous legal systems invariably deepens and entrenches discrimination against women. These grounded analyses of different Latin American realities have contributed more broadly to "de-essentializing" the study of indigenous law.

Whereas a previous generation of studies of indigenous law and legal pluralism in Latin America focused on the relations between state law and subaltern legal orders, contemporary studies mirrored concerns in the global field of legal pluralism studies with transnational forms of legal ordering. Sally Merry's concept of "vernacularization" (2006), with its focus on the ways in which transnational discourses and frameworks of human rights are taken up, under-stood, contested, and reframed in specific local contexts, thereby reshaping legal consciousness and identities, was deployed in different studies (Hernández 2016; Arteaga 2017). Emerging work on gender and indigenous law points to the vernacularization of human rights – such as the right to a life free of violence and discrimination on the basis of gender – but also the deployment of alternative epistemologies and ontologies. Actors make recourse to such framings in order to critique existing power imbalances and seek decolonized forms and languages for reimagining local law in context. Examples include the use of Andean concepts of male/female balance *chacha-warmi* (Arteaga 2017; Burman 2011) or Mayan concepts of complementarity (Macleod 2011). A concern with the possibilities offered by the judicialization and juridification of indigenous peoples' claims in national and international spheres has also led some scholars to draw on Boaventura de Sousa Santos and César Rodríguez-Garavito's concept of "subaltern cosmopolitan legalities" (2005).[5] As well as signaling the importance of non-recognized or "illegal" forms of law in counter-hegemonic struggles, Sousa and Rodríguez-Garavito emphasize the connections between law and political struggle and the importance of "bottom-up" reimaginings of the law by subaltern groups, which are played out at a range of different scales. Aragón (2015), for example, has deployed the concept in his analysis of the strategic litigation he accompanied in Cherán, Michoacán, and Sieder (2013, 2017) uses it to discuss the collabora-tive research that she and her colleagues have carried out on organized indigenous women's uses of law in Latin America.

Legality, Illegality, and Plural Constellations of Governance

Recent contributions to the field of legal pluralism studies have been concerned with the trans-national and international dimensions of legal ordering, and with the declining sovereign author-ity of states in processes of legal norm-setting. As Franz and Keebet von Benda-Beckmann and Anne Griffiths have observed: "The idea of legal pluralism draws attention to the possibility that there may be sources of law other than the nation-state and has become far more widely accepted than it was only a few decades ago" (2009a, 1). Various tenets of legal pluralism have now become common sense in the study of law, including the existence of a plurality of legal orders, the decentralization of the state, and the strengthening of non-state norms (Michaels 2009, 255). The existence of global legal pluralism is now widely accepted and its study has extended far beyond legal anthropology, with legal sociologists and social theorists analyzing the nature and relevance of a wide range of non-state forms of law (Michaels 2009; Schiff 2009).[6]

However, these more sociological appreciations of global legal pluralism still tend to approach the law in normative or institutional terms. By contrast, anthropological approaches to law and legal pluralism emphasize process and law's social constitution. They point to multiple competing and overlapping normative orders coexisting in the same social field, each encompassing distinct discourses, practices, routines, symbols, and identities. Such constructivist perspectives raise the central question of foundational debates in the anthropology of law: what is and what is not law? More importantly perhaps, they also invite us to consider more centrally the relationship between the law and that which is deemed illegal in any specific time and space. In order to have any purchase for Latin America (and for postcolonies more generally: see Comaroff and Comaroff 2006), a theory of legal pluralism needs to take into account not just the subnational, national, and international, or transnational spheres in which law operates, but also the shifting dynamics between the legal and the illegal, and between law – or the order that law purports to guarantee – and violence (see Lemaitre in this volume).[7] While the existence of multiple sources and types of law is now generally accepted, the processes underpinning changing dynamics between the "legal" and the "illegal" within these legally plural landscapes have generally been less considered. Mark Goodale has argued for a dialectical approach to legality/illegality, stating:

> the spaces of the legal are in constant motion with the spaces of the nonlegal or illegal … because legality and illegality are never finally settled discursively, but remain two necessary parts of the same conceptual framework within which 'law' itself can serve its purposes.

> *(2008, 216)*

In their introduction to a special issue of *PoLAR: Political and Legal Anthropology Review* on anthropology in contexts of supposed "illegality," Kedron Thomas and Rebecca Galenda remind us "how dominant legal discourse [be it national or international] … 'illegalizes' particular people and practices, excluding them from the moral–legal community and rendering them available for criminalization, marginalization, exploitation, and even dehumanization" (2013, 211). By focusing on the socio-political processes and power dynamics that underpin what they call "illegalization" (2013, 211), Thomas and Galenda underline the importance of analyzing the relationship between the constitution of law and the exclusion and criminalization of different subjects. In other words, they insist on one of the central concerns of critical legal studies: the analysis of how power operates through law. However, the category of illegality covers an enormous range of phenomena that merit disaggregation if we are to distinguish – and theorize – their changing roles in plural constellations of governance. While in practice the boundaries between different phenomena or social practices deemed illegal by states are often blurred, I suggest here four heuristic categories of illegality emerging from although by no means exclusive to Latin America that may contribute to such an undertaking: *informality*; *transnational criminal economies*; *corruption*; and the *criminalization of social protest*.

1 *Informality:* this category, the subject of decades of sociological debate, refers principally to non-state ordering of spheres such as commerce, employment, or the provision of social goods such as housing, justice, or security. The preponderance of informality is a long-standing feature of Latin American societies and underlines the structural exclusion of the majority of the region's population from the formal protections of the law and the ways in which existing forms of social regulation are simultaneously tolerated by the state and criminalized in practice. (See for example, Boaventura de Sousa Santos' landmark study of

alternative regulation of informal housing in a Rio de Janeiro favela [1977], or the work of
Goldstein 2004, 2012; Risør 2010; and Snodgrass 2006 on the role of vigilantism and
lynchings in the alternative provision of security)

2   *Transnational criminal economies:* such as the trafficking of narcotics or people are part of
transnational regimes of profit, prohibition, and persecution, which invariably involve
highly violent and coercive social orders. In Latin America analyzes of *la ley del narco* is a
growing area of research, albeit one fraught with ethical and methodological challenges
(Arias 2006; Maldonado 2010). Similarly, the normative dimensions of paramilitarism and
the "guerrilla justice" of the FARC (Revolutionary Armed Forces of Colombia) in Colombia, both paralegal formations intimately related to the transnational drugs economy, have
been analyzed respectively by Aldo Civico (2016) and Alfredo Molano (2001).These
violent orders have increasingly assumed explicitly para-statal forms, in effect constituting
predatory, and lethal constellations of governance across many parts of the continent

3   *Corruption:* governments across Latin America are increasingly legislating against corrupt
practices by state officials in response both to pressure from their own citizens and from
international institutions and other governments. Yet at the same time, massive corruption
and bribery scandals, such as the *Lava Jato* or "carwash" scandal in Brazil, or the case of *La
Línea* in Guatemala (both of which led to the removal of sitting presidents) highlight the
ways in which transnational criminal economies are increasingly intertwined with formal
politics and business in Latin America and across the globe.[8] (Comaroff and Comaroff 2006,
2016; see chapter by Linn Hammergren in this volume)

4   *Criminalization of social protest:* this fourth category of illegality refers to the increasing
criminalization of processes of resistance to neoliberal forms of political economy, which in
effect signals a form of politics by other means or what the Comaroffs have termed "lawfare"
(2006). This has been particularly evident in the repression of indigenous peoples' and
environmental movements across the region, repression which involves both the use of
criminal law and direct state violence in attempts to quash dissent and defend the interests
of transnational capital (Composto and Navarro 2012; Bastos and León de 2014).

Thinking across these categories of illegality can put the extant law and society literature on
"lawlessness" in Latin America in dialog with contemporary debates on legal pluralism in the
region.[9] In more functionalist or state-building framings, Latin America has often been characterized as having weak rule of law – for example, Guillermo O'Donnell's (1993) celebrated
conceptualization of the rule of law and citizenship as a kind of social and territorial heat-map,
with blue zones signifying functioning law and bureaucracy and brown zones disorder and lawlessness. Yet while state institutionality and "law on the books" may apparently be absent for
many geographical regions and populations, these places and people are ruled in practice by
highly effective, and sometimes extremely violent, coercive, gendered, and racialized normative
orders. For example, drug cartels in Mexico regularly publish their "norms" through *narco-
mantas* or in the most gruesome manifestations inscribe them directly onto the bodies of their
victims. Understanding these norms means the difference between life and death for subject
populations and facilitates control over specific geographical areas, economic activities, and
subject populations. As Boaventura de Sousa Santos reminded us, "there is nothing inherently
good, progressive or emancipatory about legal pluralism" (Sousa 1995, 114–15). Yet in the main
scholars have shied away from using theories of legal pluralism to frame more systemic analysis
of these phenomena. Aside from the ethical and political risks involved, many would argue that
extending the notion of "law" to all forms of social regulation means that law as a concept loses
all analytical purchase. Yet understanding the nature of law and its effects requires attention to

relations between the legal and the illegal. This can reveal changing dynamics within normative and institutional fields (local, national, and transnational), and also changing legal imaginations, consciousness, and identities. How do perceptions about what is legal or illegal change across time and space? How do people negotiate the often indeterminate frontiers between them and with what effects on their legal subjectivities?[10] And how do such shifts within plural constellations of governance relate to broader patterns of political economy and global legal pluralism?

In their call to put political science and anthropological perspectives on democracy into dialog, Desmond Arias and Daniel Goldstein advance the idea of "violent pluralism" as a characteristic feature of Latin America, which they define as "states, social elites, and subalterns employing violence in the quest to establish or contest regimes of citizenship, justice, rights, and a democratic social order" (2010, 4). Rather than taking debates on law or legal pluralism as their point of departure, Arias and Goldstein focus on the pervasiveness of violence in Latin America and consider what that implies for understandings of democracy. Nonetheless, by emphasizing the centrality of violence to the functioning of the region's political systems and challenging more normative understandings of politics, they invite further reflection on the relationship between law, legal pluralism, and violence. As they observe, "violence is implicated both in the institutional structure of the regimes and the ways these regimes are inserted into the international system" (2010, 13). They also point to the ways in which state institutions function more or less optimally in different contexts – echoing O'Donnell's formulation – but insist that these are intrinsically connected with each other. In other words, the securing of political order without violence in some contexts always depends on the securing of order through the direct use of violence in others, as postcolonial studies have emphasized (Mbembe 2017). These propositions lead us to ask what role different modalities of illegality and violence play in contemporary constellations of governance in Latin America, and what law and society scholarship from Latin America can contribute to their understanding. In recent years, legal orders across the region have become more formally plural, recognizing indigenous and Afrodescendant jurisdictions but also incorporating international human rights and commercial law into domestic law. International standards are increasingly important and their guarantee is demanded by citizens and social movements through different kinds of political and legal mobilization. Yet at the same time violence and illegality characterize most people's everyday experiences of the state. Can a regional theory of legal pluralism informed by more anthropological sensibilities toward law account for the shifting interplay between legality and illegality?

César Rodríguez-Garavito makes an important theoretical intervention, which potentially bridges the division in the literature between a focus on legal pluralism and indigenous peoples, on the one hand, and on the relationship between contemporary forms of governance, law, illegality, and violence on the other. Rodríguez-Garavito used the term "social minefields" to conceptualize the dynamics at play between law, extractive economies, and violence in Afrodescendant and indigenous territories in Colombia:

> I use the term "minefields" to refer to these territories and the dynamics of social interaction produced within them, including FPIC processes. They are minefields in both the sociological and the economic sense. In sociological terms, they are true social *fields*, [emphasis in original] characterized by the features of enclave, extractive economies, which include grossly unequal power relations between companies and communities, and limited state presence. They are *mine*fields [emphasis in original] because they are highly risky; within this terrain, social relations are fraught with violence, suspicion dominates, and any false step can bring lethal consequences. In this regard, they

are an indication of the volatile social relations that are associated with hybrid economies – situated at the crossroads of legality, illegality, and informality – which abound in nations of the Global South (and increasingly Global North) in times of globalization.

(2011, 5)

By pointing to what he calls "hybrid economies," Rodríguez-Garavito raises the central question of what kind of il/legal orders of governance underpin contemporary forms of accumulation in neoliberal Latin America. The social minefields he refers to in Colombia are characterized by one of the most advanced legal formulations for the recognition of cultural difference existing in the region, and the institutionalization of international legal standards for indigenous and Afrodescendant peoples, most notably processes of prior consultation to secure free and informed consent (FPIC). The fragmentation and instability of multiple forms of order, many highly violent and coercive,[11] seem to coexist with a hyperlegalization of the political, or what some have referred to as the fetishization of the law.[12] Viviane Weitzner, also working with indigenous and Afrodescendant peoples in Colombia, has proposed the concept of "raw law" to refer to the often lethal rules and regulations deployed by armed actors, an interpretation of the interplay between state regulation and violence inspired by Achile Mbembe's work on "raw economy" – the illegal shadow or "dark" economy that structures contemporary global capitalism (Weitzner 2017, 2018).

Plural Forms of Governance: Fragmented and Overlapping Sovereignties

Outside Latin America, recent contributions to the field of legal pluralism studies have also turned to the ambiguous divisions and continuities between the legal and the illegal, and on the role these dynamic and diverse il/legal configurations play in securing neoliberal forms of governance (Benda-Beckmann, Benda-Beckmann, and Ekert 2009b). Jean Comaroff and John Comaroff (2006) have rightly emphasized the need for an analytical shift within legal anthropology from concern with legal pluralism per se, to a consideration of the combined problematic of law and governance in the contemporary world, and specifically relationships between law and governance in the age of neoliberalism. The securitization of development is particularly important in this respect, with securitization paradigms increasingly favoring the partial suspension of constitutional guarantees for specific regions or populations,[13] blurring the line between the legal and the illegal and creating "gray zones" of intensified legal ambiguity. Across Latin America indigenous peoples' movements for self-determination, autonomy, and territorial defense are caught in comparable gray zones: formally recognized by national and international legal instruments and provisions yet subjected to violence and increasingly to criminalization, they inhabit a liminal space that Deborah Poole incisively described as a place "between threat and guarantee" (Poole 2004).

I want to suggest that anthropological theories of sovereignty can contribute to a regionally informed theory of legal pluralism that engages debates on illegality. Anthropologists have distinguished between legal and de facto sovereignty; for example, Thomas Blom Hansen and Finn Stepputat define legal sovereignty as "the legitimate right to govern" and de facto sovereignty as the "right over life" and "the ability to kill, discipline and punish with impunity" (2006, 296). Yet while many theorists have taken their cue from the work of Giorgio Agamben and Carl Schmitt, emphasizing the violence of both *de jure* and de facto forms of sovereignty, others have suggested an analytical focus on the situated ways of life that constitute and sustain sovereignty, rather than just conceiving it as the power of exclusion and violence (Humphrey 2007). Caroline

Humphreys's appeal speaks to the concept of indigenous sovereignties, which can be understood as claims for alternative ontologies or ways of being in the world, moral orders and constructions of law and justice "from below," subaltern forms of "legal consciousness" and identity, and forms of defense against the racialized violences visited on specific populations and territories. Indigenous sovereignties are constituted through everyday practices and projected through a range of transnationalized legal imaginations claiming autonomy as a right, yet in practice they continue to exist in a liminal space between the *de jure* and the de facto. In this way, they signal the porous and indeterminate boundaries of the legal and the illegal in Latin America; the fact that the law is inherently unstable, dynamic, and constantly contested. The mobilization of "languages of stateness" (Blom Hansen and Stepputat 2001) by indigenous movements and communities in order to stake their claims and defend their territories, natural resources, and political autonomy reflects the current global purchase of the law as a language of politics, but also its historic importance as an idiom of both elite and subaltern politics in Latin America.

These forms of claim-making occur within a broader context of fragmented or overlapping sovereignties (Randeria 2007; Sieder 2011) characterized by competition and conflict between different transnationalized actors pursuing territorial control, new forms of governance and political economy. The fragmentation of the Weberian paradigm of state legality is intimately related to the privatization and deregulation that are the hallmarks of contemporary capitalism and governance, leading to a "dispersal" or "fracturing" of state sovereignty into the plural, partial, and lateral sovereignties, which characterize twenty-first century forms of private indirect governance and produce the paradoxical "present-absence of state enforcement" (Comaroff and Comaroff 2016, 28, 39). Joshua Barker refers to "informal sovereignties," observing that "[they] are most evident at the margins of modern state power: in remote areas, squatter settlements, zones of illegality, conflict zones, domains of 'traditional' authority, privatized concessions, free trade zones." (2013, 260). Veena and Poole (2004) suggested that such margins of state power, where the hold of state power is tenuous and the state as a project is always incomplete and contested, are in fact central to processes of state formation. As Daniel Goldstein has argued, "understanding the relationship between the state and its margins, particularly in terms of justice and security making, requires us to move beyond a limited vision of the law's spatial distribution and connection with nonstate forms of ordering" (2012, 29). In other words, the constitution of the contemporary state in Latin America is characterized by rule through fragmented and overlapping sovereignties, which are both *de jure* and de facto, legal and "illegal." These multiple sovereignties are generated in part through law and particularly through legal pluralism at the global scale where human rights, commercial law, soft law mechanisms, and other globalized forms of ordering are superimposed. At the same time they are also configured through highly violent, coercive, and illegal means. As Rodríguez-Garavito (2011), Weitzner (2017, 2018) and others have signaled, this is particularly evident in disputes surrounding extractive industry projects in territories claimed by indigenous people. The actors in such disputes or "social minefields" may include transnational companies and their local allies, state institutions (national or federal and municipal authorities, the military, different police corps, etc.,), private security firms hired by the companies to police the sites of extractive developments, and illegal armed groups, or paramilitaries linked to drug cartels, generically referred to as "organized crime." Within such contexts indigenous peoples' forms of law and governance, or *derecho propio*, are increasingly "illegalized" in practice; for example, the authorities of the *policía comunitaria* in Guerrero, Mexico, who in recent years have been charged with kidnapping when they detain suspected miscreants (Sierra 2016), or community leaders in Guatemala who face criminal charges when they try to assert their rights over communal land in conflicts with mining companies (Mazariegos 2014). The boundaries between what is "the state" and what is not, and what is legal and what is illegal, are increasingly difficult to decipher. More broadly, analysis of indigenous peoples' experience with the law in Latin America indicates that what is considered illegal at one moment can become part of the formal law the next, and then again be illegalized in practice. This is clearly the case for *derecho propio*, which was marginal or outlawed, then became part of state legality through late twentieth century multicultural constitutional reforms, but has been illegalized in practice – as evidenced by indigenous authorities being subjected to criminal prosecutions for exercising their own forms of law.[14] This heightened ambiguity surrounding the legal appears to be a central factor in facilitating the processes of accumulation and dispossession that threaten the very existence of indigenous peoples across the continent.

Conclusions

In a key intervention in debates on law and legal pluralism, anthropologists Jean Comaroff and John Comaroff called for analysis of "the ways in which legally plural configurations secure different forms of governance in the age of neoliberalism" (Comaroff and Comaroff 2009, 32, 39). I have suggested here that the concept of fragmented and overlapping sovereignties may help us understand new modalities of governance and power in Latin America, allowing as it does for analysis of the dialectical relationship between plural forms of legality and illegality, between structural and other forms of violence, and between hegemonic and counter-hegemonic constructions of law. Anthropological perspectives on law have underlined the importance of exploring ethnographically how people in different contexts and historical moments conceive of law, justice, and security, and their actions to try and achieve them. Such research perspectives help us continue to evaluate the legacies of nearly three decades of multicultural legal reform in Latin America,[15] as well as the transformative potentials of different constellations of legal pluralism. As Mark Goodale has observed, a reconceptualized legal pluralism in Latin America "is both permanently shifting, and potentially subversive" (2008, 220). He argues that the fragmentary nature of law in the region – and thus the inevitable incompleteness of hegemonic, state law – opens the possibilities for non-elite sectors to experiment with a plurality of legal strategies. In line with other Latin American scholars, I emphasize the counter-hegemonic elements present in the fragmented sovereign landscape of contemporary legal pluralism, and the importance of careful ethnographic research into these configurations. Numerous examples show how neoliberal multiculturalism's limited endorsement of indigenous autonomies has opened the way for new demands and forms of self-determination, which question dominant logics of extractivism and commodification. Within plural fields of often highly violent regulatory orders, communities and social movements continue to invoke international law alongside their own ethical and moral constructions, insisting on the legality – but more importantly, the legitimacy – of their alternative practices and ontologies. In the process they generate new understandings and subjectivities, which ultimately go far beyond the languages of the law. Ethnic identity is but one dimension of these subaltern sovereignties; these fragile and contested sites of autonomy in fact constitute claims to forms of sociality, which contrast with the dominant tropes of individual advancement and ever more militarized forms of development and security promoted by national and transnational elites. In sum, in this chapter I have argued that more anthropologically informed research on fragmented sovereignties and the interplay between the legal and the illegal from Latin America makes important contributions to the broader theorization of legal pluralities and contemporary constellations of governance, and thus to law and society scholarship as a whole. Debate between empirical, positioned ethnographic research, and efforts to develop more regionally grounded theories of (i) legal pluralism continue to constitute the heart of this endeavor.

Notes

1 See for example, Chanock 1985; Griffiths 1986; Merry 1988; Moore 1996, 2005.
2 One exception is the work of Antonio Wolkmer (2015), who proposes a theory of legal pluralism to counter prevailing traditions of legal monism in the region.
3 Moore proposed that a small field, such as that observable by an anthropologist, could generate its own rules, customs, and symbols internally, but that it was "vulnerable to the rules and decisions and other forces emanating from the larger world by which it is surrounded" (1973, 720).
4 Sousa defined interlegality as:

> the conception of different legal spaces superimposed, interpenetrated and mixed in our minds, as much as in our actions, either on occasions of qualitative leaps or sweeping crises in our life trajectories, or in the dull routine of eventless everyday life. [He stated that] We live in a time of porous legality or of legal porosity, multiple networks of legal orders forcing us to constant transitions and trespassings. Our legal life is constituted by an intersection of different legal orders, that is, by interlegality.
>
> *(Sousa 1995, 473)*

5 Sousa and Rodríguez-Garavito (2005) deploy "subaltern cosmopolitan legalities" to refer to locally grounded forms of resistance and legal innovation by those most marginalized within the current global order. They also emphasize the need to give due weight to non-hegemonic or non-Western elaborations of rights and human dignity in subaltern formulations of law.
6 See for example, Cotterrell on legal transnationalism and the challenges this poses for legal sociology (Cotterrell 2009), or César Rodríguez-Garavito's call for a "post-Westphalian conception of law" (Rodríguez-Garavito 2011).
7 One important contribution, which did consider these questions for the case of Colombia, and explicitly discusses legal pluralism, is the two volumes *Caleidoscopio de las Justicias en Colombia*, edited by Mauricio García-Villegas and Boaventura de Sousa Santos (2001).
8 They also point to the ways in which accusations of corruption have become part of the idiom of political competition, as they have elsewhere in the world.
9 Goldstein's proposal of "outlawing" (2012) is a signal contribution in this respect.
10 On the relationship between perceptions of justice and legal subjectivities see the essays in the collection edited by Sandra Brunnegger and Karen Ann Faulk (2016).
11 Daniel Goldstein emphasizes the ways in which "marginal spaces are characterized not by stable forms of social ordering and by plural systems of law and legality, but by fractured, ever-shifting planes of law and lawlessness, order and chaos" (2012, 30).
12 See Lemaitre 2009.
13 See chapter by Madrazo and Pérez Correa in this volume.
14 See for example, Marc Simon Thomas's analysis of intercultural justice coordination in Ecuador (2016).
15 For an important contribution on Colombia see Chaves 2011; on Mexico see Hernández, Sierra, and Sieder 2013.

References

Aragón, Orlando. 2015. El Derecho después de la Insurrección. Cherán y el Uso Contra-Hegemónico del Derecho en la Suprema Corte de Justicia de México. *Sortuz. Oñati Journal of Emergent Socio-Legal Studies* 7(2): 71–87.

Aragón, Orlando. 2016. *De la "vieja a la nueva justicia indígena." Transformaciones y continuidades en las justicias indígenas en Michoacán.* Mexico: Universidad Autónoma Metropolitana.

Arias, Enrique Desmond. 2006. *Drugs and Democracy in Rio de Janeiro: Trafficking, Social Networks, and Public Security.* Chapel Hill: University of North Carolina Press.

Arias, Enrique Desmond and Daniel Goldstein (eds). 2010. *Violent Democracies in Latin America.* Durham: Duke University Press.

Arteaga Böhrt and Ana Cecilia. 2017. "Let Us Walk Together: *Chachawarmi* [male–female] Complementarity and Indigenous Autonomies in Bolivia," In Rachel Sieder (ed.). *Demanding Justice and Security: Indigenous Women and Legal Pluralities in Latin America.* Rutgers University Press, New Brunswick, New Jersey, and London, 150–72.

Barker, Joshua. 2013. Epilogue: Ethnographies of State-Centrism. *Oceania* 83(3): 259–64.

Barrera, Anna. 2016. *Violence against Women in Legally Plural Settings: Experiences and Lessons from the Andes.* Oxon and New York: Routledge.

Bastos, Santiago and Quimy de León. 2014. *Dinámicas de Despojo y Resistencia en Guatemala. Comunidades, Estado, Empresas.* Guatemala: Diakonía/Colibrí Zurdo.

Benda-Beckmann Von, Franz, Keebet Von Benda-Beckmann, and Anne Griffiths (eds.). 2009a. *The Power of Law in a Transnational World, Anthropological Enquiries*, New York and Oxford, Berghan Books.

Benda-Beckmann Von, Franz, Keebet Von Benda-Beckmann, and Julia Eckert (eds.). 2009b. *Rules of Law and Laws of Ruling. On the Governance of Law.* Surrey and Burlington, Ashgate.

Blom Hansen, T. and Finn Stepputat (eds.). 2001. *States of Imagination: Ethnographic Explorations of the Post-colonial State*, Durham NC, Duke University Press.

Blom Hansen, T. and Finn Stepputat. 2006. Sovereignty Revisited. *Annual Review of Anthropology* (35): 295–315.

Brunnegger, Sandra and Karen Ann Faulk (Eds.). 2016. *A Sense of Justice. Legal Knowledge and Lived Experience in Latin America.* Stanford, Stanford University Press.

Burman, Anders. 2011. Chachawarmi: Silence and Rival Voices on Decolonisation and Gender Politics in Andean Bolivia. *Journal of Latin American Studies* 43(1): 65–91.

Calla, Pamela and Susan Paulson. 2008. *Justicia Comunitaria y Género en las Zonas Rurales de Bolivia. Ocho Estudios de Caso.* La Paz: Oasis-Red de Participación y Justicia de Bolivia-Jiquisiña-Comai Pachamama.

CEJIL. 2014. *Sumarios de Jurisprudencia/Pueblos Indígenas.* Center for Justice and International Law – CEJIL, Costa Rica. Available at: www.cejil.org/sites/default/files/legacy_files/SumariosJurisprudencia_PueblosIndigenas.pdf. Accessed May 5, 2017.

Chanock, M. 1985. *Law, Custom and Social Order: The Colonial Experience in Malawi and Zambia.* Cambridge: Cambridge University Press.

Chaves, Margarita. (Comp.). 2011. *La Multiculturalidad Estatalizada: Indígenas, Afrodescendientes y Configuraciones de Estado.* Bogotá: ICANH.

Chenaut, Victoria. 2014. *Género y Procesos Interlegales.* Mexico: El Colegio de Michoacán/ CIESAS.

Civico, Aldo. 2016. *The Para-State. An Ethnography of Colombia's Death Squads.* Berkeley: University of California Press.

Comaroff, Jean and John Comaroff. 2006. "Law and Disorder in the Postcolony: An Introduction," In John L. Comaroff and Jean Comaroff (eds.), *Law and Disorder in the Postcolony.* Chicago and London: University of Chicago Press, 1–56.

Comaroff, Jean and John Comaroff. 2009, "Reflections on the Anthropology of Law, Governance and Sovereignty," In Benda-Beckmann, F. von, K. von Benda-Beckmann, and J. Eckert (eds.) *Rules of Law and Laws of Ruling: On the Governance of Law*, Ashgate, Surrey and Burlington, 31–59.

Comaroff, Jean and John Comaroff. 2016. *The Truth about Crime. Sovereignty, Knowledge, Social Order.* Chicago: University of Chicago Press.

Composto, Claudia and Mina Navarro. 2012. Estados, transnacionales extractivas y comunidades movilizadas: dominación y resistencias en torno de la minería a gran escala en América Latina. *Revista Theomi* 25: 58–78.

Condor, Eddie. 2009. *Estado de la Relación entre Justicia Indígena y Justicia Estatal en los Países Andino: Estudios de Casos en Colombia, Perú, Ecuador y Bolivia.* Lima, Perú: Comisión Andina de Juristas.

Condor, Eddie. 2010. *Experiencias de Coordinación y Cooperación entre Sistemas Jurídicos en la Región Andina.* Lima, Perú: Comisión Andina de Juristas.

Cotterrell, Roger. 2009. Spectres of Transnationalism: Changing Terrains of the Sociology of Law. *Journal of Law and Society* 36(4):481–500.

Das, Veena and Deborah Poole, (eds.). 2004. *Anthropology in the Margins of the State.* Santa Fe: SAR Press.

Franco, Rocío and María Alejandra González Luna. 2009. *Las Mujeres en la Justicia Comunitaria: Víctimas, Sujetos y Actores.* Serie Justicia Comunitaria en Los Andes: Perú y Ecuador, Vol. 3. Lima: IDL.

García, Fernando. 2002. *Formas Indígenas de Administrar Justicia. Estudios de Caso de la Nacionalidad Quichúa Ecuatoriana.* Quito: FLACSO-Ecuador.

Goldstein, Daniel. 2004. *The Spectacular City. Violence and Performance in Urban Bolivia.* Durham and London: Duke University Press.

Goldstein, Daniel. 2012. *Outlawed. Between Security and Rights in a Bolivian City.* Durham and London: Duke University Press.

Goodale, Mark. 2008. "Legalities and Illegalities," In Deborah Poole (ed.) *A Companion to Latin American Anthropology.* Malden and Oxford: Blackwell, 214–29.

Griffiths, John. 1986. What is Legal Pluralism? *Journal of Legal Pluralism* 24: 1–50.

Hernández, Rosalva. 2016. *Multiple Injustices: Indigenous Women and Legal Pluralism in Latin America*. Tucson: University of Arizona Press.

Hernández, Rosalva, María Teresa Sierra, and Rachel Sieder (eds.). 2013. *Justicias Indígenas y Estado: Violencias Contemporáneas*. Mexico: FLACSO/ CIESAS.

Humphrey, Caroline. 2007. "Sovereignty," In David Nugent and Joan Vincent (eds.) *A Companion to the Anthropology of Politics*. New York: Blackwell, 418–36.

Lang, Miriam and Anna Kucia. 2009. *Mujeres Indígenas y Justicia Ancestral*. Quito: UNIFEM.

Lemaitre, Julieta. 2009, *El Derecho Como Conjuro. Fetichismo Legal, Violencia y Movimientos Sociales*. Bogotá: Siglo del Hombre Editores y Universidad de Los Andes.

Macleod, Morna. 2011. *Nietas del Fuego, Creadores del Alba. Luchas Político-Culturales de Mujeres Mayas*. Guatemala: FLACSO.

Maldonado, Salvador. 2010. *Los Márgenes del Estado Mexicano. Territorios Ilegales, Desarrollo y Violencia en Michoacán*. Zamora: El Colegio de Michoacán.

Martínez, Juan Carlos. 2004. *Derechos Indígenas en los Juzgados. Un Análisis del Campo Judicial Oaxaqueño*. Mexico: INAH.

Mazariegos, Mónica. 2014. *Derecho a la Consulta y Disenso. Por el uso Contrahegemónico del Derecho*. Doctoral thesis, Universidad Carlos III, Madrid.

Mbembe, Achille. 2017. *Critique of Black Reason*. Durham NC: Duke University Press.

Merry, Sally. 1988. Legal Pluralism. *Law and Society Review* 22: 869–96.

Merry, Sally. 2006. *Human Rights and Gender Violence: Translating International Law into Local Justice*. Chicago, University of Chicago Press.

Michaels, R. 2009. Global Legal Pluralism. *Annual Review of Law and Social Science* 5: 243–62.

Molano, Alfredo. 2001. "La justicia guerrillera," In *El Caleidoscopio de las Justicias en Colombia: Tomo II*. Mauricio García-Villegas and Boaventura de Sousa Santos. Bogotá, Siglo del Hombre: 331–88.

Moore, Sally Falk. 1973. Law and Social Change: The Semi-Autonomous Social Field as an Appropriate Subject of Study. *Law & Society Review* 7(4): 719–46.

Moore, Sally Falk. 1996. *Social Facts and Fabrications: "Customary" Law on Kilimanjaro, 1880–1980*. Cambridge and New York: Cambridge University Press.

Moore, Sally Falk. 2005. "Certainties Undone: Fifty Turbulent Years of Legal Anthropology, 1949–1999," In Sally Falk Moore (ed.), *Law and Anthropology: A Reader*. Oxford: Blackwells: 346–67.

Nostas, Mercedes and Carmen Elena Sanabría Salmón. 2009. *Detrás del Cristal con que se Mira: Órdenes Normativos e Interlegalidad. Mujeres Quechuas, Aymaras, Sirionó, Trinitarias, Chimane, Chiquitanas y Ayoreas*. La Paz: Coordinadora de la Mujer.

O'Donnell, Guillermo. 1993. *On the State, Democratization and Some Conceptual Problems: A Latin American View with Glances at Some Post-Communist Countries*. Kellog Institute Working Paper #192. Available at: www3.nd.edu/~kellogg/publications/workingpapers/WPS/192.pdf. Accessed May 10, 2016.

Orellana, René. 2004. *Interlegalidad y Campos Jurídicos. Discurso y Derecho en la Configuración de Órdenes Semiautónomos en Comunidades Quechuas de Bolivia*. Amsterdam: Universitat von Amsterdam.

Poole, Deborah. 2004. "Between Threat and Guarantee: Justice and Community in the Margins of the Peruvian State," In Veena Das and Deborah Poole (eds.) *Anthropology in the Margins of the State*. Baltimore: Johns Hopkins University Press, 35–65.

Randeria, Shalini. 2007. The State of Globalization Legal Plurality, Overlapping Sovereignties and Ambiguous Alliances between Civil Society and the Cunning State in India. *Theory, Culture & Society* 24(1): 1–33.

Risør, Helene. 2010. Twenty Hanging Dolls and a Lynching: Defacing Dangerousness and Enacting Citizenship in El Alto, Bolivia. *Public Culture* 22(3): 465–85.

Rodríguez-Garavito, César. y Boaventura de Sousa Santos. 2005, *Law and Globalization from Below: Towards a Cosmopolitan Legality*, Cambridge and New York: Cambridge University Press.

Rodríguez-Garavito, César. 2011. Ethnicity.gov: Global governance, Indigenous Peoples, and the Rights to Prior Consultation in Social Minefields. In *Indiana Journal of Global Legal Studies* 18(1): 263–305.

Salvatore, Ricardo, Carlos Aguirre, and Gil Joseph (eds.). 2001. *Crime and Punishment in Latin America: Law and Society since Colonial Times*. Durham NC: Duke University Press.

Sánchez, Esther. 2010. *Justicia y Pueblos Indígenas de Colombia. La Tutela Como Medio para la Construcción del Entendimiento Intercultural*. 3ª edición. Bogotá: UNIJUS.

Schiff, Paul. 2009, The New Legal Pluralism. *Annual Review of Law and Social Science* 5: 225–42.

Sieder, Rachel (ed.). 2017. *Demanding Justice and Security: Indigenous Women and Legal Pluralities in Latin America*. New Brunswick: Rutgers University Press.

Sieder, Rachel and Anna Barrera. 2017. Women and Legal Pluralism: Lessons from Indigenous Governance Systems in the Andes. *Journal of Latin American Studies* 49(3): 633–58.

Sieder, Rachel and María Teresa Sierra. 2010. *Indigenous Women's Access to Justice in Latin America.* CMI working paper. Bergen, Norway: Chr. Michelsen Institute.

Sieder, Rachel. 2011. Contested Sovereignties: Indigenous Law, Violence and State Effects in Postwar Guatemala. *Critique of Anthropology* 31(3): 161–84.

Sieder, Rachel. 2013. Subaltern Cosmopolitan Legalities and the Challenges of Engaged Ethnography. *Universitas Humanística* 75: 219–47.

Sierra, María Teresa (Coord.). 2004. *Haciendo Justicia: Interlegalidad, Derecho y Género en Regiones Indígenas*, Mexico: CIESAS/ Miguel Ángel Porrúa.

Sierra, María Teresa. 2016. *Las Apuestas por la paz y la Dignidad de los Pueblos Desde la Justicia y la Seguridad Comunitaria. Pueblos Indígenas y Estado en Guerrero.* Unpublished manuscript on file with author.

Snodgrass, Angelina. 2006. *Popular Injustice: Violence, Community, and Law in Latin America*, Stanford, CA: Stanford University Press.

Sousa Santos de, Boaventura and Agustín Grijalva (Coords.). 2012, *Justicia Indígena, Plurinacionalidad e Interculturalidad en Ecuador.* Quito: Abya Yala/ Fundación Rosa Luxemburg.

Sousa Santos de, Boaventura. 1995. *Toward a New Commonsense: Law, Science and Politics in the Paradigmatic Transition.* London and New York: Routledge.

Sousa Santos de, Boaventura. 1977. The Law of the Oppressed. The Construction and Reproduction of Legality of Pasagarda. *Law and Society Review* 12(1): 5–126.

Sousa Santos de, Boaventura and Mauricio García-Villegas (coords.). 2001. *El Caledoscopio de las Justicias en Colombia*, Tomos I y II. Bogotá: ICAHN/CES/Siglo del Hombre Editores.

Sousa Santos de, Boaventura and José Luis Exeni Rodríguez (eds.). 2012. *Justicia indígena, plurinacionalidad e interculturalidad en Bolivia.* Quito: Abya Yala/ Fundación Rosa Luxemburg.

Stavenhagen, Rodolfo. 2002. "Indigenous People and the State in Latin America. An Ongoing Debate," In Rachel Sieder (Ed.) *Multiculturalism in Latin America: Indigenous Rights, Diversity and Democracy.* Basingstoke and New York: Palgrave Macmillan: 24–44.

Stavenhagen, Rodolfo and Diego Iturralde. 1990. *Entre la Ley y la Costumbre. El Derecho Consuetudinario Indígena en América Latina.* San José: Instituto Indigenista Interamericana.

Terven, Adriana. 2009. *Justicia Indígena en Tiempos Multiculturales. Hacia la Conformación de Proyectos Colectivos Propios: La Experiencia Organizativa de Cuetzálan.* Doctoral Thesis in Social Anthropology. Mexico City: Centro de Investigación y Estudios Superiores en Antropología Social (CIESAS).

Thomas, Kedron and Rebecca Galemba. 2013. Illegal Anthropology: An Introduction. *PoLAR: Journal of the Association for Political and Legal Anthropology* 36(2): 211–14.

Thomas, Marc. 2016. The Effects of Formal Legal Pluralism on Indigenous Authorities in the Ecuadorian Highlands. *Journal of Latin American and Caribbean Anthropology* 22: 46–61.

Van Cott, Donna Lee. 2000. *The Friendly Liquidation of the Past: The Politics of Diversity in Latin America.* Pittsburgh: University of Pittsburgh Press.

Weitzner, Viviane. 2017. "'Nosotros somos Estado.' Contested legalities in decision-making about extractives affecting ancestral territory in Colombia," *Third World Quarterly* 38(5): 1198–214.

Weitzner, Viviane. 2018. *Economía Cruda/ Derecho Crudo. Pueblos Ancestrales, Minería, Derecho y Violencia en Colombia.* Doctoral Thesis in Social Anthropology. Mexico City: Centro de Investigación y Estudios Superiores en Antropología Social (CIESAS).

Wolkmer, Antonio Carlos. 2015. *Pluralismo Jurídico: Fundamentos de uma Nova Cultura no Dereito.* 4th edition. São Paulo: Saraiva.

Yrigoyen, Raquel. (ed.). 2010. *Pueblos Indígenas, Constituciones y Reformas Políticas en América Latina.* Lima: Instituto Internacional de Derecho y Sociedad.

Yrigoyen, Raquel. 2011. "Derecho y Jurisdicción Indígena en la Historia Constitucional: De la Sujeción a la Descolonización," In César Rodríguez-Garavito (Coord.) *El Derecho en América Latina: Los Retos del Siglo XXI.* Buenos Aires: Siglo XXI: 139–59.

5

DISOBEYING THE LAW
Latin America's Culture of Noncompliance with Rules

Mauricio García-Villegas[1]

Latin America's culture of noncompliance with rules originated during the Spanish and Portuguese colonial period. Since then, writers, thinkers, and political leaders throughout the continent have referred to this phenomenon.[2] As far back as 1743, for example, Viceroy Eslava complained to his superiors because he felt that "the provinces of Nueva Granada were practically ungovernable" (McFarlane 1997). With the coming of independence, norms changed but the gap between law and social practices remained. In the mid-nineteenth century, Mexican President Benito Juárez lamented "the generally observed tendency among peoples to ignore obligations that the laws impose upon them" (Juárez 1987, 225). The poet Octavio Paz used to say that in Mexico people live a constitutional lie because no one ever complies with the law.

Evidence of the roots of this culture can be found in popular Latin American parlance. For example, one often hears the expressions "*hecha la ley, hecha la trampa*" ("every law has a loophole") and "*la ley es para los de ruana*" ("there is one law for the rich and another for the poor"), as well as other, more official refrains, such as "*se acata pero no se cumple*" ("one complies but does not carry out"). In Brazil, the word *jeito* refers to a way of resolving problems by going above – or outside – existing codes, norms, and laws (Rosenn 1985). There is also an old Brazilian adage that says "*manda quem pode, obedece quem quer*" ("those who can, give orders; those who want to, obey"), which offers a good reflection of the disparity between the ruling class's vision of power and law and that of their subjects. In Mexico, people often say "*para mis amigos todo, para mis enemigos la ley*" ("for my friends, everything; for my enemies, the law"), and President Benito Juárez who is popularly claimed to have stated, "*para mis amigos paz y justicia, para mis enemigos la ley*" ("for my friends, peace and justice; for my enemies, the law").

Latin American literature also contains abundant references to the culture of noncompliance, through indomitable characters who answer to nobody. *Martín Fierro*, the famous poem by Argentinean writer José Hernández, narrates the world view of a rural policeman who rebels against the prevailing order so as to capture a criminal. Also in *gaucho* country, *Don Segundo Sombra* by Ricardo Güiraldes portrays the life of characters who live proudly and freely, without the need for society and even less for the state, similar to dynamics portrayed in *El Mundo es Ancho y Ajeno*, written by Peruvian author Ciro Alegría, or *Juan Moreira* by Argentina's Eduardo Gutiérrez. In *El Chulla Romero y Flores* by Ecuadorian author Jorge Icaza, society is divided by differences in class and power, and nobody follows the rules. Similarly, in Venezuela and Peru, we find unruly characters who submit to no one, such as Ño Pernalete and Mujiquita from the novel *Doña Bárbara* by Rómulo Gallegos, and Jaguar in *La Ciudad y los Perros* by Mario Vargas Llosa. Similarly, many Latin American children's tales extol shrewdness and sharpness, often telling the story of a picaresque character who triumphs in the midst of adversity. For example, in *La Sopa de Piedras* (Brazil), *Tío Conejo y Tío Lobo* (Ecuador), *Pedro Urdemales* (Guatemala), the Peruvian story *El Bastón de Santo Lloque* (Peru), *Juan Bobo y el Secreto de la Princesa* (Dominican Republic), *Pedro Rimales, Curandero* (Venezuela), and *El rey de Hojarasca* (Nicaragua), a mischievous character emerges gracefully from a situation of oppressive impediments. However, such literature is concerned not only with the noncompliance of individuals but also with that of the state. In *Yo el Supremo* by Augusto Roa Bastos and *El Otoño del Patriarca* by Gabriel García Márquez, the state is an institution guided more by the whims of its rulers than by law on the books. The novel *El Coronel no Tiene Quien le Escriba*, also by García Márquez, tells the story of an official who waits endlessly for his pension, which has been promised but never arrives.

Although ubiquitous throughout Latin American history and literary tropes, this culture of noncompliance with rules is a little-studied phenomenon. According to Carlos Santiago Nino, "It is surprising that despite the evident Argentine tendency towards illegality, it has not been cited until now by scientists, historians and economists as a significant factor indicating Argentine underdevelopment" (2005, 28, 29).[3] Of course there are exceptions. Perhaps the most notable among them is the work of anthropologist Roberto DaMatta, for whom the manner in which Brazilians sing, dance, and celebrate is key to understanding their social system, particularly their detachment vis-à-vis power and authority (Da Matta 1987, 2002). The writings of Julio Mafud fall into this category, especially his book *Psicología de la Viveza Criolla*, which astutely describes the way in which Argentines are always trying to capitalize on their interactions with authority. In this respect Nino's book *Un País al Margen de la Ley*, in which the author, from a sociological perspective, shows the costs of noncompliance for democracy and development in Argentina, is a key reference work. Some historians of the region have also concerned themselves with identifying elements of popular culture that help explain Latin Americans' relationship with authority and the law, including José Luis Romero in Argentina, Leopoldo Zea in Mexico, and Mario Góngora in Chile.

From what has been said, noncompliance with rules in Latin America is widespread and, despite being a little-studied phenomenon, has called the attention not only of lawmakers and political leaders but also of intellectuals and writers. In Europe and in the USA, interest in legal disobedience is rather marginal among law and society scholars. Only in two cases does it seem to arouse attention: when noncompliance questions the legitimacy of the law, leading to the problem of civil disobedience,[4] which is a matter treated by legal philosophy; and when it comes to the implications and causes of crime in society, which is a subject treated by criminology.[5] In both cases, noncompliance is perceived as a dysfunctional, marginal, and exceptional social phenomenon.[6] In Latin America social and legal disobedience is often seen as a rather "normalized," or even justified social fact of both laypeople and officials, which has relevant consequences for the functioning of democracy, economic development, and citizenship. This explains why Latin America has developed a unique sociological or socio-political perspective on noncompliance that does not exist in Europe or in the USA.

In this chapter I will review some of this literature, show its originality in comparative terms, and classify it into three different perspectives, which, I think, encompass most of what has been produced in Latin America on this subject. These points are both an effort to present a general overview of Latin American works on noncompliance with rules, and a product of my own academic reflections on this subject (García-Villegas 2009, 2011, 2014a). I subsequently suggest ways in which the academic studies on noncompliance in Latin America can shed light on some of the problems that the globalized world is facing. Finally, I will present some conclusions.

Perspectives on Noncompliance in Latin America

References to Latin America's culture of noncompliance with rules can be classified under three general perspectives.[7] The first is a strategic point of view, according to which people fail to comply after calculating the costs and benefits of disobedience. Here, individuals are seen as rational actors who disobey when the negative effects deriving from that behavior – punishment, for example – can be avoided, are not grave, or are not comparable to the benefits obtained. The second point of view is political: it supposes that people's disobedience is an act of resistance to authority. According to this view, the social world is dominated by a handful of usurpers; institutions and authorities lack legitimacy, prompting subjects to refuse to do as they are ordered. The third perspective is of a contextual type. Some people disobey because they claim to have exceptional circumstances that prevent them from complying. These individuals do not question the validity or legitimacy of the rules; they simply point to their exceptional situation as exempting them from being subject to law enforcement. Each of these perspectives emphasizes a particular type of reason for noncompliance: personal interest in the case of the strategic vision; justice in the case of the political vision; and exceptional circumstances in the case of the contextual vision. Theoretically speaking, each refers to a particular non-respectful attitude toward rules.[8]

Three initial clarifications are in order. First, for reasons that I will explain later, in this review I examine not only disobedience vis-à-vis legal but also social norms (disobeying legal norms is very often the result of obeying social norms), and not only disobedience by lay people but also by officials. Second, it is very important to bear in mind that in spite of the importance of this behavior in Latin America, the majority of people, in general terms, comply with norms. Third, not only individuals disobey; the state is perhaps the first noncompliant actor in Latin America. Not just politicians, but administrators as well, promise to comply but do not (Araujo 2009; Dewey 2015; Duhau and Giglia 2008; García-Villegas 2009). But that is another story.

Strategic Disobedience

The strategic point of view on noncompliance is perhaps the most common and even accepted in Latin America. In general, it is found among authors who take positions close to methodological individualism (Arrow 1994; Olson 1965). Bearing in mind this idea of calculation, economists tend to explain the phenomenon of noncompliance as the result of incentives to not comply that derive from institutional inability to sanction deviates[9] (Bergman 2009; Cuéllar 2000; Harrison 1985; Harrison and Huntington 2000; Kalmanovitz 2001; Rubio 1997). Noncompliance is seen as the product of an individual strategy in which the costs of criminal practices are low compared to the results obtained. This being the case, the problem stems from the existence of weak institutions that are unable to impose sanctions on those who do not comply. The lack of effective sanctions is an incentive to violate the norms. Disobedience turns out to be cheap.

The protagonist of this type of disobedience is a character that in Latin America is known as *el vivo*, approximatively translated as "the shrewd." In every part of the continent, from northern Mexico to the Patagonia, *el vivo* and *la viveza* (shrewdness) are recognized, understood, and practiced. Shrewdness is an ambivalent behavior. On the one hand, it is the subject of praise because it signifies the ability to triumph in difficult situations. On the other hand, shrewdness can be something reproachable when it is used to "rip off," cheat, or take advantage of another. Former Colombian President Alberto Lleras Camargo defined shrewd people as:

people who resolve all of their problems and invite others to resolve them using means that are just barely legal, and occasionally illegal, but in such a way that it is not easy to discover. Essentially, they are people who have invented all kinds of tricks to fool the government along with all of its regulations and extremely complex formulism.

(Camargo 1992)

Yet in practice, in Latin America the difference between these two meanings of shrewdness tends to evaporate. When shrewd people achieve what they are after, they are more likely to receive praise rather than reproach for their conduct. The means are not good, but the end is achieved and that is enough. The triumph hides the means used to achieve it. If a particular play by Argentine football star Diego Maradona was ever praised by his compatriots, it was when, applying his shrewdness, he scored a goal against the British using his hand. The good result erases the memory of the bad intermediate steps. Writer Jorge Luis Borges once said that Argentines lack moral conduct but not intellectual conduct; to be considered immoral is less grave than to be viewed as dumb. In mid-twentieth century Brazil, there was a candidate for governor of São Paulo named Adhemar de Barros, who successfully used the campaign slogan "Rouba, mas faz!" ("Steals but gets things done!").

However, shrewd individuals are, above all, calculating. Their art consists of strategically meas- uring the balance between the risks of noncompliance and the benefits deriving from it. That is why studying mentalities is insufficient to predict the way in which those who do not comply are going to behave; we must also look at the contexts in which these people design their strategies. If the shrewd are calculating, their calculations do not always benefit them over the medium- and long-term. Carlos Santiago Nino uses the model of the rational actor to maintain that in Argen- tina there is a kind of anomie in social life, which he calls a "silly anomie," because it involves a type of behavior that ends up hurting everyone, or at least most of the actors involved, despite the fact that, from an individual point of view, it could be viewed as rational behavior.[10] Perhaps the best illustration can be found in automobile traffic: when, in order to arrive first, most drivers violate basic rules that require them to respect the separation of traffic lanes, they end up creating obstacles and arriving later than they would have if they had followed those rules.[11]

As stated at the beginning of this section, those who attempt to explain individuals' noncom- pliance with rules by analyzing these individuals' behavior tend to adopt a perspective of the rational actor. According to this perspective, individuals are guided by an instrumental ration- ality by which they try to maximize their interests. When it is unlikely that a sanction provided by a norm will be applied, then the individual's interest in violating that norm increases. Some Colombian economists have adopted such a perspective, allowing them to conclude that a weak state is the main cause of the country's violence. Fabio Sánchez, Daniel Mejía, Mauricio Rubio, and María Alejandra Arias, professors of economics at the Universidad de Los Andes, have each written along these lines of interpretation (Sánchez 2006; Arias et al. 2014). Colombian political scientists have also adopted this perspective, in order to analyze the possible relationships between the existence of a weak state and the development of illegal markets, such as those related to the illegal exploitation of gold and wood (Giraldo and Muñoz 2012; Correa, Silva, and Zapata 2014). These authors argue that noncompliance is the product of incentives generated by the state's inability to enforce compliance with criminal provisions. In Brazil, sociologist Michel Misse argues that an individual's decision whether to comply with a given norm is, above all, "a rational choice between the weight of [one's own] interests and the costs derived from the state's ability to transform [a particular behavior] into a crime" (2013, 14).

In a similar sense, we can consider the works of Mexican author Graciela Bensusán, who has studied noncompliance with labor standards in various Latin American countries (2006, 2007;

Bensusán and Middlebrook 2013). Her writings demonstrate how an employer's decision whether to comply with labor standards is in large measure the result of a rational calculation based on a cost-benefit ratio—that is, between what it would cost the employer to comply with the norm and the benefit that the employer would obtain by not doing so. Marcelo Bergman partially adopts this perspective in a comparative study on tax evasion in Argentina and Chile (2009). As Bergman explains, every person would rationally prefer not to pay taxes and benefit from the system as a *free-rider*; people will only comply with taxation norms if they believe there is a good chance that they will be sanctioned for tax evasion. In this sense, the decision to comply, or to cheat with tax norms is the product of a rational calculation by individuals. However, the rationality that guides this decision is a limited one, since it is impossible for most people to really foresee whether they will be caught and sanctioned or not. That is why people end up acting by imitation, or in other words doing what they believe others do. The generalized perception in Argentina is that the majority of individuals don't pay taxes and that nobody gets punished for it, while the generalized perception in Chile is that most people comply with tax duties and that those who try to cheat on them end up being sanctioned by the state. This explains the different tax cultures or "ecologies of taxation" that prevail in both countries: in Chile the process of imitation produces a "compliance equilibria," while in Argentina the same process brought about a "noncompliance equilibria." Latin American legal sociologists have criticized this instrumental perspective, common in studies that shape public policies. Two examples of such a critique can be found in Catalina Pérez's socio-legal analyzes of Mexico's penal punitivism (2008, 2011, 2012) and Rodrigo Uprimny's critique of Colombia's drug law (Uprimny, Guzmán, and Parra 2012).

Political Disobedience

The political vision of noncompliance is even more diffuse and less perceptible than the strategic one. There are only brief, passing, and isolated references among those who have a critical perception of power and law in Latin America. Two traditions can be differentiated within this perspective. The first is the old Spanish *iusnaturalism* – represented by the School of Salamanca – that puts justice above the law, and the right to resist above the obligation to accept the law. Francisco de Vitoria, Francisco Suárez, and Juan de Mariana, among other writers from this school, believed that individuals possessed the inherent right to oppose unjust laws, since such laws went against God's will and could thus not even be considered true laws. For Francisco Suárez, law that lacks this justice or righteousness is not law, nor does it oblige, or can it even be complied with. The second is the Latin American Marxist tradition that opposes written law, even progressive written law, as a deceit, devised by the dominant sectors against the poor (see, for instance, Múnera1998; Rivera 2009; Wolkmer 1995). According to this latter tradition, law is nothing more than a mechanism designed to secure political domination. The difference between "paper laws" and "real laws" is important here (Lassalle 1964); from that difference originates the justification of rebellion. "Against the authority of the *hacendado* [landlord]," says José Carlos Mariátegui, "the written law is powerless." In the light of this fact, the only alternative is a rebellion against the powerful (Mariátegui 1969).

Since the colonial period, rebelliousness has been common in Latin America. This is evident in the political arena. Some of the protagonists in Latin American history – including *gauchos* in Argentina, *charros* in Mexico, *llaneros* in Venezuela, and *bandoleros* (*cangaceiros*) in northeastern Brazil – were rebels (Pereira de Queiroz 1992). Martín Fierro, the hero of the Argentine national novel, is undoubtedly one of the best illustrations of the rebel. The difference between criminals and politicians has always been blurred among these characters. According to José Luis Romero, "the same kind of people who joined bands of highwaymen may have enlisted in the revolutionary armies" (1999, 217).

Latin American literature and popular culture often illustrate rebel behavior. One example is Pedro Malasartes, a personification of Brazilian popular culture studied by DaMatta.[12] Malasartes is a "a hero without character" – an individual who is poor but who uses tricks and jokes to make fools of those who give orders and to correct the injustices of the world. Malasartes – as narrated by Luís da Câmara Cascudo (1967) – is born into a poor family. He has a brother who goes to look for work on a *hacienda* (ranch) but falls into the hands of a despotic boss who refuses to pay him. On seeing his brother return home penniless after a year of labor, Malasartes is filled with rage and promises to avenge him. Malasartes then goes to work for the evil boss and, through shrewdness, is able to destroy him and become rich.[13] But Malasartes is not a Robin Hood who robs the rich to give to the poor. Instead, he is a burlesque, individualistic, and cynical transgressor who, seeing the injustice that he is forced to experience, rebels and "gives the devil his due." It is a story of "social ascent as a moral right" (Cascudo 1967). That is why he is a hero: because he is a bad man who has the right to be bad. "I wanted to be someone," says Chulla Romero, "someone who steals with the right to do so, like they steal, dammit" (Icaza 2005, 221). If complying with the boss's rules does not bring its due reward, then one must seek that reward through noncompliance. That is how this "cruel world" learns its lesson.

In recent years, much has been written on the phenomenon of resistance. Some works have focused on the right to resist, particularly in Argentina as a result of the events that led to the resignation of President Fernando de la Rúa in 2001. For example, Gustavo Fondevila explores whether we can effectively speak of a right to disobedience (2003, 172), and Roberto Gargarella analyzes the right of resistance in the case of street protests in Buenos Aires (2005) and the right to resist law by social actors that find themselves in situations of extreme poverty because of the incapacity – or unwillingness – of the state to guarantee their basic social rights (2008). In a similar sense, Colombian legal and political philosopher Óscar Mejía Quintana argues in defense of civil disobedience as an act of public and pacific resistance to unjust laws (2003). At a more regional level, Danilo Martuccelli studies the practice of lying in Latin America, noting that this practice is sometimes part of a repertoire of small acts of resistance in the face of power that seek to mitigate, even if symbolically, the strong social hierarchies that characterize Latin American societies. In this context, lying is an attitude that allows, behind the customary "yes, sir," for the development of an ensemble of tactics of resistance (2009).

Faced with the impossibility of openly confronting the powers that be, subaltern sectors in Latin America have resorted to hidden forms of daily disobedience and resistance (Ceceña 1999; Rivera 2009). These acts of resistance have been exercised before various types of authorities and in different periods. In the case of Mexico, for example, studies document acts of daily disobedience against both colonial authorities (Alcantara 2007) and revolutionaries of the Liberation Army of the South, led by Emiliano Zapata (Vélez Rendón 2013). In the case of Colombia, Ana María Vargas interprets street vendors' noncompliance with the law as a political act of resistance (2016). She argues that this noncompliance is not just a coping mechanism in the face of economic necessity, but also an attitude of resistance to the law.

Contextual Disobedience

In Latin America, there is a strong culture of creating exceptions to norms. This tendency – inherited from classical Spain, where prerogatives and *fueros* were common – is prevalent not only within the state, but also among individuals and society at large.[14] Very often, individuals justify their noncompliance by the fact that they are behaving under exceptional circumstances (Escalante 2004; García-Villegas 2009; Mockus and Corzo 2003; Murraín 2015). They see norms not as heteronomous impositions, but rather as autonomous patterns of behavior. Their own authority governs them; in other words, they are autarchic people.

Two types of disobedience can be differentiated here: disobedience by necessity; and disobedience by arrogance. In the first case, the noncompliant justify their actions in the particular circumstances they are confronting. An individual believes he is exempted from obeying, given that the situation he is confronting was not anticipated by the creators of the standard and therefore there is no reason for him to follow such a rule.[15] This type of justification was common in colonial times, especially with regard to the standards laid down in Spain, which were often not suited to the realities encountered in America; hence the expression, frequent among officials, *"se obedece, pero no se cumple"* ("one obeys but does not comply"), which means "Yes, I am obedient and respect authority, but in this case, I find myself unable to meet the standard" (Botero 2011a; Ots Capdequí 1967). The existence of exceptional conditions is a frequently invoked justification for noncompliance in Latin America and has contributed to the practice, originally Spanish, of creating exceptions to every rule. To that extent, Latin American legal culture is still part of that old Spanish understanding of the individual for whom a perfect life is one free from the obligation to obey authorities (Castro 1954, 1959; Genivet 1999).

This Latin American practice of exception has inspired many socio-legal studies, especially on criminal, economic, and constitutional issues.[16] One recent example is Matías Dewey's book *El Orden Clandestino*, which explores how the police in Buenos Aires allow mafias to purchase an "exception" to the application of criminal law, thus letting them carry out their business with impunity. As Dewey explains, it is not the mafias that sell security but rather the state that offers this security through the option of non-enforcement (2015). Instead of talking about a weak or absent state incapable of regulating social life, Dewey speaks of a state that regulates and is efficient – just in an illegal manner.

Lina Buchely, in a text called *activismo burocrático* (bureaucratic activism) analyzes how the women who have been hired by the Colombian Family Welfare Institute to operate "Communitarian Homes" – a government program intended to provide childcare while mothers are at work – construct a "low intensity legality" that prevails over the formal dispositions that rule the "Communitarian Homes." She shows how the formal norms to select the recipient families of state support sometimes end up being put aside in favor of informal criteria – such as friendship – introduced by the "Communitarian Mothers" (2015).

Also from a socio-legal perspective, Keith Rosenn studied the Brazilian *jeito* or *jeitinho*, a convention or "paralegal institution" that allows Brazilians to disobey the law with the approval of other citizens and even public officials if a particular situation warrants it (Rosenn 1985).[17] The penetration of *jeito* in Brazilian society is deep enough for Rosenn to consider it as a fundamental part of Brazil's legal culture. From an anthropological perspective, Lívia Barbosa explores the contradictory moral assessments of *jeitinho* in Brazilian society: while it can be seen as an equalizing practice that allows the poor to avoid the costs of complying with unjust laws, it can also be seen as a practice close to corruption (Barbosa 2005). Scholars interested in the study of business organizations have also been attracted by the *jeito*. Entrepreneurship in Brazil and its relationship with the *jeito* as a specific Brazilian cultural trait is explored by Penteado, Massukado-Nakatan, and Barón (2009), while the influence of Brazilian *jeitinho* and its Chinese counterpart *guanxi* in Brazil's and China's business environment is the subject of a recent study by the same authors (2015).

The second type is disobedience by arrogance. In this case the noncompliant individual accepts the law, at least in general terms, but considers that most of the time he should be excluded from the obligation to comply, given his particular position of power, the type of person he is, or the situation within which he acts. He believes that the law is for the "poncho people" – meaning the poor, the Indians, and the lower class – but not him. During the colonial period, Spaniards and whites were considered honorable people. To have honor was tantamount to having virtue and liberty.[18] That liberty translated into two great privileges: not having to work and not having to obey practically anyone.[19] Having to work was viewed as something for the lower classes, and obedience to God and the king – both of whom were remote, though undeniable – did not necessarily imply obedience to local authorities. The more honor one had, the freer one was. The extremes of the social scale were differentiated not only in terms of wealth, but also in terms of honor and freedom. At one end were the powerful, honorable, and free, and at the other were the slaves. In 1776, for example, a royal ruling established that family honor could be one of the judicial objections to matrimony.[20] Colonial elites shared the ideal of honor that the conquistadores had brought to America and that the Siete Partidas (the seven basic legal precepts of Alfonso X) defined as "the reputation that a man has acquired due to his rank, exploits or the valor that he demonstrates" (Durand 1953; Garrido 1997). In theory, honor could not be invoked to disobey authority. In practice, however, the elites would disobey authorities whom they considered less honorable than themselves. Cases of disobedience of local authorities based on the lesser honor of the rulers were relatively frequent in the colonial society of Nueva Granada.[21]

Faith also played an important role in fostering arrogant behavior. The Spaniards considered religion as a universal and unquestionable truth that they were obliged to disseminate, by force if necessary. "A Christian government was a government tempered by virtue and directed by divine grace" (Zea 1957, 255). This messianic ideal survived the coming of the republics, except that it was now headed by the dominant elites. That is not to say that there weren't any clashes between the republican elites and the Catholic Church. During the first years of republican life extremely conservative priests remained loyal to the Spanish crown and rebelled against the new order. Diana Herrera has written about the attempts of some Colombian clerics to promote popular rebellions against the republican order in 1823 and 1835, publicly justifying their uprisings by arguing that they were representatives of something that was beyond the earthly powers of the state (Herrera 2010, 2012). Defense of the family also tends to be above the law. Put another way, the family tends to subjugate individuals more effectively than the state. When, in *Cien Años de Soledad*, General José Arcadio Buendía, the ruthless ruler of Macondo, is about to order the execution of Don Apolinar Moscote, the general's mother appears and not only thrashes him pitilessly in front of everyone but disbands the firing squad and orders Don Apolinar to be taken safely and soundly to his home. "I dare you, murderer," she screams. "And kill me as well, son of a bad mother. Then I will not have eyes to weep from the shame of having raised such a phenomenon" (García Márquez 1970, 93).

The progress of the market and the rise of the bourgeoisie at the end of the nineteenth century were unable to banish the economic structures inherited from the colony or the lordly spirit that accompanied them. Independence from Spain removed the king but not the *caudillos* (strongmen), military personnel, chieftains (*caciques* and *curacas*), or *cabecillas* (ringleaders) (Silva Charvet 2005, 134). Many nobles transformed themselves into bourgeois while keeping the habits of their aristocratic pride. During the twentieth century, the *mestizos* made gains, even among the dominant elites. Nonetheless, the spirit of moral and political superiority of the elites made few concessions. Bourgeois and egalitarian behaviors mixed with aristocratic and lordly attitudes (Romero 1999). Status and social roles ended up becoming stronger than the law and citizenship. Since then, Latin Americans have been much more firmly guided by their roles in society than by a citizen identity with regard to the law. In Brazil, DaMatta (1987) distinguishes

73

between two types of replies in social encounters: "Do you know who I am?" and "Who do you think you are?" The first question puts hierarchy first and is very common in Latin American societies, whereas the second puts equality and citizenship first and is common in Europe and the United States. The equalizing power of general and abstract laws was never strong enough to banish the differences in a society based on hierarchy and privilege. "Doctors" replaced commanders, barons, viscounts, and imperial counselors (Freyre 1962). Those who enjoyed positions of privilege developed an entire set of strategies so that the goal of universalizing the law would be compatible with recognition of those privileges. The old and new regimes ended up coexisting and nourishing a hybrid society composed of selected spaces for modernity and tradition.

In my own work, I study noncompliance from the three perspectives noted above. But I also claim that the study of mentalities embedded in these perspectives is not enough to understand the culture of noncompliance with rules in Latin America. The study of mentalities, although important, is insufficient for understanding noncompliant behavior. This is because people change according to their context; a single individual with a well-defined noncompliance mentality can suddenly become a strict complier when changing from one context to another.

It is therefore necessary to consider two additional issues: (1) the degree of institutionalization; and (2) the quality of social reciprocity. First, the practice of noncompliance is linked to the degree of institutionalization. In Latin America, the state is not actually present everywhere (Centeno and Ferraro 2013; García-Villegas and Espinosa 2014; García-Villegas 2014b). Very often, state institutions are purely symbolic reality; reduced legal routines, behind which there is no effective power able to impose on the owners of the villages, the economic powers, or offenders. The greater the institutional weakness, the higher the degree of noncompliance with the rules. Second, people tend to imitate the behavior of others. Not only self-interest determines behavior; altruism and collaboration also play an important part. Numerous studies have shown that, for instance, people cooperate even more with the police, when they see that other people do the same (Bergman 2009; R.T. Tyler 2009; T. Tyler and Huo 2002). Quite often, individuals act as "reciprocators," not only in conditions traversed by affection or compassion, but also where economic relations are crucial. For example, companies are more generous with the workers that voluntarily work harder. And the more an individual thinks that the fraud rate increases, the more he tends to commit fraud (Gordon 1989). Against an explanation of behavior based on interest and wealth maximization, often suggested by economic theory or by so-called methodological individualism, confidence, rather than interest, is a key factor in human behavior (Bicchieri 2006; García-Villegas 2015; García-Villegas and Lejeune 2015; Murraín 2015).

Finally, each one of the three basic mentalities reflects a deficiency of the political system. Shrewdness (la viveza) is the product of the inefficacy of the state; rebelliousness is the result of the lack of legitimacy of public power; and the culture of finding exceptions to norms is the product of the absence of a culture of legality (rule of law). Thus, institutional capability is a remedy for shrewd behavior, legitimacy is a remedy against rebellious characters, and the rule of law is a remedy against arrogant conceptions and attitudes vis-à-vis legality. None of these remedies is exclusively destined to address one type of behavior. All are complementary: effectiveness may contribute to improved legitimacy; legitimacy is essential for the construction of the rule of law; and effectiveness is easier to obtain when a culture of legality exists. Remedies are therefore interconnected and influence each other reciprocally.

A Socio-Legal Field of Study

As I pointed out at the beginning of this chapter, a sociological understanding of noncompliance has developed in Latin America over the last decades. This perspective has historical roots: since colonial times, legal scholars and social scientists in the region have been astonished by the gap between written rules – often imported from Europe and the USA – and the behavior of citizens and officials. The encounter between Spanish law and indigenous customs created a kind of syncretism between the ideals embodied in legal norms and the potential imposed by social reality that has often fascinated Latin American intellectuals interested in the meaning that individuals attribute to legal standards (Basave 2011; Borges 1974).

Perhaps this Latin American perspective can help shed light on some of the most pervasive problems in today's world, most of which tend to be ones of legal disobedience, associated with the inability of law to penetrate the globalized social and economic fabric. Indeed, national and international law are unable to control the major economic and political powers that dominate the globe. Regressive legal pluralism, the spread of violence, and the rule of lawless powers are penetrating the current global arena (Lemaitre 2015). Two or three decades ago, these were typical Latin American problems. Today, the developed world is following suit. We find ourselves in a globalized world governed by weak international institutions. The decline of the nation-state, with all its implications (the erosion of sovereignty, the democratic deficit, the loss of universal values, the rise of illegal powers, the deficit of regulation, regressive legal pluralism, and so on) is an enormous challenge for future generations. The current disorder and lack of compliance with international norms is due to the fact that the law that is supposed to govern is soft law that lacks the institutional tools to ensure its enforcement.

Conclusions

Latin America's culture of noncompliance with norms is a significant social phenomenon inherited from colonial times and with important implications for economic development, the quality of democracy, and citizenship. It is also a complex phenomenon involving a number of cultural, social, and political factors. In this chapter, I have explored three different perspectives regarding this culture. Each places particular emphasis on a specific factor: the strategic perspective focuses on tactical noncompliance; the political vision analyzes the perception of illegitimacy; and the cultural view attempts to show how a belief in higher values can provide incentives for noncompliance with norms. But disobedience in Latin America is more than an exceptional and disruptive phenomenon – it is an almost normalized practice that lies at the core of sociability. This is why the study of this practice on the continent has produced a sociology of disobedience of rules that offers important insights not only for the understanding of Latin American societies, but also for the understanding of what is happening in today's world, where noncompliance has become an undeniable fact.

Notes

1 Professor at the Universidad Nacional de Colombia. This chapter draws on material from García-Villegas 2011 and 2014 ¿Cuál 2014 a ó b?

2 See, for example, Crow (1992), Elliott (2006), Keen (1996), Lipset (1986), and Morse (1974). Most of this culture has been attributed to Spain; see De Madarriaga (1928), Ganivet (1980), and Goytisolo (1969). But noncompliance is not an exclusively Latin American phenomenon; in this regard, see Ellickson (1991), Naim (2005), and Tyler (1990).

3 It might be that the lack of interest in the culture of disobedience is part of the general indolence that, until very recently, characterized Latin American social sciences regarding cultural topics, particularly people's beliefs.

4 See the classic text of Thoreau (1983); for a more recent debate, see Habermas (1990, 1997), Rawls (1987), and Zancarini (1999).
5 See Garland and Sparks (2000), Newburn (2007), and Turk (1969).
6 In the law and society movement, however, it is possible to find some exceptions, among which probably the most important is the work of Tom Tyler (Tyler 1990; Tyler and Boeckmann 2014). See also Kahn (1999).
7 These are not perspectives on the phenomenon of noncompliance itself, but rather perspectives on the relation between law and the state understood more broadly. However, given both the socio-political character of this phenomenon in Latin America, and the great variety and dispersion of practices related to this, such a classification make sense and bring about some clarity in such a complex social fact.
8 None of these three perspectives has a direct and specific interest in the study of the culture of noncompliance. They address this topic only because it sheds light on other phenomena that are deemed more important.
9 For a more general view of this perspective, see Castañeda (2011) and Harrison (1985).
10 Nino uses the celebrated "prisoner's dilemma" to show how certain rational patterns of behavior produce ineffective and unsuspected results (Nino 2005).
11 On this specific topic, see the interesting article "¿Y a mí qué me importa?" by Guillermo O'Donnell (1984).
12 In line with Clifford Geertz, DaMatta attempts to unravel the structures of power and culture in Brazilian society by studying popular culture: carnivals, parades, parties, songs, prayers, and other practices of ordinary life (DaMatta 2002).
13 A similar character is the Mexican Pito Pérez developed by José Rubén Romero in his "La vida inútil de Pito Pérez" (1963).
14 Lidia Girola describes this as "la cultura del como si" (2009).
15 For a description of this kind of justification for disobedience in Peru, see Portocarrero (2009); for a similar analysis in Chile, see Araujo (2009).
16 For a general perspective on the culture of exception in Latin America, see Basave (2011), Girola (2009), Gonzalez Jácome (2015), and Ost Capdequí, (1967). On the legal culture of exception, see Barreto (2006), Del Olmo (2002), De Soto (1987), García-Villegas and Uprimny (2006), Iturralde (2010), Loveman (1993), Nino (2005), O'Donnell (1986, 1998), Orozco (1997), and Waldmann (2007). For the Colombian case, see García-Villegas and Uprimny (2006).
17 See also de classic book of Peter Kellemen (1961).
18 In the colonial collective imagination, an association was made between honor and liberty (Caulfield, Chambers, and Putnam 2005; Garrido 1997).
19 There is a vast literature on this subject both in Spain and Latin America; see, for instance, Freyre (1975), Genivet (1999), and Lewald (1973).
20 According to Góngora, "this provision shows to what extent the policy of Charles III, far from being bourgeois, continued to be inspired by the basic concepts of status and honor" (2003, 122).
21 Gilberto Freyre, one of Brazil's greatest sociologists, explains that the state of Pernambuco was one of the most prosperous in the country thanks to its large sugar plantations and the fact that the owners of these plantations felt they were above the law and ruled over their estates as if they were feudal lords (Freyre 1922). A similar idea is developed by Germán Colmenares for the colonial period (1990); see also Andrés Botero (2011).

References

Alcantara, A. 2007. Élites ganaderas, redes sociales y desobediencia cotidiana en el sur de Veracruz a finales del siglo XVIII. *Historia Mexicana*, 56(3): 779–816.
Araujo, K. (ed.) 2009. *¿Se Acata Pero no se Cumple? Estudios Sobre las Normas en América Latina*. Santiago de Chile: LOM Ediciones.
Arrow, K.J. 1994. Methodological Individualism and Social Knowledge. *American Economic Review*, 84: 1–9.
Barbosa, L. 2005. *O Jeitinho Brasileiro. A Arte De Ser Mais Igual Do Que Os Outros*. Rio de Janeiro: Editora Campus.
Barreto, A. 2006. Normalidad y excepcionalidad: la indescifrable regularidad contemporánea de la excepción. En *Poder Ejecutivo*. Buenos Aires: Editorial del Puerto, pp. 321–37.
Basave, A. 2011. *Mexicanidad y Esquizofrenia*. México: Océano.

Bensusán, Graciela. 2006. "Diseño legal y desempeño real: México" En Graciela Ensusán (coord.), *Diseño Legal y Desempeño Real: Instituciones Laborales en América Latina*. México: UAM-X-Editorial Porrúa.

Bensusán, Graciela. 2007. *La Efectividad de la Legislación Laboral en América Latina*. Ginebra: Instituto Internacional de Estudios Laborales, Organización Internacional del Trabajo.

Bensusán, Graciela and Kevin J. Middlebrook. 2013. *Sindicatos y Política en México: Cambios, Continuidades y Contradicciones*. México: FLACSO, UAM-X, and CLACSO.

Bergman, M. 2009. *Tax Evasion and the Rule of Law in Latin America. The Political Culture of Cheating and Compliance in Argentina and Chile*. Pennsylvania: Penn State University Press.

Bicchieri, C. 2006. *The Grammar of Society. The Nature and Dynamics of Social Norms*. Cambridge: Cambridge University Press.

Borges, J.L. 1974. Nuestro pobre individualismo. En *Obras Completas*. Buenos Aires: Emecé Editores, pp. 658–59.

Botero, A. 2011. La tensión entre la justicia lega y la justicia letrada durante la primera mitad del Siglo XIX: El caso de Antioquia (Nueva Granada). En P. Salazar and G. Nares (Eds.), *Memoria del XVII Congreso del Instituto Internacional de Historia del Derecho Indiano*. Mexico: Porrúa, pp. 605–32.

Bourdieu, P. 1972. *Esquisse d'une Théorie de la Pratique, Précedé de Trois Études d'Ethnologie Kabyle*. Geneva: Droz.

Bouveresse, J. 2000. Rules, Dispositions, and the Habitus. In R. Shusterman (Ed.), *Bourdieu: A Critical Reader*. Oxford: Blackwell, pp. 46–63.

Buchely Ibarra, L.F. 2015. *Activismo burocrático. La Construcción Cotidiana del Principio de Legalidad*. Bogotá: Ediciones Uniandes.

Cascudo, C. 1967. *Contos Tradicionais do Brasil*. Rio de Janeiro: Edicoes de Ouro.

Castañeda, J. 2011. *Mañana o Pasado. El misterio de los Mexicanos*. Mexico: Aguilar.

Castro, A. 1954. *Iberoamerica. Su Historia y su Cultura*. New York: The Dryden Press.

Castro, A. 1959. *Origen, ser y Existir de los Españoles*. Madrid: Ser y Tiempo.

Caulfield, S., S. Chambers, and L. Putnam. 2005. *Honor, Status, and Law in Modern Latin America*. Durham: Duke University Press.

Ceceña, A.E. 1999. La Resistencia Como Espacio de Construcción del Nuevo Mundo. *Chiapas*, 7: 93–114.

Centeno, M.A., and A. Ferraro. 2013. *State and Nation Making in Latin America and Spain*. Cambridge: Cambridge University Press.

Colmenares, G. 1990. La ley y el orden social: fundamento profano y fundamento divino. *Boletín Cultural y Bibliográfico*, 27(22): 3–19.

Crow, J. 1992. *The Epic of Latin America*. Berkeley: University of California Press.

Cuéllar, M.M. 2000. Capital social. In *Colombia: Un Proyecto Inconcluso* (Vol. II). Bogotá: Universidad Externado de Colombia, pp. 761–873.

Da Matta, R. 1987. The Quest for Citizenship in a Relational Universe. In J. Wirth, E. de Oliveira, and T. Bogenschild (Eds.), *State and Society in Brazil. Continuity and Change*. Boulder: Westview Press, pp. 307–35.

Da Matta, R. 2002. *Carnavales, Malándros y Héroes*. Mexico: Fondo de Cultura Económica.

De Madarriaga, S. 1928. *Englishmen, Frenchmen and Spaniards*. London: Geoffrey Cumberlage.

De Soto, H. 1987. *El Otro Sendero*. Buenos Aires: Suramericana.

Del Olmo, R. 2002. ¿Por qué el Actual Silencio Carcelario? En *Violencia, Sociedad y Justicia en América Latina*. Buenos Aires: CLACSO, pp. 369–81.

Dewey, M. 2015. *El Orden Clandestino. Política, Fuerzas de Seguridad y Mercados Ilegales en la Argentina*. Madrid: Katz editores.

Duhau, E. and A. Giglia. 2008. *Las Reglas del Desorden: Habitar la Metrópoli*. Mexico: Siglo XXI.

Durand, J. 1953. *La Transformación Social del Conquistador*. Mexico: Porrúa y Obregón.

Ellickson, R. 1991. *Order without Law: How Neighbors Settle Disputes*. Cambridge, Mass: Harvard University Press.

Elliott, J.H. 2006. *Imperios del Mundo Atlántico*. Madrid: Taurus.

Escalante, F. 2004. Especulaciones a partir del concepto de anomia. En W. Bernecker (Ed.), *Transición Democrática y Anomia Social en Perspectiva Comparada*. Mexico: Colegio de México, pp. 125–47.

Fondevilla, G. 2003. Desobediencia civil en Argentina. *Signos Filosóficos*, 9: 155–72.

Freyre, G. 1922. Social Life in Brazil in the Middle of the Nineteenth Century. *The Hispanic American Historical Review*, 5(4): 597–630.

Freyre, G. 1962. *Orden e Progreso*. Rio de Janeiro: José Olimpo.

Freyre, G. 1975. *O Brasileiro Entre os Outros Hispanos*. Brasilia: Livraria José Olympio Editora.

Ganivet, A. 1980. *Idearium Español*. Madrid: Espasa-Calpe.

García Márquez, G. 1970. *Cien Años de Soledad*. Barcelona: Círculo de lectores.

García-Villegas, M. 2009. Incumplimiento, ciudadanía y democracia. En M. García-Villegas (Ed.), *Normas de Papel*. Bogotá: Dejusticia, pp. 307–36.

García-Villegas, M. 2015. *Les Pouvoirs du Droit*. Paris: L'Extenso.

García-Villegas, M. and J.R. Espinosa. 2014. *El Derecho al Estado. Los Efectos Legales del Apartheid Institucional en Colombia*. Bogotá: Dejusticia.

García-Villegas, M. 2011. Disobeying the Law. The Culture of non-Compliance with Rules in Latin America. *Wisconsin International Law Journal*, 29(2): 263–87.

García-Villegas, M. 2014a. Ineffectiveness of the Law and the Culture of Noncompliance with Rules In Latin America. In C. Rodríguez-Garavito (Ed.), *Law and Society in Latin America: A New Map*. New York: Routledge, pp. 63–80.

García-Villegas, M. 2014b. *La Eficacia Simbólica del Derecho. Sociología Política del Campo Jurídico en América Latina*. Bogotá: Random House.

García-Villegas, M. 2015. Le non-respect du droit. Sur la désobéissance aux règles en Amérique latine. *Droit et Société*, 91(3): 593–606.

García-Villegas, M. and A. Lejeune. 2015. Désobéissance et non-respect des normes juridiques. *Droit et Société*, 91(3): 563–76.

García-Villegas, M. and R. Uprimny. 2006. *El Control Judicial de los Estados de Excepción en Colombia*. Bogotá: Norma.

Gargarella, R. 2005. *El Derecho a la Protesta*. Buenos Aires: Ad-Hoc.

Gargarella, R. 2008. *De la Injusticia Penal a la Justicia Penal*. Bogotá: Siglo del Hombre.

Garland, D. and R. Sparks. 2000. *Criminology and Social Theory*. Oxford: Oxford University Press.

Garrido, M. 1997. Honor, reconocimiento, libertad y desacato. Sociedad e individuo desde un pasado cercano. En L.G. Arango, G. Restrepo, and C.E. Jaramillo (Eds.), *Cultura, Política y Modernidad*. Bogotá: Universidad Nacional, pp. 99–121.

Genivet, A. 1999. *Idearium Esapañol*. Madrid: Espasa-Calpe.

Girola, L. 2009. La cultura del "como si." Normas, anomia y transgresion en la sociedad mexicana. En *¿Se Acata Pero no se Cumple? Estudios Sobre las Normas en América Latina*. Santiago de Chile: LOM Ediciones, pp. 21–56.

Góngora, Mario. 2003. *Historia de las Ideas en la América Española y Otros Ensayos*. Medellín: Universidad de Antioquia.

Gonzalez Jácome, J. 2015. *Estados de Excepción y Democracia Liberal en América del Sur: Argentina, Chile y Colombia (1930–1990)*. Bogotá: Editorial Universidad Pontificia Javeriana.

Gordon, J.P.F. 1989. Individual Morality and Reputations Costs as Deterrents to Tax Evasion. *European Economic Review*, 33(4): 797–805.

Goytisolo, J. 1969. *España y los Españoles*. Barcelona: Editorial Lumen.

Habermas, J. 1990. Le droit et la force. Un traumatisme allemand. En *Ecrits Politiques*. Paris: CERF, pp. 88–104.

Habermas, J. 1997. *Droit et Démocratie*. Paris: Gallimard.

Harrison, L. 1985. *Underdevelopment is a State of Mind: The Latin American Case*. Harvard: Harvard University and University Press of America.

Harrison, L., and Huntington, S. 2000. *Culture Matters: How Values Shape Human Progress*. New York: Basic Books.

Icaza, J. 2005. *El Chula Romero y Flórez* (Vol. Quito). Libresa.

Iturralde, M. 2010. *Castigo, Liberalismo Autoritario y Justicia Penal de Excepción*. Bogotá: Siglo del Hombre.

Juárez, B. 1987. *México*. Mexico: Instituto Nacional de Estudios Históricos de la Revolución Mexicana.

Kahn, P. 1999. *The Cultural Study of Law: Reconstructing Legal Scholarship*. Chicago: Chicago University Press.

Kalmanovitz, Salomón. 2001. *Las Instituciones y el Desarrollo Económico en Colombia*. Bogotá: Norma.

Keen, B. 1996. *Latin American Civilization History and Society, 1492 to the Present*. Boulder Colorado: Westview Press.

Kellemen, P. 1961. *Brazil Para Principiantes*. Rio de Janeiro: Civilizacao Brasileira.

Lassalle, F. 1964 *¿Que es una Constitución?* Buenos Aires: Siglo XXI.

Lemaitre, J. 2015. Law and Globalism: Law without the State as Law without Violence. In A. Sarat and P. Ewick (Eds.), *The Handbook of Law and Society*. Malden: Wiley Blackwell, pp. 433–45.

Lewald, E. 1973. *Latinoamérica, sus Culturas y Sociedades*. Mexico: McGraw-Hill Book Company.

Lipset., S.M. 1986. Values, Education and Entrepreneurship. In P.F. Klaren and T.J. Bossert (Eds.) *Promise of Development: Theories of Change in Latin America*. Boulder: Westview Press, pp. 39–75.

Lleras Camargo, A. 1992. "El avivato," *El Tiempo* (newspaper), February 14, Bogotá.

Loveman, B. 1993. *The Constitution of Tyranny, Regimes of Exception in Spanish America*. Pittsburgh: University of Pittsburgh Press.

Mariátegui, J.C. 1969. *Siete Ensayos de Interpretación de la Realidad Peruana*. Mexico: Ediciones Solidaridad.

Martuccelli, D. 2009. Los usos de la mentira. En Araujo, K. (ed.) *¿Se Acata Pero no se Cumple?* Santiago de Chile, pp. 119–46.

McFarlane, A. 1997. *Colombia Antes de la Independencia: Economía, Sociedad y Política Bajo el Dominio Borbón*. Bogotá: Banco de la República – El Ancora editores.

Mejía Quintana, O. 2003. La desobediencia civil: un concepto problemático. *Revista de Estudios Sociales – Universidad de Los Andes*, (14): 76–87.

Mockus, A. and J. Corzo. 2003. *Cumplir para Convivir. Factores de Convivencia y su Relación con Normas y Acuerdos*. Bogotá: IEPRI – Universidad Nacional de Colombia.

Morse, R. 1974. The Heritage of Latin America. In *Politics and Social Change in Latin America: The Distinct Tradition*. Amherst, Mass.: University of Mass. Press, pp. 25–69.

Múnera, L. 1998. *Rupturas y Continuidades. Poder y Movimiento Popular en Colombia*. Bogotá: IEPRI-CEREC.

Murraín, H. 2015. La légalité et la représentation de l'autre. Une étude du rôle des normes sociales dans le respect des lois. *Droit et Société*, (91): 653–64.

Naim, M. 2005. *Illicit. How Smugglers, Traffickers, and Copycats are Hijacking the Global Economy*. New York: Doubleday Broadway Publishing Group.

Newburn, T. 2007. *Criminology*. Cullompton: Willan Publishers.

Nino, C.S. 2005). *Un País al Margen de la Ley: Estudio de la Anomia Como Componente del Subdesarrollo Argentino*. Buenos Aires: Ariel.

O'Donnell, G. 1984. *Y a mí Qué me Importa? Notas Sobre Sociabilidad y Política en Argentina y Brasil*. Buenos Aires: Centro de Estudios de Estado y Sociedad – CEDES.

O'Donnell, G. 1986. *Bureaucratic Authoritarianism: Argentina, 1966–1973*, In *Comparative Perspective*. Berkeley: University of California Press.

O'Donnell, G. 1998. *Polyarchies and the (Un)Rule of Law in Latin America*. Kellog Institute.

Olson, M. 1965. *The Logic of Collective Action*. Cambridge: Harvard University Press.

Orozco, I. 1997. *Los Peligros del Nuevo Constitucionalismo en Materia Penal*. Bogotá: IEPRI – Universidad Nacional de Colombia.

Ots Capdequí, José María. 1967. *Historia del Derecho Español en América y del Derecho Indiano*. Madrid: Aguilar.

Ots Capdequí, J.M. 1967. *Historia del Derecho Español en América y del Derecho Indiano*. Bogotá: Biblioteca Jurídica Aguilar.

Penteado, J.-P., M. Massukado-Nakatan, and F. Barón. 2009. A relação entre o jeitinho brasileiro eo perfil empreendedor: interfaces no contexto da atividade empreendedora no Brasil. *Revista de Administração Mackenzie*, 10(4): 100–30.

Pereira de Queiroz, M.I. 1992. *Os Cangaceiros. La Epopeya Bandolera del Norte del Brasil*. Bogotá: El Ancora Editores.

Pérez, C. 2008. Front Desk Justice: Inside and Outside Criminal Procedure in Mexico City. *Mexican Law Review*, 1(1): 3–31.

Pérez, C. (Ed.). 2011. *Justicia Desmedida. Proporcionalidad y Delitos de Drogas en América Latina*. Mexico: Fontamara.

Pérez, C., C. Silva, and R. Gutiérrez. 2012. Uso de la fuerza letal. Muertos, heridos y detenidos en enfrentamientos de las fuerzas federales con presuntos miembros de la delincuencia organizada. *Desacatos*, (40): 47–64.

Portocarrero, G. 2009. Moralismo, contestación y cinismo como posiciones de enunciación de los juicios morales en la juventud peruana. En K. Araujo (Ed.), *¿Se Acata Pero no se Cumple? Estudios Sobre Normas en América Latina*. Santiago de Chile: LOM Ediciones, pp. 57–88.

Rawls, J. 1987. *Théorie de la Justice*. Paris: Seuil.

Rivera, A. 2009. *La Resistencia a la Opresión un Derecho Fundamental*. San Luis de Potosi: Universidad Autónoma de San Luis Potosí.

Romero, J.L. 1999. *Latinoamérica: Las Ciudades y las Ideas*. Medellín: Editorial Universidad de Antioquia.

Romero, J.R. 1963. *Obras Completas*. Buenos Aires: Editorial Porrúa.

Rosenn, K. 1985. Brazil's Legal Culture: The Jeito Revisited. *Florida International Law Journal*, 1: 1–43.

Rubio, M. 1997. Perverse Social Capital – Some Evidence from Colombia. *Journal of Economic Issues*, 31: 805–17.

Silva Charvet, E. 2005. *Identidad Nacional y Poder*. Quito: Abya Yala.

Thoreau, H.D. 1983. *Civil Disobedience*. Middlesex: Penguin Group.

Torres, C., S. Alfinito, C.-A. Pinto, and B.-C. Yin Tse. 2015. Brazilian Jeitinho Versus Chinese Guanxi : Investigating Their Informal Influence on International Business. *Revista de Administração Mackenzie*, 16(4): 77–99.

Turk, A. 1969. *Criminality and Legal Order*. Chicago: Rand McNally.

Tyler, R.T. 2009. Legitimacy and Criminal Justice: The Benefits of Self-Regulation. *Ohio State Journal of Criminal Justice*, 7: 307–59.

Tyler, T. 1990. *Why People Obey the Law?* New Haven and London: Yale University Press.

Tyler, T. and Y. Huo. 2002. *Trust in the Law: Encouraging Public Cooperation with the Police and Courts*. New York: Russell Sage Foundation.

Tyler, T.R. and R. Boeckmann. 2014. Three Strikes and You Are Out; But Why The Psychology of Public Support for Punishing Rules Brakers. In *The Law and Society Reader II*. New York: New York University Press, pp. 223–31.

Uprimny, R., D. Guzmán, and J. Parra. 2012. La judicialización de los delitos de droga: ¿Des-proporción? Un análisis del caso colombiano. En C. Pérez Correa (Ed.), *Justicia Desmedida. Proporcionalidad y Delitos de Drogas en América Latina*. Mexico: Fontamara, pp. 105–37.

Vargas, A.M. 2016. *Outside the Law. An Ethnographic Study of Street Vendors in Bogotá*. Lund: Lund Studies in Sociology of Law.

Vélez Rendón, J.C. 2013. Expresiones de mal-estar, desacato y desobediencia en un entorno de guerra. Autonomía y protesta civil en el sur y centro de México, 1913–1917. *Historia Mexicana*, 63(1): 205–50.

Waldmann, P. 2007. *Guerra Civil, Terrorismo y Anomia Social*. Bogotá: Norma.

Wolkmer, A.C. 1995. *Introdução Ao Pensamento Jurídico Critico*. Sao Pablo: Academica.

Zancarini, J.-C. 1999. *Le Droit de Résistance, XIIe–XXe Siècle*. Fontenay-aux-Roses: ENS éditions.

Zea, L. 1957. *América en la Historia*. Madrid: Editorial Revista de Occidente.

6

LAW AND VIOLENCE IN LATIN AMERICA

Julieta Lemaitre

> In the cities were books, ideas, municipal spirit, courts, rights, laws, education, all
> the points of contact and communality that we have with the Europeans.
> *Domingo F. Sarmiento, Facundo o civilización y barbarie en las pampas argentinas*

Introduction

It is a contemporary truism that Latin America contains the most violent countries in the world,
except countries with an ongoing civil war.[1] At the same time, the region is increasingly stable,
with regular elections, and steadily developing economies. In the twenty-first century the metaphor of civilization and barbarism has returned as an explanation for the prevalence of violence.
Perhaps the most obvious example of this framing is the clash between civilized liberal societies
and organized crime financed by drug trafficking – a confrontation constantly evidenced in the
bloody news from the Mexican borders, the Colombian mountains, and the favelas of Brazil.
However, the enormous challenge that state authorities face in stemming the tide of drug-
related violence cannot disguise the fact that law is no stranger to violence: in fact, different legal
regimes and policy choices are at the root of present patterns of violence, beginning with prohibition itself. Neither can it hide the fact that large populations engaged in illegal or unregu-
lated activities, that is, whose everyday lives are outside the purview of state law, do sometimes
thrive and prosper under alternative, non-state forms of governance.

This chapter explores the rhetorical persistence of "civilization and barbarism" as a heuristic
device that locates law firmly on the side of civilization, equating as well lawlessness and
barbarism. It describes its emergence as a foundational metaphor for the republican projects of
the nineteenth century, and the changes and continuities surrounding its persistence throughout
various nation-building processes, in spite of the significant differences between Latin American
countries. These nation-building processes include the positivist liberal-conservativism of the
late nineteenth century, the social uprisings, and revolutions of the turn of the century, the
heavy imprint of the Cold War in the twentieth century, and the emergence of democracies that
elaborate both a new constitutionalism, and new concerns with crime and citizen security.

The chapter also suggests that resisting the seduction of pitting law against violence can be
quite productive for law and society studies in the region, building from the location of the two
phenomena in a single field. This would allow for the emergence of scholarship that interrogates

the relationship between law, especially liberal and progressive law, and the violence that shapes the continent. For example, it can foster complex engagements with everyday life under prohibition, with the effects of privatization of social services and security, and with popular forms of crime control such as lynching and armed self-defense, to give just some initial examples. The following sections begin by tracing the history of the persistent pull of the opposition between law and violence as a foundational trope for Latin American nations, signaling when relevant the underlying contradiction in this opposition. It then offers a brief overview of the research that can follow from examining law as both constitutive of and constituted by Latin America's violent contexts.

Civilization or Barbarism

Since independence in the early nineteenth century, Latin American elites have been engaged in a quest for national identity, and anxiety about the nation has been a persistent preoccupation. The civilizing power of law has been central to that endeavor, exemplified in national constitutions as well as through the regulation of everyday life by civil, commercial, family, and labor laws. Underlying the search for national identity through law is political liberalism's foundational metaphor: will Latin American nations be civilized, or will they fall under the sway of barbarism? The persistence of this frame can be traced to nineteenth century liberal Domingo Faustino Sarmiento's influential formulation, set out in *Facundo o Civilización y Barbarie en las Pampas Argentinas*, published in 1845. In Sarmiento's description, Argentina's violent gaucho hinterlands threatened to overcome the fledging civilization achieved in the cities, cities that represented the European heritage, materialized as *"courts, rights, laws, education."*

Independence brought the rejection of the Spanish colonial heritage, but not of the civilizing enterprise led by white men, located in cities and towns and expanding from this center to the hinterlands. In the nineteenth century elites remained haunted by the presence of what they defined as barbarism: great extensions of uncultivated land ungoverned by national laws and populated, although sparsely, with peoples uneducated in European customs. In some countries miscegenation and the myth of racial democracy represented a dialectical solution to the tension between the civilized and the barbaric; others deliberately sought out an increase in white European migrations to populate the "empty" hinterlands. The essays and novels of this period include not only concern over this internal division, between civilization and barbarism, but a persistent promise of resolution through the taming of barbarism represented by the domestication and cultivation of wild lands, and by the marriage of white men and brown women (Fuentes 1961; Sommer 1991). These processes were frequently intensely violent.

Nineteenth century liberal elites hoped that law would be instrumental in the construction of national civilizations, both as a bulwark against Spanish authoritarianism and religious fanaticism, and as protection against dictatorships by military leaders and other *caudillos*. In Colombia for example, Francisco Santander, the emblematic founding father of the new republic, expressed a regional hope for a future under the rule of law, claiming *"Colombians: arms have given us independence but only laws will us bring freedom."* Belief in republican law as a means to usher in civilization and progress was widespread among liberals, as was the call for the education of the people in the forms and substance of liberal law and democratic values. As Argentine Esteban Echavarría stated in *Dogma Socialista* (1837), a primer of Latin American liberalism: "one does not make Constitutions for the people; one shapes the people for the Constitution."[2] However, this "shaping" frequently built on intense elite mistrust and contempt for the people who needed "shaping."

Conservative reactions against liberalism also aimed to construct national civilizations, and imagined law as central to this endeavor. However, Latin American conservatives resisted the turn to France, England, and the United States for inspiration and instead coined a Hispanic nationalism that was also romantic and rebellious, and where law was natural as read by neo-scholastic theology and legal doctrine. Conservatives turned to natural law as the embodiment of civilization, and promoted the recovery of its Catholic lineage, against the liberal notion of natural rights. Rejection of the United States' influence in the region and a return to Catholicism were the banners of Conservative governments, notably in Colombia after their triumph in the civil war of 1885, and in Ecuador during the government and influence of devout Catholic Gabriel García Moreno (1861–1865 and 1869–1875). Natural law, rather than republican institutions, was the legal cornerstone of this conservative civilization, expressed in constitutions that re-established Catholicism as a State religion, and gave the church extensive powers for the administration of indigenous territories through "*misiones*" covenants.[3] The abuses committed by the church in this process are well-documented, including indigenous slavery and "orphanages" that forced indigenous families to give up their children.

By the late nineteenth century liberalism, triumphant in most of the region, was transformed by the influence of positivist philosophy and its call to both order and progress, not just liberty (as reflected in the Brazilian flag and its motto: *Ordem e Progresso*.) The influence of positivism built on the representation of elites as leading the nation from barbarism to civilization, except European civilization was now represented as the endpoint of a scientific social evolution. Liberal positivist authors in Mexico for example, equated liberalism, science, and secularism with civilization and sought to "shape" the Mexican people for civilization through education.[4] Gabino Barreda, founder of Mexico's Escuela Nacional Preparatoria, in his *Oración Cívica* (1867) justified public education for all arguing that, "the multitude will be an instrument of barbarism or civilization, following the absence or presence of an elevated moral guidance." Schools were meant to provide this guidance, and free, public elementary education for "the multitude" became an aspiration shared by elites across the continent.

Codification of legislation, especially the adoption and adaptation of Napoleon's Civil Code, was part of this evolutionary nationalistic project. Codification was "scientific" because it was systematic; "science" was also deeply racist. It demonstrated nation-building required the "improvement" of the mixed raced population through the introduction of "white blood" by miscegenation and, in some countries, through fostering white European immigration. Liberty was increasingly subordinated to "order and progress" and new limitations on suffrage reflected both the fear of popular uprisings and racist positivist science that attested to the superiority of European whites. Hence, as liberalism turned positivist, and merged with conservative defenses of racialized power hierarchies, laws enshrined both limitations to poor men's suffrage and the dissolution of collective land titles of indigenous peoples in the name of progress. The defense of slavery was also sometimes shrouded in positivist terms, and emancipation was slow to come even in those countries that had promised black soldiers their freedom during the independence wars. For positivist liberalism, the task was still first to *civilize* peoples that were indigenous and brown, peasant and heretic, physically located in the hinterlands and lawless. Civilization, in these terms, was well worth violence and authoritarian rule, as in the Mexican Porfiriato.

Resistance to this positivistic liberal rule, or to what Gargarella (2005) describes as liberal-conservative rule, came at the end of the century not through the resurgence of a more egalitarian liberalism, but through the romantic and nationalistic rejection of Anglo-American influence. Uruguayan José Enrique Rodó and Cuban José Martí represented the renewed commitment to a national identity that could overcome the tension between civilization and barbarism by articulating an authentic national civilization, different from that of North America and Europe. Law retained its centrality in this project, and the search for national identity often included the call for "authentic" or "national" laws, instead of Civil Codes based on the

Napoleonic version. Martí, for example, in *Nuestra América* (1891) argued that the new nations required "forms that could accommodate them" and that Latin America's failure to thrive came not from the people themselves but rather from those who "want to rule original peoples, of a singular and violent composition, with laws inherited from four centuries of freedom in the United States, from nineteen centuries of monarchy in France" (Martí 1891). The longing for a nationalistic resolution of the foundational metaphor required the dialectic triumph of one of its binary terms: civilization. Law remained a symbol of this triumph and therefore, its absence remained at the center of barbarism. Theses rhetorical tropes persisted at the heart of nation-building as the nineteenth century slid into to the twentieth.

The Socialist Inversion of Terms

The first half of the twentieth century in Latin America was dominated by social uprisings and challenges to the liberal political projects of the previous century. A persistent longing for progress and development among elites became embedded in a growing sense of failure. Liberals and Conservatives faced new political challenges, especially from the emerging Latin American left, whose cosmopolitan allegiances to international socialism imbricated with local rebellions, especially those of indigenous peoples demanding collective land ownership, and with the remnants of a defeated egalitarian liberalism that remained in abeyance.[5]

Emerging socialist frames did not abandon the foundational metaphor: instead they inverted the terms. Indigenous and peasant peoples were reimagined as virtuous and law-abiding, and capitalists and landowners as depraved and lawless. When the law did not defend the rights of the downtrodden, especially indigenous peasants and workers, it was denounced as barbaric and unjust: the aspiration was to enshrine laws and constitutions that would reflect the moral superiority of the poor thus, bringing progress and civilization. Liberalism was condemned for its failure to ensure the implementation of laws that (on the books) protected the poor, but that in practice did little to limit abuses and humiliation, keeping the nation in a state of barbarism.

Peruvian José Carlos Mariátegui influentially portrayed the failures of liberalism in his widely read *Siete ensayos de interpretación de la realidad peruana*, published in 1928, critiquing liberal laws as impotent before landowners' power:[6] "Gamonalismo inevitably invalidates all law or order for indigenous protection. Against its authority, validated by the environment and habit, written law is impotent" (Mariátegui 1928, 26–7). In his arguments, law's impotence reflected the unjust distribution of land titles as a result of land theft and illegal forced labor. In the early twentieth century these ideas were widely shared in Latin America where the critique of law as favoring the rich was also rooted in frustration with the lack of implementation of liberal laws (with *lawlessness*.)

Indigenous leaders of the early twentieth century echoed the theme of laws that remained on the books, the denunciation of lawlessness, as well as a defense of the moral superiority of indigenous peoples. For example, the Colombian indigenous leader Quintín Lame opposed the dissolution of collective indigenous land rights claiming *the indigenous heart rebels against unjust law*, but also demanding the implementation of existing legal protections against forcible dissolution of collective lands (Lemaitre et al. 2014). Likewise, peasant revolutionaries in Mexico also demanded the implementation of just laws, and the rejection of lawlessness fired resistance to the positivist liberal dictatorship of the *Porfiriato* in Mexico. In this spirit, peasant leader Emiliano Zuleta signed some of his letters with the slogan: *reforma, libertad, justicia y ley* ("reform, liberty, justice, and law"). His ambitious agrarian reform, the *Plan de Ayala*, redistributed the possession of agrarian property, claiming it was a reaction against land theft, and restituting the land of indigenous peasants who were the legal owners, but had been expelled by white lawlessness. Throughout the twentieth century, these views justified the carnage of revolutionary violence.

These demands for justice as the effective implementation of laws fueled not only the Revolution in Mexico, but also the emergence of a new type of liberal governments, now influenced by socialist and communist ideas. These ideas identified with civilization, rejecting traditional hierarchies and patterns of distribution as barbaric. Legal and constitutional changes adopted a "social" definition of civilization, materialized in social welfare and labor protection legislation, and aspiring to fulfill the old promises of liberty and equality. Again, these new laws often remained "in the books" generating a new wave of protest and frustration, which threatened the stability of elite rule, setting the stage for the anti-communist rhetoric of the Cold War.

The Cold War

The Cold War meant for Latin America the emergence of numerous low intensity armed conflicts as well as the renewed justification of authoritarian rule. Yet, underlying the justification of the use of violence by both Cold War liberals and by communists, remained the rhetorical use of the appeal to civilization and law.

Cold War liberalism was clearly aligned with the need to suspend laws protecting civil liberties in order to defend the nation from communism. However, civil liberties were suspended but not rejected; the rhetoric was instead of exceptionalism, a suspension but not a subversion of liberal values. These values were also expressed in the law and development nation-building projects that flourished hand in hand with anti-communist dictatorships.

Cold War liberals, both in the United States and in Latin America, frequently envisioned law as essential to the civilizing project that would save the region from communist rule. This civilizing project was closely tied to economic development, and first promoted by the Alliance for Progress and the package of legal reforms its promoters defended as necessary for development of market-friendly liberal democracies (sometimes defined as law and development reforms.) These reforms were sometimes enacted under the same authoritarian state-of-siege forms that allowed for legislation, which restricted civil liberties and under the same governments engaged in violent repression.

However, at least in an early period of the Cold War, economic development, premised on market-friendly legal reforms, was defined as necessary for the triumph of liberalism not only over communism, but also over traditional hierarchies and forms of distribution defined as the origin of poverty, inequality, and social protest. The Organization of American States' Alliance for Progress Report in 1962, for example, described the aspirations of its program as attempting to found a "civilization where spiritual and cultural values are strengthened by an ever-broadening base of material advance." To achieve this goal, social reforms, including legal reforms, were necessary:

> [P]olitical freedom must be accompanied by social change. For unless necessary social reforms, including land and tax reforms, are freely made, unless we broaden the opportunity of all of our people, unless the great mass of Americans share in increasing prosperity, then our alliance, our revolution, our dream, and our freedom will fail.
>
> *(OAS 1962, 21)*

But the 1960s saw the failure of liberal reforms and the frustration of attempts to achieve social justice within the framework of existing legal systems. The groundwork for increased political violence was set. Communist armed struggle, supported by the Soviet Union and China, seemed to be the only solution for socialists and communists that had previously actively participated in national politics. The appeal to law also persisted in the armed struggle embraced by communists, who frequently evoked the socialist inversion of terms of the earlier decades, arguing for the need for the people to take up arms to defend law against elite lawlessness. The Cuban revolution of 1959 became a symbol of the need for violence to transform unjust regimes, and Marxism built on a Catholic culture arguing that rebellion was justified by natural law, and often by the fact that laws that granted rights were never put into effect.

This frustration with law, and the need for violence in response to its failings, was influentially articulated by Fidel Castro's famous speech during his 1953 trial; widely circulated under the title: "*History will absolve me*," the speech justified Castro's rebellion by appealing to the persistent legitimacy of the Cuban Constitution of 1940, violated by Batista's dictatorship. Castro claimed the right to rebel when law was impotent before the violence of the powerful, a call that resonated across the region as young men and women formed urban and rural guerrillas and attempted to found a new nation through violence.[7]

Chilean socialist Salvador Allende's government (1970–1973) dramatically illustrated for Latin American reformers the limits of law, and the lure of political violence. Democratically elected, Allende adopted a program of radical reform of Chilean institutions within the limits of the constitution and existing laws: his minister of justice, Eduardo Novoa Monreal, described this strategy as using "*los resquicios legales*," the legal cracks, to insert socialist redistributive mechanisms within a liberal legal system. After the military coup supported by the United States – that ended Allende's life in September 1973 and exiled Novoa Monreal, the latter wrote a widely circulated book denouncing the impossibility of working within the traditional legal frame as liberal law became *an obstacle to social justice* (Novoa 1975).

The end of the 1960s brought a dramatic increase in the number of communist guerrillas in the region, the collapse of the Alliance for Progress and its reformist aspirations, and a wave of military coups, as well as nominal democracies with radically restricted civil rights under harsher state-of-siege legislation. It was a time of unabashed lawlessness, enacted as a defense of order, sometimes within the forms of the law. Support for military and state-of-siege domestic rule came both from national anti-communist movements, and from the United States in its role as regional hegemon. The defense of civilization was part of the rhetoric of the dictators, just as it had been of the Cold War liberals; legality and legal reform, however, was seldom part of this defense, suspended until it could be enjoyed once the nation was safe from communist threat.

By the 1980s, repression had engendered a wide-ranging resistance, extended beyond the proportionately small guerrillas. New alliances brought forth the regional human rights movement, which peacefully resisted the massive violation of civil and political rights. The human rights movement once more trusted the civilizing power of law against the monstrosity of dictatorships, with their mass detention centers and routine practice of forced disappearances, torture and executions of suspected communist sympathizers and subversives. Lawyers and activists defended political prisoners and denounced abuses, and eventually brought perpetrators to trial. The human rights movement and its political commitments have dominated Latin American politics – and a considerable proportion of law and society studies – since the end of the Cold War in 1989, heralding the return of a triumphant liberalism represented by the defense of human and the "new constitutionalism." The question remains whether this turn to law in the region can renounce a foundational rhetoric that identifies law with civilization, and is willing to use violence to impose it on "barbarians."

The New Constitutionalism and the New Barbarians

Latin America renewed its commitment to law and justice after the Cold War ended, placing law at the center of social movement activism and policymaking (Couso, Huneeus, and Sieder 2010). A wave of new constitutions swept the region, fanning hopes for redistribution and welfare reform (Barrett, Chávez, and Rodríguez-Garavito 2008; Santos 2010) as well as hopes for democracy and the rule of law through more liberal reforms (García 2002). With the new constitutions came the development of new constitutionalism, comprised of normative legal theories that defend liberal egalitarianism (Vásquez 2015; Arango 2012; García, Rodríguez, and Uprimny 2006; Allegre and Gargarella 2007) as the foundation of Latin American nations. Aspiration to social justice through redistributive constitutionalism has not been without its critics, and neither has the elevation of the rule of law as an end in itself. (Trubek and Santos 2006; Nader and Mattei 2008). However, despite such criticism, the increasingly hegemonic position in the continent is that the road to justice is paved with legal reform, and the civilizing power of law remains unquestioned.

The turn to left-liberal legal reform is deeply linked to the vibrant human rights movement against dictatorships. This movement was the prelude to the new constitutions, and provided much of the energy fueling the normative aspirations of the period. It garnered support from different fronts, from former insurgents to traditional liberals to United States foundations (Keck and Sikkink 1998; Meili 2001). It also gave rise to a transnational movement clamoring for trials of former dictators and abusive military officers, and to a specific branch of human rights focusing on transitions to democracy (Sikkink 2011). Other social movements, including indigenous and afro Latin Americans, women and LGBTI (lesbian, gay, bisexual, transgender, and intersex), tapped into an international turn to human rights frames for social movements and lobbying for legal reform.[8]

Social science literature on human rights in Latin America (much of it written by foreign visitors), as well as human rights reports, chronicled the traumatic effects of widespread human rights violations under military regimes or restricted democracies like those of Colombia and Mexico (Taussig 1984; Green 1994; Tate 2007).[9] Their regard, and their emphasis on violations of human rights, however, has had little comprehension of the role of law in the creation of horror, beyond the description of lawlessness as its necessary pre-condition. Instead, like liberals and socialists before them, they share an appreciation of law as civilization, and a rejection of lawlessness as a separate space of barbarism. Old tropes die hard. With the return of democracies, the experience of horror has faded, but not the rejection of lawlessness represented both by popular culture and by crime. Also persistent is the romantic description of the poor whose protection seems to require revolutionary violence against elite lawlessness.

Academic literature persistently describes lawlessness as the warp and woof of everyday life in the region. The persistent concern with lawlessness as the root of both violence and inequality echoes the nineteenth century themes of civilization and barbarism. Roberto Da Matta, for example, blamed everyday lawlessness on the persistence of hierarchical relations so embedded in culture they create social spaces impervious to both law and markets (1991, 200). He famously described the Brazilian expression "don't you know who you are talking to?" (used by the upper class to dismiss interpellations by lower class people) as an everyday expression of the power of these hierarchical social relations, beyond the law. Expanding on Da Matta, O'Donnell (1984) added that military dictatorships and restricted democracies used force to silence the egalitarian impulses that might upset these hierarchical social orders, expressed in Argentina as the response to "don't you know who you are talking to": "what the f★★★ do I care." Carlos Nino (1992) wittily and influentially linked unreflective lawlessness (*anomia estúpida*) not just as an effect, but as the root of inequality, and of underdevelopment, a conclusion widely cited by a generation of scholars engaged with corruption, underdevelopment, legal culture, and the illegitimacy of legal institutions in Latin America (see for example, Ansolabehere 2008; Cianciardo 2012; Binder 2007; Pérez 2007; García 2009).

Cultural change and the creation of a "culture of citizenship" (*cultura ciudadana*) is frequently presented as the solution for popular culture's penchant to flout the law. Exemplified and promoted by Bogotá's Mayor Antanas Mockus in the mid-1990s, *cultura ciudadana* spread across the region as a program for municipal governance, founded on its numerous successes ranging from pedestrian events (literally) such as circulation on roads and sidewalks following traffic rules, to significant decreases in the level of violence. The mechanism of these improvements was touted as the promotion of a culture that harmonized citizen rights (centered on ideas of human dignity) with popular culture and morality, generating law-abiding behaviors as well as lowering general levels of tolerance toward lawlessness (Mockus 1999; Nogeira 2009).

State-building also appears as a favored solution to the cultural problem presented by lawlessness. State-building recipes follow Guillermo O'Donnell's description of the fragmentation of state territorial control between the blue areas, controlled by the state and the police, and green or brown areas of inefficient public administration, disorder, and lawlessness (O'Donnell 1993). Green and brown areas are also the poorest, characterized by "the (un)rule of law." State weakness is the main culprit in this description: Pinheiro and Méndez point to a weak and inefficient police and criminal justice system (Méndez, O'Donnell, and Pinheiro 1999) and a state so weak it is unable to mediate social conflicts (García and Santos 2004).

Both in the cultural explanation and in the weak state explanations for lawlessness, the rule of law (if not the state itself) appears to exist in a different world from that of violence. Civilization, civility, citizenship, and law appear radically opposed to everyday lawlessness, which generates violence, chaos, and injustice. The underlying call seems to be: if only the law was obeyed, there would be justice. This call is shared by other contemporary scholars concerned with Latin American lawlessness: namely those studying the growth of criminal violence.

Criminals, especially organized criminals funded by drug trafficking, but also petty criminals, have loomed large since the 1990s as the new barbarians, as anxieties about civilization are expressed as anxieties about public safety (*seguridad ciudadana*) (Svampa 1994). Street crime and organized crime have fed a resurgence of the question of social violence as a cultural problem, where law is again firmly on the side of civilization and lawlessness is a proxy for barbarism. The enemy is rampant illegality, and concerns for public safety are not limited to the elites, as a significant sector of the public also accepts lynching, serial murders of petty criminals, and other forms of violence against criminals as just desserts. More generally, the death of young men supposedly associated with organized crime is normalized every day; they are the new "dangerous classes," the persistent presence of barbarism targeted by public safety projects (Svampa 2006).

Academic literature has signaled the danger posed by the rise of public safety projects, as well as their negative impact on the poor (Gargarella 2008; Iturralde 2009; Dammert 2007; Briceño 2007, 2012). They are part of a tradition of critical criminology that links criminality to the radical inequality of Latin American cities. This criticism has focused on demanding that criminal law remain the last resort, while still defining violent areas as places that require a state presence and equitable treatment.[10] In this light, the disaffected youth that form part of the new dangerous classes can also be seen as forms of resistance against unjust rule, or at least as a protest against poverty.

This frame evokes the socialist inversion of terms by which the elites (whites, landowners, and government) are barbaric and lawless, and bandits an expression of poor people's rebellion (Hobsbawm 1981). The rebellion of lawlessness is also present in other illegal actions, such as writing graffiti and defacing private and public property, actions, which can be seen as claims for recognition and citizenship. For example, Teresa Caldeira (2002) describes disaffected urban youth as reacting to "a long history of state disrespect for civil rights, in particular poor people's rights" and "a deep disbelief in the fairness of the justice system and its ability to function without bias" (2002, 235–63).

The link between rebellion and state disrespect for legal rights is also implicit, and explicit, in Latin America's vigorous social justice lawyering tradition, present in "liberation" lawyering (close to liberation theology) as well as in "alternative uses of law," a movement of judges and lawyers committed to obtaining justice for the poor through the use of law (for an overview, see Souza 2001). Sympathetic contemporary scholars have both supported this type of social justice lawyering, and conceptualized it as a spectrum of counter-hegemonic uses of law (Santos 2002; Santos and Rodríguez 2005; Santos and García 2004). The assumption in this literature is that law is distinct from violence, at least a certain type of law, counter-hegemonic law, and that given the right kind of law, barbarism (understood as structural violence and its wages) will be defeated.

The persistent hope in law, and the aspiration of justice, while inspiring, raises concerns insofar as it reproduces once more the dichotomy between us (the civilized, the lawful, the human rights and social justice lawyers, the poor) and them (the barbarians, the landowners, the corporations, corrupt government elites). The force of this dichotomy romanticizes the poor as much as early nineteenth century elites romanticized European culture in their use of the civilization and barbarism metaphor. Perhaps more importantly, the dichotomy silences the possibility of examining the ways laws in which is complicit with violence, as well as ways in which lawless is frequently legitimate. As such the rhetoric of civilization and barbarism becomes an obstacle for the study of law in violent contexts.

Law and Society Studies in Violent Contexts

Law and society approaches to the study of law in everyday life can productively approach the way both law and violence are mutually constitutive on the ground, as long as scholars eschew the pull of the foundational metaphor. Violence shapes state law and legal activism: the turn to human rights, for example, is a reaction against dictatorships that gave life to sections of international law and constitutional law that were previously devoid of much practical meaning. This relationship has limited the potential of human rights as a vocabulary for emancipatory aspirations, limited as they tend to be to the rejection of state violence. For example, Colombian social movement activism in the wake of the 1991 Constitution is deeply rooted in the rejection of violence during the civil war of the 1990s and 2000s. (Lemaitre 2009). Conversely, law also shapes violence, most obviously by definition: either directly (by deeming certain social practices and worlds illegal, thus shaping the exact contours of violence), or indirectly (by refusing to regulate social life where conflict is bound to happen, as in informal and illegal markets). Both moves are exemplified in twenty-first century Latin America through two phenomena directly linked to social violence: prohibition, and the reduction of the size and presence of the state as provider of social and police services.

Prohibition, a complex national and international legal regime whereby the interdiction of certain drugs is carried out through the use of military force, is directly responsible for the sharp rise both in cartel and police violence in large sections of Latin America. While the violence in Colombia in the 1980s and in Mexico in the 2000s is the most visible, prohibition is also the direct cause of elevated murder rates in Central America and the Caribbean, and contributes significantly to violence in Venezuela, Brazil, and Colombia. The militarization of interdiction generates a constant slippage of the state's use of lethal force away from the democratic constitutional frame, and into both martial law and the illegal use of state force. It also keeps the price of drugs artificially high, and the absence of taxes or any form of regulation produce enormous profits, which in turn finance corruption of state officials as well as full governance by criminal organizations in some territories.[11]

The reduction of state functions after neoliberal reforms is also clearly linked to the rise of certain types of violence. As Comaroff and Comaroff (2006) explain for Africa, neoliberal policies advocating a reduction of the state have resulted in an increase in violence as armed groups strive to dominate deregulated economies and spaces. State reduction has multiple causes: it can be linked to neoliberal structural reform programs that promote self-help (as argued for example, by Goldstein 2005), but it can also have other origins. For example, the dramatic increase in violence in Venezuela after Chavez' socialist revolution is not linked to a neoliberal reform program, but rather to the dramatic erosion of certain state institutions under socialism, particularly the police and criminal investigation units (Briceño 2012).

Furthermore, the civilization championed by liberalism can also be violent, and lawless spaces a place of refuge. Historically there is ample evidence of indigenous peoples, former slaves, and landless peasants fleeing the purview of the state into the hinterlands in order to avoid injustice, especially forced labor and conscription, but also to avoid the regulation of everyday life that comes with living under the law (Scott 2009; Clastres 1989). Within these lawless spaces however, norms emerge as do forms of regulation that are increasingly studied by social scientists, forms that signal the absorption or assumption of state functions by different organizations.

Some legal scholars who have articulated a counter-hegemonic view of law build their understanding on the idea that ordinary people self-regulate in the margins of state power, and that this is the only legitimate kind of law. De la Torre (2006), for example, argues for the existence of a law born of the people, affirming that those are "the legal norms the people themselves create to regulate their relationships and defend their just causes." Similarly, some legal scholars have also turned to legal pluralism as a framework that can represent law outside the boundaries of state law, building on the early work of Boaventura de Sousa Santos (1977). For Antonio Wolkmer (2003) and Oscar Correas (2003), legal pluralism, like De la Torre's law of the people, is at its heart emancipatory because its origin lies outside the power of the state. Other scholars make a defense of indigenous legal pluralism (Sieder 2011; Yrigoyen 2011) to argue for the presence of norms and justice in the lawless lands and social spaces populated by indigenous peoples, often implicitly or explicitly described as a better defense of constitutional values of human dignity and equality than state law.

However, as Santos has also pointed out (2001), armed non-state actors can also regulate illegal and informal social relations. In Colombia for example, guerrillas benefiting from cocaine and illegal mining markets set up their own forms of insurgent governance that include taxation and the provision of social services, conflict resolution, and sometimes also infrastructure such as roads (Arjona 2015). In Mexico cartels have also assumed similar state functions in the regions they dominate (Maldonado 2011). Similar mechanisms are at work, although with a much smaller investment in policing the boundaries, in other illegal and informal markets. Less violent than illegal markets, informal markets also suffer because of lack of state regulation (or benefit from a lack of enforcement of rules, depending on the point of view).[12] Communities often assume the functions that the state refuses to perform in markets that are not formally legal, for example, by solving conflicts through community justice mechanisms, as in Santos' example of a neighborhood association solving disputes between tenants and landowners in an informal settlement (Santos 1977; see also Godoy 2006; Goldstein 2003). There is a large social science literature in English and in Spanish describing informal markets in housing (see for example,

Fischer, McCann, and Auyero 2015), commerce and informal labor (Centeno and Portes 2006), mining and the exploitation of natural resources, and illegal economies generally. The governance of these illegal worlds remains little studied and little understood in law and society scholarship, even though there is ample evidence in political anthropology of their intersections with state law and institutions (Arias 2006; Holston 2008; Dewey and St Germain 2012).

Conclusions

In sum, if law and society scholars in Latin America face the conceptual challenges presented by violence, they will find a productive avenue in overcoming the historical pull of the dichotomy between "civilization and barbarism." They might for example explore instead the ways in which law is in fact a constitutive part of the social spaces described as lawless, and the ways in which social spaces defined as lawless are effectively regulated. They will find law in practice is not firmly located on the side of civilization as the absence of violence, nor is violence consistently an expression of barbarism located in marginal physical and social spaces. These insights, expressed in Walter Benjamin's much cited critique of violence, can undergird complex examinations of the ways in which law and violence constitute and define each other, the mutual dependency of state-controlled and so-called "lawless" lands, and the forms of governance that regulate everyday life outside the purview of the state. Political and legal anthropologists have analyzed some of these phenomena, as have political scientists studying violence in civil war and organized crime in the region. However, their focus is not the meanings and practices of law on the ground among us: it is perhaps time for law and society scholars to adopt an understanding of law, even progressive and liberal law that does not exclude its constitutive proximity to violence in a region that includes some of the most violent countries in the world.

Notes

1 See for example, the 2015 data as described by the *Guardian* www.theguardian.com/world/2015/may/06/murder-map-latin-america-leads-world-key-cities-buck-deadly-trend. Accessed April 10, 2017.
2 On liberal constitutionalism in the region in the nineteenth century see Gargarella 2005; Jaksic and Posada 2011.
3 Notably, Law 89 of 1890 in Colombia exempted indigenous peoples from criminal responsibility and from the dissolution of collective property precisely because they were "not civilized" and therefore not subjects to general laws. Similar provisions exempting indigenous people from criminal responsibility due to their "diminished responsibility" or cultural condition were common to criminal procedures codes throughout Latin America in the late nineteenth and early twentieth centuries. They coexisted with indigenous servitude and slavery-like exploitation justified by their lack of civilization.
4 For positivism in Mexico see Zea 1968 and Hale 1972.
5 For this egalitarian liberalism, also known as radical liberalism see Gargarella (2005, 2014.) He distinguishes it from liberalism proper, which he sees as an eventual ally of conservative forces through power-sharing agreements.
6 Indigenista literature, inspired in the political movement that defended indigenous rights and culture in the early twentieth century, is rife with similar references to unjust rule, as exemplified by the citation to *El Mundo es Ancho y Ajeno*.
7 Populist movements and governments also claimed a disregard for law and rights based on the primacy of popular sovereignty and the direct relationship between the government and the people, without the mediation of law. However, this review focuses on the representation of a relationship between law and violence, generally untheorized in studies of populism.
8 There is a large literature on law and social movements in the region. See Lemaitre 2009 and the chapters by Machado et al., Wilson and Gianella, and Saldivia in this volume.
9 In the 1970s, Amnesty pioneered reports on disappearances and imprisonments under military regimes in Latin America see www.amnesty.org/en/documents/amr13/083/1977/en/. Accessed May 10, 2017.

10 The dramatic rise of violence in socialist Venezuela remains a conundrum for this type of analysis.

11 Prohibition gives a market advantage to the ruthless and to those who can ensure territorial control. For a thoughtful explanation of this link see Andreas and Wallman (2009). See also Reuter (2009) linking violence to the youth of participants, the high value of the drug and the intensity of law enforcement. See Snyder and Duran-Martinez (2009) for a surprising take on the role of the state in drug-related violence.

12 For the argument that lack of enforcement is a deliberate political move, see Holland 2015.

References

Alegría, Ciro. 1941/2000. *El Mundo es Ancho y Ajeno*. Madrid: Alianza Editorial.

Allegre, Marcelo and Gargarella, Roberto. 2007. *El Derecho a la Igualdad*. Buenos Aires: Lexis Nexis.

Andreas, Peter and Joel Wallman. 2009. Illicit markets and violence: what is the relationship? *Crime Law and Social Change* 52: 225–29. 10.1007/s10611-009-9200-6.

Ansolabehere, Karina. 2008. Legalistas, legalistas moderados y garantistas moderados: ideología legal de maestros, jueces, abogados, ministerios públicos y diputados. *Revista Mexicana de Sociología* 70(2): 331–59.

Arango, Rodolfo. 2012. *El Concepto de Derechos Sociales Fundamentales*. Bogotá: Legis.

Arias, Enrique. 2006. *Drugs and Democracy in Rio de Janeiro*. Chapel Hill: University of North Carolina.

Arjona, Ana. 2015. *Rebelocracy*. Cambridge: Cambridge University Press.

Barreda, Gabino. 1867/1979. Oración cívica. *Cuadernos de Cultura Latinoamericana* 72.

Barrett, Patrick, Daniel Chávez, and Cesar Rodríguez-Garavito. 2008. *The New Latin American Left: Utopia Reborn*. London: Pluto Press.

Binder, Alberto. 2007. *La Cultura Jurídica, Entre la Tradición y la Innovación*. Ediciones Universidad.

Briceño, Roberto. 2007. *Sociología de la Violencia en América Latina*. Quito: FLACSO.

Briceño, Roberto. 2012. Three phases of homicidal violence in Venezuela. *Ciência & Saúde Coletiva* 17(2): 3233–42.

Caldeira, Teresa. 2002. The paradox of police violence in democratic Brazil. *Ethnography*. 3(3): 235–63.

Centeno, Miguel Ángel and Alejandro Portes. 2006. "The Informal Economy in the Shadow of the State." In Patricia Fernández-Kelly and Jon Shefner (Eds.), *Out of the Shadows: Political Action and the Informal Economy in Latin America*. Philadelphia: Penn State Press: 23–48.

Cianciardo, Juan. 2012. The paradox of the moral irrelevance of the government and the law: a critique of Carlos Nino's approach. *Ratio Iuris* 25(3): 368–80.

Clastres, Pierre. 1989. *Society against the State*. Cambridge MA: MIT Press.

Comaroff Jean and Jihn Comaroff. (Eds.). 2006. *Law and Disorder in the Postcolony*. Chicago: Chicago University Press.

Correas, Oscar. 2003. *Pluralismo Jurídico, Alternatividad y Derecho Indígena*. México: Fontamara.

Couso, Javier, Alexandra Huneeus, and Rachel Sieder (Eds). 2010. *Cultures of Legality Judicialization and Political Activism in Latin America*. Cambridge: Cambridge University Press.

DaMatta, Roberto. 1991. "Do You Know Who You're Talking to? The Distinction between Individual and Person in Brazil." In *Carnivals, Rogues, and Heroes: An Interpretation of the Brazilian Dilemma*. Notre Dame: Notre Dame Press: 37–97.

Dammert, Lucia. 2007. *Perspectivas y Dilemas de la Seguridad Ciudadana en América Latina*. Quito: FLACSO.

Dewey, Susan, and Tonia St. Germain. 2012. Between global fears and local bodies: toward a transnational feminist analysis of conflict-related sexual violence. *Journal of International Women's Studies* 13(3): 49–64.

Fischer, Brodwyn, Bryan McCann, and Javier Auyero. 2015. *Cities from Scratch*. Duke University Press.

Fuentes, Carlos. 1961. *La Gran Novela Latinoamericana*. Alfaguara.

García, Mauricio and Boaventura de Sousa Santos (Eds.). 2004. *Emancipación Social y Violencia en Colombia*. Bogotá: Norma.

García, Mauricio, César Rodríguez, and Rodrigo Uprimny. 2006. *Justicia para Todos Derechos Sociales, Sistema Judicial y Democracia en Colombia*. Bogotá: Editorial Norma.

García, Mauricio. 2002. Law as hope: constitutional and social change in Latin America. *Wisconsin International Law Journal*, 20(2): 352–70.

García, Mauricio. 2009. *Normas de Papel*. Bogotá: Norma.

Gargarella, Roberto. 2005. *Los Fundamentos Legales de la Desigualdad*. Buenos Aires: Siglo XXI.

Gargarella, Roberto 2008. *De la Injusticia Penal a la Justicia Social*. Bogotá: Siglo del Hombre.

Gargarella, Roberto. 2014. *La Sala de Máquinas de la Constitución. Dos Siglos de Constitucionalismo en América Latina* (1810–2010). Buenos Aires: Katz.

Godoy, Angelina. 2006. *Popular Injustice Violence, Community and Law in Latin America*. Stanford: Stanford University Press.

Goldstein, Daniel. 2003. In our own hands: lynching, justice, and the law in Bolivia. *American Ethnologist* 30(1): 22–43.

Goldstein, Daniel. 2005. Flexible justice neoliberal violence and 'self-help' security in Bolivia. *Critique of Anthropology* 25(4): 389–411.

Green, Linda. 1994. Fear as a way of life. *Cultural Anthropology* 9(2): 227–56.

Hale, Charles. 1972. *La Transformación del Liberalismo en México a Finales del Siglo XIX*. México: Fondo de Cultura Económica.

Hobsbawm, Eric. 1981. *Bandits*. London: Pantheon Books.

Holland, Alisha. 2015. *Voting for Forbearance: The Politics of Informal Redistribution in Latin America*. Available at: www.bu.edu/polisci/files/2015/03/HollandBU03.15.pdf. Accessed June 8, 2017.

Holston, James. 2008. *Insurgent Citizenship: Disjunctions of Democracy and Modernity in Brazil*. Princeton, NJ: Princeton University Press.

Iturralde, Manuel. 2009. *Castigo, Liberalismo Autoritario y Justicia Penal de Excepción*. Bogotá: Uniandes.

Jaksic, Ivan and Eduardo Posada Carbó (Ed.). 2011. *Liberalismo y Poder. Latinoamérica en el Siglo XIX, Santiago de Chile*. México: Fondo de Cultura Económica.

Keck, Margaret and Katrhyn Sikkink. 1998. *Activists Beyond Borders*. Ithaca: Cornell University Press.

Lemaitre, Julieta. 2009. *El Derecho Como Conjuro*. Bogotá: Siglo del Hombre y Uniandes.

Lemaitre, J., López, E.S., Mosquera, J.P., Sandvik, K.B., and Gómez, J.V. 2014. De desplazados a víctimas. *Estudios Justicia Global*, 7.

Machado, Marta, Ana Luiza Villela and Fernanda Matsuda. Forthcoming, 2019. "Law, gender and social movements in Latin America: moral negotiations and uneven victories in feminist legal mobilization." In Rachel Sieder, Karina Ansolabehere, and Tatiana Alfonso (Eds.), *Routledge Handbook of Law and Society in Latin America*. New York and London: Routledge.

Maldonado, Salvador. 2011. *A los Márgenes del Estado Mexicano*. Michoacán: Colegio de Michoacán.

Mariátegui, José Carlos. 1928/1979. *Siete Ensayos de Interpretación de la Realidad Peruana*. México: Ediciones Era.

Martí, José. 1939. *Nuestra América*. La Habana: Trópico.

Meili, Stephen. 2001. "Latin American Cause Lawyering Networks." In Austin Sarat and Stuart Scheingold (Eds.), *Cause Lawyering and the State in a Global Era*. Oxford: Oxford University Press: 307–33.

Méndez, Juan, Guillermo O'Donnell and Paulo Sergio Pinheiro. 1999. *The Unrule of Law and the Underprivileged in Latin America*. Notre Dame: University of Notre Dame Press.

Mockus, Antanas. 1999. *Armonizar Ley, Moral y Cultura: Cultura Ciudadana, Prioridad de Gobierno con Resultados en Prevención y Control de Violencia en Bogotá*. Washington, DC: Inter-American Development Bank.

Nader, Laura and Ugo Mattei. 2008. *Plunder: When the Rule of Law is Illegal*. London: Wiley.

Nino, Carlos 1992. *Un País al Márgen de la Ley*. Buenos Aires: Emecé Editores.

Nogeira de Oliveira, Mario. 2009. Ethics and citizenship culture in Bogotá's urban administration. *The University of Miami Inter-American Law Review* 41(1): 1–17.

Novoa, Eduardo. 1975. *El Derecho Como Obstáculo al Cambio Social*. Ciudad de México: Editorial Siglo XX.

O'Donnell, Guillermo. 1993. On the state, democratization and some conceptual problems: (A Latin American view with glances at some post–communist countries). *World Development* 21(8): 1355–70.

O'Donnell, Guillermo. 1984. *¿Y a mí, Qué me Importa? Notas Sobre Sociabilidad y Política en Argentina y Brasil*. Notre Dame: University of Notre Dame Press.

Organization of American States (OAS). 1962. *Alliance for Progress Report*. Washington, DC: OAS.

Pérez, Catalina. 2007. Desconfianza y Desobediencia: Discurso y Práctica del Derecho en México. SELA. *Derecho y Cultura*. Puerto Rico: Ediciones tal Cual.

Reuter, Peter. 2009. Systemic violence in drug markets. *Crime, Law and Social Change* 52(3), 275–84.

Ruiz, Alicia. 2001. *Identidad Femenina y Discurso Jurídico*. Buenos Aires: Editorial Biblos.

Saldivia, Laura. Forthcoming, 2019. "Society, the State, and Recognition of the Right to a Self-Perceived Gender Identity." In Rachel Sieder, Karina Ansolabehere, and Tatiana Alfonso (Eds.), *Routledge Handbook of Law and Society in Latin America*. New York and London: Routledge.

Santos, Boaventura and Mauricio García. 2004. *Emancipación Social y Violencia en Colombia*. Bogotá: Editorial Norma.

Santos, Boaventura. 2001 *La Globalización del Derecho*. Bogotá: ILSA.

Santos, Boaventura. 2002. *Toward a New Legal Common Sense: Law, Globalization, and Emancipation*. London: Butterworths.

Santos, Boaventura. 2010. *Refundación del Estado en América Latina: Perspectivas desde una Epistemología del Sur*. Plural editores.

Santos, Boaventura. 1977. The law of the oppressed: the construction and reproduction of legality in Pasargada law. *Law and Society Review* 12: 5–126.

Santos, Boaventura and César Rodríguez. 2005. *Law and Globalization from Below*. Cambridge: Cambridge University Press.

Sarmiento, Domingo. 1999. *Facundo*. Buenos Aires: ElAleph.com. Available at: http://bibliotecadigital. educ.ar/uploads/contents/DomingoF.Sarmiento-Facundo0.pdf. Accessed June 14, 2017.

Scott, James, 2009. *Art of Not Being Governed*. New Haven: Yale University Press.

Sieder, Rachel 2011. "Pueblos indígenas y derecho en América Latina." En César Rodríguez-Garavito (coord.) *El Derecho en América Latina: Los Retos del Siglo XXI*. Buenos Aires: Siglo XXI: 302–21.

Sikkink Kathryn. 2011. *The Justice Cascade*. New York: Norton.

Snyder, R. and A. Duran-Martinez. 2009. Does illegality breed violence? Drug trafficking and state-sponsored protection rackets. *Crime Law Social Change* 52: 253. https://doi.org/10.1007/s10611-009-9195-z

Sommer, Doris. 1991. *Foundational Fictions*. Berkeley: University of California Press.

Souza de, María de Lourdes. 2001. *El Uso Alternativo del Derecho. Génesis y Evolución en Italia, España y Brasil*. Bogotá: Ed. Universidad Nacional de Colombia/ILSA.

Svampa, Maristela. 2006/1994. *Civilización o Barbarie el Dilema Argentino*. Madrid: Editorial Taurus.

Svampa, Maristella. 2008. *Cambio de Época. Movimientos Sociales y Poder Político*. Buenos Aires: Siglo XXI.

Taussig, Michael. 1984. Culture of terror space of death. *Comparative Studies in Society and History* 26(3): 467–97.

Tate, Winifred. 2007. *Counting the Dead*. Berkeley: University of California Press.

Torre Rangel de la, Jesús Antonio. 2006. *El Derecho Como Arma de Liberación en América Latina. Sociología Jurídica y Uso Alternativo del Derecho*. San Luis Potosí: Facultad de Derecho de la Universidad Autónoma de San Luis Potosí.

Trubek, David and Alvaro Santos. 2006. *The New Law and Economic Development*. Cambridge: Cambridge University Press.

Vásquez, Rodolfo. 2015. *Derechos Humanos una Lectura Liberal Igualitaria*. México: Fontamara ITAM.

Wilson, Bruce and Camila Gianella. Forthcoming, 2019. "The Judicialisation of Politics in Latin America." In Rachel Sieder, Karina Ansolabehere, and Tatiana Alfonso (Eds.), *Routledge Handbook of Law and Society in Latin America*. New York and London: Routledge.

Wolkmer, Antonio. 2003. Legal pluralism: the new emancipatory framework in Latin America. *Law and Society in Latin* 26: 155–68.

Yrigoyen Raquel. 2011. El horizonte del constitucionalismo pluralista: del multiculturalismo a la decolonización. En César Rodríguez-Garavito (Coord.) *El Derecho en América Latina: Los Retos del Siglo XXI*. Buenos Aires: Siglo XXI.

Zea, Leopoldo. 1968. *El Positivismo en México*. México: Fondo de Cultura Económica.

Websites

Amnesty International. 1977. [online]. Argentina: Report of an AI Mission to Argentina November 6–15, 1976. Index number: AMR 13/083/1977. Available at: www.amnesty.org/en/documents/amr13/083/1977/en/. Accessed October 22, 2017.

Watts, Jonathan. 2015. [online]. Latin America Leads World on Murder Map, But Key Cities Buck Deadly Trend. *Guardian*. Available at: www.theguardian.com/world/2015/may/06/murder-map-latin-america-leads-world-key-cities-buck-deadly-trend#top. Accessed October 22, 2017.

7

ETHNOGRAPHY, BUREAUCRACY, AND LEGAL KNOWLEDGE IN LATIN AMERICAN STATE INSTITUTIONS

Law's Material and Technical Dimensions

Leticia Barrera and Sergio Latorre

Introduction

State institutions and practices in Latin America has been a very rich field of academic research for years. We do not have space here for a thorough review of all the literature, but it is worth noting that in general terms, the social sciences and the humanities have focused their inquiries on the constitution and development of Latin American states (Halperin Donghi 1982; Coronil 1997; O' Donnell 1985, 1996; Ribeiro 1999). More recently, though, scholarly attention has been driven to the multiple struggles that take place within Latin American societies reaching a broad scope of conflicts: from state violence and the legacy of dictatorial regimes, to indigenous rights' movements, and the effects of neoliberal reforms, among others (Brunnegger and Faulk 2016; Couso, Hunneeus, and Sieder 2010; Faulk 2013; Hetherington 2012; Tiscornia 2004, 2005; Vaisman 2014). In this chapter, we seek to advance an approach to the state and state-like legal institutions and processes in the region by looking at their mundane and everyday workings; that is, their *bureaucracies*. More concretely, our interest in the workings of state and legal bureaucracy draws specifically on a current and growing anthropological and socio-legal scholarship that, in different contexts – from financial institutions to city governance; water regulation to biotechnology; or patent ownership to legal history – focuses on the artifacts of bureaucratic knowledge-making, such as forms, documents, files, and other "legal technicalities" (Riles 2005) in the understanding that these artifacts also become *means* to build expertise, governance, and knowledge relations (Ballestero 2015; Foster 2016; Hull 2012l; Latour 2004; Richland 2013; Riles 2005, 2011; Valverde 2009; Vismann 2008).

At first glance, a scholarly engagement with legal technicalities may look somewhat awkward for a "law and society" or "law in context" audience that is more familiar with an idea of law as an instrument of social forces, or as "an expression of processes by which society maintains and reproduces itself" (Pottage 2014, 147). Consequently, in this essay we seek to unpack our approach to law and legal knowledge-making by reflecting, in the ethnographic mode, on law's mundane and material – bureaucratic – workings as encountered in two different and distant milieus of lawmaking in Latin America: the field of judicial practice in Argentina, and that of disputes over land tenure in Colombia. In both fields we came across with different documentary practices that exposed the construction of legal discourse through the making, exchange, and circulation of official (and non-official) documents, protocols, forms, and papers; a process that can be seen as ordinary to any bureaucratic action. However, in paying attention to the role that these artifacts played in our actors' daily workings within the legal body (Barrera 2012) or in their mimicking of state-like institution (Latorre 2018), we were also able to notice these instruments' capacity to impact on the (legal, and bureaucratic) discourses they mediate and the relations that take place beyond bureaucracy's (physical) boundaries (Hull 2012, 21, 23).

In taking on bureaucracy as a subject of study we wish to shift analysis away from a political and normative focus on bureaucracy's operation that frames bureaucracy as taking part into the persistent tension between how law should do (law on the books) and what law actually does (law in action). Likewise, we want to set apart any abstract theory of law and power to frame our inquiry. Accordingly, we propose a different kind of engagement with bureaucracy, which through an ethnographic lens on the technical dimension of law, reveals a different modality of how law works: one that emphasizes the law's constitution and its constitutional force "in and through documents, records, files, and other modes of bureaucratic language" (Richland 2013, 5). Ultimately, we hope that our privileging of the technical and procedural elements of bureaucratic state practices sheds new light on the workings of state institutions in Latin America, and hopefully problematizes some of the common tropes according to which power has been conceptualized in the region's social relations.

In the following section, we begin by situating bureaucracy as a subject matter that unfolds within the context of historical tensions and phenomena that make state practices in Latin America worthy of scholarly attention. In this section we also seek to place our approach to everyday legal and bureaucratic knowledge-making within a larger anthropological research agenda on the state that, according to Trouillot, should "look for state processes and effects in sites less obvious than those of institutionalized politics and established bureaucracies" (2001, 133). In the second section, we revisit the long-run discussion between law on the books and law in action by bringing the question of law's materiality center-stage. In turning legal tools into a subject of inquiry, we envision a reconsideration of the persistent gap between law on the books and law in action as a fixed category that predetermines socio-legal analysis and pursue an alternative mode of analysis not to get trapped within such dichotomy. In other words, rather than taking for granted the distance between the two dimensions of legality (text versus practice), we explore other modalities in which law is instantiated through the mundane and overlooked aspects of bureaucratic (legal) knowledge-making. In doing so, we are taking anthropologist Colin Hoag's call for studies of bureaucracy to move beyond this kind of binary relations that tend to undermine the analysis. As he argues: the challenge "is to not only write about the gap, but to find ways to write from it, looking for those aspects of the bureaucratic ecology that complicate the legal realism of bureaucratic discretion" (Hoag 2011, 85). In the last two sections we provide some vignettes drawn from our respective ethnographic studies. The sort of insights gained from our researchers have helped us elucidate the role of legal forms and instruments that we encountered in our fields in the making and circulation of legal knowledge, as well as pushing our analysis forward to interrogate the kinds of subjects, modes of agency, and power relations that those instruments reveal. In the conclusion, we argue for the importance of an ethnographic exploration of the material aspects of lawmaking as a different modality of knowing about how law is crafted, experienced, and lived.

The State and its Specters: Old Questions and Emerging Problems

The political history of Latin American countries has influenced the development of their institutions. For example, during the twentieth century political regimes often alternated between dictatorships and democratic governments. In the legal field, political instability has been reflected not only in changes to codes, statutes, and even national constitutions, but has also affected institutional practices as well as the subjectivities of individuals and groups, to the extent that the legal field and law in general is likely to be projected as a site of "indeterminacy," to quote Faulk's study on Argentina (2013, 178), contingency, and even discontinuity.

This historical perspective regarding the development of legal institutions has influenced scholarly analyzes that often approach state practices in Latin America from a normative standpoint. Accordingly, representations of the state tend to be framed within binary categories such as formal-informal, visible-invisible, legal-illegal, or functional-dysfunctional, which inevitably point to the existing gap between how state institutions *should* work and how they *actually* work (Hoag 2011, 84).

In our opinion, a reading of the legal field as contingent on political shifts in Latin America is based on two central assumptions that have characterized the legal history of institutions, and which permeate the ways in which socio-legal scholars tend to analyze the workings of the state. First, a state-centered view that conceptualizes the state as a clearly bounded and autonomous institution, that is, a unitary entity that organizes and regulates the lives of people within a given territory. And second, the state is placed above any other authority or form of social organization. According to this perspective, not only does the state stand apart from society but, more remarkably, it exists in contraposition to other forms through which social relations are lived by civil society. Therefore, culture – or rather, legal culture – is a result of the development and workings of the state and its institutions, rather than the manifestations of actors' practices, discourses, and lived experiences with the law.

The state as an encompassing analytical category has dominated legal research in Latin America. And the absence or uneven presence of the state has been the focus of most scholarly inquiry on the workings of state institutions. Two trends in Latin American socio-legal analysis pivot on the idea of the absence of the state: legal pluralism (De Sousa Santos and Garcia-Villegas 2001; Wolkmer 2003) and the instrumental efficacy of law accounts (Garcia-Villegas 1993, 2009), both theories that presuppose the idea of territories with non-state or non-official law. The former focuses on the forms of social and legal order other than the state that operate in territories excluded from institutional recognition under official law, whereas the latter emphasizes the gap between the instrumental efficacy of law – or rather, its inefficacy – and law's symbolic meaning. Central to both perspectives is their account of the failure of the state's legal apparatus (Ariza and Bonilla 2007; Buchely 2015).

The emergence of state-like institutions at both supra and subnational levels, the workings and practices of transnational corporations, the development of social movements, and shifting forms of regulation – for instance, from a state-driven economy to a more porous and fluctuating economic governance by transnational organizations such as the World Trade Organization (WTO), the World Bank, or even private market institutions – have challenged a monolithic conceptualization of the state. However, the figure of the state remains central to attempts to address some of the enduring and most pressing problems facing Latin America. And even when policies of economic liberalization promoted through transnational governance mechanisms play a significant role in shrinking state resources and altering its redistributive powers, they continue to emphasize the place of the state as the leading actor. In other words, despite the common assumption that the state and its central role might be fading through different processes of "de-nationalization," "de-statization," and internationalization, not all national state forms are necessarily retreating or eroding. Rather, those processes matter-of-factly are paving the way to new forms of supranational state-like forms and perspectives.

Latin American countries share a long prognosis of problems historically associated with the region as a whole that have been framed within a state or supra/state rubric; for instance, state violence, political authoritarianism, corruption, the lack of compliance with the law, and justice claims. Similarly, some of the contemporary and most outstanding concerns among different political actors can be read under a state (supra)-centered lens: the crisis of center-left and populist governments, extractivism affecting natural resources, human rights advocacy, minorities' struggles, and social mobilization for basic resources such as water, land, or food; issues that certainly extend well beyond the frontiers of the nation-state.

Similarly, the emergence of state-like regimes at supranational level has also made scholars to rethink the old frames of supranational state entities to capture new forms in which state practices are manifested contemporarily, that is, amid modern uncertainties and ambiguities (Ong and Collier 2005). In this vein, a long list of literature has produced counter examples of state-centered theories leading to understandings of the state not as a given (distinct and fixed entity), but rather as different arrangements that come into being in the actors' everyday life. In particular, anthropology has offered a useful lens through which to examine state formation and understand how the state (and the boundaries that keeps it apart from other social institutions) is culturally constructed (Gupta 2006). Accordingly, culture is not produced by the state or as a consequence of processes of state formation, but rather the state is produced and understood as the effects of socio-cultural processes (Trouillot 2001; Greenhouse, Mertz, and Warren 2002; Das and Poole 2004; Ong and Collier 2005; Sharma and Gupta 2006; Gluck and Tsing 2009). Moreover, new directions in anthropological research have shed light on everyday rules and processes as state-making practices. Bernstein and Mertz, for instance, have argued that "scholars interested in the workings and the effects of the state should look, at the very least, to the bureaucracies that keep it running." Bureaucracy, therefore, becomes, "another arena for social life and political action" (2011, 6–7).

Undoubtedly, a focus on the quotidian and mundane operation of the state apparatus has allowed social scientists and humanities scholars to trace disperse institutional and social networks of power, bringing together its ideological and material aspects (Foucault 1991). Certainly this line of inquiry has been a very insightful path: scholarly emphasis on state procedures and the activities through which the state is instantiated and reproduced have put under the spotlight the key role that bureaucracy may play in reproducing social inequalities, such as those of class and gender (Sharma and Gupta 2006; Buchely 2015).

Interestingly, addressing bureaucratic procedures as instantiations of state power has made it possible to apprehend the similar ways in which state entities carry out their everyday practices, regardless of their structural differences. In addition, a micro-scale perspective on the workings of the state highlights the ambivalent role of bureaucratic practices. Bureaucracies or bureaucratic knowledge-making practices can be silently applied, without drawing attention to their performative power, or sometimes they can be applied asserting their presence and power through red-letter practices. Also, the focus on bureaucratic procedures has allowed researchers to draw parallels between different actors in widely contrasting settings (for instance, bureaucrats and activists; or experts and non–experts) by engaging with those actors' ideas about the state and their relationship to it (Sharma and Gupta 2006).

For its part, the socio-legal academy in Latin America and abroad has shown that bureaucracy and bureaucratic practices and processes can be encountered at the center of state formation, governance. and exercise of power (Scott 1998). This is due to the fact that everyday practices are the arena in which people learn about the state (Gupta 2006).

Nonetheless, the critical focus on procedural practices of state-making sometimes fails to comprehend that such routine practices are much more than modes of controlling or exercising power. As our own research works have indicated, the technical and procedural practices of bureaucratically structured locations open up different analytical possibilities for exploring their esthetics, performative, and conceptual configurations, which, in turn, may reveal not just our subjects' practices as much as the technical and procedural quality of our own knowledge practices (Riles 2006). Consequently, we would like to argue here that an over-privileging of state practices as micro-politics of power relations reduces their potential of becoming themselves objects of socio-legal analysis. Conversely, the emphasis on some of the most mundane material forms of bureaucracy, such as its documents, has led anthropologists to interrogate particular types of political and ethnographic subjects; the capacity of those forms to generate authority, agency, and affect; and even work as technologies that mediate social interaction and production (Hoag 2011, 85). Consequently, it is in the subtleties of the interplay between different subjects and law's material objects (namely, its documents) that, researchers may reflect on different conceptions of law, including their own; how law works; and what kind of subjects and agency law elicits.

Also notably, a focus on the mundane and seemingly uninteresting material aspects of law, and the procedural and technical problems that arise in their engagements, renders visible other kinds of subjects; or enables new, fresh, and more complex visions of "old" subjects of inquiry, such as the victims of political conflicts, often examined in Latin America and other contexts under the rubrics of poverty, exclusion, or the dichotomy domination versus resistance, all of them under the encompassing category of power. For instance, as Abélès and Badaró note (2015, 53), resistance became an obsession in anthropological studies in the final decades of the twentieth century in contrast to anthropology's traditional enchantment with the state. According to these authors, anthropological studies of power have turned into an exploration of people's resistance to different forms of domination. This trend is in evidence in most contemporary approaches and conceptualizations of the state-resistance relationship advanced by political anthropology. This, in turn, Abélès and Badaró continue to argue, has refreshed concepts such as state dominance and sovereignty, which appeared to have been surpassed by the critique of institutional approaches to the state and ethnographic explorations of different state agencies. However, the relationships between state and resistance may assume different and multiple forms, urging anthropologists to approach them by disentangling first the automatic associations of both categories with specific forms of power and political action (Abélès and Badaró 2015).[1]

Law On The Books *Versus* Law In Action: Legal Technicalities in the Gap

After bringing the question of law's materiality center-stage in our quest on the constitution and workings of the law (Richland 2013), we would like to revisit the long-run discussion in law and society between law on the books and law in action, and advocate, following Riles' insight, for socio-legal scholars' engagement with law's material and technical dimension. Indeed, law and society scholarship is primarily interested in what the law does on the ground, and generally less concerned with what the law *is* (legal rules and procedures understood from inside the legal system) (Macaulay, Friedman, and Stooke 1995). A core tenet in law and society studies is that social and institutional practices surrounding the law are just as important as the substance of law on the books (Pound 1910). This premise encapsulates the problem of the *gap* between the legal norm and how it is actually performed, that is, law's practice.

At least two modes of inquiry in socio-legal studies have been developed to attempt to answer the question of the *gap* between law in action and law on the books, or in other words to explain the relationship of law and society. On the one hand, law is seen as an instrument through which society can be deterred, controlled, or influenced (Chambliss 1967; Gaventa 1980; Zimring and Hawkins 1971). On the other, law cannot be conceived merely as an instrument, but must also be understood as a set of conceptual categories that help construct, compose, communicate, and interpret social actions in everyday life (Sarat and Kearns 1994; Ewick and Silbey 1998). These two modes of inquiry have produced a stimulating body of work in socio-legal research: those for whom law constitutes a tool that reflects, reproduces, and modifies specific features and institutions of social life; and also those who by critiquing conceptions of society as an ontological domain separate from law[2] see in the law a constitutive element of society and direct their attention to theorizing law's relation to power and ideology, as well as law's inherent hegemonic power. For both of these influential trends of socio-legal thought, the question about how technical legal knowledge itself is created, used, circulated, or exchanged has remained undertheorized. Indeed, the material dimension of legal knowledge-making, namely, the routine and everyday tools on which the workings of law rests, have been somewhat "black boxed"[3] by socio-legal scholars' emphasis on the social forces and power relations at play in different legal arrangements. As Annelise Riles has observed, "legal technicalities" – legal instrumentalism, managerialism, procedures, the figures of legal technocrats, and the forms of legal doctrines, among others – are often seen as "profoundly uninteresting" and "too mundane" to require investigation from cultural legal studies, that tend to see them as part of "the realm of practice rather than theory" and consequently as "non-strategical" for critical socio-legal analysis (Riles 2005, 976, 974). For scholars who share a more instrumentalist approach to law (including economists, cognitive scientists, and corporate lawyers), the technical character of law becomes relevant only insofar they are useful to solve actual legal problems (Riles 2005, 974, 976). Similarly, Mariana Valverde has argued that "[l]aw is usually examined by critical legal studies and socio-legal scholarship as a key site for the reproduction and contestation of various forms of power relations." However, as she remarks, "if power works through knowledge, it should prove useful to undertake the examination of some legal events that highlights the knowledge dimension" (Valverde 2003, 1). In Valverde's project, this means observing the constitution, contestation, and circulation of certain sets of truths within legal arenas "through and in" the work of some legal actors, namely, state officials, lawyers, and judges. Riles's research agenda, for its part, has urged socio-legal scholars to shift their attention to the core aspects of legal thought, that is to the technicalities of law, and turn them into objects of humanistic inquiry:

> Indeed, it is precisely the commonsensical quality of the thing that makes the lawyer's love of tools an appropriate point of entrée for an ethnographer into contemporary law and institutions.
>
> *(Riles 2011)*

Along the same lines, by asking how socio-legal scholars can re-conceptualize the "persistent, troublesome gap between the law on the books and the law in action" that is at the heart of legal knowledge, Susan Silbey invites scholars to revitalize their theoretical approaches toward this core tenet in law and society studies. In this vein, she considers tracing legal knowledge at "the middle level between citizen and the transcendent rule of law: [namely] the ground of institutional practices" to be the most promising line of inquiry. She claims it is important "to describe the mechanisms by which legal schema are propagated, circulated, and received." Arguing that it is precisely in these places and through these mechanisms by which, "[i]n institutions, cultural meaning, social inequality, and legal consciousness are forged." According to Silbey, it is in institutions where law both promises and fails to live up to its promises (Silbey 2005, 360).

Following these scholars' insights, we believe that an ethnographic approach to law and legal knowledge that take on the technical and material aspects of law in the context where knowledge practices are created, circulated, and exchanged can be a promising line of inquiry for law and society scholars in Latin America. But what ethnographic possibilities do these material and technical aspects of law offer? Moreover, how can the researcher "appropriate" these instruments of legal knowledge-making and turn them into analytical constructs, and even, artifacts of her own knowledge? (Riles 2001, 2011; Levine 2016). The subject, as in any other ethnographical project, poses methodological, epistemological, and political challenges to the ethnographer's representational strategies. In our respective researches, access to the legal field has been through the mundane forms of bureaucratic knowledge, beginning with "legal looking" documents such as consent forms and land titles, and continuing with piles of dossiers that circulate within Argentina's maximum tribunal, as well as public deeds, certificates of registration, and other private documents, like the *cartaventa* – an informal letter that resembles some features of legal deeds encountered in rural Colombia. These artifacts are quintessential to the making of law on a daily basis and can be encountered in both formal and less formal settings. Also, we have interrogated what they have in common. From an epistemological perspective, we found that an ethnographic attention to the materiality of law (or bureaucracy) has helped us engage in our fields with bureaucratic practice "without fetishizing the bureaucratic decision" (Hoag 2011, 85) and hence, to grasp "the contingency, partiality and co-produced nature of bureaucratic knowledge" (ibid., 86). And yet, a focus on the material dimension of bureaucracy has allowed us to reflect on the state not just through its more familiar and commonsensical arrangements – namely, its political institutions, as in Leticia Barrera's research on the Argentine Supreme Court – but also to track their presence in practices, places, and languages considered to be at its margins (Das and Poole 2004), as shown in Sergio Latorre's work. As we explain further in the following section, a focus on the esthetics and informational content of the legal forms that we encountered in our respective field settings, made perceptible to us the subjects, modes of agency, knowledge, and power relations that those forms elucidate (Yablon 1990).

Legal Files as Spaces of Knowledge, Agency, and Authority

The file or *dossier* became Leticia Barrera's point of entry to the judicial institution, both materially and analytically. Files establish the basis for law's authority and account for its everyday operations. Bureaucratic (legal) knowledge moves according to scripted routines (more documents and files) (Riles 2006), which contain their own logic and hold their own progression (Vismann 2008), but these routines are not just mechanical inscriptions of words on paper. Nor are they merely a means to an end (namely, the judicial decision). In exploring files' administrative capacity, Barrera noted that they take on a certain agency: they elicit relations of knowledge (Hetherington 2008; Hegel-Cantarella 2011); mediate social interaction (Hull 2012; Latour 2004; Gordillo 2006; Jacob 2007), and are even able to create affective states within the subjects who make and trade them (Navaro-Yashin 2007).

In this light, a fine-grained analysis of the Argentine Court's "papering practices" that Barrera encountered in the field provided her with an access point to the actors who create those files, in particular law clerks, a figure typically perceived and portrayed within the bureaucratic logic as impersonal and interchangeable. However, as these subjects' documentary practices unfolded in her research, they rendered themselves visible in different forms, though not always in ways readily accessible to outsiders. Drawing on Marilyn Strathern's insight about the forms of objectification and personification that operate in two "ethnographically conceived" social domains: a Euro-American commodity-driven economy, and Melanesia's economy based on gift exchange (1988), Barrera showed that legal bureaucrats, through a process of objectification, become apparent to the external observer on a rational and objective basis. This process occurs via the subjects' own interventions in the bureaucracy; that is, through the papers – the documents – they produce and circulate. She also explained that there is another way in which these bureaucratic subjects may appear not as things but as persons themselves through the personal capacities that the documentary practices actualize. From this perspective, which the practice of judicial adjudication keeps concealed from view, each subject is differentiated as a particular person, and apprehended in her, or his specific capacities.

A similar insight about files' dual capacity of individualization of subjects and agency collectivization can be drawn from Matthew Hull's study of bureaucracy in Islamabad. In his study, bureaucracy is presented to the outsiders as "the epitome of a collective (and authoritative) social organization" – a representation advanced by the impersonal and anonymous bureaucratic discourse of public documents – yet files also articulate an "individualization" of agency that operates simultaneously to the production of bureaucracy as collective agent (Hull 2012, 127, 130).

In Barrera's research, the passage of files that circulate within the judicial apparatus became an essential component to understand actors' perceptions about their roles within the tribunal, to the extent that the circulation of files emerged in their accounts as both the engine and demise of their practices (Barrera 2008, 2012). Moreover, this finding also allowed her to grasp the subjects' understandings about the role and place of the court in contemporary Argentina. For instance, in her interactions with different law clerks, Barrera noticed that their subjects' references to the court´s caseload pervaded their descriptions of both their routines and the tribunal's workings: "There are cases that should not be here [in the court]" was a recurrent claim that she heard from bureaucrats during her fieldwork. Accordingly, through the data that she was able to collect through interviews, informal conversations, participant observation and even the experience of being herself as a claimant before the court waiting for a decision upon her request (Barrera 2008), she went on to explore a particular mode through which the court dismisses or rejects cases that are filed to it.

Barrera's analysis of this particular court's mode of excluding cases from its jurisdiction ("gatekeeping" to quote Yngvesson from another context 1998) led her to conclude that in the post-crisis context in which the court's practices that she studied unfolded, exclusion and gatekeeping, can be interpreted as a means to rebuild the court's authority and regain social prestige, in addition to them being a technique of docket management and control (Barrera 2018). Therefore, Barrera's study of the Argentine Court shows, following Hoag's insight, that understanding bureaucracy – in particular the legal one – "requires an attention to this confluence of materialities (physical structures, technologies), discourses (personal assurances, rules, laws) and the experience of time" (Hoag 2011, 86). In doing so, she furthers a growing field of socio-legal research that focuses on the central role that the artifacts of legal bureaucracy play in the constitution of law itself. Also importantly, the question of law's materiality, we should note, is taken in her analysis beyond legal thinking to inquire into its sociological effects (Barrera 2018, 91).

Unpacking Legal Technologies: Property Relations, Legal Thinking, and Bureaucracy

Sergio Latorre's work proposes an innovative approach to the issue of landownership among rural communities and peasants (*campesinos*), which lies as an alternative to the dominant scholarly focus on socio-political disputes between rural communities and elites that have the economic and legal means to consolidate their power through access and control over land (Fajardo 2002; Machado 2009; Reyes and Duica 2009).

While law in the context of land disputes is often seen as a tool that responds to broader social, political, or economic forces in contention, Latorre highlights the more complex and interesting effects the tool of law produces in land disputes by focusing on the documents and the standard routine practices involved in making and using law in everyday situations.

Central to Latorre's analysis is the emphasis he places on the title deed document that attests to landownership. Latorre's esthetical engagement (Riles 2001) with the sealed document of the land title deed allows him to conceptualize this as a legal technology engineered by law to create land as a thing to be owned (Callon 1987; Law 1991). The use of the technology of the sealed title document enables the individuation of persons, assets, and documents. It is hence, the deed title – understood as a technology – and the legal arrangements it produces, what leads us to think comfortably of land as an "already made entity" in the world.

In Latorre's account, the imprint left by the seal and the effects it elicits is what is behind "the implicit legal infrastructure" (De Soto 2000, 8) assumed to exist in projects that advocate the formalization of property rights in order to draw capital from death assets in informal markets and thereby foster development among the world´s poor (Latorre 2015).

However, the effects produced by the sealed title understood as a technology of law are not only important in the debate between property and state development for Third World countries. For Latorre, the seal stamped on the document of the land title is a form of reification of knowledge under a legal framework.[4] In other words, the seal's function is to maintain the stability and self-referentiality of the conceptual framework that operates within law regarding ownership of land. The imprint left by the seal relates to the conceptual framework legal scholars maintain and work with when thinking about law in terms of a division between public and private orders.[5] The seal contains the interrelation between the private and public orders we perceive in legal thought, providing an interesting entry point for thinking through and destabilizing this relationship.

Our conceptual image of legal knowledge is constituted by the public and private order as two separate domains and, at same time, we perceive them related to each other so we can recognize the image of the law as a whole. In landownership both spheres are present: private arrangements between parties who are the persons involved in the transaction and entitled to own land, and the public, in this case represented by the authority the state, that confers land its character as a thing to be owned by private parties.

Latorre's study explains how, in the context of the title that formalizes the relationship of land ownership, once the deed gets stamped it becomes the agreement through which we maintain and accept the cognitive constructions fabricated by the law. By accepting the seal as technology of the law, we commit our own knowledge practices to reproducing the mental imprint constituted by the interrelation of both orders.

Latorre´s ethnography also contributes to the literature on socio-legal approach to property by describing the problems and blind spots that arise from such a commitment to the technology of the sealed title. His work points to the problems that arise from land fragmentation among Colombian *campesinos*. When the formalization of land ownership is achieved and land is individualized, land can be subsequently subdivided into smaller parts that can be allocated among different persons. This has proved to be particularly troublesome for poor *campesinos* recognized as owners, who have slowly subdivided the land they owned among their descendants and other members of their community because of economic constraints. Most of these divisions are enacted informally according to the owner's desires and they are not necessarily impartial or in accordance with the law. When these new owners attempt to legalize the divided parcels, they find it incredibly difficult to deal with anti-economic fragmentation laws and other regulations that forbid them from legally attempting such divisions in the first place.

Similarly, the technology of the sealed title document, as it creates land as a thing, maintains the persistent gap between abstraction and territoriality. This detachment occurs when the representation of land in a deed title does not match the current practices over land that happen in a territory. Despite the efforts made by law to actualize the system of ownership and the registration of each transaction over land, a mismatch remains between the processes for land formalization and recording, which requires all land transactions to be recorded in chronological order at the office of registration, and the land transactions that occur spontaneously in the territory among *campesinos*. (Latorre 2015).

Latorre's study engages with the state through the unpacking of legal technologies, which leads him to other spaces of legality, lawmaking, and processes under which legal knowledge is formed and upheld. His ethnography explores spaces of lawmaking that have been undertheorized but have remarkable importance in the Latin America legal context. This is the case with the notary, which with its formal arrangements, becomes an important space of lawmaking where documents are fashioned and people are made into documents (Barrera 2008). His study describes how parties (either accompanied by a lawyer or on their own) are required to participate in the regime of formalization that occurs at the notary. The work done at the notary is not only key in understanding how land becomes a thing to be privately owned, but is also important in the formalization of many of the most important actions in our lives, such as marriage and divorce, births and deaths, and inheritance.

In Latorre's ethnography the land title deed is not the only document that is essential in the interaction of *campesinos* and bureaucrats pertaining to landownership. Contrary to an image of the rural landscape as isolated, marginalized, and far removed from modern life, it is in fact highly dynamic, characterized by the circulation and exchange of different legal documents. *Campesinos* have to learn how to deal with different kinds of papers and documents in order to interact with government institutions. Documents such as birth certificates, school attendance certificates, and perhaps the most important for *campesinos* displaced by violence, the certificates as "displaced persons," are all part of this complex setting. Relatedly, bureaucratic practices once thought to happen only in the modern state or in the most advanced institutions as part of the process of rationalization granted to bureaucratic knowledge (Weber 1946), in fact occur in multiple settings.

A number of discontinuities are discernible in bureaucrats and *campesinos'* interactions over legal documents. Both groups remained quite uncertain of each other's intentions in the use of such artifacts, as the legal document never renders the quality of the thing or person entirely complete. At the level of the meaning of the law, while bureaucrats are only confident to speak about the world once it has been transformed into written texts (Latour 2004), the experience of *campesinos* is quite different. For example, when a local court issued a judicial decision, it allowed bureaucrats to recreate in their minds an idea of law, fundamental rights, and legal procedure, very different to the idea of law *campesinos* drew from the practice of bringing a lawsuit and their experience of the law through handling paperwork. In the ruling, the discussions of rights did not speak to *campesinos*; rather than conceiving the outcome in terms of justice, they felt as if they had won a prize, much as they might win the lottery (Latorre 2012).

In summary, Latorre's work ethnographically recasts the material and technical aspects of the law in order to understand and unpack the legal technologies embedded in legal practices. This approach proves to make a fruitful intervention in some important trends in law and society scholarship regarding economic and state development in the Third World, socio-legal approaches to property, the legal institutions and processes that help shape the public-private division in legal thought, and the operations of lawmaking practices and bureaucracies in Latin America.

Conclusions: Compartmentalizing Politics – Legal Instruments in the Realm of the State

Drawing on two ethnographic explorations of the workings of legal bureaucracy – and the theoretical contributions of legal and political anthropology, social studies of science and technology, and anthropology of bureaucracy – we have proposed in this chapter that a fine-grained analysis of the most commonsensical and routine aspects of lawmaking provides a fresh and fruitful understanding of how law works. In this light, we argue that the material and mundane aspects of the law offer an analytical space from where socio-legal scholarship can orient its critical inquiry. Latin America, a region marked by political crisis and upheaval, provides a particularly admirable context for the analysis of legal instruments. Whether the focus is on access to land in Colombia or judicial decision-making in Argentina, to name two examples among many other fields of socio-legal inquiry in the region, working with technical devices shows how political debates and narratives may dissolve in practice into other kinds of conflicts.

In the context of Colombia, characterizing these debates through a flat reading of the role of law as oscillating between market-based approach that seeks to generate a competitive and efficient rural sector by creating incentives for capital investment, or alternatively, by a regulatory-state approach that aims at issuing policies with specific socioeconomic purposes through land distribution remedies, is far too simple to account for the actors' legal knowledge practices developed in their implementation of law.

By the same token, to characterize the discussion of Argentina's judicial system as formally governed rules vis-à-vis informal and discretionary judges' decision-making power at the supreme court might reduce the question of judicial adjudication to its result: the *judgment*. This understanding of judicial practice leaves aside a whole instance of knowledge-making and relationships that lies before the law's *ends*, that is, the judicial decision (Vismann 2008). In addition, a focus on the material aspects of law reveals that actors such as officials and judges are more concerned with conflicts that are of a technical, legal, institutional, procedural, or even personal kind (affecting their subjectivities and the social order of their relationships). In contrast to macro political discourses about law, legal technical devices set limits, make distinctions, and characterize the politics at play in different contexts. According to Riles, official and judges' practices of drafting legal documents or form-filling are instantiations where politics are compartamentalized. "It is through these practices that political legitimacy—the kind of legitimacy that is the hallmark of the liberal state— is created and manipulated" (Riles 2011, 65).

In fact some of the processes and technical devices deployed to collect information about land or court cases, including legal titles, certificates of registration, and court dossiers, remain for the most part materially unchanged despite political and legal transformations in Latin America's legal and judicial systems. Bureaucrats' everyday work stays constant and consists in solving the conflicts and indeterminacies of these legal technical devices, regardless of political discussions surrounding their everyday actions.

Drawing on examples from our respective research fields, it is clear that, despite the fact that the model of land distribution in Colombia has changed several times over the years, some of the technical devices used to collect information about land remain the same from one law to the next. When deciding upon a course of action, officials base their behavior on these legal technicalities more than on the regulations contained in laws drafted to regulate the state of land ownership in rural areas. Likewise, Barrera's observation of lawmaking procedures within the Argentine Court revealed that the practices of those committed to the court's day-to-day routines, such as clerks, are matter-of-factly a very stable aspect of law, in spite of the tribunal's erratic positions on similar issues over a short period of time.

Moreover, in the case of *campesinos* and their struggle to gain access to land, the experiences they had with other actors involved in the process of granting land, and their contact with a highly sophisticated set of technical devices, enabled them to develop different ideas of law and implement strategies to interact with this set of technical legal artifacts. *Campesinos* even reproduce some of the technical aspects of formal land title, as is the case of the informal "*cartaventa*" document (a handwritten document used to transfer land among them) found in rural Colombia (Latorre 2018).

Theoretical attention to the materiality of law found in the mundane and routine practices of lawmaking in places such as courts or administrative offices offers a fruitful departure from representations of law in Latin America that understand the transformations of state institutions as contingent on political shifts. Such approaches tend to accentuate the persistent gap between how state institutions actually work and how they should work (the gap between law on the books and law in action). Our focus seeks precisely to overcome what we consider to be a taken for granted distance between these two dimensions of legality (text versus practice) by exploring other modalities in which law is instantiated through bureaucratic (legal) knowledge-making.

Ethnographic exploration of the inner and mundane spaces of lawmaking enables a shift of focus from legal knowledge as a mode of surveillance and exerting power, to a focus on legal knowledge-making practices – in which subtle and complex interplays between different subjects and material objects occur. This, in turn, allows for a rich and invigorating view of the field of law and society in Latin America that expands beyond the gap. It raises questions about other spaces of lawmaking or the kinds of material objects of law that might be analytically interesting to explore in the Latin American context. Additionally, it signals the sorts of subjects and modes of agency that law can elicit and, which have often escaped our understandings of power relations in Latin America, often centered on macro (economic, political, and social) structures. Overall, it offers possibilities of deepening our understanding of "old" subjects such as poverty, resistance, or exclusion in the region. And still, different conceptions of law can therefore, contribute to better understanding of law and its interaction with the state in Latin America.

Notes

1 Abélès and Badaró advance Deleuze and Guattari's definition of the state as an "apparatus of capture" through which the most salient aspects of the state are territoriality, work or public works, and taxation (Deleuze and Guattari 2004). From this perspective, they argue, the canonical association between the state, repression, and ideology is challenged and set apart from the matter of the monopoly of violence by the state and its ideological apparatuses (Abélès and Badaró 2015, 54).

2 These authors critique the conception of society as one separate ontological domain separated from law:

> For most of the twentieth century, legal scholars had treated law and society as if they were two empirically distinct spheres, as if the two were conceptually as well as materially separate and singular. They are not. The law is a construct of human ingenuity; laws are material phenomena. Similarly, society is a fiction we sustain through hard work and mutual communication.
>
> *(Silbey 2005, 327)*

3 In Science studies, "black boxing" is used to indicate the social process through which the joint production of actors and artifacts becomes entirely opaque by its own success:

> When a machine runs efficiently, when a matter of fact is settled, one needs to focus only on
> its inputs and outputs and not in its internal complexity. Thus, paradoxically, the more
> science and technology succeed, the more opaque and obscure they become.
>
> *(Latour 1999, 183, 304)*

4 Strathern explains such process of reification as:

> The manner in which entities are made into objects when they are seen to assume a particular
> form (gift, exchange). This form in turn indicates the properties by which they are known
> and, in being rendered knowable or graspable through such properties, entities appear (in
> Euro-American idiom) as things […]. We should not lose sight of the fact, then, that the
> effort of knowing which goes into making an analysis or model of the world appear in a
> written account is a process which involves reification.
>
> *(1999, 13–14)*

5 The question that has captured the imagination of some legal scholars is where to draw the line sepa-
rating the public and private orders, or even if it makes sense to draw a line between them at all. In
Legal Theory, more broadly, the relationship between private and a public order has long been
addressed. The imbrications of private arrangements and the public enforcement of private rights has
been the object of prolific intellectual activity since legal realism, up until today in a wide variety of
areas. In Property, Contracts, Torts, Global Governance, Human Rights, and Private International
Law, we constantly observe certain kinds of relationship between both domains – whether they challenge or complement one another – to gain new insights about their multipronged relationship or, on
the contrary, to dismantle the distinction between them.

References

Abélès, Marc and Máximo Badaró. *2015. Los Encantos Del Poder. Desafíos De La Antropología Política.*
Buenos Aires: Siglo XXI editores.

Ariza, Libardo, and Daniel Bonilla. 2007. "El pluralismo jurídico: contribuciones, debilidades y retos de un
concepto polémico." *El Debate Sobre el Pluralismo Jurídico*, Bogotá: Universidad de Los Andes.

Ballestero, Andrea. 2015. The ethics of a formula: calculating a financial-humanitarian price for water.
American Ethnologist 42(2): 262–78.

Barrera, Leticia. 2008. Files circulation and the forms of legal experts: agency and personhood in the
Argentine Supreme Court. *Journal of Legal Anthropology* 1(1): 3–24.

Barrera, Leticia. 2012. *La Corte Suprema En Escena. Una Etnografía Del Mundo Judicial.* Buenos Aires: Siglo
XXI editores.

Barrera, Leticia. 2018. Gatekeeping: documents, legal knowledge and judicial authority in contemporary
Argentina. *PoLAR: The Political and Legal Anthropology Review* 41(1): 90–107.

Bernstein, Anya and Elizabeth Mertz. 2011. Introduction – symposium on bureaucracy: ethnography of
the state in everyday life. *PoLAR: The Political and Legal Anthropology Review* 34(1): 6–9.

Brunnegger, Sandra and Karen Faulk. 2016. "Introduction: making sense of justice." In Sandra Brunnegger and Karen Faulk (eds.), *A Sense of Justice. Legal Knowledge and Lived Experience in Latin America.*
Stanford, CA: Stanford University Press.

Buchely, Lina. 2015. *Activismo Burocrático. La Construcción Cotidiana del Principio de Legalidad.* Bogotá:
Uniandes.

Callon, Michael. 1987. "Society in the making; the study of technology as a tool for sociological analysis."
In W.E. Bijker, T.P. Hughes, and T.J. Pinch (eds.), *The Social Construction of Technological Systems, New
Directions in the Sociology and History of Technology.* Cambridge, MA: MIT Press.

Chambliss, William J. 1967. Types of deviance and the effectiveness of legal sanctions. *Wisconsin Law
Review* 703–19.

Couso, Javier, Alexandra Huneeus and Rachel Sieder. 2010. *Cultures of Legalities: Judicialization and Political
Activism in Latin America.* Cambridge: Cambridge University Press.

Coronil, Fernando. 1997. *The Magical State: Nature, Money, and Modernity in Venezuela.* Chicago: University of Chicago Press.

Das, Veena and Deborah Poole (eds.). 2004. *Anthropology in Margins of the State*. Santa Fe, NM: School of American Research Press.

Deleuze, Gilles and Felix Guattari. 2004. "Mil Mesetas. Barcelona, Pre-Textos (6ª edición)." Cited in Marc Abélès and Máximo Badaró. 2015. *Los Encantos Del Poder. Desafíos De La Antropología Política*. Buenos Aires: Siglo XXI editores.

De Soto, Hernando. 2000. *The Mystery of Capital: Why Capitalism Triumphs in the West and Fails Everywhere Else*. New York: Basic Books.

De Sousa Santos, Boaventura, and Mauricio Garcia-Villegas. 2001. *El Caleidoscopio de las Justicias en Colombia: Análisis Socio-Jurídico*. Bogotá: Siglo del Hombre Editores.

Ewick, Patricia, and Susan S. Silbey. 1998. *The Common Place of Law: Stories From Everyday Life*. University of Chicago Press,

Fajardo, Dario. 2002. *Tierra, Poder Político y Reformas Agraria y Rural. Cuadernos Tierra y Justicia, Número 1*. Bogotá: Instituto Latinoamericano de Servicios Legales Alternativos.

Faulk, Karen A. 2013. *In the Wake of Neoliberalism, Citizenship and Human Rights in Argentina*. Stanford, CA: Stanford University Press.

Foucault, Michel. 1991. *The Foucault Effect: Studies in Governmentality*. Chicago: University of Chicago Press.

Foster, Laura A. 2016. The making and unmaking of patent ownership: technicalities, materialities and subjectivities. *PoLAR: The Political and Legal Anthropology Review* 39(1): 127–43.

García-Villegas, Mauricio. 1993. *La Eficacia Simbólica Del Derecho: Examen De Situaciones Colombianas*. Santafé de Bogotá, DC, Colombia: Ediciones Uniandes.

García-Villegas, Mauricio. 2009. *Normas de Papel: La Cultura del Incumplimiento de Reglas*. Bogotá: Siglo del Hombre.

Gaventa, John. 1980. *Power and Participation, Power and Powerlessness. Quiescence and Rebellion in an Appalachian Valley*. Urbana, Chicago and London: University of Illinois Press.

Gluck, Carol and Anna Lowenhaupt Tsing. 2009. *Words in Motion. Toward a Global Lexicon*. Durham and London: Duke University Press.

Gordillo, Gaston. 2006. The crucible of citizenship: ID-papers fetishism in the Argentinean chaco. *American Anthropologist* 33(2): 162–76.

Greenhouse, Carol, Elizabeth Mertz, and Kay B.B. Warren. 2002. *Ethnography in Unstable Places: Everyday Lives in Contexts of Dramatic Political Changes*. Durham, NC: Duke University Press.

Gupta, Akhil. 2006. "Blurred boundaries: the discourse of corruption, the culture of politics and the imagined state." In Aradhana Sharma and Akhil Gupta (eds.), *The Anthropology of the State: A Reader*. Malden, MA: Blackwell.

Halperin Donghi, Tulio. 1982. *Una Nación Para El Desierto Argentino*. Buenos Aires: Centro Editor de América Latina.

Hegel-Cantarella, Christine. 2011. Kin-to-be: betrothal, legal documents, and reconfiguring relational obligations in Egypt. *Law, Culture and the Humanities* 7(3): 377–93.

Hetherington, Kregg. 2012. *Guerrilla Auditors. The Politics of Transparency in Rural Paraguay*. Durham: Duke University Press.

Hoag, Colin. 2011. Assembling partial perspectives: thoughts on the anthropology of bureaucracy. *PoLAR: The Political and Legal Anthropology Review* 34(1): 81–94.

Hull, Matthew S. 2012. *Government of Paper: The Materiality of Bureaucracy in Urban Pakistan*. Berkeley and Los Angeles: University of California Press.

Jacob, Marie-Andree. 2007. Form-made persons: consent forms as consent's blind spot. *PoLAR: The Political and Legal Anthropology Review* 30(2): 249–68.

Law, John. 1991. Notes on the theory of the actor–network: ordering, strategy, and heterogeneity. *Systems Practice and Action Research* 5(4): 379–93.

Latorre, Sergio. 2012. Legal Technicalities in Conditions of Political Conflict: The Case of Land Tenure Disputes in Colombia. JDS Dissertation, Cornell University.

Latorre, Sergio. 2015. The making of land ownership: land titling in rural Colombia – a reply to Hernando de Soto. *Third World Quarterly* 36(8): 1546–69.

Latorre, Sergio. 2018. "Hacia una visión institucionalizada de la propiedad: Estudio etnográfico del documento de la cartaventa en los Montes de María." En Sergio Latorre (ed.), *Conflicto Armado y Transición Hacia El Post-Conflicto: Una Aproximación Desde El Caribe*. Barranquilla, Colombia: Ediciones Uninorte.

Latour, Bruno. 1999. *Pandora's Hope: Essays on the Reality of Science Studies*. Cambridge, MA: Harvard University Press.

Latour, Bruno. 2004. *La Fabrique Du Droit. Une Ethnographie Du Conseil d'Etat*. Paris: La Decouverte/ Poche.

Levine, Amy. 2016. *South Korean Civil Movement Organisations. Hope, Crisis and Pragmatism in Democratic Transition*. New Ethnographies Series, Manchester: Manchester University Press.

Macaulay, Stewart, Lawrence M. Friedman, and John A. Stookey. 1995. *Law & Society: Readings on the Social Study of Law*. New York: W.W. Norton & Co, Print.

Machado, A. (2009). *La Reforma Rural, Una Deuda Social y Política*. Bogotá: Universidad Nacional de Colombia, Facultad de Ciencias Económicas, Centro de Investigaciones para el Desarrollo, CID.

Navaro-Yashin, Yael. 2007. Make-believe papers, legal forms and the counterfeit. affective interactions between documents and people in Britain and Cyprus. *Anthropological Theory* 7(1): 79–98.

O'Donnell, Guillermo. 1996. *El Estado Burocrático-Autoritario. Triunfos, Derrotas y Crisis*. Buenos Aires, Argentina: Editorial de Belgrano.

O'Donnell, Guillermo. 1985. "Apuntes para una teoria del Estado." En Oscar Oszlak (comp.), *Teoria De La Burocracia Estatal*. Buenos Aires: Editorial Paidós.

Ong, Aiwa and Stephen Collier. 2005. *Global Assemblages: Technology, Politics and Ethics as Anthropological Problems*. Malden, MA: Blackwell Publishing.

Pottage, Alain. 2014. Law after anthropology: object and technique in roman law. *Theory, Culture & Society* 31(2/3): 147–66.

Pound, Roscoe. 1910. Law in books and law in action. *American Law Review* 44:1.

Reyes Posada, Alejandro, and Liliana Duica Amaya. 2009. *Guerreros y Campesinos: El Despojo de la Tierra en Colombia*. Bogotá: Grupo Editorial Norma.

Ribeiro, Darcy. 1999. *El Pueblo Brasileño*. Mexico DF: Fondo de la Cultura Económica.

Richland, Justin B. 2013. Jurisdiction: grounding law in language. *Annual Review of Anthropology* 42:1–33.

Riles, Annelise. 2001. *The Network Inside Out*. Ann Arbor: University of Michigan Press.

Richland, Justin B. 2005. A new agenda for the cultural study of law: taking on the technicalities. *Buffalo Law Review* 53: 973.

Richland, Justin B. 2011. *Collateral Knowledge: Legal Reasoning in the Global Financial Markets*. Chicago: University of Chicago Press.

Riles, Annelise (ed.). 2006. *Documents: Artifacts of Modern Knowledge*. Ann Arbor: University of Michigan Press.

Sarat, Austin and Thomas R. Kearns. 1993. *Law in Everyday Life*. Ann Arbor: University of Michigan Press.

Scott, James C. 1998. *Seeing Like a State: How Certain Schemes to Improve the Human Condition have Failed*. New Haven: Yale University Press.

Sharma, Aradhana and Akhil Gupta. 2006. *The Anthropology of the State: A Reader*. Malden, MA: Blackwell Publishing.

Silbey, Susan. 2005. After legal consciousness. *Annual Review of Law and Social Science* 1: 323–68.

Strathern, Marilyn. 1988. *The Gender of the Gift: Problems with Women and Problems with Society in Melanesia*. Berkeley: University of California Press.

Strathern, Marilyn. 1999. *Property, Substance, and Effect: Anthropological Essays on Persons and Things*. London: Athlone Press.

Tiscornia, Sofia. 2004. *Burocracias y Violencia. Estudios de Antropología Jurídica*. Buenos Aires: Antropofagia.

Tiscornia, Sofia. 2005. *Derechos Humanos, Tribunales y Policias En Argentina y Brasil. Estudios De Antropología Jurídica*. Buenos Aires: Antropofagia.

Trouillot, Michel-Rolph. 2001. The anthropology of the state in the age of globalization. *Current Anthropology* 42(1): 125–33.

Vaisman, Noa. 2014. Relational human rights: shed-DNA and the identification of the 'living disappeared' in Argentina. *Journal of Law and Society* 41(3): 391–415.

Valverde, Mariana. 2003. *Law's Dream of a Common Knowledge*. Princeton, NJ: Princeton University Press.

Valverde, Mariana. 2009. Jurisdiction and scale: legal 'technicalities' as resources for theory. *Social and Legal Studies* 18(2): 139–57.

Vismann, Cornelia. 2008. *Files: Law and Media Technology*. Stanford, CA: Stanford University Press.

Weber, Max, Hans Heinrich Gerth, and C. Wright Mills. 1946. *From Max Weber: Essays in Sociology*. New York: Oxford University Press.

Wolkmer, Antonio Carlos. 2003. *Pluralismo Jurídico: Nuevo Marco Emancipatorio En América Latina*. Buenos Aires: Red de bibliotecas virtuales de Ciencias Sociales de America Latina y el Caribe, de la Red de Centros Miembros de CLACSO.

Yablon, Charles M. 1990. Forms. *Cardozo Law Review* 11(5): 1349–135.

Yngvesson, Barbara. 1998. *Virtuous Citizens, Disruptive Subjects: Order and Complaint in a New England Court*. New York, London: Routledge.

Zimring, Franklin and Gordon Hawkins. 1971. The legal threat as an instrument of social change. *Journal of Social Issues* 27: 33–48.

8

LATIN AMERICAN FEMINIST LEGAL THEORY

Taking Multiple Subordinations Seriously

Isabel Cristina Jaramillo Sierra

The use of gender to understand law as a practice with material existence is not a particularity of Latin American scholarship, nor is it generally accepted as a relevant dimension of reflection in academic work in the region. Latin Americans indeed have made no special claim to having invented gender as a category to shape or understand the law.[1] Rather, the use of gender to think about the law is still perceived by most as an eccentricity, or even a mistake, given the "real problems" that we face in our daily lives as individuals and that "we" have faced historically as nations.[2] On the other hand, nonetheless, foreign commentators on Latin America are quick to point out the ways in which legal rules are strongly involved in the production of sexual inequality, attributing the difficulty locals experience in "seeing" gender to their own conservatism and to the Catholic legacy.[3] Latin American feminist legal scholarship is best understood, thus, as constructed from a defensive position: trying at once to learn from a very well established transnational canon, without appearing as a naïve copycat; and to be attentive to local realities, without giving up on the centrality of its own claim.

In this entry, I give an account of three different ways in which Latin American feminist legal scholars have confronted these tensions between the transnational and the local, and between sexual inequality and other forms of oppression. I call these approaches "Solidaristic Feminism," "Radical Feminism *a la Latina*," and "Political Feminism."[4] I point out to the contributions that they have made to our understanding of the way in which law participates in the creation and reproduction of oppression by carefully reading their context, in four areas: the subjects that they have worked with; the doctrinal innovations they have constructed; the legal tactics they have used; and the organizational structures they have fostered. Certainly other mappings could be made in which regional thinking follows more closely the transnational, largely American, canon but that would serve other purposes such as inter-American integration or cross fertilization, among others. Hopefully, the one I use here will inspire conversations that we seldom ever have when the geopolitical focus is more external than internal.

Besides this emphasis on context and local contributions, readers will note that the list of authors whose work is mentioned here is not very long. This has to do, in general, with the absence of feminist thinking inside law schools and legal scholarship in the region: it is hard to work on an argument that is already suspicious even for progressives and leftists. Also, it is related to the enormous difficulties in obtaining works produced in other countries in the region, that is problems of circulation of printed materials, and the impact this has on the articulation of a veritable academic community in the region. Readers will also note that, thus, Colombia is somehow overrepresented in the sample of authors chosen because it is the country in which we can trace most clearly the presence and changes of the three approaches to legal feminism. Nonetheless, I am quite confident that I have been able to produce a persuasive account based not only on my research but also in my countless meetings with feminist legal scholars in the region.

Slaves of Slaves: Legal Reform as Tactics – Solidaristic Feminism

In 1981, the Latin American and Caribbean (LAC) Women's Collective articulated in a manuscript the position that many feminists in the region had adopted before and would continue to embrace thereafter: feminist should always mobilize bearing in mind the most vulnerable women (Latin American and Caribbean Women's Collective 1980). They revealed awareness of the risks involved in erasing class from their understanding of oppression, while at the same time committing to the notion that the most vulnerable in society are, lastly, women. This choice has been relevant to setting the agenda for mobilization, incidence, and theorizing, as well as to conceptualizing patriarchal harm and remedies. Although most feminists sharing this view were not legal scholars but sociologists, anthropologists, economists, and activists, they acknowledged law as a tactic and developed legal doctrines that have had lasting influence in the region, and used law for empowerment and consciousness rising.

Indeed, drawing from their own experiences, women in the LAC Women's Collective concluded that they could not think about oppression along the same lines than women in the United States; they had never met other bourgeois women in a laundry room or supermarket, they had not lived as women through their sexuality. Rather, they had lived in societies with huge inequalities in which men expropriated not only women's sexuality but also, and mainly, their labor, and in which bourgeois women expropriated other women's labor. Only by choosing the poorest of the poor, the slave of slaves, could feminists actually intervene in their own context to achieve greater freedom (Latin American and Caribbean Women's Collective 1980). This view would consolidate over the four following decades to express what could be called a view of multiple oppression as "cumulative oppression."

The poorest of the poor, the most vulnerable, however, have not always been the same. Throughout the 1980s and 1990s, the poorest of the poor were domestic servants and peasant women. At the organizational level, the struggles with these women led to the creation of unions (León 2013) and peasant organizations that last to this day (León and Deere 1997). They also started debates about the reform of exceptional legislation concerning domestic service, which reduced women's rights as workers (León, Proyecto Investigación-Acción: Trabajo Doméstico y Servicio Doméstico en Colombia 2013) and introduced the prioritization of women in agrarian reforms (Alviar 2008). They explicitly understood law as a tactic to empower subordinated women and raise the consciousness of elite women, while the political context allowed them to pursue more radical changes beyond/outside the law (León 2013). They understood that subordinated women could use certain labor and family law rules to obtain redress and were convinced that knowing about the law would increase their bargaining power (León 2013). Teaching law to the *patronas* was perceived as an effective strategy to make them aware of the rights of their *muchachas* and transform the paternal relationship into a contractual one (León 2013).

The focus changed by the early 2000s, when women living in areas affected by insurgent and counterinsurgent movements and/or organized crime became the new allies in the fight for emancipation. These women were not only deprived of basic goods and services, as they lived in remote and rural areas especially prone to occupation by non-state groups, but also found restrictions in their ability to organize, engage in political action, or even receive assistance by feminists living in other parts of the country (Casa de la Mujer 2014). In this case, showing that women are the most affected by war has become the main goal for feminists. Turning away from a maternal rhetoric that only made visible women's roles as mothers and wives, these feminists have insisted on women's sexual victimization in armed conflicts (Alviar and Jaramillo 2013). They have shown that because women are victims of sexual violence, and because this victimization needs to be added up to their structural exclusion from society, they fare worse than men in war. This idea became a doctrinal innovation in feminist legal theory: the continuum hypothesis. To show sexual victimization, which in some cases can be almost insignificant measured by traditional standards, these feminists have produced sophisticated institutional arrangements that investigate contexts of conflict and occupation in order to find patterns of sexual violence; they have developed elaborate definitions of sexual violence to include not only sexual abuse and sexual assault but also sexual slavery, forced pregnancies, forced abortions, forced domestic service, forced nudity, among others. As in the previous case, feminists have developed durable organizations to articulate the pleas of women as victims of armed conflict, and created scenarios for their participation in peace negotiations and the invention of the post-conflict society (Mantilla 2006; Corporación SISMA Mujer 2009; Corporación Humanas 2011, 2013; Casa de la Mujer 2015).

In the last decade, roughly since 2010, women who are "forced" migrants have entered the picture of the poorest of the poor (Women's Link Worldwide 2013). Apparently motivated by a concern over the living conditions of migrants originating in countries of reception, such as Spain, and a preoccupation over money laundering by international crime cartels commanded by the United States, the issue of forced migration has sparked feminist campaigns that have enriched the debate and brought about innovations in legal mobilization. On the one hand, feminists have struggled to refine the current depictions of the sex trade in order to show how most countries are both expellers and recipients of sex migrants, that not all sex work migrations are forced, that not all forced migrations of women are for sex work, and that most forced migration is not connected to international crime cartels. On the other hand, they have revealed that litigation efforts should not concentrate on home countries, where they might endanger the victims, but rather on host countries, where the human rights of victims are often violated (Women's Link Worldwide 2013). This litigation has evidenced that notwithstanding the existence of international instruments that protect the interests of forced migrants, there is plenty of abuse that is hard to pin down and redress (Women's Link Worldwide 2010). The following table (Table 8.1) sums up the approach to law and mobilization for the three different moments.

Frequently, feminists in this group do not have a theory about the role of law in the production of those layers of power and the corresponding accumulation of resources. Rather, they seem to generally share the "good law view" advanced by most socio-legal theorists and public opinion in the region (Jaramillo 2013). In its most sophisticated version, presented by Julieta Lemaitre, this view claims that the enchantment of law is an unfulfilled promise for the poorest of the poor and therefore, should still be a goal to reach through elite mobilization (Lemaitre 2008). The less elaborated versions, the pop or operative versions of the good law view, confide that instead of changing rules it is crucial to interpret, disseminate, and act upon the existing rules to obtain the promised results. Feminists in this group, in particular, have introduced several doctrines into existing law: the doctrine of the continuation of attacks in occupation (to include all acts of sexual violence committed by armed groups into the definition of war crimes), the doctrine of the need of context to appreciate the systematic character of a given action (again

Table 8.1 Slaves of Slaves

Character That Personifies Most Layers of Oppression	Doctrinal Innovation	Legal Tactics	Organizational Innovation
Domestic workers and peasants		Reform law on domestic service	Domestic service unions
		Bring suits concerning rights of domestic workers	Rural Women Organizations
		Educate *patronas* on the rights of workers	
		Include women in agrarian reform as recipients of land and/or aid	
Victims of armed conflict and military dictatorships	Continuum hypothesis	Introduce articles from the Roma Statute into national legislation	Organizations of victims
	Examination of facts according to "contexts" or systematic patterns	Investigate sexual violence in armed conflicts	"Women" sections in Truth Commissions and in Truth Reports
	"Combat" as including occupation by irregular forces	Redefine sexual violence to include forced abortions, force maternities, forced contraception, domestic slavery, and sexual slavery	
Migrant workers	Expulsion and reception of migrants not defined by jurisdiction	Domestic litigation using international standards	
	Sex work as work; forced migrations as more than white slavery	International litigation	

Source: Table created by author.

to prove that sexual violence is a war crime), the doctrine of the continuum (about the accumulation of women's factors of oppression to produced exalted vulnerability in certain women), the doctrine of multiple centers of expulsion and reception in forced migration. They have also furthered elite and popular knowledge of existing legal rules and litigated to guarantee the rights of the poorest of the poor (see Table 8.1).

It is crucial to note here, that while intimately connected to the critique of the fourth world developed by radical movements in the United States, the insistence on cumulative oppressions is different from the emphasis on intersectionality as a method that feminist legal scholars in the United States have pressed. The claim of intersectionality, as originally developed by Kimberlé

Crenshaw, was oriented to making visible the exclusions produced by legal categories of discrimination such as those included in the United States Constitution and developed by the Supreme Court of that country. (Crenshaw 1989) In particular, Crenshaw wanted to show that black women could suffer discrimination that could only be noticed when counted as black women and not exclusively as black people or as colorless women. Debates about intersectionality have grown to become a constant source of critique for feminist thinking. Participants in these debates, nonetheless, have not been interested in claiming one identity as a source of greater evil, as opposed to the solidaristic feminists I describe here, and have not been especially interested in class as a source of oppression.[5]

Radical Feminism *a La Latina*: Human Rights as Total Signifiers

With the publication of *Cuando el Género Suena, Cambios Trae* in 1992, Alda Facio gave voice to an understanding of law as embodiment of the "male point of view" that sought to interrogate and transform the "good law view" and introduced practices of legal criticism into Latin American feminist mobilization and theorization (Facio 1992). In this case, the claim to originality came in the form of an "autochthonous" production, and the answer to the problem of "intersectionality" was "total justice" in the language of human rights. This theoretical position has spread widely throughout the region and inspired a significant amount of work by scholars in the region.

Facio explains that law embodies the male point of view because it only takes into consideration and protects the interests and needs of men. This happens both because men are the main agents in the production, adjudication, and enforcement of legal rules, and because legal theory reduces the legal phenomenon to a system of norms produced by public officials (Facio 1992, 91). The overwhelming presence of men in public institutions, Facio relieves, alienate women from these institutions and prevent them both from claiming their rights and from criticizing their biases (Facio 1992, 91). Most importantly, though, the reduction of law to a system of norms turns practices of adjudication, enforcement, and negotiation into "distortions" that no one has to explain or is responsible for (Facio 1992, 92).

To engage law as a scenario of domination, but also of emancipation, Facio proposes understanding law as composed by three levels: the formal-normative, the substantive-structural, and the cultural-political (see Figure 8.1) (Facio 1992, 94–100). The first level would include the norms produced by legislators and judges. The second level, on its part, would include the peculiar interpretations that are used by lawyers, judges, and bureaucrats when arguing, adjudicating, or enforcing norms in specific cases. The third and final level includes the social knowledge about the legal system; that is, the set of beliefs concerning the norms included in the other two levels. This model evidences both how beliefs and attitudes may be incorporated into the law, and how as individuals we participate in the creation of law. Thus, it contains the key for critique but also for the transformation of gendered practices, not only for scholars and legal practitioners but for everyone.

The methodology to account for law understood in this way is composed of six steps (Facio 1992, 109–56):

1   Consciousness raising of the individual that will engage the gendered analysis of the legal phenomenon
2   Identification of the ways in which legal commentary, legal principles, and legal research exclude, erase, or subordinate women. In particular, study the operation of sexism through overgeneralizations, over specificity, double parameters, and sexual dichotomism, the insistence on sexual difference as enough explanation of a given situation

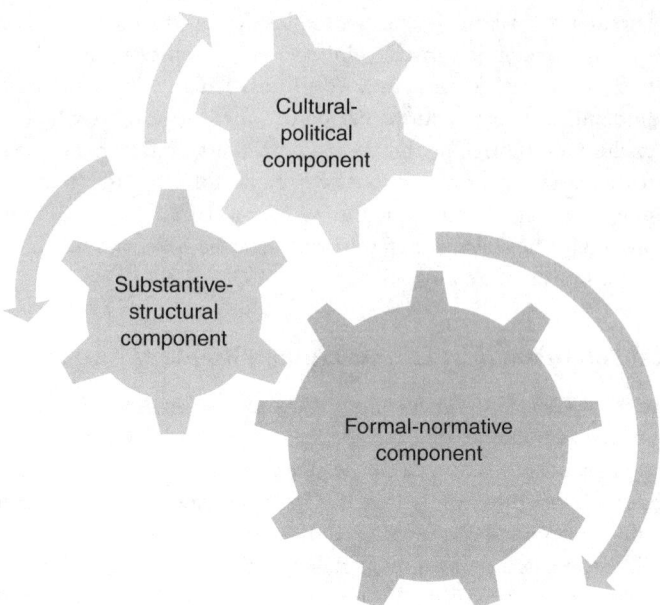

Figure 8.1 Law as a Complex Cultural Phenomenon

3 Identification of the way in which women are depicted as "other" of men, and studying of the effects on women differently situated
4 Finding which concept of women is used as basis for the norm and proposing alternatives that would help to undo inequality
5 Studying the legal element in light of the other two components that have not yet been considered
6 Making the analysis known to many women so that it might be enriched through debate and criticism.

The result of the analysis should be a conclusion about how law should be reformed, in any of its components, to bring about more equality. Furthermore, as Facio clarifies, the analysis should increase our knowledge about how sexism operates and how the law participates in producing inequality; that is, it should increase our consciousness and give us tools to overcome it. The focus, therefore, should be in the process: in the type of questions we ask, the elements we include in our reflection, the costs of producing a given analysis to women differently situated, and the amount of participation we were able to guarantee, among others.

Two additional concepts will appear in Facio's work after *Cuando el Género Suena*: (1) the notion of women's law; and (2) the idea of true universality as a consequence of integrating the male and female points of view. Facio elaborates the notion of women's law in her contribution to *Género y Derecho*, the volume she edited in 1999 with Lorena Fries (Facio and Fries 1999). In this piece, entitled: "Another Critical Theory," she engages the issue of the form that feminist reform should accept that law will not be "fixed" merely by adding women or by recognizing that law is politics (Facio 1999). She proposes using "women's law" to name all proposals that spring from a truly feminist analysis of the law, that is, analysis that reveal women's point of view, regardless of the particular content of the suggestion. She particularly studies Ana Obando's proposal of leaving aside the language of human rights to speak of relational rights and concludes that it should not be taken for granted that human rights will not bring the desired change or that relational rights will provide correct answers in every situation (Obando 1999). The idea of women's point of view as a complement necessary to achieve true universality is also developed in this text. Here she claims that justification for women's law derives from the valid human aspiration to universality, objectivity, and impartiality, though she also advances that neither point of view on its own is universal, objective, or impartial and therefore that her own analysis are always biased by her women's point of view.

It is precisely from this commitment to the universal, that Facio started to defend human rights as a scenario for social justice. In *Los Derechos Humanos Desde una Perspectiva de Género y de Políticas Públicas* she explains that the field of human rights is precisely the terrain where the universal is construed and deployed; instead of seeing human rights as a static field of exclusion, she proposes understanding human rights as a battle field over the reform of human rights law and over the enforcement of human rights at the local level (Facio 2003). The advantage of this vocabulary over others, in particular that of development, is that it starts from the premise of equality and dignity of ALL human beings at the same time, and not from the notion that some have to wait to see their situation improved (Facio 2009).

As pointed out above, Facio argues for the originality of her contribution through the localism of its production, and proposes that she pays heed to concerns over intersectionality without giving them priority over her own feminist position. Indeed, in *Cuando el Género Suena*, Facio recognizes that she got the idea of writing a book from Rhonda Copelon and learned the concept of the "male point of view" from Sandra Harding, but emphasizes that the methodology she proposes for the gendered analysis of legal phenomena represents her original contribution to feminist jurisprudence (Facio 1992, 13–15). She claims to have developed this methodology through her work at the University of Costa Rica and with several Central American women's groups and feminist scholars. Her academic activism effectively can be traced through her own efforts at citing her colleagues in this book (even unpublished manuscripts), compiling Latin American feminist scholarship (Facio and Fries 1999), editing a journal on feminist scholarship (Camacho; Facio, and Martín 1997), and consulting for a variety of international and regional organisms on issues of gender and the law.

Besides this localism in the process of theoretical production, Facio points out two ways in which her theory is Latin American: (1) the attention to multiple forms of domination and subordination; and (2) the adoption of human rights as a strategy to overcome the "male point of view." She explicitly states that Latin American feminists agree that "feminism opposes all forms of domination and oppression and not only that of men over women" (Facio 1992, 52) because they are convinced that "the subjugation of one group by other in any other level or sphere of society (in the home's privacy, for example), creates and maintains domination practices in other levels or spheres of society (in the workplace or international relations)" (Facio 1992, 52).

While not noted by Facio, this confidence in the international and the long-term bet for human rights as a language to overcome patriarchy and other forms of oppression simultaneously, does indeed set her apart from American style radical legal feminists. For them, encountering human rights has been quite a long process and forging transnational alliances has only become of interest in the last two decades.[6] Their most representative figure, namely, Catharine MacKinnon, has also insisted on the priority of patriarchy as a system of oppression and rejected demands to reflect on multiple oppressions. (MacKinnon 1991).[7]

Both Facio´s critique of law's embodiment of the male point of view and her enthusiasm about human rights have inspired an important group of feminist legal scholars in the region. Their work is available in three collections of essays: The Costa Rican Women´s Movement

(Abshagen 1997); Género y Derecho (Facio and Fries 1999); and El Género en el Derecho (Ávila; Salgado, and Valladares 2009). It includes reflections on the male point of view in criminal law, constitutional law, and family law; as well as elaborations of the possible ways in which international human rights might be of use to women. Even if they acknowledge that international human rights law in general is as tainted by the male point of view as local laws, they seem confident that the international arena will be more permeable to their claims based on the experience of CEDAW (Convention on the Elimination of all Forms of Discrimination Against Women) and of adjudication by the Inter-American Court (Facio 2009; Salgado 2009; Medina 2009).

This post-critical faith in human rights is shared by an important number of activists in the region that are not only active in the increasingly dynamic field of international litigation, but also use human rights jargon in domestic litigation, and have made scholarly contributions to the development of human rights doctrine. Among those doing this kind of work are Alicia Yamin (Yamin 2010), Lidia Casas (Casas 2013), Mónica Roa (Cabal, Roa, and Sepúlveda 2003), Lilian Sepúlveda (Cabal, Roa, and Sepúlveda 2003), Mónica Arango and Ana Cristina González (Arango and González 2016), and Paola Bergallo (Bergallo 2014). Their work has been crucial in transforming the Inter-American Court's approach to cases of abortion and gender violence (Cabal, Roa, and Sepúlveda 2003) (Yamin, Datta, and Andion 2017), in increasing the number of cases that the court studies (Cabal et al. 2006), and in providing local activists with knowledge about the content and possible uses of international law in local arenas (Jaramillo and Alfonso 2008).

Political Feminism: Distributional Analysis and the Possibility of Taking a Break from Feminism

A third group of scholars in the region has responded to the critique of rights asking for the reasons that may be driving the insistence on the rights strategy, and producing analysis that try to show how law operates, through rights, to produce women's subordination in specific confrontations that reveal their situated-ness beyond gender. Isabel Jaramillo and Tatiana Alfonso have referred to this approach as the "law as legitimation and distribution" approach (DDL for its initials in Spanish) in their book *Mujeres, Cortes y Medios* (Jaramillo and Alfonso 2008). They proposed this rubric to support an eclectic position that demanded at the same time recognizing the legitimating effects of legal arguments and the distributional consequences of law's operation. With this, they carved a distance regarding the idea that law can be used as an instrument without interrogating its rationalizing power if the interventions are discrete, as proposed by the solidaristic feminists, and with regard to the conviction that uncovering the "maleness" of law and speaking "womanese" in the human rights container will bring down the whole system, as suggested by the radicals. They acknowledge their position as eclectic in the sense that distributional analysis seems to demand, and produce, an idea of law as determinate, while legitimation analysis pushes for an idea of law as indeterminate against the grain of reification that serves the status quo. This eclecticism may be understood and justified as required by a context in which scholars not only need to do the work of critique, but also of developing the analysis that needs to be done after the critique has produced its effects of disenchantment and renewal.

In *Mujeres, Cortes y Medios*, Jaramillo and Alfonso intervene in the debate about legal mobilization oriented to the change of the status quo, by studying the case of abortion reform through constitutional litigation in Colombia (Jaramillo and Alfonso 2008). They suggest that, to understand the role of law in controlling women's abilities to make reproductive decisions it is not enough to study criminal law regarding abortion; and that to change the way in which criminal law limits women's reproductive choices it is not enough to study the text of the Penal Code. This double move inside and out of the text is inspired by the authors' interpretation of abortion as involving the stabilization of the sexual division of labor through control of women's sexual and reproductive conduct. Thus, they do not accept the criminalization of abortion as a mere historic accident or as required by the introduction of the right to life into modern constitutions. Rather, they highlight the peculiar contradiction of an inflammatory rhetoric that demands harsh punishment at the level of constitutional argumentation, and the insignificant levels of enforcement of the rules involved. They show how the debate over the right to life obscures the stakes in this contradiction, how men are empowered in the bargain over abortion by the lack of enforcement but also by legal rules concerning women's employment, child support, alimony, and divorce. According to this analysis, partial decriminalization would not produce the desired effects of reducing women's recourse to illegal abortions; this would only be possible as long as life is decentered as the main stake in abortion regulation, and women's reproductive bargaining power is not shaped by their dependency on their fathers and husbands, beyond the criminalization of the conduct.

In *Feminismo y Crítica Jurídica* (Alviar and Jaramillo 2013), Alviar and Jaramillo further develop the distributional analysis framework and deploy it in four more cases: quota laws; equal pay; conditional cash transfers; and armed conflict in Colombia. They propose a four-step method for distributional analysis and identify four feminist strategies for interrogating law's legitimation of the status quo. The four-step method for distributional analysis encompasses: (1) an account of the situation as one in which there is conflict: actors differently situated oppose each other over the control of certain resources (stakes); (2) to show what contributes to the bargaining power of each individual in this context; (3) the identification of the legal rules that ground this bargaining power, including those in the "background" and taking into consideration the way in which legal rules operate "on the ground"; and (4) to show what rule changes might introduce significant changes in distribution and bargaining power.

The four feminist strategies that the authors propose as useful to engage distributional analysis are the critique of binaries, the critique of the public/private distinction, the politization of legal conflict, and the denaturalization of legal categories. In the cases, they reveal the usefulness of denaturalizing legal categories (quota law case), foregrounding background rules and ideologies (equal pay and conditional cash transfers cases), and interrogating binaries (armed conflict case) for legal feminist analysis. They also provide tools for taking distance from feminist hyperboles and accepting the limitations of feminism even when it is attentive to multiple subordinations.

The individual works of Jaramillo (Jaramillo 2002, 2006, 2013); Buchely (2015) and Castro (2016) are worth mentioning as explicitly connected to these efforts of articulating distributional analysis as a theoretical position in law. They have provided insights into the work of exceptionalism in private law and the consequences for the entrenchment of the ideology of the family (Jaramillo 2010), explained how the ideology of the family produces bad effects for women and racializes colonial populations to produce race as an indicator of class (Jaramillo 2013), revealed the importance of thinking of bureaucracies when engaging the question of how law allocates resources (Buchely 2015) and shown how critical geography can help in comprehending "foregrounding" and "backgrounding" moves in the law, patrolling of concepts as frontiers, and identity production as territorialization (Castro 2016).

Although not intended to function on this same theoretical register, the works of Lemaitre (Lemaitre 2009) and (Gallo et al. 2010) can also be included here as reflections on the way in which law creates, or not, bargaining power for women. Using psychoanalytic frameworks, both engage the question of the effects of legal reform on women's ability to transform their lives. They arrive to quite opposite conclusions: while for Lemaitre legal fetishism, which she describes as characteristic of Colombian culture in general, produces the effect of empowerment necessary for women to change their situation; Gallo et al. point to the permanence of sacrificial logics and the satisfaction they provide women with, to explain why most women do not see their bargaining power as modified by the introduction of legal reforms in the realm of constitutional rights. This last work goes as far as to claim that the sacrificial logic also explains female mobilization and the emphasis on the poorest of the poor: it is the sacrifice for the other that has nothing that may replace the sacrifice for the child.

Empirical work attempting to explain how certain areas of the law operate could also be included here in so far as it illuminates the way in which law may be allocating resources. Paola Bergallo and Beatriz Cohen have led the way in collecting data and interpreting the situation of women in the judicial system. In her 2006 work on women in the judicial system in Argentina, Bergallo showed how the apparently "neutral" and "meritocratic" selection mechanisms for judges systematically privileged men by overvaluing male contributions to the profession and not making any consideration of the difficulties women face to accommodate reproductive work and have a career in law. Her interest in studying the role of women in the judicial system is founded on a firm belief that judges are key actors in the democratization of modern societies and the absence of women in the highest positions operates against this goal (Bergallo 2006, 152). Cohen, on her part, shows how the fact that women are overrepresented as family law judges, bears some relationship to the reproduction of the sexual division of labor and does not introduce changes favoring women. Indeed, according to the author, the judges interviewed – both men and women – explained that they believed that individuals chose to be judges over firm lawyers because it allowed them to fulfill other duties, such as tending to their children and other members of the family. This would also explain why they were not interested in moving along the hierarchy, but more interestingly, why the overwhelming presence of women did not change the results significantly (Cohen 2008). More recently, Bergallo and Moreno have published data on the City of Buenos Aires that is quite promising in its suggestions as to how to move ahead in terms of achieving gender justice through the judiciary (Bergallo and Moreno 2017).

This work has not been oblivious to the question of the tension between the transnational and the local, though it is by far less apologetic and bolder in its conclusions. Authors in this group have been educated in law schools in the United States and have a strong sense of their ability to contribute to the transnational discussion without claiming their locale – the "south" – or commitments – to the poorest of the poor – as a brand. Their work has in common, though, that it is geographically and historically situated, oriented to an audience of Latin American scholars, and cognizant of that audience as composed by true interlocutors that deserve mention in footnotes and endnotes. Their intervention in the multiple subordinations debate avoids the pitfalls of the cumulative and total oppression narratives by demanding always distance from total explanations and emphasis on contextual narratives.

Themes for a New Agenda

Notwithstanding the concern over multiple oppressions, feminist legal scholars in the region have not articulated yet an innovative point of view on the situation of Afro-Americans and indigenous women that transcends to legal scholarship.[8] On the one hand, women affiliated to these groups remain to a large extent at the margins of society, academia, and the legal profession. On the other hand, their situation seems to be constantly relegated to the confines of society, politics, or culture, instead of law, in a literature that replicates the colonial gaze in every invocation of the "good law" view.

Indeed, for all the calls for caring for multiple oppressions among Latin American feminists, ethnic identity has eluded legal analysis as a worthy concept: either ethnicity is counted as just another layer of oppression similar in every way to the others (as in solidaristic feminism), or is masked by the claim that the male point of view is oppression for all women in the same way (as in radical Latin American feminism). The contexts that distributional analysis scholars have engaged are not mainly populated by women of African or Indigenous descent, with the exception of Jaramillo's work on family law that proposes understanding race as a careful result of the operation of colonial work, and calls for contemporary studies that take seriously the importance of race for modern understandings of family and of family law for the production of race (Jaramillo 2013). These studies of the family and family law are still to be written.

The absence of African and indigenous women in Latin American legal academia for sure is related to the difficulties in articulating their point of view. Thus, not only efforts to understand the role of law in their oppression is crucial, but also efforts to incorporate these women should be part of the new agenda. Resources donated to the Racial Discrimination Observatory by the Ford Foundation for the education of African Colombian lawyers in the United States are an example of actions that could be undertaken to influence the composition of local academies and their research agendas. Unfortunately, this program has had no intention of centering gender as a concern.[9]

The critique of the colonial twist to legal liberalism that frequently exacerbates interest in the "natives" from the social scientific gaze seems also relevant for shaping a research agenda within the law. Some projects along this line could include studies on the construction of the Indian as male by the courts in cases of military service, exploitation of land, religious dissidence, etc.; the importance of the "cultural" excuse in cases of violence against women; the reappearance of female genital mutilation in cultures materially deprived; the role of Indian judges in reproducing or interrogating colonialism; the racial and ethnic silences of debates on domestic service and land reform; the role of law in producing territorial segregation and as a consequence racial poverty; among others.

Conclusions

Latin America's colonial past and totalitarian present have inspired many reflections that contribute to transnational debates about the role of law in society. Finding a voice for feminist legal theory in this context has been hard both because of transnational feminist claim to a universal theory, therefore not susceptible of being enriched by the situated-ness of authors, and because of local accusations of alliances of feminists with the status quo. Latin American legal theorists have even stated explicitly their distrust of feminism. This entry suggests, nonetheless, that these difficulties have inspired contributions that are highly attentive to multiple subordinations, taking class, racial, and ethnic inequalities very seriously. Three positions about subordination were identified in Latin American feminist thinking of the last 40 years: the solidaristic; radical; and political. The first, is attributed to feminists that claim that mobilization and legal action should engage the "poorest of the poor," in the understanding that to become such individual "multiple layers of oppression" should be liable of being traced to your body. The second, to those who believe that all oppressions are connected structurally and through our bodies in such a way that you may not "fix" one without fixing the other, and you will make things worse for some if you make things worse for others. The third, political feminists, have demanded a return to context to understand how in relation to particular issues women may end up differently situated vis-à-vis each other and with regards to men.

Each position has been tied up to a mode of understanding the role of law and society. For the first group, law may be used to enhance the situation of the poorest of the poor within the status quo without meaningfully changing it. They have engaged in massive litigation campaigns, consciousness rising for the oppressors through law, and the reform of statutes directly connected to the rights of women that have been identified as the poorest of the poor in different moments in time. For the second group, the ideological critique of the maleness of law and the construction of a female law that might be incorporated in the idiom of human rights are crucial to female emancipation. For the third group, legal feminists advocating distributional analysis of the law have produced situated analysis about law reform that takes seriously the role of law in the reproduction of male privilege but is aware of other ideological stakes and other material resources that might be involved in particular contexts.

This rich body of ideas however, is only starting to gain recognition and the projects it inspires are just about to gain momentum. At this point, the call to strengthen legal academies and, especially women of color within these legal academies seems particularly relevant. Not because women of color will necessarily bring with them interest and resources to conduct research on the subordination of women of color, but because their agendas eventually will help us understand the subordination of women of color.

Notes

1 It would be wrong to say that Latin Americans have not made any claims to "originality," *passim* Diego López Medina's depiction of the region as an impoverished context of consumption of legal knowledge produced in other locales (López 2004). Latin American scholars, for example, attribute to the geniality of Mexicans the introduction of "social" clauses in modern constitutions (Diaz 1953) and believe that Chilean, Argentinian, and Colombian scholars have produced a regional version of international law (Obregón 2012). Latin Americans lawyers have also been recognized as key actors in the creation of international instruments on human rights (Glendon 2003; Carozza 2002; Morsink 2000), and more recently, as innovators in constitutional drafting and adjudication (Tushnet 2015).
2 It is impossible to quote any scholarly work that has tried to sustain this point. It does come through in two ways in contemporary scholarship: (1) as a critique of feminist reform, for not being aware of the class divisions existing in society and the way in which feminists favor conservative elites; and (2) by failing to mention women's legal mobilization when accounting for legal mobilization in the region.
3 Oquendo's work on Latin American law, for example, takes sexual inequality for granted when speaking of Latin America (Oquendo 2006).
4 I use these categories, rather than the more frequently used of equality and difference feminism, or liberal, socialist, and cultural feminism, to stress the difference that context has made in feminist legal thinking in the region. I have used the mainstream classification in a previous work; see Jaramillo (1999).
5 For a recent compilation of works on intersectionality, see the volume of SIGNS edited by Sumi Cho, Kimberlé Crenshaw, and Leslie Call (volume 38, no. 4, 2013).
6 On the worldwide spread of one version of radical feminism see Halley (2007).
7 Though also in many ways she has recanted her positions from 15 years ago; see Mackinnon (2013).
8 Ochy Curiel from the Gender School at Universidad Nacional de Colombia has worked hard to articulate an African Colombian position within feminism, for example. How this position translates into law is still to be announced. In the same vein, the studies of Maria Teresa Sierra regarding the interlegality lived by indigenous Mexican women is still short of contributing a legal theory. See, in general, (Curiel 2007; Sieder and McNeish 2013).
9 See their webpage: www.odr.org. Accessed June 7, 2017.

References

Abshagen Leitinger, Ilse. 1997. *The Costa Rican Women's Movement: A Reader*. Pittsburgh: Pittsburgh University Press.

Alviar, Helena. 2008. *Derecho, Desarrollo Y Feminismo En América Latina*. Bogotá: Temis.

Alviar, Helena and Isabel Cristina Jaramillo Sierra. 2013. *Feminismo Y Crítica Jurídica: El Análisis Distributivo Como Alternativa Crítica al Legalismo Liberal*. Bogotá: Universidad de Los Andes, Siglo del Hombre.

Ávila Santamaría, Ramiro, Judith Salgado, and Lola Valladares. 2009. *El Género en el Derecho*. Quito: Ministerio de Justicia y de Derechos Humanos del Ecuador.

Bell, Christine and Catherine O'Rourke. 2007. Does feminism need a theory of transitional justice? An introductory essay. *The International Journal of Transitional Justice* 1: 23–44. Esta referencia no tiene cita en el texto.

Bergallo, Paola. 2006. "¿Un techo de cristal en el poder judicial? La selección de jueces federales y nacionales en Argentina." En *Más Allá del Derecho: Justicia y Género en América Latina*, Luisa Cabal and Cristina Motta, 145–218. Bogotá: Siglo del Hombre, Center for Reproductive Rights, Universidad de Los Andes.

Bergallo, Paola. 2014. "The struggle against informal abortion rules in Argentina." In *Abortion Law in Transnational Perspective: Cases and Controversies*, Rebecca, Erdman, Joana, Bernard, Dickens Cook. Philadelphia: Penn University Press.

Bergallo, Paola and Aluminé Moreno. 2017. *Hacia Políticas Judiciales de Género*. Buenos Aires: Jusbaires.

Bernal, Carolina and Miguel Larrota. 2012. *El Delito de Inasistencia Alimentaria*. Bogotá: DeJusticia. Esta referencia no tiene cita en el texto.

Buchely Ibarra and Lina Fernanda. 2015. *Activismo Burocrático – La Construcción Cotidiana del Principio de Legalidad*. Bogotá: Universidad de Los Andes.

Cabal, Luisa, Mónica Roa, and Lilian Sepúlveda. 2003. What role can international litigation play in the promotion and advancement of reproductive rights in Latin America? *Harvard Health and Human Rights Journal* 7(1): 51–88.

Cabal, Luisa, Mónica Roa, and Lilian Sepúlveda. 2006. "El litigio internacional en la promoción y el avance de los derechos reproductivos en América Latina." En *Más Allá del Derecho: Justicia y Género en América Latina*, Luisa Cabal and Cristina Motta, 379–414. Bogotá: Siglo del Hombre, Center for Reproductive Rights, Universidad de Los Andes.

Camacho, Rosalía, Alda Facio, and Ligia Martín. 1997. "The Group La Ventana: an assessment" In *The Costarrican Women's Movement: A Reader*, de Ilse Abshagen Leitinger, 13–19. Pittsburgh: University of Pittsburgh Press.

Carozza, Paolo. 2002. From conquest to constitutions: retrieving a Latin American idea of human rights. *Human Rights Quarterly* 24.

Casa de la Mujer. 2014. *Gestando la Paz, Haciendo Memoria*. Bogotá: ONU Mujeres, Cumbre mujeres por la paz.

Casa de la Mujer. 2015. "Propuestas de la Cumbre Nacional de Mujeres y Paz a la Mesa de Negociación." *Paz – Documentos*. February. Available at: http://media.wix.com/ugd/ff58cd_98df4c62dd8d437fbec64 1e2cf8c92e3.pdf. Accessed April 13, 2015.

Casas, Lidia and Leita Vivaldi. 2013. "La penalización del Aborto como violación de los derechos humanos." En *Informe Anual Sobre Derechos Humanos En Chile 2013*, de Universidad Diego Portales Centro de Derechos Humanos. Santiago: Universidad Diego Portales.

Castro Cristancho, María Victoria. 2016. *Derecho, Espacio y Poder: Contribuciones de la Geografía Crítica al Análisis Distributivo del Derecho*. Tesis Doctoral.

Centro Nacional de Memoria Histórica, Dirección de Acuerdos de Verdad. 2014. *Yo Aporto A La verdad, ACUERDOS DE CONTRIBUCIÓN A LA VERDAD Y LA MEMORIA HISTÓRICA. Mecanismo No Judicial Decontribución a la Verdad, la Memoria Histórica y la Reparación, Ley 1424/2010*. Bogotá: Imprenta Procesos Digitales. Esta referencia no tiene cita en el texto.

Cohen, Beatriz. 2008. *El Género en la Justicia de Familia*. Buenos Aires: Ad-Hoc.

Corporación Humanas and UNIFEM. 2005. *Riesgos Para la Seguridad de las Mujeres en Procesos de Reintegración de Excombatientes*. Bogotá: Humanas. Esta referencia no tiene cita en el texto.

Corporación Humanas. 2013. *Mujeres en Territorios Urbanos de Inseguridad*. Bogota: Anthropos.

Corporación Humanas. 2007. *Mujeres Entre Mafiosos y Señores de la Guerra*. Bogotá: Ediciones Anthropos. Esta referencia no tiene cita en el texto.

Corporación Humanas. 2011a. *Violencia Sexual en Conflicto Armado. Caracterización de Contextos y Estrategias Para su Judicialización: Contexto del Accionar de Hernán Giraldo Serna Comandante del Bloque Resistencia Tayrona*. Bogotá: Humanas. Es recomendable poner letras a y b para diferenciar las dos referencias en las citas. Favor de poner la letra en la cita correcta.

Corporación Humanas. 2011b. *Violencia Sexual en Conflicto Armado. Caracterización de Contextos y Estrategias Para Su Judicialización: Contexto en el Que se Inscriben Las Acciones de la Violencia Sexual llevadas a Cabo Por el Bloque Catatumbo en Norte de Santander 1999–2004*. Bogotá: Humanas. Es recomedable poner letras a y b para diferenciar las dos referencias en las citas. Favor de poner la letra en la cita correcta.

Corporación SISMA Mujer. **(Year?)** *Mas Allá de las Cifras*. Bogotá: Corporación SISMA Mujer, 2008. Esta referencia no tiene cita en el texto.

Corporación SISMA Mujer. 2009. *Mujeres en Conflicto: Violencia Sexual Y Paramilitarismo*. Bogotá: Corporación SISMA Mujer.

Crenshaw, Kimberlé. 1989. Demarginalizing the intersection of race and sex: a black feminist critique of antidiscrimination doctrine, feminist theory and antiracist politics. *University of Chicago Legal Forum*: 139–67.

Curiel, Ochy. 2007. La crítica postcolonial desde las prácticas políticas del feminismo antirracista. *Revista Nómadas* 96: 92–101.

Diaz Guijarro, Enrique. 1953. *Tratado de Derecho de Familia*. Buenos Aires.

Facio, Alda. 1992. *Cuando el Género Suena, Cambios Trae*. San José: ILANUD.

Facio, Alda. 1999. "Hacia otra teoría crítica del derecho." En *Género y Derecho*, Alda Facio and Lorena Fries, 201–29. Santiago de Chile: LOM, CIMA, American University.

Facio, Alda. 2009. "La carta magna de todas las mujeres." En *El Género en el Derecho,* Judith Salgado, Lola Valladares and Ramiro Ávila Santamaría, 541–58. Quito: Ministerio de Justicia y Derechos Humanos.

Facio, Alda. 2003. Los derechos humanos desde la perspectiva de género y de políticas públicas. *Otras Miradas* 15–26.

Facio, Alda and Lorena Fries. 1999. *Género y Derecho*. Santiago de Chile: LOM, CIMA, American University.

Gallo, Héctor, Ángela María Jaramillo Burgos, Rubén López and Mario Elkin Ramírez Ortiz. 2010. *Feminidades: Sacrificio y Negociación en Tiempos de Derechos*. Medellín: Editorial Universidad de Antioquia.

Glendon, Mary Ann. 2003. The forgotten crucible: the Latin American influence in the universal human rights idea. *Harvard Human Rights Journal* 16: 27.

González Vélez, Ana and Simone Diniz. 2007. Inequality, Zika epidemics, and the lack of reproductive rights in Latin America. *Reproductive Health Matters* 24: 57–61.

González Vélez, Ana C and Laura Castro. 2016. *Barriers to Access to Legal Abortion Services in Colombia,* Edited by La Mesa por la Vida y la Salud de las Mujeres. (Original title in Spanish: Barreras de Acceso a la Interrupción Voluntaria del Embarazo en Colombia). Bogotá. Digital Document, available at: www.despenalizaciondelaborto.org.co/wp-content/uploads/2017/05/Barreras_IVE_vf_WEB.pdf. Accessed August 24, 2017.

Halley, Janet. 2007. *Split Decisions. How to Take a Break from Feminism*. Princeton: Princeton University Press.

Jaramillo Sierra, Isabel Cristina. 1999. "La critica feminista al derecho." En *Género y Teoría del Derecho*, 10–55. Bogotá: Universidad de Los Andes y Siglo del Hombre.

Jaramillo Sierra, Isabel Cristina. 2002. "Instrucciones para salir del discurso de los derechos." En *La Crítica a los Derechos*, Isabel Cristina Jaramillo Sierra. Bogotá: Siglo del Hombre, Instituto Pensar, Universidad de Los Andes Facultad de Derecho.

Jaramillo Sierra, Isabel Cristina. 2006. "Reforma legal, feminismo y patriarcado: El caso de la ley de cuotas para mujeres en cargos de alto nivel de la Rama Ejecutiva." En *Más Allá del Derecho*, de Luisa Cabal y Cristina Motta, 59–144. Bogotá: Siglo del Hombre Editores.

Jaramillo Sierra, Isabel Cristina. 2010. The social approach to family law: conclusions from the cannonical family law treatises of Latin America. *American Journal of Comparative Law* 843–73.

Jaramillo Sierra, Isabel Cristina. 2013. *Derecho y Familia. Historias de Raza, Género y Propiedad, 1560–1980*. Bogotá: Universidad de Los Andes.

Jaramillo Sierra, Isabel Cristina and Tatiana Alfonso. 2008. *Mujeres, Cortes y Medios: La Reforma Judicial del Aborto*. Bogotá: Universidad de Los Andes.

Latin American and Caribbean Women's Collective. 1980. *Slaves of Slaves: The Challenge of Latin American Women*. New York: Zed Books.

Lemaitre Ripoll, Julieta. 2008. *El Derecho Como Conjuro*. Bogotá: Universidad de Los Andes y Siglo del Hombre.

Lemaitre Ripoll, Julieta. 2009. *El Derecho Como Conjuro: Fetichismo Legal, Violencia y Movimientos Sociales*. Bogotá: Siglo del Hombre y Universidad de Los Andes.

León, Magdalena. 2013. Proyecto investigación-acción: trabajo doméstico y servicio doméstico en Colombia. *Revista de Estudios Sociales* 45: 198–211.

León, Magdalena and Carmen Diana Deere. 1997. La mujer rural y la reforma agraria en Colombia. *Cuadernos de Desarrollo Rural* 7–23.

López Medina, Diego. 2004. *La Teoría Impura del Derecho*. Bogotá: Legis.

MacKinnon, Catharine. 1991. From practice to theory, or what is a white woman anyway? *Yale Journal of Law and Feminism* 4(3): 13–22.

Mackinnon, Catharine. 2013. Intersectionality as method, a note. *Signs* 38(4): 1019–30.

Mantilla, Julissa. 2006. "La perspectiva de género en la búsqueda de la verdad, la justicia y la reconciliación: el caso del Perú." En *Más Allá del Derecho: Justicia y Género en América Latina*, Luisa Cabal and Cristina Motta, 415–44. Bogotá: Siglo del Hombre Editores, Center for Reproductive Rights, Universidad de Los Andes.

Medina, Cecilia. 2009. "Hacia una manera más efectiva de garantizar que las mujeres gocen de sus derechos humanos en el Sistema Interamericano." En *El Género en el Derecho*, Ramiro Ávila Santamaría; Judith Salgado and Lola Valladares, 559–92. Quito: Ministerio de Justicia y de Derechos Humanos Ecuador.

Morsink, Johannes. 2000. *The Universal Declaration of Human Rights: Origins, Drafting, Intent*. Pittsburgh: University of Pensilvania Press.

Obando, Ana Elena. 1999. "Las interpretaciones del derecho." En *Género y Derecho*, Alda Facio and Lorena Fries, 163–86. Santiago de Chile: LOM, Cima, American University.

Obregón, Liliana. 2012. Regionalism constructed: a short story of Latin American international law. *Selected Proceedings of the European Society of International Law* (Hart Publishing) 4: 25–38.

Oquendo, Angel. 2006. *Latin American Law*. New York: Foundation Press.

Ruta Pacífica de las Mujeres. 2006. *Nuevas Formas De Resistencia Civil de lo Privado a lo Público. Movilizaciones de la Ruta Pacífica 1996–2003*. Bogotá: Cooperacio, SUIPPCOL.

Salgado, Judith. 2009. "Género y derechos humanos." En *El Género en el Derecho*, Ramiro Ávila Santamaría; Judith Salgado and Lola Valladares, 165–80. Quito: Ministerio de Justicia y Derechos Humanos del Ecuador.

Sieder, Rachel and John McNeish. 2013. *Gender Justice and Legal Pluralities: Latin American and African Perspectives*. New York: Routledge.

Tushnet, Mark. 2015. Peasants with pitchforks, and toilers with Twitter: constitutional revolutions and the constituent power. *International Journal of Constitutional Law* 13(3): 639.

Women's Link Worldwide. 2013. *La trata y la explotación en Colombia: no se puede ver, no se quiere hablar. Informe de derechos humanos*, Bogotá: Women's Link Worldwide.

Women's Link Worldwide. 2010. *Los Derechos de las Mujeres Migrantes: Una Realidad Invisible. Informe de Derechos Humanos*. Madrid: Women's Link Worldwide.

Yamin, Alicia. 2010. Toward transformative accountability: a proposal for rights-based approaches to fulfilling maternal health obligations. *Sur* 7: 95–122.

Yamin, Alicia, Neil Datta, and Ximena Andion. 2017. Behind the curtain: the roles of transnational actors in legal mobilization over sexual and reproductive rights. *Georgetown Gender and the Law*. Forthcoming.

9

AFRODESCENDANTS, LAW, AND RACE IN LATIN AMERICA

Tanya Katerí Hernández

Law and society research in and about Latin America has been particularly beneficial in elucidating the gap between the ideals of racial equality laws in the region and the actual subordinated status of its racialized subjects. This chapter maps recurring research themes in the race-related socio-legal literature, mostly focusing on studies about Afrodescendant populations and the ways in which states throughout the region have dealt with ideas of race and racial discrimination. I organize this literature according to the analysis of what Latin American states have achieved – or not – in addressing racial inclusion, racial discrimination, and racial equality through reparations and affirmative action. As a result, I identify three sets of socio-legal debates: the limits of multicultural constitutional reform for full political participation; the limits of the Latin American emphasis on criminal law to redress discriminatory actions; and the challenges to implementing race-conscious public policies such as affirmative action. Following my mapping of the field, I signal the resistance of legal systems to enforcing anti-discrimination measures in order to show that future research should interrogate the judicial presumption that racial violence does not and has not existed in Latin America, and the resulting social disempowerment of not naming violence as racial.

Limits of Multicultural Constitutional Reforms

Law and society literature has documented the advent of multicultural constitutions. For instance, Jean Muteba Rahier's work points to the ways in which the "Latin American multicultural turn" since the 1980s has rightfully celebrated indigenous and Afrodescendant contributions to nation-states that were historically ignored and/or not fully valued (Rahier 2014, 105); other authors have argued that the multicultural constitutional turn created new forms of citizenship in nations composed by ethnically diverse populations (Yashar 2005; Loveman 2014). However, Tianna Paschel notes that, for the case of Afrodescendants, the existing scholarship on Latin America tends to collapse policies of collective rights and race-based affirmative action into a singular "multicultural turn" rather than distinguishing between the two varied developments (Paschel 2016, 20).

Disaggregating the development of multiculturalist collective land rights from affirmative action and anti-discrimination laws helps to illuminate the limits on their reach and enforcement and how they can reproduce racialized color hierarchies (Rahier 2014, 105). In fact, the literature regarding multicultural constitutions is roughly made up of two subcategories, where one focuses on the rise of indigenous political activism and the other on the recognition of racial discrimination against Afrodescendants. Within the indigenous rights literature indigeneity is not for the most part examined as a matter of racial identity for which racial discrimination laws are paramount (Sieder 2002). This could very well be because indigenous leaders themselves have not usually engaged with discourses centered on racism and discrimination (Beck, Mijeski, and Stark 2011, 102–25).

In contrast, racial identity has been the primary focus regarding the examination of Afrodescendant communities (Hooker 2005, 285–310). Juliet Hooker's work has suggested that not all multicultural constitutions similarly situate Afrodescendant communities. She aptly notes that because Latin American states have primarily envisioned multicultural rights as pertaining to indigenous peoples, who are viewed as deserving "ethnic" group members, Afrodescendants have often been excluded as distinct "racial" subjects without an ethnic identity needing constitutional protection (Hooker 2009, 80–2). For instance, Hooker lists Colombia, Brazil, Ecuador, and Peru as those jurisdictions where Afrodescendants have obtained some multicultural constitutional rights, but not to the same extent as indigenous communities.

The dichotomy drawn between deserving "ethnic" indigenous persons and the undeserving "racial" Afrodescendants overlooks both the racialization of indigenous peoples as well as the cultural identities of Afrodescendant communities. For this reason, Colombia stands out as a jurisdiction that has included Afrodescendants while also exemplifying the limitations of a nation equating multicultural rights with ethnic group status (Ng'weno 2007a). Colombia thus provides an illustrative contrast to countries like Mexico and Venezuela that completely exclude Afrodescendants from their multicultural rights landscape. Colombia also compares with those countries that have accorded Afrodescendants the same collective rights to land and culture, such as Guatemala, Honduras, and Nicaragua.

The Colombian Constitution states that it "recognizes and protects the ethnic and cultural diversity of the Colombian nation." Transitory Article 55 of the 1991 Constitution mandated that laws recognizing Afrodescendants' rights to collective property be enacted. The constitutional provisions have thus been augmented by specific legislation. In order to implement the mandate of Article 55, in 1993 Ley 70 (Law 70) was enacted to provide protection for traditional landholdings of Afro-Colombians as an essential element of their ethnic identity, recognizing their right to organize collectively through their own traditional authorities and apply for collective title. Article 7 of Ley 70 provides that collective titles are inalienable, protected from seizure, and exempt from statutes of limitations. The law was originally devised for black communities in the Pacific Coast but as the Afro-Colombian movement and black identity gained ground since the 1990s, black communities in different regions of the countries have made claims for land. Black rights to collective land have been extended (via jurisprudence) to other areas, especially the Caribbean coast, wherever communities defend a self-ascribed black identity, collective organization, and traditional forms of land settlement and use. Law 70 requires that only lands deemed to be *tierras baldías* (state-owned vacant land) can be passed on to collective ownership: urban areas; indigenous territories; national park areas; and regions reserved for national security and defense are not deemed apt for collective titling. Yet Afro-Colombians are regionally and ethnically diverse and do not all live on *tierras baldías*. Furthermore, the land titling process is particularly demanding in that it requires the production of historical, demographic, economic, and cartographic studies of the community claiming collective ownership. What this effectively means is that vast numbers of urban Afrodescendants are excluded from the benefits of collective title because they are not viewed as having firmly-rooted ties to specific parcels of land, as – by contrast, is the case with indigenous communities' collective land titles (Ng'weno 2007b). Ley 70 thus, addressed the needs of only one type of Afro-Colombian.

In addition, Jaime Arocha observes that many Afro-Colombians have been dissuaded from pursuing the land titling process by the violence of paramilitary groups and the Colombian Army (Arocha 1998, 70–89). Similarly, Kiran Asher describes how Afro-Colombian community organizers seeking collective ownership have seen themselves labeled as guerrillas or terrorists and have then been targeted for violence by government agents interested in controlling resource-rich Afro-Colombian areas for corporate development (Asher 2009). In addition, right-wing paramilitary squads long enmeshed in drug trafficking are similarly involved in land grabs (Rosero 2002, 547–59). Indeed, at least one study found that 33 percent of all Afro-Colombians have been expelled from their lands by armed groups (Hernández 2013, 117). Afro-Colombians represent the largest percentage of those displaced because of the civil war (Hernández 2013, 117): an Afro-Colombian is 84 percent more likely to be displaced than a mestizo. Of the Afro-Colombian population with registered collective property titles in 2007 alone, 79 percent had been forcibly dispossessed of their lands (Rodríguez, Alfonso, and Cavelier 2008, 34–5). So significant has been the displacement of Afro-Colombians (and indigenous communities as well) that in 1999, the United Nations officially put the Colombian government on notice to address it as a form of racial discrimination (CERD 1999). Thereafter, Colombia's Constitutional Court evaluated the government's policy for dealing with the plight of the many dispossessed and held that the policy was inadequate and unconstitutional in its violation of the fundamental rights of Colombian citizens (Constitutional Court of Colombia, 2004). Since that court order, the government has been obligated to design policies to prevent the forced removal of landowners, in addition to ameliorating the poor living conditions of the dispossessed. In a subsequent decision the constitutional court assessed the particular and specific impact of the armed conflict and forced displacement on Afro-Colombians as a targeted group and concluded that for these communities, displacement was a result of the structural exclusion of this population.

In contrast to the situation regarding land, the government has been willing to focus upon Afro-Colombians as a group with respect to educational reform. In 1998, President Ernesto Samper, in compliance with the dispositions of Law 70 of 1993 on protection of cultural identity and the obligation to establish Afro-Colombian studies as a permanent part of the school curriculum, passed a presidential decree mandating that schools teach Afro-Colombian history and culture (Decree No. 1122 1998). The general law of education (Law 115 of 1993) in Article 160, provides that the board of each education district must include a member representing the local Afro-Colombian community, if such a local community exists.

However, the promise of multicultural constitutions and new laws will need to confront the long embedded history of racially exclusionary politics in Latin America. For example, César Rodríguez-Garavito describes how in the Colombian context even though the legislation for the "multicultural protection" of the constitution requires that government authorities consult Afrodescendant communities before making decisions that affect their communal lands, Afro-Colombians confront barriers to the consultation process because the government must first officially recognize a pre-established community council of Afrodescendants before they are entitled to be consulted (Rodríguez-Garavito 2011, 263–305). The official recognition process has thus been perceived as overly bureaucratic and restrictive (Rodríguez 2008). Nevertheless, in her review of multicultural constitutions Donna Lee Van Cott notes that after so many years of marginalization, even the symbolic constitutional recognition of the importance of Afrodescendants is indeed some measure of progress (Van Cott 2000).

Limits of the Emphasis on Criminal Law to Redress Discriminatory Actions

The law and society literature has been helpful in illuminating how the vast majority of countries in Latin America have focused on criminal law as the vehicle for addressing racial discrimination. This literature has highlighted that such approaches, while sending a message about state commitment, leave structural and institutional causes of racial discrimination untouched. Moreover, the emphasis on criminal sanctions tends to create a gap between the mere existence of the norm and its implementation, just as in the classical gap between law on the books and law in action.

César Rodríguez-Garavito and Carlos Baquero Díaz note that all Latin American countries except for Paraguay have passed laws to criminally punish acts of racial discrimination (Rodríguez and Baquero 2015, 68). Given the long histories of ignoring the existence of racism and discrimination in Latin America, it is understandable that the strongest state sanction that criminal law provides would be sought as the symbol of the state's new commitment to recognizing societal discrimination. Robert J. Cottrol thus, rightfully notes that criminal law sanctions are often the default anti-discrimination approach because they contain a strong normative message that the state condemns racism (Cottrol 2013, 290).

Relatively few criminal prosecutions have been brought since the social justice advocacy for recognition of racial discrimination of the 1990s. In 2013, Claudia Dary reported that six court cases had been brought by indigenous Maya persons in Guatemala since the nation's enactment of its discrimination criminal code provision in 2002 (Dary 2013, 140). Peru convicted an individual for racial discrimination against an Afro-Peruvian for the first time in 2015 (Sentencia No. 479-2015-2JPL-PJ-CSJJU). Similarly, Ecuador issued its first prison sentence for racial discrimination against an Afro-Ecuadorian only in 2016 (Corte Nacional de Justicia de Ecuador, Proceso No. 17124-2014-0585).

The public focus on criminal law conflicts with fully addressing the sources of racial inequality. For instance, further entrenching the focus on criminal law provisions has been the notion that Latin American nation-states are innocent of racial wrongdoing. Tanya Katerí Hernández notes that given the absence of state mandated Jim Crow segregation in the region, the legal stance toward racism has been to view it as an aberration rather than a systemic part of a national culture (Hernández 2013, 104). As a result, the legal response has been to treat racism as the work of isolated individuals, who are presumably abnormal in their prejudices. In short, racists are criminals rather than representatives of longstanding racist cultural norms. Rodríguez and Baquero conclude that the use of criminal law individualizes racism and fails to challenge the structural causes of racial inequality (Rodríguez and Baquero 2015, 92). This also helps to explain why the large majority of hate speech laws in Latin America are part of the criminal codes in the region. Yet limiting the idea of racism to biased words uttered by those labeled as aberrant racists overlooks the structural and institutional aspects of discrimination that operate in the absence of racist commentary. The work of Carlos de la Torre has exemplified these law and society insights with respect to the plight of Afro-Ecuadorians. For instance he notes that "[r]educing racism to the hostile words and actions of ignorant, ethnocentric, and parochial individuals, a view that was dominant in American sociology until recently, does not take into account power relations" (de La Torre 2005).

Tanya Katerí Hernández's work in particular has documented how some countries in Latin America maintain a singular criminal approach to discrimination (Hernández 2013). For example, in the Dominican Republic, the 1997 Ley contra la Violencia Intrafamiliar ("Law against Interfamily Violence") makes it a crime to inflict unequal or humiliating treatment based on race or ethnicity. Persons found guilty of the crime of discrimination can be imprisoned for one year and one month and be subject to a fine of two to three times the minimum wage (Ley No. 24–97). In Nicaragua, the criminal code penalizes the obstruction of a constitutional right because of race or ethnicity (Ley No. 641). The penalty is six months to one year of imprisonment. If the racially motivated obstruction of a constitutional right is found to have been publicly promoted, an additional fine can be imposed. The criminal code also authorizes the augmentation of a penalty for other crimes when they are racially motivated (Crim. Code Art. 36.5).

What the law and society literature on the criminalization of racial discrimination underlines is that even though criminal sanctions suggest a strong normative commitment to the eradication of discrimination, they may in practice have had the ironic effect of making the legal system less capable of dealing with the problems of inequality and discrimination. Criminal cases require stronger evidence and a higher burden of proof than civil cases. For instance, an analysis of experiences of filing a criminal complaint of discrimination in Peru found that the evidentiary standard for discrimination cases was high and that it was often difficult for a victim to prove that he/she had experienced discrimination. The report described the case of an individual who lodged a complaint against the police department alleging discrimination for the inappropriate issuance of a traffic ticket because of his race. The public prosecutor deemed that this complaint did not merit a criminal investigation or action because the evidence presented was insufficient. Yet the complainant had submitted an affidavit and that of a family member who witnessed the incident: it is difficult to fathom what more he could have submitted in order to support his allegations (Defensoría del Pueblo, República Del Perú 2007, 119).

In addition to the reluctance of prosecutors to proceed with racial discrimination cases, judges are reluctant to impose criminal sanctions. Latin American criminal justice systems are overloaded with traditional crimes of violence and crimes against property. In a system plagued with case overload and systemic inefficiencies, the crimes of racism, and racial discrimination are likely to continue to have a low priority.

Moreover, entrusting the enforcement of the criminal law to public authorities, risks having the law undermined by the complacent inaction of public officials who may harbor the same racial bias as the agents of discrimination. Indeed, commentators have noted that Latin American police officers are often the perpetrators of racial violence against persons of African descent because they see their role as protecting society from "marginal elements" by any means necessary without regard to the rule of law (Pinheiro 1999, 1–16). This is a particular danger in Latin America, where police officers consistently discourage Afrodescendants from filing racial discrimination complaints and are often themselves the perpetrators of discrimination and violence (Brinks 2008, 49–54; Mitchell and Wood 1999, 1001–20).

Seth Racusen notes that a civil framework can provide for broader theories of discrimination and less burdensome evidentiary standards (Racusen 2002, 87–8, 2004). In addition, the civil context carries less risk of selective enforcement whereby vulnerable populations are disproportionately targeted for prosecution. This is because, unlike in criminal prosecutions, the state need not be the primary enforcer of the legislation. Yet because of the prevalent notion that criminal laws against discrimination show how serious the state is about racism, the development of civil law measures has been slow and their reach has been modest.

Reparations and Affirmative Action

In contrast to the United States' narrow vision of reparations as limited to state-based apologies and financial compensation for specific harms, the Latin American conception of reparations has been depicted in the law and society literature as broadly encompassing not only multicultural constitutional land rights provisions but also policies of affirmative or positive action (Rodriguez and Baquero 2015, 93). Claudia Mosquera Rosero-Labbé and Luiz Claudio Barcelos in particular, set out the varied possibilities for formulating demands for reparations in Latin America (Mosquera Rosero-Labbé and Barcelos 2007). They note that the regional discussion about reparations includes affirmative action policies, redistribution of wealth and power, state protection of cultural forms, protection and compensation for territorial expulsions, legal recognition and title for ancestral lands, and studies for the recognition of the harms of subtle implicit bias.

In the specific case of Colombia, Rodríguez-Garavito and Lam suggest that the frame of reparations is a better lens for redressing the collective injustices that ethnic populations have incurred as a consequence of being displaced from their lands, displacement that often occurred with state support (Rodríguez and Lam 2011, 13). With Afro-Colombians followed by indigenous groups as the largest numbers of displaced persons, the racialization of their expulsions is marked and necessitates the racially-conscious lens of reparations discourse (Rodríguez, Alfonso, and Cavelier 2009a, 7). Yet, as previously noted, Colombia has been slow to respond to the racially specific occurrences of land displacement with reparations-like racial specificity. This may be due to some extent to the great variation in understandings on the part of government actors about what constitutes affirmative action (Mosquera Rosero-Labbé, Díaz, and Morales 2009, 350).

However, in Colombia and other nations that have broached the issue of affirmative action, states have been more willing to consider racially targeted policies. In fact the recent growth in race-related law and society literature regarding Latin America is centered on the topic of affirmative action (Htun 2016). For instance, Rocío Martínez describes the national government's consideration of affirmative action and the implementation of its strategies at municipal level in the city of Bogotá (Martínez 2013, 207–26). Indeed Bogotá's municipal movement on affirmative action stands in marked contrast to Colombia's national failure to implement effective legislation (Rodríguez, Alfonso, and Cavelier 2009b, 325).

Brazil's wider implementation of affirmative action policies across various sectors means it is the country where law and society analysis of racial discrimination is most focused (Reiter and Mitchell 2009). Ollie A. Johnson III and Rosana Heringer's 2015 collection on affirmative action provides a comprehensive picture of the complexities involved in legislating affirmative action policies in Brazil (Johnson III and Heringer 2015). As a whole this literature has highlighted how affirmative action is pursued as a means to address racial exclusion, even when that racial exclusion continues to operate when socioeconomic status is the same across races (Telles 2004).

However, whenever the issue of racial and ethnic empowerment is raised as a political issue for Latin America, the inevitable critique is voiced that such concerns are not relevant to such a racially mixed context. Socioeconomic status is still understood to be the most salient factor for understanding inequality in the region. However, law and society scholarship has documented how indigenous and Afrodescendant social justice activists with very different perspectives have successfully lobbied for ethnic and racial policies of inclusion in Brazil. It has also shown how Brazilian officials have managed to administer affirmative action programs that creatively operate in the midst of racial fluidity by using various combinations of non-white race proxies, such as public secondary school attendance and low-income status, along with racial self-declarations of being black or brown, photographs, and interviews for determining program participation (dos Santos and Lobato 2003).

Moreover, the literature indicates that Brazilian affirmative action programs are relatively successful. For instance, a study of student outcomes at the State University of Campinas found that students from socioeconomically and educationally disadvantaged backgrounds performed relatively better than those from a higher socioeconomic and educational level (Pedrosa 2007).

The study concluded that the need for hard work when striving for greater opportunity (as in preparing for the university admission examination when coming from an under-resourced public secondary school) creates an "educational resilience" that improves educational performance once a student is admitted to university. The educational resilience of the less privileged students resulted in higher grade point averages of the affirmative action students after only one year of university study in 31 of the 55 possible undergraduate courses of study and the success rate improved over the course of their years at the university. Overall, the relative performance of the affirmative action students was higher in 48 of the 55 courses. Equivalent studies at the University of Brasilia, the State University of North Fluminense, the Federal University of Bahia, the State University of Rio de Janeiro, and the Federal University of Espirito Santo found similar outcomes (Velloso 2009; Brandão and da Matta 2007; Queiroz and dos Santos 2006; Vieira 2011; Ford 2011). In other words, affirmative action students succeed once provided the opportunity of admission.

The law and society literature shows that growing numbers of Brazilians and program beneficiaries have come to view affirmative action as positive. In fact, the most common student stereotype about the program beneficiaries is that they are "cones" (nerds) who prefer to work all the time rather than party (Cicalo 2012). The general student body's respect for the program participants is illustrated by the following reflection by a University of the State of Rio de Janeiro law student:

> I can tell you that I'm in the third year and I don't see any real difference between the marks of the quota and non-quota students. Many cotistas [quota students] do very well, and they definitely deserve to be here; this fact has made me change my [negative] opinion of quotas in the last few years.
>
> *(Cicalo 2012, 256–57)*

Similarly, in a 2007 study of 557 university instructors, the vast majority considered that affirmative action had contributed to democratizing the academic space by having it more accurately reflect Brazilian society (Petruccelli 2007).

At the same time that the law and society research has traced the evolving shift in Latin American attitudes regarding the suitability of presumably United States-like race-conscious policies of inclusion, it has also documented judicial resistance to the notion that racial discrimination exists in Latin America simply because its manifestations are deemed to be inconsequential compared to the "real discrimination" of the racially violent United States. The next section addresses the legal system's resistance to enforcing anti-discrimination laws.

Legal System Resistance to Anti-Discrimination Enforcement: The Case of Racial Violence

Ariel Dulitzky, was one of the first legal scholars to assess the region-wide phenomenon of denying the existence of racial discrimination because of the assertion that "the serious incidence of racism and racial discrimination" more accurately exists in the United States (Dulitzky 2005, 39). This observation was based upon an analysis of official nation-state reporting responses to human rights violation claims before the United Nations Committee on the Elimination of Racial Discrimination. Despite evidence that racial discrimination permeates every realm in the region including social, political, education, labor, culture, and public health sectors, government responses downplayed its significance as inconsequential compared to the legal violence of the USA.

Dulitzky's general insight has also accorded with country-specific studies that describe legal systems, which treat racial discrimination claims as lacking merit because of the belief that Latin America is not a region with "real racism." For instance, in the Brazilian context, Antonio Guimarães found that judges frequently dismissed such claims based on the notion that Brazilian culture is immune from racial bias (Guimarães 1998). For instance, Guimarães quotes one representative case in which the judge explicitly stated: "We do not have the rigorous and cruel racism observed in other countries, where non-'whites' are segregated, separated and do not have the same rights. That is racism" (Guimarães 1998, 35).

While not all judges are so explicit about how a particular comparison to the United States limits the full recognition of racism in Latin America that should be legally regulated, other country-specific studies have observed a similar refusal to acknowledge the existence of racism in the enforcement of equality laws. For instance, in the Justice Studies Center of the Americas' examination of Colombia, the Dominican Republic, and Peru, it was found that each of these countries suffered from a limited legal response to the issues of racial discrimination (Judicial Studies Center of the Americas 2004). Similarly, Carlos de la Torre's inquiry into the Ecuadorian legal system discovered that the Ecuadorian government had a constrained view of racism as solely a problem of isolated verbal expressions of infrequent individual bigotry (de la Torre 2005). Even apparent victories in court that recognize that racial discrimination exists can be premised on problematic understandings of racism. For instance, in his analysis of Colombian Constitutional Court case findings, Jorge González Jácome concludes that the court confines its understanding of racism to the acts of individuals with overtly manifested intent to discriminate in ways that problematically shields from consideration the ways in which pervasive structural discrimination operates (González Jácome 2006). The focus on individual intent is yet another articulation of the vision of discrimination as exceptional in Latin America.

Given continued resistance to recognizing the gravity of racial discrimination in Latin America, emerging law and society literature could most productively turn to empirical evaluations of how structural racial discrimination operates in practice. Such studies could be instrumental in disrupting judicial attitudes of racial innocence that interferes with the enforcement of anti-discrimination laws. This could be achieved most directly by interrogating the presumption that racial violence does not and has not existed in Latin America, along with examining the social disempowerment that occurs when violence is not named as racial.

For instance, in João Costa Vargas's analysis of violent police practices in Brazil, he readily identifies the racialized aspects of policing in the poor regions, despite the Brazilian norm of treating poverty as the sole basis for social differentiation unaffected by racism (Costa 2004, 459). Rather than accept at face value the traditional Latin American explanation of racial disparities in police violence as solely emblematic of socioeconomic class distinctions, Costa Vargas digs deeper to demonstrate how "urban space became a metaphor, a code concept for blackness, in the same way that the *favela* was rendered a code word for blacks" that justifies racialized violence (Costa 2004, 455). Similarly, Carlos de la Torre describes a parallel dynamic of racialized police practices in Ecuador where police "conceive of their mission as protecting citizens from the 'danger' of blacks. These blacks are not viewed as citizens but rather as violent intruders that invade the cities" (de la Torre 2002, 33). A study of police practices in Cali, Colombia also notes that Afro-Colombians perceive law enforcement as targeting the Afro-Colombian community with physical mistreatment (Lam and Ávila 2013, 35). Examples of state violence extend beyond law enforcement officials to instances of state complicity in the contemporary massacre of ethnic populations. Aurora Vergara Figueroa describes such an instance in the 2002 massacre of Afro-Colombians in Bellavista, Colombia (Vergara 2011). More recently, an

133

Afrodescendant student was repeatedly physically attacked by his classmates and was ultimately burned with acid as racist slurs were uttered (LaFM 2013).

Nor are Colombia, Ecuador, and Brazil the only countries in the region with reported instances of racialized violence. In Argentina, a young female Senegalese street vendor was physically attacked and kicked in the stomach by a doorman as he shouted: "I don't want to see a black woman when I walk out of the door of this building" and "go back to your country you shitty black woman" (IARPIDI 2014). In Uruguay, a Nigerian man was beaten and thrown out of a dance club by four club doormen as they shouted, "get this shitty negro out of here" (Lima and Delgado 2011). The beating was so brutal that the victim lost vision in one eye. In each reported attack, those interviewed asserted how common such racial violence is in the region.

In the future, a law and society race-related research agenda could productively explore the role that racial violence plays in subordinating vulnerable populations in Latin America, as well as deconstructing the judicial premise that violence in Latin America is unrelated to racial discrimination.

References

Arocha, Jaime. 1998. "Inclusion of Afro-Colombians: Unreachable National Goal?" *Latin American Perspectives* 25 (May): 70–89.

Asher, Kiran. 2009. *Black and Green: Afro-Colombians, Development, and Nature in the Pacific Lowlands.* Durham, NC: Duke University Press.

Beck, Scott H., Kenneth J. Mijeski, and Meagan Stark. 2011. "Qué es racismo? Awareness of Racism and Discrimination in Ecuador." *Latin American Research Review* 46: 102–25.

Bernard and Audre Center for Human Rights and Justice. 2007. "A Report on the Development of Ley 70 of 1993 Submitted to the Inter-American Commission on Human Rights." 8. Available at: www.utexas.edu/law/academics/centers/humanrights/students/FINAL%20REPORT.pdf. Accessed August 5, 2017.

Brandão, André and Ludmila Gonçalves da Matta. 2007. "Avaliação da Política de Reserva de Vagas na Universidade Estadual do Norte Fluminense: Estudos dos Alunos Que Ingressarem em 2003." En *Cotas Raciais No Brasil: A Primeira Avaliação*, edited by André Augusto Brandão, 46–80. Rio de Janeiro: DP&A.

Brinks, Daniel M. 2008. *The Judicial Response to Police Killings in Latin America: Inequality and the Rule of Law.* Cambridge: Cambridge University Press.

Cicalo, André. 2012. "Nerds and Barbarians: Race and Class Encounters through Affirmative Action in a Brazilian University." *Journal of Latin American Studies* 44(2): 235–60.

Committee on the Elimination of Racial Discrimination: Colombia, United Nations. 1999. "Concluding Observations of the Committee on the Elimination of Racial Discrimination: Colombia." CERD: United Nations, August 20, 1999. Available at: www.unhchr.ch/tbs/doc.nsf/(Symbol)/c318bd791cc8 a6ea8025686b0043560f?Opendocument. Accessed August 6, 2017.

Corte Constitucional de Colombia. 2004. *Sentencia T-025 de 2004.*

Corte Nacional de Justicia de Ecuador. 2016. *Proceso No. 17124–2014–0585, July 5, 2016 (crime of discrimination against Michael Arce Méndez).*

Costa Vargas, Joao. 2004. "Hyperconsciousness of Race and its Negation: The Dialectic of White Supremacy in Brazil." *Identities: Global Studies in Culture and Power* 11: 443–70.

Cottrol, Robert J. 2013. *The Long, Lingering Shadow: Slavery, Race, and Law in the American Hemisphere.* Athens: University of Georgia Press.

Código Penal. Art. 36.5. Nicaragua.

Dary, Claudia. 2013. "Acknowledging Racism and State Transformation in Postwar Guatemalan Society." In *Central America in the New Millennium: Living Transition and Reimagining Democracy*, edited by Jennifer L. Burrell and Ellen Moodie, New York: Bergahn Books: 131–45.

Decreto 1122. 1998. Colombia.

De la Torre, Carlos. 2002. *Afroquitenos: Ciudadanía y Racismo.* Quito: Centro Andino de Acción Popular.

De la Torre, Carlos. 2005. "Afro-Ecuadorian Responses to Racism: Between Citizenship and Corporatism." In *Neither Enemies Nor Friends: Latinos, Blacks, Afro-Latinos*, edited by Anani Dzidzienyo and Suzanne Oboler. New York: Macmillan.

Defensoría del Pueblo, República Del Perú. 2007. *La Discriminación en el Perú: Problemática, Normatividad y Tareas Pendientes*. Perú: Defensoría del Pueblo, República Del Perú. 119.

Dos Santos, Renato Emerson and Fátima Lobato, (eds.) 2003. *Ações Afirmativas: Políticas Públicas Contra As Desigualdades Raciais*. Rio de Janeiro: Lamparina Editora.

Dulitzky, Ariel E. 2005. "A Region in Denial: Racial Discrimination and Racism in Latin America." In *Neither Enemies Nor Friends: Latinos, Blacks, Afro-Latinos*, edited by Anani Dzidzienyo and Suzanne Oboler. 39–60. New York: Palgrave Macmillan.

Ford, Clara (Kaya). 2011. *The Impact of Socioeconomic Quotas on Student Retention: The Case of a Brazilian University*. Ph.D. diss., Capella University.

Guimarães, Antonio Sergio. 1998. *Preconceito e Discriminação: Queixas de Ofensas e tratamento Desigual Nos Negros No Brasil*. Bahia: UFBA Ed. Novos Toques.

Hernández, Tanya. 2013. *Racial Subordination in Latin America: The Role of The State, Customary Law, and the New Civil Rights Response*. Cambridge: Cambridge University Press.

Hooker, Juliet. 2005. "Indigenous Inclusion/Black Exclusion: Race, Ethnicity and Multicultural Citizenship in Latin America." *Journal of Latin American Studies* 37(2): 285–310.

Hooker, Juliet. 2009. *Race and the Politics of Solidarity*. Oxford: Oxford University Press.

Htun, Mala N. 2004. *Dimensiones de la Inclusión y Exclusión Política En Brasil: Género y Raza*. Serie de Informes Técnicos del Departamento de Desarrollo Sostenible. Washington, DC: Banco Interamericano de Desarrollo. 2004. www.iadb.org/IDBDocs.cfm?docnum=361865.

Htun, Mala. 2016. *Inclusion without Representation in Latin America: Gender Quotas and Ethnic Reservations in Latin America*. Cambridge: Cambridge University Press.

IARPIDI, Instituto Argentino para la Igualdad, Diversidad e Integración. 2014. *Fuerte y Brutal Ataque Racista a Una Joven Senegalesa En Buenos Aires*. August 9. Available at: http://iarpidi.org/2014/08/09/fuerte-y-brutal-atauqe-racista-una-joven-senegalesa-en-buenos-aires/. Accessed August 5, 2017.

González Jácome, Jorge. 2006. "Esclavitud Perpetua: Construyendo Una Perspectiva De Raza en el Derecho Constitucional Colombiano." *Universitas* 111: 313–35.

Johnson III, Ollie A., and Rosanna Heringer, (eds.) 2015. *Race, Politics, and Education in Brazil: Affirmative Action in Higher Education*. New York: Palgrave Macmillan.

Judicial Studies Center of the Americas. 2004. *The Judicial System and Racism Against People of African Descent: The Cases of Brazil, Colombia, The Dominican Republic and Peru*. Santiago: Centro de Estudios de Justicia de las Américas.

LaFM. 2013. *Por Ser Negro Niño Es Quemado Por Sus Compañeros*. July 10 2013. Available at: www.lafm.com.co/noticias/por-ser-negro-nino-es-quemado-141347. Accessed August 20, 2017.

Lam, Yukyan and Camilo Ávila Ceballos. 2013. *Orden Público y Perfiles Raciales: Experiencias De Afrocolombianos Con La Policía En Cali*. Bogotá: Ediciones Antropos.

Ley 70. 1993. Colombia.

Ley 115. 1993. Colombia.

Ley 24. 1997. República Dominicana.

Ley 641. Nicaragua.

Lima, Maria and E. Delgado. 2011. "Uruguay: Marcharon Contra el Racismo y, En Especial, por el Nigeriano Golpeado." *El Pais*, June 2011. Available at: www.elpais.com.uy. Accessed August 20, 2017.

Loveman, Mara. 2014. *National Colors: Racial Classification and the State in Latin America*. New York: Oxford University Press.

Martínez, Rocio. 2013. "Acciones afirmativas para población afrocolombiana en Bogotá: Historia de la formulación de una política pública." En *Estudios Afrocolombianos Hoy: Aportes a Un Campo Transdisciplinario*, edited by Eduardo Restrepo. Popayán: Editorial Universidad del Cauca: 207–26.

Mitchell, Michael J. and Charles H. Wood. 1999. "Ironies of Citizenship: Skin Color, Police Brutality, and the Challenge to Democracy in Brazil," *Social Forces* 77: 1001–20.

Mosquera Rosero-Labbé, Claudia, Luiz Claudio Barcelos, and Andrés Gabriel Arévalo Robles. 2007. "Contribuciones a los debates sobre las Memorias de la Esclavitud y las Afro-reparaciones en Colombia desde el campo de los estudios afrocolombianos, afrolatinoamericanos, afrobrasileros, afroestadounidenses y afrocaribeños." En *Afro-reparaciones: Memorias de la Esclavitud y Justicia Reparativa Para Negros, Afrocolombianos y Raizales*, edited by Claudia Mosquera Rosero-Labbé, and Luiz Claudio Barcelos. Bogotá: Universidad Nacional de Colombia: 13–69.

Mosquera Rosero-Labbé, Claudia, Ruby Esther León Díaz and Margarita María Rodríguez Morales. 2009. "Las Acciones Afirmativas vistas por distintos actors(as)." En *Acciones Afirmativas y Ciudadanía Diferenciada Étnico-Racial Negra, Afrocolombiana, Palenquera y Raizal*, edited by Claudia Mosquera Rosero-Labbé and Ruby Esther León Díaz. Bogotá: Universidad Nacional de Colombia: 347–426.

Ng'weno, Bettina. 2007a. "Can Ethnicity Replace Race? Afro-Colombians, Indigeneity and the Colombian Multicultural State." *Journal of Latin American and Caribbean Anthropology* 12: 414–40.

Ng'weno, Bettina. 2007b. *Turf Wars: Territory and Citizenship in the Contemporary State*. Stanford: Stanford University Press.

Paschel, Tianna S. 2016. *Becoming Black Political Subjects: Movements and Ethno-Racial Rights in Colombia and Brazil*. Princeton: Princeton University Press.

Pedrosa, Renato H.L., J. Norberto, W. Dachs, Rafael P. Maia, Cibele Y. Andrade, and Benilton S. Carvalho. 2007. "Academic Performance, Students' Background and Affirmative Action at a Brazilian University." *Higher Education Management and Policy* 19: 1–20.

Petruccelli, José Luis. 2007. *A Cor Denominada: Estudos Sobre a Clasificação Étnico-Racial*. Rio de Janeiro: DP & A Editores.

Pinheiro, Paulo Sérgio. 1999. "The Rule of Law and the Underprivileged in Latin America: Introduction." In *The (Un)Rule of Law and the Underprivileged in Latin America*, edited by Juan E. Méndez, Guillermo O'Donnell, and Paulo Sérgio Pinheiro. Notre Dame, IN: University of Notre Dame Press. 1–16.

Queiroz, Delcele Mascarenhas and Jocelio Teles dos Santos. 2006. "Sistema de Cotas: Um Debate: Dos Dados a Manutencao de Privilegios e de Poder." *Educação e Sociedade* 27: 717–37.

Racusen, Seth. 2002. *A Mulato Cannot Be Prejudiced: The Legal Construction of Racial Discrimination in Contemporary Brazil*. Ph.D. dissertation, Massachusetts Institute of Technology. 87–8.

Racusen, Seth. 2004. "The Ideology of the Brazilian Nation and the Brazilian Legal Theory of Racial Discrimination." *Social Identities* 10(6): 775–809.

Rahier, Jean Muteba. 2014. *Blackness in the Andes: Ethnographic Vignettes of Cultural Politics in the Time of Multiculturalism*. New York: Palgrave Macmillan.

Reiter, Bernd and Glady L. Mitchell (eds.) 2009. *Brazil's New Racial Politics*. Boulder: Lynne Rienner.

Rodríguez, Garavito César. 2011. "Ethnicity.gov: Global Governance, Indigenous Peoples, and the Right to Prior Consultation in Social Minefields." *Indiana Journal of Global Legal Studies* 18(1): 263–305.

Rodríguez, Garavito César and Carlos Baquero. 2015. *Reconocimiento Con Redistribución: El Derecho Y La Justicia Étnico-Racial En América Latina*. Bogotá: Dejusticia.

Rodríguez, Garavito César and Yukyan Lam. 2011. *Etnorreparaciones: La Justicia Colectiva Étnica y la Reparación a Pueblos Indígenas y Comunidades Afrodescendientes En Colombia*. Bogotá: Dejusticia.

Rodríguez, Garavito César, Tatiana Alfonso, and Isabel Cavelier. 2008. *El Derecho a no Ser Discriminado: Primer Informe Sobre Discriminación Racial y Derechos de la Población Afrocolombiana (Versión Resumida)*. Bogotá: Universidad de Los Andes.

Rodríguez, Garavito César, Tatiana Alfonso, and Isabel Cavelier. 2009a. *El Desplazamiento Afro*. Bogotá: Universidad de Los Andes.

Rodríguez, Garavito César, Tatiana Alfonso, and Isabel Cavelier. 2009b. "El Derecho Ausente: Ni Legislación Ni Políticas Contra la Discriminación." In *Raza y Derechos Humanos En Colombia: Informe Sobre Discriminación Racial y Derechos de la Población Afrocolombiana*, edited by César Rodríguez-Garavito, Tatiana Alfonso, and Isabel Cavelier, 307–31. Bogotá: Universidad de Los Andes.

Rodríguez, Gloria Amparo. 2008. "Continúa La Exclusión y la Marginación de las comunidades negras Colombianas." *Revista Diálogos de Saberes* 29: 215–38.

Rosero, Carlos. 2002. "Los Afrodescendientes y el Conflicto Armado en Colombia: La Insistencia en lo Propio Como Alternativa." En *Afrodescendientes En Las Américas: Trayectorias Sociales e Identitarias, 150 Años de la Abolición de la Esclavitud en Colombia*, edited by Claudia Mosquera, Mauricio Pardo, and Odile Hoffman. Bogotá: Universidad Nacional de Colombia, 547–59.

Sieder, Rachel, ed. 2002. *Multiculturalism in Latin America: Indigenous Rights, Diversity and Democracy*. Houndmills: Palgrave Macmillan.

Sentencia No. 479-2015-2JPL-PJ-CSJJU (Peru) Segundo Juzgado Penal Liquidador –Sede Central [Penal Court] November 13, 2015 (crime of discrimination against Azucena Asunción Algendones).

Telles, Edward E. 2004. *Race in Another America: The Significance of Skin Color in Brazil*. Princeton: Princeton University Press.

Van Cott, Donna Lee. 2000. *The Friendly Liquidation of the Past: The Politics of Diversity in Latin America*. Pittsburgh: University of Pittsburgh Press.

Vieira, Márcia. 2011. "Médicos da Uerj Põem á Prova Sistema de Cotas." *O Estado de São Paulo*, May 8.

Velloso, Jacques. 2009. "Curso e Concurso: Rendimento No Universidade e Desempenho en um Vestibular Com Cotas da UnB." *Cadernos de Pesquisa* 39: 621–44.

Vergara Figueroa, Aurora. 2011. *Ripped from the Land, Shipped Away and Reborn: Unthinking the Conceptual and Socio-Geo-Historical Dimensions of the Massacre of Bellavista.* Master's Thesis, University of Massachusetts-Amherst.

Yashar, Deborah. 2005. *Contesting Citizenship in Latin America: The Rise of Indigenous Movements and the Postliberal Challenge.* Cambridge: Cambridge University Press.

10

AN AGENDA FOR LATIN AMERICAN "LAW AND DEVELOPMENT"

Pedro Fortes

Beyond Self-Estrangement

Although the death of the "law and development movement" was solemnly proclaimed four decades ago (Trubek and Galanter 1974), this was clearly premature (Tamanaha 1995). The relationship between law and socioeconomic development continues to stimulate various governmental projects, legislative reforms, judicial trainings, and academic debates. Particularly in Latin America, the movement is relevant for the transformation of legal education, professional lawyering, and developmental reforms (Steiner 1971; Tamanaha 1995; Dezalay and Garth 2002; Perez-Perdomo 2006). Innovative law schools were inaugurated in Argentina, Brazil, Chile, Colombia, and Mexico, whose methodologies, materials, and research provided transformative perspectives for Latin America's legal academia (Steiner 2012; Alviar 2014; Vargas 2014). On one hand, the influence of these reforms in legal education was limited and traditional formalism, dogmatism, and doctrinal approaches are still prevalent throughout the region (Alviar 2008). On the other, the success of a legal elite trained according to these innovative pedagogical methods transformed the legal market and professional lawyering (Dezalay and Garth 2002).

Moreover, the insight that law is relevant for the rise of capitalism (Trubek 1972; Weber 1978) also influenced developments in Latin America. The project of social modernization through liberal legalism generated novel models of corporate, constitutional, and criminal law (Galanter 1966; Tamanaha 1995). Additionally, the mid-twentieth century agenda of import substitution industrialization led to protection of local industry, closed markets, and limited participation in international trade in an attempt to overcome the asymmetries of power between Latin American countries and the wealthier nations of the North Atlantic (Tamanaha 1995; Trubek 2006). The collapse of the Soviet Union and the end of the Cold War gave a false impression of the victory of liberalism (Fukuyama 2006), but the promises of liberal legalism and the developmental recipes offered by the Washington Consensus did not produce the expected results across the globe. On the contrary, with limited democracy, weak courts, and rule by law, the Chinese economy experienced impressive growth in the twenty-first century (Kennedy and Stiglitz 2013; Kennedy 2013; Tamanaha 2004). Because attempts to engineer legal transplants from the USA in China had previously failed, some commentators condemned projects of "law and development" as a futile exercise (Kroncke 2015). However, this critique seems disingenuous at best. Law definitely matters – even if legal transplants did not produce the expected results in China or elsewhere.

Instead of abandoning reflection on how to design a normative architecture that may positively influence the social and developmental environment (Galligan 2006), the agenda for Latin American "law and development" requires a rethink. One of the challenges consists in promoting the comprehensive transformation of legal education beyond the few innovative elite law schools, such as Torcuato di Tella (Argentina), Diego Portales (Chile), and Los Andes (Colombia) (Trubek 2012). Another important issue involves the transformation of professional lawyering into an activity connected to socio-legal realities with the potential to positively influence social life (Tamanaha 1997; Twining 2012; Merryman and Perez-Perdomo 2007). Additionally, there is the persistent challenge of institutional strengthening through the development of democracy, rule of law, and constitutional government. Latin America also needs to position itself in the global economy, competing not only with Europe and the USA, but also with China, India, and other emerging economies. What then should be included in the contemporary agenda for "law and development"?

This chapter explores a few possibilities. First, I revisit the project of legal development through the transformation of legal education and professional lawyering. Despite the initial pessimism of some United States-based scholars, Latin America has developed some centers of excellence in legal education and the challenge involves the expansion and democratization of innovative teaching, transformative methodologies, and empirical research beyond these few elite institutions. The potential impact on professional lawyering is significant, but this requires both resources to fund high quality legal education and power to overcome the resistance of traditional scholars. Second, I point to important lessons of law and development regarding the embedded character of formal state law, which is interconnected with a web of social interactions, power dynamics, and economic incentives that influence how the legal architecture may shape the socioeconomic environment in order to favor development. Third, I analyze how institutional quality influences the establishment of a democratic rule of law, emphasizing not only the role of courts and judges, but also of the police, the ombudsmen, and the attorney general's office. Fourth, I discuss the role of law in developing market regulations, property regimes, and industrial policies. Finally, I conclude with a brief comment on conceptions of development, the importance of legal indicators, and the complexity of law and development.

Legal Education and Professional Lawyering

Originally, the law and development movement was an effort to transform Latin American legal education. These initiatives included the "Chilean Law Project" and the "Center for Teaching and Research on Law (CEPED)" initiative in Brazil. In both cases, North American academics trained elite Latin American lawyers (Merryman 2000; Steiner 2012; Trubek 2012). In Chile, the focus was primarily on training law professors, who would eventually have a multiplying effect with their classroom activities, academic writing, and pedagogical methods (Merryman 2000). In Brazil, legal training was provided for hundreds of young law graduates, who became prominent corporate lawyers and developed national commercial legislation (Lacerda 2012; Falcão 2012). This initiative was terminated not because of its failure, but actually due to its complete success – a new generation of elite Brazilian lawyers had already been trained and there was no one else to participate in CEPED (Dezalay and Garth 2002). The proximity between the North American professors and these Latin American lawyers increased their academic exchange and generated a constant flow of lawyers from the Global South pursuing their graduate studies in Harvard, Stanford, and Yale, in turn importing legal ideas into Brazil, Chile, Mexico, and Argentina (Dezalay and Garth 2002; Fortes 2014).

As part of this process of globalization of legal education, a few boutique law schools were opened under the tenets of the elite United States law schools (Dezalay and Garth 2002). The case of Fundação Getúlio Vargas (FGV) Law School is a prodigious example of this trend. The FGV is a Brazilian think-tank founded in the 1940s. Originally, it did not have a law department, but rather focused on economics, management, political science, and international relations. Yet even without a law faculty or an institute for legal research, FGV hosted the CEPED in the 1970s and provided the opportunity of elite training for a generation of Brazilian lawyers (Lacerda 2012; Falcão 2012). In 2002, FGV decided to revive the CEPED experience by opening two new law schools in Rio de Janeiro and São Paulo.

The FGV Law Schools became references in Brazil for innovative teaching, research, and lawyering (Falcão 2012; Vieira, Lima, and Ghirardi 2014). The academic curricula, pedagogical materials, and methodologies are inspired by the United States experience (Unger 2010), but focus on Brazilian legal issues. Professors were trained in Harvard, Stanford, and Yale, experiencing the case method, pursuing empirical legal studies, and adopting the pragmatism, legal realism, and policy-oriented legal reasoning so different from the Latin American legal tradition (Merryman and Perez-Perdomo 2007). On the other hand, reflection, teaching, and research is focused on contemporary Brazilian problems, such as the proceedings of the Brazilian Supreme Court (Falcão 2013), the accountability of judges through the National Council of Justice (Fortes 2015), and the capacity of the criminal justice system to reduce torture and other episodes of police violence (Fortes 2017).

Therefore, legal education is simultaneously global and local (Falcão 2014). Teaching is based on concrete problems and their potential legal solution is discussed with the participation of students. However, observers suggest that the influence of these elite Latin American law schools is marginal and that high costs will prevent the dissemination of this model to other law faculties (Trubek 2012; Dezalay and Garth 2002). Consequently, one important issue on the agenda for Latin American "law and development" is the challenge of providing excellent legal education beyond the elites educated at FGV, Torcuato di Tella, Diego Portales, and Los Andes. High quality education is expensive. Should we expect governments to invest in the democratization of legal education? Or develop a model of private financing with scholarships and subsidized loans for talented students who cannot afford to pay for legal education in their youth? In many Latin American countries, the suggestion that students should cover the expenses of their studies in public universities is a taboo – especially because it involves the reallocation of resources.

In addition to the financial issue, there are also cultural and political dimensions that pose challenges for the transformation of legal education and professional lawyering. The majority of lawyers in the region would need to revise their own conceptual toolboxes, analytical frameworks, and traditional perspectives. Path dependency therefore constitutes a major obstacle for such reforms, especially because the acceptance of new legal knowledge by some traditional Latin American lawyers would probably reduce their power (Prado and Trebilcock 2009; Dezalay and Garth 2002). Established faculties of law in the region tend to criticize more United States-inspired trends as alien, imperialistic, and incompatible with legal science and the civil law tradition. Consequently, students are deprived of forms of legal knowledge that could open their horizons and improve their skills.

Overall, professional lawyering remains predominantly formalistic, dogmatic, and doctrinal. Many lawyers consider their legal activity as primarily an interpretative work of textual exegesis, refusing to reflect on legal problems from an interdisciplinary perspective that considers the economic incentives, policy impact, and social consequences of a particular ruling. Therefore, professional lawyering related to issues of socioeconomic development is often disconnected from social reality. For instance, legislation may prohibit police violence and corruption, but the normative architecture is not realistically designed to shape the socio-legal environment in a way that deters corrupt and violent behavior in practice Hammergren 2019; Dammert 2019. Likewise, the constitutional social rights typical of Latin American constitutionalism are often not implemented and legally enforced because of practical obstacles (Gargarella 2013). In short, legal education influences professional lawyering and this in turn has a considerable impact over institutions and the rule of law.

The Lessons of Law and Society

The initial efforts of the law and development movement suffered from theoretical premises and ideological positions that were unable to offer solutions for all developmental challenges. Modernization through liberal legalism fell prey to the limits of enlightenment, hyperrationalism, and reality checks provided by historical circumstances and social conditions (Prado and Trebilcock 2009; Scott 1998; Horkheimer and Adorno 2002). And dependency theory suffered from the shortsighted and reductionist perspective of Marxist orthodoxy, which denied that law had a relevant role in society and failed to analyze conflict beyond that between labor and capital (Tamanaha 1995; Cotterrell 2003; Collins 1982).

The lessons of law and society perspectives could remedy these failures. First, instead of promising utopian dreams, transcendental ideals, and generalized revolutions, law and development projects should be designed to achieve practical improvements, grounded in concrete problems and pragmatic objectives, and with a focus on incremental reforms. To date, ambitious legal provisions in pursuit of perfection have far outweighed an emphasis on quasi-optimal outcomes. Yet a reading of Latin American constitutions and legislation suggests that many promises simply cannot be delivered.

Law should therefore be understood beyond its conceptual ontology, hermeneutical meaning, and formal validity as a positive source of rules and principles (Hart 2012; Dworkin 1986). In terms of its potential impact on socioeconomic development, we should examine the law as a phenomenon embedded in society (Polanyi 2001; Tamanaha 2011a): law does not exist autonomously as an exclusive product of the legal system (Kelsen 1941; Luhmann 2004). On the contrary, it is a social phenomenon constituted through social interactions, power dynamics, and economic incentives.

Jurists sometimes ignore this interconnectedness of law or consider it to be irrelevant (Tamanaha 2011a; Prado and Trebilcock 2009); however, the institutionalization of law – its capacity to define the rules of the game in a given society – depends precisely on the relationships between its content, on the one hand, and multiple institutional actors on the other. The law is not simply the written text, but also what society makes of it (Twining 2009; Tamanaha 2001). In many cases, relevant stakeholders simply ignore, dismiss, or abandon a law; in others, the law is embraced and implemented. Sometimes the implementation of a law depends on formal organizations that perform the role of enforcement agents – the police, prosecutors, courts, and other state agencies (Galligan 2006), while in others, informal institutions prevail.

Importantly, law on the books is invariably shaped, influenced, or interpreted according to customs, habits, culture, religion, and other sources of informal norms. For instance, contrast the recognition of reproductive rights in Europe and North America with the generalized prohibition of abortion in many Latin American countries (Gargarella 2013). There is little doubt about the influence of religion over the rules of the game. Likewise, consider the extreme violence in areas controlled by drug lords and the informal "law of silence" imposed over potential witnesses by these criminals. Such experiences contradict the suggestion made by adepts of Latin American *garantismo* about the force of state law and instead signal that hyper-liberal criminal procedures have not sufficed to enforce law, protect social goods, and deter criminals (Gargarella 2016).

Likewise, courts are influenced by legal education and the mindset established by traditional practice. For instance, the innovative model of Latin American *Civil Public Action* may produce progressive rulings against corporations for collective wrongdoings (Oquendo 2008; Gomez 2012), but consumers rarely receive individual compensation because of judicial formalism in the execution of these sentences (Barroilhet 2012). Laws should always be examined as a social phenomenon within the context in which they will be applied, interpreted, and implemented (Tamanaha 2011a); the failure or success of legislative reforms is usually attributable to informal social rules that affect law in practice (see for example Daniel Brinks's research pointing to the informal license to kill violent criminal suspects enjoyed by the police in Buenos Aires, São Paulo, and Salvador: Brinks 2006).

An oft-emphasized feature of developed societies is the quality of their institutions. However, institutions can mean many things. For some, institutions mean "organizations" (Trebilcock and Prado 2011, 2014); so the police, attorney general's office, and human rights nongovernmental organizations (NGOs) are examples of institutions. However, others consider that institutions are the "rules of the game" – the normative guidance for behavior that shapes the conduct of social actors through an adequate regime of incentives and sanctions (North 1990). It seems that both semantic meanings are correlated, because organizations are often instruments for the constitution of rules. In numerous instances the emergence of rules depends on organizations that set standards, implement rules, and enforce the law. Without organized means for compliance, rules may simply be inoperative in practice.

One tragic example is provided by police violence in Buenos Aires and São Paulo. In theory, police officers are prohibited from executing criminal suspects. However, in practice, the informal rules of game are different (Brinks 2006). Killings committed by the police are normally not investigated. Although overview and control organizations do exist (the internal affairs and the attorney general's office), public prosecutors normally receive the official communication about killings committed by the police only after considerable time has passed, when it is practically impossible to find witnesses and conduct a proper prosecutorial investigation (Fortes 2006). These cases are usually registered as "killings committed in self-defense" and the police investigation is limited to the testimony of the police officers as the victims of the crime of unlawful resistance (Fortes 2006).

The explanation for this institution of extrajudicial executions is not just limited to the legal culture and an intersubjective belief that authorizes an informal death penalty (Brinks 2006); rather, the absence of an adequate organizational structure within the justice system for overview and accountability of killings committed by the police prevents prosecutors from investigating these cases and courts from convicting violent police officers (Fortes 2006). This is a clear case in which the "rules of the game" are the result not only of a regime of incentives and sanctions, but also of organizational design. Evidence to support this claim comes from an institutional reform in Salvador, Bahia, that not only changed the organization of the justice system, but also the "rules of the game" regarding extrajudicial executions of minors due to the establishment of a new structure within the judiciary and the attorney general's office for control and accountability of these cases (Brinks 2006).

This problem of institutionalized violence is also relevant for setting the agenda for law and development in Latin America, especially with regards to the war on drugs. A first essential focus should be on constitutionalism, rule of law, and democracy. The widespread violence in the region demonstrates that enacting a constitutional text and maintaining regular elections is necessary but insufficient for instituting a democratic rule of law (Prado, Trebilcock, and Hartford 2012). A second essential point is the establishment of regulated markets, especially because of the potential polarization in several Latin American countries between liberals and radicals (Gargarella 2013), which may become a "palace war" between adepts of laissez-faire liberalism and interventionists (Dezalay and Garth 2002). In this dispute of extreme ideological perspectives, it is fundamental to empirically assess how laws, regulations, property, and contract regimes may support economic development. There is simply no silver bullet or benchmark formula for success (Hammergren 2003; Trubek 2013).

Constitutionalism, Rule of Law, and Democracy

The enactment of a constitutional text is the point of departure – not of arrival – for the establishment of a constitutional democracy. In its origins, the idea of constitution was connected to the organization of the political body of a particular society (Galligan 2013), establishing mechanisms of coordination for the organization of power and society in particular ways that generate efficient government (Galligan and Versteeg 2013). Additionally, the republican tradition precludes domination over citizens, guaranteeing that individuals will have opportunities to exercise their power, rights, and freedoms (Pettit 1997, 2012; Skinner 2008). However, the constitutional text is a necessary but insufficient condition for this coordination and protection against domination. The institutionalization of the rules of the game depends on a complex set of social and political practices that leads to effective government of people and lawful regulation of social life. The practice of constitutionalism therefore depends on the gradual implementation of constitutional rules and principles through the development of policies, exercise of powers, and protection of rights. In Latin American constitutional history, these objectives of political coordination and anti-domination suffered considerable obstacles due to a combination of extremely strong executive branches, and highly unequal societies (Gargarella 2013). In this context, the emergence of the judiciary as a political actor in the twenty-first century reduces the concentration of power, especially when courts provide constitutional control over the executive branch. However, judicial review is not necessarily positive for governance or egalitarianism. Courts may affect political governability by considering a program or a particular policy to be unconstitutional. Likewise, judicial decisions often have economic consequences and may lead to unequal redistribution of resources among citizens, in fact preventing the adoption of redistributive policies that could reduce unequal treatment. Therefore, courts may negatively affect constitutional democracy and worsen social equity (Sieder, Schjolden, and Angell 2005). Moreover, because of the potentially negative effects over other citizens who will be denied state protection for analogous legal interests that may be left unprotected, rights-enhancing decisions are not necessarily always positive. On the other hand, judicial intervention may also secure the democratic and inclusive character of a governmental policy. Consequently, as a reviewer of the executive, the role of the judiciary in contemporary Latin America is fundamental – even if we have to analyze concrete cases and may disagree with the content and outcomes of particular judicial decisions.

The concept of the "rule of law" requires the limitation of power by the constitution and legislation. Even if there are multiple variations of this concept (Santos 2006), the common denominator is the limitation of state power (Tamanaha 2004). This idea is different than the use of law to justify governmental action without any constraints or limits over state power – so-called "rule by law" (Tamanaha 2004). Therefore, in contrast to the Bolivarian model that inspired Latin American hyper-presidentialism (Gargarella 2013), the existence of checks and balances over the executive branch is essential for the constitution of a democratic rule of law.

Contemporary Latin American states have developed multiple instances of reciprocal controls for the establishment of democratic institutions. Courts are an important part of this developmental effort and the judiciary received assistance, training, and funding over past decades (Hammergren 2003). However, other institutions are also extremely important. For instance, most individuals have limited contact with courts, but regular interaction with police forces on the streets. Nonetheless, the Latin American police force is often undemocratic, in the sense that police officers operate outside the limits imposed by the "rule of law" (Prado, Trebilcock, and Hartford 2012). Even after political democratization, the police may still be subordinate to the party in government (authoritarian police), protect the interests of organized crime (criminal police), or follow its own internal code of conduct shaped by corporatism and internal interest (autarkic police) – instead of representing the will of the people expressed in the constitution and laws (Prado, Trebilcock, and Hartford 2012).

Likewise, Latin American countries have attributed the power to supervise and control other state actors to some special organs. In addition to the human rights ombudsmen, the model of *defensores del pueblo* was adopted in Argentina, Colombia, Peru, and other countries. Brazil incorporated this supervisory power into the functions of the attorney general's office and public prosecutors have exercised this role of general ombudsmen and defenders of society since the 1980s. The regular interactions of these special bodies with citizens, courts, and the state may have significant impacts on the implementation of laws, the recognition of rights, and the promotion of public policies (McAllister 2008).

Moreover, the effective constitution of the democratic rule of law depends on the active participation of citizens and civil associations. Latin America has experienced several periods of dictatorial governments and totalitarian states within two centuries of constitutionalism (Gargarella 2013). Historically, courts and lawyers often offered little or no resistance to authoritarianism (Perez-Perdomo 2006). This situation changed since the 1970s; for example, the Brazilian bar association was a pivotal actor in the process of redemocratization (Dezalay and Garth 2002). In Venezuela and Peru, individuals and human rights groups have challenged actions taken by very powerful presidents (Perez-Perdomo 2006). In terms of legal architecture, most countries adopted powerful judicial remedies inspired by the Mexican *amparo* and the Brazilian collective action (Oquendo 2008; Gómez 2016). However, the success of these legal measures depends also on a strong civil society capable of defending its democratic institutions (Dahl 1971, 2015).

Finally, the concept of rule of law in most Latin American countries is not just the "thin" conception of formal legality, but rather a "thick" conception that includes a series of positive rights (Tamanaha 2002). Constitutions in the region were innovative in the adoption of social rights (Gargarella 2013), protecting labor, housing, healthcare, and education. Yet for many years, governments rarely implemented social rights and these clauses remained merely aspirational (Gargarella 2013). However, in recent decades, courts have become more active in the adjudication of social rights. Some consider that courts have an important role to play as a catalyst for incremental progress (Young 2012; King 2012), but further empirical research is necessary, especially to investigate the impact of these economic, social, and cultural (ESC) rights on inequality reduction.

Regulated Markets, Protective Regimes, and Industrial Development

The establishment of regulated markets remains an important challenge for Latin American countries. One of the difficulties is ideological. Historically the region has suffered from ideological disputes between extreme views of the economy – state interventionism versus neoclassical liberalism (Dezalay and Garth 2002). Because markets are embedded in society, their functioning is subject to the dynamics, complexities, and failures typical of any social phenomenon (Polanyi 2001). Therefore, well-functioning markets depend on effective regulation and institutional quality. Even if many Latin American countries emulated the United States Independent Regulatory Agencies (IRAs) in their market reforms, there is also no single recipe for success – capture and "revolving doors" are potential pathologies in every regulatory scheme (Ayres and Braithwaite 1991; Makkai and Braithwaite 1992). Likewise, the historical development of antitrust and market regulation incorporated ideas from the North Atlantic, but experienced several local adaptations to the regional political structure (Dezalay and Garth 2002; Palacios 2017; Mendoza 2017).

Capitalism presents itself in various forms. An important variation of capitalism often absent in Latin American debates is the German *Ordoliberalism*, which developed a theory of the social market with a strong role for the state in regulating the economy and pursuit of social justice through prices, taxes, social securities, and pensions. This ordered variation of capitalism led to the German economic miracle, the reconstruction of the country after the Second World War, and the development of a more balanced and fair society. The promises of German social welfare were delivered through a combination of legal reforms, political action, social participation, and economic development. This alternative model is interesting, because Latin America's fundamental development challenge is to overcome inequality.

Some commentators suggest that the region has also developed a variation of capitalism through a "new developmental state" (Trubek, Coutinho, and Shapiro 2013). In their opinion, this model of state activism resulted from the combination of liberal macroeconomic policies combined with state-supported industrial policies, and the expansion of social policy through social protection and anti-poverty programs (Trubek, Coutinho, and Schapiro 2013). Governments expected to support and provide guidance for local industry through a broad range of public-private partnerships financed by the development banks (Rojas 2013; Schapiro 2013). Ambitious cash transfer programs were used not only to reduce economic inequality (Coutinho 2013), but also with populist intentions (Alviar 2013).

At least in Brazil, the initial success of such a formula under the Lula administration evaporated during the government of Dilma Rousseff, culminating with economic recession and the impeachment of the president in 2016. Empirical research is needed to investigate the reasons underlying the failure of the Brazilian Government's developmental strategies, but potential explanations for the negative growth, high unemployment, dismantling of industry, and spike in inequality that were experienced may include a host of factors, among them fiscal indiscipline, regulatory interventionism, anti-competitive measures, limited innovation, insufficient infrastructure, a fall in commodity prices, political corruption, unsustainable public and social policies, unbalanced social pensions, and poor institutional quality. It is important to highlight the interdependence of multiple factors and the fact that "development" does not result from the prophecy of a grand visionary (Elias 1995).

Another idea that has been adopted to try and foster socioeconomic development through law is the establishment of special zones. Argentina, Brazil, Chile, and Peru all established so-called Special Economic Zones with low taxation to promote their industries and international trade. This kind of special legal regime might also include the establishment of charter cities, areas with special legislation designed to overcome political corruption, path dependence, and other obstacles for the development of institutions conducive to socioeconomic development (Romer 2016). In 2011, there was an attempt in Honduras to authorize the creation of these "special development regions," but the project was prematurely discontinued without any possibility of assessing its developmental potential (Miller 2012). At least in theory, charter cities could function as a means to bypass national institutional and legislative deficiencies (Prado 2017). For instance, instead of reforming the entire social security, taxation, and labor regime to reduce costs and become competitive in the global economy, a country could keep its legislation and simply create a charter city with a particular legal system with the aim of fostering socioeconomic development. Likewise, instead of transforming the entire judicial system, a charter system could promote international arbitration or other mechanisms for alternative dispute resolution (ADR).

Property rights are also a central part of the contemporary agenda of law and development. De Soto has argued that informal titles of property in Latin America inhibit economic development because they cannot be used as collateral for bank loans; he recommends recognition of title for informal sector housing as a means to increase their value and their occupants' legal security (De Soto 2000). Nonetheless, commentators recommend caution about predicting the effects of formalization of property rights (Kennedy 2013; Tamanaha 2011b). First, informal mechanisms of exchange of possession already exist in marginalized sectors of cities via non-legal markets (Gómez 2014; Santos 1977). Second, the process of formalization of property rights is not neutral, but has consequences for the allocation of resources and access (Kennedy 2013). It may in fact facilitate the purchase and eventual gentrification of areas currently inhabited by the urban poor (Tamanaha 2011b). Additionally, the titling process may involve gender biases, favoring male heads of household and worsening the position of women (Prado and Trebilcock 2014). Yet although the formalization of property rights may not in fact solve the housing problem in Latin America, the agenda for law and development should definitely investigate potential solutions. Empirical research should also investigate the hypotheses of social rental and subsidized rentals as potential substitutes for mortgages or donation of houses by the state. There are multiple ways of organizing the market and responding to the social demands of capital and labor. The agenda should also include trade agreements and protections for foreign investment, contractual regimes, and arbitration.

Conclusions: Conceptions of Development and Legal Indicators

Traditionally development has been identified with gross domestic product (GDP) growth, but the elimination of poverty, enhancement of freedom, and improvement of quality of life also constitute conceptual elements of socioeconomic development (Trebilcock and Prado 2014). Obviously, growth matters, but it is not a panacea for development, because strong political actors may concentrate the benefits without redistributing them (Easterly 2002). Latin American countries should also develop policies aimed at the empowerment of individuals, improvement of human capabilities, and elimination of practices of domination (Sen 2001). The region still suffers from modern forms of slavery, subemployment, and exploitation of workers. For instance, many agricultural workers still experience conditions of debt servitude. Millions of domestic workers receive very low salaries, sacrificing their own family life in order to guarantee the comfort of the middle and upper classes. Many workers in the region perform tasks that could be undertaken by technology or consumers themselves, indicating a loss of resources and human capital that needs to be empirically mapped. Latin America faces the challenge of reducing inequality and providing opportunities for everyone to live a better life. Progress may be evaluated, measured, and quantified through the contemporary technology of governance – legal indicators (Restrepo 2015). Courts, judges, and procedures are already analyzed through quantitative data and mathematical formulas that assess judicial performance, procedural traffic jams, and duration of cases (Fortes 2015). Legal indicators can evaluate the quality of rule of law through indexes and rankings that provide easily accessible information about perceptions of legal institutions (Urueña 2015). These instruments have a clear political dimension and critics warn of their limitations for capturing more complex conceptions of development (Uribe 2015). Nonetheless, legal metrics have established a mathematical turn in the discourse and practice of law and development, facilitating evidence-based reforms and continuous evaluation of their progress (Restrepo 2017).

Finally, the agenda of law and development experiences constant transformation because of the complexity of social objectives and conflicts. Understandings, together with forms of oppression change over time, and developmental efforts require new action and transformation of the agenda. This chapter has recommended an empirical approach to the mission of transforming Latin America, arguing that the quest for utopia be substituted by the incremental reform of our dystopian societies – extremely violent, highly unequal, and with low human capital. Without a comprehensive transformation of legal education and professional lawyering, the low quality of institutions – organizations and rules of the game – will continue to negatively affect the democratic rule of law, industrial and market regulations, and human development. On the other hand, the interactive dynamics between institutional actors may also become positive (Alviar 2017), generating a normative architecture that stimulates a developmental environment. Development is a complex interactive process with uncertain outcomes. A law and development agenda fit for purpose in twenty-first century Latin America will require continuous action, interaction, and evaluation.

References

Alviar, Helena. 2008. "Classroom and the Clinic: The Relationship between Clinical Legal Education, Economic Development and Social Transformation." *UCLA J. Int'l L. & Foreign Aff.* 13: 197.

Alviar, Helena. 2014. Quando Ideias Viajam: Algumas Reflexões Sobre Globalização do ensino jurídico E A Circulação da Crítica. in Fortes, Pedro (ed.). *Globalização do Ensino Jurídico*. Rio de Janiero: FGV.

Alviar, Helena. 2013. "Social Policy and The New Development State: The Case of Colombia." In David Trubek, Helena Alviar Garcia, Diogo R. Coutinho and Alvaro Santos (eds.), *Law and the New Developmental State: The Brazilian Experience in Latin American Context*. Cambridge: Cambridge University Press.

Alviar, Helena. 2017. "The Evolving Relationship Between Law and Development: Proposing New Tools." In Pedro Fortes, Larissa Borati, Andrés Palacios Lleras, and Tom Gerard Daly (eds.), *Law and Policy in Latin America: Transforming Courts, Institutions, and Rights*. London: Palgrave Macmillan.

Ayres, Ian and John Braithwaite. 1991. "Tripartism: Regulatory Capture and Empowerment." *Law & Social Inquiry* 16(3): 435–96.

Barroilhet, Agustin. 2012. "Class Actions in Chile." *Law & Bus. Rev. Am.* 18: 275.

Brinks, D. 2006. "The rule of (Non) Law." In Gretchen Helmke and Steven Levitsky (eds.), *Informal Institutions and Democracy in Latin America*. Baltimore, Johns Hopkins University Press.

Collins, Hugh. 1982. *Marxism and Law*. Oxford: Oxford University Press.

Cotterrell, Roger B.M. 2003. *The Politics of Jurisprudence: A Critical Introduction to Legal Philosophy*. University of Pennsylvania Press, 2nd edition.

Coutinho, Diogo R. 2013. "Decentralization and Coordination in Social Law and Policy: The Bolsa Família Program." In David Trubek, Helena Alviar Garcia, Diogo R. Coutinho, and Alvaro Santos (eds.), *Law and the New Developmental State: The Brazilian Experience in Latin American Context*. Cambridge: Cambridge University Press.

Dahl, Robert A. 2015. *On Democracy*. New Haven, CT: Yale University Press.

Dahl, Robert Alan. 1973. *Polyarchy: Participation and Opposition*. New Haven, CT: Yale University Press.

Dammert, Lucía. 2019. "Problems of Police Reform in Latin America." In Rachel Sieder, Karina Ansolabehere, and Tatiana Alfonso (eds.), *Routledge Handbook of Law and Society in Latin America*. New York and London: Routledge.

Dezalay, Yves and Bryant G. Garth. 2002. *The Internationalization of Palace Wars: Lawyers, Economists, and the Contest to Transform Latin American States*. Chicago: University of Chicago Press.

Dworkin, Ronald. 1986. *Law's Empire*. Cambridge, MA: Harvard University Press.

Easterly, William. 2001. *The Elusive Quest for Growth: Economists' Adventures and Misadventures in the Tropics.* Cambridge, MA: MIT Press.

Elias, Norbert. 1995. "Technization and Civilization." *Theory, Culture & Society* 12(3): 7–42.

Falcão, Joaquim. 2014. "Ensino Jurídico Local-Global." In Pedro Fortes (ed.). *Globalização do Ensino Jurídico.* Rio de Janiero: FGV.

Falcão, Joaquim (ed.). 2013. *Mensalão: Diário De Um Julgamento: Supremo, Mídia e Opinião Pública.* Rio de Janeiro: FGV.

Falcão, Joaquim. 2012. "Reforma Da Educação Jurídica: Continuidade Sem Continuísmos." En Lacerda, Gabriel, Joaquim Falcão, and Tânia Rangel (eds.). *Aventura e Legado No Ensino Jurídico.* Rio de Janiero: FGV.

Fortes, Pedro. 2006. *O Direito à Vida.* O Globo, Opinião, p. 3–3, 25 maio.

Fortes, Pedro. 2014. "Admirável Mundo Novo Pós-Colonialista: Descolonizando O Ensino Jurídico Global." En Pedro Fortes (ed.). *Globalização do Ensino Jurídico.* Rio de Janiero: FGV.

Fortes, Pedro. 2015. "How Legal Indicators Influence A Justice System and Judicial Behavior: The Brazilian National Council of Justice and 'Justice in Numbers.'" *The Journal of Legal Pluralism and Unofficial Law* 47(1): 39–55.

Fortes, Pedro. 2017. "Human Rights and Remains: A Policy Proposal to Prevent Human Rights Violations in Brazil." In Pedro Fortes, Larissa Borati, Andrés Palacios Lleras, and Tom Gerard Daly (eds.), *Law and Policy in Latin America: Transforming Courts, Institutions, and Rights.* London: Palgrave Macmillan.

Fukuyama, Francis. 2006. *The End of History and the Last Man.* New York: Free Press.

Galanter, Marc. 1996. "The Modernization of Law." In Weiner Myron (ed.) *Modernization: The Dynamics of Growth.* New York and Berkeley: Basic Books: 153–65.

Galligan, Denis. 2006. *Law in Modern Society.* Oxford: Oxford University Press.

Galligan, Denis. 2014. "The People, the Constitution, and the Idea of Representation." In Denis Galligan and Mila Versteeg (eds.), *Social and Political Foundations of Constitutions.* Cambridge: Cambridge University Press.

Galligan, Denis and Mila Versteeg. 2013. "Theoretical Perspectives on the Social and Political Foundations of Constitutions." In Galligan, Denis and Mila Versteeg (eds.). *Social and Political Foundations of Constitutions.* Cambridge: Cambridge University Press: 3.

Gargarella, Roberto. 2013. *Latin American Constitutionalism, 1810–2010: The Engine Room of the Constitution.* Oxford: Oxford University Press.

Gargarella, Roberto. 2016. *Castigar el Prójimo: Por Una Refundación Democrática Del Derecho Penal.* Siglo Veintiuno Editores.

Gil, Diego. 2015. "The Political Economy of Land Use Governance in Santiago, Chile and Its Implications for Class-Based Segregation." *The Urban Lawyer* 47(1).

Gómez, Manuel A. 2012. "Will the Birds Stay South? The Rise of Class Actions and Other Forms of Group Litigation Across Latin America." *The University of Miami Inter-American Law Review* 43(3): 481–521.

Gómez, Manuel A. 2014. "Tower of David: Social Order in a Vertical Community." *FIU L. Rev.* 10: 215.

Gómez, Manuel A. 2016. "Smoke Signals from the South: The Unanticipated Effects of an 'Unsuccessful' Litigation on Brazil's Anti-Tobacco War." In Deborah R. Hensler, Christopher Hodges and Ianika Tzankova (eds.), *Class Actions in Context: How Culture, Economics and Politics Shape Collective Litigation.* Cheltenham and Northampton, MA: Edward Elgar.

Hammergren, Linn. 2003. "International Assistance to Latin American Justice Programs: Toward an Agenda for Reforming the Reformers." In Erik Jensen and Thomas Heller (eds.), *Beyond Common Knowledge: Empirical Approaches to the Rule of Law.* Cambridge: Cambridge Univeristy Press.

Hammergren, Linn. 2019. "New Influences on Legality and Justice in Latin America: Corruption and Organised Crime." In Rachel Sieder, Karina Ansolabehere and Tatiana Alfonso (eds.), *Routledge Handbook of Law and Society in Latin America.* New York and London: Routledge.

Hart, Herbert Lionel Adolphus. 2012. *The Concept of Law.* Third edition. Oxford: Oxford University Press.

Horkheimer, Max and Theodor W. Adorno. 2002. *Dialectic of Enlightenment: Philosophical Fragments.* Standford, CA: Stanford University Press.

Kelsen, Hans. 1941. "The Pure Theory of Law and Analytical Jurisprudence." *Harvard Law Review* 55(1): 44–70.

Kennedy, David. 2013. "Some Caution about Property Rights as a Recipe for Economic Development." In Kennedy, David and Joseph E. Stiglitz, (eds.), *Law and Economics with Chinese Characteristics: Institutions for Promoting Development in the Twenty-First Century*. Oxford: Oxford University Press.

Kennedy, David and Joseph E. Stiglitz. 2013. "Introduction." In Kennedy, David and Joseph E. Stiglitz, (eds.), *Law and Economics with Chinese Characteristics: Institutions for Promoting Development in the Twenty-First Century*. Oxford: Oxford Universtiy Press.

King, Jeff. 2012. *Judging Social Rights*. Cambridge: Cambridge University Press.

Kroncke, Jedidiah J. 2015. *The Futility of Law and Development: China and the Dangers of Exporting American Law*. Oxford: Oxford University Press.

Lacerda, Gabriel. 2012. "CEPED – Um Debate Que Dura Há Quase Meio Século." En Lacerda, Gabriel, Joaquim Falcão, and Tânia Rangel (eds.), *Aventura e Legado No Ensino Jurídico*. Rio de Janiero: FGV.

Langston, Joy. 2006. "The Birth and Transformation of the Dedazo in Mexico." In Gretchen Helmke and Steven Levitsky (eds.), *Informal Institutions and Democracy: Lessons from Latin America*. Baltimore, MA: John Hopkins University Press: 143–59.

Luhmann, Niklas. 2004. *Law as a Social System*. Oxford: Oxford University Press.

Makkai, Toni and John Braithwaite. 1992. "In and Out of the Revolving Door: Making Sense of Regulatory Capture." *Journal of Public Policy* 12(1): 61–78.

McAllister, Lesley. 2008. *Making Law Matter: Environmental Protection and Legal Institutions in Brazil*. Standford, CA: Stanford University Press.

Mendoza, Jose Miguel. 2017. "Convergence, Coordination and Collusion in Securities Regulation: The Latin American Integrated Market." In Pedro Fortes, Larissa Borati, Andrés Palacios Lleras, and Tom Gerard Daly (eds.), *Law and Policy in Latin America: Transforming Courts, Institutions, and Rights*. London: Palgrave Macmillan.

Merryman, John Henry. 2000. "Law and Development Memoirs I: The Chile Law Program." *The American Journal of Comparative Law* 48(3): 481–99.

Merryman, John Henry and Rogelio Pérez-Perdomo. 2007. *The Civil Law Tradition: An Introduction to the Legal Systems of Europe and Latin America*. Standford, CA: Stanford University Press.

Miller, Michael Castle. 2012. "The Governance Market: A New Vision for Paul Romer's Charter Cities Concept." Available at: *SSRN 2458669*.

North, Douglass, C. 1990. *Institutions, Institutional Change and Economic Performance*. Cambridge: Cambridge University Press.

Oquendo, Angel R. 2008. "Upping the Ante: Collective Litigation in Latin America." *Colum. J. Transnat'l L* 47: 248.

Palacios, Andres. 2017. "A Counterhistory of Anti-Trust in Latin America." In Pedro Fortes, Larissa Borati, Andrés Palacios Lleras, and Tom Gerard Daly (eds.), *Law and Policy in Latin America: Transforming Courts, Institutions, and Rights*. London: Palgrave Macmillan.

Pérez-Perdomo, Rogelio. 2006. "Rule of Law and Lawyers in Latin America." *The ANNALS of the American Academy of Political and Social Science* 603(1): 179–91.

Pettit, Philip. 2012. *On the People's Terms: A Republican Theory and Model of Democracy*. Cambridge: Cambridge University Press.

Pettit, Philip. 1997. *Republicanism: A Theory of Freedom and Government*. Oxford: Oxford University Press.

Polanyi, Karl. 2001. *The Great Transformation: The Political and Economic Origin of Our Time*. Second edition. Boston, MA: Beacon Press.

Prado, Mariana. 2017. "Institutional Bypasses in Brazil: Overcoming Ex-Ante Resistance to Institutional Reforms." In Pedro Fortes, Larissa Borati, Andrés Palacios Lleras, and Tom Gerard Daly (eds.), *Law and Policy in Latin America: Transforming Courts, Institutions, and Rights*. London: Palgrave Macmillan.

Prado, Mariana and Michael Trebilcock. 2009. "Path Dependence, Development, and the Dynamics of Institutional Reform." *University of Toronto Law Journal* 59(3): 341–80.

Prado, Mariana Mota, Michael Trebilcock, and Patrick Hartford. 2012. "Police Reform in Violent Democracies in Latin America." *Hague Journal on the Rule of Law* 4(2): 252–85.

Restrepo, David. 2015. "Legal Indicators, Global Law and Legal Pluralism: An Introduction." *The Journal of Legal Pluralism and Unofficial Law* 47(1): 9–21.

Restrepo, David. 2017. "Transnational Legal Indicators: The Missing Link in an Era of Law and Development." In Pedro Fortes, Larissa Borati, Andrés Palacios Lleras, and Tom Gerard Daly (eds.), *Law and Policy in Latin America: Transforming Courts, Institutions, and Rights*. London: Palgrave Macmillan.

Rojas, Shunko. 2013. "Understanding Neo-Developmentalism in Latin America: New Industrial Policies in Brazil and Colombia." In David Trubek, Helena Alviar Garcia, Diogo R. Coutinho and Alvaro Santos (eds.), *Law and the New Developmental State: The Brazilian Experience in Latin American Context*.

Romer, Paul. 2016. *Charter Cities: New Cities, More Choices, Better Rules*. Available at: https://paulromer.net/charter-cities-new-cities-more-choices-better-rules/. Accessed November 20, 2016.

Santos, Alvaro. 2006. "The World Bank's Uses of the 'Rule of Law' Promise in Economic Development." In David and Alvaro Santos (eds.) *The New Law and Economic Development: A Critical Appraisal*. Cambridge: Cambridge University Press.

Santos, Boaventura. 1977. "The Law of the Oppressed: The Construction and Reproduction of Legality in Pasargada." *Law and Society Review* 5–126.

Scott, James C. 1998. *Seeing Like a State: How Certain Schemes to Improve the Human Condition have Failed*. New Haven, CT: Yale University Press.

Schapiro, Mario. 2013. Rediscovering the Developmental Path? Development Bank, Law, and Innovation Financing in the Brazilian Economy. In David Trubek, Helena Alviar Garcia, Diogo R. Coutinho, and Alvaro Santos (eds.), *Law and the New Developmental State: The Brazilian Experience in Latin American Context*. Cambridge: Cambridge University Press.

Sen, Amartya. 2001. *Development as Freedom*. Oxford: Oxford University Press.

Sieder, Rachel, Line Schjolden, and Alan Angell (eds). 2005. *The Judicialization of Politics in Latin America*. New York: Palgrave Macmillan.

Skinner, Quentin. 2008. *Hobbes and Republican Liberty*. Cambridge: Cambridge University Press.

Steiner, Henry J. 2012. "Meio Século Depois: Um Olhar sobre Mudanças na Educação Jurídica Brasileira e Americana." In Lacerda, Gabriel, Joaquim Falcão, and Tânia Rangel (eds.), *Aventura e Legado No Ensino Jurídico*. Rio de Janiero: FGV.

Steiner, Henry J. 1971. "Legal Education and Socio-Economic Change: Brazilian Perspectives." *The American Journal of Comparative Law* 39–90.

Tamanaha, Brian Z. 1995. "The Lessons of Law-and-Development Studies." *American Journal of International Law*: 470–86.

Tamanaha, Brian Z. 1997. *Realistic Socio-Legal Theory: Pragmatism and a Social Theory of Law*. Oxford: Oxford University Press.

Tamanaha, Brian Z. 2001. *A General Jurisprudence of Law and Society*. Oxford: Oxford University Press.

Tamanaha, Brian Z. 2004. *On the Rule of Law: History, Politics, Theory*. Cambridge: Cambridge University Press.

Tamanaha, Brian Z. 2011a. Primacy of Society and the Failures of Law and Development." *Cornell Int'l LJ* 44: 209.

Tamanaha, Brian Z. 2011b. "The Rule of Law and Legal Pluralism in Development." *Hague Journal on the Rule of Law* 3(1): 1–17.

Trebilcock, Michael J. and Mariana Mota Prado. 2011. *What Makes Poor Countries poor? Institutional Determinants of Development*. Cheltenham: Edward Elgar Publishing.

Trebilcock, Michael J. and Mariana Mota Prado. 2014. *Advanced Introduction to Law and Development*. Chelthenham: Edward Elgar Publishing.

Trubek, David M. 1972. "Max Weber on Law and the Rise of Capitalism." *Wis. L. Rev.* 720.

Trubek, David M. 1972. "Toward a Social Theory of Law: An Essay on the Study of Law and Development." *The Yale Law Journal* 82(1): 1–50.

Trubek, David M. 2012. "Reabrindo o Arquivo do CEPED: O Que Podemos Aprender De Um 'Caso do Arquivo Morto?'" En Lacerda, Gabriel, Joaquim Falcão, and Tânia Rangel (eds.), *Aventura e Legado No Ensino Jurídico*. Rio de Janiero: FGV.

Trubek, David M. 2013. "Law, State, and the New Developmentalism: An Introduction." In David Trubek, Helena Alviar Garcia, Diogo R. Coutinho, and Alvaro Santos (eds.), *Law and the New Developmental State: The Brazilian Experience in Latin American Context*. Cambridge: Cambridge University Press.

Trubek, David. 2006. "The 'Rule of Law' in Development Assistance: Past, Present, and Future." In David Trubek and Alvaro Santos (eds.), *The New Law and Economic Development: A Critical Appraisal*. Cambridge: Cambridge University Press.

Trubek, David M., Diogo R. Coutinho, and Mario G. Schapiro. 2013. "New State Activism in Brazil and the Challenge for Law." In David Trubek, Helena Alviar Garcia, Diogo R. Coutinho and Alvaro Santos (eds.), *Law and the New Developmental State: The Brazilian Experience in Latin American Context*. Cambridge: Cambridge University Press.

Trubek, David M. and Marc Galanter. 1974. Scholars in self-estrangement: some reflections on the crisis in law and development studies in the United States. *Wis. L. Rev.*: 1062.

Twining, William. 2009. *General Jurisprudence: Understanding Law from a Global Perspective*. Cambridge: Cambridge University Press.

Twining, William. 2012. *Karl Llewellyn and the Realist Movement*. Cambridge: Cambridge University Press.

Unger, Roberto. 2010. "Uma Nova Faculdade De Direito No Brasil." In Caio Farah Rodriguez and Joaquim Falcão (eds.), *O Projeto da Escola de Direito Rio da FGV*. Rio de Janeiro: FGV.

Uribe, María Angélica Prada. 2015. "The Quest for Measuring Development." In Sally Engle Merry, Kevin E. Davis, and Benedict Kingsbury (eds.), *The Quiet Power of Indicators: Measuring Governance, Corruption, and Rule of Law*. Cambridge: Cambridge University Press.

Urueña, René. 2015. "Indicators and the Law: A Case Study of the Rule of Law Index." In Sally Engle Merry, Kevin E. Davis, and Benedict Kingsbury (eds.), *The Quiet Power of Indicators. Measuring Governance, Corruption, and the Rule of Law*. Cambridge: Cambridge University Press.

Vargas, Daniel. 2014. Jurista Criativo. In Fortes, Pedro (ed.). *Globalização do Ensino Jurídico*. Rio de Janeiro: FGV.

Vieira, Oscar Vilhena, Maria Lúcia L.M. Pádua Lima e José Garcez Ghirardi. 2014. "Ensino do Direito para um Mundo em Transformação: A Experiência da FGV Direito SP." In Fortes, Pedro (ed.). *Globalização do Ensino Jurídico*. Rio de Janeiro: FGV.

Weber, Max. 1978. *Economy and Society: An Outline of Interpretive Sociology*. California: University of California Press.

Young, Katharine G. 2012. *Constituting Economic and Social Rights*. Oxford: Oxford University Press.

11

MARXIST PERSPECTIVES ON LAW AND THE STATE IN LATIN AMERICA

Carlos Rivera Lugo

What are we dealing with when we speak of the relationship between law and the struggle against inequality in Latin America? In order to understand the fundamental reason behind this pervasive and pernicious condition, it is imperative that we focus on one of its most decisive structuring relationships: that between the state, capital, and law, in its concrete historicity and, particularly, from Marxist perspectives.

Marxism has been undoubtedly the foremost strategic deconstruction of the capitalist grand-narrative. According to the distinguished Argentinean-Mexican legal scholar Oscar Correas (1943), Marxism, as a theoretical corpus, is "the major and best attempt made by human intelligence for explaining how capitalism functions and how it can be displaced in order to establish a society founded on the community" (Ferreir, 2011, 34). In the same line, the Swiss sociologist Razmig Keucheyan (1975) proposes the hypothesis that historically Marxism has proven to be unsurpassed as a theory of capitalism, its expansive logics of exploitation and accumulation, and, more importantly, its innate tendency toward crisis, such as the one in which the capitalist world economy has been staggering through since 2008. Said author understands the present crisis to be of an organic nature, thus affecting the system in its totality. However, non-Marxist or so-called post-Marxist perspectives have proven to be quite silent or deficient in explaining its root cause and the historical need to develop alternative modes of collective existence in light of the capitalist world economy's insurmountable contradictions (Keucheyan 2016, 51).

Once again we are confronted with the inescapable fact that the capitalist system has shown that it is not willing to reconcile different class interests. Its ultimate objective is not the general well-being of society. It is an antagonistic system that exists for the main purpose of securing the particular interests of the capitalist class through its permanent and expansive enrichment. This explains why it is characterized by recurrent cyclical crisis. Inequality and, therefore, crisis are inherent to the capitalist system. Presently we are talking about a crisis of overaccumulation, monopolization, and concentration as the result of a structural negation of any possibility of conciliation between capital and labor. This produces a vicious cycle of capital accumulation under which overexploitation of labor by capital and its ensuing inequality is its cornerstone. In this chapter, I trace the various Marxist approaches to the law and the state and identify how Latin American scholarship has appropriated them and produced novel understandings that are promising for a Marxist socio-legal agenda. In particular,

I focus my attention in the so-called New Latin American Constitutionalism and its recognition of communal forms of organization as the clearest example of a legal or normative communism.

The Two Faces of the Present Crisis

The prominent Italian political economist and sociologist Giovanni Arrighi (1937–2009) sustains that since 2008 we are witnessing a "terminal crisis" of the capitalist system due to the increasing exhaustion of possibilities for restructuring under what he defines as the present descending phase of the most recent systemic cycle of capitalist accumulation inaugurated in 1945, after the end of the Second World War, under the hegemony of the United States of America. Building on Marx's theory regarding the cyclical crisis that is inherent to capitalism due to the antagonistic contradictions of its social processes of production, exchange, and accumulation, Arrighi sustains that since its inception capitalism has experienced a series of systemic cycles characterized by phases of expansion, stagnation, and decline. Accordingly, what characterizes the current autumn of capitalism, under neoliberalism, is that it has returned to its previous logic of accumulation of the late nineteenth century and early twentieth century, another highly turbulent and descending phase of the previous systemic cycle of accumulation, based on the idea that its objectives can only be obtained through the increasing exploitation and dispossession of workers, as also the violent repression of its struggles (Arrighi 2010, 371–86). This attempt to suppress capitalism's inherently antagonistic social contradiction between capital and labor has increased structural asymmetries, social polarization, antagonisms, and inequality throughout the planet, particularly in Latin America.

The resulting structural turbulence that we are now witnessing throughout the capitalist world as a result of the logics and effects of the present stage of capitalist globalization under neoliberalism (Laval and Dardot 2013) is an expression of said "terminal crisis." In the best-case scenario, this poses a unique opportunity for radical systemic change. In the worst-case scenario, it could conclude in an increasing systemic gridlock or chaos, including the permanent presence of violent conflicts, both social and international. Wolfgang Streek (1946), Emeritus Director of the prestigious Max Plank Institute for Social Research, proposes that the latter scenario may result in a lasting *interregno*, a period of indeterminacy and disorder resulting from the lack of a collective agent of structural change in the midst of a system wrought with a structural crisis characterized by an apparently insurmountable dialectic of inequality, stagnation, and debt (Streek 2016, 12–18). In light of this, it would not be far-reaching to propose that behind the counterrevolutionary, autocratic, or neofascist trends that we are presently witnessing in various parts of the world as, for example, in the United States and Europe, there is usually a lost or failed anti-systemic or revolutionary opportunity, as Walter Benjamin (1892–1940) of the Frankfurt School affirmed.

In this regard, one of the main problems of legal and social theory since the end of the twentieth century has been a kind of reformist institutionalized critique based on the struggle for a more broader democracy from within the framework of the present bourgeois state and legal forms. This strand of critical thought assesses the present crisis of capitalism, under neoliberalism, as a condition that can be overcome by gradual reforms of a regulatory nature, under the illusion that a reaffirmation or return to the Keynesian social or welfare state is still possible. The idea of systemic or revolutionary change of a transcapitalist nature is discarded or, what is worse, not even seriously considered. However, what is needed is precisely a more profound strategic critique that focuses on the main contradictions of the present capitalist political economy (Mascaro 2016, 1–2). In that sense, we are in the midst of a *crisis within the crisis* that has to do with the crisis of the idea of revolution, that is, of the need and the concrete possibility of the construction of another social and world order that takes humankind beyond capitalism.

The present neoliberal political economy, in which inequality is foundational for capital reproduction and accumulation, has become the new *raison d'état* and its principal material source of normative prescription. Capital, in its present stage of development, has embarked on a real colonization of means and forces of production, including those it previously ignored or merely appropriated marginally in our region. However, more importantly, the continuous expansion of capital has required it to finally become the state, as the influential French historian Fernando Braudel (1902–1985) anticipated (Braudel 1977, 92). The law is equally implicated in this process of real and total subsumption under capital's logics of reproduction. This is why Marx's conviction that only through our understanding of the political economy can we comprehend both the nature of the legal form and its changes under capitalism, holds a particular significance in the present situation.

In this sense, it once again becomes evident that the political economy is the normative matrix of capitalist society. It is in this strategic context that we need to approach our understanding of the correlative changes experienced by the historically specific rule of law in Latin America, particularly its relation to social and economic exclusion; the criminalization of those who protest, which includes the use of torture, disappearances, officially sanctioned assassinations, and extrajudicial executions; the effective immunity of the powerful or privileged; the class and racial bias of present penal policies and practices; or its general insensitivity to the exploitative and oppressive conditions under which too many in society are forced to work and live in. However, it also includes the valuation of those new developments in favor of an alternative and counter-hegemonic mode that promotes social, economic, and political inclusion in the region. Such is the case with the *New Latin American Constitutionalism* in countries such as Venezuela, Ecuador, and Bolivia, where there has been a conscious attempt to revitalize and relegitimize the rule of law. Another example is the constitutive normative force of autonomous societal and communal actions as, for example, in Mexico that goes beyond the inherent limitations of a liberal capitalist legality.

The Gordian Knot of the Transition to a New Society

Before we continue, it is imperative that we clarify that by Marxist perspectives we are referring to the plurality of understandings of Marxism that have prevailed since its inception, not only in Latin America, but throughout the world. For if there can be no future without Marx, as sentenced by the well-known French Deconstructionist and Postmodern philosopher Jacques Derrida (1930–2004), we must be aware of the fact that we are referring to a certain Marx whose thought has transcended its own specific authorship and concrete historicity (Derrida 1994, 13). As such we are forced to recognize as Marxist all those perspectives that in one way or another recognize the impossibility of approaching any kind of socio-historical critique of the present capitalist society and world economy, including the subjects of law and inequality, without referring directly or indirectly to Marx's specific theoretical propositions and categories, as also those developed by others in the subsequent and continuous development of Marxist thought (Sánchez Vázquez 1998, 11). We also include those theoretical horizons that contribute to the enrichment of critical theory and, although generally considered non-Marxist, are nevertheless, recognizably influenced by Marxist thought. This is the case, for example, of the French philosopher Michel Foucault (1926–1984) and his paradigmatic discourse on the subject and power relations, as also his strategic perspective of the law and governmentality in the present under neoliberalism, all considered major contributions to contemporary critical theory.

Marxist thought has thus been de facto the result of a constellation of diverse sources and arenas, which has also included academia and research centers not directly connected to specific political and social organizations or movements and their practices, but more broadly associated with the historical anticapitalist proposition of socialism or communism. In the specific case of Latin America, present Marxist thought has also been the result of what many times has been a dissenting, decolonizing, and creative endeavor toward its enrichment and development beyond its European origins, thus reflecting a desire for a more authentic perspective duly inscribed in its own historical context and conditions (Bosteels 2013; Lowy 1992).

However, more specifically there is a major discussion on which we should delve due to its centrality for the present chapter. It revolves around the specific nature and function of the law and the state as historically particular modes of social regulation, structuring, and political-economic governance. More precisely, it deals with the question of articulating the theoretical and practical framework necessary to effectively encounter the transitioning process from capitalism to communism as a new transcapitalist communal mode of social production and relations, governance, and regulation. It also entails confronting what has been labeled as the pervasive fetishism of the state and legal forms that has historically limited the horizons of any real or substantive possibilities of systemic or civilizational change under past historical socialist experiences. The problematic character of the transition to a new society has been the Gordian knot that Marxism has been unable to untangle insofar as it has not been capable of breaking away from the normative framework of the capitalist world economy. Thus, there is a dire need for the development of a theory of its social constitutive process that finally breaks with bourgeois legal discourse, including its language, categories, practices, and institutions.

One of the main difficulties confronted for the development of an alternative Marxist theory of the constitutive process of norm prescription, social regulation, and structuring has been the fact that the prevailing Marxist perspective of the law has been an instrumental understanding in which the law, as well as the state, ultimately serve the interests of the ruling class in society. Accordingly, under capitalism, they essentially represent the political and normative framework of a dictatorship of the dominant class dedicated to furthering its class interests. Nevertheless, as an instrument, they are not without their contradictions, which allegedly explain their relative autonomy from its infrastructural base: the capitalist economy. This creates the possibility of their use by the working class and other subaltern social groups, thus exploiting to their advantage their political and juridical contradictions in order to pave the way for a gradual systemic transformation.

One of the most important contributors to this particular view of the law was initially the soviet jurist Andrey Vichinsky (1883–1954), the most important intellectual influence on the Stalinist conception of the state and the law. As Stalin's attorney general and major legal theorist, his would be the dominant perspective on the subject throughout most of the communist movement and the so-called concrete historical experiences of *real socialism* in the twentieth century in different parts of the world. Thus, if the state and the law are basically instruments in the service of class domination, the same could be said in the case of the coming to power of the proletariat. It could be used in favor of its own dictatorship over the bourgeois class. Even bourgeois private property would cease to exist once it is legally transferred into the hands of the "Proletarian State," as if transfigured magically by the legal form. In this sense, law is reduced to state-centric norms, rules, and procedures of a transcendent nature, that is, external to the individual, or community. Its strict compliance is guaranteed, if need be, by coercive means. This perspective represented the abandonment of the initial ideal of the Bolsheviks in favor of the immediate abolishment of the bourgeois state and legal power and its substitution with immanent constitutive social processes, that is, self-determined processes of normative prescription and structuring in the hands of the soviets, in which considerations of justice would be paramount over the law and its formalities. The Marxian proposition in favor of the "withering away of the State and the Law" was to be the result of the immediate construction of a soviet system of self-governance, something that was abandoned under Stalinism and so-called *real socialism*.

Marxism's *Normativity of the Real*

Marxian thought regarding the law is nevertheless much richer and complex. In a series of five articles published in 1842 in the *Rheinische Zeitung*, on a legal controversy at the time regarding the appropriation of wood from the forests by the poor, a young Marx inquires as to how liberal private law supplanted a universal customary law during capitalism's primitive accumulation in Europe. He was referring to a societal customary normativity not only limited to the customary laws of the privileged elites but also the customary norms of those who have no other patrimony and thus no other law but their own customs. Liberal positive law thus constitutes a unilateral and exclusionary recognition of the customary norms of the privileged elites, in particular the ascending bourgeoisie, and the existing relations of domination. For Marx, modern law is nothing more than the customs of property owners and their private interests, which are codified as law and guaranteed by the state, therefore ceasing to be considered mere customs like the rest of the existing customary norms of society. In contrast, Marx refers to the customary normativity of the poor as invisibilized in terms of its own positivity and rationality, although it is this normativity that rightly has a claim to be considered a universal law. In any case, it is the customs of the rich that should be illegalized and not the customs and actions of the dispossessed. A selfish individualist economic calculus prevails as law over the common good, marginalizing in the process a significant portion of society from the material possibilities of guaranteeing its own existence. (Marx and Bensaid 2015; Laval and Dardot 2015, 367–414; Roux 2009). Marx's view reflects an initial search for a common societal normative foundation that is independent of bourgeois positive law, an approach that is particularly relevant in the present with regard to the current reassessment of the normative force of community usages and customs in Latin America as part of an historically alternative mode of social structuring and regulation. The denial of the binding force of this societal and communal normativity leads to the state and market-centric despotic legal exceptionalism that we are presently living under. It is therefore imperative that we recover this immanent normativity of which society and the community has been dispossessed.

Marx later proposed that the focal point of a radical conception of the state and the law be the concrete human being and its material reality. It is in this material context, with its concrete social and power relations, that we have the basis for any possibility of radical change. He insists that the only way to overcome any type of oppression is overcoming every form of servitude in general, especially bourgeois private property. Although he comprehended that his total critique of capitalist society could not be reduced to the economy, nonetheless, Marx understood that his critique of political economy, its concepts and categories, also served to reveal the reality behind both the political and the juridical (Holloway and Picciotto 1978, 17–18; Bonnet, Holloway, and Tischler 2006, 46).

In the context of his major writings on the political economy of capital, Marx expresses his understanding that only through our appraisal of the contradictions that are produced in the economic base of society can we grasp the nature and the constant changes concretely experienced under the political and legal forms, as also their historical possibilities or limitations. We should cease to depend on fictions and appearances and finally realize that the specific contents and applications of the political and the legal in capitalist society are the result of power relations. Thus, normativity cannot be founded on an idea, but in reality itself, strategically contextualized. Marx proposes a *normativity of the real* that necessarily constitutes the permanent overcoming of the bourgeois legal form. In particular, it is through a comprehensive grasp of the dialectics between economic relations and legal relations, that we can witness the so-called laws of the capitalist market display an exceptional and dominating constitutive force that determines the horizon of bourgeois law, under which efficacy ultimately constitutes the criteria for legitimacy. The political economy of capital, in particular its intrinsic social relations based on the value form, constitutes the material source of the bourgeois state and its law, as also its *raison d'être*. From Marx's dialectical perspective, form and substance are inseparable. Form structures empirical reality.

The Bolshevist legal scholar Eugeny Pashukanis (1891–1937) followed in Marx's footsteps. His critical theory of the revolutionary imperative to go beyond the existing classist and coercive legal form would prove to be a paradigmatic contribution. It stood in stark contrast to Vichinsky's revisionist or reductionist conception. Pashukanis asserts that the legal form essentially legalizes, through a series of coercive mechanisms, the commodity form as its normative matrix, including its mode of valuation of commodities and their exchange in the capitalist market. This has constitutive effects for the creation of a subordinate subjectivity that is a direct expression of historically concrete social relations, more specifically, as relations between subjects engaged in the production and exchange of commodities, including labor, under the capitalist mode of production.

Rules and norms are derived from specific social relations and practices. As Pashukanis would correctly state: in material reality a specific social relation and its facticity will always prevail over the abstract norm and its concrete content and application. That is why Marx was correct in saying that "between equal rights, force decides" (1990, 344). The rationale of the commodity form is essentially responsible for the structuring of the legal form, in terms of its ordering function as well as its mediating function with regard to the conflicts inside capitalist society.

Pashukanis also warned of the inescapable fact that the social relations entailed in the process of commodity production and exchange, together with their normative underpinnings, as represented by the state and legal forms, are essentially the foundation of both liberalism and capitalism in general. The continuing presence of these during the transition period from capitalism to communism would transmit also their major contradictions. This would prove to be fatal, since their structuring and regulative effects impinges everyday life at all levels, as well as constituting an alienated subjectivity. The legal form cannot disembrace itself from its hierarchical and adversarial normative matrix that demands strict compliance and obedience. Pashukanis reaffirmed Marx's proposition on the historical need for the eventual extinction of the legal form as the dominant mode of social regulation, and its replacement with a new non-legal mode based on the self-determination of the working people, under the communal or communist form (Pashukanis 1976; Freitas and Feitosa 2012, 205–25; Mascaro 2012, 466–78; Rivera Lugo and Correas 2013, 128–38; Rivera Lugo 2014, 164–70). Of course, his ideas ran contrary to the prevailing Stalinist instrumental conception of the state and the law, a fact that would eventually lead to his purge as the Bolsheviks' most creative and critical legal scholar. However, it is important that we underline that his seminal theoretical contributions have proven to be particularly influential among many contemporary Marxist jurists in Latin America and elsewhere.

For example, the contributors to what has been labeled the *Marxist State Derivative Debate* (Holloway and Picciotto 1978; Hirsch 2010; Caldas 2015) tend to coincide with Pashukanis in that they also derive the state and legal forms from the specific character of capitalist social relations of production, exchange, and accumulation. According to the Brazilian jurist Camilo Onoda Caldas, the theoretical proposition that derives the law from the capitalist political economy and its inherent socioeconomic relations "rejects the idea that the Law, as also the State, are simply neutral instruments – that can be used for any purpose – managed freely by the political decisions of those who occupy certain positions inside the state apparatus." This means that mere changes or reforms "do not result in a destructuring of the capitalist mode of production and its common socioeconomic consequences, including in the political and legal spheres" (Caldas 2015, 255–56). However, the distinguished Brazilian legal scholar Alysson Leandro Mascaro alerts to the need of avoiding any oversimplification of the relation between the law and the economy. As a socioeconomic form, the law is not totally identical to the economic logics and processes it helps to structure. Thus, it is vital to understand that the legal form has its nuances that must be identified and taken into account (Mascaro 2013).

On Law's Apparent Relative Autonomy

Another valuable Marxist perspective of law is George Lukács' *ontological critique of the Law* (Sartori 2010). Also following in Marx's line of thought from an unorthodox and critical perspective, the Hungarian philosopher (1885–1971) was most probably the preeminent Marxist thinker outside of the Soviet Union in times of Stalin. Lukács recognizes the articulations between the law and socioeconomic facticity: "The Law is a specific form of reflection and reproduction in the conscience of that which actually happens in economic life." The law is not in itself an effective and total instrument for the solution of every conflict in society. For this reason the law requires its interiorization by the members of society. Bourgeois legality thus, has a double character: a reified abstraction that promotes the illusion of law's autonomy and a manipulative prescription ontologically dependent on the concrete and extra-legal reality of the political economy. The law depends on this social process that imposes a concrete form of sociality. Legal relations are therefore, the product of the material reproduction of the total social complex and, as such, are imbued by specific class interests and contradictions.

For Lukács, the idea of the law as the principal mode of social regulation is a manifestation of a reductionist legal fetish. The law in its dual reflective and manipulative functions only serves to reduce social regulation to the defense of hegemonic class interests. Therefore, once these limitations of the present mode of social regulation are overcome, there arises the concrete possibility, in a society of equals, of the extinction of the legal sphere as dominant mode of social regulation (Sartori 2010; Fortes 2014).

A quite different version of the relative autonomy of the state and law with regard to the economy was the structuralist perspective of the Greek Marxist and political sociologist, Nicos Poulantzas (1936–1979), whom together with the reformist vision of the renowned German social theorist, Jürgen Habermas (1929), share the idea of a prioritization of the political and the juridical, as also the class structure and relations, in abstraction of a more complete understanding of the complex articulations of these with the political economy. Their emphasis tends to promote the previously mentioned false illusion as to the historical possibilities of gradual systemic change under the so-called social or welfare state and the alleged opportunities offered by its liberal representative democracy.

Of course, as to the historical possibilities of change under the bourgeois rule of law, the British Marxist historian E.P. Thompson (1924–1993) warned that Marxists should avoid any structural reductionism. Beginning with the constitution and the orderly solution of conflicts, the rule of law constitutes a universal historical accomplishment, he emphasized. It represents a set of limitations on the exercise of naked power. For Thompson, whose view was to be highly regarded in Marxist circles, what originally emerged as an instrument in favor of the bourgeois class, imbued within the very basis of capitalist relations of production, also represents an instrument against the arbitrary acts of de facto powers. It serves to mediate existent class relations and, thus, constitutes a battleground between the existing plurality of class interests. Thompson admonishes that for the rule of law to be effective and recognized as legitimate by all members of society, its ideological rhetoric cannot be empty nor can its dominant class objectives be transparent. It must at least appear to be independent of the social, political, economic context. Of course, he recognizes that in a society characterized by flagrant class inequalities, the law would always appear to be a charade. However, he insists that any contradiction between what is formally proclaimed and what is effectively practiced should be denounced and fought without attacking the principle itself of the rule of law. Otherwise, we would be abandoning a major instrument of struggle against the arbitrary exercise of power (Beirne and Quinney 1982, 130–7).

The *New Latin American Constitutionalism* tends to share this view of the relative autonomy of the law and of its material reality as a field of struggles, believing it can construct its *Socialism of the Twenty-First Century* through legal means. A previous historical experience, the case of Chile under the government of Salvador Allende (1970–1973) and its attempt to produce a peaceful and orderly transition from capitalism to socialism, under the prevailing bourgeois rule of law, ended in a bloody *coup d'état*, which provided the initial opportunity for the launching of the global neoliberal counterrevolution. As in the case of Chile, the current endeavors to construct a new society through constitutional means have also encountered attempts, with foreign support, to destabilize and finally defeat these.

The Argentinean-Mexican philosopher Enrique Dussel is correct when he emphasizes that the political economy is always imbued with historically determined normative principles, of an ethical nature, sometimes referred to as "laws," which serve to structure and regulate its operation. For example, take the normative foundation of the capitalist institution of private property, which is also recognized by the new constitutions of Venezuela, Bolivia, and Ecuador, although accompanied by other more cooperative or socialized forms of property such as the community form. It is private property as an "inalienable and natural right," recognized as such under the rule of law that, legitimizes and guarantees, through its universal binding and co-active force, the capitalist's "right" to privately appropriate and use, as he or she sees fit, any surplus value produced. In this sense, all aspects of the capitalist political economy are in a normative relation, expressive of a social and power relation, protected under the bourgeois rule of law. For this reason, Dussel insists that the law is more properly of an infrastructural nature, and not superstructural as sustained traditionally by many Marxists. Under capitalism, law serves a structuring, and not only a prescriptive or regulative function (Dussel 2014, 61–3). This in part explains the difficulties encountered by these countries in developing a new political economy that effectively breaks with the *dialectics of dependence* (Marini 1973), including their continuing reliance on *extractivism* as a development strategy.

We cannot ignore the fact that the modern rule of law and its liberal constitutional ideal and practice have essentially revolved around bourgeois rights: private property, contractual freedom, free enterprise, free markets and, as their corollary, the autonomy of the will to establish contractual relations and obligations, and individual freedom, particularly to sell and alienate one's labor force to capital. In this sense we have to ask ourselves if perhaps inequality and discrimination have always been inherent to the prevailing bourgeois rule of law whose normative matrix is to be found in the social production, valuation, and accumulation of capital, a reality generally invisibilized under our pervasive fetishism of the legal form. That is the reason why, for example, it has refused to recognize the right not to be exploited as a fundamental human right. Of particular relevance in this sense is Giorgio Agamben's (1942) insistence that the central concern under neoliberalism is not on the citizen as a subject of rights but as *homo eco-nomicus* or, as the contemporary Italian philosopher would prefer, *bare life* under which rights are dictated by the current political economy.

Another important contribution in this regard is that of the Italian Marxist, Antonio Negri (1933), one of the most influential contemporary political philosopher's. He defines the present condition of the rule of law as a process of fragmentation, a constituent excess that is "constituent of a biopolitical fabric." What does he mean by this? This biopolitical fabric is defined by "powers that operate transversally to determine (through relations of force, epistemic relations, voluntary, technical and productive acts) behavioral and normative contexts" (Negri 2008, 338). Here we are outside the accustomed categories of Modern legal discourse, even from a traditional Marxist view. Positive constitutive facts and actions reveal themselves, on the one hand, as part of capital's offensive in favor of *real subsumption*, that is, total dominance and, on the other hand, as resistance and the affirmation of new possibilities. Instances of self-regulation and self-governance multiply due to the asymmetrical and critical presence of these incontinent normative flows and instances of autonomy and self-determination, which also result in the production of new subjectivity. In this sense, capital is not a monolithic reality but a dynamic social relation characterized dialectically both by domination and struggle.

In that sense, we may also speak of a *biojuridical fabric* under which capital, according to Negri and Michael Hardt (USA 1960), "functions as an impersonal form of domination that imposes laws of its own, economic laws that structure social life and make hierarchies and subordinations seem natural and necessary" (Hardt and Negri 2009, 7). This *biojuridical fabric* is imposed and guaranteed with a violence that is accepted as something normal. Capital's oppressive controls over our lives depend on its laws being internalized as natural. This Marxist phenomenology of bodies opposes any ideological reification of the rule of law, including the subject of rights. Instead, it invites us to examine the dynamic of struggles and their immanent constituent force for the creation of a new political economy. This includes its normative foundations whose matrix is a democratically empowered common, not reduced to the public or private spheres, but going beyond these as obsolete modes of social organization that strategically and historically need to whither away.

For his part, Foucault warns that the creation and construction of an alternative mode of social structuring, regulation, and governance is highly contradictory, thus forcing us to live and struggle both within and beyond the state and the law as long as they exist as dominant modes (Domínguez González and Alhambra Delgado 2012, 99). However, the well-known French philosopher Alain Badiou (1937) would tend to warn, from a Communist perspective, that in order to articulate a new affirmative anti-systemic proposition you must be outside the state and the law, otherwise you are reduced to the figure of opposition that must act inside of the logics of the bourgeois political and legal framework, which are contrary to those of anti-systemic movements or organizations (Badiou 2013, 10).

The Alternative Normative Impulse of the Communal Form

Marx was right in insisting that the bourgeois state was nothing more than an "illusory community" and that behind its apparently neutral laws and rules, that purportedly offer liberty and justice for all, lies a series of economic norms and relations, based on the institution of capitalist private property and relations, which materially structure and determine the existence of its subjects as an isolated and solitary monad. Consequently, his insistence on the need for the law's gradual extinction as the predominant mode of social regulation and structuring (Guastini 1976).

While some have dismissed this theoretical proposition as wishful thinking, more recently there has been an upsurge of those that, outside of any alleged structural reductionism, consider it a profound empirically validated truth whose time has come (Rivera Lugo 2014, 123–61). What is needed is a more concrete proposition as to the alternative normative principles and constitutive processes, arising from concrete factual experiences, on which the new should be founded and developed.

More recently it has been recognized that the communal form was the main focus of attention for Marx in his later years, for which he even put aside his work on Volumes 2 and 3 of his major work *Capital*, ultimately leaving them unfinished. He undertook a critical evaluation of the historical significance of the Paris Commune of 1871, and an extensive study of the Russian rural commune, among other communal experiences that included those of indigenous peoples of Latin America. Marx was convinced that the commune represented a historically alternative mode of autonomous social production and governance to capitalism, which made the existence of the state superfluous. He had finally found his non-state model of governance to complete his thesis on the withering away of the bourgeois state form. What was left was to realize its historical potential. His studies and thinking regarding the commune as an alternative form of governance made him introduce an important theoretical addition to the *Communist Manifesto*, in his Preface to the 1872 German edition. For him, the experience of the Paris Commune had shown that "the working class cannot simply lay hold of the ready-made state machinery, and wield it for its own purposes." Afterwards, in the 1882 Preface to the Russian Edition, Marx more openly suggested the communal form, in the case of Russia, as a potential "starting point for a communist development" and an alternative to the Western European experience under capitalism (Bosteels 2014, 53–5, 60–8).

Marx was convinced that, among other things, the commune had to overcome its tendency to reduce its scope to the local, a fact that if not corrected would eventually facilitate its destruction at the hands of capital's onslaught (García Linera 2008, 38). His observation has a special relevance now that capital's aspirations of real and total subsumption have targeted specifically this alternative community or communal form in order to dispossess indigenous peoples of the natural resources contained in their territories. It has presented the historical necessity of rising above an ancestral identity prone to reduce its struggles to the local and to ignore the broader strategic framework in which they are being forced to act.

Hence, the importance that in most recent struggles, for example, in Bolivia, Ecuador, and Mexico, we have witnessed the emergence of a new subjectivity and militancy that transcends the immediate community setting, demonstrating the growing potential for radicalization of the community form. Furthermore, the political influence of indigenous peoples and communities has grown to the point where they have been able to play a major part in the constituent processes of the *New Latin American Constitutionalism*, becoming one of its most significant material sources of normative principles and provisions. They have also introduced new ideas to theoretical debates on the transition to an alternative future that includes a civilizational transformation beyond a systemic rupture with the present capitalist order. This is the case with the Andean indigenous principle of *sumak kawsay* (the good living) as an alternative mode of sociality based on the community form.

As to the *New Latin American Constitutionalism*, it is representative of a potentially new normative subjectivity: the people as constituent power. Likewise, it represents, at least, the potential emergence of a new legal *episteme* that proposes to socialize and multiply the major material sources of valid normativity, with their autonomous constitutive force beyond the constituted governmental power. This of course poses a unique challenge for each, filled with the potential for tensions, due to the fact that societies are not homogeneous and symmetric wholes but, instead, heterogeneous, asymmetric, and contradictory totalities. These constitutions are, in the end, total constitutive processes of a potentially expansive participatory character that go beyond their texts and their interpretation under the prevailing bourgeois legal culture. In these cases, we may well be talking about the need to forge a *new constituent normativity*, which exceeds the possibilities of the present framework of constitutional law. In this regard, there are critics that warn that, in the case of Bolivia and Ecuador, the new constitutional order may finally represent a new form of domination if it does not open up to the normative force of these participatory and constitutive societal and communitarian processes. They emphasize that the respective processes of civil rebellion that led to the prescription of a new constitution were mostly committed to more autonomous forms of the political than those that are being practiced in the present (Tapia 2011, 167–85; Noguera and Navas 2016, 23–7, 213–54). In the case of Venezuela, before his untimely demise, Hugo Chávez (1954–2013), as president and founder of the Bolivarian revolutionary project, insisted on the need to aggressively develop a new communal power structure throughout the country, as a new form of governance beyond and in substitution of the existing state form. In absence of this, he underlined, their radical undertaking would surely suffer the same dire fate as the European *real socialism* (Chávez 2012).

As to the historical potential represented by the *New Latin American Constitutionalism* in other contexts, such as present day Mexico, the young legal anthropologist Orlando Aragón Andrade – a member of the militant Collective *Emancipaciones* of Michoacán, Mexico, dedicated to the Critical Study and Practice of the Law – extends its transformative impulses to the constitutive effects of the autonomous struggles of local indigenous communities, as in the case of San Francisco Cherán. He refers to this as a *new transformative constitutionalism from below* with a normative constitutive force not limited to the local sphere but also with transformative possibilities on a national scale (Aragón Andrade 2016). I have referred to this elsewhere as *societal and communal constitutionalism*, which has to do with the progressive autonomization of the constitutive processes and their extended normative impulse beyond the state and its law (Rivera Lugo 2016). This contrasts with the state-centric constitutionalization of indigenous peoples rights, encumbered by its limited horizon in which the inalienable liberties they represent are basically normalized under the bourgeois–colonial legal form.

According to the Italian legal researcher Massimo Fichera, presently "constitutionalism's soul must be looked for at the local level." He adds: "What lies ahead is a field of possibilities for a form of communal constitutionalism" (Fichera 2016). This refers to the empirically identifiable trend toward the recognition of the whole of society as the site of a plurality of constitutive processes that are independent of the state-centric constitutional order. It is here that lays the real new historical possibility initially potentiated by the *New Latin American Constitutionalism* as a dynamic and participatory social process of normative prescription that is permanently impregnated from a constitutive plurality of contexts and sources.

An example of these *communal constitutions* are the autonomous normative regimes of indigenous peoples and communities, in as much as they are representative of an effectively consensual agreement among its members that is constitutive of a specific mode of participatory political organization, with its own institutions and processes of norm production (Correas 2007, 67). Thus, we are referring to much more than what is commonly referred to as legal pluralism. More accurately, we are alluding to the existence and interplay of a plurality of normative orders that include both the community and the state, as also the processes of social production and commodity exchange, among others, all of which are struggling for normative legitimacy in the midst of the present structural crisis of capitalism. This decisive normative plurality mirrors the increasing breakdown of systemic integration under the present crisis, resulting in an increasingly evident paradigmatic shift regarding social regulation and structuring outside of its state-centric institutional framework.

The Specter of Normative Communism

Antonio Gramsci (1891–1937) was right in insisting that ultimately norm creation is not the exclusive prerogative of the state. According to the well-known Italian Marxist, the whole of society, its associations and institutions, are also material sources of normative prescriptions:

> Every man, in as much as he is active, i.e., living, contributes to modifying the social environment in which he develops (to modifying certain of its characteristics or pre-serving others); in other words, he tends to establish "norms," rules of living and of behaviour.
>
> *(Gramsci 1971, 265–6)*

In this sense, everyone is potentially a legislator of norms and rules, with the caveat that under the present bourgeois dichotomy between political and civil society, the first has been provided with the ideological and coercive instruments to legitimize and secure universal compliance with its norms. This explains the struggle waged, on the one hand, for control over the law and its concrete meanings and applications and, on the other hand, the struggle to establish authoritative positions for norm creation that can alter the real balance of forces that ultimately determines the law's real existence. It is a question of developing a new normative order in which the distinction between political and civil society is gradually erased.

It is for this reason that one of the most important developments for critical socio-legal research and thought in Latin America is the study of the different historical experiences of the common or communal, from the Marxist, the Anarchist and those of the indigenous peoples of Latin America, among others. Keeping in mind that the most important object of Marxist thought is not merely to obtain a better understanding of reality but to radically transform it, one of our major challenges today is perfecting our critical thought or perspective on the subject in light of our current and ever-changing reality. Thus, we need to go beyond a mere diagnostic of the current situation so as to establish an alternative theoretical and practical framework based on the real societal and communal normative experiences and principles that have been surfacing, including the *New Latin American Constitutionalism*. It is a question of potentiating a process of continuous creative and critical construction and transformation, with the objective of contributing to the production of a new hegemonic mode of social regulation and structuring. This will certainly require the deconstruction and defetichization of prevailing concepts and categories, as well as the creation of new theoretical constructs that can effectively mirror these alternative normative experiences, some of which we have proposed in this chapter. Above all, there is a need to go beyond a mere valuation of the differences that characterize the diverse conceptions and experiences of the common and identify their strategic affinities and possibilities for developing a collective agency in favor of the construction of the previously mentioned revolutionary transcapitalist alternative, including the normative foundations of its political economy. For the Marxists in the region, this situation poses a unique opportunity to finally overcome its "abstract communism" (Echeverría 1986, 179–95) through the comprehension of the strategic implications of Marx's wager in favor of the revolutionary possibilities of the communal or community form, therefore radically breaking with the pervasive Eurocentric understanding of Latin America's concrete historicity under Capitalism (Cueva 2008).

In this respect, the Zapatista movement in Mexico represents a positive convergence between Marxist perspectives and the Mayan worldview that proposes to dispute the present social and power relations, not only in their communities, but also elsewhere. They believe that a real revolutionary anticapitalist change can only be the result of the autonomous institution, from below, of new social and power relations based on the community or communal form. That is the case with the establishment of the Councils of Good Government and the institution of an autonomous administration of justice. The latter, with the successful application of the community's own norms, rules, and procedural practices, effectively operates outside the control of the central government. Experiences such as these have proven the concrete possibility of providing for democratically empowered governance, via decisional processes channeled through assemblies, with the direct representation of the members of the community. They have also shown the feasibility of a self-determined and relational community justice based on a participatory process of conflict resolution, whose terms are collectively structured and enunciated in an accord of a reparative nature.

This phenomenon represents an empirically verifiable example of Marx's aforementioned understanding of communism as the permanent becoming of those historical communal impulses and experiences that not only engage in the negation of the present state of things but, more importantly, actively affirm a new historical opening for an alternative form of normativity that has been described as *legal or normative communism* (Negri 2003, 11–12; Rivera Lugo and Correas 2013, 13–27). This includes the possibility of a proletarian non-law (Badiou 2009, 184) or a societal and communal non-law (Rivera Lugo 2014, 123–61) as potentially alternative forms of normativity, social regulation, and structuring beyond and in place of the present market and state-centric bourgeois law. By non-law I am referring to the self-determined normative framework under which social and community movements operate, as well as revolutionary movements and organizations. It is also the tacit or informal normative framework of all human relations and associations founded on a cooperative or solidarity-based reciprocity, quite alien to bourgeois law. These experiences forge, one by one, a cumulative logic of a constitutive power for the institution of an alternative mode of life that already is present, at least in *potentia*. They are proof that there is space not only for resistance but, more importantly, for seeking new possibilities outside of capital and its normative underpinnings.

According to the distinguished Cuban legal philosopher and historian, Julio Fernández Bulté (1937–2008), the end of European *real socialism* constitutes an historical opportunity to revisit the Marxist understanding both of the state and the law, through the effective recognition of the increasing production of a non-state-centric normativity and the corollary reduction of the prescriptive function and sphere of the state. This should not be understood as a mere circumstantial alteration in regard to the material sources of the law but a manifestation of a structural mutation in how the law or social normativity in general is produced and how it expresses itself in these times (Matilla Correa 2009, 206–7). It's the specter of *real normative communism* that is presently haunting the juridical world and that ultimately poses a challenge to the legal form as an historically determined, limited, and increasingly superseded form of social regulation and structuring.

References

Aragón Andrade, O. 2016. "Transformando el constitucionalismo transformador. Lecciones desde la experiencia político-jurídica de Cherán, México." *Seminario de estudios críticos del Derecho y las Humanidades* (Colectivo Emancipaciones/UNAM: Morelia).

Arrighi, G. 2010. *The Long Twentieth Century* (London/New York: Verso).

Badiou, A. 2009. *Theory of the Subject* (New York: A&C Black).

Badiou, A. 2012. *The Rebirth of History* (London/New York).

Badiou, A. 2013. "Affirmative Dialectics: From Logic to Anthropology," *The International Journal of Badiou Studies* Vol. 2, No. 1, Brooklyn, New York.

Beirne, P. and Quinney, R. (1982) *Marxism and Law* (New York: John Wiley and Sons).

Bensaid, D. 2015. "Karl Marx, los ladrones de leña y los derechos de los desposeídos," en Marx, K. and Bensaid, D. *Contra el expolio de nuestras vidas* (Madrid: Errata Naturae).

Bonnet, A., Holloway, J., and Tischler, S. 2006. *Marxismo abierto: Una visión europea y latinoamericana Volumen I* (Caracas: Monte Ávila).

Bosteels, B. 2013. *El marxismo en América Latina: Nuevos caminos al comunismo* (La Paz: Vicepresidencia del Estado Plurinacional).

Bosteels, B. 2013. *"The Mexican Commune."* Available at: www.academia.edu. Accessed September 17, 2017.

Bosteels, B. 2014. "Estado, comuna, comunidad," *Revista Boliviana de Investigación*, Vol. 11, No. 1.

Braudel, F. 1977. *Afterthoughts on Material Civilization and Capitalism* (Baltimore: Johns Hopkins University Press).

Caldas, C.O. 2015. *A teoria da derivação do estado e do direito* (São Paulo: Outras Expressões/Dobra).

Cerroni, U. 1975. *Marx y el Derecho moderno* (México, DF: Grijalbo).

Chávez, H. 2012. *Golpe de timón* (Caracas: Correo del Orinoco).

Correas, O. 2000. *Introducción a la crítica del Derecho moderno* (México, DF: Fontamara).

Correas, O. n.d. *"Marxismo, Derecho y Crítica Jurídica,"* Available at: www.yumpu.com/es/document/view/14533775/para-una-critica-juridica-marxista-seminario-critica-juridica. Accessed March 20, 2019.

Correas, O. 2007. *Derecho indígena mexicano I* (México: CEIICH-UNAM/Coyoacán).

Cueva, A. 2008. "El marxismo latinoamericano: Historia y problemas actuales," en *Entre la ira y la esperanza y otros ensayos de crítica latinoamericana* (Buenos Aires/Bogotá: CLACSO/Siglo del Hombre).

Derrida, J. 1994. *Specters of Marx* (New York/London: Routledge).

Domínguez González, D.J. and Alhambra Delgado, M. 2012. "El hilo rojo de Foucault," *Youkali* No. 13.

Dussel, E. 2014. *16 tesis de economía política* (México: Siglo XXI).

Echeverría, B. (1986) *El discurso crítico de Marx* (Mexico: Ediciones Era).

Fereira, E. 2011. "Entrevista a Oscar Correas," *Revista Jurídica Direito & Realidade*, Vol. 1, No. 1, January-June 2011.

Fernández Bulté, J. 2008. "El socialismo del Siglo XXI," *Revista Jurídica del Ministerio de Justicia*, La Habana, Tercera época, Año 1, Número 1, Enero-Junio 2008.

Fichera, M. 2016. *The Paradox of Liberal Constitutionalism: A Call for Communal Constitutionalism, VerfBlog*, November 10, 2016. Available at: http://verfassungsblog.de/the-paradox-of-liberal-constitutionalism-a-call-for-communal-constitutionalism/. Accessed August 2, 2018.

Freitas, L. and Feitosa, E. 2012. *Marxismo, realismo e direitos humanos* (Paraíba: Universidad Federal da Paraíba).

García Linera, A. 2008. *La potencia plebeya* (Buenos Aires: CLACSO/Prometeo). English translation: García Linera, A. 2014. *Plebian Power: Collective Action and Indigenous, Working-Class and Popular Identities in Bolivia* (Leiden: Brill).

García Linera, A. 2009. *Forma valor, forma comunidad*, (La Paz: CLACSO/Muela del Diablo/Comuna).

Guastini, R. 1976. *"Sobre la extinción del Estado,"* Available at: www.juridicas.unam.mx/publica/librev/rev/critica/cont/1/teo/teo3.pdf. Accessed June 17, 2018.

Hardt, M. and Negri, A. 2009. *Commonwealth* (Cambridge: Harvard University Press).

Harvey, D. 2004. "The 'New' Imperialism: Accumulation by Dispossession," *Socialist Register*, Vol. 40, pp. 63–87.

Holloway, J. and Picciotto, S. ed. 1978. *State and Capital* (London: Edward Arnold).

Jaramillo, R. 2008. *Karl Marx: Escritos de juventud sobre Derecho. Textos 1837–1847* (Barcelona: Anthropos).

Keucheyan, R. 2016. "Las mutaciones de la teoría crítica," *Nueva Sociedad*, No. 261, enero-febrero de 2016.

Laval. C. and Dardot, P. 2013. *The New Way of the World: On Neoliberal Society* (London/New York: Verso).

Laval. C. and Dardot, P. 2015. *Común* (Barcelona: Gedisa).

Löwy, M. 1992. *Marxism in Latin America from 1909 to the Present: An Anthology* (Amherst, New York: Humanity Books).

Marini, R.M. 1973. *Dialéctica de la dependencia* (Mexico: Ediciones Era).

Marx, K. 1842. "En defensa de los ladrones de leña," en Marx, K. and Bensaid, D. (2015) *Contra el expolio de nuestras vidas* (Madrid: Errata Naturae).

Marx, K. 1990. *Capital*, Vol. 1 (London: Penguin Classics).

Marx, K. and Zasulich, V. 1881. "Correspondence," Available at: www.marxists.org/archive/marx/works/1881/zasulich/. Accessed June 2, 2018.

Mascaro, A.L. 2013. *Estado e forma política* (São Paulo: Boitempo).

Mascaro, A.L. 2016. "Democracia e crise do capitalismo atual: Aportes teóricos," paper presented to the Conference *Constitucionalismo, Derechos Humanos y Democracia: Análisis de los conflictos y debates en Nuestra América* (Quito: CLACSO/IAEN/UASB).

Matilla Correa, A. coord. 2009. *Panorama de la Ciencia del Derecho en Cuba, Estudios en homenaje al profesor Dr. C. Julio Fernández Bulté* (La Habana/Palma de Mallorca: Universidad de La Habana/Lleonard Muntaner).

Naves, M.B. 2000. *Marxismo e direito: um estudo sobre Pachukanis* (São Paulo: Boitempo)

Naves, M.B. 2014. *A questão do direito em Marx* (São Paulo: Outras Expressôes/Dobra).

Negri, A. 1994. *Labor of Dionysus: A Critique of the State-Form* (Minneapolis: University of Minnesota Press).

Negri, A. 2003. *La forma-Estado* (Madrid: Akal).

Negri, A. 2008. "Philosophy of Law Against Sovereignty: New Excesses, Old Fragmentations," *Law Critique*, Vol. 19, pp. 335–43.

Noguera, A. and Navas, M. 2016. *Los nuevos derechos de participación en Ecuador, ¿Derechos Constituyentes o Derechos Constitucionales? Estudio del modelo constitucional de 2008* (Valencia: Tirant Lo Blanch).

Pashukanis, E. 1976. *La teoría general del derecho y del marxismo* (México, DF: Grijalbo).

Rajland, B. and Benente, M. coords. 2016. *El Derecho y el Estado. Procesos políticos y constituyentes en Nuestra América* (Buenos Aires: CLACSO/FISYP).

Rivera Lugo, C. and Correas Vázquez, O. coords. 2013. *El comunismo jurídico* (México: UNAM-CEIICH).

Rivera Lugo, C. 2014. *¡Ni una vida más para el Derecho! Reflexiones sobre la crisis actual de la forma-jurídica* (Aguascalientes/San Luis Potosí: Centro de Estudios Jurídicos y Sociales Mispat y Programa de Maestría en Derechos Humanos de la Universidad Autónoma de San Luis Potosí).

Rivera Lugo, C. 2015. "La dialéctica afirmativa de lo común," en Conde Gaxiola, N. coord. *Teoría crítica y derecho contemporáneo* (México: Ediciones Horizontes).

Rivera Lugo, C. 2016. "La normatividad societal de lo común," en Rajland, B. and Benente, M. coords., *El Derecho y el Estado. Procesos políticos y constituyentes en Nuestra América* (Buenos Aires: CLACSO/FISYP).

Rivera Lugo, C. 2016. "El constitucionalismo societal y comunitario: Apuntes para una teoría del proceso constitutivo," paper presented before the *Meeting on Constitutionalism, Human Rights and Democracy*, Research Work Group on Legal Critique of the Latin American Council of the Social Sciences/Andean University Simon Bolivar/National Institute of Higher Studies, Equador.

Roux, R. 2008. "Marx y la cuestión del despojo. Claves teóricas para iluminar un cambio de época," *Revista Herramienta*, No. 38, Buenos Aires.

Sánchez Vázquez, A. 1988. "El marxismo en América Latina," *Dialéctica*, No. 19.

Sartori, V.B. 2010. *Lukács e a crítica ontológica ao direito* (São Paulo: Cortez).

Streek, W. 2016. *How Will Capitalism End?* (London/New York: Verso).

Tapia, L. 2011. *El estado de derecho como tiranía* (La Paz: CIDES/UMSA).

PART II

New Constitutional Models and Institutional Design

12

JUDICIAL POLITICS IN LATIN AMERICA

Juan F. González-Bertomeu[1]

Introduction

One cannot but welcome the opportunity to review the ever-growing, burgeoning field of Latin American judicial politics. The field is chockfull of valuable, and often novel, work. It continues to build from past efforts, offering empirically-sound and methodologically state-of-the-art contributions as well as conceptually- and theoretically-grounded ones. Over the last decades, many Latin American courts have reclaimed the stage by increasingly asserting their power against manifold actors and partaking in meaningful collective conversations, and the scholarship tracing their determinants and trajectories has risen to the challenge. The abundance of good-quality production is therefore cause for celebration as well as a challenge for writing a short review.

This chapter offers a reading of the field as organized around five questions. It reviews relatively recent work[2] on Latin American courts –particularly those exercising constitutional adjudication – in an illustrative fashion. The aim is not to achieve elucidation, since explanations often rival one another, but highlight the field's representative contributions and challenges. The first question, tackled in section 1, is conceptual – what we mean when we talk about judicial "independence" and "power"? The second question (section 2) concerns court empowerment – why and under what conditions do political actors delegate power to courts? The third question is what explains judges' behavior on the bench? What are (some of) the motivational factors that influence their decisions? Section 3 explores two sets of candidates – judges' attitudes and strategic considerations – while section 4 offers a discussion of the law and legal ideas or cultures. The final two questions (section 5) regard the relevance and determinants of, on the one hand, court activation and, on the other, compliance with decisions. The chapter concludes by offering some insights into the challenges lying ahead.

Studying courts is a difficult endeavor. The reasons partly revolve around the main points this chapter addresses but reach beyond them. Courts' decisions can potentially carry different political and social implications. Save for instances of ex officio review, courts' main mission is to solve disputes. Yet their judgments can result in the protection or weakening of rights; the legitimization or weakening of a political regime; the accountability (or lack thereof) of officials; the successful or unsuccessful mediation of conflicts between factions, and so on. In many cases, it is hard to grasp whether courts intend these outcomes or whether they are just the unexpected or (what is not the same) unintended consequences of their actions. Also, institutional components as well as political, social, cultural, and professional traits can affect the extent that courts bring about one or more of those outcomes. A chapter can only tackle so many questions, and many are left unaddressed. In particular, the chapter assumes away the potentially enormous influence of courts' structure and internal rules on judges' caseload, deliberation, and judgments.[3]

The chapter's emphasis is on projects at the intersection of political science, sociology, and the law with a tilt toward measurable explanations, some involving mixed methods. This is not to deny the relevance of entirely qualitative analysis (some such contributions are indeed included).[4]

Concepts

While the chapter's focus is not concepts, a discussion in passing may be beneficial. The field of Latin American judicial politics developed against the background of political systems that were transitioning from authoritarianism to democracy, and where courts faced political pressure and other serious challenges (which some still do), so it is only natural that scholars reflected on courts' roles, condition, and status.

An inveterate debate concerns the notion of judicial *independence* – what it is and whether it is useful (Kornhauser 2002; Shapiro 1981; Tate and Vallinder 1995; Larkins 1996; the list is lengthy). As Brinks has said, given the variegated use of "independence," it is noteworthy that scholars agree that Latin American courts largely do not have it (2005, 596). In the region, independence has been conceptualized as a judge's freedom to "reflect their preferences in their decisions without facing retaliation" (Iaryczower et al. 2002, 699). This cannot be totally right. No acceptable theory claims that a judge with far-fetched preferences should have absolute freedom to do what she wants (Kapiszewski and Taylor 2008). Also, a partisan judge may not "prefer" to ever oppose the government.

A better way to conceive of independence is that judges should be "authors of their decisions," without undue influence or threats (Korhauser 2002, 48; Staton 2010). Notice, however, that "threats" may come in all stripes, and not all of them will be "undue" but only those that lead to a loss of impartiality (Brinks 2005). A promising attempt at concept-building is Brinks' distinction between *decisional* independence and *preference* independence (ibid.). The former is compromised with undue interference in the decision-making process favoring one party. The latter is compromised with unilateral factional capture of the appointment process. In a non-plural process that selects like-minded, partisan judges, a case outcome may be *ex ante* preordained given the preference correspondence of judges and one of the parties; it does not matter whether undue interferences exist (ibid.). While independence is compromised if either of those dimensions is lacking, a system may have decisional independence without preference independence and the other way around (ibid.).

Judicial power is a less charged concept. It has been analyzed in its legal and factual nature. The former is the bundle of rules structuring adjudication, including type of review, effects of decisions, and access (Ríos-Figueroa 2011; Staton 2010). Notice that a weak court in this sense can be independent in either of the dimensions above (Kornhauser 2002). The latter, more connected to independence, is a court's ability to "cause by its actions" certain preferred outcomes, mainly ensuring compliance (Staton 2010, 9). Along these lines, the more neutral and increasingly employed *assertiveness* (Kapiszewski and Taylor 2008) can usefully replace the also charged *activism*.

Empowerment

Courts can either solidify or weaken their power through their actions. Yet their ability to operate (the type of cases they hear, the legal effects of their decisions, the tenure requirements that may reinforce or weaken their power) largely depends on decisions made by external actors, prominently including the government. It often is the case that the government decides to strengthen that ability in some way via institutional reform, which it can open up channels for it to be held accountable.[5] A puzzle many scholars have addressed is what determines this seemingly self-defeating action on the part of a ruling coalition (Finkel 2004; Ingram 2015). At least five explanations of *strategic* motivation can be identified.[6] To varying degrees, they assume that the strategy is attempted within a context of perceived weakness, either in the form of foreseeable electoral defeat or divided government.[7] Notice that all explanations try to capture *motivations*, which are hard to pinpoint. (Ingram 2016 attempts to unpack motivations as stemming from material and non-material incentives.) Scholars aim at reconstructing them by analyzing the behavior of actors and the information deemed available to them, though a number of potentially questionable assumptions are often built into the explanations, such as the actors' non-myopic behavior. Also, whatever the motivations explaining their emergence, institutions often take on a life of their own once in operation (Mahoney and Thelen 2009).

A first, well-known explanation is *insurance* theory (Ramseyer 1994; Ginsburg 2003; Finkel 2008). A ruling coalition that fears losing power will strengthen courts to entrench its policies into the future (thus protecting them from reversal) or allow it to contest the incumbent when in the opposition (ibid.). The coalition pays a premium (a reinforced judiciary that may presently control it) to be subsequently insured if so needs it. Connected to the first in its underscoring of electoral competition, another explanation is *power balance* (Chavez 2004a, 2004b). The government has an incentive to strengthen the judiciary when power is shared with other parties over time and no party tends to dominate both the executive and the legislature. In such scenarios, the courts "can emerge as [arbiters] among political actors." (Chavez 2004b, 465) Chavez conceives of power balance, for a long period lacking in Argentina, as necessary for independence. The explanation can be extended from the government's *tolerance* of independent courts to the active *reinforcement* of them.[8]

The third is *legitimization*. Through court empowerment, a regime perceived as weak, authoritarian, and/or lacking transparency may seek to signal its renewed commitment to the rule of law (Landry 2008). Ruibal rightly attributes to this the changes made to the supreme court of Argentina's appointment system in the early 2000s.[9] The fourth is rather a compendium of explanations involving *coalition-preserving* or coalition-strengthening strategies. Enabling a third party may be a way for the government to consolidate power – because it has lost its ability to arbitrate intra-coalition conflicts, to avoid making decisions in sensitive cases, or to overcome obstructions in agenda implementation (Voigt and Salzberger 2002; Whittington 2005; Hirschl 2006).[10] The fifth is a *bargaining chip* explanation (Finkel 2008). The government may strengthen the judiciary in exchange for measures it values more. In Argentina, an amendment in 1994 whose main aim was to allow President Menem's reelection could only pass muster when the government agreed to other changes, including a new judicial council (Finkel 2008).[11]

One would expect these motivations to match the proper institutional manifestation.[12] For example, if the legitimacy deficit stems from a perception of weak rights enforcement, one would probably observe rights adjudication capabilities being reinforced through concrete adjudication in *amparo*-like proceedings, as it happened in 1991 Colombia.[13]

Mexico

Mexico provides fertile ground for exploring these theories. In 1994, against the background of 65 years of continued rule by the PRI Party (Institutional Revolutionary Party), a severely delegitimized political system, and local electoral defeats, Ernesto Zedillo, a PRI economist, reached power promising a judicial reform. Shortly thereafter, Zedillo had a constitutional amendment passed expanding the supreme court's jurisdiction and changing its personnel. The supreme court was assigned the ability to arbitrate inter-organ conflicts through the *constitutional controversy* mechanism and to hear direct challenges to rules through the *constitutional action*. Further, it was reduced from 26 to 11 justices and its membership was replaced under a new plural procedure (Finkel 2004; Magaloni 2008). A few scholars tried to account for these events.

Finkel (2004) saw Zedillo's move as the archetypical insurance-buying strategy in a context where the PRI was no longer able to control elections. Looking into the mid-term, Zedillo and his advisors sought to create a "hedge against the loss of office" (Finkel 2004, 87). Zedillo put forward a weaker version of the bill than the one ultimately approved, but part of the opposition (the right-wing National Action Party [PAN]; the left-leaning Party of the Democratic Revolution [PRD] voted against), whose votes were needed, pushed "for greater judicial empowerment" (ibid., 102). This is the first explanation above, with traces of the fifth. Magaloni (2008) had a different take. The author resorted to game-theoretical analysis pitting two politicians disputing a nomination against each other, with the president making final decisions. While the PRI effectively monopolized nominations, whatever decision the president made was complied with. As new electoral avenues opened, the cost of challenging the leadership decreased, and the president lost the ability to guarantee compliance either in favor or against his allies. The solution was to externalize decisions, the fourth explanation.

Inclán (2009) shared Magaloni's view but embraced the third explanation. Both agreed that what inspired Zedillo was more immediate than Finkel allowed – to keep the PRI's grip on power. Inclán disputed that the insurance model fitted the Mexican case. For it to be the explanation, either the reform proposal or its implementation should have been delayed until a later stage of Zedillo's tenure, when the possibility of a PRI defeat was clearer. When Zedillo implemented it, the climate was of "political victory," not expectable defeat (Inclán 2009, 755; Woods and Hilbink 2009). Also, if defeat was seen as likely, the party with the largest chance to reach power, the PAN, should probably have *opposed* the reform, while the small PRD should have favored it (ibid.). The reverse happened. In Inclán's view, Zedillo wanted to clean the party's image, first to convince voters to support it, then to signal it would govern in a transparent way, and third, as in Magaloni, to prevent the erosion of power by externalizing arbitration.[14]

Some of the explanations in this fruitful dialog can be integrated into a 'more complex motivation. Yet parsimony advises researchers to focus on simpler accounts, and the evidence might help tell them apart. In sum, the five strategic explanations above predict that empowerment occurs in contexts of relatively weak government, although identifying which was at play at a particular juncture depends on the relevant political conditions as well as the information and rationality of political actors. Unsurprisingly, this is challenging.

Decision-Making

The preceding discussion focused on the *external* determinants of court empowerment, holding the courts constant. Probably the bulk of contemporary studies analyze instead the factors behind courts' and judges' decision-making on the bench. This section offers preliminary considerations for discussing judicial behavior, outlines potential drivers of it, highlights relevant contributions, and points out some challenges.

As some scholars have noted, studying the behavior of judges as isolated from the aftermath of their decisions has the advantage of letting researchers focus on a small set of issues, but it is somewhat artificial. Judges' predictions about compliance might influence their decisions regarding case outcomes and their choice of remedies, particularly in cases involving the government (Kapiszewski and Taylor 2013; Staton 2010). One can imagine judges taking into consideration the societal impact of decisions even beyond compliance. We can also go backward, asking who activated the courts' intervention in a case and how is it that the parties "were able to gain access to the court" in the first place? (Ingram 2015, 256)

Attitudes

In the early twentieth century, American Legal Realists disputed the prevalent view that judges in their decisions applied the law. A closer look revealed that judges responded "primarily to the stimulus of the facts of the case, rather than to legal rules and reasons" (Leiter 2002). This was partly because the law was indeterminate; legal reasons did not justify a single decision (ibid.). Accompanying this trend, in the late 1940s, Pritchett (1948) started a "paradigm shift" in the study of courts by political scientists (Cameron and Kornhauser 2015). Instead of interpreting *opinions*, Pritchett turned to judges' *votes* (ibid.). In the ensuing decades, Pritchett was joined by others (prominently including Schubert and Spaeth) in an ambitious research agenda, labeled "attitudinalism," that looked into the attitudes of judges in response to case facts (ibid.). In the United States, a multiplicity of studies has attempted to measure the attitudes of judges, mainly to capture the weight of their policy preferences in adjudication along a liberal-conservative dimension, and novel methods have been employed for it.

Judges' policy or ideological attitudes have only been studied in a handful of works on Latin American courts. Among them is Scribner's study (2011) of the supreme courts of Chile and Argentina (in the periods 1932–1999 and 1946–1999, respectively), finding that the Argentine justices considered as liberal by a host of experts were around 15 percent more likely to vote to protect expressive rights than conservative justices under democratic rule; she did not find any effect in Chile. Another contribution is Basabe-Serrano's study of the Ecuadorian Constitutional Court's decision-making in its abstract jurisdiction (2012). Based on experts' rankings of justices on a left-right dimension both concerning state intervention and labor flexibilization and justices' party leanings, the author regressed each justice's votes (in cases involving those areas) on the ideology indicator. He found some effect of "ideology" thus-defined.

Tests of attitudinal models have usually scaled judges' preferences by attributing them the preferences of the appointing official (typically the president) or, as above, by resorting to experts' views. Though these methods can be very useful, and often are the only ones available, they come with some caveats. The former is an indirect measure, while the latter is endogenous to the experts' knowledge of judges' past behavior, sometimes in the very cases that are under scrutiny. A few studies have tried to circumvent these issues by directly inferring judges' "ideal points" from their *revealed* behavior in court (Martin and Quinn 2002), though they also come with caveats whose significance will vary depending on the type of project for which ideal points are employed.[15] One such study focused on *constitutional controversies* and *constitutional actions* at the supreme court of Mexico (Sánchez et al. 2011). The authors inferred two-dimensional estimates of justices' preferences; independent from one another, the dimensions are a liberal-conservative one and a legalist-interpretativist one. The authors defined "interpretivism" as a position in favor of expanding the court's jurisdiction by overturning judicial precedents limiting it, engaging in nonliteral interpretation, and offering a generous interpretation of standing ("legalism" was the opposite). They found that justices "not only divide … along the prevailing ideological cleavage …" but also "with respect to judicial philosophy or forms of legal interpretation …" (ibid.).

Another ideal-point estimation study is González-Bertomeu et al. (2016). The authors centered on the supreme court of Argentina's justices' votes in rights and political-process cases in the period 1984–2007, placing them along a liberal-conservative dimension. Justices divided fairly neatly along this dimension – and those appointed by the most conservative president clustered together casting conservative opinions. Also employing judicial ideal points, Desposato et al. (2015) studied the Brazilian *Supremo Tribunal Federal* from 1989–2010, finding that a combination of both reforms enhancing the policymaking authority of the court and an increase in the number of judges appointed by the *Partido dos Trabalhadores* (PT) created a new "partisan cleavage" on the court.

Strategies

Surely judges value other things apart from implementing their policy preferences – to keep their job or get promotions, not be overruled, achieve notoriety, and so on. Under the umbrella of "strategic" approaches, a second branch of studies claim that, in their quest to advance their preferences, judges are constrained by, and take into consideration, a host of factors that may impinge upon some of those goals. The factors are related either to the political environment surrounding judges – e.g., the degree of unity of the elected branches and public support for the government – or to some form of peer pressure. As has been noted, it is no surprise that scholars in Latin America have been more concerned with strategic studies than with attitudinalism (Helmke and Ríos-Figueroa 2011). The region's political instability translated into judges' *tenure* instability and attempts to undermine courts' power.

A standard strategic approach, based on separation of powers models, posits in its simplified form that judges' assertiveness grows as the party in the executive is less able to assert control over the legislature (Gely and Spiller 1990, Ferejohn and Weingast 1992, Ferejohn 1999). While the explanations rely on many assumptions, the central notion is that more unified elected branches are better able to coordinate to overturn "hostile" judicial interpretations, discipline judges, or strip courts. Relevant considerations include whether the decision was announced on constitutional or statutory grounds,[16] the type of legislative majorities needed to enact each of those measures, and the timing of actions.

Latin American scholars have tested such approaches. Iaryczower et al. (2002) studied the Argentine Supreme Court in the period 1935–1998. Among the authors' findings, the probability that the court struck down a rule significantly increased when the executive did not control the legislature. In her study of Argentina, Chavez argued that courts become autonomous when "no highly disciplined party sustains control of both the executive and legislative branches" (2004b, 451). Chavez (2003) took advantage of subnational political variation in the country, comparing the electorally competitive Mendoza province with the monolithic San Luis province and showing that a degree of judicial independence is only observed in the former.[17] Ríos-Figueroa (2007) centered on the Mexican Supreme Court's decisions against federal and local PRI governments from 1994 to 2002, finding that the probability of a vote against the PRI increased as the party first lost a legislative majority and then the presidency.[18]

Inter-branch interaction was the crux of some contributions involving Brazil. One is Kapiszewski's careful work on decision-making in economic policy cases by Brazil's and Argentina's high courts from 1985–2004 (2012, 2013). Another is by Brinks (2011) highlighting the implications a fragmented political context has for judicial appointments. Fragmentation leads to the selection of judges who "faithfully serve" the regime, not just "the current power holder," and that are autonomous on disputes that do not involve it. What is in the regime's interest is "colored" by the preferences of those controlling appointments, especially the president (ibid.). Kapiszewski (2013) agreed, seeing the professionalized Brazilian court as a "cooperative," "statesman" court compared to the more "volatile" Argentinian court. Additionally, in his study of Paraguay, Basabe-Serrano (2015) claimed that fragmentation is a necessary but insufficient condition for independence, since *informal* institutions can also be an obstacle.

Other studies have operationalized the government's strength via public support for it – sufficiently popular governments will be able to confront courts while weathering potential backlash. They include Rodríguez-Raga's exploration of abstract adjudication at the Colombian Constitutional Court in *public actions of unconstitutionality* (2011). Among its interesting results, the study did not find that public support for the president *directly* affected the court's decision-making, although a rule in a case decided at the beginning of a president's term was "less likely to be struck down" than one in a case decided toward the end. Tiede and Ponce (2011) looked at *amparo* claims decided by the Peruvian Constitutional Court. The court was more likely to decide against the government as the level of support for it deteriorated (and as the share of congressional seats held by the president's party decreased).

Three theoretically-novel approaches bear mentioning. Two emerged from the seemingly perplexing observation that, despite threats to their independence, judges in Latin America frequently "confront" the government. One is well-known – Helmke's strategic defection model (2002, 2005, 2006). In contexts of insecure tenure, judges defer to the incumbent, except when doing so jeopardizes their standing vis-à-vis the incoming government (ibid.). When judges ascertain that, with sufficiently high probability, a government of a different political sign will take power, they will rationally "defect." They will challenge the incumbent, thus signaling the incoming government that their allegiance does not lie with the former. The author found some evidence of defection on the supreme court of Argentina in 1976–1999, with decisions against the government crowding at the end of its period. However, a cross-national empirical replication of the theory (Sanchez-Uribarri and Songer) has cast doubts on its generalizability. Also, following the model, votes against the government should decrease once the new government takes office, something that Helmke did not investigate.

Basabé-Serrano studied justices' "conviction" voting in contexts of "extreme institutional instability" (2012). The author bought into strategic explanations but with an important twist. Justices respond to instability by strategically deferring to the government, though "only up to a certain point." If they know their tenure is radically doomed, justices will consider it a fleeting experience and use their time at the bench to, among other things, vote their convictions. In this way, they approach the behavior of judges in stable settings; the most "strategic" judges are those in contexts of medium levels of stability. (Phrased differently, the voting function is not linear – instability encourages strategic voting – but curvilinear. [134]) Basabé-Serrano found evidence of this at the Ecuadorian Constitutional Court.

Staton combined decision-making and compliance and focused on public support *for courts* (2010). The study resonates with Hamilton's claim that courts lack the "sword" to enforce decisions, which is relevant when the enforcer, namely, the government, is the one whose compliance is called for. A court is more likely to rule against the government when it believes the public is more likely to become informed about noncompliance (ibid.; Vanberg 2005; Tiede 2011). In the case of the Mexican Supreme Court, the court itself can influence knowledge. The public gains information about a case from newspapers, and coverage is partly a function of the court's decision to issue a press release. Staton found that an anti-government ruling was more likely as newspaper coverage increased *and* that the court was more likely to issue a press release when it struck down a rule, shielding its position with public support. This is consistent with other findings, including Helmke's cross-country study of courts in Latin America (2011). Public support for courts seems central to minimize attacks against judges.

Prudence Versus Assertiveness

Apart from the previous insights, what can explain Latin American courts' occasional challenge to the government in contexts of (real or perceived) instability? Further, if support for courts is crucial, what does it take to build it? In the context of the United States, it has been suggested that a short-term strategy of prudence, of piecemeal intervention, is key (Bickel 1986). Staton and Helmke (2011) argued that, in Latin America, excessive prudence may not be appropriate. It risks constructing "inaccurate beliefs about judicial preferences," showing future litigants that the court is "partisan" or "unwilling to defend rights." (325) This is intuitive. As a function of factors including political expectations and institutional design, the Colombian Constitutional Court and the Costa Rican Constitutional Chamber are the opposite of prudent, and yet they are fairly well-respected bodies. Latin American high courts may partly construct their legitimacy by asserting their power, especially if the public comes to regard their contribution as directly or indirectly beneficial. At the same time, these strategies are surely precarious, since political retaliation remains a risk in the process (Castagnola and Pérez-Liñán 2011).

Judges' Utility

The question of what motivates judges is complex, and one can be certain that a comprehensive theory of behavior should account for numerous factors and adjust to the local landscape. The law (however defined) and other institutional considerations can certainly be part of the mix, but also can be ideological, political, social, and economic considerations as well as professional idiosyncrasies and proclivities (including an interest in maximizing leisure time or avoiding peer conflict) (Cameron and Kornhauser 2015). Since social scientists aim to achieve elucidation of complex phenomena, they often restrict their explanatory variables to a minimum. The flipside is oversimplification, though the open question is whether this is the price to pay for (admittedly partial) elucidation.

Exceptions to such parsimony include Kapiszewski (2011b). The author offered a multivariate theory of behavior – labeled "tactical balancing" – inductively derived from the Brazilian Supreme Federal Tribunal's decision-making. Justices in politically crucial cases balance six considerations: their ideology, judicial interests, government preferences, the expected economic or political consequences of judgments, popular opinion, and the law. Studying a set of carefully selected decisions, the author claimed that variation in the relevance of those considerations in different cases leads courts "to shift between challenging and endorsing" the government (473). Through balancing, justices weigh and prioritize "the different roles high courts can play in a democracy" (ibid.).[19]

Decision-Making and the Law

Mostly High Courts

A usual remark is that judicial politics studies mostly focus on high courts from only a handful of countries (Shapiro 1981; Kapiszewski and Taylor 2008). Regarding Latin America, the former rings more true today than the latter. While the list of countries that elicit scholarly attention has expanded, the lens on high courts keeps being the norm (exceptions include Ingram [2016], and Ingram and Kapiszewski [forthcoming]). High courts are politically salient institutions, and therefore are appealing to study. Also, if high court's publication systems are usually not thorough, they are radically deficient, or non-existent, in the case of most other national or subnational courts. Often, high courts are not low-hanging fruit but the only hanging fruit.

One cost of this lopsided focus is that it affects our understanding of how courts and judges handle the law relative to other considerations. The American Realists typically qualified their claim that judges were insufficiently constrained by the law by arguing that this was especially so at the appellate level, and particularly at the United States Supreme Court, where legal questions are relatively open-ended and novel (Friedman 2006; Cameron and Kornhauser 2015). The same may be true of constitutional decision-making in at least some Latin American high courts, but things might be different in the case of ordinary courts confronting non-constitutional issues, where the law may be more determinate. Two other features might explain differences between high courts and lower courts. As Cameron and Kornhauser have argued within the United States context (2015), the outcomes of *judicial selections* may vary at different levels of the judiciary. Because of the political stakes involved in high courts' decision-making, it is likely that more "political" judges concentrate there, and that legal technicians tend to populate the lower echelons (ibid.). Also, *hierarchical control* of judges may be higher as one descends in the judiciary's pyramid (ibid.). In sum, looking at high courts can yield a biased picture of how judges generally handle the law. A fruitful line of research may be to compare courts at different levels of the judicial hierarchy, with proper consideration of each court's role and structure.

Law

The law seems one big elephant in the room. Positive scholars often present the "legal" model of decision-making as rival of the others above (Segal and Spaeth 2002). Yet, as has been noted (Friedman 2006; Cameron and Kornhauser 2015; Landau 2005; Kapiszewski 2013), the legal model is often identified with a mechanistic view of adjudication that no legal scholar really espouses. The basic question of what the law *is* still elicits the attention of legal philosophers. Nonetheless, few dispute that, together with clear-cut rules, the law's arsenal includes less clear rules as well as principles subject to interpretation (Dworkin 1977). The law is not a site for mechanistic behavior but a public practice of "reasoned justification" that embraces disagreement (Friedman 2006, 266; Dworkin 1986; Kapiszewski 2013). Accommodating this view into a legal model of decision-making makes it more difficult for scholars to test whether the law sufficiently constrains judges, but it can offer a more accurate rendering of how the latter should, and do, operate (Friedman 2006).

Is the "legal model" compatible with other explanations of behavior, particularly "attitudinalism"? One way to answer would be that it is – what looks like judges' policy preferences really are a component of their legal philosophy (Friedman 2006). Now, while some legal scholars may perceive judgments as manifestations of that philosophy, positive researchers may insist that they are determined by judges' narrower preferences. If so, semantics would block progress. Perhaps, however, there is some difference between, on the one hand, a judge's ideological and relatively exogenous preferences and, on the other, her "preferences" about how to approach legal materials and the judicial function. The latter may partly be endogenous to the judge's training, her understanding of what the institution she is part of requires, and the evolving norms of the profession.

Should this distinction survive scrutiny, preferences about the law (i.e., a judge's "judicial philosophy") may be able to be embraced by the legal model broadly conceived, while more clearly ideological preferences may not. Ideological preferences would tend to dictate a case outcome given some facts, while preferences about the law would work as meta-issues regarding how to identify and interpret legal materials and the judicial role (Friedman 2006). An illustration of the latter may be the interpretivism/legalism dimension in Sánchez et al. (2011). Other examples include Landau (2005) and Ansolabehere (2008). Landau distinguishes between two "worldviews" about the law, a positivistic stance that, in his view, is typical of career judges and the principle-oriented ("new constitutionalist") tendency of legal scholars of late. Although the distinction between ideology and legal philosophy may be useful, it is also imperfect. The legal system itself often dictates an outcome or hints at one.[20] And, at a more general level, the two types of "preference" may be intertwined. A judge's judicial philosophy may be colored by her own ideology, and what we think of as the judge's ideological, exogenous preferences may in turn be influenced by her training and legal ideas.

In sum, what the attitudinal model consists of and its links to the law depend both on what we think the law is *and* what we think attitudes about the law are. There are two further issues concerning the always suggestive challenges to the notion that the law sufficiently constrains. One is a simple methodological issue that most empirical studies of decision-making confront. Even if a well-specified model showed that an extra-legal variable accounts for some of the observed variation in the dependent variable, it is crucial not to lose sight of effect size. If the variable were to explain, say, 15 percent of such variation, this would hardly mean that judges are unconstrained by the law – they may or may not be – since the remaining variation would be left unexplained. A similar point applies to studies that discard unanimous opinions for not conveying useful information about judges' preferences (Pritchett 1948; Cameron and Kornhauser 2015), like those inferring judges' "ideal points."[21] This is entirely appropriate insofar as the studies avoid drawing clear-cut conclusions regarding the weight of preferences in decision-making. Unanimity might mean that the case is not ideologically salient, but it might also just mean agreement in legal reasoning.

The other issue is what do we look at when studying behavior? Positive studies, in Latin America and beyond, usually consider case outcomes or *dispositions* without paying much attention to *opinions* (Friedman 2006). This is completely understandable. Doing so is simpler and it might seem to reflect what judges "really do" (ibid.). The content of opinions, however, is central to the law. Dispositions are inextricably tied to a set of relevant facts – at least in instances of concrete review – and the doctrines announced (ibid.; Cameron and Kornhauser 2015). The content of opinions may reflect that law "does have an influence in structuring analysis and organizing outcomes" (Friedman 2006, 266). Also, even assuming that judges are driven by ideology, two judges with a conflicting ideology may find themselves sharing a disposition. Judges' preferences over rules, principles, or policies (theoretically central for the attitudinal model) may not always translate into preferences over dispositions (Cameron and Kornhauser 2017). Positive studies would benefit from more seriously engaging with opinions. In other words, if studying judges' votes instead of opinions was considered a crucial step in the study of courts, a new step forward would be to recover the value of opinions.

Ideational Factors

Latin American legal studies are devoting increasing attention to the sources of ideas, languages, or "cultures of legality" (Huneeus et al. 2010) and the way they shape "judicial power and social relations" (Ingram 2016, 252; Hilbink 2012; Ansolabehere 2008; Nunes 2010; Landau 2005).

In their valuable work, Huneeus et al. claim that legal ideas and paradigms of interpretation are in flux, currently "undergoing dramatic change" away from the prototypical civil law formalism, and that a new set of repertoires "accompany, cause, and are a consequence of the judicialization of politics" (2010, 3–4). Among other issues, studies have traced the origin and evolution of legal ideas and have stressed the role of legal networks in their dissemination (Ingram 2015, 2016; Couso 2010; Hilbink 2007, 2012).

Contributions like these greatly enhance our understanding of the law's operation. They bring their own complexities as well. Huneeus et al. claim that "ideas and non-strategic action matter to political outcomes" (2010, 5), which is correct. Yet the "genealogy" of ideas may be difficult to ascertain. Judges' and lawyers' notions about the law are probably formed by training but also by the social, institutional, and political milieu in which they interact and, as noted, their own ideology. Specifically, it may be hard to discern what is strategic and what is not. A host of relevant studies has highlighted the Chilean judiciary's apoliticism and passivity (Couso and Hilbink 2011). This stance has been taken to reflect illiberal cultural traces in the country's history (Hilbink 2007). However, Couso and Hilbink have pointed out that such apoliticism was a survival strategy of a judiciary that had unsuccessfully confronted the government in the past. Once bitten, twice shy.

Indeed, "legal culture" may partly be shaped by institutions and politics themselves. An intriguing example is the notion of court "character" or "profile." Kapiszewski (2012, 2013), and Ansolabehere (2007), among other authors, have argued that institutional and political traits concerning such factors as judges' selection, stability, professional profile, and level of cohesion help define the character or profile of a court, which in turn affects the way a court interacts with other actors. This is fascinating, although, if character is a function of those traits, a valid question is whether we can attribute a distinct causal role to it. In sum, as Huneeus et al. (2010) acknowledge, changes in ideational factors can be both a cause and consequence of judicialization and, more specifically, judicial behavior. Those changes can also be mediated by other factors, including institutional ones.

Activation and Compliance

This final section briefly discusses who effectively access courts and under what conditions, as well as what compliance is and what determines it.[22] The centrality of activation cannot be overstressed. The Inter-American Court of Human Rights was created in 1979 but, for want of cases, it only decided a controversy almost a decade later. Following Epp and Galanter, Smulovitz has shown how changes in the support structure in Argentina triggered judicialization even in the face of citizens' negative perceptions about the judiciary – i.e., a weak legal culture (2005, 2008, 2010). This is compatible with reports of diverse social groups instrumentally "appropriating" the law to litigate their perceived grievances (Ingram 2015; Gomez 2010; Domingo 2010; Rueda 2010).

Also crucial are impact and compliance. In their much-needed discussion of compliance – what it is, what it is not, and how to measure it – Kapiszewski and Taylor (2013) claim that impact and compliance should be distinguished. Impact is broader and goes beyond "the actions or policy changes that directly result" from a ruling (807); it includes effects on society, public policy, or the behavior of institutions even in the absence of compliance (ibid.). Impact's dimensions go beyond the scope of this contribution, including a symbolic one (see Pou's chapter in this volume) and a redistributive one (Brinks and Gauri 2014; Ferraz 2011).

Compliance, particularly by political authorities, has been conceptualized as the "full execution of the action ... called for (or prohibited) in one or more court rulings," though most instances of compliance "will fall somewhere along the continuum" between full compliance and noncompliance (Kapiszewski and Taylor 2013, 805–6). To help measure compliance, Kapiszewski and Taylor provide four dimensions of public authorities' response to a ruling: the *actor* who responds to it (whether the one identified in the ruling or a different one); the type of *action* (whether it corresponds to the mandate); the *timing* of action; and the *persons reached* by the response (whether the people mandated in the ruling or more or fewer than mandated) (ibid.).

Staton and collaborators (Staton and Vanberg 2008; Staton and Romero 2012; Gauri et al. 2015) have connected government's compliance to court judgments' clarity in the design of a remedy. Compliance is partly determined by clarity; the clearer the remedy, the harder it will be to ignore it while escaping criticism (2008). Yet, the less expected government compliance becomes, the vaguer the court's remedy will be.[23] As in Staton (2010), this emphasizes the courts' available strategies at self-empowering.

Both court's activation and compliance can (and probably should) be part of a theory of decision-making, only that this makes such a theory more complex. One interesting attempt is Helmke and Staton (2011), incorporating litigants into a model of inter-branch interaction. A more comprehensive example is Gauri and Brinks' framework of social and economic rights' litigation (2008) as a multidimensional process of "policy legalization."[24] The authors posit that "the life cycle of public-policy litigation" reflects four key stages: (1) legal mobilization, which partly depends on the support structure for litigation; (2) the judicial decision, reflecting the theories discussed above; (3) a response by a bureaucratic, political, or private party; and, in some cases, (4) follow-up litigation. Each stage "involves a choice by one or more strategic actors" (ibid.). For example, potential litigants anticipate the proclivities of judges, the likelihood of compliance, and "their own capacity to conduct any necessary follow-up," while judges decide with an eye to compliance (20). The legal, institutional, and political landscape also affect the form and impact of legalization (14–20). The availability of remedies will be key as will also be the breadth of the constitutions' rights provisions. Another valuable multidimensional framework that combines demand-side and supply-side factors is Gloppen et al. (2010), addressing the "accountability functions of courts."

Conclusions

Latin American judicial politics is a rich, well-trodden field, with progress surely to be made in the coming years. Like any other field, the path forward is also riddled with challenges, some of which are interspersed in the discussion above. They are both methodological and theoretical. The field can benefit from more data-driven projects employing fresh datasets. For works employing court decisions, focusing on subject matters that are appropriate to answer the relevant questions is key. Also, although this is more easily said than done, it would be felicitous if the list of courts receiving scholarly attention were expanded, and if more comparative projects were tackled, of courts at different levels within a judiciary and from different countries. Additionally, the institutional variation of constitutional adjudication in the region (Navia and Rios-Figueroa 2005) is still underexploited.

Methodological advances in the scaling of judges' preferences are promising. Yet more energy can be devoted to the question of what occupies judges' minds besides policy preferences and tenure stability. Notably, our understanding of the law as well as other potentially relevant institutional considerations is still in an embryonic stage. And, since the main approach has been to study judgments, not opinions, we are depriving ourselves from the insight we could gain from reviewing patterns of cases in sets of subject matters. Save for valuable exceptions, we also tend to overlook the law's interpretive and cultural dimensions, which, for all their complexities, offer great potential rewards. Although not reviewed here, also extremely promising are studies of potential gender, racial, and class biases in decision-making and the extent that they are a function of, but also affect, judges' recruiting processes, and training.

Efforts to both integrate different aspects of the legal process and take the law and other institutional traits more seriously can push knowledge forward. Of course, models alone cannot do the job without a firm theoretical grounding. There is still much to discuss concerning the roles courts can and should play in a democracy, and these discussions can keep informing positive scholarship.

Notes

1 The author has benefited from such reviews as Ingram (2015) and Kapiszewski and Taylor (2013), and wishes to thank the editors, Matthew Ingram, Lewis Kornhauser, and Raúl Sánchez-Urribarri for their very helpful remarks. Theo Baizabal helped identify contributions. Any remaining errors are the author's.
2 All contributions reviewed in this chapter appeared before 2018.
3 See, among others, Pou (2017), Brinks (2011), and Kapiszewski (2010).
4 Valuable studies not reviewed include ethnographic explorations like Barrera's (2012). The chapter does not analyze the proper role of courts in a democracy (see Pou's chapter), it does not study strategic voting within a court, and it does not delve into specific methodological issues. The study of the relationship between domestic courts and the Inter-American adjudicatory bodies is crucial (Huneuus 2011), but focusing on the former is intricate enough.
5 Studies of "court empowerment" typically attempt to explain institutional changes of a non-transient nature (e.g., a change in appointment procedures) instead of political strategies without an institutional manifestation (e.g., the appointment of judges perceived as independent).
6 *Non*-strategic explanations include the diffusion of constitutional ideas.
7 Although, perhaps, as Bodin suggested, even relatively strong rulers may see it in their interest to cede power, especially to administer "bad news" to citizens (Holmes 1995).
8 This might be one equilibrium in a repeated game.
9 Ruibal (2009) thus explains newly-elected President N. Kirchner's decision in 2003 to tie the government's hand when nominating by setting up a prior consultation procedure. Kirchner had taken power with 22 percent of the vote, and took advantage of society's perception of the court as partisan as a way to "obtain social cooperation and legitimacy" (70).
10 The latter may be the result of governance problems generated by federalism or multiple branches of government (Ginsburg and Versteeg 2014).
11 For the motivations to bear fruit, the first, second, and fourth explanations require that the relevant court is able to operate independently. For the third, it suffices that actors *believe* courts are able to operate independently. See note 14.
12 Surely, one needs to be careful not too easily to assign motivations backward from outcomes.
13 Abstract review with the possibility of challenges by the opposition can be an option to dispute policies.
14 Inclán denies that Zedillo mainly intended to create a positive international image.
15 As Martin and Quinn say (2005), circularity can be a problem if ideal points (based on judges' votes) are used as the explanatory variable in a regression model with the *same* votes as the dependent variable.
16 Save for exceptions, only in instances of statutory interpretation is the legislature legally authorized to override a ruling.
17 Bill Chavez et al. (2011) compared the supreme courts of the United States and Argentina.
18 Sánchez et al. (2010) partly disagree. The court continued to favor the PRI in *constitutional controversies* even after the PRI's power became fragmented (ibid., 198).
19 This section reviewed theories of *decision-making*. Examples of multidimensional explanations of the entire litigation or "legalization" process are discussed below.
20 The former is exemplified by a rule prohibiting smoking in restaurants and the latter by a ban on "cruel" punishment.
21 Sánchez et al. (2011), Desposato et al. (2015), and González-Bertomeu et al. (2016).

22 See Wilson's chapter.
23 An unexplored option is a precise but less demanding remedy (Lewis Kornhauser suggested this point).
24 Defined as the extent that courts and lawyers become relevant actors, and legal language and categories become relevant, in the design and implementation of policy (ibid., 4).
25 Only cited works are listed.

References[25]

Latin America

Ansolabehere, Karina (2008). "Legalistas, legalistas moderados y garantistas moderados." *Revista Mexicana de Sociología* 70(2) (April–June), 331–59.

Ansolabehere, Karina (2007). *La política desde la justicia: cortes supremas, gobierno y democracia en Argentina y México*. FLACSO México, Fontamara.

Barrera, Leticia (2012). *La Corte Suprema En Escena*. Buenos Aires, Siglo Veintiuno Editores.

Basabe-Serrano, Santiago (2015). "Informal Institutions and Judicial Independence in Paraguay, 1954–2011." *Law & Policy* 37: 350–78.

Basabe-Serrano, Santiago (2012). "Judges without Robes and Judicial Voting in Contexts of Institutional Instability: The Case of Ecuador's Constitutional Court, 1999–2007." *Journal of Latin American Studies* 44.1 (Feb 2012), 127–61.

Brinks, Daniel M. (2005). "Judicial Reform and Independence in Brazil and Argentina: The Beginning of a New Millennium?" *Texas International Law Journal* 403, 595–622.

Brinks, Daniel M. (2011). "'Faithful Servants of the Regime': The Brazilian Constitutional Court's Role under the 1988 Constitution." In: Helmke, Gretchen and Julio Ríos-Figueroa. *Courts in Latin America*. New York, Cambridge University Press, 128–53.

Brinks, Daniel M. and Varun Gauri (2014). "The Law's Majestic Equality?" *Perspectives on Politics* Vol. 12, No. 2, 375–93.

Castagnola, Andrea and Aníbal Pérez-Liñán (2011). "Bolivia: The Rise (and Fall) of Judicial Review." In: Helmke and Ríos-Figueroa. *Courts in Latin America*, 278–305.

Chavez, Rebecca Bill (2003). "The Construction of the Rule of Law in Argentina: A Tale of Two Provinces." *Comparative Politics* Vol. 35, No. 4, 417.

Chavez, Rebecca Bill (2004a). *The Rule of Law in Nascent Democracies: Judicial Politics in Argentina*. Stanford, CA: Stanford University Press.

Chavez, Rebecca Bill (2004b). "The Evolution of Judicial Autonomy in Argentina: Establishing the Rule of Law in an Ultrapresidential System." *Journal of Latin American Studies* Vol. 36, No. 3, 451–78.

Chavez, Rebecca Bill, John A. Ferejohn, and Barry R. Weingast (2011). "A Theory of the Politically Independent Judiciary." In: Helmke and Ríos-Figueroa. *Courts in Latin America*, 219–47.

Couso, Javier A. (2005). "The Judicialization of Chilean Politics: The Rights Revolution that Never Was." In: Sieder, Rachel, Line Schjolden, Alan Angell (eds). *The Judicialization of Politics in Latin America*, New York: Palgrame Macmillan.

Couso, Javier A. (2010). "The Transformation of Constitutional Discourse and the Judicialization of Politics in Latin America." In: Couso, Javier A., Alexandra Huneeus, and Rachel Sieder. *Cultures of Legality: Judicialization and Political Activism in Latin America*, New York, Cambridge University Press, 141–60.

Couso, Javier A. and Lisa Hilbink (2011). "From Quietism to Incipient Activism: the Institutional and Ideological Roots of Rights Adjudication in Chile." In: Helmke and Ríos-Figueroa. *Courts in Latin America*, 99–127.

Da Silva, V.A., and F.V. Terrazas (2011). "Claiming the Right to Health in Brazilian Courts: The Exclusion of the Already Excluded?" *Law & Social Inquiry* Vol. 36, No. 4, 825–53.

Desposato, Scott, Matthew C. Ingram and Osmar Lannes, Jr. (2015). "Power, Composition, and Decision Making: The Behavioral Consequences of Institutional Reform on Brazil's Supremo Tribunal Federal." *Journal of Law, Economics, & Organization* Vol. 31, No. 3, 534–67.

Domingo, Pilar (2005). "Judicialization of Politics: The Changing Political Role of the Judiciary in Mexico." In: Sieder, Schjolden and Angell. *The Judicialization of Politics in Latin America* 21–46.

Domingo, Pilar (2010). "Novel Appropriations of the Law in the Pursuit of Political and Social Change in Latin America." In: Couso, Huneeus and Sieder. *Cultures of Legality* 254–78.

Ferraz, Octavio Luiz Motta. 2011. "Harming the Poor through Social Rights Litigation: Lessons from Brazil." *Texas Law Review* Vol. 89, 1643–68.

Finkel, Jodi S. (2004). "Judicial Reform as Insurance Policy in Mexico in the 1990s," *Latin American Politics and Society* Vol. 47, No. 1, 87–113.

Finkel, Jodi S. (2008). *Judicial Reform as Political Insurance Argentina, Peru, and Mexico in the 1990s.* Notre Dame, IN: University of Notre Dame Press.

Gauri, Varun, Jeffrey K. Staton, and Jorge Vargas Cullell (2015). "The Costa Rican Supreme Court's Compliance Monitoring System." *Journal of Politics* Vol. 77, No. 3, 774–86.

Gauri, Varun and Daniel M. Brinks (2008). "Introduction." In: *Courting Social Justice. Judicial Enforcement of Social and Economic Rights in the Developing World.* Cambridge University Press, 1–37.

Gloppen, Siri, Bruce M. Wilson, Roberto Gargarella, Elin Skaar and Morten Kinander (2010). *Courts and Power in Latin America and Africa.* New York, Palgrave Macmillan.

Gomez, Manuel A. (2010). "Political Activism and the Practice of Law in Venezuela." In: Couso, Huneeus and Sieder, *Cultures of Legality: Judicialization and Political Activism in Latin America,* 182–206.

González-Bertomeu, Juan F., Nuno Garoupa and Lucia Dalla Pellegrina (2016). "Estimating Ideal Points in Latin America: The Case of Argentina." *Review of Law and Economics,* Issue 2.

Helmke, Gretchen (2002). "The Logic of Strategic Defection: Court-Executive Relations in Argentina under Dictatorship and Democracy." *The American Political Science Review* Vol. 96, No. 2, 291–303.

Helmke, Gretchen (2005). *Courts under Constraints: Judges, Generals, and Presidents in Argentina.* Cambridge, UK; New York: Cambridge University Press.

Helmke, Gretchen (2011). "Public Support and Judicial Crises in Latin America." 13 *U. Pa. J. Const. L.* 397.

Helmke, Gretchen and Jeffrey K. Staton (2011). "The Puzzling Judicial Politics of Latin America." In: Helmke and Ríos-Figueroa. *Courts in Latin America,* 306–31.

Helmke, Gretchen and Julio Ríos-Figueroa (2011). "Introduction." In: Helmke, Gretchen and Julio Ríos-Figueroa. *Courts in Latin America,* Cambridge; New York: Cambridge University Press.

Helmke, Gretchen and Mitchell S. Sanders (2006). "A Method for Inferring Judicial Goals from Behavior." *Journal of Politics* Vol. 68, No. 4, 867–78.

Hilbink, Lisa (2007). *Judges Beyond Politics in Democracy and Dictatorship: Lessons from Chile.* New York: Cambridge University Press.

Hilbink, Lisa (2012). "The Origins of Positive Judicial Independence." *World Politics* Vol. 64, No. 4, 587–621.

Huneeus, Alexandra (2011). "Courts Resisting Courts: Lessons from the Inter-American Court's Struggle to Enforce Human Rights." 44 *Cornell Int'l L.J.* 493.

Huneeus, Alexandra, Javier Couso, and Rachel Sieder (2010). "Cultures of Legality: Judicialization and Political Activism in Contemporary Latin America." In: Couso, Huneeus and Sieder, *Cultures of Legality* 3–24.

Iaryczower, Matías, Pablo Spiller, and Mariano Tommasi (2002). "Judicial Independence in Unstable Environments, Argentina 1935–1998." *American Journal of Political Science* Vol 46, No. 4.

Inclán Oseguera, Silvia (2009). "Judicial Reform in Mexico: Political Insurance or the Search for Political Legitimacy?" *Political Research Quarterly* Vol. 62, No. 4, 753–66.

Ingram, Matthew C. (2015). "Judicial Power in Latin America." *Latin American Research Review* Vol. 50, No. 1, 250–60.

Ingram, Matthew C. (2016). *Crafting Courts in New Democracies.* New York: Cambridge University Press.

Ingram, Matthew C. and Diana Kapiszewski (forthcoming). *Beyond High Courts.* Notre Dame: University of Notre Dame Press.

Kapiszewski, Diana (2010). "How Courts Work: Institutions, Culture, and the Brazilian Supremo Tribunal Federal." In: Couso, Huneeus and Sieder, *Cultures of Legality,* 51–77.

Kapiszewski, Diana (2011b). "Tactical Balancing: High Court Decision Making on Politically Crucial Cases." *Law and Society Review* Vol. 45, 471–506.

Kapiszewski, Diana (2012). *High Courts and Economic Governance in Argentina and Brazil.* New York: Cambridge University Press.

Kapiszewski, Diana (2013). "Economic Governance on Trial: High Courts and Elected Leaders in Argentina and Brazil." *Latin American Politics and Society* Vol. 55, No. 4, 47–73.

Kapiszewski, Diana and Matthew M. Taylor (2008). "Doing Courts Justice: Studying Judicial Politics in Latin America," *Perspectives on Politics* Vol. 6, No. 4: 741–67.

183

Kapiszewski, Diana and Matthew M. Taylor (2013). "Compliance: Conceptualizing, Measuring, and Explaining Adherence to Judicial Rulings." *Law and Social Inquiry,* Vol. 38, No. 4, 803–35.

Landau, David (2005). "The Two Discourses in Colombian Constitutional Jurisprudence: a New Approach to Modeling Judicial Behavior in Latin America." *George Washington International Law Review* Vol. 373, 687–744.

Larkins, Christopher M. (1996). "Judicial Independence and Democratization: A Theoretical and Conceptual Analysis." *The American Journal of Comparative Law* Vol. 44, No. 4, 605–26.

Larkins, Christopher M. (1998). "The Judiciary and Delegative Democracy in Argentina." *Comparative Politics* Vol. 30, 423–43.

Magaloni, Beatriz (2008). "Enforcing the Autocratic Political Order and the Role of Courts: The Case of Mexico." In: Ginsburg, Tom and Tamir Moustafa (eds.), *Rule by Law: The Politics of Courts in Authoritarian Regimes,* Cambridge University Press, 180–206.

Navia, Patricio and Julio Ríos-Figueroa (2005). "The Constitutional Adjudication Mosaic of Latin America." *Comparative Political Studies* Vol. 38, No. 2, 189–217.

Nunes, Rodrigo M. (2010). "Ideational Origins of Progressive Judicial Activism: The Colombian Constitutional Court and the Right to Health." *Latin American Politics and Society* Vol. 52, No. 3, 67–97.

Pou Giménez, Francisca (2017). "Changing the Channel: Broadcasting Deliberations in the Mexican Supreme Court." In: David, Richard and David Taras (eds.). *A Global Perspective on Justices and Journalists,* Cambridge University Press.

Ríos-Figueroa, Julio (2007). "Fragmentation of Power and the Emergence of an Effective Judiciary in Mexico, 1994–2002." *Latin American Politics and Society* Vol. 49, No. 1, 31–57.

Ríos-Figueroa, Julio (2011). "Institutions for Constitutional Justice in Latin America." In: Helmke and Ríos-Figueroa. *Courts in Latin America,* 27–54.

Ríos-Figueroa, Julio and Mathew M. Taylor (2006). "Institutional Determinants of the Judicialization of Policy in Brazil and Mexico." *Journal of Latin American Studies* Vol. 38, No. 4, 739–66.

Rodríguez-Raga, Juan Carlos (2011). "Strategic Deference in the Colombian Constitutional Court, 1992–2006." In: Helmke and Ríos-Figueroa. *Courts in Latin America,* 81–98.

Rueda, Pablo (2010). "Legal Language and Social Change during Colombia's Economic Crisis." In: Couso, Huneeus and Sieder, *Cultures of Legality,* 25–50.

Ruibal, Alba M. (2009). "Self-Restraint in Search of Legitimacy: The Reform of the Argentine Supreme Court." *Latin American Politics and Society* Vol. 51, No. 3, 59–86.

Sánchez, Arianna, Beatriz Magaloni, and Eric Magar (2011). "Legalist versus Interpretativist: the Supreme Court and the Democratic Transition in Mexico." In: Helmke and Ríos-Figueroa. *Courts in Latin America,* 187–218.

Sánchez-Urribarri Raúl and Donald R. Songer (2006). "A Cross-National Examination of the 'Strategic Defection' Theory." APSA 2006.

Scribner, Druscilla L. (2011). "Courts, Power, and Rights in Argentina and Chile." In: Helmke and Ríos-Figueroa. *Courts in Latin America,* 248–77.

Scribner, Druscilla L. (2013). "Distributing Political Power: The Constitutional Tribunal in Post-authoritarian Chile." In: Kapiszewski, Diana, Gordon Silverstein, and Robert A. Kagan. *Consequential Courts: Judicial Roles in Global Perspective,* Cambridge University Press.

Sieder, Rachel (2010). "Legal Cultures in the (Un)Rule of Law: Indigenous Rights and Juridification in Guatemala." In: Couso, Huneeus and Sieder, *Cultures of Legality,* 161–81.

Smulovitz, Catalina (2005). "Petitioning and Creating Rights: Judicialization in Argentina." In: Sieder, Schjolden and Angell. *The Judicialization of Politics in Latin America,* 161–86.

Smulovitz, Catalina (2010). "Judicialization in Argentina: Legal Culture or Opportunities and Support Structures?" In: Couso, Huneeus and Sieder, *Cultures of Legality,* 234–53.

Staton, Jeffrey K. (2006). "Constitutional Review and the Selective Promotion of Case Results." *American Journal of Political Science* Vol. 50, No. 1, 98–112.

Staton, Jeffrey K. (2010). *Judicial Power and Strategic Communication in Mexico.* New York: Cambridge University Press.

Staton, Jeffrey K. and Alexia Romero (2012). "Clarity and Compliance in the Inter-American Human Rights System." Manuscript.

Staton, Jeffrey K. and Georg Vanberg (2008). "The Value of Vagueness: Delegation, Defiance, and Judicial Opinions." *American Journal of Political Science* Vol. 52, No. 3, 504–19.

Taylor, Mathew M. (2006a). "Beyond Judicial Reform: Courts as Political Actors in Latin America." *Latin American Research Review* Vol. 41, No. 2, 269–80.

Taylor, Mathew M. (2008). *Judging Policy: Courts and Policy Reform in Democratic Brazil*. Stanford University Press.

Tiede, Lydia Brashear (2011). "Review." *The Journal of Politics* Vol. 73, No. 3, 957–58.

Tiede, Lydia Brashear and Aldo Fernando Ponce (2011). "Ruling Against the Executive in *Amparo* Cases: Evidence from the Peruvian Constitutional Tribunal." *Journal of Politics in Latin America* Vol. 3, No. 2, 107–40.

Wilson, Bruce M. (2005). "Changing Dynamics: The Political Impact of Costa Rica's Constitutional Court." In: Sieder, Rachel, Line Schjolden, Alan Angell. *The Judicialization of Politics in Latin America*, New York: Palgrame Macmillan.

Wilson, Bruce M. and Juan Carlos Rodríguez Cordero (2006). "Legal Opportunity Structures and Social Movements: The Effects of Institutional Change on Costa Rican Politics." *Comparative Political Studies* Vol. 39, No. 3, 325–51.

Wilson, Bruce M. and Roger Handberg (1999). "From Judicial Passivity to Judicial Activism: Explaining the Change within Costa Rica's Supreme Court." 5 *NAFTA Law & Bus. Rev. Am.* 522.

Woods, Patricia J. and Lisa Hilbink (2009). "Comparative Sources of Judicial Empowerment: Ideas and Interests." *Political Research Quarterly* Vol. 62, No. 4, 745–52.

Other

Bickel, Alexander (1986). *The Least Dangerous Branch*. Yale University Press.

Cameron, Charles M. and Lewis A. Kornhauser (2015). "Rational Choice Attitudinalism?" *Eur J.Law Econ*, doi:10.1007/s10657-015-9512-1.

Cameron, Charles M. and Lewis A. Kornhauser (2017). "Theorizing the U.S. Supreme Court." Forthcoming, *Oxford Research Encyclopedia of Politics*.

Dworkin, Ronald (1977). *Taking Rights Seriously*. Harvard University Press.

Dworkin, Ronald (1986). *Law's Empire*. Belknap.

Epp, Charles R. (1998). *The Rights Revolution*. University of Chicago Press.

Epstein, Lee and Jack Knight (1998). *The Choices Justices Make*. CQ Press.

Epstein, Lee and Jack Knight (2000). "Toward a Strategic Revolution in Judicial Politics: A Look Back, a Look Ahead." *Political Research Quarterly* Vol. 53, No. 3, 625–61.

Ferejohn, John (1999). "Independent Judges, Dependent Judiciary: Explaining Judicial Independence." *Southern California Law Review* Vol. 72, No. 2–3, 353–84.

Ferejohn, John and Barry Weingast (1992). "A Positive Theory of Statutory Interpretation." *International Review of Law and Economics* Vol. 12, 263–73.

Friedman, Barry (2005). "The Politics of Judicial Review." 84 *Tex. L. Rev.* 257.

Friedman, Barry (2006). "Taking Law Seriously." New York University Public Law and Legal Theory Working Papers, Paper 21.

Galanter, Marc (1974). "Why the 'Haves' Come out Ahead: Speculations on the Limits of Legal Change." *Law and Society Review* Vol. 9, No. 1, 95–160.

Gely, Rafael and Pablo T. Spiller (1990). "A Rational Choice Theory of Supreme Court Statutory Decisions with Applications to the *State Farm* and *Grove City* Cases." *Journal of Law, Economics and Organization* Vol. 6, 263–300.

Ginsburg, Tom (2003). *Judicial Review in New Democracies: Constitutional Courts in Asian Cases*. Cambridge University Press.

Ginsburg, Tom and Mila Versteeg (2014). "Why Do Countries Adopt Constitutional Review?" *Journal of Law, Economics and Organization* Vol. 30, 587.

Hirschl, Ran (2006). "The New Constitutionalism and the Judicialization of Pure Politics Worldwide." *Fordham Law Review* Vol. 75, No. 2, 721–54.

Holmes, Stephen (1995). *Passions and Constraint*. University of Chicago Press.

Kornhauser, Lewis A. (2002). "Is Judicial Independence a Useful Concept?" In: Burbank, Stephen B. and Barry Friedman (eds.), *Judicial Independence at the Crossroads,* SAGE.

Landry, Pierre (2008). "The Institutional Diffusion of Courts in China: Evidence from Survey Data." In Ginsburg, Tom and Tamir Moustafa (ed.). *Rule by Law: The Politics of Courts in Authoritarian Regimes,* Cambridge University Press.

Leiter, Brian (2002). "American Legal Realism." University of Texas Law, Public Law Research Paper No. 42.

Martin, Andrew D. and Kevin M. Quinn (2002). "Dynamic Ideal Point Estimation via Markov Chain Monte Carlo for the U.S. Supreme Court, 1953–1999." *Political Analysis* Vol. 10, 2.

Pritchet, Herman (1948). *The Roosevelt Court*. Macmillan, New York.

Ramseyer, J. Mark (1994). "The Puzzling (In)dependence of Courts: A Comparative Approach." *Journal of Legal Studies* Vol. 23, No. 2, 721–47.

Segal, Jeffrey and Harold J. Spaeth (2002). *The Supreme Court and the Attitudinal Model Revisited*. Cambridge University Press.

Shapiro, Martin (1981). *Courts, a Comparative and Political Analysis*. University of Chicago Press.

Tate, C Neal and Torbjörn Vallinder (1995). *The Global Expansion of Judicial Power*. New York University Press.

Thelen, Kathleen and James Mahoney (2009). *Explaining Institutional Change: Ambiguity, Agency, and Power*. Cambridge University Press.

Vanberg, Georg (2005). *The Politics of Constitutional Review in Germany*. Cambridge University Press.

Voigt, Stefan and Eli Salzberger (2002). "Choosing not to Choose: When Politicians Choose to Delegate Powers." *Kyklos* Vol. 55, 289–310.

Whittington, Keith (2005). " 'Interpose Your Friendly Hand': Political Supports for the Exercise of Judicial Review by the United States Supreme Court." APSR, v. 99 No. 04, 583–96.

13

SUPREME AND CONSTITUTIONAL COURTS

Directions in Constitutional Justice

Francisca Pou Giménez

Introduction

Constitutional courts are a distinctive feature of contemporary democracies all over the world, and legal and socio-legal literature on courts is now boundless. This chapter analyzes the richness and frequent novelty of constitutional justice developments in Latin America, identifying what are clearly distinctive regional trends, such us the combination of judicial review models at the level of institutional design, the importance apex courts have placed on social communication and creating direct bonds with the citizenry, the salience of inter-court interaction and judicial dialog, and the vitality of debates about the social impact of judicial action.

Perceptions about the role of the judiciary in Latin America have changed enormously in recent years, and the image of subservience to the executive and relative irrelevance within the political system has been left far behind (Rodiles 2016, 153). The burgeoning literature on "judicial politics," "judicialization" or "judicial roles" in the region attests that, following a global trend (Boulanger 2015; Hirschl 2004; Stone 2000, 2012; Tate and Vallinder 1995), its supreme and constitutional courts have become vastly consequential political players (Kapiszewsky, Silverstein, and Kagan 2013; Helmke and Ríos 2011; Gianella and Wilson in this volume). The legal academy, for its part, pays ever-increasing attention to legal developments in courts, compared to those occurring in the other branches.

This chapter privileges analysis of the courts' institutional structure and performance over causal inquiry focused on explaining why courts behave as they do. Developed in combination with waves of studies about the rule of law and democratization in Latin America, the literature trying to ascertain the empirical determinants of courts' performance and survival is vast and rich. Studies on judicial independence – a classic theme – have been more recently supplemented with others that set forth models of judicial behavior and ponder what elements might explain why courts end up privileging certain directions –protecting rights, guarding interbranch peace, favoring social transformation, securing economic and legal stability, or defending their professional interests – over others. Illuminating as it is, I do not engage in a systematic assessment of the literature on empirical determinants, which is addressed elsewhere in this volume (see the chapter by González-Bertomeu 2012). Instead, I privilege description of what the region's constitutional and supreme courts arguably do, and how they do it, over inquiry into why they do it. I survey the institutional and procedural structures that organize their performance, and single out some of the traits that point to their roles and functions in contemporary Latin American democracies.

For reasons of space, this chapter does not cover all apex courts and countries with the same intensity, focusing explicitly or implicitly on developments in Colombia, Argentina, Brazil, and Mexico. Apex courts of Central America and the Caribbean, of South American countries like Paraguay, Uruguay, Chile, or Peru, or the group of three that mark a distinctive current within the region's constitutionalism – the "new Latin American constitutionalism" of Bolivia, Ecuador, and Venezuela (Viciano and Martínez Dalmau 2011; Couso 2014; Gargarella 2012) – will receive cursory references at most. While there is no excuse for gaps that enlarged research could fill, there is no denying either that the most discussed, well-known, and readily available literature in the areas covered here disproportionately focuses on that handful of countries. This immediately marks pending research agendas, since unbalance attention deepens South–South asymmetries, no less harmful than the North–South asymmetries that have traditionally pervaded the production and diffusion of socio-legal knowledge (Bonilla 2016). In short, rather than offering a comprehensive comparative appraisal, this chapter attempts to identify the most salient and influential directions and developments in the region's constitutional justice.

The chapter is structured as follows: the first section analyzes Latin American apex courts as institutions, underlining the remarkable quantity and variety of procedural paths they have been conferred to fulfill their constitutional functions. Second, it surveys salient aspects of their relations with civil society. The way Latin American courts have understood their public role, their quest for transparency, their taste for public exposure, and the manner in which interaction between activists, litigants, and judges has molded the latter's political position and created new forums of democratic debate no doubt singularizes judicial developments in the region. The third section addresses the relations apex courts maintain among themselves and with other courts, at both national and supranational levels. In recent decades Latin America has witnessed a revolution in interpretive methods and general understandings of the law: new paradigms of normative legitimacy have emerged in a continental-wide judicial space in which courts sometimes depict themselves as a kind of deliberative community. I consider how the dialogic paradigm has been progressively advanced and contested, and address some of the questions it poses in relation to democracy in the continent. The final section addresses an issue of primordial importance, given the intersection between transformation-oriented constitutions, activist courts and grossly unfair background social structures, namely, the debate on the efficacy of judicial rulings and the relations between law and social change more generally, which has generated illuminating, and innovative scholarly work.

Institutional Design: The Mosaic Re-Visited

Latin American countries played a pioneering role in setting up judicial review procedures in the nineteenth century. Mexico created the *amparo* writ in 1847 to guard fundamental rights against state encroachments, when nobody could predict this procedure would become a staple of post-Second World War constitutionalism. Colombia and Venezuela, for their part, were pioneers with regards to abstract review of legislation – which many people wrongly assume was invented much later in Europe by Hans Kelsen. These two countries created in 1850 and 1859, respectively, public actions of unconstitutionality allowing citizens to challenge the validity of general acts enacted by subnational entities before the supreme court (Fernández 2012, 169–76; Ortiz 1997). Sometime later in Colombia, the famous 1907 Act Number 3 extended this possibility to national statutes and decrees (Giacomette 2008; Rodríguez Peñaranda 2007). These developments were path breaking not only because such a review could lead to the total invalidation of statutory provisions, but also because ordinary citizens were given standing – something that continues to be remarkable viewed from contemporary eyes. At different points during the nineteenth century, several countries adopted systems of diffuse review of legislation along the lines followed in the United States after 1803, even if the region's legal systems and culture were – and continue to be – continental, not common law (Fix-Zamudio 2001; Saba 2008). Nonetheless, the centrality of judicial review of legislation at that time should not be overrated. Under prevailing understandings in the nineteenth century constitutions were not directly applicable, as they are today. Courts had many legality-review responsibilities – often under the frame of "cassation" – and their performance was marked by the fact that statutes, not the constitution, were at the center of the law, and also by strong direct or indirect executive influence (see Navia and Ríos-Figueroa 2005, exploring the elements that allegedly influenced the historic behavior of regional judiciaries).

Things have changed radically in recent decades, with the global advance of a rights-based modality of democracy that confers core responsibilities on the judiciary. In comparative studies, contemporary Latin American systems of judicial review are portrayed as "hybrid" (Frosini and Pegoraro 2008) or "mixed" (Brewer-Carías 1990). This means they combine traits from two ideal types: the diffuse or decentralized system along the lines adopted in the USA, and the concentrated, or centralized model theorized by Hans Kelsen at the beginning of the twentieth century. In a stylized centralized model, review of legislation is performed exclusively by a dedicated institution – the constitutional court – whose members are appointed through special procedures, the review is principal (not incidental), abstract (not concrete), *ex ante* or *ex post* (before or after the statute has entered into force) and culminates in a decision with general effects: unconstitutional provisions are struck from the books. In a prototypical decentralized model, by contrast, any court of law can review the constitutionality of legislation and review is carried out in the course of ordinary procedures; it is therefore incidental, concrete, *ex post*, and has inter parts effects: the unconstitutional provision is merely set aside in the case at hand.

Almost all contemporary regulations make for hybrid models. Different groups of hybrids, however, exhibit identifiable family traits. Thus, European hybrids may be described as centralized systems with a few elements of decentralization, the latter represented by the possibility of ordinary judges to pose a "question of unconstitutionality" and activate review by the constitutional court. Latin American hybrids, by contrast, are more fairly described as decentralized systems with a few elements of centralization, or as systems that superimpose the two models. Thus, in Argentina any judge can set aside a statute in the course of ordinary adjudication, but the supreme court has areas of exclusive jurisdiction (sec. 117 C. Argentina) and decides the "extraordinary recourse" (sec. 280 Civil Proc. Code) in several hypotheses interpretively controlled through a certiorari system (Dalla 1997; Sagüés 2002). In Colombia, the constitutional court concentrates abstract review, being the sole institution allowed to decide unconstitutionality actions, but there is diffuse review through the "exception of unconstitutionality," which allows any judge (including the constitutional court) to set aside a statute she may find unconstitutional while resolving a case. And Mexico, after constitutional amendments in 2011, now has three tiers of review: centralized review through actions of unconstitutionality and constitutional controversies, semi-centralized review through the writ of *amparo*, and diffuse review in the hands of all ordinary judges.

Beyond this, available surveys (Roa 2015; Frosini and Pegoraro 2008; Navia and Ríos-Figueroa 2005) document that the region's apex courts are quite varied along almost all relevant dimensions of design: number and status of courts; appointment procedures; areas of jurisdiction; effects of the rulings; and so forth. Thus, while some countries have supplemented the pre-existing scheme by creating a constitutional court, others have kept a single supreme court, and still others have created a specialized constitutional chamber within the former court. In some places – Mexico, Brazil, or Argentina – a single court concentrates a huge amount of functions, while in others – Colombia or Peru – the same package of responsibilities is distributed among several apex courts. Some appointment systems follow the traditional North American path of having the president and the senate share responsibility for designations, while others feature more innovative mechanisms. Thus, Colombian justices are elected by the senate from candidates proposed, in turns, by the Council of State, the president, and the constitutional court itself. In Bolivia, the members of the Supreme Tribunal of Justice are elected by popular vote (sec. 182, C. Bolivia); the same system is used in the appointment of the Pluri-National Constitutional Tribunal members, which must moreover respect pluri-nationality criteria and assure representation of both Ordinary Justice and Indigenous Native Peasant Justice (sec. 196–201, ibid.). To appoint the members of the constitutional court of Ecuador, the legislative, executive, and social supervision branches each designate two people to integrate a qualifying commission, which, respecting gender parity, then appoints the justices from candidates pre-selected by them in a process of public examination that must allow citizens to raise public challenges (sec. 434 C. Ecuador).

As regards areas of jurisdiction, existing overviews underline two main traits: the importance of ancillary powers (Frosini and Pegoraro 2008) and the prevalence of rights-protective writs or individual complaints (Uprimny 2015; Ferrer 2006). Ancillary powers are those other than judicial review of legislation. Latin American courts hold many; from participating in the appointment of other public officials, to deciding the validity of elections or conducting impeachment procedures. To put it in Kelsenian jargon, Latin American courts have not been designed to be "pure" (Ferreres 2009), but to crown multifunctional systems where the judiciary has quite varied responsibilities.

The second trait is the number, variety and reach of individual complaints for the protection of rights. I would in fact point to a more general regional characteristic, namely, the procedural openness of Latin American constitutional justice to society, well beyond what we find in the USA or Europe. Thus, *amparo*-style procedures are flexible and far-reaching in the region. In contrast to the German or Spanish *amparos*, most Latin American writs can be used to challenge statutes or even treaties – not only state conduct and executive and administrative regulations – and even conduct by private actors. This last trait, the extension of constitutional rights enforcement in the private domain – often called by its German tab, *drittwirkung*, or simply "horizontal effect" – is indeed one of the leading themes in contemporary constitutional law (Gardbaum 2013) and a crucial bolster of constitutional efficacy in scenarios where private power is sometimes overwhelming. Also important has been the existence of collective *amparo*, which in countries like Argentina has extraordinarily invigorated rights litigation and, more generally, the fact that these writs tend to operate under loose procedural strictures –Colombian and Costa Rican *tutelas* being paradigmatic in this regard (Restrepo 2003, 81–3; Wilson 2011, 59–60). An additional element of openness is that several countries – among them Colombia, Ecuador, El Salvador, Bolivia, Guatemala and, less generously, Peru – following the historical precedents mentioned above, have set up public actions of unconstitutionality allowing individuals to challenge statutes and obtain their permanent invalidity. In Colombia, far from over-burdening the court, this channel means court has generated doctrine about extraordinarily relevant issues that in all probability would not have been raised by the institutions that enjoy standing under traditional *organklage* Kelsenian models. An additional factor is, of course, the content of regional last-wave constitutions, which include distinctively extensive bills of rights and are allegedly concerned about speaking to the needs of the people.

This quite impressive institutional stage opens up many lines of inquiry. An immediate one, within the field of comparative scholarship, is to develop theoretical work and "new grounds of classification" (Frosini and Pegoraro 2008) capable of accounting for the rich and nuanced mosaic portrayed by the region's supreme and constitutional courts. These analyzes must be advanced with new lenses. As critical comparative scholarship has noted (Esquirol 2014; Bonilla 2015; López 2016), accounts of Latin American institutions and developments have been too often permeated by appallingly asymmetric assumptions about the value of different legal traditions. So, the ample spectrum and frequent superimposition of institutional elements we have just documented should not be portrayed as "curious," "kitsch" or "exceedingly complex"; rather, it reflects the sheer geographical dimensions of Latin America, core chapters of different national and regional history, important features of Latin American constitutionalism, and distinctive developments that should be studied on their own terms – not in function of something else.

A more specific line of inquiry might ascertain in what ways the multiplicity of apex courts' responsibilities and the panoply of channels available to reach them is (or is not) related to the heightened profile – "activism" – they are generally attributed. While institutional factors have long been counted as central is explaining court's delivery, further work is called for to map out what sort of institutional choices are found in correlation with different outcomes (González-Bertomeu 2012). Some theorists have argued, for instance, that European centralized models have an in-built activist bias: since constitutional courts are set up exclusively to review legislation, being very passive could suggest they are actually not systemically required and raise doubts about their continuation, in contrast with North American style apex courts, which "earn their salary" while discharging their ordinary duties within the judiciary regardless of how often they strike down statutes (Ferreres 2009, 79–80). The fact that Latin American courts, however, are generally dealing with an upsurge in litigation and have an image of activism, despite their multi-layered and busy jurisdictional menu, could suggest otherwise – or could simply help illuminate new analytical approaches, from pursuing more refined models to construe and measure core notions ("activism," "constitutional enforcement"), to finding new ways of mapping out the legal, cultural, institutional, and political interactions that convene around courts.

Latin American Courts and the People: Building Up Legitimacy Through Social and Judicial Action

The extensive literature on judicialization – which inquires how and why courts are established and what elements influence their survival and performance – accords great weight to courts' relations with the other branches. Insurance, strategic defection, fragmentation, attitudinal, or strategic theories, to name a few, all focus on how courts situate themselves vis-à-vis the position and exercise of power of the other branches, in turn regularly portrayed as having different or even opposing interests.

Yet regardless of what may be found to occur at the level of deeper motivations, Latin American courts have seemingly obsessed not about the other branches, but about the people. In one sense, in line with the transformative mandates of last-wave constitutions and perhaps following the activist drive built into the set of procedural tools just surveyed, contemporary regional courts have striven to cement their political position by building a privileged relation with the citizenry, and by favoring inter-branch cooperation over conflict, sometimes along the lines favored by weak-form, dialogic forms of judicial review (Gargarella 2014a; Tushnet 2008; Roach 2004). These dynamics have delivered important outcomes in many areas, but most noticeably three in particular: social rights; sexual and reproductive rights; and indigenous and environmental rights.

In the area of social rights, interaction between litigants and courts cannot be understood without first referring to an intervening doctrinal element: the fact that Latin American scholars have been pioneers in developing theories about the judicial enforceability of social rights, and about the democracy-reinforcing potential of judicial intervention in contexts marked by highly exclusionary majoritarian politics. Thus, in an early articulation of the main arguments, Christian Courtis and Víctor Abramovich convincingly discredited traditional constructions about the structural or otherwise "natural" differences between civil and political rights, on the one hand, and social, economic, and cultural rights, on the other, and stressed their continuities in terms of state obligations, positive and negative dimensions, and costs (Abramovich and Courtis 2003). In so doing they were joining an international trend that, in close connection with the work of the two United Nations 1966 Rights Covenants Committees, developed doctrines about transversal state obligations to respect, protect, and guarantee rights and about the multiple dimensions of rights enjoyment. A practice of "unpacking rights" along these lines progressively emerged, creating a battery of analytical and argumentative tools that bolstered opportunities for social advocacy and litigation in both national and international fora. This strand of literature argues that remaining difficulties for the enforceability of social rights should be met by transforming existing procedural frameworks and further notes that judicial intervention in public policy is not necessarily anti-democratic. In the context of often elitist, paralyzed and deeply captured legislative chambers (and provided they operate with well-crafted and carefully administered remedies), courts can vastly contribute to attain crucial democracy-reinforcing goals, such as taking the political branches out of inaction, forcing them to correct discrimination, or securing the enforcement of already recognized entitlements (Abramovich and Courtis 2003; Abramovich 2009; Bergallo 2006; Gargarella 2006).

These views have been absorbed by wide sectors of the academy and, albeit not uncontested, have gained ground within the judiciary and other institutional spaces – it is remarkable, for instance, that Section 1 of the Mexican Constitution as amended in 2011 now enshrines transversal state obligations to respect, protect, and guarantee rights and the principles of universality, indivisibility, interdependency, progressivity and *pro persona* interpretation. In a region where constitutions – let alone social rights – had been mere "pieces of paper" for so long, new tools and a new general "state of mind" have been installed, fostering the enforceability of even their most transformative provisions.

Changes at the level of ideas were propelled by the extraordinary expansion of national and transnational networks of socio-legal activism and public interest litigation (Rodríguez- Garavito 2011a). In many countries, people first organized to denounce impunity for the mass-scale atrocities perpetrated by the military juntas in the 1970s and 1980s – litigation being part of a wider set of efforts later theorized under the framework of "transitional justice" (De Greiff 2012; Saffon and Uprimny 2007; Teitel 2000). Efforts in this area went back and forth in national jurisdictions and before the Inter-American System, pointing to the potential of litigation in other domains. Thus, well-equipped, well-funded, and high-profile nongovernmental organizations (NGOs), joined by an increasing number of public interest university clinics, have assured the continuous engagement of Latin American courts.

While some topics have been litigated mostly at the national level (see, for instance, surveys of national experiences in health rights in Lamprea 2014; Bergallo 2013; Yamin and Parra 2010, and the chapters on Latin American countries in Langford 2008, which cover other social rights as well), in others the action of transnational networks has been crucial. Transnational action has been particularly visible in the domain of sexual and reproductive rights, where litigation has delivered legal changes of variable reach – more weighty with regards to sexual orientation, less spectacular but nonetheless real in abortion law (see Restrepo 2011; Cook, Erdmann, and Dickens 2014; Bergallo and Ramón 2016; Gianella and Wilson 2016). More recently, advocacy and litigation networks have entered the area of indigenous and environmental rights. Litigation that vindicates respect for the right to prior consultation and denouncing the effects of extractive economic projects – often result of the combined efforts by communities, lawyers, sociologists, and anthropologists (Rodríguez-Garavito 2011b, 2015a) – has marked news bonds between law and indigenous populations and has supplemented the developments occurring at the national level under the pluri-cultural or pluri-national provisions of last-wave constitutions (Bonilla 2006; Yrigoyen 2015; Ramírez and Maisley 2016; Rodríguez-Garabito 2015b).

Courts have reacted to litigation by advancing new doctrines and forms of adjudication. Attention should be paid, for instance, to normative doctrines such as "unconstitutional state of affairs," "connexity," or "*vía de hecho,*" famously crafted by the Colombian Constitutional Court and imported by some others. In declaring an "unconstitutional state of affairs," the Colombian Court signals social problems that are multi-causal, and that generate multiple and mutually reinforcing violations of rights. The concept allows for a thicker description of unconstitutional realities, to which the court responds with special remedies calling for the joint action of a wide number of social actors and public authorities. Thanks to the "connexity" doctrine – now officially abandoned, but only after the court declared permanent many of the gains obtained under it – the court allowed certain second-tier rights claims to be treated as first-tier, *tutela*-protected claims, when a sufficient connection between the two could be established, thus reinforcing the idea of rights interdependency and multiplying access and protection in crucial domains such as healthcare, social security, or environmental protection. The "*vía de hecho*" construct (and similarly occurs with "*arbitrariedad*" in Argentina) allows apex courts to correct exercises of judicial adjudication on constitutional grounds beyond the possibilities available under standard rules. Evolving conceptions about rights damage and wrongs have ultimately meant that new doctrinal conceptions about remedies and reparations – often inspired by Inter-American doctrines – are increasingly permeating national practice.

Other innovations are procedural, such as the admission of amicus and the celebration of public hearings where apex courts listen to experts, parties, and civil society, gathering elements to decide on thicker grounds – a novelty in civil law systems – and, markedly, the crafting of non-traditional participatory, dialogical, or structural remedies (Bergallo 2006; Gargarella 2014a). As scholars have noted (Rodríguez-Garavito 2011a), Latin American structural rulings may be considered a second-generation that intend to learn from what happened with first-generation ones, issued, paradigmatically, by the United States Supreme Court in the 1950s and 1960s in domains such as school desegregation or prison reform. In contrast with the "command and control" remedial style of the latter – which includes detailed orders and pre-fixed schedules, making courts the key decision-makers and supervisors of compliance, the structural rulings of the Colombian or the Argentinian Courts are flexible and try to engage a wide array of social and political actors, summoned to act under the supervision of the court. In the execution of the famous T-25 of 2004 ruling on internally displaced people, for instance, the Colombian Court set down very loose guidelines for the making of public policy that was largely non-existent, and required the concurrence of government agencies, civil society – including Colombian universities, who were asked to help produce some of the expert knowledge – and victim's representatives, under a strong supervision scheme that required the creation of a special office inside the court (Rodríguez-Garavito 2009).

These developments would have less chances of success were they not complemented by a feature peculiar to Latin American apex courts: the way they strive to render their tasks highly visible, appear accessible and transparent, and generally display a high public profile. Strategies of social communication have included unprecedented initiatives, such as the broadcasting of judges' deliberations on the merits of cases in Brazil and Mexico (Falcão and Oliveira 2013; Hübner Mendes 2017; Pou 2017b). These initiatives are strictly intertwined with the broader vision about the relationship between courts and society highlighted here. Cultivating an image of transparency and openness has been considered key to the courts' effort to distinguish themselves from the often discredited majority branches, and instrumental to sustain a dynamic relation with social actors (Screibner 2016). This publicity-mediated interaction becomes crucial in getting issues discussed before the courts, securing the efficacy of the rulings, and of course maintaining the sort of public image that courts find appealing. As has been cautioned, however (Silva 2013, 2015; Pou 2017a), it is crucial to examine the impact internal rules such as the broadcasting of the sessions have on the deliberative quality of judicial decisions and more generally on the courts' capacity to successfully meet their role as articulators of public reasons. At a more general level, whether the courts' "transparency revolution" is genuine or rather includes excessive "marketing" and strategic moves – which might even decrease our capacity to hold them accountable for what really matters – remains to be seen and should be carefully monitored.

Future research agendas should engage legal and socio-legal scholars in the systematic identification and critical analysis of the doctrinal areas where the region's apex courts have made distinctive contributions. The first regional casebook, edited by Juan González-Bertomeu and Roberto Gargarella (2016) surveys regional judicial doctrine on 13 areas – including equality rights, religious freedom, free speech, rights of prisoners, LGBTI (lesbian, gay, bisexual, transgender, and intersex) people, indigenous people, the environment, economic regulation, and the separation of powers – constituting a first, giant step in that regard. Ongoing monitoring should carefully survey developments in the domain of non-traditional rights (i.e., the right to peace, the right to food, and the rights of the earth) without neglecting doctrines generated outside the realm of rights, where there are allegedly less developments to be registered, but some of them identifiably distinctive from the comparative perspective – Latin American doctrines about the unconstitutionality of constitutional amendments being, for instance, a case in point.

Latin American Courts and Their Peers: The "Judicial Community"

By some accounts, over the last decade Latin America has witnessed the emergence of a regional "judicial space" distinguished by the force of the interpretivist turn, the centrality of the idea of judicial dialog, and the salience of Inter-American sources of law in judicial reasoning. In contrast to other regions of legal integration such as Europe, Latin America is distinctive in that such tendencies occur in a region where the bonds of political integration are weak, thus inviting a debate about the potential and possible risks of integration based almost exclusively on courts and rights adjudication practices.

Last-wave democratic constitutions in the region have taken life in parallel with a radical change in traditional understandings of law, legal reasoning, and legal culture – a dimension that, quite appropriately, is gaining increasing weight in overall accounts of judicial power (Couso, Huneeus, and Sieder 2010). In the past, variably (dis)empowered Latin American judges would carry out their jobs as described under the "legislative state" paradigm (Zagrebelsky 2003; Aguiló 2004): putting rules – not principles – at the center of the law, they resolved disputes by applying statutes – not the constitution – and assumed a relatively detached relationship between the constitution and the wider legal system. Years later, both legal theorists and sociologists

(Carbonell 2011; Esquirol 2011; Couso 2010; Rodríguez-Garavito 2011a) signal Latin America as a champion of legal "interpretivism," or of "neo-constitutionalism," understood as a version of the "constitutional state" paradigm. Under this paradigm, law comprises principles, values and rules, the constitution is directly applicable and paramount in judicial adjudication, and basic constitutional rights and principles shape the wider legal system (Pozzolo 2015).

The "neo-constitutional" label has progressively faded into non-use, as for some it signals nothing "new" – only constitutionalism, taken seriously – and for others it captures an objectionable variety of it: one that is hyper-elitist and accords judges a messianic role, paving the way to an exceedingly anti-majoritarian administration of the new constitutions of the region. Yet beyond labels and emphasis, there is no denying that regional courts operate under the pretty much globalized paradigm articulated around the idea of rights supremacy, supported in the series of conceptual argumentative structures that comparative scholars have called "generic constitutional law" (Law 2005). In the context of these emerging patterns of "global constitutionalism," two features distinguish Latin American judicial discourse: first, the thematic and argumentative emphases mentioned above, and second, the openness of judicial discourse to international sources and institutions, particularly Inter-American ones, which in turn demonstrate a distinctive willingness to influence national practices. Both the "internationalization of constitutional law" (Chang and Yeh 2012) and the "constitutionalization of international law" (Klabers, Peters, and Ulfstein 2009; Acosta 2015) are perceptible in contemporary Latin America.

Underlying these trends we find, on the one hand, constitutions that accord a preeminent hierarchical position – supra-legal or even constitutional – to international sources, particularly in the domain of rights, and a court that nurtures a distinctive stance vis-à-vis its own functions: the Inter-American Court of Human Rights. The Inter-American Court of Human Rights – itself a highly interpretivist court – has progressively crafted a model of interaction with national courts that departs from standard expectations under international law. Ariel Dulitzky calls it the "integration model," in opposition to the prior "subsidiarity model" that still prevails in other human rights systems (Dulitzky 2015). Under a classic subsidiarity model, first, states must secure observance of the treaties but need not accord them any particular hierarchical position within the system of legal sources; second, the duty to honor international commitments falls on the shoulders of the state understood as a single entity, without imposing duties as to how the goal will be met; third and accordingly, international courts can only be reached after exhausting internal remedies, precisely because the state must be given full opportunity to comply and international institutions must come into play only when it fails; and fourth, when the international court or body detects an infringement of the treaty, it declares the state to have incurred in "international responsibility," without making specific qualifications about the legal status of particular state acts or norms (Dulitzky 2015, 52–4). By contrast, beginning in 2008 and at least until 2013, the Inter-American Court progressively crafted the "conventionality review" theory, which almost inverts the aforementioned tenets: it declared that the full efficacy of Inter-American sources must "prevail," suggesting they must be accorded supremacy; second, the court asserted that treaty efficacy must be guaranteed by "all state authorities, within their areas of jurisdiction," with repeated emphasis on the judiciary, which is explicitly directed to engage in conventionality review while discharging its ordinary duties; third, the requirement of exhausting internal remedies has been relaxed when ineffectivity can be presumed; and fourth, the court, far from stopping at the traditional "international responsibility" declaration, directly pronounced the "invalidity" of domestic statutes and acts, and directed judges to change particular doctrinal strands, suggesting that there is little space for states not to treat Inter-American human rights sources as paramount within the legal system (Dulitzky 2015, 54–9). Dulitzky believes we are facing a new paradigm of integration and suggests the court increasingly operates in the manner of an Inter-American *Constitutional* Court.

"Conventionality review" has triggered disparate reactions. In the academy, a group of scholars, with historic links with the Max Planck Institute in Heidelberg and remarkable influence among the upper levels of the national judiciaries, wholeheartedly embraced this evolution; it has registered the progressive emergence of a sort of "Latin American *Ius Constitutionale Commune*," hoping that this signals the articulation of a community of Latin American judges collectively committed, for the first time, to the enforcement of a common set of fundamental values (Bogdandy 2013, 2015; Bogdandy, Ferrer, and Morales 2010). While these scholars strongly favor recognizing the Inter-American Court's interpretive supremacy – whose powers of "concentrated conventionality review" would guarantee the coherence and closure of the system (Ferrer 2011) – they also place much emphasis on "judicial dialog" and the idea that judges, including the Inter-American Court, learn from each other and decide within this wider community of peers (Ferrer and Herrera 2013; Acosta 2015; Ferrer 2015). Other scholars have been more moderate, or less enthusiastic. Jorge Contesse (2014, 106, 111–20), for instance, defends the need to privilege the domestication of Inter-American standards and duties through national deliberative processes, advanced before national judicial forums, and argues that the Inter-American Court of Human Rights should replace a maximalist, cassation-like attitude with a genuinely dialogical approach that recognizes spaces of state discretion and treats national courts as equal partners (see also Basch and Contesse 2016). Roberto Gargarella (2014b, 2015) warns on his part that this judge-made "shared amalgam of fundamental rights law" should not escape a democracy-sensitive evaluation. He points out that Inter-American institutions exhibit a clear democratic deficit – given current appointment procedures and other institutional features – and that state actions and norms are not always equal in terms of democratic pedigree. For example, Gargarella questions the uncompromising views on the invalidity of amnesty laws expressed by the Inter-American Court in rulings like *Barrios Altos*, *Almonacid*, *Gomes Lund,* or *Gelman*, for not being sensitive enough to the nature of the national processes that led to their adoption and treating indecorous self-amnesties and carefully debated pieces of legislation alike. "Of course, judges are an integral part of the democratic process, and should help us in the construction of democratic laws," Gargarella concedes, "[b]ut the content of democratic laws should be fundamentally the product of collective, 'horizontal agreements,' and not the result of 'vertical impositions' of the judicial or political type" (2015, 119). Uprimny, Sánchez, and Sánchez (2014, 24–6) have identified several elements to determine the reach and contours of the internationally mandated state duty to investigate and sanction in a context of negotiated peace process, thus proposing a more careful and democratically sensitive balance between national and international commitments.

How have supreme and constitutional courts reacted to this self-proclaimed Inter-American leadership, and to the idea of "judicial dialog" more generally? Regional apex courts seem at ease holding periodic meetings at various seminars and summits, where they debate recent developments and issues of common concern, sometimes in combination with courts from other regions (Pérez and Hernández 2014) or with the Inter-American Court, which sometimes celebrates public audiences in countries parties to the system and reserves space for seminars with members of the wider legal community. Assessing what happens when these judges sit down and write their rulings is less straightforward. There is some work registering, commenting, or trying to systematize different modalities of incorporation of Inter-American sources (Filippini and Rossi 2010; Rodiles 2016) – analogous work on comparative law sources is largely pending – and a general interest in more closely documenting how and to what extent, beyond judicial comity, engagement with foreign and international courts in fact occurs. Regarding the Inter-American Court and its demands, the general view is that national courts have not offered open resistance; recent debates in the Colombian Constitutional Court about the normative force of the interpretive doctrines set down in the *Kimel* or *López Mendoza* cases (see, for instance, C-442 of 2011) and similar events in Costa Rica around *Atala* and again *López Mendoza* – suggest that a more fine-grained interaction is starting to emerge.[1] In short, this is a crucial area where more comprehensive findings should soon become available.

Analysis of how apex courts relate to one another and with the institutions of the Inter-American System should be supplemented with analysis of their interactions with lower judges in each country. This is an area where more research is in order. Scholars often fall prey to an "availability bias" and tend to develop work focused on what occurs at the highly visible level of the upper judiciary, whose rulings and activity are typically public and readily available. By contrast, monitoring and analyzing developments in the lower levels of the judiciary is logistically more complex and time-consuming. In any case, over time thicker descriptions of intra-judicial dynamics should become available, identifying some of the main patterns. For instance, have all countries crowned with a plurality of apex courts faced a "train crash," as was the case for some time in Colombia (as far as the doctrines of the supreme court and the constitutional court were concerned)? What elements have been helpful in avoiding or overcoming frictions? Has the constitutional system opening to international legal sources influenced traditional relations between upper and lower judges, and if so how? Does the impact vary depending on whether the traditional structure of the judiciary reflects a hierarchical model or a coordinated one, in Damaška´s terms (1986)? And how do different degrees of internal independence influence legal developments?

Finally, analysis of regional judiciaries should pay attention to a development that – regrettably – seems likely to gain more prominence in the times to come: the rise in non-traditional forms of pressure on judges. As political branches replace traditional attacks (court packaging, open defiance) with a new repertoire – from Bolivarian presidents' criticism to Inter-American judicial imperialism (Couso 2016), to more nuanced, underhand strategies such as nomination of government-friendly judges, low-quality execution of rulings, or economic strangling of the courts – it will be interesting to inquire what sort of designs or dynamics help preserve the autonomy of the judiciary, and which do not. Jan Boesten (2016) has argued, for instance, that institutional design that includes several apex courts – as in Colombia – makes it harder for an assertive executive to co-opt the judiciary. Another relevant line of inquiry could try to ascertain whether internationalization and the new transnational texture of the Latin American judiciary – the alleged existence of an incipient "Latin American judicial community" – makes any difference in terms of resisting these new forms of pressure.

Constitutional Adjudication, Efficacy, and Social Transformation

Contemporary Latin American constitutional courts enjoy an unprecedented position in the political and legal system. They have a multifaceted and diversified functional menu, although their role as ultimate rights guardians is paramount. Regional constitutions stand out for the robustness of the substantive program they enshrine, providing the transformative cue for regional apex courts that have created innovative doctrines. They have tried to build a direct relationship with citizens and social groups, progressively asserting their systemic position, often conceiving themselves as operating in a wider judicial space in which they have won an uncontestable space for political and legal action.

To what extent, however, have these courts actually succeeded in changing the world – which is, allegedly, what Latin American constitutions instruct them to do (García 2013)? The central question of the efficacy of rulings must then be faced. This is more pressing than in other contexts because of the interplay between transformative constitutions and socioeconomic backgrounds that include millions of people in deprivation, and because analysis proceeds at a point in time when there is no way to sidestep certain arguments and debates – those developed around the United States "rights revolution" (Rosenberg 1991; McCann 1994), for instance, or the powerful "critique of rights" in the American legal academy (Jaramillo 2004). On the flip-side, the debate can build on the careful and sophisticated scholarship about the efficacy of the law in Latin America, which is path breaking in many respects, and illuminate aspects largely overlooked in analyzes from the Global North (García 2009, 2010; and the chapter in this volume; Böhmer 2011).

The first thing regional scholars have noted is that the efficacy or inefficacy of rulings looks radically different depending on whether one adopts an instrumental or a constitutive theory of the relations between law and society (Restrepo 2003; Rodríguez–Garavito 2011a; Parra 2014). From an instrumental stance, law and social realities are conceived as conceptually separate, and legal efficacy is gauged in terms of whether a particular legal product directly generates the outcome it was intended to have. A good part of the Global North literature on constitutional efficacy – for instance, the theories that define efficacy as "text-reality-congruence" (Kokott and Kaspar 2012) – seems to be permeated by this stance. According to a constitutive vision, by contrast, law and social realities cannot be seen as conceptually separate, since law is a social artifact with continuities with all others, which shapes and is shaped by them in different and not always predictable manners. From a constitutive perspective, the indirect and symbolic effects of rulings are as significant as direct and instrumental ones (Restrepo 2003).

Along these lines, socio-legal scholars César Rodríguez and Diana Rodríguez have argued that it is necessary to develop new methodological and theoretical lenses capable of more adequately capturing a wide range of indirect effects. The analytical framework they develop – and then apply to case studies – detects at least five types of indirect effects of rulings (material or symbolic). These include: the reframing effect, by which certain problems start to be perceived as human rights questions and enter public agendas; the unblocking and public policy effect, which reinforce a country's institutional capabilities to deal with complex socioeconomic problems; the participatory effect, associated with the way rulings favor the creation of activist social coalitions that foster deliberation and may participate in the process of implementation of the rulings; and the socioeconomic effect, which favors collective debate over management of complex problems of redistribution (2015, 37). They additionally argue that potential effects depend on three different dimensions of the rulings: the legal force they accord to the right (weak or strong rights, in Tushnet's sense), but also – and critically – the sort of remedy (weak or strong) crafted by the court, and the type of supervision mechanism (weak or strong) devised to assure compliance. According to their findings, courts multiply the general effects of their rulings when engaging in exercises of dialogical decision-making that result from the combination of strong rights, intermediate remedies, and strong supervision schemes; these rulings respect the division of powers, promote efficacy, and favor participatory compliance processes that engage a plurality of social actors, thus reinforcing public deliberation (2015, 37). Similarly illustrating the relevance of indirect effects, David Landau has argued that, while Latin American social rights adjudication seems to have largely favored middle class, majoritarian interests and failed to be really transformative (Landau 2012), it has also displayed effects of another sort that must be definitely counted, such as guaranteeing public services and correcting regulatory failures in states with serious bureaucratic dysfunctions, representing somehow the popular mandate in view of the representative shortcomings of parliaments, or fostering the development of "constitutional culture" in the region (Landau in press).

The impact Latin American apex courts have exerted in recent years, in short, cannot be measured exclusively in terms of the number of technical, procedural, or doctrinal novelties we find in case law, nor by measuring compliance formalistically, or trying to correlate rulings with economic or political indicators. That would miss many of the social, cultural, and political effects of constitutional adjudication and the wider processes it encourages, or emerges from. In particular, it would miss the social import judicial intervention has often had. As Esteban Restrepo remarks, through *amparos, tutelas,* or *mandados,* over the last decades Latin American courts have attended the demands of ordinary people on an unprecedented scale, putting the spotlight on issues – violence, poverty, racism, and discrimination of all sorts, material depriva-tion, land mismanagement, and hundreds of others – that had previously received little political attention (Restrepo 2015, 6–8). As in other countries of the Global South (Bonilla 2013), oppressed social groups have knocked at the judges' door and judges have answered, expressing confidence in the power of constitutional adjudication to wipe out indignity, thus assuming a central role in modern struggles for social emancipation (Restrepo 2015, 8).

Of course not all regional courts understand themselves under this role, and a more sophist-icated methodological apparatus would facilitate the heightened detection of pernicious effects and dynamics, as much as virtuous ones. A full and geographically comprehensive assessment of gains and losses has yet to be undertaken and is perhaps overly ambitious. But if the task is more modestly to identify significant and distinctive developments in constitutional justice, no doubt paramount among them is the fact most supreme and constitutional courts in the region have recently succeeded – probably for the first time – at rendering the constitution relevant to the ordinary citizen.

Conclusions

In recent decades the judiciary has greatly strengthened its constitutional position. In Latin America this has been particularly notorious because traditionally judges had not been politically weighty, and the constitution did not figure large in everyday legal and political dynamics. Last-wave Latin American constitutions have been innovative at many levels, including the design of the judicial branch, which has been assigned a wide menu of functions, powers, and respons-ibilities. The apex courts of the region have understood that the founding documents confer them important public roles and have generally not refrained from deploying them.

Latin America is a huge area and a comparative appraisal of judicial developments should account for the variety we encounter. But for several reasons – including a relatively simultane-ous reinstallation of democracy, similarities in socioeconomic background, and the existence of self-perceived and externally attributed family traits among the countries of the region – there are many dynamics with a truly transnational dimension that somehow gloss over the absence of political integration at the subcontinental level.

This chapter has surveyed distinctive regional developments in constitutional adjudication. They are grounded in identifiable traits of institutional design and illustrate the performance of apex courts from perspectives that reveal an intense concern about their interaction with civil society and the other courts. An analysis bent on identifying trends and novelties naturally over-emphasizes certain aspects and underemphasizes others. The existence of novelties does not erase in itself the many things that remain the same: "dialogical" developments do not deny the persistence of huge areas of adjudication shaped by different parameters; nor does the emergence of new channels of access to justice erase those where the situation remains inertial; and so essentially closed. Yet such caveats notwithstanding, what stands out is the amazing dynamism of the region in the areas we have surveyed and the amount of developments future research agendas should carefully register and analyze.

Note

1 I thank Óscar Parra-Vera for extremely useful information and references about these developments, which he is exploring in ongoing research on national courts patterns of compliance and margins of dissent with Inter-American doctrines.

References

Abramovich, Víctor and Christian Courtis. 2003. *Los derechos sociales como derechos exigibles*. Madrid: Trotta.

Abramovich, Víctor. 2009. "El rol de la justicia en la articulación de políticas y derechos sociales" In Víctor Abramovich and Laura Pautassi (Comp.). *La revisión judicial de las políticas sociales. Estudio de casos*. Buenos Aires: Editores del Puerto.

Acosta, Paola. 2015. *Diálogo judicial y constitucionalismo multinivel. El caso interamericano*. Bogotá: Universidad Externado de Colombia.

Aguiló, Josep. 2004. *La constitución del estado constitucional*. Bogotá and Lima: Temis-Palestra.

Basch, Fernando and Jorge Contesse. 2016. "International law and domestic adjudication." In Juan F. González-Bertomeu and Roberto Gargarella (Eds.) *The Latin American Casebook*. New York: Routledge.

Bergallo, Paola. 2006. "Justicia y experimentalismo: la función remedial del poder judicial en el litigio de derecho público en Argentina." En *Derecho y pobreza. SELA 2005*. Buenos Aires: Editores del Puerto.

Bergallo, Paola. 2013. *Unleashing Health Rights in Argentinian Courts: From the Myth of Rights to the Politics of Rights*. JSD Dissertation, Stanford University.

Bergallo, Paola, and Agustina Ramón Michel. 2016. "Abortion." In Juan F. González-Bertomeu and Roberto Gargarella (Eds.). *The Latin American Casebook*. New York: Routledge.

Boesten, Jan. 2016. *Between democratic security and democratic legality: discursive institutionalism and Colombia's Constitutional Court*. Ph.D. Dissertation, University of British Columbia. Available at: https://open.library.ubc.ca/cIRcle/collections/ubctheses/24/items/1.0224798. Accessed May 22, 2017.

Bogdandy, Armin von. 2013. "Ius Constitutionale Commune Latinoamericanum: Una aclaración conceptual desde una perspectiva europea." En Luis Raúl González Pérez and Diego Valadés (Coords.). *El constitucionalismo contemporáneo. Homenaje a Jorge Carpizo*. Mexico City: Instituto de Investigaciones Jurídicas, UNAM.

Bogdandy, Armin von. 2015. Ius Constitutionale Commune en América Latina: Observations on *Transformative Constitutionalism*, 109 AJIL Unbound.

Bogdandy, Armin von, Eduardo Ferrer Mac-Gregor, and Mariela Morales Antoniazzi. 2010. *La justicia constitucional y si internacionalización: ¿Hacia un ius constiutionale comune en América Latina?* Mexico City: Instituto de Investigaciones Jurídicas UNAM, Instituto Iberoamericano de Derecho Constitucional, Max Planck Institut.

Böhmer, Martín. 2011. "Lursus naturae." En César Rodríguez-Garavito, *El Derecho en América Latina. Un mapa para el pensamiento jurídico del Siglo XXI*. Buenos Aires: Siglo Veintiuno Editores.

Bonilla, Daniel. 2006. *La Constitución multicultural*. Bogotá: Siglo del Hombre Editores.

Bonilla, Daniel. 2013. *Constitutionalism of the Global South*. New York: Oxford University Press.

Bonilla, Daniel. 2016. "La economía política del conocimiento jurídico." En Daniel Bonilla Maldonado (Ed.) *El constitucionalismo en el continente americano*. Bogotá: Uniandes, Siglo del Hombre Editores, Universidad EAFIT.

Boulanger, Christian. 2015. *Role Theory, Democratization and Comparative Constitutionalism: Constitutional Courts as "Guardians," "Umpires" and "Founders"* (unpublished paper, on file with author).

Brewer-Carías, Alan. 1990. "Judicial Review in Comparative Perspective." *Columbia Law Review* 90(5):1449–52.

Carbonell, Miguel. 2011. *Neo-constitucionalismo(s)*. Madrid: Trotta.

Chang, Wen-Chen and Jiunn-Rong Yeh. 2012. "Internationalization of Constitutional Law." In Michel Rosenfeld and Andras Sajó (Eds.). *The Oxford Handbook of Comparative Constitutional Law*. Oxford: Oxford University Press.

Contesse, Jorge. 2014. "¿La última palabra? Control de convencionalidad y posibilidades de diálogo con la Corte Interamericana de Derechos Humanos." En Marisa Iglesias, J. Couso, D. Dyzenhaus, J.A.F. Estrada, R. Gargarella. *Derechos humanos: posiblidades teóricas y desafíos prácticos. SELA 2012*. Buenos Aires: Libraria Ediciones.

Cook, Rebecca, Joanna Erdmann, and Bernard Dickens. 2014. *Abortion Law in Transnational Perspective. Cases and Controversies.* Philadelphia: The University of Pennsylvania Press.

Couso, Javier. 2010. "Los desafíos de la democracia constitucional en América Latina: entre la tentación populista y la utopía neoconstitucional." En *Anuario de Derechos Humanos 2010.* Santiago de Chile: Universidad de Chile, pp. 33–47.

Couso, Javier. 2014. "Las democracias radicales y el nuevo constitucionalismo latinoamericano." En Marisa Iglesias, J. Couso, D. Dyzenhaus, J.A.F. Estrada, R. Gargarella. *Derechos humanos: posiblidades teóricas y desafíos prácticos. SELA 2012.* Buenos Aires: Libraria Ediciones.

Couso, Javier. 2016. "¿Regreso al futuro? El retorno del 'principio de no intervención en los asuntos internos de los Estados' en el constitutucionalismo radical latinoamericano." En Bradley Hayes, Luís Roberto Barroso, Renata Bregaglio Lazarte, Javier Couso, Iñigo de la Maza Gazmuri, Alberto do Amaral Junior, Fiona Doherty, Roberto Gargarella, Chloé S. Georas, Diego Gil McCawley, Bradley Hayes, Eleonora Lozano Rodríguez, Vivian I. Neptune Rivera, Ezequiel Nino, Paulina Ochoa Espejo, Catalina Pérez Correa, Aline Rezende Peres Osorio, Daniela Salazar, Constanza Salgado Muñoz. *La Desigualdad. SELA 2015.* Buenos Aires: Libraria Ediciones.

Couso, Javier, Alexandra Huneeus, and Rachel Sieder. 2010. *Cultures of Legality.* New York: Cambridge University Press.

Dalla, Alberto. 1997. "La Justicia Constitucional en Argentina." En *Anuario Iberoamericano de Justicia Constitucional.* Madrid: Centro de Estudios Constitucionales.

Damaška, Mirjan. 1986. *The Faces of Justice and State Authority. A Comparative Approach to the Legal Process.* New Haven, CT: Yale University Press.

De Greiff, Pablo. 2012. "Theorizing Transitional Justice." In Melissa Williams, Rosemary Nagy and Jon Eslter (Eds.). *Transitional Justice.* Nomos Vol. LI. New York: New York University Press.

Dulitzzky, Ariel. 2015. "An Inter-American Constitutional Court? The Invention of the Conventionality Control by the Inter-American Court of Human Rights." *Texas International Law Journal* 50(1):45–93.

Esquirol, Jorge. 2003. "Continuing Fictions of Latin American Law." 55 *Florida Law Review* 41.

Esquirol, Jorge. 2011. "The Turn to Legal Interpretation in Latin America." 26 *American University International Law Review* 1031.

Esquirol, Jorge. 2014. *Las ficciones del derecho latinoamericano.* Bogotá: Siglo del Hombre Editores, Uniandes.

Falcão, Joaquim and Fabiana Luci de Oliveira. 2013. O STF e a agenda pública nacional: de outro desconhecido a supremo protagonista? *Lua Nova* 87: 429.

Fernández, Francisco. 2012. *Del control político al control jurisdiccional. Evolución y aportes a la justicia constitucional en América Latina. Pensamiento Constitucional* XII(12).

Ferrer, Eduardo. 2006. "Breves notas sobre el amparo iberoamericano (desde el derecho procesal constitucional comparado)." En Héctor Fix-Zamudio and Eduardo Ferrer Mac-Gregor (Eds.) *El derecho de amparo en el mundo.* Mexico City: UNAM, Porrúa, Konrad Adenauer Stiftung.

Ferrer, Eduardo. 2011. "Interpretación conforme y control difuso de convencionalidad. El nuevo paradigma para el juez constitucional mexicano" In Miguel Carbonell and Pedro Salazar (Eds.). *La reforma de derechos humanos del 2011: un nuevo paradigma.* Mexico City: IIJ UNAM.

Ferrer, Eduardo. 2015. "Conventionality Control: The New Doctrine of the Inter-American Court of Human Rights." 109 *AJIL Unbound* 93.

Ferrer, Eduardo and Alfonso Herrera García. 2013. *Diálogo jurispurdencial en Derecho Humanos entre Tribunales Constitucionales y Cortes Internacionales.* Mexico City: Tirant lo Blanch.

Ferreres, Víctor. 2009. *Constitutional Courts and Democratic Values. A European Perspective.* New Haven, CT: Yale University Press.

Filippini, Leonardo and Julieta Rossi. 2010. "El derecho internacional en la justiciabilidad de los derechos sociales: el caso de Latinoamérica." En Pilar Arcidiácono, Nicolás Espejo Yaksic and César Rodríguez-Garavito (Eds.) *Derechos sociales: justicia, política y economía en América Latina.* Bogotá: Siglo del Hombre Editores, Uniandes, U. Diego Portales, CELS y LAEHR.

Fix-Zamudio, Héctor. 2001. "La justicia constitucional en América Latina." En Héctor Fix-Zamudio, *Justicia constitucional, ombudsman y derechos humanos.* México City: CNDH.

Frosini, Justin and Lucio Pegoraro. 2008. Constitutional Courts in Latin America: A Testing Ground for New Parameters of Classification? *Journal of Comparative Law* 3(39).

García, Mauricio. 2009. *Sociología y crítica del derecho.* Mexico City: Ediciones Fontamara.

García, Mauricio. 2010. *Normas de papel. La cultura del incumplimiento de reglas.* Bogotá: Siglo del Hombre Editores, DeJusticia.

García, Mauricio. 2013. Constitucionalismo aspiracional. *Araucaria. Revista Iberoamericana de Filosofía, Política y Humanidades*15(29).

Gardbaum, Stephen. 2013. "The structure and scope of constitutional rights." In Tom Ginsburg y Rosalind Dixon (Eds.). *Comparative Constitutional Law*. Cheltenham: Edward Elgar.

Gargarella, Roberto. 2006. "Should Deliberative Democrats Defend the Judicial Enforcement of Social Rights?" In Samantha Besson and José Luis Martí (Eds.). *Deliberative Democracy and its Discontents*. Burlington, VT: Ashgate.

Gargarella, Roberto. 2012. "Latin American Contitutionalism Then and Now: Promises and Questions." In Detlef Nolte and Almut Schilling-Vacaflor (Eds.) *New Constitutionalism in Latin America. Promises and Practices*. Ashgate Publishing.

Gargarella, Roberto (Ed.). 2014a. *Por una justicia dialógica. El poder judicial como promotor de la deliberación democrática*. Buenos Aires: Siglo Veintiuno Editores.

Gargarella, Roberto. 2014b. "Sin lugar para la soberanía popular. Democracia, derechos y castigo en el caso *Gelman*." En *Derechos Humanos: posibilidades teóricas y desafíos prácticos. Seminario en Latinoamérica de Teoría Constitucional y Política (SELA) 2013*. Buenos Aires: Libraria Ediciones.

Gargarella, Roberto. 2015. Democracy and Rights in Gelman v. Uruguay. *AJIL Unbound* 109:115–19.

Giacomette, Ana. 2008. "Acción pública de inconstitucionalidad de las leyes." En Eduardo Ferrer Mac-Gregor and Arturo Zaldívar (Comp.). *Estudios en homenaje a Héctor Fix-Zamudio en sus cincuenta años como investigador del derecho. Tomo VIII. Procesos constitucionales orgánicos*. UNAM, IMDC, Marcial Pons.

Gianella, Camilla and Bruce Wilson. 2016. "LFBTI Rights." In Juan F. González-Bertomeu and Roberto Gargarella (Eds.). *The Latin American Casebook. Courts, Constitutions and Rights*. New York: Routledge.

González-Bertomeu, Juan. 2012. *Constitutional Adjudication in Non-ideal Scenarios. The case of Argentina and Colombia*. JSD Dissertation, NYU School of Law.

González-Bertomeu, Juan and Roberto Gargarella. 2016. *The Latin American Casebook. Courts, Constitutions and Rights*. New York: Routledge.

Helmke, Gretchen and Julio Ríos-Figueroa. 2011. *Courts in Latin America*. New York: Oxford University Press.

Hirschl, Ran. 2004. *Towards Juristocracy. The Origins and Consequences of the New Constitutionalism*. Harvard, MA: Harvard University Press.

Jaramillo, Isabel. 2004. "Estudio preliminar." En *La crítica de los derechos*. Bogotá, Siglo del Hombre Editores.

Kapiszewsky, Diana, Gordon Silverstein, and Robert A. Kagan. 2013. *Consequential Courts. Judicial Roles in Global Perspective*. New York: Cambridge University Press.

Klabers, Jan, Anne Peters and Geir Ulfstein. 2009. *The Constitutionalization of International Law*. Oxford, Oxford University Press.

Kokott, Julianne and Martin Kaspar. 2012. "Ensuring Constitutional Efficacy." In Michel Rosenfeld and András Sajó, *The Oxford Handbook of Comparative Constitutional Law*. Oxford: Oxford University Press.

Lamprea, Everaldo. 2014. "Colombia's Right-to-Health Litigation in a Context of Health Care Reform." In Coleen Flood and Aeyal Gross (Eds.). *The Right to Health at the Public/Private Divide. A Global Comparative Study*. Cambridge: Cambridge University Press.

Landau, David. 2012. The Reality of Social Rights Enforcement. *Harvard Law Review* 53(1):190–247.

Landau, David. (in press). "Socioeconomic rights without social transformation in Latin America. Theorizing courts favorable to majoritarian social ideas" In Colin Crawford and Daniel Bonilla Maldonado (Eds.). *Constitutionalism in the Americas*. Cheltenham, UK & Northampton MA, USA: Edward Elgar.

Langford, Malcolm. 2008. *Social Rights Jurisprudence: Emerging Trends in International and Comparative Law*. Cambridge: Cambridge University Press.

Law, David. 2005. Generic Constitutional Law. *Minnesota Law Review* 89: 652.

López, Diego. 2016. "Reposicionando América Latina y el Caribe en los mapas del Derecho constitucional comparado." En Daniel Bonilla Maldonado (Ed.). *El constitucionalismo en el continente americano*. Bogotá: Siglo del Hombre Editores.

McCann, Michael. 1994. *Rights at Work: Pay Equity Reform and the politics of Legal Mobilization*. Chicago: The University of Chicago Press.

Mendes, Hübner. 2017. "The Brazilian Supremo Tribunal Federal." In András Jakab, Arthur Dyevre and Giulio Itzcovich (Eds.). *Comparative Constitutional Reasoning*. Cambridge, Cambridge University Press.

Navia, Patricio and Julio Ríos-Figueroa. 2005. The constitutional adjudication mosaic of Latin America. *Comparative Political Studies* 38(2):189–217.

Ortiz, Julio César. 1997. "El nuevo sistema de control constitucional en Colombia. De la supresión de las funciones de control constitucional de la Corte Suprema a la creación de la Corte Constitucional." En *La Justicia Mexicana hacia el Siglo XXI*. Serie Estudios Doctrinales, No. 183. Mexico City: IIJ UNAM.

Parra, Óscar. 2014. "El impacto de las decisiones interamericanas. Notas sobre la producción académica y una propuesta de investigación en torno al empoderamiento institucional." En Armin von Bogdandy, Héctor Fix-Fierro and Morales Antoniazzi, Mariela (Eds.). *Ius Constitutionale Commune en América Latina. Rasgos, potencialidades y desafíos*. IIJ UNAM, Max Planck Institute, IIDC.

Parra, Óscar and Alicia Ely Yamin. 2010. Judicial Protection of the Right to Health in Colombia; from Individual Demands to Individual Claims to Public Debates. *Hastings International and Comparative Law Review* 33(2): 101–29.

Pérez,, Carlos and Javier Hernández Valencia (Eds.). 2014. *A Dialogue Between Judges. Writings of the Summit of Presidents of Constitutional, Regional and Supreme Courts (Mexico, 2012)*. Mexico City: Suprema Corte de Justicia de la Nación, Office of the UN High Commissioner for Human Rights.

Pou, Francisca. 2017a. "Constitutional Change and the Supreme Court Institutional Architecture: Decisional Indeterminacy as an Obstacle to Legitimacy." In Andrea Castagnola and Saúl López Noriega (Eds.). *Judicial Politics in Mexico: The Supreme Court and the Transition to Democracy*. New York, Routledge.

Pou, Francisca. 2017b. "Changing the Channel: Broadcasting Deliberations in the Mexican Supreme Court." In Richard Davis and David Taras (Eds.). *Justices and Journalists: The Global Perspective*. New York: Cambridge University Press.

Pozzolo, Susanna. 2015. "Apuntes sobre neoconstitucionalismo." En *Enciclopedia de Filosofía y Teoría del Derecho*, Jorge Fabra and Álvaro Núñez (Eds.). Vol. I. Mexico City. Available at: http://biblio.juridicas. unam.mx/libros/libro.htm?l=3875. Accessed February 22, 2018.

Ramírez, Slivina and Nahuel Maisley. 2016. "The Protection of the Right of Indigenous Peoples." In Juan F. González-Bertomeu and Roberto Gargarella (Eds.). *The Latin American Casebook*. Burlington, VT: Ashgate Publishing.

Restrepo, Esteban. 2003. "Reforma constitucional y progreso social: la constitucionalización de la vida cotidiana en Colombia." En Roberto Saba (Ed.), *SELA 2002. El derecho como objeto e instrumento de transformación*. Buenos Aires: Editores del Puerto.

Restrepo, Esteban. 2011. "Advancing Sexual Health and Reproductive Rights in Latin America and the Caribbean." Working paper prepared for the World Health Organization. Geneva. Available at: www. ichrp.org/files/papers/183/140_Restrepo_LAC_2011.pdf. Accessed February 22, 2018.

Restrepo, Esteban. 2015. *Constitutional Agonism*. JSD Dissertation, Yale Law School.

Roa, Jorge Ernesto. 2015. La justicia constitucional en Amércia Latina. *Serie Cuadernos de Trabajo*, No. 34, Universidad Externado de Colombia.

Roach, Kent. 2004. *Dialogic Judicial Review and Its CriticsSupreme Court Law Review* 23: 49–104.

Rodiles, Alejandro. 2016. "The Law and Politics of the Pro Persona Principle in Latin America." In Helmut P. Aust and Georg Nolte (Eds.). *The Interpretation of International Law by Domestic Courts. Unity, Diversity, Convergence*. Oxford: Oxford University Press.

Rodríguez-Garavito, César. 2009. (dir.). *Más allá del desplazamiento: políticas, derechos y superación del desplazamiento forzado en Colombia*. Bogotá: Uniandes, Acnur, ASDI.

Rodríguez-Garavito, César. 2011a. Beyond the Courtroom: The Impact of Judicial Activism on Socioeconomic Rights in Latin America. *Texas Law Review* 89: 1669.

Rodríguez-Garavito, César. 2011b. Ethnicity.gov: Global Governance, Indigenous Peoples, and the Right to Prior Consultation in Social Minefields. *Indiana Journal of Global Legal Studies* 18: 263.

Rodríguez-Garavito, César. 2015a. "Remapping law and society in Latin America: Visions and topics for a new legal cartography." In César Rodríguez-Garavito (Ed.). *Law and Society in Latin America. A New Map*. New York: Routledge.

Rodríguez-Garavito, César. 2015b. (dir.). *Human Rights in Minefields. Extractive Economies, Environmental Conflicts, and Social Justice in the Global South*. Bogotá: Center for the Study of Law, Justice and Society, DeJusticia.

Rodríguez-Garavito, César and Diana Rodríguez Franco. 2015. *Radical Deprivation on Trial: The impact of Judicial Activism on Socioeconomic Rights in the Global South*. New York: Cambridge University Press.

Rodríguez, María Luisa. 2007. *Minorías, acción pública de inconstitucionalidad y democracia deliberativa*. Bogotá: Universidad Externado de Colombia.

Rosenberg, Gerald. 1991. *The Hollow Hope: Can Courts Bring About Social Change?* Chicago: The University of Chicago Press.

Saba, Roberto. 2008. Constitutions and Codes: A Difficult Marriage. The Unusual Merging of the American Constitutional Law Tradition with The Continental Law Tradition. *Revista Jurídica de la Universidad de Puerto Rico* 77: 285.

Saffon, María Paula and Rodrigo Uprimny. 2010. "Uses and Abuses of Transitional Justice in Colombia." In Morten Bergsmo and Pablo Kalmanovitz (Eds.). *Law in Peace Negotiations*. Torkel Opsahl Academic Publishing.

Sagüés, Néstor. 2002. *Derecho procesal constitucional. Recurso extraordinario*. Buenos Aires, Astrea.

Screibner, Druscilla. 2016. "Judicial Communication: (Re)constructing Legitimacy in Argentina" In Richard Davis and David Taras (Eds.). *Justices and Journalists: The Global Perspective*. New York: Cambridge University Press (in press).

Silva, Virgílio Alfonso da. 2013. Deciding without Deliberating. *International Journal of Constitutional Law* 11(3).

Silva, Virgílio Alfonso da. 2015. Um Voto Qualquer? O Papel do Ministro Relator Na Deliberaçao No Supremo Tribunal Federal. *Journal of International Studies/Revista Estudios Institucionais* 1(1).

Stone, Alec. 2000. *Governing with Judges. Constitutional Politics in Europe*. Oxford: Oxford University Press.

Stone, Alec. 2012. "Constitutional Courts." In Michel Rosenfeld and Andras Sajó (Eds.). *The Oxford Handbook of Comparative Constitutional Law*. Oxford: Oxford University Press.

Tate, Neal and Torbjorn Vallinder. 1995. *The Global Expansion of Judicial Power*. New York: New York University Press.

Teitel, Ruti. 2000. *Transitional Justice*. Oxford: Oxford University Press.

Tushnet, Mark. 2008. *Weak Courts, Strong Rights. Judicial Review and Social Welfare Rights in Comparative Constitutional Law*. Princeton: Princeton University Press.

Uprimny, Rodrigo, Luz María Sánchez Duque, and Nelson Camilo Sánchez León. 2014. *Justicia para la paz. Crímenes atroces, derecho a la justicia y paz negociada*. Bogotá: Dejusticia.

Uprimny, Rodrigo. 2015. "The recent transformations of constitutional law in Latin America: trends and challenges." In César Rodríguez-Garavito (Ed.). *Law and Society in Latin America. A New Map*. New York: Routledge.

Viciano, Roberto and Rubén Martínez Dalmau. 2011. El nuevo constitucionalismo latinoamericano: fundamentos para una construcción doctrinal. *Revista General de Derecho Público Comparado* 9.

Wilson, Bruce. 2011. "Enforcing Rights and Exercising an Accountability Function: Costa Rica's Constitutional Chamber of the Supreme Court" In Gretchen Helmke and Julio Ríos-Figueroa (Eds.). *Courts in Latin America*. New York: Oxford University Press.

Yamin, Alicia and Óscar Parra-Vera. 2010. Judicial Protection of the Right to Health in Colombia: From Social Demands to Individual Claims to Public Debates. *Hastings Int'l & Comp. L. Rev.* 33:431.

Yrigoyen, Raquel. 2015. "The panorama of pluralist constitutionalism: from mlticulturalism to decolonization." In César Rodríguez-Garavito, (Ed.). *Law and Society in Latin America. A New Map*. New York: Routledge.

Zagrebelsky, Gustavo. 2003. *El derecho dúctil. Ley, derechos, justicia*. Madrid: Trotta.

14

PUBLIC PROSECUTOR'S OFFICES IN LATIN AMERICA

Verónica Michel

Criminal prosecutions have to be recognized as part of a two-stage process that involves: (1) the investigation and prosecution of a crime; and (2) adjudication (Ríos–Figueroa 2006, 2012). This two-stage process involves actually two different institutions within a judicial system: the prosecutorial office (that investigates and prosecutes); and the judiciary (that adjudicates). Thus, a successful criminal prosecution depends on a good investigation conducted by a state's prosecutorial organ that is ultimately in charge of the investigation and prosecution of crime. The discretion to decide to prosecute or not makes the prosecutorial organ a key gatekeeper to the judicial system given that prosecutors have an enormous unilateral power to dictate what, when, and whom to prosecute and bring to trial.[1] Only cases that are investigated and prosecuted will make it to a court. Given the power invested in this office, it is quite surprising that until very recently law and society scholars began to study the role of this institution in the relationship between law, society, and the state.

The chapter thus explores recent scholarship that has emerged around this previously unstudied institution. The chapter begins with a brief historical overview of the prosecutorial organ within the context of criminal procedural law in Latin America, and explains important recent reforms that transformed the role of this institution within criminal justice systems in the region. The next section describes the varying institutional design that we currently observe in prosecutorial organs across the region. A third section provides a review of the empirical research that has emerged in the literature, assessing the importance that independent and accountable prosecutorial organs have on the functioning of a constitutional democracy, buttressing the provision of legal certainty, the protection of individual rights, and strengthening the rule of law. The chapter concludes with some suggestions for future research.

What's in the Name? The Origins of Prosecutorial Organs in Latin America

The antecedents of what we now know as a public prosecutor's office (PPO) can be traced back to the emergence of criminal law in modern states. Historically, criminal law appeared in the modern era as arguably the crudest legal expression of the coercive power of the sovereign state, entitling the state to assign guilt and determine punishment (Dubber 2006, 2014). Before the centralization of prosecutorial powers in the hands of the state took place, for centuries societies settled their conflicts through local private means, like revenge, mediation, forgiveness, or personal reconciliation (Ma 2008). Gradually, the centralization of coercive power in the hands of the state led to the definition of some offenses as issues of public concern, with prosecution and punishment to be administered by the state. Thus, with the emergence of the modern state, crime became a social (not private) matter, making prosecution and punishment a prerogative of the state, not the individual. Prosecutorial discretion, in particular the decision not to prosecute, is best understood as a vivid display of sovereign power (Sarat and Clarke 2008).

Although the centralization of prosecutorial power was a slow and uneven process across countries and legal systems, most countries began creating state prosecutorial institutions by the nineteenth century, and Latin America was not an exception.[2] We know little about the actual performance of these early prosecutorial organs, because for many years this institution, like the judicial branch in general, escaped the curiosity of scholars probably because it was considered epiphenomenal to politics. Most publications on prosecutorial organs in Latin America tend to be mostly descriptive and historical in nature, most often part of criminal procedure textbooks (for example, Castro 2008; Gimeno, Moreno, and Cortés 1999; Horvitz and López 2002). This literature, however, is quite important to understand the historical background of this institution in the region, as well as their overall function within the state. From this early scholarship we know that Latin America's newly independent states inherited the legal institutions imposed by Spain and Portugal during colonialism (Barahona, Cerón, Peroti 2010; Fix-Zamudio 2002; Suárez 1995), and it took about a century for the newly independent countries to achieve the political and economic stability necessary for criminal justice reforms to take place (Aguirre and Salvatore 2001, 3–4).[3]

Although all countries in the region inherited a civil law tradition, each country dealt in different ways with the centralization of prosecutorial powers. All newly independent countries maintained inquisitorial principles, but some, like Chile, introduced a "pure inquisitorial model," where Instruction Judges (*Jueces de Instrucción*) investigated, prosecuted, and adjudicated at the same time (Duce 2009). Other countries, like Mexico or Argentina, instead followed the "French model" of criminal prosecution and concentrated the monopoly of prosecution in the hands of a prosecutorial organ, the *Ministerio Público*, introducing a "mixed model" that separated prosecution from adjudication, but that was still based on inquisitorial principles (e.g., secrecy and written proceedings) (Castro 2008; Garro 2000).

It is important to briefly mention the role of prosecutors in the two different models of criminal prosecution. Inquisitorial systems were designed under the assumption that criminal "truth" is discovered through an official investigation or inquiry conducted by a neutral party (Instruction Judge or public prosecutor). In contrast, adversarial or accusatorial systems function under the assumption that truth is discovered through the contestation between defense and prosecution, where a judge plays the role of a neutral arbiter (Bradley 2007). Perhaps the most criticized aspect of "pure" inquisitorial systems is the concentration of investigation and adjudication in the hands of one judge, the Instruction Judge (*Juez de Instrucción*). This makes one judge responsible for conducting investigations, assigning guilt, and adjudicating the case.

Many other characteristics that also present in the "mixed" inquisitorial model have also been criticized. In inquisitorial systems the procedure is mostly written, making it slow and rather obscure. The required secrecy throughout the proceedings leaves crucial actors in Kafkaesque-type scenarios: unaware of the stage of the proceedings or even their role in them, for example, by not making public the identity of individuals under investigation. During the stage of investigation, defendant's rights can be potentially affected in other ways. In an inquisitorial system, the main objective is the discovery of "truth" through a criminal investigation, where confession is regarded as a key component of the official inquiry. Furthermore, the defense has virtually no role in producing evidence, which is mostly gathered by the Instruction Judge or the public prosecutor.

Since the 1980s, most countries in Latin America have radically changed the role of the PPO in criminal proceedings through reforms that have implemented a more accusatorial or adversarial model of criminal procedure. In contrast to inquisitorial systems, the responsibility to gather evidence in adversarial systems is shared by both the defense and the prosecutorial organ. Furthermore, proceedings are now public and oral, and there is a clear separation of investigation and adjudication roles (as explained in Table 14.1). To make this transition possible, important legal and institutional changes were required. First, new criminal procedure codes had to be enacted. Second, probably one of the most radical changes occurred in countries that

Table 14.1 Comparisons Between Inquisitorial and Adversarial Criminal Procedure Systems

	Inquisitorial Criminal System	*Adversarial Criminal System*
Assumptions about how the pretrial process can avoid false convictions	Based on the assumption that false convictions can be avoided through a lengthy pretrial investigation. The truth is assumed to be found through official inquiry	Assumption that false convictions can be avoided through contestation. The truth is assumed to be found through competition between defense and prosecution
Responsibility to gather evidence	Responsibility is overseen by the prosecutorial organ (i.e., the public prosecutor, or the instruction judge). In purely inquisitorial systems, the instruction judge investigates, and prosecutes. In mixed inquisitorial systems, the public prosecutor presents the evidence in court	Responsibility to gather evidence is shared between defense and prosecutors. The evidence introduced by both parties has to be presented before a judge, who decides if it is accepted or not
Trial proceedings	Judicial decisions are submitted in writing to the parties involved. The trial is in the hands of the judge. Adjudication is made by the instruction judge based on the official inquiry	Oral proceedings. All parties participate, interrogate, and cross examine. Pretrial hearings and trial are public and always mediated by the presence of a control judge (*juez de garantías*). The trial is mediated by a judge panel (*tribunal de sentencia*), and adjudication is made by such panel or by jury
Defendants' rights	Right to a fair trial	Right to a fair trial. Right to silence is also perceived as providing stronger protections to the accused in some countries
Victims' rights	Inquisitorial systems tend to provide reparation and participation rights to victims, granting them the status of party during the pretrial and trial stages	Adversarial systems that come from a common law tradition tend to eliminate participation and reparation rights within criminal proceedings, and only recognize the victim as a witness. Mixed systems or recently reformed systems from civil law countries tend to offer more reparation and participation rights to victims during the pretrial and trial

Source: Table created by author.

moved away from a pure inquisitorial system, like Chile. The creation of a new prosecutorial organ, the *Ministerio Público*, empowered public prosecutors with the discretion to investigate and prosecute, and left judges with the sole responsibility of implementing the law and adjudicating cases. And finally, the introduction of oral trials, with the attempt to make the proceedings more open and less secretive, has required extensive training and restructuring of court systems. The result, however, has been not a pure accusatorial process, but a mixture of both models, resembling more the type of criminal procedure existing today in continental Europe (Merryman and Pérez-Perdomo 2007). To this day, only Brazil and Uruguay have not yet reformed toward an adversarial model of criminal procedure.

The relevance of the reforms previously described cannot be understood without taking into account the context in which these emerged: the process of transition from authoritarianism toward democracy. As part of the process of democratic transition, Latin American countries were in a way forced to implement a series of judicial reforms that aimed to address the historical failure to enforce the rule of law in the region (Adelman and Centeno 2002). The wave of reforms that began in the mid-1980s has since targeted the entire justice sector, understood here as wide range of public and private sector entities "and the formal and informal rules governing their conduct. At a minimum this would include the courts, public prosecution and defense, police, prisons, the private bar, law schools, and various civil society groups" (Hammergren 2002a, 1).

Judicial reforms have been buttressed on strong assumptions about the role of the judiciary as a guarantor of the rule of law, which has been at the same time considered a necessary, though not sufficient, element for the consolidation of democracy and the functioning of the markets (Thome 1998; Ansolabehere 2007). Hence, judicial reforms can be distinguished analytically as being focused on three goals:

1   Independence of the judiciary: two interrelated objectives are advanced here, one is to strengthen the judicial branch, and the other one is to abandon the traditional role the judiciary played as a subordinate and politicized branch of government
2   Efficiency: efforts in this area include modernizing dated legislation through normative changes in the civil and criminal procedural codes. Other efforts to improve efficiency have included the creation of alternative dispute resolution (ADR) mechanisms, as well as an expanded budget allocated to the justice system, the modernization of the courts, and the professionalization of the bench and bar, for example, through the creation of judicial schools
3   Access to justice: some measures have addressed structural problems of the legal systems to improve access to justice, like the introduction of ADR mechanisms (Thome 1998; Messick 2002). However, the creation of public defenders programs, the expansion of victims' rights and the development of offices to serve victims, where free legal council is offered, are solely about increasing access to justice to the more disadvantageous groups of society.

Observing the momentous changes that were taking place in Latin America, scholars initially focused their attention on the causes of democratic transition, and on assessing the new electoral and participatory machineries (Collier and Collier 1991; Murphy 1993; O'Donnell, Schmitter, and Whitehead 1986; Putnam 1993; Schmitter and Karl 1991). By the 1990s, however, when the expected democratic benefits failed to materialize in new democracies (Zakaria 1997), there was a scholarly shift to study democratic quality, shifting the focus away from "vertical accountability" toward issues of "horizontal accountability" and rule of law (Brinks, Leiras, and Mainwaring 2014; Guarnieri 2003; Mainwaring and Welna 2003; O'Donnell 1999; Schedler, Diamond, and Plattner 1999). In contrast to keeping a government accountable of its actions through vertical mechanisms, like elections, horizontal accountability requires the existence of:

state agencies that are legally enabled and empowered, and factually willing and able, to take actions that span from routine oversight to criminal sanctions or impeachment in relation to actions or omissions by other state agents or agencies of the state that may be qualified as unlawful.

(O'Donnell 1999, 38)

This shift toward studying horizontal accountability in constitutional democracies made the judicial branch an object of inquiry itself to understand democratic governance.[4]

As noted earlier, judicial reforms enacted in Latin America have shown a lot of variation across countries and have targeted several areas of the justice sector, but initially scholars focused mostly on reforms that aimed to improve the independence of the judicial bench. The questions that seemed to attract most scholars was why would political actors empower an institution that could in the future rule against them and how lack of independence impacted democratic governance (Ferejohn 1999; Inclan and Inclan 2005; Skaar 2001; Tiede 2006). Given the traditional use of courts as a political tool in the region, scholars and policymakers alike soon advocated on the need of reforms that guaranteed judicial independence, access to justice, and judicial efficiency (HiiL 2007; O'Donnell 2004; Peerenboom 2004; Schedler, Diamond, and Plattner 1999), and soon some scholars in American academia began advocating for research on prosecutorial organs (Kapiszewski and Taylor 2008).

Latin American legal scholars, however, were the first to identify that judicial reforms had to focus not only on the courts, but also on prosecutorial organs. Since the 1980s, legal scholars in the region urged for reforms of the criminal justice system that would support democratic governance and protect human rights (Binder 2000; Zaffaroni 1986; Zaffaroni 2000). In particular, they noted the use of prosecutions as a tool of repression by previous authoritarian regimes, and highlighted the need to improve the independence not only of judges, but of prosecutorial organs as well. Thus, parallel to discussions about the role of judicial independence within the courts in Latin America (Hammergren 2002a, 2002b; Prillaman 2000; Skaar 2002), early discussions about prosecutorial organs focused on issues of prosecutorial independence (Garro 2000; Heymann 1995; Sadek and Cavalcanti 2003). Not surprisingly, thus, the focus centered on issues of institutional design as I explain in more detail below.

Prosecutorial Organs in Latin America Today

As the wave of criminal procedure reforms swept the region in the mid-1990s (Binder 2000; Duce 2009; Langer 2007), scholars began to pay closer attention to prosecutorial organs. Probably one of the first questions that emerged was why were countries reforming their prosecutorial organs institutions in the first place, although most of these discussions have been framed within the overall discussion of criminal procedure reform. For some, the reform of PPOs in the region is best understood as part of the overall criminal justice reform processes that were taking place in the region (Duce 2009; Duce and Perez Pérdomo 2003), that had the main objectives of making justice more transparent, efficient, and more attuned to democratic governance (Domingo 1999; Pereira 2003). Some authors have further explained that political incentives created by electoral competition best explain why politicians would seek such ambitious reforms of the criminal justice system (Ingram 2008, 2016). And yet other scholars have explained the trend to reform toward an adversarial model as the product of policy diffusion across Latin America, where legal scholars played a key role disseminating a Model Code of criminal procedure, which explained why so many countries in the region implemented such similar codes (Langer 2007).

Leaving aside the reasons or causes for the implementation of these ambitious reforms, today the PPO receives many names across Latin American countries. For instance, some countries call it the *Ministerio Público* (Guatemala), others call it the *Procuraduría General* (México), while others refer to it as *Fiscalía General* (Chile). Regardless of nomenclature issues, a prosecutorial organ fulfills the following criteria, as defined by Van Aaken, Salzberger, and Voigt (2004, 6): it is a state's organ that: (1) has the competence and authority to investigate a crime (by gathering information/evidence or instructing the police to gather such information/evidence); (2) has the competence to indict or press charges; and (3) and most important, it represents the interests of the public (i.e., state). Thus, by constitutional mandate, most PPOs in the region share the mission to enforce the law and defend the interests of the state, to prosecute crime, and to protect the rights of citizens (Payne, Zovatto, and Mateo 2006,144).

Probably the first thing we have learned about prosecutorial organs in the region is that, despite performing a similar functional role within a judicial system, these organs are still quire diverse in their institutional design. For instance, there is vast variation regarding who actually conducts the criminal investigation. In some countries, the PPO has an investigative branch (e.g., the *Procuraduría General de la Republica* of Mexico has the *Agencia de Investigación Criminal*, or the PPO in Guatemala has the DIGICRI [*La Dirección General de Investigación Criminal*], which is also in charge of criminal investigations); in other countries the police force has a department in charge of conducting criminal investigations on behalf of the PPO (e.g., the *Policía de Investigaciones de Chile*, which depends on the Interior Ministry). Regardless of variations on what institution conducts the investigation of the crime, criminal prosecution is always in the hands of the prosecutorial organ.

More important are variations that can potentially shape how much independence prosecutors enjoy in their discretion to prosecute. Similar to previous measures of judicial independence (Ferejohn 1999; Ríos-Figueroa 2006; Staton and Ríos-Figueroa 2009), here I conceptualize *prosecutorial independence* as the capacity of the PPO to translate its own preferences into actions, without external political pressures. The literature has noted that a PPO can enjoy *de jure* independence, depending on how the laws created the institution, or de facto independence, which reflects how these laws are actually implemented (Maggetti 2007; Van Aaken, Salzberger, and Voigt 2004). Given the difficulty to measure de facto independence (Ríos-Figueroa 2015), in this section I address issues that have been noted to influence *de jure* prosecutorial independence.

One important institutional design factor that can impact prosecutorial independence is the actual location of the PPO. Historically, legislators have located the PPO in different branches of government or have given the institution full functional autonomy (see Table 14.2). We can observe that across time, the PPO has been located within the executive branch (as in Mexico or Uruguay, and similar to the United States), within the judiciary (as in Costa Rica), or it has been designed as autonomous (as in Chile, Guatemala, or Brazil). PPOs that lie within the executive are more likely to be subordinated to political pressures from the incumbent government. Hence, in PPOs dependent on the executive, there is a higher risk that the office not only represents the interests of the "state" but, instead, of the ruling elite. So prosecution of some cases, for example, human rights cases, will depend more heavily on the willingness of the executive to prosecute these. In contrast, when the PPO is within the judiciary, public prosecutors should "enjoy the same degree of independence from government as judges do" (Ríos-Figueroa 2012, 198). In other words, the independence of prosecutors in this case is the same as that enjoyed by judges. In theory, therefore, an autonomous PPO by design should be less likely to be under political pressures from the executive, as well as free from any threats to judicial independence that may be suffered by judges. Interestingly, Table 14.2 makes clear that establishing an autonomous PPO has become the norm in the region (with the exceptions of

Table 14.2 Diversity in Institutional Design of Prosecutorial Organs in Latin America

	Location Previous PPO	Location Current PPO	Head of PPO Appointed By	Prosecutorial Discretion	Judicial Review
Argentina	n/a	Auto (1949)	Executive (with 2/3 senate approval)	0.85	1
Bolivia	Exe (1947–1994)	Auto (1995)	Congress	0.6	0
Brazil	Exe (1968–1988) Jud (1967)	Auto (1988)	President (with senate approval)	0.2	0.33
Chile	Jud (1949–1996)	Auto (1997)	President (from list provided by supreme court, approved by senate)	n/a	n/a
Colombia	Jud (1949–1995)	Auto (1996)	Senate (from list provided by president, supreme court, and state council)	0.75	1
Costa Rica	Exe (1949–1972)	Jud (1973)	Supreme court	0.55	0.66
Ecuador	Exe (1945–1977)	Auto (1978)	Congress	0.9	1
El Salvador	Exe (1950–1982)	Auto (1983)	Congress	n/a	1
Guatemala	Exe (1956–1992)	Auto (1993)	President	0.75	1
Honduras	n/a	Auto (1957)	Congress	n/a	0.66
Mexico	n/a	Exe (1949)	President (ratified by senate)	0.35	0.66
Nicaragua	Exe (1948–1999)	Auto (2000)	Congress (from list provided by president and congressmen)	n/a	n/a
Panama	Exe (1972–1982)	Auto (1983)	Executive (approved by congress)	0.75	1
Paraguay	Jud (1992–1999), Auto (1967–1991)	Auto (2000)	Executive (approved by senate, from a list provided by judiciary)	0.6	1
Peru	Exe (1947–1978)	Auto (1979)	Junta de Fiscales Supremos	0.2	0.33
Uruguay	n/a	Exe (1952)	Executive (approved by senate)	n/a	n/a
Venezuela	n/a	Auto (1947)	National assembly (from a list provided by Poder Ciudadano)	0.6	1

Sources: Location of PPO data based on past and current organic laws. The year reflects when the reform to the current location took place (and it is not necessarily the last reform of an organic law). Appointment data from Carrillo Flores, 2006. Judicial review and discretion data from Van Aaken, Feld, and Voigt, 2008.*

Notes

n/a = information not available; Auto = autonomous design; Exe = within the executive; Jud = within the judiciary; PPO = Public Prosecutor's Office.

* The data from Van Aaken, Feld, and Voigt (2008) are drawn from a survey questionnaire distributed across countries to local experts. The variable "discretion" asked respondents if: (1) the mandatory principle existed in the law; and (2) if there are exceptions introduced to the mandatory principle due to the opportunity principle. The variable "judicial review" asked respondents if the judiciary had the competence to review: (1) charges brought by the prosecutor; (2) the decision to prosecute a crime; (3) the decision not to prosecute a crime due to legal or factual deficiencies; and (4) the use of the opportunity principle.

Mexico and Uruguay, that have kept the PPO within the executive branch, and Costa Rica, that has kept it within the judicial branch).

The location of the PPO, however, is not the only factor that affects the independence with which public prosecutors make decisions regarding which cases are investigated and reach the courts. The independence of prosecutors is also greatly shaped by *rules of appointment, promotion, and tenure*. When the executive has a stronger say on the career of a prosecutor, the likelihood that the prosecutor will behave according to the preferences of the incumbent are higher. There is also variation across countries on the rules that determine the career of a prosecutor. In some countries, decisions are made between the executive and the legislative branches, in others it is between the executive and the judiciary, while in others decisions are made within the judicial branch (see for example, Aguiar 2012).

There are, however, other factors beyond the institutional location that can make the PPO more or less constrained on discretionary powers. In many countries, these powers can be stronger when criminal procedure law bounds the PPO to the opportunity principle (or principle of selective prosecution). In contrast to the legality principle (or principle of mandatory prosecution) that forces the PPO to investigate/prosecute every case for which there is enough evidence of an offense, the opportunity principle allows more discretion to the PPO when deciding to prosecute or not (Van Aaken, Feld, and Voigt 2008, 10). The opportunity principle, in contrast, then allows for the PPO not only to decide if the report or claim actually constitutes a crime, but also if the case merits a prosecution. When mandatory prosecution is imposed, usually the decision not to prosecute is subject to judicial review. Although selective prosecution can help reduce backlog and allocate resources to cases that merit attention (CEJA 2005; Horvitz and López 2002), in theory it can also give a legal resource for a PPO to systematically dismiss certain cases more speedily when prosecutors are influenced by politics or by incentives created by rules of promotion/tenure makes them risk averse (Garoupa 2009). In practice, today there is a preference for the implementation of opportunity principle to make systems more effective. Nonetheless, there exists variation in how countries use these two principles. For example, some countries require mandatory prosecution for felonies, but selective prosecution for misdemeanors.

When confronting the vast variation in the institutional design of prosecutorial organs, and in a way echoing research on judicial independence, a key question has focused on trying to understand the choices among different institutional designs. Why are some PPOs designed to be more independent? Why others are designed to depend more on the executive or the judiciary? Scholarship that has emerged on this issue again highlights the importance of political competition. For instance, there has been research at the regional level (comparing data across countries in the region, for example, Ríos–Figueroa and Pozas-Loyo 2010) and at the subnational level (comparing reforms across states within a country, for example, Ingram [2016]), that has found that legislators are more likely to design and implement reforms for more independent judicial institutions when there are at least two different parties in congress. The explanation behind this appears to be that when there is electoral competition, politicians want to design and create institutions that will be neutral and fair, rather than easily politicized. However, it has also been suggested that, despite electoral democratization, the lack of a meaningful commitment toward the ideals of democratic governance and rule of law can explain why some countries, like Mexico, have been reluctant to provide more functional autonomy to the PPO (Aguiar 2015).

Probably more interesting is that as scholars looked more into the work of PPOs they have found that *de jure* prosecutorial independence does not easily translate into de facto independence. Furthermore, an additional obvious concern has emerged: not only are PPOs important for their potential role as key actors in providing horizontal accountability in a constitutional democracy, but prosecutorial organs should also be required to be held accountable on any misuse or abuse of prosecutorial discretion. In any constitutional democracy, prosecutors are assumed to be not only independent from external pressure, but also neutral in how they make their prosecutorial decisions (Green and Zacharias 2004). Prosecutors, when they decide if and what to prosecute, act as "quasi-judicial" actors and this "combination of power in one actor is troubling because it puts prosecutors in a position to judge their own cause – the classic threat to the rule of law" (Barkow 2008, 883).

Thus, in a country that upholds the rule of law and supports democratic governance, it is imperative that the state organ in charge of prosecuting crime is *both* independent and accountable. *Prosecutorial accountability* is conceptualized here as the institutionalized oversight of prosecutorial decisions. Drawing on previous definitions, here prosecutorial accountability "implies not only answerability, but also the *legal obligation* [original emphasis] to answer or the institutionalized right of an agent of accountability to impose sanctions" on public officials (Mainwaring 2003, 5). In the next section of this chapter I will elaborate on the impact of having an independent and accountable PPO.

Assessing the Importance of Prosecutorial Organs

The importance of prosecutorial independence and prosecutorial accountability is best understood when we consider the type of failures or miscarriages of justice a judicial system can produce at the prosecutorial stage. Systemic failures can be categorized into two types, depending on to whom the system is failing, the defendant or the victim (see Table 14.3). But also, we must acknowledge the intentionality behind such failures. Thus, failures can be the intentional result of a direct mandate or policy, which I label here failure "by commission," or prosecutorial failures can result from lack of resources, capacity, or training, which are better described as failures "by omission."[5]

Empirically, we can provide examples of these four types of failures. We observe systematic failures "by commission" with the politicized use of prosecutorial discretion, for instance, when a system unfairly targets particular individuals or groups, or when it protects certain wrongdoers from prosecution for political reasons. Latin American governments not only have a history of

Table 14.3 Type of Systemic Failures in Criminal Justice at the Prosecution Stage

	To Defendant	*To Victim/Society*
Failure by "omission" (state incapacity/training)	Poor/inefficient criminal investigations that lead to prosecutions of innocent individuals	No investigations/no prosecutions resulting in "systemic impunity" for wrongdoers (failure to prosecute)
	Racial/class prejudice or stereotyping may lead to similar systemic injustice	
Failure by "commission" (political will or mandate)	Prosecutorial power used as tool for repression against dissidents and/or to maintain order	"Selective impunity": de facto or *de jure* prosecutorial policy that excludes prosecution of some crimes (e.g., white collar crimes, corruption, human rights cases)

Source: Table created by author.

using murder and torture as tool for political repression (Green 2015; Kritz 1995; McAdams 1997; Nino 1996), but there is also evidence that governments have used prosecutorial powers as a means to maintain order and repress political opponents. For example, human rights research has shown that political prisoners were quite common during authoritarian rule in the region (Aguayo 1998; Gibney 1987; Lessa 2013; Lutz and Sikkink 2003). After the transition to democracy, some have observed a worrying tendency to criminalize social protest (Abal Medina and Ortega Breña 2011; Müller 2012). Similarly, there is research among historians that shows that prosecutions and imprisonments have long been used as a way to "clean" society from unwanted populations (prostitutes, homosexuals, and gangs) or as a means to repress social rebellion (Monterroso 2008; Piccato 2001; Salvatore, Aguirre, and Joseph 2001). More recently, scholars have also criticized anti-gang policies implemented in Brazil or Central America for curtailing due process rights against youths suspected as gang members (Bruneau 2014; Lambert 2012).

By mandate or political will, there is also vast evidence that certain groups or individuals are purposely shielded from prosecution, establishing a de facto policy of "selective impunity" (Binder 2000, 81), which can impact victims' rights. This has been most clearly evidenced in human rights research. For instance, amnesty laws emerged in the region as a way to shield state agents from prosecutions for human rights abuses committed during authoritarian rule (Lessa and Payne 2012; Roht-Arriaza and Gibson 1998), which can be described as a *de jure* policy of selective impunity. Furthermore, the research on human rights prosecutions has also suggested that prosecuting high-ranking officials has proven to be more difficult when compared to prosecuting low-ranking officials (Lutz and Sikkink 2001; Lutz and Reiger 2009).

On the other hand, criminal justice systems can also produce systemic failures "by omission" when prosecutions are inefficient and/or biased and they disproportionly target minorities or marginalized groups, severely affecting defendants' rights. Also, there can be important failures to victims' rights and society at large when the criminal justice system is just incapable of prosecuting crime, producing "systemic impunity." Probably some of the most severe criticisms against most criminal justice systems in Latin America focus on their abysmal failure to protect defendant's rights. Although scarce, there is empirical research that condemns some countries in the region that practice arbitrary arrests and detentions, rely on (coerced) confessions for prosecutions, fail to guarantee and provide proper legal counsel, and abuse pretrial detention (Lopes 2016; McGrath 2000; Méndez, O'Donnell, and Pinheiro 1999; Riego and Duce 2009; Ríos-Figueroa 2012; Tiede 2012).

However, criminal justice systems in the region have probably been most severely criticized for their incapacity to prosecute and punish crime, creating a safe-haven for criminals (Ungar 2002, 2011), producing a context of "systemic impunity," which severely impacts victims' rights and society at large. It has been noted that sometimes this type of failure against victims' rights may result not so much from explicit policies, but from deep-ingrained prejudices and biases that end up producing systemic failures. For instance, recent research assessing the failure of legal systems to investigate and prosecute gender violence suggests that most often than not, the lack of prosecutorial interest in the cases rests on misogyny and discrimination against women (Sanford 2008; Wright 2011). In the next section on p. 215 I will address how systemic impunity impacts society at large because, contrary to the other type of failures identified here, systemic impunity has generated empirical research that explicitly looks into the role of prosecutorial organs.

The four types of failures described on p. 213 either reflect tyrannical rule or signal an erosion of the rule of law. Therefore, understanding prosecutorial independence and prosecutorial accountability on the misuse or abuse of prosecutorial powers is vital. Although little empirical research has emerged on these issues, on pp. 215–216 I provide a summary of an emerging empirical research agenda that aims to assess the importance and impact that prosecutorial organs can have on the rule of law. First, I address research that highlights how and when a prosecutorial organ can have a positive or negative impact on the rule of law, and then second, I focus on how prosecutorial organs can be made more accountable for their misuse or abuse of powers.

The Impact of PPOs on the Rule of Law

It is quite encouraging to learn about what happens when judicial reforms work to help reduce historical inequalities. For instance, reforms introduced to the PPO of Brazil make evident that sometimes a prosecutorial can work as an agent of accountability and social change. After transition to democracy and with the enactment of the Federal Constitution of 1988, the Brazilian PPO was endowed with stronger independence. One of its main roles has been the oversight and control over public administration, and in such role, scholars have pointed out that it has emerged as a key political actor promoting social rights, including children's rights, by bringing claims to the courts that aim to enhance the enforcement of such rights (Sadek and Cavalcanti 2003; Silva 2000).

As important as it is to know how or when a PPO works well and advances social change, most empirical scholarship has instead focused on instances where prosecutorial organs fail. A common cause behind systemic prosecutorial failures, as noted earlier, comes from low capacity, lack of resources, and poor inter-agency or inter-institutional coordination (Monterroso 2008; Payne 2008; Zepeda 2004). There has also been research that highlights the overall failure to properly implement reforms, for instance, by failing to properly train and provide resources to judicial actors, including prosecutors, on how to operate under the new rules of an adversarial system (CEJA 2005; Hammergren 2008; Lopes 2016; Rodríguez Ferreira and Shirk 2015).

Also, some prosecutorial failures may be blamed on institutional design. Prosecutorial independence, guaranteed by institutional design, has been identified as a key factor explaining corruption (Ríos-Figueroa 2006, 2012; Van Aaken, Feld, and Voigt 2008, 2010; Van Aaken, Salzberger, and Voigt 2004). The main reason for this is that prosecutors that are not independent enough from politics may be less likely to bring charges against politicians. Similar to corruption cases, human rights violations put the state in the uncomfortable position of prosecuting its own agents. The first empirical work to highlight this problem in Latin America focused on cases of police accountability providing evidence from Argentina and Brazil (Brinks 2003, 2008). This research noted the importance that institutional design plays in the impunity enjoyed by policemen accused of human rights violations, given that those in charge of gathering the information for the prosecution, i.e., the police, have preferences that are closer to the accused (i.e., fellow policemen). Qualitative research from Mexico has also identified similar obstacles to prosecuting state agents for their participation in the recent spike of homicides and disappearances in the country (OSF 2016), noticing that the appointment process generates low independence among prosecutors (Aguiar 2012, 2015).

The impact that prosecutorial failures can have on rule of law offers strong warnings from recent scholarship that focuses on impunity. For example, the systematic failure of many countries to investigate, prosecute, and punish the killers of journalists and human rights activists in the region (for interesting examples see, CIDH 2011; Green 2015; Sack, Shapiro, and Castro 2015), has been shown to decrease the overall trust in the legal system and in democratic institutions (Fernandez and Kuenzi 2010). Also, not surprisingly some have found that systematic impunity not only increases perceptions of insecurity (Duce and Perez Pérdomo 2003), but it may also increase overall violence and crime (Imbusch, Misse, and Carrión 2011), given that the deterrent effect of "punishment" is never perceived (CAF 2014). For example, some have argued that the lack of justice for victims of domestic violence actually increased the incidence of femicide in Guatemala (Benítez 2007). Similarly troubling is that when citizens fail to trust and rely on courts to channel grievances, this increases the emergence of private means of justice, like lynching (Godoy 2006; Malone 2012).

When All Fails, How to Improve Prosecutorial Accountability?

Given the importance of prosecutorial organs to provide certainty and security, support the rule of law, and buttress democratic governance, it is not surprising that slowly scholars are venturing into exploring if and how prosecutorial accountability can be achieved. As explained earlier, PPOs require a mix of both independence and oversight to ensure that prosecutorial discretion is not abused or misused, and to provide accountability when failures of commission or omission occur. Just like variation in the design of the prosecutorial organ can impact how independent a PPO is, recent scholarship has found that by design legislators can also introduce mechanisms of control over the discretionary powers of the prosecutor that can bring some accountability on prosecutorial decisions.

A very obvious way in which the prosecutorial powers of the PPO can be kept "accountable" is introduced by design when criminal procedure law allows *judicial review* of decisions made by the PPO, usually the decision to prosecute or not to prosecute, the charges made, as well as the decision to use the opportunity principle. There is, however, another way in which institutional design can introduce certain mechanisms that can potentially serve as an accountability tool, and in the process help avoid arbitrary (and perhaps politically driven) decisions not to investigate or prosecute crimes or to dismiss a case.

Research that has focused on "prosecutorial accountability" has highlighted the different legal tools that are available for societal actors to push for prosecutions. For a long time it was noted by human rights scholars that an unwilling or incapable prosecutorial organ can be pushed to do its work as a result of actions initiated by citizens (Burt 2013; Peruzzotti and Smulovitz 2006; Sikkink 1993). But until very recently it was identified that private prosecution rights provided the legal mechanism through which societal actors were able to exert such impact on prosecutorial decisions (Collins 2009, 2010; Michel and Sikkink 2013).

Although a PPO is usually designed to hold the monopoly the power to prosecute, this monopoly can be made porous by granting the right to private prosecution to victims, their relatives, or nongovernmental organizations (NGOs) working on behalf of such victims. The introduction of private prosecution in criminal offenses serves as such an institutional mechanism that in theory can keep the PPO accountable regarding its duty to investigate and prosecute crime. The right to private prosecution allows victims and their lawyers, sometimes even domestic human rights organizations, to open a criminal investigation and actively participate throughout every stage of the investigation and prosecution. Private prosecution can be *auxiliary*, where the private party is only allowed to adhere to the prosecution of the state, or private prosecution can be *autonomous*, where the private party has the power also to press different charges from those introduced in the indictment of the public prosecutor. Private prosecution also serves as a check because this actor is usually granted the right to appeal key decisions the public prosecutor makes. In some countries, for instance, private prosecutors can usually request a judge to review every key decision that puts an end to a case at any stage of the proceedings. Empirical scholarship has found not only that private prosecution rights, when used by societal actors, can serve as an important accountability tool against prosecutorial organs that are unwilling to prosecute state agents for human rights violations (Dancy and Michel 2016; Michel and Sikkink 2013). Interestingly, it has also been found that private prosecution works as an accountability tool when facing a PPO incapable of prosecuting common crime (e.g., due to lack of resources) (Michel 2018).

Final Comments and Suggestions for Future Research

This chapter aims to have shown that the research on prosecutorial organs, despite being quite recent, has already proven the urgent need we face to study prosecutorial organs in the region. The role of this institution in the overall functioning of a judicial system, and in buttressing democratic governance and rule of law, makes this imperative. Overall, future research on prosecutorial organs should also help us better understand the distinction between de facto and *de jure* independence, as well as help us understand the factors that help improve prosecutorial accountability. Although this is a burgeoning area of research, there are many areas that are virtually understudied and that need to be addressed by future research. Drawing on the four types of systematic failure produced at the prosecutorial stage (as explained in Table 14.2) in this final section, I will highlight some areas that require more empirical and comparative research.

On the area of failures "by omission," we need to know more about how and when a prosecutorial organ works or does not work. Although currently we have some empirical research showing some factors that allegedly make prosecutorial organs inefficient as well as research on the overall impact of impunity at large, we need to know more to be able to provide policy advice on how to reduce the systematic failures that lead to impunity. We need more systematic empirical research that helps us understand the impact of racial, class, or gendered prejudice on producing both inefficient and/or biased prosecutions, as well as on how these factors may influence prosecutorial inaction and produce impunity. This lacuna in research also highlights the need to study the role of the police in the criminal investigation stage, as well as on their relationship with prosecutors. Although some scholars have already ventured studying the role of the police in prosecutorial failures (Brinks 2008; Lopes 2016; Monterroso 2008), there remains an urgent need for more empirical and theoretical research on the police force in the context of Latin America (Macaulay 2007).

On the area of failures "by commission," we should consider as a good starting point the human rights scholarship that has helped us understand when prosecutorial power was used as a tool for repression of political opponents during authoritarian rule, as well as when prosecutorial discretion has been used for selective impunity, protecting state agents from prosecutions for human rights abuses. However, we know little about prosecutions for current human rights violations, or about when or why prosecutorial powers are being used to maintain order through the criminalization of social process or as a tool of social cleansing. Similarly, although human rights scholarship provides a good starting point on explaining impunity for past human rights abuses, there is little we know about conditions that foster or inhibit the prosecution of corruption cases, or the prosecution of white collar crime.

Notes

1 There is a longer history of research focused on prosecutorial organs among scholars that focus on common law countries or continental Europe. The risks inherent to prosecutorial powers have long been noted in such scholarship, for example, Abrams (1971), Krug (2002), and Moley (1929).
2 For historical accounts on the development of prosecutorial organs in common law countries see: Langbein (1973); Ma (2008); and Ramsey (2002).

3 I use the term "Latin America" to refer to only those Spanish and Portuguese speaking countries of Central and South America that are based on a civil law tradition, excluding all Caribbean and common law countries.

4 Besides the judiciary, that through judicial review has an important role in upholding the constitution and the rule of law, other important state agencies and institutions that have mandates with horizontal accountability functions are: audit institutions (like a comptroller's office) entrusted to oversee budgeting and expenditure); human rights ombudsman offices; and PPO or the Attorney General's Office. (For a discussion of these different agencies in the region see: Payne, Zovatto, and Mateo [2006].)

5 Empirically, of course, a country's criminal justice system may in fact present one or all of the four types of judicial failures.

References

Abal, Paula and Ortega, Mariana. 2011. Thoughts on the Visual Aspect of the Neoliberal Order and the Piquetero Movement in Argentina. *Latin American Perspectives, 38*(1): 88–101.

Abrams, Norman. 1971. Internal Policy: Guiding the Exercise of Prosecutorial Discretion. *UCLA Law Review, 19*(1): 1–58.

Adelman, Jeremy and Centeno, Miguel Angel. 2002. Between Liberalism and Neoliberalism: Law's Dilemma in Latin America. In Y. Dezalay and B.G. Garth (Eds.), *Global Prescriptions: The Production, Exportation, and Importation of a New Legal Orthodoxy*, 139–61. Ann Arbor: The University of Michigan Press.

Aguayo, Sergio. 1998. *1968: los archivos de la violencia*. México: Grijalbo: Reforma.

Aguiar Aguilar, Azul América. 2012. Institutional Changes in the Public Prosecutor's Office: The Cases of Mexico, Chile, and Brazil. *Mexican Law Review, IV*(2), 262–90.

Aguiar Aguilar, Azul América. 2015. La Procuración de Justicia: El Talón de Aquiles del Estado de Derecho en México. *Revista Mexicana de Análisis Político y Admistración Pública, IV*(1), 159–72.

Aguirre, Carlos and Salvatore, Ricardo. 2001. Introduction: Writing the History of Law, Crime, and Punishment in Latin America. In Ricardo Salvatore, Carlos Aguirre and Gilbert Joseph (Eds.), *Crime and Punishment in Latin America: Law and Society Since Late Colonial Times*, 1–32. Durham: Duke Univesity Press.

Ansolabehere, Karina. 2007. *La política desde la justicia. Cortes Supremas, gobierno y democracia en Argentina y México*. Ciudad de México: FLACSO y Fontamara.

Barahona, Carlos, Cerón, Roberto, and Peroti, Felipe. 2010. El Ministerio Público y el Fiscal en Chile. Notas para el Estudio de su Historia Institucional. *Revista Chilena de Historia del Derecho, 22*, 735–98.

Barkow, Rachel. 2008. Institutional Design and the Policing of Prosecutors: Lessons from Administrative Law. *Stanford Law Review 61*(4): 869–922.

Benítez, Inés. 2007. Rights Guatemala: Impunity Fuels Violence Against Women. *Inter Press Service News Agency*.

Binder, Alberto. 2000. *Ideas y Materiales para la Reforma de la Justicia Penal*. Buenos Aires: Ad-Hoc.

Bradley, Craig. 2007. *Criminal Procedure: A Worldwide Study* (second edition). Durham, NC: Carolina Academic Press.

Brinks, Daniel. 2003. Informal Institutions and the Rule of Law: The Judicial Response to State Killings in Buenos Aires and São Paulo in the 1990s. *Comparative Politics, 36*(1): 1–19.

Brinks, Daniel. 2008. *The Judicial Response to Police Killings in Latin America: Inequality and the Rule of Law*. Cambridge: Cambridge University Press.

Brinks, Daniel, Leiras, Marcelo, and Mainwaring, Scott. 2014. *Reflections on Uneven Democracies: The Legacy of Guillermo O'Donnell*. Baltimore: Johns Hopkins University Press.

Bruneau, Thomas. 2014. Pandillas and Security in Central America. *Latin American Research Review, 49*(2): 152–72.

Burt, Jo-Marie. 2013. The New Accountability Agenda in Latin America: The Promise and Perils of Human Rights Prosecutions. In Katherine Hite and Mark Ungar (Eds.), *Sustaining Human Rights in the Twenty-First Century: Strategies for Latin America*, 101–41. Baltimore and Washington, DC: Woodrow Wilson Center Press and The Johns Hopkins University Press.

CAF. 2014. *Towards a Safer Latin America: A New Perspective to Prevent and Control Crime*. Bogotá Colombia: Development Bank of Latin America.

Castro, Juventino. 2008. *El Ministerio Público en México* (15a ed.). México: Editorial Porrúa.

CEJA. 2005. *Desafíos del Ministerio Publico Fiscal en America Latina*. Chile: Centro de Estudios de Justicia de las Américas.

CIDH. 2011. *Segundo Informe sobre la Situación de las Defensoras y los Defensores de Derechos Humanos en las Américas*. Washington, DC: Comisión Interamericana de Derechos Humanos.

Collier, Ruth and Collier, David. 1991. *Shaping the Political Arena: Critical Junctures, the Labor Movement, and Regime Dynamics in Latin America*. Princeton, NJ: Princeton University Press.

Collins, Cath. 2009. Human Rights Trials in Chile during and after the 'Pinochet Years.' *The International Journal of Transitional Justice, 4*(1): 67–76.

Collins, Cath. 2010. *Post-Transitional Justice: Human Rights Trials in Chile and El Salvador*. University Park, PA: Penn State Press.

Dancy, Geoff and Michel, Verónica. 2016. Human Rights Enforcement From Below: Private Actors and Prosecutorial Momentum in Latin America and Europe. *International Studies Quarterly*, 60(1), 173–188.

Domingo, Pilar. 1999. Rule of Law, Citizenship and Access to Justice in Mexico. *Mexican Studies, Winter*, 151–91.

Dubber, Markus. 2006. Comparative Criminal Law. In Mathias Reimann and Reinhard Zimmermann (Eds.), *The Oxford Handbook of Comparative Law*, 1287–1325. New York: Oxford University Press.

Dubber, Markus. 2014. *Foundational Texts in Modern Criminal Law*. Oxford, United Kingdom: Oxford University Press.

Duce, Mauricio. 2009. Criminal Justice Reform in Latin America: A Panoramic and Comparative Perespective Examining Its Development, Contents, Results, and Challenges. *UDP Public Policy Series: Working Papers*, No. 3.

Duce, Mauricio and Perez Pérdomo, Rogelio. 2003. Citizen Security and Reform of the Criminal Justice System in Latin America. In Hugo Frühling, Joseph Tulchin, and Heather Golding (Eds.) *Crime and Violence in Latin America: Citizen Security, Democracy, and the State*, xii, 284. Washington, DC, Baltimore: Woodrow Wilson Center Press; Johns Hopkins University Press.

Ferejohn, Jonh. 1999. Independent Judges, Dependent Judiciary: Explaining Judicial Independence. *Southern California Law Review*, 72(2–3): 353–84.

Fernandez, Kenneth and Michele Kuenzi. 2010. Crime and Support for Democracy in Africa and Latin America. *Political Studies*, 58(3): 450–71. doi:10.1111/j.1467-9248.2009.00802.x

Fix-Zamudio, Héctor. 2002. *Función Constitucional Del Ministerio Público: Tres Ensayos y Un Epílogo*. México: Universidad Nacional Autónoma de México-Instituto de Investigaciones Jurídicas.

Garoupa, Nuno. 2009. Some Reflections on the Economics of Prosecutors: Mandatory vs. Selective Prosecution. *International Review of Law and Economics, 29*(1): 25–8. doi:10.1016/j.irle.2008.07.001

Garro, Alejandro. 2000. Staffing the Judiciary and Prosecutorial Offices in Argentina: Trials and Tribulations in Search of Merit, Integrity, and Accountability. *Southwestern Journal of Law and Trade in the Americas, 7*: 349–447.

Gibney, Mark 1987. Well-Founded Fear of Persecution, A. *Hum. Rts. Q., 10*: 109.

Gimeno, Vicente, Moreno, Víctor and Cortés, Valentín. 1999. *Derecho Procesal Penal*. Madrid, España: Editorial Colex.

Godoy, Angelina. 2006. *Popular Injustice: Violence, Community, and Law in Latin America*. Stanford, CA: Stanford University Press.

Green, Bruce and Zacharias, Fred. 2004. Prosecutorial Neutrality. *Wisconsin Law Review*, 837–904.

Green, Jonh. 2015. *A History of Political Murder in Latin America: Killing the Messengers of Change*. Albany, NY: SUNY Press.

Guarnieri, Carlo. 2003. Courts as an Instrument of Horizontal Accountability: The Case of Latin Europe. In José María Maravall and Adam Przeworski (Eds.) *Democracy and the Rule of Law*. Cambridge, UK: Cambridge University Press.

Hammergren, Linn. 2002a. Do Judicial Councils Further Judicial Reform? Lessons from Latin America. In C.E.F.I. Peace (Ed.), *Working Papers*, 28. Washington, DC.

Hammergren, Linn. 2002b. *Fifteen Years of Judicial Reform in Latin America: Where We Are and Why We Haven't Made More Progress*. From USAID Global Center for Democracy and Governance.

Hammergren, Linn. 2008. Twenty-Five Years of Latin American Judicial Reforms: Achievements, Disappointments, and Emerging Issues. *The Whitehead Journal of Diplomacy and International Relations, 9*(1): 89–104.

Heymann, Philip. 1995. Should Latin American Prosecutors Be Independent of the Executive in Prosecuting Government Abuses? *University of Miami Inter-American Law Review, 26*: 535–611.

HiiL. 2007. *Rule of Law Inventory Report: Academic Part*. Hague Institute for the Internationalisation of Law.

Horvitz, María Inés and López, Julián. 2002. *Derecho Procesal Penal Chileno, 1*. Santiago de Chile: Editorial Jurídica de Chile.

Imbusch, Peter, Misse, Michel, and Carrión, Fernando. 2011. Violence Research in Latin America and the Caribbean: A Literature Review. *International Journal of Conflict and Violence, 5*(1): 88–154.

Inclán, María and Inclán, Silvia. 2005. Las reformas judiciales en America Latina y la rendicion de cuentas del Estado. *Perfiles Latinoamericanos, 12(26)*: 55–82.

Ingram, Matthew. 2008. *Subnational Judicial Change in New Democracies: Elections, Ideology, and Elite Voluntarism in Three Mexican States*. Paper presented at the Prepared for research workshop at CIDE, Centro de Investigación y Docencia Económicas, Mexico City.

Ingram, Matthew. 2016. Mandates, Geography, and Networks: Diffusion of Criminal Procedure Reform in Mexico. *Latin American Politics and Society, 58*(1): 121–45. doi:10.1111/j.1548-2456.2016.00301.x

Kapiszewski, Diana and Taylor, Matthew. 2008. Doing Courts Justice? Studying Judicial Politics in Latin America. *Perspectives on Politics, 6*(4): 741–67.

Kritz, Neil. 1995. *Transitional Justice: How Emerging Democracies Reckon with Former Regimes*. Washington, DC: United States Institute of Peace Press.

Krug, Peter. 2002. Prosecutorial Discretion and Its Limits. *The American Journal of Comparative Law, 50*: 643–64. doi:10.2307/840893

Lambert, Peter. 2012. National Identity, Conflict, and Political Violence: Experiences in Latin America. In Marie Breen-Smyth (Ed.) *The Ashgate Research Companion to Political Violence*. London and New York: Routledge.

Langbein, Jonh. 1973. The Origins of Public Prosecution at Common Law. *The American Journal of Legal History, 17*: 313–335.

Langer, Máximo. 2007. Revolution in Latin American Criminal Procedure: Diffusion of Legal Ideas from the Periphery. *The American Journal of Comparative Law, 55*: 617–76.

Lessa, Francesca. 2013. *Memory and Transitional Justice in Argentina and Uruguay*. New York: Palgrave Macmillan.

Lessa, Francesca and Payne, Leigh. 2012. *Amnesty in the Age of Human Rights Accountability: Comparative and International Perspectives*. Cambridge, New York: Cambridge University Press.

Lopes, Ludmila. 2016. *Problemas de la Investigación Penal de Delitos de Cierta Complejidad en Brasil*. Biblioteca Virtual CEJAS. Available at: http://biblioteca.cejamericas.org/handle/2015/3146. Accessed September 6, 2017.

Lutz, Ellen and Sikkink, Kathryn. 2001. The Justice Cascade: The Evolution and Impact of Foreign Human Rights Trials in Latin America. *Chicago Journal of International Law, 2*(1): 1–33.

Lutz, Ellen and Reiger, Caitlin. 2009. *Prosecuting Heads of State*. Cambridge, New York: Cambridge University Press.

Lutz, Ellen and Sikkink, Kathryn. 2003. International Human Rights Law and Practice in Latin America. *International Organization, 54*(3): 633–59.

Ma, Yue. 2008. Exploring the Origins of Public Prosecution. *International Criminal Justice Review, 18*.

Macaulay, Fiona. 2007. Knowledge Production, Framing and Criminal Justice Reform in Latin America. *Journal of Latin American Studies, 39*(3): 627–51. doi:http://dx.doi.org/10.1017/S0022216X07002866.

Maggetti, Martino. 2007. De Facto Independence After Delegation: A Fuzzy-Set Analysis. *Regulation and Governance, 1*(4): 271–94.

Mainwaring, Scott. 2003. Introduction: Democratic Accountability in Latin America. In Scott Mainwaring and Christoper Welna (Eds.), *Democratic Accountability in Latin America*. New York, NY: Oxford University Press.

Mainwaring, Scott and Welna, Christoper. 2003. *Democratic Accountability in Latin America*. Oxford, New York: Oxford University Press.

Malone, Mary Fran. 2012. *The Rule of Law in Central America: Citizens' Reactions to Crime and Punishment*. New York, NY: Continuum International Pub. Group.

McAdams, James. (Ed.). 1997. *Transitional Justice and the Rule of Law in New Democracies*. Notre Dame: University of Notre Dame Press.

McGrath, Luke. 2000. Presumed Guilty?: Criminal Justice and Human Rights in Mexico. *Fordham International Law Journal 24*(3): 801–88.

Merryman, Jonh and Pérez-Perdomo, Rogelio. 2007. *The Civil Law Tradition: An Introduction to the Legal Systems of Europe and Latin America* (third edition). Stanford, CA: Stanford University Press.

Messick, R.E. (2002, March). Judicial Reform: The Why, the What, and the How. In *World Bank Thematic Group on Legal Institutions. Conference on Strategies for Modernizing the Judicial Sector in the Arab World*, Marrakech, Morocco, March (pp. 15–17).

Michel, Verónica. 2018. *Prosecutorial Accountability and Victims' Rights in Latin America*. New York, NY: Cambridge University Press.

Michel, Verónica and Sikkink, Kathryn. 2013. Human Rights Prosecutions and the Participation Rights of Victims in Latin America. *Law and Society Review, 47*(4). 873–907.

Moley, Raymond. 1929. *Politics and Criminal Prosecution*. New York: Minton, Balch.

Monterroso Javier. 2008. *Investigacion Criminal: Estudio Comparativo y Propuesta de un Modelo de Policía de Investigación en Guatemala* (second edition). Guatemala: ICCPG.

Murphy, William. (1993). Constitutions, Constitutionalism, and Democracy. In Douglas Greenberg (Ed.) *Constitutionalism and Democracy: Transitions in the Contemporary World*, 3–25. New York: Oxford University Press.

Méndez, Juan, O'Donnell, Guillermo, and Pinheiro, Paulo (Eds.). 1999. *The (Un)Rule of Law and the Underprivileged in Latin America*. Notre Dame, IN: University of Notre Dame Press.

Müller, Markus-Michael. 2012. The Rise of the Penal State in Latin America. *Contemporary Justice Review, 15*(1): 57–76. doi:10.1080/10282580.2011.590282

Nino, Carlos. 1996. *Radical Evil on Trial*. New Haven, CT: Yale University Press.

O'Donnell, Guillermo. 1999. Horizontal Accountability in New Democracies. In A. Schedler, L. Diamond and M.F. Plattner (Eds.), *The Self-Restraining State: Power and Accountability in New Democracies*.

O'Donnell, Guillermo. 2004. Why the Rule of Law Matters. *Journal of Democracy, 15*(4): 32–46.

O'Donnell, Guillermo, Schmitter, Philippe, and Whitehead, Laurence. 1986. *Transitions From Authoritarian Rule in Latin America*. Baltimore: Johns Hopkins University Press.

OSF. 2016. *Undeniable Atrocities: Confronting Crimes Against Humanity in Mexico*. New York, NY: Open Society Foundations.

Payne, Mark, Zovatto, Daniel, and Mateo, Mercedes. 2006. *La Política Importa: Democracia y Desarrollo en América Latina*. Washington, DC: Banco Interamericano de Desarrollo/Instituto Internacional para la Democracia y la Asistencia Electoral.

Payne, Leight. 2008. *Unsettling Accounts: Neither Truth Nor Reconciliation in Confessions of State Violence*. Durham: Duke University Press.

Peerenboom, Randall. 2004. *Human Rights and Rule of Law: What's the Relationship?* bepress Legal Series Paper, 355.

Pereira, Anthony. 2003. Explaining Judicial Reform Outcomes in New Democracies: The Importance of Authoritarian Legalism in Argentina, Brazil, and Chile. *Human Rights Review, 4*(3): 3–16.

Peruzzotti, Enrique and Smulovitz, Catalina. 2006. *Enforcing the Rule of Law: Social Accountability in the New Latin American Democracies*. Pittsburgh, PA: University of Pittsburgh Press.

Piccato, Pablo. 2001. *City of Suspects: Crime in Mexico City, 1900–1931*. Durham, NC: Duke University Press.

Prillaman, William. 2000. *The Judiciary and Democratic Decay in Latin America*. Westport, Connecticut; London: Praeger.

Putnam, Robert. 1993. *Making Democracy Work: Civic Traditions in Modern Italy*. Princeton, NJ: Princeton University Press.

Ramsey, Carolyn. 2002. The Discretionary Power of "Public" Prosecutors in Historical Perspective. *American Criminal Law Review, 39*: 1309–93.

Riego, Cristián and Duce, Mauricio. 2009. *Prisión Preventiva y Reforma Procesal Penal en América Latina: Evaluación y Perspectivas*. Santiago, Chile: CEJA-JSCA.

Ríos-Figueroa, Julio. 2012. Institutional Design and Judicial Behavior: Constitutional Interpretation of Criminal Due Process Rights in Latin America. In D. Nolte and A. Schilling-Vacaflor (Eds.), *New Constitutionalism in Latin America: Promises and Practices*. Farnham, Surrey; Burlington, VT: Ashgate Pub.

Ríos-Figueroa, Julio. 2015. Judicial Institutions. In J. Gandhi (Ed.), *Routledge Handbook of Comparative Political Institutions*, xiii, 448. Milton Park, Abingdon, Oxon; New York, NY: Routledge.

Ríos-Figueroa, Julio and Pozas-Loyo, Andreas. 2010. Enacting Constitutionalism: The Origins of Independent Judicial Institutions in Latin America. *Comparative Politics, April*, 293–311.

Ríos-Figueroa, Julio. 2006. *Judicial Independence: Definition, Measurement, and Its Effects on Corruption. An Analysis of Latin America*. PhD Dissertation. New York: Department of Political Science, New York University.

Ríos-Figueroa, Julio. 2012. Justice System Institutions and Corruption Control: Evidence from Latin America. *The Justice System Journal, 33*(2): 195–214.

Rodríguez, Octavio and Shirk, David. 2015. *Criminal Procedure Reform in Mexico 2008–2016: The Final Countdown for Implementation.* San Diego, CA: Justice in Mexico/University of San Diego.

Roht-Arriaza, Naomi and Lauren Gibson. 1998. The Developing Jurisprudence on Amnesty. *Human Rights Quarterly, 10*(4): 843–85.

Sack, Jon, Shapiro, Adam, and Castro, Lucha. 2015. *La Lucha: The story of Lucha Castro and Human Rights in Mexico.* London, Brooklyn, NY: Verso.

Sadek, María Tereza and Batista, Rosângela. 2003. The New Brazilian Public Prosecution: An Agent of Accountability. In Scott Mainwaring and Christoper Welna (Eds.) *Democratic Accountability in Latin America,* 201–27. New York: Oxford University Press.

Salvatore, Ricardo, Aguirre, Carlos, and Joseph, Gilbert. 2001. *Crime and Punishment in Latin America: Law and Society Since Late Colonial Times.* Durham: Duke University Press.

Sanford, Victoria. 2008. *Guatemala: Del Genocidio al Feminicidio.* Guatemala: F&G Editores.

Sarat, Austin and Clarke, Conor. 2008. Beyond Discretion: Prosecution, the Logic of Sovereignty, and the Limits of Law. *Law and Society Inquiry, 33*(2): 387–416.

Schedler, Andreas, Diamond, Larry, and Plattner, Marc. 1999. *The Self-Restraining State: Power and Accountability in New Democracies.* Boulder: Lynne Rienner Publishers.

Schmitter, Philippe and Terry, Karl. 1991. What Democracy Is and Is not. *Journal of Democracy,* 75–88.

Sikkink, Kathryn. 1993. Human Rights, Principled Issue-Networks, and Sovereignty in Latin America. *International Organization, 47*(3): 411–41.

Silva, Cátia. 2000. *Brazilian Prosecutors and the Collective Demands: Bringing Social Issues to the Courts of Justice.* Paper presented at the Annual Meeting of the Latin American Studies Association, Miami, FL, March 16–18.

Skaar, Elin. 2001. *Judicial Independence and Human Rights Policies in Argentina and Chile.* Bergen: Chr. Michelsen Institute.

Skaar, Elin. 2002. *Judicial Independence: A Key to Justice. An Analysis of Latin America in the 1990s.* PhD Dissertation, Department of Political Science, University of California, Los Angeles.

Staton, Jeffrey and Ríos-Figueroa, Julio. 2009. *Unpacking the Rule of Law: A Review of Judicial Independence Measures.* Paper presented at the Measuring Democracy: A Multi-Dimensional, History Approach, Boston University, Boston MA.

Suárez, Santiago. 1995. *Los Fiscales Indianos: Orígen y Evolución del Ministerio Público.* Caracas: Academia Nacional de la Historia.

Thome, J.R. 1998. Searching for Democracy: The Rule of Law and Legal Reform in Latin America. In *Workshop on Reforma Judicial: Motivaciones, Proyectos, Caminos Recorridos, Caminos por Recorrer.* Spain. Instituto Internacional de Sociología Jurídica

Tiede, Lydia. 2006. Judicial Independence: Often Cited, Rarely Understood. *Journal of Contemporary Legal Issues, 15*: 129–61.

Tiede, Lydia. 2012. Chile's Criminal Law Reform: Enhancing Defendant's Rights and Citizen Security. *Latin American Politics and Society, 54*(3). doi:10.1111/j.1548-2456.2012.00165.x

Ungar, Mark. 2002. *Elusive Reform: Democracy and the Rule of Law in Latin America.* Boulder: L. Rienner Publishers.

Ungar, Mark. 2011. *Policing Democracy: Overcoming Obstacles to Citizen Security in Latin America.* Washington, DC, Baltimore: Woodrow Wilson Center Press; Johns Hopkins University Press.

Van Aaken, Anne, Feld, Lars, and Voigt, Stefan. 2008. *Power Over Prosecutors Corrupts Politicians: Cross Country Evidence Using a New Indicator.* Paper presented at the CESifo Working Paper No. 2245, Center for Economic Studies (CESifo Group), Munich, Germany.

Van Aaken, Anne, Feld, Lars, and Voigt, Stefan. 2010. Do Independent Prosecutors Deter Political Corruption? An Empirical Evaluation Across Seventy-Eight Countries. *American Law and Economics Review, 12*(1): 204–44.

Van Aaken, Anne, Salzberger, Eli and Voigt, Stefan. 2004. The Prosecution of Public Figures and the Separation of Powers. Confusion within the Executive Branch: A Conceptual Framework. *Constitutional Political Economy, 15*(3): 261–80.

Wright, Melissa. 2011. Necropolitics, Narcopolitics, and Femicide: Gendered Violence on the Mexico-U.S. Border. *Journal of Women in Culture and Society, 36*(3): 707–31.

Zaffaroni, Eugenio. 1986. *Sistemas Penales y Derechos Humanos en América Latina.* Retrieved from Buenos Aires.

Zaffaroni, Eugenio. (Ed.) (2000). *Sistema Penal y Derechos Humanos Brasil, Costa Rica, El Salvador, Guatemala, Honduras, México, Nicaragua, Panamá, Espana* (second edition). México, DF: Editorial Porrúa-Secretaría de Gobernación–ILANUD–Comisión Europea.

Zakaria, Fareed. 1997. The Rise of Illiberal Democracy. *Foreign Affairs* (November/December).

Zepeda Guillermo. 2004. *Crimen Sin Castigo: Procuración de Justicia Penal y el Ministerio Público en México.* México, DF: CIDAC–Fondo de Cultura Económica.

15

HUMAN RIGHTS OMBUDSMEN IN LATIN AMERICA

Fredrik Uggla

One of the most dynamic areas of legal reform in Latin America during recent decades has been the establishment of national human rights institutions in the form of ombudsmen for human rights (see for overviews, Reif 2004; Cardenas 2014). Almost all countries in the region have seen the creation of such entities, typically known as *Defensores del Pueblo or Procuradores de los Derechos Humanos*. These are state agencies whose task it is to promote citizens' rights vis-à-vis other state entities and in society at large; either by handling complaints relating to violations committed by state agents, or by promoting human rights through training, information campaigns, and legislative proposals.

Accessibility, informality of procedure, and application of general human rights principles rather than exact legal formulations, mean that the ombudsman can be a promising invention to broaden access to justice and safeguard the rights of disadvantaged groups. Yet, the ombudsman also has another characteristic; it lacks formal sanctioning power to enforce its decisions and resolutions. Most of its work consists in arbitration, persuasion, or provision of information. Even when the ombudsman emits formal resolutions, such verdicts are recommendations, which the entities concerned can choose to disregard. This means that there is a permanent risk that what is often promoted as an instrument to improve access to justice and enforcement of human rights, may end up producing few concrete results.

In spite of their lack of enforcement powers, several of the ombudsmen of Latin America have become important actors in the legal, political, and social landscapes of their respective countries. Ombudsmen have successfully challenged leading politicians and advanced rights-based agendas, provided civil society groups with ways to access the state, offering people in general an institution that they can believe in and, which takes their demands seriously. Yet, the role of the ombudsman differs between countries, and even vis-à-vis different state institutions. Whereas some ombudsmen are indeed forceful defenders of human rights, others are all but disregarded.

This chapter traces the history of human rights ombudsmen in Latin America, and sketches out their respective structures and mandates. Beyond such formal aspects, it also discusses how "these institutions function" in practice, as well as how the general public perceives them. Two areas of theoretical debate relevant to the ombudsman are addressed; first, whether the actions of an institution without sanctioning power can really be expected to be effective (efficacy), and; second, what the broader implications of an ombudsman's office are for the legal and political environment in which it is active (accountability). Finally, I discuss possible future areas for research in relation to these institutions.

The History of the Latin American Ombudsmen

A "justice ombudsman" (*justitieombudsman*) was included in the Swedish Constitution of 1809 as an instrument to receive citizens' complaints against public authorities, and in the twentieth century, similar offices were established in parts of Western Europe (Jägerskiöld 1961). Its inclusion in the democratic constitution of Spain of 1978 most probably provided the spur for its transfer to Latin America (Cardenas 2014), where the first ombudsman, the *Procurador para los Derechos Humanos*, was established in the Guatemalan Constitution in 1985 and became functional in 1987.

During the following decades Latin America would witness a virtual explosion of similar institutions, as shown in Table 15.1.

By the end of 2015, Chile stood out as the only Latin American country without an ombudsman's office, and in several cases separate ombudsmen had also been created at the regional or local levels, for example, in Mexico and in Argentina where the first regional ombudsmen were created already in 1986 (Reif 2004).

Scholars have advanced different explanations for the widespread introduction of ombudsmen, and why politicians presiding over widespread and persistent violations of civil and social rights – which is the case in virtually all Latin American countries – would choose to create a human rights office with diffuse and untested powers (Cardenas 2014). Some of these explanations stress the relevance of the ombudsmen in settings with a non-functioning judicial system and an abusive bureaucracy. Accordingly, the first ombudsmen were created by states that had recently escaped the clutches of authoritarian government and civil conflict. In such settings, the idea of setting up an institution to safeguard and promote human rights must have had an evident appeal (Popkin 2000, 166). But the ombudsman can also be seen as a solution to a potentially more pressing problem: the need to establish a bureaucratic oversight to guarantee the functioning of democratic delegation. Hence, rather than performing costly permanent supervision, an ombudsman can be seen as a "fire-alarm" kind of oversight (Lupia and McCubbins 1994), which relies on third parties (the citizens) to bring bureaucratic transgressions to the attention of elected politicians.

In addition to explanations related to memories of past abuses or administrative necessities, more cynical accounts of the institution's emergence emphasize the fact that an ombudsman, in contrast to a constitutional court for instance, does not have the power to compel a certain course of action. Accordingly, establishing an ombudsman may have seemed an easy and not too politically costly way of demonstrating political commitment to democracy and human rights (Ungar 2002, 37; Pegram 2008). Indeed, it has been noted how the creation of ombudsmen has corresponded to a need to placate international actors (Maiorano 2001; see Finkel 2012 on Mexico).

Once created, most Latin American ombudsmen would evolve in a rather similar fashion. In the first place, and as can be seen in Table 15.1, in several cases there was a significant time lag between the legal or constitutional introduction of the ombudsman, and the actual establishment of the institution. This would lend support to the idea that their establishment often owed more to the need to demonstrate support for the human rights as a principle, rather than to any perceived urgency to improve the human rights situation in the country in question. That seems to have been the case in Peru and Paraguay, for instance, where the establishment of the institution occurred several years after its constitutional recognition. Conversely, where the institution was created in constitutional reform processes aimed at ending violent conflict (as in El Salvador

Table 15.1 Name, Creation, and ICC status (2014) of Different Latin American Ombudsmen

Country	Name	Created	Operational	Internationally Accredited By the ICC*
Guatemala	Procurador de los Derechos Humanos	1985	1987	1999: B 2000: A(R) 2013: A
El Salvador	Procurador para la Defensa de los Derechos Humanos	1991	1992	2006: A
Colombia	Defensor del Pueblo	1991	1992	2001: A
Costa Rica	Defensor de los Habitantes	1992	1993	1999: A
Honduras	Comisionado Nacional de los Derechos Humanos	1992	1995	2000: B 2007: A 2011: B
Paraguay	Defensoría del Pueblo	1992	2001	2003: A
Mexico**	Comisión Nacional de los Derechos Humanos	1992/1999	(1990)	1999: A
Peru	Defensor del Pueblo	1993	1996	1999: A
Argentina	Defensor del Pueblo de la Nación	1994	1994	1999: A
Bolivia	Defensor del Pueblo	1994	1998	1999: B 2000: A
Nicaragua	Procurador para la Defensa de los Derechos Humanos	1995	1999	2006: A
Ecuador	Defensor del Pueblo	1996	1997	1999: A(R) 2009: A
Panama	Defensor del Pueblo	1997	1997	1999: A
Venezuela	Defensor del Pueblo	1999	1999	2002: A
Uruguay	Institución Nacional de Derechos Humanos y Defensoría del Pueblo	2008	2012	(under way)

Sources: Cárdenas 2014; Reif 2004; Uggla 2004; International Coordinating Committee of National Institutions for the Promotion and Protection of Human Rights (ICC) 2014.

Notes

* Refers to the ICC status of each institution; A = compliance with the Paris Principles; B = not fully in compliance with the Paris Principles; A(R) = insufficient documentation to confer A status; ICC = International Coordinating Committee.
** The convoluted chronology of the Mexican ombudsman responds to the gradual development of the institution.

or Colombia), it became operational much more rapidly. In the latter set of cases, however, the ombudsman was part of a broader set of reforms in the same direction, and not a special priority (Cardenas 2014).

The majority of the ombudsman institutions were thus created almost on a whim, and with little regard for what they would need in terms of resources and support from other state powers. But in spite of slow beginnings and limited mandates, early ombudsmen in many cases managed to convert the institution into an independent, legitimate, and relatively forceful advocate for citizens' rights. Such a development has been noted in Peru, Honduras, El Salvador, and Bolivia for instance (Pegram 2011; Uggla 2004; Popkin 2000). More concretely, the accessibility of the ombudsmen, possibly combined with relatively quick processes, seems to have contributed to their credibility, evidenced by rapidly increasing caseloads and high degrees of confidence in the institution (Ungar 2002). This support, often combined with substantial levels of external donor funding, would in turn eventually allow the institution to confront even the highest echelons of the state. In Peru, for instance, the ombudsman created by Alberto Fujimori in 1993, played a key role in the supervision of the 2000 elections, conferring "moral weight to the opposition" in a process that contributed to Fujimori's downfall (Pegram 2008, 78).

But as success led the institution into conflict with powerful state interests in many countries, there were also attempts to limit the ombudsmen's independence and strength. Typically, such attacks were related either to the processes of nomination of new ombudsmen or to the approval of the institution's budget. Thus, in Peru, congress abstained from naming a new titular to the office, and in El Salvador and Bolivia, partisan or incompetent candidates were designated to lead the office (Popkin 2000; Domingo 2006). In El Salvador the ombudman's assertiveness also led to budgetary repercussions and in Nicaragua the office's budget was cut by 40 percent after it adopted positions opposed to the government (Popkin 2000; The Economist 2001). Hence, during the first years of the current century, a number of the Latin American ombudsmen, including several of the most successful ones, found themselves going through periods of flux or decline (Pegram 2011).

During the second decade of the twentieth century, such turbulence has diminished, and several of the region's ombudsmen today appear as relatively consolidated institutions that provide citizens with a way to seek redress for maltreatment, and that – through information campaigns, public communiqués and trainings – serve as a kind of "moral consciousness" of the nation, even if this implies taking unpopular positions with the public or the government. However, as Pegram (2011) has noted, if direct attacks on the ombudsman have become rarer, that may also be because many ombudsmen today appear less openly combative, and possibly less independent from either government or political parties. Examples of the latter include the recent ombudsmen in Nicaragua (Omar Cabezas 2004–2016) and Venezuela (Tarek William Saab 2014–2017); both known partisans of the governing parties in these countries. In other cases, recent nominations have led to concerns that even strong and independent ombudsman institutions can be thwarted by the actions of new titulars perceived as standing closer to the government (Página Siete 2017). Furthermore, in several countries long delays in the designation of new ombudsmen have persisted. For instance, in Paraguay a new ombudsman was elected in 2016 after seven years of delay and in Argentina, congress had in 2017 not yet named a new ombudsman to substitute for the one who resigned in 2009. While partisan differences may account for some of these delays, it is also possible to see in some of them machinations to weaken the institution by depriving it of leadership and legitimacy. Accusations regarding nominations and lack of autonomy vis-à-vis the government were indeed at the center of the 2014 suspension of the Paraguayan ombudsman from the International Coordinating Committee for National Institutions for the Promotion and Protection of Human Rights (ICC), and the 2016 decision to designate the Venezuelan ombudsman as only partially compliant with international standards on national human rights institutions (ICC 2014, 26f.; GANHRI 2016, 51ff.).

In terms of thematic focus, the evolution of Latin America's ombudsmen reflects broader trends with regard to human rights in their respective countries. Whereas most of them were created in countries in which gross abuses by state agents of the most fundamental human rights were still common, such violations have become rarer in most of the countries in which they operate. Instead, new issues such as social rights, good governance, and increased visibility for minorities have come to the fore. Today, such matters generate the majority of cases for most ombudsmen in the region. Accordingly, whereas the image of the ombudsman is often that of a high-profile defender of civil and political rights threatened by the state, much of the institution's work now relates either to less dramatic interactions between state and citizens, or promoting consciousness regarding previously neglected social or cultural rights. Accordingly, although police forces and elements of the judiciaries still feature prominently in the work of the majority of the region's ombudsmen, they are equally or more likely to relate to entities such as social security institutions, municipalities, or the public in general.

What the Ombudsman Is

The term "ombudsman" does not translate easily into non-Nordic languages. Whereas the meaning of the Swedish word "ombud" is representative or agent, most Latin American terms focus on the protective character of the institution and normally involve the terms "Procurador" or "Defensor" in combination with "*Pueblo,*" "*Habitantes,*" or in some cases explicitly: "*Derechos Humanos.*" No matter the exact term, however, these institutions reflect a common model: They are state entities that receive and handle complaints from citizens relating to violations of their rights committed by public authorities. While most of these complaints are dealt with directly, the ombudsmen may also emit non-binding recommendations or issue reports that present their findings. In certain cases, the ombudsmen may also act legally as prosecutors or advocates. In no case, however, do the actions or opinions of the ombudsman constitute legally binding judgments or resolutions for other state entities. Rather, they are recommendations that such parties can choose to comply with or not.

While the above definition captures what ombudsmen have traditionally done, their tasks and functions have evolved over time. Thus, Linda Reif (2011) has noted a distinction between the "classical ombudsman" and the "hybrid ombudsman." The former term denotes "an institution that uses 'soft powers' of persuasion and cooperation to control conduct rather than coercive or adjudicative means." As such, it provides a "non-judicial alternative for over-seeing public administration" (Reif 2011, 270). But the Latin American ombudsmen are examples of the "hybrid ombudsman," which combines the tasks of the classical ombudsman with a broader function that consists in the protection and promotion of human rights through information campaigns, studies, advice, training, and legislative proposals. These latter functions are of course tasks that are commonly associated with a national human rights institution (Cardenas 2014), and as noted in Table 15.1, most of the Latin American ombudsmen are internationally recognized as the relevant national human rights institutions in accordance with the Paris Principles. However, this recognition is incomplete. Some Latin American ombudsmen have never become members of the ICC, the coordination body that awards such accreditation (Brazil, for example), and others have lost the accreditation (Honduras) or been demoted to "B-status" (Venezuela), meaning that they are only partly compliant with the Paris Principles (ICC 2017).

Presenting the ombudsmen as national human rights institutions indicates the close connection that exists between the ombudsmen and the global human rights system. In several cases, the ombudsman serve as a conduit for the introduction and application of human rights norms on the domestic stage or as a national representative of human rights at the global and regional level (Pegram 2015). For instance, Costa Rica, Nicaragua, and Mexico use their national ombudsmen as national rapporteurs on the Optional Protocol to the United Nations Convention Against Torture, while the Inter-American Court of Human Rights has in a number of cases relied on ombudsmen as expert witnesses (Reif 2004).

The Structure of the Ombudsman

Common origins and the diffusion effects evident in their establishment have left the ombuds-man offices of Latin America with structures that are highly similar in formal terms. Accord-ingly, the typical ombudsman's office is a constitutionally established, formally autonomous entity with a high degree of independence to structure its work and set priorities. Its exact posi-tion in the administrative hierarchy may vary; whereas in some countries the office forms part of a larger entity, for example, in Colombia and El Salvador, where it is part of the Ministerio Público or public prosecutor's office, in most countries it is either located under the legislature or has a fully autonomous position.

In keeping with its name and history, the ombudsman is an essentially personalist institution, the indisputable center of which is its titular ("the ombudsman"), who is named by congress, typically by a qualified majority. Beyond the titular, most ombudsmen's offices have rather elaborate structures with decentralized offices to enhance accessibility and separate branches for different themes in order to allow for more specialized attention, examples include: women's rights; rights of indigenous people; sexual diversity; and workers' rights. Ambitious administra-tive structures require sufficient funding. Still, the allocation of resources replicate the paradox present at the ombudsman's creation; whether or not governments can be expected to give suf-ficient support to an institution that will supervise and criticize their conduct. As signaled above, retribution through the budget is not unknown to the Latin American ombudsmen. In order to minimize this risk, most enjoy a degree of budgetary autonomy from the government, and typically receive their allocations directly from the legislature, rather than through the govern-ment's budget. But in many cases this has been insufficient to ensure adequate funding (Pegram 2011). Instead, foreign donor support has become important to sustain several of Latin Ameri-ca's ombudsmen, particularly in poorer countries such as Bolivia or Peru.

The personalized character of the ombudsman makes it highly dependent on the personal qualities of its incumbent. Hence, while a committed and popular ombudsman can raise the institution's public standing and ensure a higher degree of respect for its work from other state entities, an incompetent ombudsman can all but destroy the institution. The vulnerability this implies is readily recognized in Latin America, where upcoming nomination procedures are often viewed with apprehension (Página Siete 2017). Alternatively, congresses may abstain from nominating new ombudsmen, and it is not uncommon for the post to be left vacant for years, with the corresponding loss of visibility and leadership.

What the Ombudsman Does

As noted above, the tasks of the ombudsman fall into two categories (Reif 2011). On the one hand is the protective and primarily reactive work related to the handling of individual cases of possible human rights violations by state agents and institutions; on the other hand, the ombuds-man is supposed to promote knowledge and acceptance of human rights by means of informa-tion campaigns, legislative proposals, and reports and opinions on current events (Cardenas 2014). In contrast to the first set of tasks, the ombudsman's promotion activities are not nor-mally confined to state authorities, but rather target society as a whole.

Protective Work

Even though all ombudsmen have the explicit mandate to handle citizens' complaints against the public bureaucracy (and in many cases, private companies that provide public services), the exact definition of this task varies between countries. For instance, the Argentine ombudsman can neither investigate the legislature nor the judiciary, nor military and security entities, nor the authorities of Buenos Aires (which has its own ombudsman) (Law 24.284, Article 16); by contrast the Bolivian ombudsman faces none of these restrictions apart from the limitation that it cannot intervene in ongoing trials (Law 1818, Article 24:2). In general, however, Latin American ombudsmen have relatively unrestricted mandates, which allow them to act vis-à-vis the public bureaucracy in general, with possible exceptions for the judiciary (in Mexico, for instance) or ongoing legal cases. But even as the ombudsman normally has the right to undertake investigations on its own initiative – sometimes as part of the explicit task to inspect prisons and detention facilities that several ombudsmen fulfill – the vast majority of cases handled by the institution are the result of complaints or petitions presented by individual citizens.

The total number of such cases brought before the ombudsman is considerable. For instance, the Colombian ombudsman claimed to have received close to 85,000 cases in 2013 (Defensor del Pueblo [Colombia] 2014), and the Peruvian ombudsman over 115,000 in 2014 (Defensor del Pueblo [Peru] 2015). Yet, for most ombudsmen a large part of such petitions do not fall within their protective mandate, and only require guidance to redirect plaintiffs to the relevant public entity. In terms of concrete complaints against state institutions, these amounted to some 17,000 and 32,000 respectively in the above cases.

When a complaint is brought before the ombudsman, the institution investigates it and normally initiates direct contact with the public entity concerned. In most countries, public authorities are under a legal obligation to answer the ombudsman. If this contact does not produce results in the form of a cessation of the violation, the ombudsman can proceed to elevate the case to their bureaucratic superiors and, ultimately, to congress. In such cases, a formal resolution is emitted, and the case is reported in the ombudsman's annual report to legislature. In addition, most ombudsmen also have the right to present cases before the courts to demand actions of protection, habeas corpus, or similar.

Yet, the vast majority of complaints lead to neither formal resolutions nor court actions. Most complaints are solved by relatively informal means, typically in the form of a direct appeal to the public entity involved. For instance, in 2013 the Bolivian ombudsman received 15,004 complaints from citizens, of which slightly over half were found to be within its mandate (i.e., they concerned a possible abuse by a public entity or a private enterprise acting in a public function). According to its own account, of the 8,136 cases eventually taken on, 4,992 were solved in direct contact between the ombudsman and the relevant state entity. In a further 1,322 cases, the relevant authority retook the case following the ombudsman's petition, while 741 were solved by other means and 688 were found to be groundless (Defensor del Pueblo [Bolivia] 2014). Hence, in Bolivia the vast bulk of the ombudsman's protective work occurred through low-key contacts and mediation efforts, rather than through open accusations, action in court or the involvement of congress or the press (Uggla 2011). The latter courses of action tend to be reserved for the most difficult or serious cases. In fact, the Bolivian ombudsman only emitted 16 resolutions in 2013, while 18 of the above cases were eventually brought before the constitutional court, either by the plaintiff or by the ombudsman office itself. Bolivia is not exceptional in this regard: for most ombudsmen the annual numbers of resolutions run into dozens or, at most (as in El Salvador) hundreds, whereas complaints normally come in thousands or tens of thousands.

This distribution reflects the aforementioned fact that even though the ombudsman is often associated with high-profile cases of human rights violations by state agents, most of their work tend to relate to more mundane issues that are often of an administrative character, or tasks that come closer to those of the "classical ombudsman" in Reif's (2011) description. Problems such as delays in pension payments or uncommunicative bureaucrats rarely require formal resolutions or public denunciations in order to be resolved.

Indeed, if the ombudsmen's own accounts are correct, the institution is actually quite successful in solving the cases that citizens bring to it. As noted, the Bolivian ombudsman reports that over half of the cases taken on were quickly solved after having been accepted by the institution. Such a rate of cooperation and compliance is not unique to Bolivia. In its annual reports, the Peruvian ombudsman gives similar figures regarding compliance. For instance, it reports that of 23,638 cases handled by the institution in 2014, the entities concerned responded in a "relevant and appropriate" way in 16,500 instances; that is in almost 70 percent of cases (Defensor del Pueblo 2015). Roughly similar figures have been reported from Honduras and El Salvador (Comisionado Nacional de los Derechos Humanos 2015; Procurador para los Derechos Humanos 2015).

Such figures may appear surprising in view of the formal powerlessness of the ombudsman. But, again, it should be remembered that for most ombudsmen, the majority of the cases received and handled actually tend to relate to administrative complaints and issues related to social services, rather than to the kind of cases that one may normally associate with human rights protection (although complaints against police and prison authorities also feature frequently among the cases brought before the ombudsman in most countries). This is illustrated in Table 15.2, which shows the rights and issues that feature most prominently among complaints to the ombudsman in different countries.

Even though it is difficult to compare figures between countries (due to different definitions of what constitutes a case or a particular right), it is evident that social rights and administrative complaints feature prominently among the cases brought before the ombudsmen. Even in a country such as Colombia in 2014, when gross violations of fundamental rights were still frequent, the most frequent complaint concerned the right to health and the lack of sufficient attention in hospitals. While complaints relating to civil rights – for instance personal integrity or prisoners' rights – are common in most cases, it is only in El Salvador and Uruguay that they top the list. Likewise, although the police force is often the single public entity that features most frequently among complaints to most ombudsmen, for some ombudsmen, such as in Mexico and Peru, public institutions responsible for social security feature prominently among the complaints (Comisión Nacional de Derechos Humanos 2016; Defensor del Pueblo [Peru] 2015).

Promoting Human Rights

As was noted above, in addition to their protective functions, ombudsmen in Latin America generally take on a broader set of proactive tasks relating to the promotion of human rights both in society in general and in the public sphere. Accordingly, most ombudsmen have an explicit duty to make legislative proposals related to human rights and concerning the ratification and implementation of international human rights treaties, as well as providing information and human rights training. Whereas the protective work of the ombudsman is to a high degree reactive and driven by the complaints and demands of plaintiffs, the institution is freer to choose the focus of its promotional activities. Accordingly, it is primarily through this kind of work that the ombudsman can make a strategic push to emphasize or introduce particular rights.

Alternatively, the ombudsman can use the experiences and documentation gathered in the process of handling complaints to raise more general issues about the status of human rights in the country, as normally happens in the annual reports that all ombudsmen have to present to their respective parliaments. Apart from documenting the ombudsman's activities, these reports

Table 15.2 The Issues and Rights That Feature Most Frequently in the Cases and Complaints Brought Before the Ombudsman in Different Countries (Percentages in Parenthesis)

Argentina 2015	Colombia 2014	Costa Rica 2015	El Salvador 2014–2015	Guatemala 2015*	Peru 2015	Uruguay 2015
Consumers, public services, taxes (55.2)	Right to health (29.5)	Admin. delays or negative responses (34)	Personal integrity (19.9)	Children and youth (19.8)	Due admin. process (31.1)	Personal integrity (14.6)
Social security and work (18.9)	Right of petition (14.3)	Health services (20)	Due admin. process (7.9)	Health (12.5)	Right of petition (9.5)	Work (13.4)
Health, social protection, education, and culture (11.9)	Rights of displaced persons (9.3)	Social security (12)	Personal security (7.4)	Women's rights (6.3)	Labor rights (9.4)	Children and youth (8.6)
General human rights (9.7)	Prisoners' rights (6.7)	Education (5)	Work (7.3)	Security (6.1)	Access to justice (9.1)	Discrimination (8.3)
Special rights (3.2)	Right to life (5.8)	Environment (5)	Access to justice (5.6)	Consumer rights (6.1)	Right to health (8.9)	Freedom and personal security 5.1

Sources: Defensor del Pueblo de la Nación (Argentina) 2016; Defensor del Pueblo (Colombia) 2015; Defensoría de los Habitantes (Costa Rica) 2016; Procurador para los Derechos Humanos (El Salvador) 2015; Procurador de los Derechos Humanos (Guatemala) 2016; Defensor del Pueblo (Peru) 2016; Institución Nacional de Derechos Humanos y Defensoría del Pueblo (Uruguay) 2016.

Note

* For Guatemala, only admitted cases.

often also group and present cases, visibilizing broader patterns of human rights abuses and opening wider societal discussions on particular topics. Likewise, several ombudsmen also make extraordinary reports concerning current or past abuse of human rights, an activity that has often contributed to their credibility and moral standing. Finally, tasks related to information and training often constitute a substantial part of the ombudsman's work. In Bolivia in 2013, for instance, the ombudsman reported having conducted more than 1,000 training events, of which almost half were aimed at schools, and a quarter at the population in general (with the remainder being reserved for civil servants and public entities) (Defensor del Pueblo [Bolivia] 2014).

The Ombudsman in Society

As the data on p. 230 show, citizens often look to the ombudsman for help and guidance, both when it comes to concrete complaints, but also for help with contacts with public authorities in general, a fact that is demonstrated by the high number of cases that simply call for orientation or help. This possibly reflects the generally high degree of popular confidence in the ombudsman, which is often considerably higher than for comparable public institutions, as illustrated in Table 15.3, which reports public opinion data from the Latin American Public Opinion Project.

As can be seen in Table 15.3, ombudsmen generally inspire more confidence than both the judicial system and the police force. This finding is remarkably consistent and statistically significant across the 11 Latin American countries for which comparable data exist. There are only a few exceptions, most notably in Honduras in which no statistically significant difference can be found between the three institutions.

Table 15.3 Popular Confidence (1–7) in the Ombudsman, the Judicial System, and the National Police (Standard Deviations in Parenthesis)

Country/Year	Confidence Ombudsman	Confidence Judicial System	Confidence National Police
Argentina (2010)	3.8 (1.81)	3.2 (1.70)★★★	2.8 (1.71)★★★
Bolivia (2014)	4.1 (1.47)	3.3 (1.50)★★★	3.2 (1.58)★★★
Colombia (2010)	4.8 (1.64)	4.2 (1.70)★★★	4.4 (1.78)★★★
Costa Rica (2010)	5.1 (1.73)	4.3 (1.81)★★★	3.9 (1.90)★★★
Ecuador (2010)	4.1 (1.74)	3.6 (1.72)★★★	4.2 (1.77)
El Salvador (2012)	4.6 (1.96)	4.0 (1.89)★★★	4.2 (1.97)★★
Guatemala (2012)	4.1 (1.57)	3.8 (1.54)★★★	3.1 (1.70)★★★
Honduras (2014)	3.9 (1.86)	3.7 (1.85)	3.8 (1.94)
Paraguay (2010)	3.8 (1.66)	3.2 (1.73)★★★	3.2 (1.89)★★★
Peru (2014)	3.8 (1.66)	3.0 (1.54)★★★	3.3 (1.68)★★★
Venezuela (2010)	3.8 (1.96)	3.3 (1.95)★★★	3.1 (1.95)★★★

Source: The Americas Barometer by the Latin American Public Opinion Project (LAPOP), www.lapop surveys.org.

Notes
★★ Significant at the 0.01 level.
★★★ Significant at the 0.001 level.
NB: The figures represent means on a scale between 1 and 7, in which the latter indicates more credibility. The significance levels refer to the difference between the figure in question and the confidence in the ombudsman.

With regard to which groups that are more likely to express confidence in the ombudsman, there is little evidence of any systematic relationship between trust in the institution and individual factors such as income, social marginalization, gender, or education. There is some indication that victimization, either in the form of crime or encounters with corrupt bureaucrats, leads to declining confidence in the institution, but this evidence is relatively weak (for two countries, the negative relationships between confidence in the ombudsman and victimization fall just below conventional levels of statistical significance). Instead, and as Table 15.4 shows for the five countries for which recent data exist – and which are also countries in which the institution has or has had a relatively prominent position – the two factors that appear most significant for explaining confidence in the ombudsman is youth (relevant in three out of five countries) and – particularly – approval of government.

This last finding may seem paradoxical, given that the ombudsmen are often held up as bulwarks against the government. But it may be easier to believe in the ombudsman and its ability to alter state behavior by means of persuasion if one has a more favorable view of the government to begin with. Likewise, this finding also has to be seen in light of the fact that the protective work of the ombudsman generally deals with misconduct by individual bureaucrats, rather than state policy more generally. Overall, however, the low explained variance of these equations shows that trust in the ombudsman largely escapes explanations based on factors such as the ones included in Table 15.4.

Beyond individual expressions of confidence in the ombudsman, it is notable that its high legitimacy in combination with its versatility and broad mandate has in many cases allowed the institution to work closely together with groups in civil society, to an extent that would be impossible for most other state agencies. Some ombudsmen have thus become important for ensuring a favorable state response to demands from civil society, by serving as an amplifier or a channel of their demands. As Peruzzotti notes in a study of how environmental groups in Argentina have acted in concert with the ombudsman to defend a protected area (2011, 265): "For civil society actors, the Defensor provides an accessible entry point to the horizontal network of accountability agencies within the state, serving as a bridge between social accountability initiatives and the intrastate network of horizontal agencies."

This relationship can work in both directions, as some ombudsmen also try to build support in society for its positions by addressing public opinion through proclamations, press releases and the like, in the hope that this may shame targeted state entities into corrective action (Pegram 2011). An extreme but vivid example of this can be found in the Guatemalan ombudsman's response to the attempted auto-golpe by President Serrano in 1993. The ombudsman refused to accept the president's actions, and called for popular mobilizations against the attempted coup. This, notes one observer, turned the ombudsman into "the leader of civil society's efforts to restore constitutional rule," which eventually met with success (Villagrán de León 1993; Dodson and Jackson 2004).

Yet although several examples of mutual cooperation between the ombudsman and groups in civil society exist, the inverse situation – of ombudsmen coming into conflict with non-state actors – has also occurred. In some cases, this situation arises when ombudsmen take positions at odds with public opinion, as with the defense of the human rights of suspected criminals (Pegram 2011; Collins 2008). In other cases, non-state human rights defenders have ended up in conflict with ombudsmen who they accuse of being government stooges (see Finkel [2012] on Mexico; Caldera [2007] on Nicaragua; and ABC Color [2010] on Paraguay). In some of these conflicts, an element of competition over attention and resources may be involved. For instance, Cardenas (2014, 159, 344) has claimed that the creation of an ombudsman in Colombia was "an astute means of stealing the thunder from (and in some cases foreign funding of) human rights NGOs [nongovernmental organizations]" (Goodman and Pegram 2011).

Table 15.4 Explanations For Confidence in Ombudsman. Figures are Unstandardized b-Values with Standard Deviations in Parentheses

Factor	Guatemala (2012)	El Salvador (2012)	Bolivia (2014)	Honduras (2014)	Peru (2014)
Constant	4.638 (0.449)***	5.539 (0.568)***	4.516 (0.357)***	4.100 (0.481)***	4.060 (0.644)***
Female respondent	0.077 (0.091)	0.290 (0.108)**	−0.038 (0.062)	−0.073 (0.100)	0.110 (0.104)
Age	−0.002 (0.003)	−0.012 (0.004)***	−0.010 (0.002)***	−0.009 (0.011)*	−0.006 (0.003)**
Rural dweller	0.245 (0.102)*	0.184 (0.129)	0.095 (0.070)	0.247 (0.108)*	0.088 (0.128)
Higher income bracket	−0.027 (0.015)**	−0.049 (0.020)*	−0.001 (0.010)	0.009 (0.013)	0.047 (0.013)***
Years of schooling	0.029 (0.013)*	−0.031 (0.015)*	−0.010 (0.008)	−0.022 (0.014)	−0.014 (0.015)
Not a victim of crime	0.162 (0.113)	0.262 (0.142)**	0.137 (0.073)**	0.504 (0.131)***	0.005 (0.112)
Has been asked for a bribe by public servant	−0.129 (0.217)	−0.145 (0.363)	−0.369 (0.104)***	−0.125 (0.214)	−0.401*
Does not have identification card	−0.393 (0.132)*	0.209 (0.247)	0.320 (0.239)	0.079 (0.199)	0.711 (0.437)
Disapproves of president/government	−0.291 (0.063)***	−0.503 (0.059)***	−0.215 (0.040)***	−0.397 (0.059)***	−0.395 (0.071)***
Adj. R²:	0.031	0.097	0.034	0.060	

Source: The Americas Barometer by the Latin American Public Opinion Project (LAPOP), www.lapopsurveys.org.

Notes

* Significant at the 0.05 level.
** Significant at the 0.01 level.
*** Significant at the 0.001 level.

Debates About the Ombudsman

During their first decade of existence, the ombudsmen of Latin America largely escaped scholarly attention. But recent years have seen the appearance of a number of studies that have examined the institution from different theoretical angles. Given the ombudsman's combination of a lofty mandate and few formal means to enforce its positions and resolutions, it is not surprising that the issues with which scholars most often grapple are related to the institution's relevance and effectiveness (Cardenas 2014).

Compliance/Efficacy

As repeatedly mentioned above, a defining feature of the ombudsman is that it lacks sanctioning power as its findings and resolutions only constitute recommendations. Even though the institution often has the additional ability to present or initiate legal action in order to protect citizens' rights, neither this power, nor its investigation of complaints should be confused for any real power to emit or enforce binding decisions. Accordingly, and in spite of the positive figures on compliance reported above, the effectiveness of the ombudsman is relative and will ultimately depend on the will of other institutions. It follows that compliance will vary between targets/sectors and also across different country contexts. This is likely to have contributed to the difference in scholarly estimations of the institution's relative value. While skeptics tend to point to the absence of visible change in the human rights situation of a given country (Brett 2011), the limited nature of its successes (Cardenas 2014) or an absence of combativeness on part of the ombudsman (Finkel 2012), believers in the institution's effectiveness tend to emphasize high-profile cases in which the ombudsman's actions contributed to the eventual outcome (Pegram 2008) or how their handling of individual complaints seems to produce effects (Uggla 2011). The few statistical studies that do exist tend to show a degree of effectiveness, although this is far from complete. It should be noted, however, that such studies are either based on an aggregate material with little relation to the actual operation of the institution (Moreno and Witmer 2015; Moreno 2016) or on data from a single country (Uggla 2011).

Apart from the question of whether the ombudsman can make a difference, there is the issue of what factors may contribute to such possible effectiveness or its absence (Reif 2004). While some observers have claimed that variables related to institutional design, such as the length of term or the form of nomination, are relevant in this regard (Moreno 2016; Moreno and Witmer 2015), others have looked toward the political context in which it functions (Finkel 2012), its support in public opinion or the media (Uggla 2004; Pegram 2011) or to the broader set of relationships set up by the ombudsman's office either in society (Peruzzotti 2011) or in the state apparatus (Uggla 2011).

Given the differences in respect for human rights between countries, it is difficult to provide a general assessment of the ombudsman's effectiveness. Furthermore, perceptions of efficacy may not always reflect the ombudman's actual work. If one looks only toward the high-profile cases or aggregate human rights scores, the institution could seem much less effective than it would be if seen from a perspective of the more mundane complaints that constitute the bulk of the caseload. Likewise, the factors that contribute to success may also vary between the different types of issue at hand. While close relations with the bureaucracy can help solve administrative complaints, support from media or civil society may be necessary to take on state policy or high-level cases of corruption or abuse.

Contribution

Beyond the question of whether the ombudsman's actions produce effects with regard to individual complaints, there is the issue of what the broader implications of the ombudsmen are for the political and legal systems in which they are active. Even an effective ombudsman may amount to little more than a democratic enclave in a setting that continues to be characterized by abuse and disrespect for citizens' rights (Gilley 2010). Conversely, an ombudsman whose resolutions are permanently ignored by other parts of the state may yet have a broader impact on how public opinion views the legal system.

A first question in this regard is thus how the introduction of the ombudsman has affected the legal systems of Latin America. Even as the relationships between the ombudsmen and the legal systems of their respective countries are seldom collaborative (Pegram 2011), there are some indications that the ombudsmen have had an effect by introducing new legal interpretations and themes in their respective legal systems, particularly with regard to the constitutional courts (Domingo 2006; Pegram 2011) to which many ombudsmen can present actions of nullity or protection. Similarly, ombudsmen may have an impact by serving as a conduit for the introduction of international norms and treaties into the national legal system (Pegram 2015; Pegram 2014). The fact that many, but not all, ombudsmen have the right to process complaints against the judiciary opens a distinct possibility in this regard. Still, no systematic evidence exists on the ombudsmen's impact and the lack of references to the ombudsman in many debates on judicial development in Latin America may well reflect a real absence of influence and the difficulty that many ombudsmen have had in finding ways in which to cooperate with the judicial system (Pegram 2011) (but see Ungar 2013 on police oversight in Latin America for an exception).

With regard to the impact of the ombudsman on the political system, this question has often been posed in relation to the "accountability deficit" in the Latin American state (O'Donnell 1994, Mainwaring 2003). Accordingly, the ombudsman has been proposed as an institution that may limit executive dominance (Ungar 2002, 36; Pegram 2008; Uggla 2011). The discussion on the ombudsman's possible role in this regard is partly conceptual. Thus, Moreno and her co-authors, argue that:

> we do not consider the ombudsman's provision of information regarding human rights abuses committed by officials of the executive branch (including the police and the armed forces) to be a relationship of accountability, for there may be no consequences of the revelation of the information. [...] Only with sanctioning has the actor been held accountable, but if the actor who reveals the information does not impose the sanctions, then that actor is not holding the abusers accountable.
>
> *(2003, 81)*

Ultimately, however, the question of whether the ombudsman can contribute to accountability is to a large extent empirical (Mainwaring 2003) and success in this regard is likely to relate to the same factors as its effectiveness in ensuring compliance. In particular, factors such as legitimacy, popular support and alliances in society may prove decisive, as demonstrated by emblematic Peruvian and Guatemalan cases mentioned on pp. 227 and 234, and the role played by the Bolivian ombudsman during the turbulent 2000–2005 period, for instance. As such cases demonstrate, the personal qualities of the titular ombudsman are also likely to be of importance. A more combative ombudsman who takes a broader view of the institution's competences and acts accordingly may well enhance its role as an agent of horizontal accountability (Pegram 2011), both by enhancing popular confidence in the institution and by being ready to hold the government to account. Yet, while most overviews of the institution mention this factor (Reif 2004; Cardenas 2014) it remains under-theorized (Pegram 2008), and systematic comparative studies tend to overlook this crucial factor in favor of institutional or contextual factors.

The ombudsman's contribution to accountability is also intimately related to its autonomy (Uggla 2004): an ombudsman controlled by the executive cannot be expected to generate accountability. Even though constitutional provisions are supposed to shield the institution from such undue influence, the extent to which they have succeeded is relative. As signaled previously, many ombudsmen have had to face government attempts to control or limit their operations, and such attempts have not always been unsuccessful. Furthermore, it is important to remember that while the ombudsman can, on the one hand, be a bulwark against government power it can, on the other hand, also be an instrument to strengthen government by providing oversight over the state bureaucracy or by providing legitimacy to dubious decisions. While the Latin American ombudsmen can typically fulfill either of these functions, it seems that the balance is in many cases tipping toward the latter one.

If that is so, this could also be the effect of broader political transformations. As discussed above, many ombudsmen were created soon after transitions to democracy, and often had to challenge the highest echelons of executive power in order to counter authoritarian legacies. But as democracies became more entrenched, open confrontations with government have become rarer for many ombudsmen. Instead, they focus on more proactive advancement of a broader rights agenda or target misbehaving bureaucrats who refuse to comply with existing laws, international norms, or government regulations. Although in some cases such developments reflect co-optation of the ombudsman by the government (particularly through naming more pliant titulars), it may also reflect a strategic choice by the institution.

In addition to the question of accountability is the related question of what the ombudsman may do to change the state's overall respect for human rights. There is evidence to suggest that the institution is often effective in correcting individual instances of abuse by state authorities, and several ombudsmen have been successful in broadening the debate and conception of human rights in their respective countries. But some authors note that the overall effects of the ombudsman in this regard may be limited, particularly when it comes to the most serious human rights violations (Cardenas 2014; Brett 2011). In a related argument, the ombudsman is sometimes presented as a façade that the state can present to cover such abuses (Cardenas 2014), and which can be used to divert public and international attention (including donor funding) from civil society to the state. According to such perspectives, the ombudsman's impact on state respect for human rights is negligible.

Even if not so dramatic, it appears that in countries where the ombudsman is accused of standing too close to the government (e.g., Venezuela), the institution often focuses on social or collective rights, rather than on the more politically contentious civil or political rights. While this may well broaden the conception of human rights, it may also lead the institution to a more limited role with a corresponding decrease in its overall impact.

Finally, there is the question of the ombudsman's broader effects on society and public opinion. In this regard, one can note how ombudsmen have in many cases fought to break down social taboos and make human rights for all acceptable to the majority (Cardenas 2014). While there is no definite evidence in this regard, the fact that ombudsmen have often been at the forefront of issues such as rights for sexual minorities, rights for migrants, or environmental rights indicates that the institution may have a more general importance as an agenda-setter in the area of human rights (Domingo 2006; Ungar and Hite 2013).

Summing up, it is evident that most scholarly debates regarding the ombudsman have dealt with its potential as a human rights institution, thereby addressing the question of how well the institution performs with regard to the protection of fundamental human rights and in providing a balance to other state powers (the government in particular). This is not surprising given that most studies have built on perspectives from human rights or democratization studies. But such a focus may also overlook those aspects of the ombudsman's work that correspond to its role as a public ombudsman whose tasks include oversight of the bureaucracy and mediation between state and citizens. As shown above, such issues feature prominently in the work of most ombudsmen, and while they are not at odds with their functions as a human rights institution, they have not received the same amount of scholarly attention. This risks overlooking crucial parts of the ombudsmen's work and their possible contributions. As argued here, several of Latin America's ombudsmen possess a remarkable thematic versatility combined with high popular confidence. Potentially, this could give them an important role as state-society relations are being redrawn and discriminatory social practices are challenged. Yet, shifts in theoretical perspectives may be needed in order to address such aspects of the ombudsman's work.

Areas for Future Research

Research on the Latin American ombudsman is still incipient, and has to a large extent been oriented toward description of the institution and a discussion about its possible effectiveness. While this focus is natural for a relatively new institution, there is a lack of systematic studies that put the ombudsman into its broader institutional and political context. As I have argued in this chapter, the impact of the ombudsman is ultimately dependent on other institutions; either those to which the ombudsman directly relates (e.g., parliaments, and bureaucratic entities) or those that may help it increase its effectiveness (such as the mass media or the judicial system). Hence, there is a promising area of enquiry that would look beyond the ombudsman per se in order to study its interaction with other institutions and actors. In relation to this, the ombudsman's role as mediator between state and citizens may be of particular interest, as it is likely both to add information about state-society relations in general and illustrate how the ombudsman can contribute to improved governance.

Systematic comparative studies aside, there is also a need for more case study-based insights. Apart from the most visible cases of intervention, very few scholarly studies have dealt with just how the ombudsman acts in individual cases, and how such choices are made in interaction with other agents and institutions. Such a process- or case-based approach may actually yield more information than statistical studies on the crucial but puzzling question of how the ombudsman – without any formal powers of sanction – can make a difference, and why popular confidence in the institution is relatively high (Uggla 2011). Likewise, qualitative case studies can complement more statistical enquiries as previous research has shown that human rights interventions can have paradoxical effects. For instance, Finkel et al. (2006) found that international support for human rights could have a significant negative impact on human rights situations, a fact that they attribute to the positive relationship between resources and detection of violations. In this regard, how the ombudsman works to promote awareness and build consciousness regarding human rights is another possible area for further studies.

Finally, and not forgetting the ombudsman's role as the national human rights institution, there is a promising area of research that sees the ombudsman as a link between international human rights norms on the one hand, and domestic realities on the other. This issue has been partly explored by Thomas Pegram (2014, 2015), but there is scope for further work in this area. Such studies could explain how and with what effect human rights norms can be applied in a particular setting. But they could also take a broader view and study how human rights norms may foment possible synergies between international and domestic action (Keck and

Sikkink 1998). Being the national human rights institution, the ombudsman stands at the center of such processes, and could therefore, provide an empirical entry point to study them in their totality.

Conclusions

Ombudsmen were introduced in Latin America with a mixture of illusion and indifference. Whereas in a country such as Argentina, the establishment of the institution was the conclusion of a long struggle to create an institution to prevent state abuses (Cardenas 2014), in others the institution seems to have been created more on a whim (see e.g. Pegram 2008 on Peru).

Similar tensions have continued to characterize the development of Latin America's ombudsmen. A public institution that is supposed to serve as a defender of the citizens against state arbitrariness and abuse, the ombudsman typically provides both the functions associated with the classical ombudsman (providing a mechanism for handling complaints about administrative behavior), and the ones that correspond to a national human rights institution (promoting human rights, serving as a kind of moral arbitrator for the nation). While it can be seen as a potentially important ally for groups in civil society as well as a crucial component in the domestic implementation of international human rights norms, its nomination and budget are in the hands of national politicians with little interest in furthering those roles. Moreover, even though it typically has a broad range of lofty tasks attributed to it by the constitution, it cannot legally enforce its decisions or positions.

Traits such as these make the institution inherently volatile and subject to broader political and social circumstances. They also make it difficult to emit a general judgment on its relevance and effectiveness. As signaled here neither the power nor the impotence of the ombudsman can be taken for granted. Likewise, it is important to note that the actual work of most ombudsmen do not always correspond to the image of the institution as a forceful opponent to government attempts to thwart fundamental political and civil rights. Rather, the bulk of the ombudsman's cases involve actions such as seeking administrative redress or mediation between citizens and the bureaucracy.

Still, such observations should not lead us to dismiss the institution. Rather, its peculiarities make the ombudsman all the more interesting to consider for students of law and society in Latin America. This is partly because the study of an institution that depends on third parties for its effectiveness could inform us about political will and the readiness of state entities to accept criticism, as well as the willingness of different public and legal institutions to adapt to domestic and international human rights norms. But it is also because of the popular confidence deposited in the ombudsman, and the role that the institution can potentially fulfill as an intermediary between citizens and state institutions.

References

Brett, Roddy. 2011. Confronting Racism from within the Guatemalan State: The Challenges Faced by the Defender of Indigenous Rights of Guatemala's Human Rights Ombudsman's Office. *Oxford Development Studies*, 39: 205–28.

Caldera, Marciela. 2007. A Omar Cabezas le "da asco" el Cenidh. *El Nuevo Diario*. June 26. Available at: http://archivo.elnuevodiario.com.ni/nacional/213781-omar-cabezas-le-da-asco-cenidh/. Accessed September 6, 2017.

Cardenas, Sonia. 2014. *Chains of Justice: The Global Rise of State Institutions for Human Rights*. Philadelphia: University of Pennsylvania Press.

Collins, Cath. 2008. The (Re)judicialisation of Human Rights Accountability in Chile and El Salvador. *Latin American Perspectives*, 35: 20–37.

Comisión National de Derechos Humanos. 2016. *Informe de Actividades 2015 del 1 de enero al 31 de diciembre*. Mexico: CNDH.

Comisionado Nacional de los Derechos Humanos. 2015. *Informe al Honorable Congreso Nacional de la República Año 2014*. Tegucigalpa: CONADEH.

Defensor del Pueblo (Bolivia). 2014. *XIV Informe a la Asamblea Legislativa Plurinacional*. La Paz: Defensoría del Pueblo.

Defensor del Pueblo (Colombia). 2014. *Vigésimo primer Informe del Defensor del Pueblo al Congreso de la República*. Bogotá: Defensoría del Pueblo.

Defensor del Pueblo (Colombia). 2015. *Vigésimo Segundo Informe del Defensor del Pueblo de Colombia al Congreso de la República*. Bogotá: Defensoría del Pueblo.

Defensor del Pueblo (Peru). 2015. *Decimonoveno Informe Anual de la Defensoría del Pueblo: enero-diciembre 2014*. Lima: Defensoría del Pueblo.

Defensor del Pueblo (Peru). 2016. *Decimoctavo Informe Anual de la Defensoría del Pueblo: enero-diciembre 2014*. Lima: Defensoría del Pueblo.

Defensor del Pueblo de la Nación (Argentina). 2016. *Informe Anual 2015*. Buenos Aires: DPN.

Defensoría de los Habitantes (Costa Rica). 2016. *Informe Anual de Labores 2015–2016*. San José: Defensoría de los Habitantes.

Dodson, Michael and Donald W. Jackson. 2004. Horizontal Accountability in Transitional Democracies: The Human Rights Ombudsman in El Salvador and Guatemala. *Latin American Politics and Society*, 46: 1–27.

Domingo, Pilar. 2006. "Weak Courts, Rights and Legal Mobilisation in Bolivia." In Roberto Gargarella, Pilar Domingo, and Theunis Roux (Eds.). Courts and Social Transformation in New Democracies, 233–54. Aldershot: Ashgate.

Finkel, Jodi. 2012. Explaining the Failure of Mexico's National Commission of Human Rights (Ombudsman's Office) After Democratization: Elections, Incentives, and Unaccountability in the Mexican Senate. *Human Rights Review*, 13: 473–95.

Finkel, Steven, Aníbal Pérez-Liñan, and Mitchell A. Seligson. 2006. *Effects of U.S. Foreign Assistance on Democracy Building: Results of a Cross-National Quantative Study*. Report. Vanderbilt University.

Gilley, Bruce. 2010. Democratic Enclaves in Authoritarian Regimes. *Democratization*, 17: 389–415.

Global Alliance of National Institutions for the Promotion and Protection of Human Rights (GANHRI). 2016. *Report and Recommendations of the Session of the Sub-Committee on Accreditation (SCA)*, Geneva, May 9–13, 2016. Report.

Goodman, Ryan and Thomas Pegram. 2011. "National Human Rights Institutions, State Compliance, and Social Change." In Ryan Goodman and Thomas Pegram (Eds.) *Human Rights, State Compliance, and Social Change: Assessing National Human Rights Institutions*, 1–27. Cambridge: Cambridge University Press.

Institución Nacional de Derechos Humanos y Defensoría del Pueblo (Uruguay). 2016. *IV Informe Anual a la Asamblea General*. Montevideo: Institución Nacional de Derechos Humanos y Defensoría del Pueblo.

International Coordinating Committee of National Institutions for the Promotion and Protection of Human Rights (ICC). 2014. *Report and Recommendations of the Session of the Sub-Committee on Accreditation (SCA)*, Geneva, October 27–31, 2014. Report.

International Coordinating Committee of National Institutions for the Promotion and Protection of Human Rights (ICC). 2017. *Accreditation Status as of 26 May 2017*. Unpublished manuscript.

Jägerskiöld, Stig. 1961. The Swedish Ombudsman. *University of Pennsylvania Law Review*, 109: 1077–99.

Keck, Margaret and Kathryn Sikkink. 1998. *Activists Beyond Borders: Advocacy Networks in International Politics*. Cornell University Press.

Lupia, Arthur and Mathew McCubbins. 1994. Learning from Oversight: Fire Alarms and Police Patrols Reconstructed. *Journal of Law, Economics and Organisation*, 10: 96–125.

Mainwaring, Scott. 2003. "Introduction: Democratic Accountability in Latin America." In Scott Mainwaring and Christopher Welna (Eds.) *Democratic Accountability in Latin America*, 3–33. Oxford: Oxford University Press.

Maiorano, Jorge Luis. 2001. El Defensor del Pueblo en América Latina. Necesidad de Fortalecerlo. *Revista de Derecho*, 12: 191–98.

Moreno, Erika. 2016. The Contributions of the Ombudsman to Human Rights in Latin America, 1982–2011. *Latin American Politics and Society*, 58: 98–120.

Moreno, Erika, Brian F. Crisp, and Matthew Soberg Shugart. 2003. "The Accountability Deficit in Latin America." In Scott Mainwaring and Christopher Welna (Eds.) *Democratic Accountability in Latin America*, 79–131. Oxford: Oxford University Press.

Moreno, Erika and Richard Witmer. 2015. The Power of the Pen: Human Rights Ombudsmen and Personal Integrity Violations in Latin America, 1982–2006. *Human Rights Review,* 17(2): 143–64.

O'Donnell, Guillermo. 1994. Horizontal Accountability in New Democracies. *The Journal of Democracy,* 5: 55–69.

Página Siete. 2016. Defensor: El Gobierno adormeció su conciencia por ambición de poder. 2016. *Página. Siete,* April 10, 2016.

Página Siete. 2017. Albarracín cree que se convirtió a la Defensoría del Pueblo en "secretaría de un partido." *Página Siete,* June 7, 2017.

Pegram, Thomas. 2008. Accountability in Hostile Times: The Role of the Peruvian Human Rights Ombudsman 1996–2001. *Journal of Latin American Studies,* 40: 51–82.

Pegram, Thomas. 2011. "National Human Rights Institutions in Latin America: Politics and Institutionalization." In Ryan Goodman and Thomas Pegram (Eds.) *Human Rights, State Compliance, and Social Change: Assessing National Human Rights Institutions,* 210–40. Cambridge: Cambridge University Press.

Pegram, Thomas. 2014. *Compliance Agents: National Human Rights Institutions and the Inter-American Human Rights System.* Paper presented for the Latin American Studies Associations Annual Conference, Chicago, May 24.

Pegram, Thomas. 2015. Global Human Rights Governance and Orchestration: National Human Rights Institutions as Intermediaries. *European Journal of International Relations,* 21: 595–620.

Peruzzotti, Enrique. 2011. "The Societalization of Horizontal Accountability: Rights Advocacy and the Defensor del Pueblo de la Nacion in Argentina." In Ryan Goodman and Thomas Pegram (Eds.) *Human Rights, State Compliance, and Social Change: Assessing National Human Rights Institutions,* 243–69. Cambridge: Cambridge University Press.

Popkin, Margaret. 2000. *Peace Without Justice: Obstacles to Building the Rule of Law in El Salvador.* University Park: The Pennsylvania State University Press.

Procurador de los Derechos Humanos (Guatemala). 2016. *Informe Anual Circunstanciado: Situación de los Derechos Humanos y Memoria de Labores 2015.* Guatemala: PDH.

Procurador para los Derechos Humanos. El Salvador. 2015. *Análisis Situacional de los Derechos Humanos: Informe de Labores de la Procuraduría para la Defensa de los Derechos Humanos Junio 2014–Mayo 2015.* San Salvador: PDDH.

Reif, Linda. 2004. *The Ombudsman, Good Governance and the International Human Rights System.* Martinus Nijhoff Publishers: Leiden.

Reif, Linda. 2011. Transplantation and Adaptation: The Evolution of the Human Rights Ombudsman. *Boston College Third World Law Journal,* 31: 269–310.

Repudiaron a Páez Monges en un acto en el Parlamento. 2010. *ABC Color (Paraguay),* June 1. Available at: www.abc.com.py/edicion-impresa/politica/repudiaron-a-paez-monges-en-un-acto-en-el-parlamento-110880.html. Accessed September 6, 2017.

The Economist. 2001. Arnoldo Alemám. Nicaragua: Democracy's Next Battleground. *The Economist,* December 14, 2001.

Uggla, Fredrik. 2004. The Ombudsman in Latin America. *Journal of Latin American Studies,* 36: 423–50.

Uggla, Fredrik. 2011. "Through Pressure or Persuasion" Explaining Compliance with the Resolutions of the Bolivian Defensor del Pueblo." In Ryan Goodman and Thomas Pegram (Eds.) *Human Rights, State Compliance, and Social Change: Assessing National Human Rights Institutions,* 270–94. Cambridge: Cambridge University Press.

Ungar, Mark and Katherine Hite. 2013. "The Arc of Human Rights." In Katherine Hite and Mark Ungar (Eds.) *Sustaining Human Rights in the Twenty-First Century: Strategies from Latin America,* 9–33. Baltimore: The Johns Hopkins University Press.

Ungar, Mark. 2002. *Elusive Reform and the Rule of Law in Latin America.* Boulder: Lynne Reinner.

Ungar, Mark. 2013. "Crime, Society, and the Challenge to Human Rights." In Katherine Hite and Mark Ungar (Eds.) *Sustaining Human Rights in the Twenty-First Century: Strategies from Latin America,* 195–217. Baltimore: The Johns Hopkins University Press.

Villagrán de León, Francisco. 1993. Thwarting the Guatemalan Coup. *Journal of Democracy,* 4: 117–24.

16

PRISONER CAPTURE

Welfare, Lawfare, and Warfare in Latin America's Overcrowded Prisons

Fiona Macaulay

Introduction

This chapter focuses on the forms of legality and illegality produced by, and within, prison systems in Latin America. The region saw prison populations surge in every country from the early 1990s (see Table 16.1), rising well over fivefold in some, and leading to a serious structural crisis in the criminal justice system. There was, of course, immense variation in the experience and management of incarceration. Some countries did not have overcrowding in their system and in these, indeed even in those with serious problems, many individual penal institutions resembled the average North American or European prison, under the full control of the authorities and compliant with fundamental human rights norms. However, in a significant number of countries, rocketing incarceration rates led to severe overcrowding and a loss of state control of individual facilities. There the state either committed violence against prisoners, permitted violence between prisoners, or ceded the carceral space to the prisoners themselves.

The chapter develops the concept of "prisoner capture," a double-sided phenomenon of illegality in the state's practices of detention, on the one hand, and informal, or parallel, governance exercised by those that it detained, on the other. State authorities held tens of thousands of people in extended and legally unjustifiable pretrial detention, and frequently denied convicted prisoners their legal rights, including timely release. This officially sanctioned form of kidnapping created such overcrowding and underinvestment in prisons that national, constitutional, and international minimum norms on detention standards were routinely, systematically, and grossly violated. These multiple illegalities on the part of the state in turn encouraged the emergence of prisoner self-defense and self-governance organizations. This resulted in "prisoner capture" of a different kind, when inmates took over the day-to-day ordering of prison life. In turn, this produced a parallel normative and pseudo-legal world in which inmates adjudicated on and disciplined other inmates in the absence of state officials within the prison walls.

In what follows I open by signaling what the study of Latin American prisons and penal practices can add to the field of socio-legal studies in the region. I then examine the reasons for prisoner capture by the state, proceeding to discuss the consequences of prisoners' increasing control of the carceral space, including the implications of this phenomenon for the dominant socio-legal literature on prisons and imprisonment.

Table 16.1 Incarceration Levels and Rates in Latin America 1992–2017

Country	No. of Prisoners		Rate of Increase	Current Occupancy Rate★ (%)	Percent Pretrial Prisoners	Imprisonment Rate		Rate of Increase
	1992★ (a)	2014–2016 (b)	b/a			1992 (a)	2014–2016 (b)	b/a
Argentina (December 2015)	21,016	72,693	3.46	106	50.1	63	167	2.65
Bolivia (July 2016)	5,412 (1996)★★	14,598	2.70	254 (February 2016)	59.0	71	130	2.06
Brazil (July 2017)	114,377	657,680	5.75	164 (January 2017)	36.9	74	318	4.29
Chile (July 2017)	20,989	42,807	2.04	111 (September 2013)	35.0	155	236	1.52
Colombia (July 2017)	33,491	116,773	3.49	148 (July 2017)	32.1	100	230	2.30
Costa Rica (September 2014)	3,346	17,440	5.21	139	17.2	105	352	3.35
Ecuador (June 2016)	7,998	26,421	3.30	114	48.8	74	160	2.16
El Salvador (June 2017)	5,348	38,410	7.18	348 (August 2016)	33.7	99	590	5.96
Guatemala (July 2017)	5,476	22,184	4.05	296 (December 2015)	49.9	56	130	2.32
Honduras (August 2016)	5,717	17,253	3.02	163	53	110	200	1.82

Country							
Mexico (July 2016)	85,712	233,469	2.72	112	39.6	98	192	1.96
Nicaragua (October 2014)	3,375	10,569	3.13	128 (September 2010)	12.3	85	171	2.01
Panama (November 2016)	4,428	17,165	3.88	121	62.6 (December 2014)	178	426	2.39
Paraguay (December 2015)	2,972 (1995)**	12,741	4.29	179	77.9	60	180	3.00
Peru (April 2017)	15,718	83,639	5.32	233	42.2	71	262	3.69
Uruguay (2016)**	3,037	10,228	3.37	113	65.0	97	297	3.06
Venezuela (2016)**	23,200 (1993)**	54,738	2.36	154 (2016)**	71.3	111	173	1.56
Average			3.78					2.71

Source: Table created by author with data from the Institute for Criminal Policy Research, World Prison Brief, available online at: www.prisonstudies.org/info/world brief/?search=southam&x=South%20America

Notes

The month and year of the data are given under the country, or under the different data items, if different.

The benchmark data are from 1992 unless indicated otherwise.

Argentina: 1992 figures included prisoners in police custody, whereas 2015 data do not include prisoners in police custody.

* Occupancy rate = number of detainees relative to the official capacity of the prison system. Over 100 percent indicates overcrowding.

** Information on the specific month is not available.

Prisons and Socio-Legal Studies in Latin America

Throughout the twentieth century, writing on prisons and penal systems was generally produced by jurists, in abstract and positivist debates about the possible or proper interpretation of the relevant legal codes. Other literature laid out, descriptively, the prevailing structures and formal provisions for the governance of an individual penal system, or the region's penal systems, but generally without reference to the *actual* functioning of penal institutions and the social influences on the behavior of the actors within them (see, for example, Rico 1997). However, as mass imprisonment started to accelerate through the end of the 1990s, a gray literature produced by local and international human rights bodies began to document the immense void between the law and its application, both in the social selectivity of the criminal justice system's processes, and in the administration of penal establishments. Reports on appalling conditions of detention, poor governance, and illegal practices by the police, courts, and prisons were based on extensive empirical data gathered in field visits and interviews with inmates and government officials (IACHR 2011). Sadly, such advocacy-oriented research did little to halt the march of mass incarceration. Researchers based in nongovernmental organizations (NGOs) or multi-lateral bodies and academics following penal policy tried to map the changing composition of the burgeoning prison population through data analysis and quantitative survey methods, demonstrating the impact of drug sentencing, and noting the rise in the proportion of women prisoners and the high levels of pretrial and illegal detention (PNUD 2013). Some also attempted to interpret the changing practices of incarceration within dominant national, regional, and global political trends such as democratization and neoliberalism (Müller 2016), or within more hybrid, alternative concepts such as "authoritarian liberalism" (Iturralde 2016) and "Bolivarianism" (Antillano et al. 2016).

As the state lost effective control of many penal facilities, a new generation of anthropologists and socio-legal researchers began to examine the complex forms of self-governance developing in prisons in the face of state absence (Darke and Garces 2017; Biondi 2016; Carter 2014; Cerbini 2012, 2017; Dias 2013).[1] Such richly nuanced research was slow to emerge in socio-legal studies partly as a result of the field environment: Latin American prisons could be unpleasant and dangerous, and often the prison authorities were unhelpful in relation to access. However, while the lived experience of prisoners in contexts of abandonment and illegality became somewhat better understood, relatively little was known about the sociology and organizational culture of the justice institutions that created this situation. Empirical work on the attitudes and decision-making processes of different cohorts of justice sector actors remained incipient. One of Brazil's leading law schools, the *Fundação Getúlio Vargas*, created a journal of empirical law studies only in 2013.[2] The key question, perhaps, was why those institutions and actors charged with upholding the rule of law so routinely perpetrated and sustained illegal practices. Prisons can reflect the immediate ideology of the government of the day, but also refract and magnify deeper social and political ideologies that contradict the former. A clear tension persists, and not only in Latin America, between "guarantee-ism" (the commitment to protect individual human rights, including those of offenders) and "social defense" (the notion that decent society requires protection against socially disruptive elements), and this is played out in the legalized, and illegal, practices of mass incarceration.

Prisoner Capture by the State

The surge in incarceration levels across Latin America was the result of primary penal expansionism, which involved increasing the number and type of crimes on the statute books, combined with secondary penal toughening (making maximum or mandatory custodial sentences longer or less flexible, and applying custodial sentences to a wider number of offenses), both of which were trends across the region since the 1980s, and generally went hand in hand. For example, in Brazil, between 1985 and 2016, more than 115 crime-related laws were passed, putting around 550 new offenses on the already overcrowded statute books; a clear example of expansionism.[3] In terms of toughening, the 1990 Heinous Crimes bills (*Lei de Crimes Hediondos*) made several types of serious crime, including drug trafficking, ineligible for bail, provisional release, pardons, amnesties, commutations, and progression to minimum security prisons. It also lengthened the period of eligibility for parole. As "drug trafficking" was not precisely defined, the prison system, especially the maximum security facilities, quickly became clogged up with street-corner dealers that police, prosecutors, and judges had decided, at their discretion, were serious criminals. Brazil's prison population jumped from 90,000 in 1990 to 148,760 in 1995, and more than doubled every decade, reaching 650,956 in early 2017 (DEPEN 2016, 15). Attempts were made to change the law but it continued to appeal to penal populists. What, then, were the underlying political, ideological, and socio-legal drivers behind this penal expansion?

Welfare, Lawfare, and Warfare

Criminologists concur that incarceration rates are not correlated with reported crime rates per se, or the distribution of particular types of crime, but rather with how society and criminal justice institutions decide to treat criminal suspects. For example, Table 16.1 shows that in 2016 Panama, Costa Rica, Uruguay, and Chile had imprisonment rates above the regional median of 192, but had average to low homicide rates (9.3 and 11.8 per 100,000 in the two Central American countries, and 7.6 and 3.6, respectively, in the South American ones).[4] Thus a number of socio-legal theories attempt to explain how incarceration emerged as a policy preference in recent decades, connecting it to political economy, the demise of other policies for social inclusion, such as labor market intervention and redistributive safety net policies, and social and legal anxieties about those whose existence threatens the social order. This section examines three interconnected ideas – welfare, lawfare, and warfare – that can explain how the state has shifted its responses toward an economically and often racially excluded underclass. A later section examines how the informal governance structures developed by inmates themselves have come to mirror these same rhetorics and functions.

Welfare suggests a duty of care on the part of the state. This can involve the targeted or universalist policies aimed at meeting the basic needs of the poorest in the population that were developed in the modern period in order to prevent the poor from engaging in undesirable (criminal) activity to meet those needs, thus constituting a strategy to divert the vulnerable away from the criminal justice system. Within prisons, welfare is a core function of administering the carceral population, from which the state has visibly withdrawn in many Latin American prisons, with the result that families and organized inmate groups have increasingly taken over this role.

Lawfare is a term with several distinct meanings. For some it has a positive meaning close to "judicialization" of social relations or politics, when less powerful actors such as social movements promote a social justice agenda by challenging government policy in the courts. A more negative meaning is the aggressive use of legal strategies in the courts against an opponent by entangling them in vexatious litigation. Yet others use it to mean the way in which legal measures are deployed in the service of national or international security. This chapter uses an idea of lawfare that is closest to this third sense, that is, "the resort to legal instruments, to the violence inherent in the law, to commit acts of political coercion, even erasure" (Comaroff and Comaroff 2006, 30). Criminal law is deployed against those social groups deemed to pose an existential threat to domestic security, state, and society. Latin American politicians – both legislators and those in the executive branch – found that harsher laws were a good symbolic way of making crime pay politically and electorally, even when their policing strategies were clearly failing to reduce crime or insecurity. Rising numbers of arrests and detentions played well in "statistical politics" (Müller 2016, 233), and enabled states to "govern through crime" (Simon 1997). A later section examines the role of judicial actors in this lawfare.

Warfare refers here to a securitizing discourse that invokes "wars on" various objects of social and moral panics – for example, terrorism, narcotics, or crime. First, this legitimizes the direct use of lethal force, which in Latin America is generally wielded by security sector agents, including the armed forces and the predominantly militarized police forces. Second, "war talk" is used by legislators and judges in order to justify the lawfare visible in the penal expansionism mentioned above. Latin American critical criminologists, such as Zaffaroni (2006), have turned to the most authoritarian strands of German legal philosophy in order to understand the "deep logic" of their own penal systems and the prevailing preference for incarceration of certain populations. Carl Schmitt, the Nazi jurist, and later Günther Jakobs both adhered to the idea of "criminal law of the enemy," which divided the populace into "citizens" and "enemies" (Schmitt 2007 [1932]). For Jakobs, the latter must be excluded and stripped of personhood by law to protect the former and the body politic (Jakobs 2014 [2010]).

One of the key theorists of the global spread of the "punitive common sense" forged in the United States in recent decades is French sociologist Loïc Wacquant, who sees the decline of welfare as directly connected to the rise in lawfare. He argued that, as the neoliberal state slashed the budget for social welfare, rejecting intellectually its social integration functions, it turned to incarceration as an alternative means of disciplining the marginal sections of the post-industrial working class, especially ethnically discriminated groups (Wacquant 1999, 2009). This was accompanied by ever harsher discourses on crime and a criminalization of more minor offenses (for example, policies of zero tolerance, or the notorious "three strikes and you're out" rule in the USA). Wacquant noticed Brazil's exploding prison system, and he and others began to extend this analysis to the region (Wacquant 2003). Müller notes that in Latin America "the prison has become the central state institution in charge of warehousing urban marginality" (Müller 2012, 72). Wacquant's earliest and most accessible statement of this thesis, *Prisons of Poverty* (1999), influenced significant intellectual and criminal justice communities desperate to contest the importation of neoliberal penal prescriptions into both Brazil and Argentina.

However, in some Latin American countries, especially those governed by the new, often populist, center-left, a more complex relationship played out between incarceration, neoliberalism, and redistributive policies. In Venezuela, prisoner numbers certainly soared in the 1980s, especially after the financial crash in 1983, doubling from 12,000 in 1980 to 29,000 in 1989 (Antillano et al. 2016, 198–9). But during the harshest years of neoliberal adjustment, from 1989 to 1998, inmate numbers remained relatively static and even declined by about 15 percent at one point. In the first few years of the Chávez government, numbers were reduced dramatically to only 14,000 due to "explicit rejection of past policies that criminalized the poor, advances in human rights rhetoric, legal reforms and an emphasis on the reduction of social inequalities to combat growing violence and crime" (Antillano et al. 2016, 200). More commonly, however, welfare provision and incarceration actually expanded *in tandem* because there are structural limits to redistribution and the ability of globalized economies to provide low-skilled work.[5] The Latin American left often seemed paralyzed in relation to security and crime issues, which were historically a right-wing, authoritarian, and military domain. Yet it also appreciated that law and order and crime ranked high among the public's concerns and had an electoral impact. Thus the governments of Brazil under the Workers' Party (PT), Venezuela under Chavismo, and Mexico City under the *Partido de la Revolución Democrática* (PRD) offered welfare support to the "deserving poor" (for example, through conditional cash transfer schemes such as the *Bolsa Escola* and *Oportunidades*, now *Prospera*) but also resorted to preventive imprisonment for the "bad" or undeserving poor. The left's structural analysis of crime, which leads it to prefer, in principle, a welfare approach to social marginality, is often quickly replaced by a moral panic rhetoric on crime, which in turn leads to lawfare. Venezuela's prison population rose only slightly from 2000–2008, but then took off, climbing from 19,257 in 2006 to 24,069 in 2008, to 40,825 in 2010 and reaching an all-time high of 51,256 in 2014, as the Bolivarian government framed criminals as threats to the revolution (Antillano et al. 2016).[6] Yet, there are still few systematic analyzes of whether or how left and left-populist governments in Latin America approach penal policy and prisons distinctively.

Both left- and right-wing governments adopted United States style zero tolerance policies, which mapped conveniently onto deep historical elite antipathies to the poor disrupting the social order and urban space. Mexico's General Law of the National Public Security System, enacted in the mid-1990s, introduced the unspecified category of "anti-social behavior" into that country's criminal code. The PRD introduced more than 500 amendments to Mexico City's penal code in 2002, inserting new crimes and increasing prison terms for others, resulting in a 40 percent increase in the local prison population in the space of three years (CDHDF 2005). Following a high-profile consultancy by former New York Mayor Giuliani, it then enacted the Civic Culture Law (LCC) in 2004, which detailed 43 misdemeanors, generally informal economic activity such as street vending, or disruption of urban space such as noise, graffiti, and public consumption of drugs or alcohol. These were punishable through monetary fines or detention for between 6 and 36 hours. Detentions related to violations of the LCC rose from 49,205 in 2006 to 134,732 in 2011 (Müller 2013, 456–7).

If the center-left combined welfare with lawfare, the right preferred warfare as its justification for mass incarceration. The "War on Drugs" urged on the continent by the USA in its conditional bilateral aid agreements, and by the prohibitionist positions of the United Nations and the Organization of American States (which it influenced), resulted in draconian provisions for small-scale drug use and possession in the anti-narcotics laws of the region (Metaal and Youngers 2010). Increased arrests and detention for drug offenses became one of the crude metrics of success in this war and pushed up incarceration rates significantly in several countries. A condition of United States-Ecuadorian bilateral agreements on anti-drug cooperation reportedly included a target increase of 12 percent in persons detained and tried for drug offenses under the 1991 Law of Narcotic Drugs and Psychotropic Substances (Edwards 2010, 51). Law 108 also mandated pretrial detention, and a minimum sentence of ten years.[7] Similarly, Bolivia's Law 1008, regulating the production of coca and other controlled substances, was informally designed by United States agents. Mexico's penal laws similarly underwent inflation and toughening due to the "wars" on drugs and organized crime. The Federal Criminal Code was reformed in 1994 to raise the penalties for the production, trafficking, and supply of drugs to a minimum of ten years and a maximum of 25 years in prison, and in 1996 the Federal Organized Crime Law substantially increased the prison terms for any even potentially related activities (Müller 2016, 231). The government of Felipe Calderón (2006–2012) then introduced indefinite sentences for what were deemed serious crimes. In consequence, the population of Mexico's federal prisons jumped from 23,286 to 41,647 between 1995 and 2000 (Zepeda Lecuona 2012, 26).[8]

United States-style warfare/lawfare policies played out most dramatically in El Salvador due to government policies intended to deal with two violent street gangs, known collectively as *maras*. Teenage children of the many Central American refugees who fled the United States-funded civil wars of the 1980s got involved in, or set up, Los Angeles street gangs. The 1996 Illegal Immigration Reform and Immigration Responsibility Act, intended to expel non-citizens sentenced to a prison term of a year or more and foreign-born United States naturalized felons once they had served their prison terms, led the United States government to deport an estimated 46,000 convicts and 160,000 illegal immigrants to Central America between 1998 and 2005 (Rodgers and Muggah 2009, 306). Many of these young men recreated local affiliates of the *Mara Salvatrucha* and the *Calle 18* gangs as a means of survival in a strange land. Thus United States foreign policy created mass flight and vulnerability, which led to mass detention (capture) under domestic penal laws, and mass expulsion under anti-terrorism and immigration laws, as part of a "war" on gangs and illegal aliens (Rodgers et al. 2009). The right-wing Alianza Repúblicana Nacional (ARENA) government in El Salvador responded with its own legalized "war" on the resultant gang violence with the notorious *mano dura* ("Iron Fist") policy. Introduced in July 2003, this effectively criminalized the bodies of anyone over the age of 12 who possessed a gang tattoo or flashed gang symbols in public, an offense punishable by two to five years in jail. The subsequent *Super Mano Dura* package of anti-gang measures increased the maximum term to nine years for leaders and to five years for ordinary gang members, who were many more in number. In 2002, the incarcerated population was 10,907. It then rose steadily, with a steeper rise after 2006 and as of early 2017 stood at 37,244, a nearly sevenfold rise over 25 years. The rate of imprisonment jumped from 130 per 100,000 in 2000 to 574 in 2017, also the highest in the region.[9]

The rhetoric of warfare justifies the legalized capture of the enemy, although as Postema et al. (2017) point out, criminal detainees are not afforded even those legal protections due to prisoners-of-war under the Geneva Conventions. War talk instead justifies states of exception, which are overlaid on top of the standing criminal codes, criminal procedures, and constitutional guarantees. Prisons are often "zones of legal silence" (Garces 2014): the legal grounds for detention are unchallengeable, the burden of proof shifts onto the accused (presuming guilt rather than innocence) yet once an individual is detained such proof is almost impossible to provide,[10] legal counsel is not supplied, and, in the increasing number of super-max facilities in the region, judicial and civil society oversight is resisted. Agamben's (1998) thesis of "bare life" extends Foucault's notion of biopolitics to understand how modern states create normalized, Schmittian states or spaces of exception (the concentration camp being the ultimate example), in which those assigned to them are simultaneously subject to the law and exempted from its protection. Many of Latin America's prisons are such spaces of internment (Birkbeck 2011) and abandonment, where the state uses penal law and judicial discretion to imprison, but has demonstrated little interest in using local legal institutions to enforce adherence either to the guarantees in the country's law and constitution, or to the international human rights conventions to which the states are party.

Pretrial and Illegal Detention

Excessive pretrial detention is the clearest form of prisoner capture and a key enabler of the prisoner takeover of the carceral space. It results partly from tougher criminal laws that prohibit bail or conditional release, and partly from the discretionary, and often illegal, practices of judicial actors, that is, from primary and secondary forms of lawfare. Globally about one-third of all detainees, that is, some 3.2 million individuals, were awaiting trial in 2017. However, some Latin American countries were world leaders: Paraguay ranked third with 77.9 percent of its prisoners awaiting due process while Bolivia was close behind with 69 percent. Yet, within the continent there was a very wide range: just 12.3 percent of Nicaragua's and 17.2 percent of Costa Rica's prisoners were on remand (Table 16.1), indicating that the practice is clearly the result of state commission or omission.

Often the period of pretrial detention exceeded any reasonable, or legally stipulated, period for the authorities to conclude their investigation and preparation of charges. This was frequently accompanied by a lack of information about the actual charges that would be, or had been, brought against detainees, denial of access to legal counsel, and lack of information about when they would eventually be brought before a judge for the first time. In many cases, individuals were held on remand on charges that were not subject to custodial sentences, or for a period beyond the maximum custodial sentence that could be imposed. Brazil's National Justice Council (*Conselho Nacional de Justiça* – CNJ), set up as a watchdog body for the nation's judiciary in 2004, began a systematic review of all case files in 2008 in order to correct the thousands of illegal detentions decreed and sustained by the country's circuit judges. By 2016, its volunteer judges, prosecutors, and public defenders had examined over 400,000 case files, and awarded overdue earned legal entitlements (such as transfer to a lighter prison regime, or parole) to 80,000 inmates, over 45,000 of whom were immediately released from prison, having exceeded their sentence.[11]

In some cases, the state legalized this excessive detention without due process. In Mexico the Federal Organized Crime Law introduced the practice of *arraigo*,[12] which allowed for the preventive detention of a suspect for up to 80 days without charge. This was subsequently incorporated into the Mexican Constitution, thus creating a legal paradox as it violated a number of constitutional guarantees such as the right to legal counsel, the presumption of innocence, and protection from torture, which is inevitably encouraged by prolonged pretrial or preventive detention without charge as officials try to extract information to prepare a legal case or about criminal or terrorist activities. However, like more run-of-the-mill forms of pretrial detention, it contributed little to reducing crime. Officials reported that of around 4,000 people detained under *arraigo* in 2011–2014, only 129 (3.2 percent) were successfully prosecuted (Deaton and Rodríguez Ferreira 2015, 23).

Between 2006 and 2009, some 43,153 people were detained for drug possession (under crimes against health) in the Mexican state of Jalisco, but only 3,500 had charges brought and only 2,173 were convicted (Hernández 2010, 66). In El Salvador, despite a new requirement of some proof of criminal activity for an arrest, the *Super Mano Dura* package of anti-gang measures created a revolving door for the thousands who were often released due to lack of evidence (Savenije and van der Borgh 2014). A Brazilian study found that 37.2 percent of prisoners remanded in 2011 did not receive a prison sentence for their offense, with around half of those being acquitted (IPEA 2014). These very low rates of subsequent conviction demonstrate that, rather than having a rational-instrumental crime-inhibiting purpose, mass pretrial detention has a symbolic, communicative, and spectacular value; that is, it is intended to demonstrate the state's coercive power and impunity.

Any pretrial detention without charge, without counsel, or for excessive and unjustifiable periods amounts to kidnap by the state. It violates both constitutional norms in the respective countries, as well as innumerable articles in the international human rights conventions to which these states are parties: the Universal Declaration of Human Rights, the American Convention on Human Rights, and the International Covenant on Civil and Political Rights, among others. The Inter-American Commission on Human Rights has been a persistent critic of these practices, from both a human rights and a rule of law perspective. Remand prisoners were often held in the worst conditions within the prison system as there is no requirement for the state to provide education and work, to which convicted offenders are entitled. They were thus perhaps the most ill-treated and frustrated group of prisoners and quickly became reliant on organized inmate groups to provide them with basic necessities. Thus pretrial detention both undermined the legitimacy of the justice system and led to loss of control of penal institutions by the authorities (IACHR 2013). The commission's concerns led to the launch of a practical guide for countries in the region to reduce pretrial detention as a matter of urgency (IACHR 2017).

Discretionary Judicial-Bureaucratic Actors

Another driver of illegal pretrial detention is that, despite the prescriptive and positivist nature of the civil law legal systems used in Latin America, criminal justice actors continue to exercise a great deal of discretion in relation to whom they arrest, arraign, detain, and sentence, and on what charges. Sometimes the discretionary element is embedded into the laws themselves, in open-ended wording such as "antisocial conduct," drug possession "for personal use," and activity "potentially" linked to organized crime. These "street-level bureaucrats" often share a powerful collective worldview as a result of passage through the same legal training institutions and professional acculturation. Many see their role not as merely applying the law, but having a higher mission to protect the public. They use their powers of secondary lawfare to do so, and often resist counter-measures.

Very occasionally, judges challenge mass detention practices. In the first 12 months of the Mano Dura policy in El Salvador, 19,275 presumed gang members were arrested and held. Some 95 percent were later released when the law was declared illegal (FESPAD and CEPES 2004). However, judges more frequently uphold detention laws of questionable legality: between 2007 and 2012 only 7 percent of requests by prosecutors to detain under *arraigo* in Mexico were denied (Deaton and Rodríguez Ferreira 2015, 22). Similarly, Brazil's Heinous Crimes bill was repeatedly upheld as constitutional between 1990 and 2006 until there was a shift in the supreme court and a number of its articles were overturned (Boiteux 2010, 32). Often, judicial actors use their discretion in favor of detention and against the spirit of the law. Recognizing the futility of imprisoning drug users, a number of countries passed laws aimed at decriminalizing simple possession and diverting users away from the criminal justice system, specifically from prison. Yet these laws often did not have the intended impact as judges were still able to make subjective decisions in relation to the offender and the offense: the decade after the 2006 reform of the drug law in Brazil, intended to offer treatment, not prison, to drug users, saw a more than threefold *increase* in the number of those detained for drug "trafficking," and the percentage of those arrested on drugs charges in the prison population from 9 percent in 2005 to 32.6 percent in 2017.[13]

In April 2011, the Brazilian government attempted to reduce remand numbers by passing the Precautionary Measures Bill (*Lei de Medidas Cautelares*), giving circuit judges a wider range of options, such as house arrest, regular reporting to the court, electronic monitoring, night-curfew at home, payment of bail, and prohibition of particular activities. However, it was met by an effective boycott: in Rio de Janeiro 98 percent of those accused of drug offenses remained in remand (Lemgruber et al. 2013). The same was true of 90 percent of cases involving illegal ownership of a firearm (for which bail conditions are set out in the law) and for well over 50 percent of non-violent offenses against property such as theft and receiving stolen goods (Lemgruber et al. 2013, 10). The CNJ then took another tack and in late 2015 instituted custody hearings, a mechanism whereby an individual arrested *in flagrante* must be brought within 24 hours before a judge to determine whether they should be remanded in custody or released pending trial. Although this resulted in around half the suspects being released pending trial, detention remained the default position of most judges. Most prisoners did not have the means to challenge these decisions and, even when a judicial decision or omission was clearly illegal and was overturned by a body such as the CNJ, the "deep principle" of judicial autonomy seemed to protect these actors from any form of consequence or discipline.

Prisoners Capturing the Carceral Space

The result of this mass prisoner capture was the creation of carceral zones of legal exception and silence where prison authorities were forced either to share governance with organized prisoner groups, or to effectively relinquish control over the prison population. In response, prisoners themselves took over from the state both the regulation of prison life, creating their own complex, pseudo-legal behavioral codes of conduct and punishments, and exerting coercive force over other inmates.

Mass incarceration reached a tipping point in the early 1990s, changing the dynamics of prison governance among prisoners and between prisoners and staff. The influx of thousands of young inmates, unaware of the complex social systems in jail, combined with unprecedented overcrowding, appalling conditions of detention, and systemic human rights violations, led to rising, unpredictable violence. A common state response to prison unrest in the region was violent militarized intervention, that is, warfare to contain the consequences of lawfare. Yet this generally had a radicalizing, rather than subduing, effect on this carceral mass. In the early 1990s Venezuela militarized its overcrowded prisons, placing them under the purview of the National Guard. Riots and violence soared, and became endemic within the Venezuelan prison system. Fires in Honduran prisons in 2003 and 2004 killed scores, with rumors that those fleeing were fired on by the police. This led to the *maras* being given their own, segregated units to self-govern and develop their own "gothic sovereignty," to protect them as much from the illegal violence of the state as from each other (Carter 2014). São Paulo state's major criminal network, First Capital Command (Primeiro Comando da Capital, PCC), was founded in the early 1990s as an inmates' union to demand better conditions of detention in response both to the extrajudicial execution of 111 prisoners by military police during a riot in the notorious Carandiru prison in 1992, and to the stringent security conditions and brutality in Taubaté maximum security prison (Dias 2013; Biondi 2016).

The lives of many inmates were reduced to "bare life" as the authorities retreated to the perimeter of many prisons, and the Panopticon was replaced by the ghetto (Cerbini 2017). This prompted prisoners to resist these necropolitics and to organize for their own survival, using their own power in numbers to play "inside the dialectic of law and disorder" (Comaroff and Comaroff 2006, 31). As many prison systems gave up the pretense that incarceration was intended to include (that is, provide welfare) rather than exclude, prisoners themselves came to the conclusion that they would be better off administering themselves as a surplus and excluded population, building a collective identity around their marginalization, and providing for their own welfare needs.

The ethnographies cited above uncovered how prisons were being informally governed by their inmates. The mode of self-organization varied considerably and ranged from survival-oriented prisoner mutual aid (and collaboration with guards), to violent, rent-seeking prisoner groups that ran protection rackets inside jails and used access to prisoners to recruit for their criminal activities on the outside (Macaulay 2017). The variables included: the degree of collective autonomy of the prisoners from the prison authorities; who exercised coercive control and ability to use violence, even lethal force, within the prison walls; the degree of structure, hierarchical organization and reach of prisoner syndicates (whether within a single facility, networked across several facilities in the prison system, or operational outside the prisons as well as within); and finally the material resources (goods brought into the prison, or necessities inherent to imprisonment, that could be traded or used to extract rents and encourage loyalty) and immaterial resources (legitimacy, trust, or fear) available to such entities, enabling them to maintain dominance in relation both to the prisoners and to the prison authorities.

At the mutual aid end of the spectrum, Bolivia's San Pedro prison became infamous for functioning as a barely bounded penal colony. The majority of the 2,300 inmates is awaiting trial, and must survive within a prison order where everything is commodified and traded: cells; healthcare; food; security; and narcotics. Although the authorities are absent, no group of individuals dominates the prison, which exists in a finely balanced equilibrium. There are clear social hierarchies among the prisoners, its complex economy is based on secure, pseudo-legal property rights (Skarbek 2010), and violence is regulated by the community sufficiently that entire families live inside the prison (Cerbini 2017).

Toward the more rent-seeking, violent end of the spectrum Venezuela's prisons developed armed self-rule in the 1990s, and governing groups (or *carros*) imposed their rules and hierarchies on the prison population: "thugs" generally controlled the *carro* through a monopoly on violence, which included firearms, paid for by a tax – *la causa* – which they levied on the other inmates, who were divided into workers and drones, evangelical Christians and, at the bottom, the dispossessed, and the outcasts (Antillano et al. 2016).

The existence of prison-based racketeering organizations that extract rents from prisoners and their families beyond the prison walls means that "violent crime increasingly counterfeits government, not least in providing fee-for-service security and social order" (Comaroff and Comaroff 2006, 5). Their provision of the welfare or survival goods such as food and security that the state is unwilling to supply binds the ordinary inmate to these organizations, which they control through the implicit threat of violence against those who break the rules (prisoners and guards) or threaten the status quo (the prison authorities).

Prison life was paradoxical in such contexts: it was at once hyper-codified and pseudo-legal – with highly detailed social rules about clothing, contact with others, sexuality, debts, drugs, language, movement – as a means of reducing interpersonal violence (which was generally outlawed, as disputes were adjudicated through pseudo-juridical conflict resolution processes), and yet also constantly underpinned by the threat of violence or exclusion by the governing group. São Paulo state prison authorities stopped sending data on deaths in custody in its prisons to the federal authorities as the PCC strengthened its grip, as many were actually executions carried out by the group's cadres inside the prisons. Like the Venezuelan *carros*, it imposed a social hierarchy, a highly codified ethos, and pseudo-judicial disciplinary system (Dias and Salla 2017).

The PCC was unusual in holding a monopoly of power not just in one jail, but across a very large jurisdiction, controlling around 95 percent of the prisons and prisoners in São Paulo State, with an increasing reach across Brazil. Unlike the Central American *maras*, who were given carceral space through draconian penal policies, the PCC was born within the prison system. While in Rio de Janeiro the various criminal networks, or *comandos*, engaged in turf warfare on the streets and had to be segregated in separate wings or units of the prison system, the PCC successfully became a hegemonic and bureaucratic organization (Dias and Darke 2016). Moreover, having extended its activities beyond the prison walls, it then acquired a dominant presence, as an organized crime cartel, in many low-income urban communities. Their governance of the carceral space enabled them to provide welfare goods to the mass of inmates, thus assuring its own survival as an organized crime syndicate. The churning of the prison population – the revolving door of arrest, detention, and release – meant that around one million individuals passed through the Brazilian prison system every year (DEPEN 2016, 23), providing a steady stream of new recruits to pay for protection inside prison, and work for it outside. The PCC was able to impose a "pax monopolista" (Biderman et al. 2014) regulating the use of violence by its members and those under its purview, and thus allegedly reducing the homicide rate in the prisons and neighborhoods where it operated. However, it functioned as a parallel "legal" and adjudicating power not in the absence of the state authorities in these sphere, but rather with their acquiescence in a "deadly symbiosis" (Denyer Willis 2009).

It was also highly convenient for the authorities that riots, which occurred on a weekly basis in Brazil in the late 1990s, generally stopped and that violence in the prisons reduced greatly. On the other hand, the state's ceding of the prisons and other areas was toxic to its legitimacy and ability to hold a monopoly on force, as a key component of rule of law. Policy on the PCC oscillated between an unspoken deal tolerating its governance of the prisons, to attempts to isolate its leadership in super-maximum security prison regimes or units. However, in May 2006 the latter led to a mass, orchestrated protest in prisons across the state, with a wave of violence in São Paulo city that shocked the authorities back to the perverse symbiosis policy.

Prisoner capture of the carceral space also challenges the state's monopoly on force and enables criminal groups to push back politically in relation to state lawfare and warfare. Rather than deterring gang membership, detention of the *maras* in El Salvador galvanized them when their locus of control moved from the streets to the prisons. The pattern of mass capture and release from 2003 onwards led to a growing social base for the gangs (van der Borgh and Savenije 2015, 156). Meanwhile the core of gang leaders that stayed in prison enabled heads of local "cliques" affiliated to either Mara Salvatrucha (MS) or the Dieciocho to meet and develop a gang structure that had hitherto been very loose and federated. From September 2004, prisons were designated exclusively by membership of the two gangs, helping each to consolidate their own identity and hardening the rivalry between them (Whitfield 2013, 8). It also provided a negotiating platform for the attempted gang truce after 2009. Their leaders were able to demand the removal of military presence in the jails and the transfer of leaders back into the main prisons, where they regained control over younger members. This helped them to offer a truce predicated on better opportunities for their members inside and outside prison. In short, the gangs were able to use their occupation of the carceral space first as leverage against the state's coercive force – the lawfare directed at them – and then to protest at the lack of state welfare inside and outside the prison.

Conclusions

The study of Latin American prisons can contribute greatly to socio-legal studies in the region not just by demonstrating the persistent illegalities perpetrated in the name of law, but also by uncovering how legal operators create and maintain these spaces of legal exception, and how they are experienced by prisoners and guards. As I have shown in this chapter, developments in the region's carceral regimes also upset some of the dominant Western socio-legal theories about the purpose and functioning of prisons (Darke and Karam 2016). Foucault's notion of the constantly watching and disciplining Benthamite Panopticon is challenged when the state cedes the carceral space, meaning that surveillance and micro-disciplining of inmates' behavior is more often carried out by their peers. Goffman's idea of the "total institution" is inapplicable to Latin American prisons, which are highly permeable socially and economically. The economic activity conducted inside jails – whether survival- or rent-oriented – draws on, and contributes to informal and illegal (as well as legal) economic activity outside, creating complex relationships between prisons and prisoners and the immediate locality, and with inmates' families and neighborhoods. Excessive and legally questionable incarceration has nourished certain kinds of crime (such as trafficking) rather than inhibiting it. Thus, as I have underlined here, the overreliance of many political and judicial actors on legally and practically unsustainable incarceration produced through forms of warfare and lawfare has ended up undermining the rule of law and producing a plurality of regulatory orders, whereby the captured have seized back some degree of control over their lives, in the face of state indifference to the welfare of those trapped in its carceral machinery.

Notes

1 These were prefigured by the engaged sociology of the 1970s, for example, Ramalho (1979) an ethnographic account of the social order in the São Paulo House of Detention (also known as Carandiru), and Lemgruber (1983), a study of the Talavera Bruce women's prison in Rio de Janeiro.
2 Attitudinal surveying of judicial actors was pioneered in Brazil by Maria Teresa Sadek in the think-tank CEDEC in the 1990s. This laid the groundwork for further, deeper research in political science, anthropology, and sociology departments. Law departments remain, however, highly formalistic and positivistic in their approach. A leading exponent of legal anthropology in Brazil is Roberto Kant de Lima at the Fluminense Federal University of Rio de Janeiro
3 http://emporiododireito.com.br/o-excesso-punitivo-e-mais-um-erro-legislativo/Consulted September 15, 2017.
4 www.insightcrime.org/news-analysis/insight-crime-2016-homicide-round-up Consulted September 15, 2017.
5 In addition, rising incomes do not decrease crime: on the contrary, there are more opportunities for acquisitive crimes.
6 World Prison Survey database www.prisonstudies.org/country/venezuela Consulted September 15, 2017.
7 Raised by congress to 12 years in 2003.
8 The rate of increase in the federal system in this period was 78 percent, compared to a 60 percent rise in the state-based prison system.
9 World Prison Survey database www.prisonstudies.org/country/el-salvador Consulted September 15, 2017.
10 Ecuador's Law 108 required all judicial decisions in drug cases to be reviewed by the supreme court, ostensibly to avoid circuit judges being bought off by drug dealers. The effect was to virtually guarantee a guilty verdict (Edwards 2003).
11 www.cnj.jus.br/sistema-carcerario-e-execucao-penal/pj-mutirao-carcerario Consulted September 15, 2017.
12 This translates as having a "hold" on someone or something.
13 http://g1.globo.com/politica/noticia/um-em-cada-tres-presos-do-pais-responde-por-trafico-de-drogas.ghtml. Consulted September 15, 2017.

References

Agamben, Giorgio. 1998. *Homo Sacer: Sovereign Power and Bare Life*. Stanford: Stanford University Press.
Antillano, Andrés, Iván Pojomovsky, Verónica Zubillaga, Chelina Sepúlveda, and Rebecca Hanson. 2016. The Venezuelan prison: from neoliberalism to the Bolivarian revolution. *Crime, Law and Social Change*, 65: 195–211.
Biderman, Ciro, Renato Lima, João Manoel Mello, and Alexandre Schneider. 2014. *Pax Monopolista and Crime: The Case of the Emergence of the Primeiro Comando da Capital in São Paulo*, Brasília: CAF Working paper No. 2014/03 07/15/2014.
Birkbeck, Chris. 2011. Imprisonment and internment: comparing penal institutions North and South. *Punishment and Society,* 13(3): 307–32.
Biondi, Karina. 2016. *Sharing This Walk: An Ethnography of Prison Life and the PCC in Brazil*, Chapel Hill: University of North Carolina Press.
Boiteux, Luciana. 2010. "Drugs and prisons: the repression of drugs and the increase of the Brazilian penitentiary population." In Pien Metaal and Coletta Youngers (Eds.). *Systems Overload: Drug Laws and Prisons in Latin America*, Washington, DC: Washington Office on Latin America, 30–38.
Carter, Jon Horne. 2014. Gothic sovereignty: gangs and criminal community in a Honduran prison. *The South Atlantic Quarterly*, 113(3): 475–502.

Cerbini, Francesca. 2017. The Panopticon to the anti-Panopticon: the 'art of government' in the prison of San Pedro (La Paz, Bolivia). *Prison Service Journal*, 229: 31–34.

Cerbini, Francesca. 2012. *La Casa de Jabón. Etnografía de una Cárcel Boliviana*. Barcelona: Edicions Bellaterra.

Comisión de Derechos Humanos del Distrito Federal (CDHDF). 2005. *Informe Especial Sobre la Situación de los Centros de Reclusión del Distrito Federal*. Mexico City: CDHDF.

Comaroff, Jean and John Comaroff. 2006. "Law and disorder in the postcolony: an introduction." In Jean Comaroff and John Comaroff (Eds.). *Law and Disorder in the Postcolony*, Chicago: University of Chicago Press: 1–56.

Cortés Amador, Ernesto and Demaluí Amighetti López. 2014. "Políticas de drogas y derechos humanos: reformas en Costa Rica." En *Perspectivas* 4, San José: Friedrich Ebert Stiftung Costa Rica.

Darke, Sacha and Chris Garces. 2017. Surviving in the new mass carceral zone. *Prison Service Journal*, 229: 2–9.

Darke, Sacha and Maria Lucia Karam. 2016. "Latin American prisons." In Yvonne Jewkes, Ben Crewe and Jamie Bennett (Eds.). *Handbook on Prisons*. Abingdon: Routledge: 460–74.

Deaton, Janice and Octavio Rodríguez Ferreira.2015. *Detention Without Charge: The Use of Arraigo for Criminal Investigation in Mexico*. San Diego: University of San Diego/Justice in Mexico Project.

Denyer, Graham. 2009. "Deadly symbiosis? The PCC, the state and the institutionalization of violence in São Paulo." In Dennis Rodgers and Gareth A. Jones (Eds.). *Youth Violence in Latin America*, New York: Palgrave: 167–81.

DEPEN. 2016. *Levantamento de Informações Penitenciárias InfoPen 2014*. Brasília: Departamento Penitenciária Nacional DEPEN Brazilian Ministry of Justice.

Dias, Camila Caldeira Nunes. 2013. *PCC: Hegemonia Nas Prisões e Monopólio da Violência*. São Paulo: Saraiva.

Dias, Camila Caldeira Nunes and Fernando Salla. 2017. Formal and informal controls and punishment: the production of order in the prisons of São Paulo. *Prison Service Journal*, 229: 19–22.

Dias, Camila Caldeira Nunes and Sacha Darke. 2016. From dispersed to monopolized violence: expansion and consolidation of the Primeiro Comando da Capital's hegemony in São Paulo's prisons. *Crime, Law and Social Change*, 65: 213–25.

Edwards, Sandra. 2003. *Illicit Drug Control Policies and Prisons: The Human Cost*, Washington, DC: Washington Office on Latin America.

Edwards, Sandra. 2010. "A short history of Ecuador's drug legislation and the impact on its prison population." In Pien Metaal and Coletta Youngers (Eds.). *Systems Overload: Drug Laws and Prisons in Latin America*, Washington, DC: Washington Office on Latin America: 50–9.

Fundación de Estudios para la Aplicación del Derecho (FESPAD) and Centro de Estudios Penales de El Salvador (CEPES). 2014. *Informe Anual Sobre Justicia Penal Juvenil El Salvador*. San Salvador: FESPAD.

Garces, Chris. 2014. Ecuador's 'black site': On prison securitization and its zones of legal silence. *Focaal: Journal of Global and Historical Anthropology*, 68: 18–34.

Hernández, Ana Paula. 2010. "Drugs legislation and prison system in Mexico." In Pien Metaal and Coletta Youngers (Eds.). *Systems overload: Drug Laws and Prisons in Latin America*, Washington, DC: Washington Office on Latin America: 60–70.

IACHR. 2011. *Report on the Human Rights of Persons Deprived of Liberty in the Americas*. Washington, DC: Inter-American Commission on Human Rights.

IACHR. 2013. *Report on the Use of Pretrial Detention in the Americas*. Washington, DC: Inter-American Commission on Human Rights.

IACHR. 2017. *Report on Measures Aimed at Reducing the Use of Pretrial Detention in the Americas*. Washington, DC: Inter-American Commission on Human Rights. Rapporteurship on the Rights of Persons Deprived of Liberty.

IPEA (Instituto de Pesquisa Econômica Aplicada). 2014. *A Aplicação de Penas e Medidas Alternativas*. Brasília: IPEA.

Iturralde, Manuel. 2016. Colombian prisons as a core institution of authoritarian liberalism. *Crime, Law and Social Change*, 65: 137–62.

Jakobs, Günther. 2014. "On the theory of enemy criminal law." In Markus D. Dubber (Ed.). *Foundational Texts in Modern Criminal Law*, Oxford: Oxford University Press (translated from German original) "*Zur Theorie des Feindstrafrecht*." In Henning Rosenau and Sanyun Kim (Eds.), *Straftheorie und Strafgerechtigkeit* (Augsburger Studien zum Internationalen Recht, 2010), vol. 7, 167–82.

Lemgruber, Julita. 1983. *Cemitério dos Vivos: Análise Sociológico de Uma Prisão de Mulheres* (second edition, Rio de Janeiro: Forense, 1999).

Lemgruber, Julita, Marcia Fernandes, Ignacio Cano and Leonarda Musumeci. 2013. *Usos e Abusos da Prisão Provisória No Rio de Janeiro: Avaliação do Impacto da Lei 12.403 2011.* Rio de Janeiro: Associação Pela Reforma Prisional/Centro de Estudos de Segurança e Cidadania.

Macaulay, Fiona. 2017. The policy challenges of informal prisoner governance. *Prison Service Journal,* 229: 51–6.

Metaal, Pien and Coletta Youngers (Eds.). 2010. *Systems Overload: Drug Laws and Prisons in Latin America,* Washington, DC: Washington Office on Latin America.

Müller, Markus-Michael. 2012. The Rise of the Penal State in Latin America. *Contemporary Justice Review,* 15(1): 57–76.

Müller, Markus-Michael. 2013. Penal statecraft in the Latin American city: assessing Mexico City's punitive urban democracy. *Social and Legal Studies,* 22(4): 441–63.

Müller, Markus-Michael. 2016. Penalizing democracy: punitive politics and neoliberal Mexico. *Crime, Law and Social Change,* 65: 227–49.

PNUD. 2013. *Estudio Comparativo de Población Carcelaria.* New York: Programa de las Naciones Unidas para el Desarrollo.

Postema, Mirte, James Cavallaro and Ruhan Nagra. 2017. Advancing security and human rights by the controlled organisation of inmates. *Prison Service Journal,* 229: 57–62.

Ramalho, José Ricardo. 1979. *O Mundo do Crime: A Ordem Pelo Avesso* (second edition, São Paulo, IBCCrim 2002).

Rico José. 1997. *Justicia Penal y Transición Democrática en América Latina.* Mexico City: Siglo Veintiuno Editores.

Rodgers, Dennis, Robert Muggah, and Chris Stevenson. 2009. *Gangs of Central America: Causes, Costs and Interventions.* Geneva: Occasional Paper of the Small Arms Survey, May 2009.

Rodgers, Dennis and Robert Muggah. 2009. Gangs as non-state armed groups: the Central American case. *Contemporary Security Policy,* 30(2): 301–17.

Savenije, Wim and Chris van der Borgh. 2014. Anti-gang policies and gang responses in the Northern Triangle: the evolution of the gang phenomenon in Central America. *The Broker,* July 3, 2014.

Schmitt, Carl. 2007. *The Concept of the Political.* Expanded Edition (1932), trans. by G. Schwab, Chicago: University of Chicago Press.

Simon, Jonathan. 2007. *Governing Through Crime: How The War on Crime Transformed American Democracy and Created a Culture of Fear.* New York: Oxford University Press.

Skarbek, David. 2010. Self-governance in San Pedro prison. *The Independent Review,* 14(4): 569–85.

Van der Borgh, Chris and Wim Savenije. 2015. De-securitising and re-securitising gang policies: the Funes Government and gangs in El Salvador. *Journal of Latin American Studies,* 47(1): 149–76.

Wacquant, Loïc. 1999. *Les Prisons de la Misère,* Paris: Raisons d'agir.

Wacquant, Loïc. 2003. Towards a dictatorship over the poor? Notes on the penalization of poverty in Brazil. *Punishment and Society,* 5(2), 197–205.

Wacquant, Loïc. 2009. *Punishing The Poor: The Neoliberal Government of Social Insecurity.* Durham, NC: Duke University Press.

Whitfield, Teresa. 2013. *Mediating Criminal Violence: Lessons From the Gang Truce in El Salvador,* Oslo: Oslo Forum Papers No. 1, June 2013, Centre for Humanitarian Dialogues.

Zaffaroni, Eugenio. 2006. *El Enemigo en el Derecho Penal.* Madrid: Dykinson.

Zepeda, Guillermo. 2012. "Diagnóstico del sistema penal mexicano." In Antonio Sánchez Galindo (Ed.). *La Transformación del Sistema Penitenciario Federal: Una Visión de Estado.* Mexico City: Centro de Investigación y Estudios en Seguridad.

Websites

Gagne, David. 2017. *InSight Crime's 2016 Homicide Round-up. InSight Crime, Investigation and Analysis of Organized Crime.* Available at: www.insightcrime.org/news-analysis/insight-crime-2016-homicide-round-up. Accessed September 17, 2017.

Mutirão Carcerário. *Conselho Nacional de Justiça.* Available at: www.cnj.jus.br/sistema-carcerario-e-execucao-penal/pj-mutirao-carcerario. Accessed September 17, 2017.

Velasco Clara, Rosanne D'Agostino and Thiago Reis. 2017. *Um em cada três presos do país responde por tráfico de drogas. Dados inéditos se referem a 22 estados; 5 não possuem os números. Com a Lei de Drogas, percentual de presos pelo crime foi de 8,7% em 2005 para 32,6% agora.* São Paulo. Available at: http://g1.globo.com/politica/noticia/um-em-cada-tres-presos-do-pais-responde-por-trafico-de-drogas.ghtml. Accessed September 17, 2017.

17

CHALLENGES OF POLICE REFORM IN LATIN AMERICA

Lucía Dammert

Introduction

Police forces in Latin America have experienced multiple processes of reform over recent decades. Since the return to democracy in the 1980s the region has faced an increasing problem of crime and violence that affects governments and citizens alike. In most cases there is a general consensus that police institutions are not well prepared, equipped, or trained to deal with the increasing complexities of the criminal world and the illicit markets that are rapidly developing.

For centuries the police were perceived as a tool of twisting the law in favor of the powerful and for the repression and containment of the vulnerable (O'Donnell 1998). In most cases, police work involved high levels of violence and low levels of accountability that configured a scenario in which the police were perpetrators of violence instead of being the arm of the justice system to control and prevent crime (Arias and Goldstein 2010). Most Latin American govern-ments lacked a concept of democratic policing, despite the fact that "how the police treat people has an important effect on whether they will perceive their government as fair, equitable and efficacious" (Bayley 1995, 5). In fact, most police institutions in the region are widely perceived to deploy high levels of violence, demonstrate low levels of effectiveness, and pursue general policing strategies based on profiling those most disadvantaged in society.

The literature on police in Latin America is very limited. During the transition to demo-cracy, in the 1980s, multiple research was carried out on police duties, their link with human rights violations, and legal reform processes that were necessary to improve their capacity to prevent and control crime; later on these lines of analysis lost importance. Although police and, specifically policing, has not been part of the main research agenda of law and society in Latin America; it is quite clear that there is a need to continue debating into the meanings of law, the importance of legal institutions as well as legal practices. Besides police culture and institutional challenges, "citizen´s experiences with the police and the ways in which such experiences influ-ence perceptions of legitimacy, and public willingness to comply with legal directives" (Wood 2015, 184) is another area of research that needs to be strengthened.

Furthermore, there are consolidated traditions of research straddling not only public policy and public administration issues but also a range of social sciences topics. In general, two focuses of research on the police can be identified: the most traditional is concerned with an institutional perspective linked to governance, legal frameworks, and political institutions related to the police (Reiner 1992). More recently, different approaches have been developed mainly concerned with what police officers do, how they do it, and how this shapes policing behavior overall (Sharp 2005). Both traditions have developed significant literatures that shed light on important issues that impact not only police forces but also society in general.

In Latin America, most analysis on the police is produced by entities with a reformist agenda to specifically tackle police violence, corruption, and ineffectiveness. However, since the 1990s an increasing number of researchers have developed more rigorous analysis on the institution and the processes of reform implemented to date (Ungar 2011; Serrano-Berthet 2016; Sabet 2014; Ortega 2016). In most cases, these studies have pointed to the failures of the political sphere to consolidate police forces able to tackle violence, crime, and citizens' perceptions of insecurity. They have also developed institutional analyzes that deepen our understanding of how policing policies are designed and implemented and the increasing role of non-state actors (both legal and illegal) in the security realm.

The central objective of this chapter is to analyze the reasons why police reforms in Latin America have had little success and to signal a future research agenda on police in the region. The chapter is organized in five sections: The first section briefly describes police institutions in Latin America, marked by their multiple differences at the national and subnational levels of government. The second section emphasizes the political context in which public security policies are developed and points to the importance of punitive populism in police reform initiatives. Reforming the police is a political issue more than a technocratic one and the way political debate develops signals the boundaries of policy implementation. The third section focuses on areas of police reform that are grouped according to three themes: institutional modernization; militarization of public security; and the expanding presence of the private sector in the provision of security. The focus on measures that impact police service means that many areas of reform are not addressed here; for example, changes to police health systems or administrative procedures. The fourth section presents a hypothesis that seeks to explain the limited results that police reform initiatives have had in the recent past. As I have signaled, political calculations have inhibited the full implementation of reforms. The final section signals a future research agenda, which should enable us not only to better understand existing police reform processes, but also to design and implement more successful initiatives.

The Police in Latin America

Police institutions in Latin America vary substantially. Most countries have national centralized institutions that are either in charge of crime prevention (Carabineros in Chile), crime investigation (Investigative Police in Chile or Civil Police in Brazil) or both (national police institutions in Peru, Uruguay, El Salvador, Honduras, and Ecuador). Furthermore, some countries have regional (Argentina and Venezuela) and even local police institutions (Mexico and Brazil). In terms of organizational structure, police institutions are both civil (Brazil, Chile, and El Salvador) and military (Chile, Colombia, and Mexico). However, any characterization across the region is necessarily dynamic since many institutions are changing their missions, structure, and even type of educational programs.

Despite the differences, almost all police institutions in Latin America share high levels of citizen distrust based on their low effectiveness, increasing corruption, and excessive use of force (Bobbea 2012; Bonner 2009; Brinks 2016; Cruz 2015; Dammert 2012). Lack of trust in the police has a long history that is linked to their prominent involvement in the civil wars and dictatorships that occurred during the 1970s and 1980s. Since the return to democracy during the 1990s, two processes occurred that directly impacted the police: increasing levels of street crime; and the growing presence of organized crime throughout the region. In fact, Latin America has become one of the most violent regions, with the region registering ten of the 15 highest homicide rates of the world (Silva 2016). Countries that were traditionally considered safe, such as Ecuador, Costa Rica, Uruguay, and Chile, have in the last decade faced a public outcry for more policies to deal with crime and insecurity (Lagos and Dammert 2012).

Lack of public investment, limited resources to consolidate professional institutions, and weak political will to enforce reforms have had a strong impact on the abilities of the police to tackle crime. This has also facilitated the growth of the private security industry. In fact, in most Latin American countries there is no state monopoly on coercive force, since the private sector has more guards, better infrastructure, and many more weapons (Ungar 2007). A wide array of internal problems has not been fully addressed in Latin America. In fact most police forces have institutional arrangements based on codes of silence, internal use of violence, discretionary decision-making processes, limited gender participation, and lack of evidence-based policy design. While many policies were implemented during the 1990s to separate the duties of the armed forces from the police, the fight against crime has at least partially reversed this trend (Diamint 2015). An increasing militarization of the public response to organized crime is evident in Mexico (Main 2014; Torres and Azaola 2014) and Central America (Johnson et al. 2016), societies that are facing extreme levels of violence mostly linked to drug trafficking. Growing military involvement in patrolling and crime control initiatives is also observable in Peru, Brazil, Ecuador, and Argentina (Ungar 2013; Glanc 2014).

Both processes, the growth of private security provision and militarization, are playing a major role in redefining police institutions not only due to the incorporation of other state and non-state actors to crime control and prevention, but also in terms of redefining police roles. These trends are being contested by those police forces that have developed new strategies to consolidate their principal role in crime control and crime prevention, increasing their technological capabilities in order to augment effectiveness (Alves and Arias 2012; Cano 2016). Corruption is widespread and ranges from everyday acts of bribery to the penetration of the police by organized crime (Brinks 2016; Corbacho et al. 2015; Dudley 2016). For instance, in 2015 Transparency International reported that the police were considered to be among the most corrupt institutions in Mexico, Bolivia, and Venezuela (Transparency International 2015). Furthermore, a national victimization survey implemented in Brazil in 2013 showed that 7.2 percent of Rio de Janeiro's citizens have been the victims of police corruption (CRISP and Datafolha 2013). In many countries, corruption is a systematic practice closely linked to organized crime (Dudley 2016; Dammert 2016). In Peru, there is evidence that police officers located in the Amazon River areas protect illegal miners and drug traffickers (Dammert forthcoming). In Argentina, after the government of Cristina Fernandez de Kirchner (2007–2015) multiple cases of political-police corruption linked not only to drug trafficking but also to money laundering cases were the subject of judicial enquiries (Sain 2012; Bonner 2015). The most violent area of the region, the Northern Triangle in Central America (Guatemala, Honduras, and El Salvador), is plagued by cases of police involvement in criminal activities, extending to killings to protect drug cartels (Cruz 2015). Unfortunately, these are not isolated situations but rather part of a general framework of police activities in the region that also reveal close links between criminal activities and political networks. The notable case of the 43 students that were kidnapped and allegedly killed in Ayotzinapa (Mexico) by the police is a grim example of illicit networks formed by organized crime, politicians, and police officers (Jimenez 2016).

Excessive use of force is another common element of policing practices in the region (Zavaleta 2016). In countries such as Brazil, the situation has reached atrocious proportions; in Rio de

Janeiro alone more than 640 people died at the hands of on-duty police officers in 2015 (HRW 2015). Moreover, during the first semester of 2016 the Venezuelan Ministry of Justice reported that police committed some 20 percent of all violent crime (Carroll 2010). In Argentina, Glanc (2014) links contemporary police violence directly to the dictatorial experiences of the past, underplaying the possible effects of different reform initiatives. In 2012, Seri reported that 3,390 people have been killed by the police since 1983 (Seri 2012, 146). Furthermore, over 1,000 complaints of torture by police forces of the Buenos Aires Province were registered in 2014 (Insight Crime 2015). Social protest throughout the region has challenged police officers to respond with strategies that are not violent. Unfortunately evidence shows that this has not been the case: for example, in Chile (Hathazy 2013) and Venezuela (Antillano 2014) the police have used disproportionate force to deal with social protest (IEP 2015). Police use of force in scenarios of social protest has directly and negatively affected public trust in the institution, consolidating a vicious circle that is growing stronger in most of the region (Ortega 2016). While citizens request urgent and swift state responses to crime and violence, they also lack trust in the police and perceive impunity as widespread. The metaphor of the criminal justice system as a revolving door that never punishes criminals is widely cited by citizens and politicians alike. Long-term police reform initiatives do not seem to respond to the crucial need of citizens and ongoing political crises of legitimacy do not allow for a rigorous and sound policy debate.

Lack of policy alternatives have consolidated a process that has granted police forces extensive new powers to deal with newly emerging threats, but with limited oversight and training to ensure quality of service for citizens (Frühling 2009). Political discourse has centered on initiatives linked to crime control, increasing police powers and punishment, while systemic reforms have disappeared from the political agenda. Punitive populism is one of the main barriers to implementing reformist agendas in order to address the problems signaled above (Fenwick 2013; Miyazawa 2008).

Punitive Populism

Although violence has been present in Latin America for decades, crime has only recently emerged as a public policy issue. The continuous use of violence by state and non-state actors has been a topic of profound analysis in the history of the region, with many authors emphasizing the recent past of civil wars and military dictatorships (Arias and Goldstein 2010; Sozzo 2016). Crime was considered to be an issue to be dealt with by the police and the justice system, and in most countries prevention and rehabilitation were neither part of the public policy discourse, nor the concern of citizens. Furthermore, with the return to democracy increasing crime levels of crime were primarily analyzed through an ideological lens. Crime became a topic of electoral debate, with the political right using rational choice perspectives to analyze criminal decision-making and the left emphasizing socioeconomic inequalities as the main explanation for criminal activity (Lagos and Dammert 2012; Mota et al. 2012; Neumann 2013). New democracies needed to demonstrate their ability to quickly tackle crime and threats to security. Yet most police institutions were not prepared to understand, prevent, or even combat crime in its various manifestations. The concept of "citizen security" emerged in the public discourse to emphasize the role of prevention, the multidimensional characteristics of the problem, and the impossibility of dealing with crime solely through police action (Dammert 2012). Yet public financing is still highly concentrated in crime control and police budgets have grown steadily for many years.

Lack of expertise within the public sector, increasing levels of insecurity, and a general perception of impunity have prompted a public debate based on myths, hard policies, and an importation of ideas that seem to have succeeded in other continents. Although this is not unique to Latin America, the elements of punitive populism should be analyzed within the context of a deep political crisis. In Latin America, punitive populism emerged marked by: (i) distrust of officials in all branches of government, as well as experts; (ii) erosion of traditional barriers between electoral politics and criminal justice policy; (iii) equating effective punishment with severity; and (iv) the emotive nature of political rhetoric. There are multiple cases and initiatives throughout the region that demonstrate the prominence of this agenda (Dammert and Salazar 2009), which has resulted in increasing levels of imprisonment, higher police budgets, and harsher punishment for criminals. As mentioned by Garland in the analysis of the USA at the beginning of the twenty-first century, there is "a distinctly populist current in penal politics that denigrates expert and professional elites and claims the authority of 'the people,' of common sense, of 'getting back to the basics'" (2001, 13).

Although the review of the literature on penal populism shows it to be a malleable term that encompasses a number of interconnected but conceptually distinct aspects (Pratt 2007), in Latin America it has mainly been a form of political rhetoric about crime designed to bolster electoral support for political elites. Associated with this has been a policy program of tough criminal justice measures that were linked to a "zero tolerance" and "iron fist" (*mano dura*) mentality, specifically in Central America, aimed at tackling youth gangs and, which have had little or no positive results (Bruneau et al. 2011). In other contexts, penal populism has been seen as a process in which new actors emerge and influence criminal justice debate and policy (Fenwick 2013). In Latin America, this trend has taken different paths that involve victims and victims' advocates becoming national leaders who demand more public security, as well as the emergence of security experts with military or police backgrounds. In general, community participation in crime issues has not sparked a process of consolidation of social capital; on the contrary, it has increased levels of distrust in public institutions and consolidated the fear of "the other" (Garland 2001). In this sense populism should be seen as a case of democratic deficit and not as a surplus; a popular movement without the kind of social capital that would lead to constructive engagement in criminal justice policymaking (Dzur 2012). Although in countries like Japan, penal populism has been interpreted as an element that opens up the debate on crime control policies by including new actors (Miyazawa 2008), in Latin America the results of this rhetoric have impacted public perceptions about democracy, fear of crime, and the increasing use of punishment as the only tool to confront violence and crime. It has also inhibited most reform proposals that were designed to enhanced police effectiveness and limit corruption or excessive use of force by labeling them as "soft on crime" and even "pro-criminal" (Sain 2008; Dammert 2012; Sabet 2013).

As previously noted, in most countries in Latin America public perceptions about police work are negative (Ungar 2011; Frühling 2012; Swanson 2013). The police institution is generally seen as corrupt, ineffective, and abusive. Unfortunately, these perceptions are based on a reality marked by poor training, limited results, erratic reforms, and increasing cases of excessive use of force. Paradoxically, public discourse still highlights the need for a greater police presence and increased levels of police patrol that have prompted anxiety on the part of politicians to increase the number of police officers and develop new policing strategies. But in most cases, increasing the number of police officers has not coincided with better training, which has resulted in a vicious circle of negative perceptions and results.

In other words, police reform has become a central issue in the punitive populist agenda by emphasizing the importance of police presence, increasing functions, and new policing strategies that would supposedly be more effective especially in controlling crime. It should be noted that not all police reform initiatives have been part of political campaigns or political rhetoric; in fact, many countries have developed multiple initiatives aimed at improving the quality of police services without much public debate. It is impossible to develop a sound reformist agenda while political debate is mostly rooted in myths and stigmatization. In the following section, several reform initiatives will be presented and discussed with the aim of identifying the elements behind failures and successes.

Police Reforms

The literature on police reform has two main sources. On the one hand, influential international nongovernmental organizations (NGOs) and think tanks have developed a focus on this issue since the 1990s. In the United States and Europe there are several such institutions, among them the Latin American Program of the Woodrow Wilson Center for Scholars, which have published multiple reports, books, policy briefs, and articles on the process of reforming the police in Latin America.[1] The Washington Office for Latin America (WOLA) also has a long tradition of policy-oriented research as well as public policy reports.[2] The International Crisis Group has also highlighted the challenges of police reform, specifically in Central America, Mexico, and Colombia.[3] Human Rights Watch has become an advocate for reform in Latin America, publishing reports and policy briefs on the acute problem of police abuses.[4] The Center for Strategic and International Studies[5] in 2012 published a report on the implications of police reform in Latin America for United States foreign policy.[6] And in Latin America *Fundación Ideas para la Paz in Colombia*,[7] the United Nations Development Program[8] (in Central America) and the Inter-American Development Bank[9] have played important roles in mainstreaming police reform as a key problem for development and the rule of law.

On the other hand, there is a continuous and growing body of academic literature on police reform that has focused on multiple national cases and topics. Unfortunately, the strong academic tradition of social science in Latin America is hardly known and recognized by many researchers in North America. Besides this evident lack of communication between the literatures from the North and South, there is a constant flow of research being published in both contexts. Yet, although there is more research on police reform, it is highly concentrated in some countries, such as Mexico, Brazil, Argentina, and Colombia (Hinton 2006; Ungar 2011; Mota 2012). There is almost no information for other countries, such as Paraguay, Bolivia, and Uruguay, although several changes to the police have been enforced in those nations during the last decade.

It is important to note that while in countries such as the United Kingdom the pressure for police reform "came initially from a desire by the conservative government of the day to bring about greater control and financial discipline" (Sharp 2005, 453), in Latin America increasing levels of expenditure on public security has never been an issue. In any case, throughout the region "the process of police reform is a notoriously difficult and labored task, in part because of inherent contradictions between the police role and the ideals of democracy" (Hinton 2006, 3). While analyzing the Argentine experience Sain states "reforming the police implies reforming politics, in fact, changing the traditional ways between political leaders (governmental authorities) and the police" (2008, 49), signaling a problem that affects most countries with different degrees of political involvement within police and policing.

Police reform is an increasingly complex process that includes political, economic, social, and even criminal challenges since "the police instead of being the most important instance to resolve this group of complex problems (criminality), is part of the problem" (Sain 2008, 46). Although several reforms have been implemented since the 1990s, the democratic process "has brought only a semblance of democratic policing to Argentina and Brazil" (Hinton 2006, 191).

The same conclusion relates to most countries in Latin America that have struggled to reform institutions but still face many authoritarian legacies (Sozzo 2016).

As mentioned above, the three most important barriers to police reform initiatives are: societal violence intrinsic to the way countries were formed and developed; internal police reaction to initiatives considered "foreign" to their culture and critical of their internal organization; and punitive populism that tends to erode any longer term reform initiatives.

Institutional Modernization

Almost all presidential candidates in the region have included plans to reform the police as part of their electoral programs. Most governments have developed reforms at either national or specific subnational levels. In Central America many police institutions experienced structural changes after the end of the civil wars. Previously police officers were trained almost exclusively to handle armed insurgency and to cooperate with the military in maintaining internal order. This situation was at the expense of education and training for crime control, let alone prevention (Dudley 2016; Johnson 2016, Main 2014). An end to armed conflict brought profound changes to police forces, initially showing elements of success. Yet low levels of confidence among citizens, perceptions of corruption, and the increased use of military-like strategies to maintain order undermined the reforms (Cruz 2015). The challenges for police forces in Central America are immense. The intense presence of organized crime and its direct infiltration into organizations with evident shortcomings have highlighted the difficulties of structural or global reforms with little long-term investment in human capital, training, and infrastructure.

In spite of the importance of overall structural changes, most cases of police reform in Latin America have specific objectives. In general, the origins of these initiatives lie either in policy design or scandal. Unfortunately, most cases respond to the latter scenario in which the media plays a key role. In particular, cases of police corruption, misconduct, and excessive use of force have ignited reform processes across the region. Less attractive to media attention are areas of police training, social protection schemes for police officers, gender mainstreaming or even changes in policing strategies. Furthermore, reform in those areas has sometimes been easier to implement since they do not directly affect the institution's internal power structure. Another axis to analyze these processes of police reform relates to the main forces that were behind the proposed plan, either internal or external to the police force itself. After two decades of democratization it is clear that those reforms that were planned without the involvement of the police met with little or no success.

In Argentina, several waves of programs to reform the Greater Buenos Aires Police (well known as *La Bonaerense*) have consistently failed (Sozzo 2016; Hathazy 2016; Colvin 2016; Sain 2008). As Sain (2008) and Sozzo (2016) explain, police links to political actors that have developed corrupt practices are the basis of such failures and setbacks. The Greater Buenos Aires police is a good example of what Arias and Goldstein term "violent pluralism" (2010), where state and non-state actors are linked by a complex network of violent practices.

In Peru, an important process of reform of the National Police was developed in 2001, but resistance on the part of high-ranking police officers and the impatience of citizens urging quicker results had a greater impact than presidential support for the initiative (Costa and Basombrio 2008). Although the team of civilians that designed and started to implement the process was removed, some results included the creation of a police ombudsman, changes in disciplinary codes, and higher importance of police stations that developed direct links with the citizens. Unfortunately, internal forces subsequently eliminated almost all those changes and police reform again occupied the center of the agenda for the 2016 presidential election.

Not all experiences are negative. In fact many specific processes of reform have shown significant progress: for example, the consolidation of systems of internal affairs aimed at improving internal management in the police investigations of Chile (Dammert 2012); the modernization process of police training in various institutions of Brasilia (Dammert 2012), and the consolidation of information systems of the Ecuadorian national police (García 2016). These are just some examples where progress has been achieved in regard to the modernization of police work. Angarita's (2014) research on policing strategies being implemented in Colombia also points to successes, specifically the *Plan Nacional de Vigilancia Comunitaria por Cuadrantes* (beat policing) that aims to achieve a better relationship with the community and higher effectiveness in terms of crime control and prevention. Also, in Brazil the UPP (Police Policing Units) is the best-known police strategy developed in recent decades, implemented since 2008 in Rio de Janeiro with the objective of regaining territories that were controlled by criminal organizations (Cano et al. 2016). Although UPP has had mixed results, those favelas where it was implemented have experienced a clear reduction of street violence (Serrano-Berthet 2013).

A wide range of initiatives has addressed policing strategies. Frühling (2012) has analyzed diverse community policing programs in Latin America and although difficult to implement, these demonstrate an interest on the part of governments and police officers to change their relationships with citizens. Furthermore, Riccio et al. (2013) studied a community police program implemented in two of the most vulnerable areas of Rio de Janeiro and their findings suggest that it is possible for the police to improve quality of life and reduce concerns about crime even in areas harder hit by violence and crime. Besides community policing, Ungar – analyzing the cases of Bolivia, Honduras, and Argentina (2012) – proposes a move from traditional (centralized, hierarchical, and forced-based) policing to what he calls "problem-oriented policing," that he defines as "the process of grouping criminal acts together to identify and address their causes" (2012, 5). In the same vein, Wilson and Parks (2011) analyzed a specific policing strategy implemented in Trinidad and Tobago focusing on five police stations, which registered positive results by reducing crime, and increasing public confidence in the police. Finally, Jaitman and Galiani (2016) posted a policy brief on the Inter-American Development Bank's web page presenting some positive results of policing changes in Montevideo (Uruguay) that supports the use of targeted or "hot spot policing."

Most countries in Latin America show mixed results in their efforts to reform their police institutions. In most cases, specific programs directed to implement a new policing strategy have had better results than those aimed at entirely rebuilding the institution. International aid has played a role in this type of innovation, since most "good practices" arrived in the region as proposed solutions to the crime and violence crisis. Community policing, for instance, has been a model of policing supported by major donors and multilateral agencies. The importation of concepts and its effects is an issue that requires further research, as in most cases the lack of adjustment to country-specific contexts has undermined results.

Another area that has experienced important changes is the police educational system (CAF 2015). Firstly, at the beginning of the 1990s many police institutions' requirement for enrollment was primary school. By 2016, however, that changed to secondary school in most cases, opening up new possibilities for police education and training. Most institutions have also modified their curricula, including human rights among the topics of study. New policing strategies are being discussed and learned in countries such as Colombia and Chile. However, the participation of teachers linked to civil society organizations or that are not part of the institution is a different issue. In fact, there is little progress in this area and some institutions directly reject the possibility of opening their classrooms to independent knowledge. Hierarchical institutions with strict disciplinary codes have to learn to open spaces to genuine debate, disagreement, and critique of policy decisions. Most education and training programs still need to face that challenge without the fear that debate entails lack of discipline.

Finally, one issue that has not been fully addressed but where important advances have been made is that of gender mainstreaming.[10] In fact many police forces had two different administrative scales (one for men and another for women), rarely opening posts for women and then mostly in "family problems" or administrative duties (Debert and Brocksom 2015; Colvin 2016; UN Women 2016). This evidently discriminatory administration has been changing in most of the region, allowing for better professional development perspectives for women in the force. Yet the increasing numbers of women in police forces are still concentrated around administrative issues or operational areas linked to children's problems or family issues. There is no doubt in the literature that creating a representative and more effective police service will increase effectiveness and efficiency. That includes increasing the representation of female police officers in all operational areas of the service (Pita 2015).

Gender-based violence is an issue that has been only partially recognized in Latin America. Traditionally considered as part of the patriarchal culture, violence against women was (and still is) overlooked in many contexts. In some countries one of the first state responses to the increasing rates of gender-based violence was the implementation of women's police stations or specialized units (UN Women 2016). In countries such as Peru the coverage of those units is still limited and they remain underfinanced given the magnitude of the problem. Paradoxically a social problem such as gender-based violence was considered part of the police's remit, but little has been done in order to tackle gender-based violence and discrimination within the institution (Azaola 2006). Research in Buenos Aires has shown that female officers did not report significant levels of institutional discrimination but did report informal disparaging treatment, including sexual harassment (Pita 2015). But in Mexico Azaola (2006) demonstrated high levels of police misconduct toward policewomen, including sexual harassment and physical and psychological violence. In Uruguay multiples changes have occurred since 2010 to deal with gender discrimination in the national police, including a complete review of protocols and procedures to develop programs to address gender-based violence within the institution, along with specific initiatives to address gender-based violence, such as women's police stations or specialized units.

Militarization of Police Work

The armed forces are part of crime control policies in most Latin American countries. Despite not being trained or educated to deal with problems such as organized crime, street patrolling, or community relations, in many countries politicians and citizens prefer them to do this type of work since there is little trust in police capacities. In fact, the following figure (Figure 17.1) shows the percentage of citizens that agreed that the armed forces should combat crime (Zechmeister 2014). Even in Chile and Uruguay, the countries with the lowest homicide rates in the region, more than half of the population favored bringing the army back on the streets to fight crime.

In many countries the armed forces' involvement in crime control and prevention was seen as a last resort, since police institutions were facing important challenges and reforms. For instance, in Mexico due to precarious institutionalization and the clear penetration of organized crime in some state police forces and many local police organizations, the military was deployed as a temporary solution (Main 2016; Brinks 2016). During the administration of Felipe Calderon (2006–2012) the military increased their budget and role in combating drug cartels. Mexican police institutions have experienced diverse processes of reform, but the military´s role has

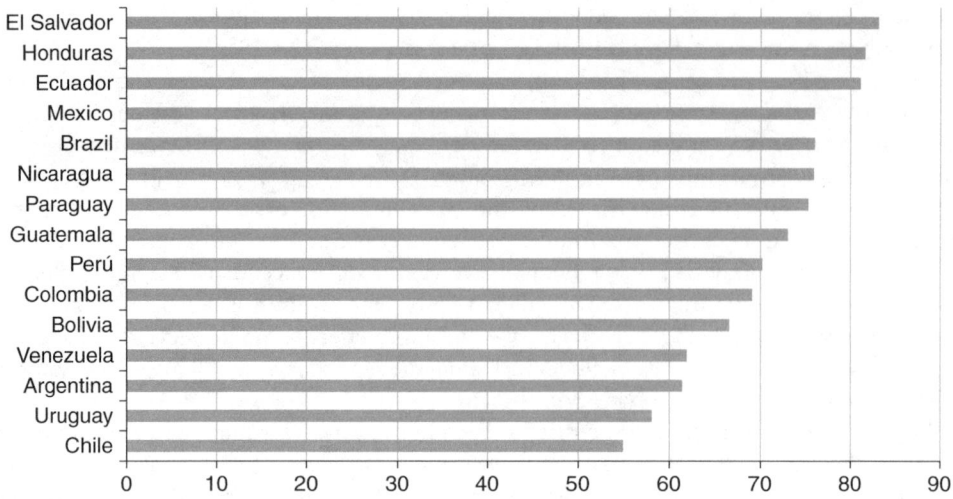

Figure 17.1   Percentage That Agreed That the Armed Forces Should Combat Crime, 2014

continued to consolidate. President Peña Nieto (2012–2018) at the start of his term in office stated that policing was the role of the police, but in fact policy did not change.

In Central America the situation is very similar. In El Salvador, Honduras, and Guatemala military forces have been deployed in the main urban areas to fight and control the increasing presence of gang violence. In those countries, police institutions are facing a process of constant reform linked to corruption scandals that involve high-ranking officers, something that in turn has opened the door to a greater involvement of the military. (In Honduras, for example, an army general was appointed to the post of minister of security). But militarization is not solely a Central American trend. In the last decade Venezuela, while reforming the police ensure protection of the political regime, has assigned high-ranking armed forces officials to public security areas. As Antillano (2014) states, policies implemented by former President Hugo Chavez (1999–2013) varied widely from social to "iron fist" policies at the end of his administration. In fact, Chavez stated that crime is a moral problem based on the values of capitalism and the criminal becomes an enemy of the revolution; a narrative of war that also helps to consolidate a military perspective. In Ecuador, the decentralized model of policing that was developed until 2008 was changed by President Rafael Correa (2007–2016), who decided to fully centralize public security strategies and in 2013 brought the armed forces onto the streets to patrol (Garcia 2014). In Argentina, President Menem in April 1999 called for the National Guard and the Argentine Navy to be "put on the streets" in order to reduce the level of urban insecurity in Buenos Aires (Sozzo 2016).

This same tendency is evident in Brazil with greater intensity. An anti-gang offensive was developed in Rio de Janeiro that counted on the participation of the police and the military and diverse interventions were made in the country's favelas. The National Public Security Force was created with the objective of responding to serious problems of insecurity and includes personnel from the armed forces dedicated to specific tasks, such as recovering firearms stolen from military arsenals. Additionally, a federal law was approved, which allows state governments to directly summon the armed forces in those cases where their support is required to fight organized crime, as well as the unfolding of other localized threats. Finally, the Brazilian government has authorized the massive use of the army to confront rural violence in the Brazilian Amazonia.

Unfortunately, the initiatives previously described are not exceptions in Latin America. On the contrary, they reflect a gradual process of incorporation of the army in tasks associated with public security, crime control, and even crime prevention. The lack of professionalism in the police has established a fertile zone where the militarization of public security looks set to become a semi-permanent element in Latin American politics. Military involvement in crime control has not been a success. In fact, in most countries that have experienced heavy military involvement in this area there are multiple cases of corruption being investigated and even more cases of human rights violations. The consequences of public security militarization for police forces are evident. First, it has increased the use of military-style weapons, uniforms, and behavior among policemen deployed in high crime areas. Second, it has sharpened tensions within the police educational system due to the clash between military and community policing doctrines. Third, it has limited professionalization of police forces that are under the leadership of military personnel who concentrate their effort on crime control rather than investigation or prevention.

A Growing Role for the Private Sector in Security Provision

In recent decades private security has grown exponentially in Latin America. In most countries the number of private guards outnumbers police officers and in some cases private guards are allowed to use heavy weapons to patrol houses, businesses, or people. This situation is not unique to the region and has generated important theoretical debates regarding the concept of policing and the need to include a notion that captures the provision of security by state and non-state actors. Thus, the concept of security governance has been widely used as an analytical tool worldwide (Wood and Font 2007). But in Latin America research on this topic is scant (Ungar 2007) and lacks the basic information needed in order to characterize the process, the industry, and the thin line that divides the state from non-state organizations. In fact, as Zedner states, "hybrid forms of 'state-corporate symbiosis' or 'grey policing' further blur the distinction between public and private" (Zedner 2009, 101).

At least three elements of the increasing trend toward private security provision directly affect the police in Latin America. First, the industry is not well regulated (Dammert 2012). In most countries the rapid development of security threats and the general perception of lack of police effectiveness heralds new modalities almost daily. For instance, the use of heavily armed bodyguards for the protection of banks, schools, and even neighborhoods. Lately, the development of technological tools has also opened the market to new devices such as crime control drones, cameras, and smartphone applications. In most countries the government's capacity to fully regulate the market is weak, allowing for increasing problems since there is little control over the qualification of guards and the use of private information.

The second element is the increasing presence of an informal sector linked to security services that involves everything from neighborhood watch-type services to private detectives and bodyguards. Informality in the security sector is a high risk since it could become a window for organized crime to penetrate communities, increase violence, and even consolidate vigilantism. Estimates vary widely, but in some countries more than half of the estimated size of non-state security actors is informal, which points to the need for further debate on the security governance concept previously alluded to.

The third element is police involvement in private provision of security. In some countries such as Argentina, Uruguay, and Peru, police officers are allowed to work as private guards in their spare time. Although in the last five years these programs have been changed (the *222 Program* in Uruguay and *24x24* in Peru) in order to limit the amount of hours that the police officer can work as a private guard, and to regulate the use of police guns and uniforms during private activities, financial incentives for police officers to work in the private provision of security continue to exist. In countries such as Mexico and Brazil specific police forces have been created to protect the private sector, but the scope of their duties is constantly being enlarged.

Reforms with Limited Results

Police reforms in Latin America display more challenges than results. The development of knowledge about the police in the region has direct implications in the research on law and society. Not only because of the crisis of legitimacy of the state monopoly of the use of force, but also the need to increase institutional capacities that improve the relationship with the community and the effectiveness of police work.

Many structural elements substantially limit almost all substantive initiatives to reform the police. There are problems linked to lack of expertise, professionalization, and even modernization in the public security sector, both inside police institutions and in civil society organizations. But police reform is mostly a political issue and for that reason the main barrier to developing sound initiatives is the lack of political will to face the massive economic and political challenges that they imply. Analyzing the Mexican case, Alvarado (2014) states that, the Mexican government has largely failed in confronting organized crime and underlines the fact that the ruling class is not willing to assume the high political and social costs that pursuing more effective policies would entail. Since crime and violence have become key electoral topics entrenched within a punitive populist narrative, there is little room for governments to fully implement the changes needed to enhance police work. Furthermore, in Argentina, Hathazy summarizes the problems of police reform when he states "personalism and institutional weakness of the Argentinean party system got easily transmitted to the bureaucracy producing discontinuity of reforms and very limited change" (2013, 34). Also, the politicization of police forces that are used, as "guards" of the administration is an ongoing process that increases impunity, decreases internal control, limits transparency, and undermines reform initiatives. In fact, the trajectory of police reforms is intimately linked to national political and bureaucratic structures (Hathazy 2013), not only in Argentina but also throughout the region.

Not all police reform initiatives are structural. In some cases importation of concepts without the proper investment in police training or infrastructure has eroded their possibilities of success. That is the case of community policing initiatives developed in the last two decades that were inaugurated with prominent media coverage but, which in the end did not include processes of decision-making decentralization or real interest in enhanced relations with the community (Frühling 2012; Wilson and Parks 2011). Another area is that of crime statistics; although reliable statistics are vital for policy design, there have been limited results in terms of transparency and data quality. In most countries, today there is widespread lack of trust of official data, although in many institutions several programs have been developed to build monitoring mechanisms and enhance crime statistics.

The police reform scenario in Latin America is challenging but not impossible. In fact, there are five elements that could shed some light on the possibilities for further developing changes in the security arena. First, initiatives to reform the police are being designed and implemented constantly. A consensus exists that police institutions need to be reformed from within the force, and the political world and public opinion will continue to be present in each and every political debate on institutional reform in the region. Second, international aid is concentrating efforts on enhancing police performance indicators, including areas that for many decades were forgotten, such as investigative results and crime analysis. Third, promising results in specific areas such as the modernization of educational systems or the development of successful policing strategies have shown internal and external stakeholders that it is possible to change, although clearly not at the pace that many experts would argue is needed. Nonetheless, there are at least signals of possible changes in the areas most important for police officers. Fourth, new generations of police officers perceive that increasing militarization and the growing role of the private sector in security provision are trends that directly affect their relevance in the administration of justice. In some countries a new leadership among younger generations with higher educational levels is concerned about the problems faced by their institutions and are willing to discuss specific reforms. Finally, there is a systemic crisis of criminal justice in Latin America than involves the judiciary, the police and the prisons. There is little room for innovation in dynamics where impunity, insecurity, and fear characterize citizens' interactions with the criminal justice system, along with increasing violence, lack of effectiveness, and corruption. Thus, reforms of the justice system will definitely impact police forces.

Future Agendas for Research

Police reform is a relatively new area of law and society research in Latin America. In recent decades growing attention has been focused on police work due to increasing levels of violence and crime that at times have appeared to be impossible to overcome. Although police forces participated in human rights violations in the 1970s and 1980s, little attention was focused on the need to reform them with the return to democratic elections. In fact, most forces became the backbone of new regimes that faced increasing social unrest and criminality as problems greatly affecting citizens.

Since the 1990s, a growing concern about police performance has emerged from NGOs, think tanks, and civil society organizations working on corruption and human rights abuses. The academy subsequently developed a research agenda on the topic from multiple disciplinary perspectives and contexts that are only marginally integrated. In fact, most research carried out in the United States and Europe hardly ever has an impact on public policy decisions in Latin America or is even known among South American researchers. There is a myth that issues such as "zero tolerance," "compstat," "community policing," or "problem-oriented policing" are good practices for police forces in the South. But in most cases little empirical information has been gathered to fully understand the context-specific elements that are central to ensuring proper implementation.

Research related to police reform is also limited due to low levels of transparency of institutional information. For instance, the police strategy developed by the Carabineros in Chile, Plan Cuadrante, has not been researched due to barriers to gathering information. Therefore, constant budget increases are based on anecdotal evidence rather than serious information about impact or even results. By the same token, the impact of strategies to deal with gender-based violence has only marginally been studied due to police officers' general unwillingness to participate in research designs.

As mentioned, official data is fragile and generally not open to the public. Even homicide rates generate doubts regarding their accuracy. Based on his ethnographic work in Brazil, Denyer (2016) raises doubts over homicide rates, signaling that in most cases these are not related to better policing strategies but rather to definitions of criminal organizations that determine when, where, and why to kill. Such trends limit the possibility of further developing an empirically-based research agenda that would better characterize the problems of crime and violence being faced by specific groups and territories in Latin America. Moreover, the possibility of developing databases capable of concentrating information from the police and the justice and prison systems is minimal, limiting researchers' possibilities of developing more sophisticated research designs.

Although multiple issues could be the center of future research agendas, some elements can be considered fundamental. First, militarization and the increased presence of the private sector in security provision, and the impact of both of these phenomenon on police work, is key. Not only because this impacts police mission and doctrine, but also because it affects the police's relationship with the community. Both processes are redefining the roles of state and non-state actors in the security arena, something that undoubtedly requires further consideration.

Corruption and excessive use of violence cannot be treated as regular elements of police work. In fact, research is needed in order to better understand the linkages with the political sphere that allow both problems to be endemic. Policing strategies are basically unknown to the police reform literature on Latin America. Innovations in other contexts are overlooked or poorly implemented, let alone evaluated. Most police forces rely heavily on randomly patrolling the streets, although there is empirical evidence that the patrolling police officer has only a marginal impact on the incidence of crime and disorder and that this is an extremely inefficient and ineffective method of detecting crime. There is a need for an applied criminological research agenda to evaluate specific reforms linked to policing in order to define what does and doesn't work in the field.

Finally, more research is needed inside the police force. Little is known regarding police officers and their relationship with the community, or about the gender differences in policing, and challenges toward crime control and crime prevention, among other issues. Clearly more specific analysis is required in order to better understand the internal forces that could become barriers for leaders of institutional change. After more than two decades of initiatives to reform the police one issue is clear: changes require leaders and internal support in order to offset the inevitable counter-reforms.

Notes

1 Wilson Center: www.wilsoncenter.org/program/latin-american-program. Accessed October 8, 2017.
2 WOLA: www.wola.org/issue/police_reform. Accessed October 8, 2017.
3 International Crisis Group: www.crisisgroup.org/en/regions/latin-america-caribbean/guatemala/043-police-reform-in-guatemala-obstacles-and-opportunities.aspx. Accessed October 8, 2017.
4 Human Rights Watch: www.hrw.org/es/americas. Accessed October 8, 2017.
5 Center for Strategic and International Studies: www.csis.org/analysis/police-reform-latin-america. Accessed October 8, 2017.
6 https://csis-prod.s3.amazonaws.com/s3fs-public/legacy_files/files/publication/120228_Johnson_Police Reform_web.pdf. Accessed October 8, 2017.
7 *Fundación Ideas para la Paz*: www.ideaspaz.org/. Accessed October 8, 2017.
8 United Nations Development Program: www.latinamerica.undp.org/. Accessed October 8, 2017.
9 Inter-American Development Bank: www.iadb.org/es/temas/seguridad-ciudadana/iniciativa-de-seguridad-ciudadana,7251.html. Accessed October 8, 2017.
10 Gender mainstreaming is the process of assessing the implications for women and men of any planned action, including legislation, policies or programs in all areas and at all levels.

References

Aitchison, Andy and Blaustein, Jarret. 2013. "Policing for democracy or democratically responsive policing? Examining the limits of externally driven police reform." *European Journal of Criminology,* 10(4): 496–511.

Alvarado, Arturo. 2014. "La criminalidad y las políticas de seguridad en México." En *Cuestiones de Sociología*, 10. Available at: www.cuestionessociologia.fahce.unlp.edu.ar/article/view/CSn10a10. Accessed June 1, 2016.

Alves, Márcia and Arias, Enrique Desmond. 2012. "Understanding the Fica Vivo programme: two-tiered community policing in Belo Horizonte, Brazil." *Policing and Society*, 22(1): 101–13.

Antillano, Andrés. 2014. "Crimen y castigo en la revolución bolivariana." En *Cuestiones de Sociología*, 10. Available at: www.cuestionessociologia.fahce.unlp.edu.ar/article/view/CSn10a19. Accessed June 1, 2016.

Arias, Enrique and Goldstein, Daniel (eds.). 2010. *Violent Democracies in Latin America*. Durham: Duke University Press.

Azaola, E. 2006. *Imagen y Autoimagen de la Policía de la Ciudad de México*. Mexico: Edición Coyoacan.

Bayley, David. 1985. *Patterns of Policing: A Comparative International Analysis*. New Brunswick, NJ: Rutgers University Press.

Bayley, David. 1995. "A foreign policy for democratic policing." *Policing and Society*, 5: 79–93.

Bobea, Lilian. 2012. "The emergence of the democratic citizen security policy in the Dominican Republic." *Policing and Society*, 22(1): 57–75.

Bonner, M. 2009. "State discourses, police violence and democratization in Argentina." *Bulletin of Latin America Research*, 28(2): 227–45.

Bonner, M. 2015 "Rethinking debates on media and police reform in Argentina." *Policing and Society*, 19. Accessed June 4, 2016. doi:10.1080/10439463.2014.993632

Brinks, Daniel. 2016. *The Judicial Response to Police Killings in Latin America. Inequality and the Rule of Law*. New York: Cambridge University Press.

Bruneau, Thomas, Dammert, Lucía, and Skinner, Elizabeth. 2011. *Maras: Gang Violence and Security in Central America*. Austin, TX: University of Texas Press.

CAF. 2014. *Programa sobre Uso de la Fuerza y Empleo de Armas de Fuego. Resumen de Evaluación de Impacto*. Caracas: CAF. Available at: http://scioteca.caf.com/handle/123456789/455. Accessed June 3, 2016.

CAF. 2015. *Proyecto 'Puntos Calientes' Colombia*. Caracas: CAF. Available at: http://scioteca.caf.com/handle/123456789/804. Accessed June 3, 2016.

CAF. 2015. Capacitación, Percepcón de Riesgo y Actuación Policial en *Resumen de Políticas Públicas. Seguridad Ciudadana*. CAF. Available at: http://scioteca.caf.com/bitstream/handle/123456789/689/ResumenDePolitica_Polic%C3%ADa%20Federal.pdf?sequence=1&isAllowed=y. Accessed June 1, 2016.

Cano, Ignacio, Trindade, Claudia, Borges, Doriam, Ribeiro, Eduardo, Rocha, Lia, Barros, Cintia, Araújo, Emanuelle, Frossard, Marcele, Ansel, Pedro, and Andrade, Sandra 2012. *Os Donos do Morro; Uma Avilacao Exploratória do Impacto das Unidades de Polícia Pacificadora (UPPs) no Rio de Janeiro*. Rio de Janeiro: Relatorio do LAV-CAF. Available at: www.lav.uerj.br/docs/rel/2012/RelatUPP.pdf. Accessed June 3, 2016.

Carroll, Rory. 2009. "Deadly force: Venezuela's police have become a law unto themselves." *Guardian*, September 6. Available at: www.theguardian.com/world/2009/sep/06/venezuela-police-law-themselves. Accessed June 6, 2016.

Colvin, Roddrik. 2016. "Female police officers and their experiences: the metropolitan police of Buenos Aires context." *Women and Criminal Justice*, 16: 1–16.

Corbacho, Ana, Phillpp, Julia, and Ruiz-Vega, Mauricio. 2015. "Crime and erosion of trust: evidence for Latin America." *World Development*, 70: 400–15.

Costa, Gino and Basombrio, Carlos. 2008. *Liderazgo Civil en el Ministerio del Interior*. (mimeo). Lima: IDL.

CRISP and Datafolha. 2013. *Pesquisa Nacional de Victimizaçao*. Sumário Executivo SENASP. CRISP and Datafolha. Available at: www.interconect.com.br/clientes/pontes/blog/pnv.pdf. Accessed June 4, 2016.

Cruz, José Miguel. 2015. "Police misconduct and political legitimacy in Central America." *Journal of Latin American Studies*, 47(2): 251–83.

Dammert, Lucía. 2012. *Fear and Crime in Latin America: Redefining State-Society Relations*. New York: Routledge.

Dammert, Lucía. 2016. "The Peruvian Perfect Storm: State Fragility, Corruption and Organized Crime." In *Fragile States in the Americas*, Kassab, H. and J. Rosen (eds.), Washington, DC: Lexington Books: 78–101.

Dammert, Lucia and Salazar, Felipe. 2009. *¿Duros Con El Delito? Populismo e Inseguridad En América Latina*. Santiago de Chile: FLACSO. Available at: https://scela.wordpress.com/2009/11/02/duros-con-el-delito-populismo-e-inseguridad-en-america-latina-lucia-dammert-y-felipe-salazar/. Accessed January 13, 2016.

Debert, G. and Brocksom, S. 2015. "Gender violence and administration of justice in Brazil: the case of São Paulo." *Journal of Feminist, Gender and Women Studies,* 21–9.

Denyer, Graham. 2016. "Police, 'Police' and the Urban." In *The SAGE Handook of Gobal Policing,* Ben Bradford, Beatrice Jauregui, Ian Loader and Jonny Steinberg (eds.). London: SAGE Publication: 479–96.

Diamint, Rut. 2015. "A new militarism in Latin America." *Journal of Democracy,* 26(4): 155–68.

Dudley, Steven. 2016. How drug trafficking operates, corrupts in Central America. *Insight Crime,* July 6, 2016. Available at: www.insightcrime.org/news-analysis/how-drug-trafficking-operates-corrupts-in-central-america. Accessed July 6, 2016.

Dzur, Albert W. 2012. "The Myth of Penal Populism." In Dzur, A. (ed.) *Punishment, Participatory Democracy, and the Jury,* Oxford Scholarship Online. 21–40.

ECLAC. 2015. *Panorama Social de América Latina.* Santiago de Chile: Naciones Unidas, CEPAL.

El Achkar, Soraya. 2012. "Police reform in Venezuela: an ongoing experience." *Policing and Society,* 22(1): 89–100.

Fenwick, M. 2013. "Penal Populism and Penological Change in Contemporary Japan." *Theoretical Criminology* 17(2): 215–31.

Früling, Hugo. 2012. "A realistic look at Latin America community policing programmes." *Policing and Society,* 22(1): 76–88.

Frühling, Hugo. 2001. "Las estrategias policiales frente a la inseguridad ciudadana en Chile." En *Policia, Sociedad y Estado. Modernización y Reforma Policial en América del Sur,* A. Candina and H. Fruhling (eds.), Santiago de Chile: CED. 17–37.

Frühling, Hugo. 2003. "Police reform and the process of democratization." In *Crime and violence in Latin America,* Frühling, Hugo, Tulchin J. and Golding H. (eds.). Washington, DC: Woodrow Wilson Center Press and Johns Hopkins University Press: 15–44.

Frühling, Hugo. 2009. "Recent police reform in Latin America." In *Policing Insecurity. Police Reform, Security and Human Rights in Latin America,* Niels Uldriks, Landham: Lexington: 21–47.

Fohrig, Alberto and Pomares, Julia. 2013. "La seguridad pública en 30 años de democracia." *Revista SAAP,* 7(2): 283–88. Available at: www.scielo.org.ar/scielo.php?script=sci_arttext&pid=S1853-19702013000200006&lng=es&nrm=iso. ISSN 1853-1970. Accessed June 5, 2016.

Garland, D. 2001. *The Culture of Control: Crime and Social Order in Contemporary Society.* Oxford: Oxford University Press.

García, Berta. 2014. "En la encrucijada: ¿Hacia dónde va la cuestión policial ecuatoriana?" En *Cuestiones de Sociología,* 10. Available at: www.cuestionessociologia.fahce.unlp.edu.ar/article/view/CSn10a07. Accessed June 4, 2016.

Glanc, G. 2014. "Caught between soldiers and police officers: police violence in contemporary Argentina." *Policing and Society,* 24(4): 479–96.

Goldstein, Daniel. 2012. *Outlawed: Between Security and Rights in a Bolivian City.* Durham: Duke University Press.

Hathazy, Paul. 2013. "Fighting for a democratic police: politics, experts and bureaucrats in the transformation of the police in post-authoritarian Chile and Argentina." *Comparative Sociology,* 12: 1–43.

Hinton, Mercedes. 2006. *The State on the Streets. Police and Politics in Argentina and Brazil.* Denver: Lynne Rienner.

HRW. 2016. *World Report 2016.* New York: Human Rights Watch. Available at: www.hrw.org/sites/default/files/world_report_download/wr2016_web.pdf. Accessed June 5, 2016.

IEP. 2016. *Global Peace Index.* Sydney: IEP. Available at: http://static.visionofhumanity.org/sites/default/files/Global%20Peace%20Index%20Report%202015_0.pdf. Accessed June 7, 2016.

IEP. 2015. *Global Peace Index 2015.* Sydney: Institute for Economics and Peace. Available at: http://static.visionofhumanity.org/sites/default/files/Global%20Peace%20Index%20Report%202015_3.pdf. Accessed June 3, 2016.

Insight Crime. 2015. *Buenos Aires Police Torture Cases Indicate Institutional Problem.* Available at: www.insightcrime.org/news-briefs/buenos-aires-police-torture-cases-indicate-institutional-problem. Accessed June 3, 2016.

Jaiman, Laura and Sebastian Galiani. 2016. *La Teoría Detrás de la Reforma de la Policía en Montevideo.* Available at: http://blogs.iadb.org/sinmiedos/2015/12/17/economia-del-crimen-aplicada-el-caso-de-montevideo/. Accessed June 3, 2017.

Jimenez, Marco. 2016. "Ayotzinapa 43: the criminal corruption of the Mexican State." *Educational Philosophy and Theory,* 48(2): 119–22.

Johnson, Stephen, Mendelson, Johanna, and Bliss, Katherine. 2012. *Police Reform in Latin America. Implications for U.S Policy.* Washington, DC: CSIS. Available at: https://csis-prod.s3.amazonaws.com/s3fs-public/legacy_files/files/publication/120228_Johnson_PoliceReform_web.pdf. Accessed June 6, 2016.

Lagos, Marta and Dammert, Lucía. 2016. "La Seguridad Ciudadana: El Problema Principal De América." *Latinobarometro,* June 12, 2016. Available at: www.latinobarometro.org/documentos/LATBD_La_seguridad_ciudadana.pdf. Accessed June 3, 2017.

Main, Alexander. 2014. "The U.S. remilitarization of Central America and Mexico." *NACLA.* June 17, 2014. Available at: https://nacla.org/article/us-re-militarization-central-america-and-mexico. Accessed June 1, 2016.

Marshall, Geoffrey. 1978. "Police accountability revisited." In Butler, D. and H, Halsey (eds.). *Policy and Politics,* London: Macmillan: 51–65.

Miyazawa, Setsuo. 2008. "The politics of increasing punitiveness and the rising populism in Japanese criminal justice policy." *Punishment and Society,* 10(1): 47–77.

Mota, Mariana, Trebilcock, Michael, and Hartford, Patrick. 2012. "Police reform in violent democracies in Latin America." *Hague Journal on the Rule of Law,* 4(2): 252–85.

Neumann, P.J. 2013. "(un)exceptional violence(s) in Latin America." *Latin American Politics and Society,* 55: 168–75.

O'Donnell, Guillermo. 1994. "Delegative democracy." *Journal of Democracy,* 5: 55–69.

O'Donnell, Guillermo. 1998. *Polyarchies and the (Un)rule of Law in Latin America.* Working paper 254. Kellogg Institute for International Studies.

O'Donnell, Guillermo, Vargas Cullel, Jorge, and Lazzetta, Osvaldo. 2004. *The Quality of Democracy: Theory and Applications.* Notre Dame: University of Notre Dame Press.

Ortega, Daniel. 2016. "Effectiveness versus legitimacy: use of force and police training in Latin America." *Brookings.* Available at: www.brookings.edu/2016/01/05/effectiveness-versus-legitimacy-use-of-force-and-police-training-in-latin-america/. Accessed June 6, 2016.

Pita, J.M. 2015. "Analysis, systematizing and elaboration of proposals of improvement in the treatment of cases of violence against the woman in application of the norms of the penal new procedural." *LEX,* 10(9): 387–416.

Pontón, Daniel. 2007. "El proceso de reforma policial en Ecuador: Un tema relegado al olvido." *URVIO Revista Latinoamericana de Seguridad Ciudadana,* 2: 37–56.

Pratt, John. 2007. *Penal Populism: Key Ideas in Criminology.* London: Routledge, Taylor & Francis Group.

Reiner, Robert. 1992. *The Politics of the Police.* Hemel Hempstead: Harvester Wheatsheaf.

Riccio, Vicente, Aurlio, Ruediger, Dutt, Marco, Ross, Steven, and Skogan, Wesley. 2013. "Community policing in the Favelas of Rio de Janeiro." *Police Practice and Research: An International Journal,* 14(4): 308–18.

Rojas, José Luis and Morán, Teresita. 2015. "Síndrome de burnout y satisfacción de vida en policías ministeriales Mexicanos." *Archivos de Criminología, Seguridad Privada y Criminalística,* 15: 1–17.

Rojido, Emiliano. 2014. "Políticas de Seguridad en el Brasil de los mega-eventos." *Cuestiones de Sociología,* 10. Available at: www.cuestionessociologia.fahce.unlp.edu.ar/article/view/CSn10a05. Accessed June 5, 2016.

Ruiz Torres, Miguel and Azaola Garrido, Elena. 2014. "Cuadrar el delito: Corrupción institucional y participación de policías en el secuestro en México." *Perfiles latinoamericanos,* 22(44): 91–112. Available at: www.scielo.org.mx/scielo.php?script=sci_arttext&pid=S0188-76532014000200004&lng=es&tlng=es. Accessed June 2, 2016.

Ruiz Vásquez, J.C. 2012. "Community police in Colombia: an idle process." *Policing and Society,* 22(1): 43–56.

Sabet, D.M. 2013. "Corruption or Insecurity? Understanding Dissatisfaction with Mexico's Police." *Latin American Politics and Society,* 55: 22–45.

Saín, Marcelo. 2008. *El Leviatán Azul. Policía y Política en la Argentina.* Buenos Aires: Siglo XXI.

Saín, Marcelo. 2012. "Es la política, estúpido. El Gobierno Federal frente a la reforma policial en Argentina." *COMUNES,* 135–64.

Sanguinetti, Pablo and Ortega, Daniel. 2015. "Towards a Safer Latin America. A new perspective to prevent and control crime." Bogotá: CAF. Available at: http://scioteca.caf.com/bitstream/handle/123456789/708/RED2014-english-towards-a-safer-latin-america.pdf?sequence=3&isAllowed=y. Accessed June 5, 2016.

Silva, Hector. 2016. *Corruption in El Salvador: Politicians, Police and Transportistas*. Bogotá: Insight Crime. Available at: www.insightcrime.org/images/PDFs/2016/InSight_Crime_El_Salvador_Police_Corruption_Special%20Report.pdf. Accessed June 3, 2016.

SENASP. 2013. *Pesquisa Nacional de Vitimizacao*. SENASP. Available at: www.interconect.com.br/clientes/pontes/blog/pnv.pdf. Accessed June 4, 2016.

Seri, Guillermina. 2012. *Seguridad: Crime, Police Power, and Democracy in Argentina*. New York: Continuum International Publishing Group.

Serrano-Berthet, Rodrigo. 2013. *O Retorno do Estado às Favelas do Rio de Janeiro: Uma Análise da Transformacao do Dia a Dia das Comunidaes Após o Processo de Pacificacao das Upps*. World Bank. Available at: http://documentos.bancomundial.org/curated/es/760411468227666514/pdf/760110ESW0P12300Rio0de0Janeiro02013.pdf. Accessed June 3, 2016.

Sharp, Douglas. 2005. "Who needs theories in policing? An introduction to a special issue on policing." *The Howard Journal*, 44(5): 449–59.

Silva, Héctor. 2016. Corruption in El Salvador: Politicians, Police and Transportistas. Bogotá: Insight-Crime. Available at: www.insightcrime.org/images/PDFs/2016/InSight_Crime_El_Salvador_Police_Corruption_Special%20Report.pdf. Accessed June 5, 2016.

Sozzo, Máximo. 2016. "Policing after Dictatorship in South America." In Ben Bradford, Beatrice Jauregui, Ian Loader and Jonny Steinberg (eds.). *The SAGE Handbook of Global Policing*, London: SAGE Publications: 337–55.

Swanson, Kate. 2013. "Zero tolerance in Latin America: Punitive paradox in urban policy mobilities." *Urban Geography*, 34(7) 972–88.

Tello, Nelia. 2012. "Police reforms: the voice of police and residents in Mexico City." *Policing and Society*, 22(1): 14–27.

Terpstra, Jan and Fyfe, Nicholas. 2015. "Mind the implementation gap? Police reform and local policing in the Netherlands and Scotland." *Criminology and Criminal Justice*, 15(5): 527–44.

Transparency International. 2015. *Corruption Perceptions Index 2015*. London: Transparency International. Available at: www.transparency.org/cpi2015. Accessed June 2, 2016.

Ungar, Mark and Salomón, Leticia. 2012. "Community policing in Honduras: local impacts of a national programme." *Policing and Society*, 22(1): 28–42.

Ungar, Mark. 2011. *Policing Democracy: Overcoming Obstacles to Citizen Security in Latin America*. Baltimore, MD: Johns Hopkins University Press.

Ungar, Mark. 2007. "The privatization of citizen security in Latin America: from elite guards to neighborhood vigilantes." *Social Justice*, 34:20–37.

Ungar, Mark. 2013. "The rot within: security and corruption in Latin America." *Social Research: An International Quarterly*, 80(4): 1187–212.

UN WOMEN. 2011. *Women's Police Stations in Latin America Case Study: An Entry Point for Stopping Violence and Gaining Access to Justice (Brazil, Peru, Ecuador and Nicaragua)*. New York: UN WOMEN. Available at: www.endvawnow.org/uploads/browser/files/security_wps_case_study.pdf. Accessed June 1, 2016.

Willis, Graham. 2016. "Before the body count: Homicide statistics and everyday security in Latin America." *Journal of Latin American Studies*, 49(1): 29–54.

Wilson, D. and Parks, R. 2011. "The impact of police reform on communities of Trinidad and Tobago." *Journal of Experimental Criminology*, 7: 375–405.

Wood, Jennifer, and Font, Enrique. 2007. "Crafting the governance of security in Argentina: Engaging with global trends." In Andrew Goldsmith and James Sheptycki (eds.). *Crafting transnational policing: Police capacity-building and global policing reform*, Oxford: Hart: 329–56.

Wood, Jennifer. 2015. "Police and policing." In Austin Sarat and Patricia Ewick (eds.). *The Handbook of Law and Society*, West Sussex: Wiley Blackwell: 183–96.

Zavaleta, Alfredo, Kessler, Gabriel, Alvarado, Arturo, and Zaverucha, Jorge. 2016. "A bibliographical essay on the relationships between police forces and the youth in Latin America." *Política y Gobierno*, 23(1): 201–29.

Zedner, Lucia. 2009. *Security*. London: Routledge.

Zechmeister, Elizabeth (ed.). 2014. *The Political Culture of Democracy in the Americas: Democratic Governance Across 10 Years of the Americas Baromete*r. Washington, DC: USAID. Available at: www.vanderbilt.edu/lapop/ab2014/AB2014_Comparative_Report_English_V3_revised_011315_W.pdf. Accessed June 2, 2016.

Websites

BID. "Seguridad Ciudadana." Available at: www.iadb.org/es/temas/seguridad-ciudadana/iniciativa-de-seguridad-ciudadana,7251.html. Accessed June 6, 2016.

Center for Strategic and International Studies. Available at: www.csis.org/analysis/police-reform-latin-america. Accessed June 6, 2016.

Fundación Ideas para la Paz. Available at: www.ideaspaz.org/. Accessed June 6, 2016.

Human Rights Watch. "Americas." Available at: www.hrw.org/es/americas. Accessed June 6, 2016.

UNDP. "United Nations Development Program in Latin America and the Caribbean." Available at: www.latinamerica.undp.org/. Accessed June 6, 2016.

Wilson Center. "Latin American Program." Available at: www.wilsoncenter.org/program/latin-american-program. Accessed June 6, 2016.

18

LEGAL PROFESSIONALS IN LATIN AMERICAN IN THE TWENTY-FIRST CENTURY

Manuel A. Gómez

The Influence of Latin American Legal Professionals

It is difficult to imagine a group with a greater influence than legal professionals on the organization and development of the modern Latin American state. By legal professionals I am not only referring to those licensed to practice law and represent clients, but also the judges, magistrates, law enforcement officials, and other individuals formally trained whose professional occupation is to liaise between the formal legal system and society at large. By this measure, law students should also be considered legal professionals, albeit their role and contribution is arguably different and more limited than the one performed by judges, lawyers, and others.

Legal professionals have been vital to many activities associated with the functioning of the formal legal system, including lawmaking, interpreting laws, adjudicating disputes, offering legal advice, and obviously participating in the enforcement of judicial and administrative decisions. Legal professionals have also been at the heart of the political process and the functioning of the state, since colonial times (Pérez-Perdomo 2006). Lawyers are commonly found in many government agencies, and public offices, across the spectrum of the state's bureaucracy throughout the region (Falçao 1984, 1988; Fix-Fierro and López Ayllón 2003). The contribution of Latin American legal professionals to society goes beyond the public sphere, as they have also been key players in the private sector (Gómez and Pérez-Perdomo 2017a). From the traditional roles of legal advisors, and in-house counsel, generally reserved to lawyers; legal professionals also act as corporate officers, political brokers, and lobbyists. Moreover, certain fields like the protection of the environment or human rights have also been primarily shaped by the work of legal professionals through their involvement in policymaking, advocacy, and activism (Gómez 2010; Rodríguez-Garavito 2010; Dezalay and Garth 2002).

It is important to acknowledge, however, that the relationship between legal professionals and society is not one-sided or unilateral, but rather complex and multidimensional. As I just said, legal professionals have contributed to create, shape, and transform institutions, customs, norms, and processes, and have had a noticeable impact on society, politics, and the economy. In turn, these realms have also influenced the development, and transformation of the legal profession. As a result, the relationship between society and legal professionals is an uninterrupted cycle where one influences and transforms the other, and vice versa.

Given the significance of Latin American legal professionals, one would expect the academic scholarship to pay considerable attention to them, but unfortunately that has not been the case. With some exceptions, most of the academic research dealing with the legal systems of Latin American countries still pays more attention to the formal rules and institutions than to the individuals who create, interpret, apply, and enforce those rules. The scant literature on legal professionals in the region has been mostly centered on judges, and much of it has emerged parallel or in relation to the judicial reform agendas promoted by the World Bank, the Inter-American Development Bank and some countries during the nineties (Hammergren 2007; Dakolias 1996).

Except for the still small but growing law and society literature on Latin American judges (Hilbink 2015; Azuela and Cancino 2014; Rodríguez-Garavito 2014; Helmke and Ríos-Figueroa 2011; García-Villegas 2008) and lawyers, the existing inventory has also tended to be mostly prescriptive or normative (Hartmann, 2007), thus relegating any descriptive analysis to a second plane. Authors have paid more attention to how the judges and lawyers fulfill – or fail to fulfill – their role in the formal legal system, but have neglected looking at them as social actors interconnected with the economic, social, and political context.

This chapter attempts to counterbalance such oversight, by focusing on Latin America's professional legal actors but as members of a distinct social group, and by bringing them to the front and center of the discussion. Given that other chapters of this book focus specifically on judges (González-Bertomeu, in this volume), and the institutions whose functioning is entrusted to them (Pou, in this volume), this chapter will be centered on three distinct but interrelated categories of professional legal actors: legal scholars; law students; and lawyers. The analysis offered here engages with the – still scarce, but increasingly important – contemporary law and society scholarship on legal professionals in the region, and also tries to provide critical assessment of the breadth and scope of such literature. Furthermore, this chapter situates the scholarship on Latin American legal professionals within the comparative debate on the relationship of professional legal actors vis-à-vis the social, political, and economic realities where they operate. Aligned with the general scope of this Handbook, this chapter hopes to contribute to the intellectual discussion about the relationship between institutional patterns, law, politics, and society in Latin America vis-à-vis legal professionals as a defined social group.

Legal Professionals in Latin America: A Definitional Hurdle

One could say that a legal professional or a professional legal actor (I use these names interchangeably) is any person whose main occupation concerns the operation of the official legal system, by performing a specific role that requires expert knowledge, familiarity, and/or formal training. As a result, legal professionals usually undergo some formal training leading to a title, license, or academic degree that proclaims their knowledge, expertise, or familiarity with the official legal system. Taking into account these two elements: *occupation;* and *title*, the most visible examples of legal professionals are the judges and lawyers; although the legal profession also includes law enforcement officers, bailiffs, law clerks, and other government officials whose main professional occupation is to deal with the legal system of the state. The formal training and occupation also helps distinguishing legal professionals from ordinary citizens, even though the latter may also be regarded as legal actors insofar their interaction with the legal system influences and shapes its operation, too.

In general terms, and based on the general description just offered, the definition of legal professionals seems simple and straightforward. Notwithstanding, such definition becomes less clear once we consider the differences that emerge both from the historical and other contextual variations that occur along the region, and the dissimilar regulation of professional legal actors from country to country. As Pérez-Perdomo (2006) has pointed out in the case of Latin American lawyers, one of the most salient subgroups of legal professionals, the requirements for becoming a lawyer are different across countries, and the role of the bar associations and similar entities may also differ. Moreover, being a lawyer in any Latin American city during the eighteenth century was very different from being a lawyer in those same places today. These variations are not trivial. They affect the definition of legal professionals in each country, and also pose certain methodological difficulties to their study.

Take for instance, the difference among national legal systems regarding who can be considered – and counted – as a lawyer. In some countries, anyone who obtains a university degree in law is automatically deemed a lawyer; in others, there are additional requirements like undergoing some practical training, working as an intern, passing a state administered examination, and/or joining a professional organization. Also, not all those who hold a professional qualification or title automatically become employed as lawyers or are otherwise engaged in the practice of law. Think of a congressperson, a public official, or a company executive who despite having graduated from a law school has never joined a bar association, or practiced law. And what about those who practiced law for a period of time, but not anymore? Some might still consider them legal professionals, while others would probably exclude them. The landscape is obviously complex and nuanced, therefore affecting how we define and study professional legal actors.

Aside from the differences among those who are counted as lawyers, there are also variances regarding, which institution or organization – if any – is in charge of tracking and gathering demographic data on lawyers and other legal professionals, the methodology used, and the availability of such data. In the majority of Latin American countries, the existing statistical data on lawyers (and professional legal actors in general) is flimsy at best. Unlike the United States where an array of institutions ranging from the universities to state bar associations have been compiling and disseminating statistics on law graduates for years; Latin American countries have not had such tradition, thus making it difficult to obtain an accurate picture of the professional legal actors in the region. Furthermore, the almost exclusive attention placed on judges and lawyers, and the subsequent marginalization and neglect of other professional legal actors has led to an incomplete representation of Latin American legal professionals in the contemporary academic literature.

With these caveats in mind, I now turn to address the current debates of professional legal actors in the region through a critical overview of the leading law and society literature on the topic. Consistent with a broad and inclusive definition of professional legal actors, the discussion offered here will focus on three important categories of professional legal actors: legal scholars; law students; and lawyers. I will center my discussion here on a description of the general landscape as well as the theoretical and empirical debates about each category according to the relevant socio-legal literature. Whenever possible, I will also offer a critical assessment of the state of the research in the region.

Re-Drawing the Landscape of Professional Legal Actors in Latin America

Legal Scholars as Legal Professionals

Most studies on legal professionals rarely consider legal scholars and law students as part of that group. Regarding the former, the general perception is that – unlike practicing attorneys and judges – legal scholars are disengaged from the daily operation of the legal system and their professional activities have neither practical impact nor carry any significant weight compared to judges and practicing attorneys. Furthermore, some have even connected the existence of legal scholars to their purported inability to practice, as if the reason why they teach is precisely because "they cannot do" (Cohen 2004). Very much as in the conventional imagery of the ivory tower, legal scholars are commonly regarded as inhabitants of a cloistered and insulated world primarily concerned with abstract and theoretical ideas about the law.

The term legal scholar primarily applies to those with expert knowledge about the law; who are professionally devoted to teach, do research, write, publish their work, and participate in other related intellectual activities exempted from professional practice. Most legal scholars nowadays are both teachers and researchers. Notwithstanding, there are also law teachers who do not write, and legal researchers who do not teach; but they all have in common that their occupation is mostly intellectual or scholarly, and not practical. To make things even more complicated, the dissemination of legal knowledge has not always been an exclusive activity of law teachers, researchers, or legal authors. There have been individuals whose contribution to the dissemination of legal knowledge is undeniable, despite not having published their work, or taught law in an academic setting. In fact, historical research has shown that the jurists of antiquity mainly communicated their ideas orally, and written scholarship is relatively recent (Pérez-Perdomo 2009).

In any case, there is no doubt that legal scholars are important actors in society. They possess specialized knowledge about the legal system, and are responsible for disseminating it. Legal scholars not only comment or discuss the laws, but also contribute to the process of creating law by proposing, drafting, advising, and consulting with lawmakers and other public officials. Because of the close connection between law and politics, it is not uncommon for some legal scholars to also pursue a career in government or public service. The history of Latin American countries is filled with examples of legal scholars who have remained closely connected to the political establishment, which has enabled them to play an even greater role in the formation of the state, the development of legal institutions, and more recently the consolidation of democracy.

One such influential legal scholar was Andrés Bello, the Venezuelan-born humanist whose prolific intellectual career during the nineteenth century left a long-lasting mark throughout Europe and South America. In addition to writing authoritative texts on grammar and being an accomplished poet, Bello was a renowned legal scholar. He drafted the first Chilean Civil Code in 1852, which was later adopted by Ecuador and Colombia, and served as important reference to the then-nascent legislation of several other Latin American countries. There is an abundance of publications about Bello and his work, focusing mainly on Bello's exceptional qualities as a humanist, and on the scholarly value and substance of his intellectual output (Jaksic 2001). Something similar can be said about other Latin American legal scholars of similar caliber like Carlos Calvo from Argentina, Antonio Sánchez de Bustamante from Cuba (Obregón 2017), or Rui Barbosa from Brazil (Coates 2016; Gonçalves 2000); to name just a few.

So far, the interest about Latin American legal scholars has either focused on the legal concepts, ideas, theories, or thoughts espoused by those scholars in their work; or their biographies, as a way to pay homage to them, celebrate their careers, and highlight their intellectual accolades. What is lacking, however, is the study of legal scholars as a distinct social group regarding their unique traits, relationships with other legal actors, the rest of the legal system, and with society as a whole. As Pérez-Perdomo has pointed out, the interest on studying legal scholars as a subcategory of professional legal actors has – unfortunately – been scant. It is puzzling to see how legal scholars have neither occupied the attention of their peers, nor other social science researchers. Both Pérez-Perdomo's own work regarding Venezuelan legal scholars (2009, 2014, 2015a, 2015b) and the work of Fix-Fierro (2014) about Mexican legal scholars are – to my knowledge – the only works geared to understand the role of legal scholars in Latin American societies, including the impact of culture, politics, and other factors that affect the operation of the legal system.

The treatment of legal scholars as a social group has routinely fallen outside the radar of researchers and commentators, but their publications and other intellectual contributions have not. The work of legal scholars is often scrutinized and criticized by their peers, learned and memorized by law students, and sometimes relied upon by policymakers or litigants in order to support their arguments or validate their positions in real-life cases and other situations. In fact, one could venture to say that a significant portion of what legal scholars do is precisely that. Notwithstanding, the format, style, and breadth of the intellectual product of legal scholars – often termed "legal scholarship" – vary greatly.

The most common contemporary vehicle for the dissemination of the academic work of legal scholars are written publications that appear in specialized academic journals, books, and other print media mainly geared to the members of the legal community. The format and style also tends to vary depending on the subject and the scope of the work, although the approach is almost invariably normative. Latin American legal scholarship in its most traditional form gravitates around the interpretation of official laws, legal institutions, court decisions, or the underlying theories and principles that inform the official legal system. Traditional scholars tend to focus on whether a particular court case was decided correctly (i.e., in accordance with certain interpretation of the relevant laws), or whether a legal provision conforms or not with a higher normative order or principle. There is also great interest on the discussion of theories, and abstract concepts that underlie the official legal system, its institutions, and actors.

With some exceptions, this traditional view portrays law as an independent and self-referenced discipline isolated from its surroundings or social context. Questions about the impact of the law on society and vice versa, tend to be largely ignored by this type of scholarship. A perusal of the catalog or table of contents of any major Latin American specialized legal journal and most law-related books may help proving this point, but unfortunately, the observation would only be anecdotal. The only systematic effort that we know of, geared to explore the relationship between the social, economic, and political realities and Latin American legal scholarship is the research of Pérez-Perdomo (2014) regarding Venezuelan law reviews. After researching a universe of more than 1,000 articles published in the seven leading law reviews of that country between 2000 and 2013, Pérez-Perdomo found an interesting correlation between legal scholarship and the then-current political situation of Venezuela. In more concrete terms, he found an upsurge of academic articles that considered the impact of the recent political, social, and economic developments on the operation of the law. This also meant a departure from the purely normative analysis of specific legal rules and principles that defines the traditional legal scholarship, as I mentioned earlier.

Pérez-Perdomo also reported the presence of a small cadre of interdisciplinary legal studies with empirical focus that also rely on social sciences methodologies, but mainly produced in the field of criminology. One specific journal, *Capítulo Criminológico* seemed particularly aligned to what we generally regard as law and society scholarship. Many of the works published there, were centered on *law in action* problems, rather than the *law on the books*. That is, they paid special attention to the *actual* operation of the criminal justice system, its interplay with the political, economic, and social reality that affects it, and the behavior of the different actors involved. Despite these interesting developments, a significant portion of the Venezuelan legal scholarship analyzed by Pérez-Perdomo was still traditional and self-referential.

Law reviews are by no means the only vehicles for the dissemination of legal scholarship in Latin America, but are certainly one of the most salient. Legal scholars also write books that are published by university-owned presses or by commercial publishing houses that serve the legal community. Latin American legal scholars also propagate their work through other media, including electronic and online publications, which have the advantage of spreading academic work much faster than other traditional means, and are also widely accessible to readers from all over the world. With certain exceptions hailing from institutions and academic publishers from Argentina, Chile, Colombia, and Mexico, which have embraced and disseminated important Latin American law and society research; most of the publishers from the region seem to be still interested in supporting only traditional legal scholarship. The case of the Instituto de Investigaciones Jurídicas of UNAM in Mexico is particularly noteworthy, because it houses an incredibly active publishing unit with a fast growing collection of both traditional and socio-legal empirical literature, several periodicals (some bilingual), and a catalog that is completely accessible online. The Instituto is also a stronghold of legal scholars with more than 100 affiliated researchers, and a very active presence in the local and global law and society communities.

Regarding the audience of legal scholarship, as happens in most other scientific and professional arenas it is mainly limited to those in the field, although it occasionally permeates to the general public. Given the connection between law and other disciplines such as politics, government affairs, history, literature, and the like; it is not unusual for legal scholars to write, publish, and have some impact in those areas as well. Unfortunately, there is no inventory, general catalog, unitary database, or directory that can give us an idea of how big or small the production of Latin American legal scholars is or has been during a particular time period. Even a web search would yield incomplete results. In any case, our perception is that the inventory is immense.

Every Latin American nation brandishes its own crop of legal scholars usually comprised by university professors, researchers, and practitioners who combine their professional lives with a limited academic activity. In terms of scope and geographical breadth, our hypothesis is that the bulk of Latin American legal scholarship is still confined to the national or subnational levels. There are also works that address legal problems more abstractly without any spatial or temporal reference. Comparative works, on the other hand, tend to be the exception unless when a scholar makes reference to the laws, legal principles, and classical commentaries about certain European nations like Italy, France, and Spain; which are still seen by many as the historical forbearers of most – if not all – national legal systems of the region. Curiously, the scholarly works of French, Italian, and Spanish commentators of the nineteenth and early twentieth centuries still find followers around Latin America. Showing familiarity with such foreign work can be seen as a sign of erudition and worldliness.

On the other hand, the comparative scholarship that only focuses on countries of the region seems to be less common. The interest in comparing, say, a particular aspect of the criminal system of Colombia with its Costa Rican counterpart is not nearly as attractive as the one from Italy, Spain, Germany, and even the United States. The same can be said about statutory interpretation, and other traditional legal analysis. Paradoxically, most of the comparative analyzes done about different Latin American jurisdictions and their legal systems have come from outside of the region.

Indeed, a sizable amount of the contemporary scholarship *about* Latin American legal systems is produced in other countries and published in languages other than Spanish or Portuguese, the two most widely spoken languages in the region. This is especially true in the case of the law and society scholarship, which seems to have flourished mainly through English-speaking publications; although the simultaneous or parallel publishing in both English and Spanish is not unusual. This book, and others such as Couso, Huneeus, and Sieder's *Cultures of Legality* (2010), Helmke and Rios-Figueroa's *Courts in Latin America* (2011), Friedman and Pérez-Perdomo's

Legal Cultures in the Age of Globalization (2013), Rodriguez-Garavito's *Law and Society in Latin America* (2014), and several others, are good examples of that phenomenon. Furthermore, there are also scores of book chapters, and academic articles about law and society in Latin America being routinely published in English outside the region, and then republished in Spanish or Portuguese.

One might wonder why this is so, and I think there are two plausible answers. First, that English has become the *lingua franca* of law and legal actors, and thus the main language of conferences, meetings, and academic publications in the socio-legal field (Friedman, Pérez-Perdomo, and Gómez 2011, 7). A second explanation is that law and society – as a distinct field – not only originated in the English-speaking world but has also continued to develop prominently outside of Latin America, mainly in places such as the United States and Europe where many of the leading Latin American law and society scholars still connect, forge their collaborations, and develop their academic projects (Friedman 1986; Silbey 2002; Trubek 1990; Garth 2016). The universities, research institutions, and professional associations of those countries are also more supportive of law and society research and scholarship than their Latin American counterparts.

Notwithstanding the obvious dominance of United States and European institutions in the field, some Latin American efforts to promote law and society studies are noteworthy. Both regarding their current success and the promises they hold, some Latin American universities such as UNAM and CIDE (Centro de Investigación y Docencia Económicas) in Mexico, Los Andes in Colombia, UNIMET (La Universidad Metropolitana) in Venezuela, Fundaçao Getulio Vargas in Brazil, and Diego Portales in Chile have become or are becoming bastions of interdisciplinary and empirical socio-legal research in the region. The list also includes research institutions such as Facultad Latinoamericana de Ciencias Sociales (FLACSO), Centro de Investigaciones y Estudios Superiores en Antropología Social (CIESAS), Coosejo Latinoamericano de Ciencias Sociales (CLACSO), DeJusticia, Laboratorio Venezolano de Violencia, Consejo Latinoamericano de Derecho y Desarrollo, and the Laboratorio de Analise da Violencia. More recent initiatives include the Rede de Pesquisa Empírica em Direito (REED), and the Red Latinoamericana de Derecho y Sociedad (RELADES), and several other informal but similarly robust groups of like-minded scholars interested in exploring the life and impact of the law in its social, economic, and political context in Latin America and beyond.

This exposure to an intellectual environment that values and supports interdisciplinary and empirically-based research that looks at the impact of law on society and vice versa, has been pivotal in the formation of many Latin American law and society scholars. They have, in turn, influenced the development of the field in the region and have also contributed to infuse legal education with innovative approaches, methods, and content. We now turn to describe this ongoing phenomenon through the lens of another understudied group of legal actors: the law students.

Law Students as Legal Professionals

Following the Western European tradition from which most Latin American countries derive their legal systems, the law curricula offered by the universities have been the main vehicle for the training of future lawyers. The historical importance of legal education in the region is such that law schools were among the first university departments in the Spanish colonies of the Americas. That was certainly the case of the Universidad de Santo Domingo (Dominican Republic) created in 1538, the Universidad Nacional Mayor de San Marcos (Peru), and the Real y Pontificia Universidad (Mexico), both founded in 1551. The high importance given by the Spanish monarchy to law, its institutions, and professional actors as means to consolidate its power, and ensure the governability and adequate control of its colonies explains in part why legal education was promoted so early in the territories that we now call Latin America (Pérez-Perdomo 2006). The case of Brazil was very different because the Portuguese monarchy opted instead for limiting the availability of legal education to the seat of the crown in Portugal, which forced the Brazilian elite to travel overseas and enroll at the Universidade de Coimbra in order to become lawyers (Venáncio Filho 1977; Bastos 2000; Pérez-Perdomo 2006).

Since colonial times and throughout the first and a half-century that followed the independence and subsequent creation of most Latin American states, legal education in the region was reserved to the male offspring of the local elites. In the former period, universities commonly barred from their student body those whose blood was not pure or lacked high social status (Pérez-Perdomo 2006; Bergoglio 1993). Becoming a lawyer was not seen as a path toward the practice of a lucrative professional occupation like in the Anglo-American tradition, but rather as an intellectual platform for maintaining or advancing one's social, economic, and political status.

The modernization of the state, the expansion of educational opportunities beyond secondary education, the growth of urban life, and more recently the democratization of education, led to an upsurge in the interest of pursuing a formal legal education among those who had been otherwise precluded from doing so (Pérez-Perdomo 2006). The twentieth century witnessed both an expansion in the number of law schools, and a growth in the amount of law students throughout the region. The admission of women into law schools, and the legal profession in general, was particularly noteworthy during this period. By the end of the nineteenth century, for example, only a handful of women were enrolled in law schools, and became lawyers (Mendieta and Nuñez 1956; Roche 2001; Pérez-Perdomo 2006).

A century later, women comprised the majority of the law student population and also had a significant presence in the legal profession throughout the region (Pérez-Perdomo 2003, 2006; Gómez and Pérez-Perdomo 2017a). Even in countries such as Cuba, where the legal profession and legal education suffered an important setback during the first decades of the revolution, by the mid-nineties women accounted for more than 70 percent of the total law student population (Bermúdez 2001; Zatz 1994).

In terms of structure and scope, Latin American legal education has generally followed a uniform path. Law is offered as an undergraduate degree that admits those who have obtained a high school diploma. Many law schools also offer specializations, masters, doctorates, and other graduate programs, which have become very popular during the last few decades. For the most part, the law career takes five years to complete, and the main course offerings tend to cover both traditional areas of law such as criminal law, civil law, commercial law, administrative law, international law, and constitutional law. In addition, many law schools still offer courses in legal philosophy, political economy, and Roman law, as these subjects have been traditionally deemed very important elements of the intellectual foundation that legal education is supposed to offer, despite their little or no practical use in the professional life. The most innovative schools, however, have been moving away from the traditional curriculum by shifting their focus to more practice-oriented components similar to the ones commonly found in United States legal education, as I now turn to explain.

The growing economic interdependence between Latin America and the United States during the last several decades, and the increasingly common exposure of Latin American lawyers to the legal professions and legal education of the United States; has invigorated the debate about the need to modernize and transform legal education in the region (Pérez-Perdomo and Gómez 2008). It is important to clarify that not all innovative ideas regarding legal education reform have come from abroad (Gonzales Mantilla 2008), and that the region has produced some laudable initiatives in the realm of interdisciplinary studies, bilingual legal education, and transnational legal studies (Gómez 2017). Notwithstanding, the general perception throughout Latin America still seems to be that both the legal education and legal professions of the United States are a reference of modernity and pragmatism that ought to be emulated (Vides, Gómez, and Pérez Hurtado 2011; Gómez 2017). This is particularly salient in areas such as criminal law, criminal procedure, and alternative dispute resolution (mostly mediation or conciliation, and arbitration), in part due to the fact that those are precisely the focus of most recent judicial and legal reform agendas promoted throughout the region (Gómez 2007).

In the case of criminal law and procedure, the recent adoption by some Latin American countries of features typically present in the Anglo-American criminal justice system, such as the jury trial and plea bargaining, has piqued the comparative interest of Latin American policy-makers, government officials, law school authorities, and legal scholars. A similar interest has developed regarding the field of alternative dispute resolution, caused in part by the enactment of national mediation and arbitration statutes, the ratification of related treaties, and other policies geared toward the institutionalization of these mechanisms (Gómez 2007; Gómez and Pérez-Perdomo 2006). The impact of these developments on legal education is palpable.

First, an increasing number of Latin American law schools are incorporating courses and other innovative curricular initiatives that address the substantive and procedural changes brought by the aforementioned reform efforts. More and more, Latin American law curricula include redesigned substantive courses on criminal law and procedure focused on the adversarial nature of the new legislation. Courses on mediation, arbitration, negotiation, and other dispute resolution processes have also become staple components of many law curricula throughout the region (Gómez 2017; Pérez-Perdomo 2004). Other innovations include mock trials, moot court and arbitration competitions, and other programs designed to teach students the fundamentals of oral advocacy, persuasive writing, and client counseling skills (Gómez 2017).

Clinical legal education has also been revamped to provide law students opportunities to work on real cases of high social and political impact such as those involving human rights, consumer protection, environmental issues, discrimination and other civil right issues, and other complex matters (Londoño Toro 2008). Even though the general trend among Latin American law schools has been toward the strengthening of clinics devoted to public interest, and strategic or impact litigation; in some schools like the Diego Portales Law School in Chile, the offering has been expanded to other areas such as labor and employment, criminal justice, and family law (Gómez 2017).

Legal clinics have played an important role in fostering collaboration among law students across different universities both at the national and transnational levels. An example of the former is Colombia's Asociación Nacional de Clínicas y Asistencia Jurídica (ASOCLIVA). At the regional level, we find the Red Latinoamericana de Clínicas Jurídicas (RLCJ) founded in 1996, which current membership comprises 18 schools from Argentina, Chile, Colombia, Ecuador, Mexico, and Peru. RLCJ members have in turn, entered into cooperation agreements with several law schools from the United States including Harvard, Columbia, American, and George Washington University.

Predictably, legal scholars and law professors have been at the epicenter of the debate on innovations and reform of legal education in Latin America. Through academic writings, scholars have weighed in the pros and cons of adopting certain pedagogical strategies common in the Anglo-American legal education such as the *case method* (Wassermann 1999; Lazo González 2011), clinical and experiential learning (Abramovich 1999), and oral advocacy skills (Alvarez 2008). Regional dialogs, sometimes sponsored from abroad, have fostered opportunities to engage in in-depth analyzes of the successes and challenges of innovative policies and pedagogical strategies advanced by law schools around the region (Pérez-Perdomo and Rodriguez Torres 2006; Pérez-Perdomo and Gómez 2008). The findings regarding innovative practices are promising, but unfortunately, most of the positive changes have taken place in a limited number of elite law schools. These happen to be institutions whose leaders and key faculty members maintain affiliations or close connections to foreign universities and transnational academic networks, most commonly as a result of their own scholarly projects, teaching assignments abroad, and/or graduate studies pursued in foreign law schools.

A foreign graduate law degree obtained at a European or American university has been always seen as an important asset in Latin America. Until the mid-twentieth century, many prominent Latin American law professors had masters or doctoral law degrees from prominent European universities under their belts. Such credentials were signs of erudition, intellectual depth, and sometimes even helped them attain a higher status in their respective academic communities. In a more practical sense, the exposure to a foreign legal system, its legal education, scholars, and practitioners, helped Latin American lawyers improve their foreign language skills, expand their substantive knowledge and gain expertise in a particular field, and learn firsthand about another culture. The foreign experience was also the source of important professional connections that helped advance or even catapult the scholarly career of the members of the transnational networks that emerged as a result. Starting in the second half of the twentieth century, the United States became the most desired destination for Latin American lawyers who enrolled in the increasingly common Master of Laws (LLM) program. Such predilection has remained strong to the present (Vides, Gómez, and Pérez Hurtado 2011).

The offering of graduate programs to foreign lawyers by United States law schools has increased significantly during the last few decades. According to the latest data obtained from the American Bar Association (2017), there are more than 300 LLM programs in the country. The academic offering varies greatly, from those that simply offer a general exposure to American law to the ones specialized in a particular field such as intellectual property, international human rights, or corporate governance. Although most LLM programs initially attracted foreign lawyers who would habitually return to their countries of origin upon graduation; some chose to remain in the United States, become eligible to practice law in a state that allowed foreign lawyer (usually New York or California), and join the legal profession. During recent years, the amount of LLM candidates interested in remaining in the United States has grown, thus compelling American law schools to retool their academic offerings, and invest more resources in helping their foreign graduates succeed and become more competitive in an increasingly difficult American job market.

Among those Latin American lawyers who return to their countries, many resume their professional legal practice in the private sector or in government, while others join legal academia. Unfortunately, there are no available statistics that allows us to know with precision how many legal professionals fall in each category. What we know from anecdote, however, is that those in academia have become key players in the efforts to transform and innovate legal education in the region, taking advantage both of their foreign-acquired knowledge and professional networks (Gómez 2017).

Lawyers as Legal Professionals

As I mentioned earlier, aside from the judges, lawyers are the most widely studied category of Latin American legal professionals in the academic literature. A vast number of studies have focused on their history (Pérez-Perdomo 1981, 2004; Mirow 2004; Bravo Lira 1998; Coelho 1999; Cutolo 1964; González Echenique 1954; Lira González 1984; Uribe-Urán 2000), while a smaller subset have chosen to pay attention to analyze the occupation and roles of lawyers in contemporary society (Gómez 2010; Pérez-Perdomo 2001). Similar to what has occurred in the case of legal scholars, national studies about lawyers seem to abound, whereas those regional or comparative in scope are still the exception (Pérez-Perdomo 2015b, 2006; Gómez and Pérez-Perdomo 2017b). The academic literature on Latin American lawyers is also scattered throughout myriads of books, law journals, and other publications around the world.

Regarding the type of lawyers that occupy the attention of scholars, despite the undeniable importance of the Latin American lawyers who practice in the fields of criminal justice, human rights (Gómez 2010; Santamaría and Vecchioli 2008), and civil litigation (Bergoglio 2007) and their numeric superiority vis-à-vis those who practice in other fields, the literature devoted to them is scarce. Business lawyers, on the other hand, seem to have garnered much more attention from legal scholars (Pérez-Perdomo 2001; Gómez 2003; Dezalay and Garth 2002; Bergoglio 2007; Engelmann 2008; Gómez and Pérez-Perdomo 2017b, 2017c), industry analysts (Latin Lawyer 2016), and the general media. Furthermore, the most recent comparative literature on lawyers, mainly hailing from the Anglo-American and Western European countries, has also devoted a great deal of attention to the lawyers that operate in the corporate world (Hensler et al. forthcoming). After all, the business sector is one of the building blocks of the modern state, and a main contributor to the phenomenon that we call globalization.

In social and economic terms, Latin America – as the rest of the world – has been impacted by *globalization*. At the core of this phenomenon is the vanishing of commercial, cultural, and technological barriers, and the convergence toward *one world*, to paraphrase the famous commercial airline industry slogan. The idea of globalization is usually associated with progress and innovation. Little or no boundaries are generally viewed as beneficial for the development of trade and commerce, and for society in general. A similar claim has been made regarding culture, technology, and most other areas of human knowledge, including law. Ironically, the lifting of commercial, technological, and cultural barriers, and the opening of geographical borders has also made societies more vulnerable to certain *global* threats such as terrorism, drug trafficking, cyberattacks, the spread of diseases, and environmental disasters. This negative dimension of globalization has also made the legal system, and the lawyers in particular, more important than ever. Law is called upon to devise solutions to tackle these problems, and lawyers are the ones tasked to ponder, and carry out the responses on its behalf.

Many challenges are the same across the globe and warrant similar reactions from the state, but most official laws are still the product of each country's own legislative process, and a reflection of its local culture. Their scope of application also remains largely confined to the territory where those laws were enacted. The regulations of the legal profession, including the requirements to enroll in law school, become licensed to practice law or to be a judge, are also local. Notwithstanding, the mark of globalization is indelible and too important to ignore; even the most parochial legal systems have been affected by it, and are increasingly compelled to respond accordingly. We see some examples of such responses in the innovations taking place in Latin American legal education described earlier in this chapter. Unfortunately, the academic literature devoted to Latin American lawyers has done very little to explicate their role in this changing reality.

What we know, however, from some empirical evidence offered in recent research (Gómez and Pérez-Perdomo 2017b, 2017c; Bergoglio 2017; Conti 2017; de la Maza et al. 2017; Taboada 2017; Lamprea 2017; Meneses and Caballero 2017; González 2017; Gómez 2017) is that the demands of a globalized and multifaceted environment have forced Latin American lawyers to acquire certain skills not necessarily offered by traditional law schools, such as learning other languages, become versed on dispute resolution techniques such as mediation and arbitration, and familiarizing themselves with foreign and comparative legal institutions such as punitive damages, strict liability, and procedural mechanisms for obtaining evidence abroad. Globalization has also affected how lawyers organize themselves (for example, through law firms, professional service networks, or other organizational forms), how their profession is governed (for example, by state organs, bar associations, and voluntary associations), and how they relate to other professional legal actors, to the legal system, and to society in general.

Conclusions

A proper assessment of the status of Latin American legal professionals merits much more than the pages devoted to this chapter, which have only scratched the surface. The landscape of professional legal actors is vast and deep, and in dire need of more law and society research that helps explain the past, understand the present, and anticipate trends toward the future. More research could contribute to better understanding the changing nature and social structure of legal professionals in the region, their internal dynamics, and relationship with other social groups. As mentioned earlier, lawyers and judges are the two most widely studied categories of professional legal actors in the region, but there is still more to be explored about them. So far, the leading literature on lawyers and judges in Latin America has primarily focused on elite groups such as "Big Law" or corporate lawyers, supreme court judges, and other highly visible members of the profession. The choice to study them is understandable, but perhaps it is time to expand and deepen the research agenda toward lesser-known groups of legal practitioners, their interaction with their clients, and other social groups.

Small law firm lawyers, solo practitioners, and lower court judges are key components of the profession, and their impact is important, too. As Heinz et al. (2005) showed through a rich and contextualized study of urban lawyers from Chicago, there are valuable lessons to learn from looking at the social stratification of lawyers, their professional autonomy, and integration with other social groups. Something similar could be said about judges.

The need to deepen the study of Latin American legal scholars is also warranted, and perhaps more urgent than expanding the research on lawyers or judges. We still know very little about legal scholars in Latin America both as a social group vis-à-vis society at large, and internally in terms of their stratification, career paths, and interaction with their peers. Not all research, however, should be focused on who they are and how they relate with other groups, but should also investigate what they do and what impact their actions have on other legal professionals.

Finally, the question of impact is less apparent when we look at law students, whose main role has been that of receivers instead of contributors. The traditional view is that students are merely recipients of specialized knowledge and nothing else. If we look more carefully, however, students are also important contributors to the development of the legal profession, and are instrumental in helping disseminate the values of the legal system to the rest of society. The increased focus of contemporary legal education on practical skills and hands-on learning has allowed law students to interact directly with other legal actors, clients, and the rest of society, and therefore contribute to shaping the profession. Legal clinics and similar initiatives are at the core of this phenomenon. Fortunately, for the field of law and society, the interest in studying Latin American legal professionals is moving in the right direction. A thorough exploration of this field is very important not only for understanding the current state of Latin American professional legal actors and the challenges they face, but even more so, to help envisage the future of the legal profession in the region.

References

Abramovich, Víctor E. 1999. *La Enseñanza del Derecho en las Clínicas Legales de Interés Público*, Cuaderno de Análisis Jurídico, Ed. Universidad Diego Portales, Santiago.

Alvarez, Graciela E. 2008. La Enseñanza del Discurso Jurídico Oral y Escrito en la Carrera de Abogacía, 6(11) *Revista Sobre Enseñanza del Derecho*, p. 1667.

Azuela, Antonio and Miguel Angel Cancino. 2014. *Jueces y Conflictos Urbanos en América Latina*, Editorial Ink, Mexico.

Bastos, Aurélio Wander. 2000. *O Ensino Jurídico No Brasil*. Second edition. Lumen Juris, Río de Janeiro.

Bergoglio, Maria Inés. 2017. Law firms in Argentina: challenges and responses to a crisis in Latin America and Spain: 1990–2015, in M. Gómez and R. Pérez-Perdomo (eds.), *Big Law in Latin America and Spain: Globalization and Adjustments in the Provision of High-End Legal Services*. Palgrave Macmillan, Basingstoke.

Bergoglio, Maria Inés. 2009. Diversidad y Desigualdad en la Profesión Jurídica: Consecuencias sobre el papel del Derecho en América Latina, *Revista Vía Iuris*, p. 10.

Bergoglio, Maria Inés. 2007. El Papel del Abogado Litigante, in Luis Pásara (ed.) *El Papel de los Actores en la Justicia Latinoamericana*, pp. 57–86.

Bergoglio, María Inés. 1993. Castas y estamentos en Córdoba, 3 *Revista de la Universidad Blas Pascal*.

Bermúdez, Carlos M. 2001. *Studying Law in Cuba: a Law Student's Perspective*. Unpublished manuscript.

Bravo Lira, Bernardino. 1998. Estudios jurídicos y estado modernizador: La cultura de abogados en Chile 1758–1998, 25, *Revista Chilena de Derecho*, Santiago, pp. 641–655.

Coates, Benjamin Allen. 2016. *Legalist Empire: International Law and American Foreign Relations in the Early Twentieth Century*, Oxford University Press, Oxford.

Coelho, Edmundo Campos. 1999. *As Profissões Imperiais: Medicina, Engenharia e Advocacia No Rio de Janeiro, 1822–1930*, Record, Río de Janeiro.

Cohen, Amy B. 2004. The dangers of the ivory tower: the obligation of law professors to engage in the practice of law, 50 *Loyola Law Review*, p. 623.

Conti Craveiro, Mariana. 2017. Big Law in Brazil: rise and current challenges, in M. Gómez and R. Pérez-Perdomo (eds.) *Big Law in Latin America and Spain: Globalization and Adjustments in the Provision of High-End Legal Services*, Palgrave Macmillan, Basingstoke.

Cutolo, Vicente Osvaldo. 1964. El primer abogado criollo que actuó en Buenos Aires, 3 *Revista Chilena de Historia del Derecho*, Santiago.

Dakolias, Maria. 1996. *The Judicial Sector in Latin America and the Caribbean,* World Bank Technical Paper 319, The World Bank, Washington, DC.

Dezalay, Yves and Bryant Garth, 2002. *The Internationalization of Palace Wars: Lawyers, Economists, and the Contest to Transform Latin American States*, University of Chicago Press, Chicago.

De la Maza, Iñigo Rafael Mery and Juan Enrique Vargas. 2017. Big law in Chile: a glance at the law firms, in M. Gómez and R. Pérez-Perdomo (eds.) *Big Law in Latin America and Spain: Globalization and Adjustments in the Provision of High-End Legal Services*, Palgrave Macmillan, Basingstoke.

Engelmann, Fabiano. 2008. *A Legitimação dos Juristas de Negócios no Brasil nas Décadas de 90 e 2000: Uma Análise Preliminar*, Colóquio Saber e Poder, UNICAMP, Sao Paolo.

Falcão, Joaquim. 1988. Lawyers in Brazil, in Richard L. Abel and Phillips Lewis (eds.) *Lawyers in Society: The Civil Law World*, University of California Press, Berkeley, CA.

Falcão, Joaquim. 1984. *Os Advogados: Ensino Jurídico e Mercado de Trabalho*, Fundação Joaquim Nabuco/ Ed. Massangana, Recife.

Fix-Fierro, Héctor. 2014. *Los Juristas Académicos del Instituto de Investigaciones Jurídicas de la UNAM y las Nuevas Instituciones Democráticas* Instituto de Investigaciónes Jurídicas, Mexico.

Fix-Fierro, Hector and Sergio López Ayllón. 2003. "Faraway, so close!" the rule of law and legal change in Mexico, 1970–2000, in Lawrence M. Friedman and Rogelio Pérez-Perdomo (eds.) *Legal Cultures in the Age of Globalization, Latin America and Latin Europe*, Stanford University Press, Stanford: 285–351.

Friedman, Lawrence M. 1986. The law and society movement, 38(3) *Stanford Law Review*, p. 763.

Friedman, Lawrence M., Rogelio Pérez-Perdomo, and Manuel A. Gómez (eds.) 2011. *Law in Many Societies: A Reader*. Stanford University Press.

García-Villegas, Mauricio. 2008. *Jueces sin Estado: La Justicia Colombiana en Zonas de Conflicto Armado*, Siglo del Hombre Editores, Bogotá.

Garth, Bryant. 2016. Brazil and the field of socio-legal studies: globalization, the hegemony of the US, the place of law, and elite reproduction, 3(1) *Revista de Estudos Empíricos em Direito*, p. 12.

Gómez, Manuel A. and Rogelio Pérez-Perdomo (eds.) 2017a. *Big Law in Latin America and Spain: Globalization and Adjustments in the Provision of High-End Legal Services*, Palgrave Macmillan, Basingstoke.

Gómez, Manuel A. and Rogelio Pérez-Perdomo. 2017b. Corporate lawyers and multinational corporations in Latin America and Spain: 1990–2015, in Manuel A. Gómez and Rogelio Pérez-Perdomo (eds.), *Big Law in Latin America and Spain: Globalization and Adjustments in the Provision of High-End Legal Services.*, Palgrave Macmillan, Basingstoke.

Gómez Manuel A. and Rogelio Pérez-Perdomo, 2017c. Big law in Venezuela: from globalization to revolution, in Manuel A. Gómez and Rogelio Pérez-Perdomo (eds.) *Big Law in Latin America and Spain: Globalization and Adjustments in the Provision of High-End Legal Services*, Palgrave Macmillan, Basingstoke.

Gómez, Manuel A. 2017. Innovaciones en la educación jurídica latinoamericana y políticas públicas en tiempos de globalización, in *La Enseñanza del Derecho como Política Pública*, Editorial Palestra, Lima.

Gómez, Manuel A. 2010. Political activism and the practice of law in Venezuela, in J. Couso, A. Huneeus and R. Sieder (eds.) *Cultures of Legality: Judicialization and Political Activism in Latin America*, Cambridge University Press, Cambridge and New York: 182–206.

Gómez, Manuel A. and Rogelio Pérez-Perdomo. 2006. Justicias alternativas en Venezuela, 7 *Reforma Judicial*, Universidad Nacional Autónoma de México, Mexico: pp. 161–90.

Gómez, Manuel A. 2003. Los abogados de negocios en Venezuela, *125 Revista de la Facultad de Ciencias Jurídicas y Políticas*, Universidad Central de Venezuela, Caracas: 23–50.

Gonçalves, João Felipe. 2000. *Rui Barbosa. Pondo as Idéias no Lugar*, Editora FGV, Sao Paolo.

González Echenique, Javier. 1954. *Los Estudios Jurídicos y la Abogacía en el Reino de Chile*. Imprenta Universitaria, Santiago.

Gonzales Mantilla, Gorki. 2017. Lawyers and globalization in Peru (1990–2014), in M. Gómez and R. Pérez-Perdomo (eds.) *Big Law in Latin America and Spain: Globalization and Adjustments in the Provision of High-End Legal Services*, Palgrave Macmillan, Basingstoke.

Gonzales Mantilla, Gorki. 2008. *La Enseñanza del Derecho o los Molinos de Viento: Cambio, Resistencias y Continuidades*. Colección Derecho PUCP Monografías No. 6, Palestra, Lima, Peru.

González, Patricio Lazo. 2011. Formación jurídica, competencias y métodos de enseñanza: premisas, 17(1) *Revista Ius et Praxis*, p. 249.

Hammergren, Linn. 2007. *Envisioning Reform: Improving Judicial Performance in Latin America*, Penn State Press, Pennsylvania.

Hartmann Arboleda, Mildred. 2007. Apuntes sobre las experiencias de reforma judicial en América Latina, in Klaus Bodemer and Fernando Carrillo Flórez (eds.) *Gobernabilidad y Reforma Política en América Latina y Europea*, GIGA, BID, REDGOB, Plural editores, La Paz: 241–54.

Heinz, John P., Robert L. Nelson, Rebecca L. Sandefur, and Edward O. Laumann. 2005. *Urban Lawyers: The New Social Structure of the Bar*, University of Chicago Press, Chicago.

Helmke, Gretchen and Julio Ríos-Figueroa. 2011. *Courts in Latin America*, Cambridge University Press, Cambridge and New York.

Hensler, Deborah R., Patrick Hanlon, Molly Selvin, Manuel A. Gómez and Rogelio Pérez-Perdomo. Forthcoming. *Reconstructing Big Law*. Edward Elgar, Gloucestershire.

Hilbink, Lisa. 2015. *Jueces y Política en Democracia y Dictadura: Lecciones desde Chile*, FLACSO, Santiago,

Jaksic, Iván. 2001, *Andrés Bello: Scholarship and Nation-Building in Nineteenth-Century Latin America*, Cambridge University Press Cambridge and New York.

Latin Lawyer 250. 2016. *Latin America's Leading Business Law Firms*.

Lamprea, Everaldo. 2017. The rise of big law in Colombia, in Manuel A. Gómez and Rogelio Pérez-Perdomo (eds.), *Big Law in Latin America and Spain: Globalization and Adjustments in the Provision of High-End Legal Services*. Palgrave Macmillan, Basingstoke.

Lira González, Andrés. 1984. Abogados, tinterillos y huizacheros en el México del Siglo XIX, in *Memoria del III Congreso de Historia del Derecho Mexicano*, UNAM, Mexico.

Mendieta y Núñez, Lucio. 1956. *Historia de la Facultad de Derecho*. Universidad Nacional Autónoma de México, México.

Meneses, Rodrigo and José Antonio Caballero. 2017. Global and traditional: a profile of corporate lawyers in Mexico, in Manuel A. Gómez and Rogelio Pérez-Perdomo (eds.), *Big Law in Latin America and Spain: Globalization and Adjustments in the Provision of High-End Legal Services.*, Palgrave Macmillan, Basingstoke.

Mirow, Matthew C. 2004. *Latin American Law: A History of Private Law and Institutions in Spanish America*, University of Texas Press, Austin.

Obregón, Liliana. 2017. The third world judges: neutrality, bias or activism at the Permanent Court of International Justice and International Court of Justice, in William A. Schabas and Shannonbrooke Murphy (eds.), *Research Handbook on International Courts and Tribunals*, Edward Elgar, Camberley: 81–200.

Pérez-Perdomo, Rogelio. 2015a. Las transformaciones de la producción y divulgación del conocimiento jurídico en la Venezuela de la segunda mitad del siglo XX, in Salvador A. Millaleo Hernández, Juan Carlos Oyanedel, Daniel Palacios Olmedo and Hugo Rojas (eds.), *Sociología del Derecho en Chile: Libro Homenaje a Edmundo Fuenzalida*, Ediciones Universidad Alberto Hurtado, Santiago: 49–72.

Pérez-Perdomo, Rogelio. 2015b. Las revistas jurídicas Venezolanas en tiempos de revolución (2000–2013), 142 *Boletín Mexicano de Derecho Comparado*: 223–74.

Pérez-Perdomo, Rogelio. 2014. *Los Juristas Académicos de Venezuela: Historia Institucional y Biografía Colectiva*, Universidad Metropolitana, Caracas.

Pérez-Perdomo, Rogelio. 2009. A plea for the social study of legal scholars: The case of XIX century Venezuela, *Sociología del Diritto* XXXVI: 67–92.

Pérez-Perdomo, Rogelio and Manuel A. Gómez. 2008, Innovaciones en la educación jurídica de América Latina, derecho y democracia II, 15 *Cuadernos Unimetanos*, Universidad Metropolitana, Caracas.

Pérez-Perdomo, Rogelio and Julia Rodriguez Torres. 2006, *La Formación Jurídica en América Latina: Tensiones e Innovaciones en Tiempos de la Globalización*, Universidad Externado de Colombia, Bogota.

Pérez-Perdomo, Rogelio. 2006. *Latin American Lawyers: A Historical Introduction*, Stanford University Press, Stanford.

Pérez-Perdomo, Rogelio. 2003. Venezuela, 1958–1999: the legal system in an impaired democracy, in Lawrence M. Friedman and Rogelio Pérez-Perdomo (eds.) *Legal Cultures in the Age of Globalization, Latin America and Latin Europe*, Stanford University Press, Stanford: 414–78.

Pérez-Perdomo, Rogelio. 2001. Oil lawyers and the globalization of Venezuelan oil business, in *Rules and Networks: The Legal Culture of Global Business Transactions*, Hart, Oxford.

Roche, Carmen Luisa. 2001. *The Feminization of the Legal Profession in Venezuela: It's Meaning for the Profession and for Women Lawyers*. Paper presented at the LSA-RCSL Joint International Meeting in Budapest. Unpublished manuscript.

Rodríguez-Garavito, César, (ed.) 2014. *Law and Society in Latin America: A New Map*, Routledge, New York.

Rodríguez-Garavito, César. 2010. Beyond the courtroom: the impact of judicial activism in socioeconomic rights in Latin America, 89 *Texas Law Review*, p. 1669.

Santamaría, Angela and Virginia Vecchioli (eds.). 2008. *Derechos Humanos en América Latina: Mundialización y Circulación Internacional del Conocimiento Experto Jurídico*, Universidad del Rosario, Bogota.

Silbey, Susan S. 2002. Law and society movement, in Herbert M. Kritzer (ed.) *Legal Systems of the World: A Political, Social and Cultural Encyclopedia*, v. II: E-L, ABC CLIO, Santa Barbara: 860–63.

Taboada, Carlos. 2017. Big law in Central America and the Dominican Republic: growth strategies in small economies, in Manuel A. Gómez and Rogelio Pérez-Perdomo (eds.), *Big Law in Latin America and Spain: Globalization and Adjustments in the Provision of High-End Legal Services*, Palgrave Macmillan, Basingstoke.

Trubek, David M. 1990. Back to the future: the short, happy life of the law and society movement, 18(1) *Florida State University Law Review*, p. 4.

Uribe-Urán, Victor. 2000. *Honorable Lives. Lawyers, Family and Politics in Colombia, 1870–1850*. University of Pittsburg Press, Pittsburg.

Venáncio Filho, Alberto. 1977. *Das Arcadas ao Bachalerismo: 150 de Ensio Jurídico No Brasil*. Perspectiva, São Paulo.

Vides, Marta, Manuel A. Gómez and Luis F. Pérez Hurtado. 2011. The American way: los abogados latinoamericanos como estudiantes de maestría en los estados Unidos de América, 130 *Boletín Mexicano de Derecho Comparado*, p. 351.

Wassermann, Selma. 1999. *El Estudio de Casos como Método de Enseñanza*, Amorrotu Editores, Buenos Aires.

Zatz, Marjorie S. 1994. *Producing Legality: Law and Socialism in Cuba*. Routledge, New York.

19

LEGAL INSTITUTIONS AS ARENAS FOR PROMOTING HUMAN RIGHTS

Karina Ansolabehere

Introduction: Legal Institutions as Arenas for Promoting Human Rights

There is nothing new in the fact that legal institutions are arenas in which important disputes are resolved. Numerous studies have pointed to the emergence of domestic judiciaries as powerful political actors (Shapiro and Stone Sweet 2002; Tate and Vallinder 1997; Hirschl 2009; Kapiszewski, Silverstein, and Kagan 2013; Sieder et al. 2005). The judicialization[1] of human rights protection and their recognition in the judicial arena are manifestations of this tendency. Latin America has not been an exception in this regard. The purpose of this chapter is to map the research agendas that derive from this judicial process.

The study of domestic judicial powers as arenas for promoting and protectiong human rights has three different research agendas that we discuss below: enforcement of the law and strengthening international human rights institutions (specifically the Inter-American System); legal responsibility for human rights violations; and social justice for disadvantaged groups.

This judicialization strategy has been of such importance that the judiciary and quasi-judiciary institutions in charge of resolving conflicts in this regard have increased in number.[2] We shall not be concerned here with all of these institutions, simply those of domestic courts. We consider these to merit special attention because that is where most of the legal disputes in human rights matters occur.

In many Latin American countries, judicialization of human rights has occurred frequently (Helmke and Ríos-Figueroa 2011; González Ocantos 2016; Ansolabehere Sesti 2014).[3] This phenomenon cannot be decontextualized from the diverse events that the region experienced and that altered expectations and the functions of the judicial powers.

The following is a list of topics that researchers in this field have emphasized: the democratization process (and reversals thereof); market-friendly structural reforms implemented together with economic liberalization (and efforts to develop post-Washington Consensus policies); and, last but definitely not least, constitutional changes that include comprehensive rights declarations and changing legal opinions characterized by the growing appreciation that the constitution is a binding legal instrument (see Pou and Gargarella in this volume). These changes have led the courts to take on a proactive role as constitutional interpreters.

Accordingly, a human rights movement is developing and consolidating (López Pacheco 2015; Saldivia 2003) whose foremost strategies include litigation.

Nonetheless, it is important to stress that Latin America is not a uniform area. There are 17 different countries in the region, excluding the Caribbean, and when agendas are contested different outcomes ensue; these agendas also express the dynamics within certain countries better than in others. Yet in an effort to review the innovative studies on law and society in the region, the aspects highlighted here are illustrative of new trends in the field.

Although these three research agendas coincide on the importance of legal institutions, they each have distinguishing traits. The agenda dealing with the uptake of international human rights treaties and the importance of the Inter-American System cannot be considered separately from the concern over the enforcement of international law (see Alexandra Huneeus's chapter in this volume). The agenda dealing with the legal responsibility for human rights violations in authoritarian regimes or post-armed conflict contexts is linked to how trials in search of truth, justice, and reparations for human rights violations have fared (see the chapter by Martínez Barahona and Gutiérrez in this volume.) Last, the social justice agenda that seeks legal protection for social rights is connected to resistance movements struggling against neoliberal reforms in the region and in favor of reducing disadvantaged groups' asymmetrical share of power.

The following analysis highlights the traits of each agenda and their intersections. We seek to shed light on the coincidence of some questions posed by two of the classic topics from the research agenda of the law and society movement: the gap between law in the books and law in practice and the relationship between law and social change (Abel 2010). We highlight the intersection between the agenda of enforcement of international human rights law and the other two agendas, and a quasi-convergence between the legal responsibility agenda and the social justice agenda. We also analyze the studies' methodological peculiarities and recommend exploring research designs that incorporate mixed methods. Last, we discuss the fact that the analysis of judicial powers as arenas has overlooked the study of the consequences that this dynamic has had in the organization of the judicial branch and the way it reaches decisions. The latter is proposed here as an emerging research topic in this field, since in Latin America the study of the judicial branch's influence in human right protection has been emphasized, sidelining to an extent an exploration of how exercising these functions has impacted the judicial structure itself.

The questions to be answered in this chapter are: What are the topics and dilemmas that have caught the attention of researchers from/of Latin America? What are their methodologies and what countries have they covered? What pending issues remain? For this purpose, we have structured the chapter as follows: First, we undertake a review of the literature pertinent to each of the agendas. Second, we analyze the traits shared among the agendas and their methodological peculiarities. Lastly, we discuss the conclusions and identify future lines of research.

In the following sections we will expand on the principal contributions of these agendas by considering three dimensions: First, how the roles of the judicial powers are conceived; second, the conditions of the judiciary as an emerging arena; and third, an analysis of the consequences brought about by new judicial roles.

The Judicial Powers as Arenas for Enforcement of International Human Rights Law

If the use of judicial powers as an arena to enforce international human rights law is problematized, it cannot be uncoupled from the growing dissemination of these in the Latin American region and the increasing importance of the Inter-American Human Rights System. Latin America is characterized by traditionally subscribing to international human rights treaties, by constitutional processes that follow transitions to democracy that incorporate international treaties as sources of law that are equivalent to the constitution (see Pou's chapter in this volume). Latin America has also developed a regional set of rules on human rights that has become especially important in the past two decades. Notwithstanding this regional tendency, we find a mosaic of circumstances among the countries, which we will not delve into here for lack of space. For example, according to information systematized in the database on Institutionalization and Enjoyment of Human Rights in Latin American Democracies located at FLACSO-Mexico, in 2011, of the 17 countries in the region (excluding the Caribbean), 11 constitutionally recognize and give constitutional rank to international human rights treaties. Nicaragua, Peru, El Salvador, and Paraguay constitutionally recognize international human rights treaties and give it a hierarchy below that of the constitution. Panama and Uruguay make no mention in their constitutions of the hierarchy of international human rights treaties within the countries' legal system.

Given these particularities, the diffusion of international human rights law, focused mainly on the relationship between the Inter-American System and domestic courts, in light of how important the Inter-American Human Rights System has become in the past two decades in most countries of the region. This growing importance is evident in the increase in the number of cases litigated, the breath of topics covered (Engstrom and Hurrell 2013), and the efforts to generate a conventionality control system that involves the different levels of justice. This means bringing together concerns related to international relations, specifically the enforcement of treaties and the strengthening of international institutions. Constitutionalism implies both the internationalization of constitutional law and the constitutionalization of international law (Nunes 2010). Lastly, we review the studies on legal policy that focus on factors that facilitate understanding of the changes in judicial powers, insofar as enforcement of international law is strengthened through its use as a source for domestic law.

In keeping with the outline presented in the previous section, first we review the conditions that made it possible for the judicial powers in Latin America to become an arena for airing disputes dealing with enforcement of international human rights law and, second, we examine the consequences arising from transforming the judiciary into an arena for this agenda.

Conditions That Made it Possible to Establish the Arena: The Receptiveness of International Human Rights Law by Domestic Judicial Powers

The receptiveness of international human rights law into the decision-making mechanisms of domestic judicial powers involves these legal instruments as sources of domestic law and their relation to observance of international treaties. Although not presented in the literature as such, this encompasses addressing the problem of the gap between the law in the books and the exercise of rights in this particular area, which is not limited to Latin America, but which has received special attention in the region.

Indeed, we should recall that, over the past four decades, countries in Latin America have implemented numerous constitutional changes, a consequence of which was the constitutionalization of a comprehensive catalog of rights (Ugalde and Ansolabehere 2012). In many cases, this led to granting constitutional hierarchy to international human rights treaties. These changes to the legal framework created new legal opportunities (Sikkink 2008), both for legal practitioners and the human rights movement.

The studies that demonstrated that judicial powers could be arenas for enforcing international human rights law sought to answer the following question: *What factors and processes helped domestic judicial powers acquire importance in implementing international human rights treaties and strengthen relationships with the Inter-American Court?*

The answers refer to two types of approaches. One emphasizes ideational factors, i.e., changes in the legal and professional thought of judges and members of the judiciary; another stresses mobilization of international human rights law by domestic and transnational actors. Both address the concerns that arise in law and society studies in general: courts, judges, judging, and legal mobilization.

According to the first approach, the answer lies in the changes in legal thought (Nunes 2010), judges' professional ideology (Hilbink 2006), and incorporation of new legal tools into domestic law (Salazar 2012). The new legal and professional thought influenced by the constitutionalization of the legal framework operates as adequate grounding for receptiveness of international human rights law as a relevant source for domestic law.[4]

For the approach that stresses transnational and domestic mobilization, the key factor for understanding the establishment of a legal arena is the use of international law by the different actors who can access the legal arena, among others, to enforce rights that have been promulgated internationally (Keck and Sikkink 1998).

Summarizing, the studies reviewed here reveal how changes in legal and professional thought and transnational and domestic mobilization modified the structure of legal opportunities (Sikkink 2005), both for social movements and for judges themselves, enabling the legal space to become an arena for disputes having to do with the receptivity of international human rights law.

The Consequences of Judicial Powers Becoming Arenas for Enforcement of International Human Rights Law

Another concern arising from the enforcement of international human rights law are the consequences of having the judicial powers as arenas. The question posed by the studies that articulate this concern is: What happens when the conditions exist such that domestic judicial powers can enforce international law?

Once again, ideational factors facilitate the use of international human rights law, yet other types of factors intervene. For example, the political interests of the executive branch, the building of alliances for enforcement of international law, and relations between the Inter-American Court of Human Rights and domestic courts. The relationship between national courts and the Inter-American System of Human Rights, and specifically the Inter-American Court, have been at the center of discussion.

The studies that stress the ideational factors have focused on judges' use of international law as a new source of law. Incorporation of these sources is viewed as a means to achieve other objectives, i.e., seeking justice for past violations, etc. The use of international human rights law takes on different connotations. On the one hand, it is viewed as a technical tool transferred to judges by organizations specializing in strategic litigation of human rights in order to try cases of complex violations. This is addressed by Ezequiel González Ocantos in his study on the processes that sued for accountability for human rights violations in Peru and Argentina (González Ocantos 2014). From another viewpoint, this is understood as a professional ideology that opens the door for the exercise of positive judicial independence (Hilbink 2012) by local judicial powers, as discussed by Lisa Hilbink and Javier Couso in the case of Chile (Couso and Hilbink 2011). A third perspective stresses that new legal thought regarding law sources does not necessarily translate immediately into reducing the levels of impunity of human rights violations, as Karina Ansolabehere (2016) analyzes in the case of Mexico.

The second approach is clearly focused on the extent to which domestic judicial powers enforce sentences handed down by the Inter-American Court of Human Rights (Couso 2013),

(Kapiszewski and Taylor 2013) (Ansolabehere Sesti 2014). We find two views on this matter. One that prioritizes domestic political factors, specifically the interests of the executive branch, and another that stresses the relationship between the Inter-American Court and domestic courts.

In the first approach, the extent to which judgments are enforced is considered to be a function of the interests of the executive branch and its ability to build pro-human rights alliances with the legislative and judicial branches (Hillebrecht 2014). Although here the interests of the executive branch have precedence, the approach recognizes the importance of the legislative and judicial branches for enforcing sentences handed down by the regional tribunal. An example of these degrees of autonomy is the way the Mexican Supreme Court handled decisions after Mexico received a condemnatory sentence from the Inter-American Human Rights Court in the case of Radilla Pacheco,[5] which provoked tension with the executive branch (Corte Interamericana de Derechos Humanos 2010a).

The second perspective places less importance on the executive branch and finds that the analytic key to enforcement lies in the relationship between the Inter-American Court and domestic courts, which then involves the study of relationships among courts (Haire 2010). As the influence of the Inter-American Court on Human Rights increases in the region (Popovski et al. 2008) and the topics it hears vary, its influence on domestic courts becomes a focus of interest (Basch et al. 2010.) Alexandra Huneeus's insight (Huneeus 2011) was able to position the topic, i.e., the national agencies that most failed to enforce sentences of the Inter-American Court of Human Rights are the judicial powers. She argues that enforcing sentences handed down by international tribunals and the inclusion of jurisprudence is a function of the type of relationship that the Inter-American Court establishes with domestic courts. Thus, the Inter-American Court needs to create support among domestic judicial powers by establishing a dialog with them.

Furthermore, while acknowledging the enforcement problems that exist within domestic courts, another perspective emphasizes the balance between the ability to audit and the need for legitimacy of the Inter-American Court vis-à-vis the domestic courts (Staton and Romero 2011), as measured by the clarity of sentences.

Lastly, in accordance with the reflection on the characteristics of relationships among the courts, a new question emerges that shifts the focus from the Inter-American Court to domestic courts: How do local courts adapt the overall standards of Inter-American criteria to local contexts? The response presumes the existence of a space in which emphasis is placed on legal studies that undertake a solid empirical analysis. Issues at the center of the debate (Contesse 2013; Von Bogdandy 2015) are: identifying how and to what extent criteria emanating from the Inter-American Court of Human Rights are used by local courts (Serrano García 2017); and the discussions regarding the pertinence, or lack thereof, of an adequate degree of discretion among local courts vis-à-vis those same criteria. Foreseeably, this topic will create a productive space in which to continue studies with an emphasis on law and society that account for the particularities of this relationship and its implications for the Inter-American System.

As we can see, this set of papers is far-reaching. However, a more exhaustive empirical analysis is missing regarding the different types of relationships established between the Inter-American Court of Human Rights and local courts, especially an analysis that delves into the factors that could lead to a more consistent use of the Inter-American criteria by domestic tribunals.

Legal Institutions and Accountability for Human Rights Violations

Latin America has received special attention in studies regarding legal responsibility for human rights violations. This region has shown the greatest progress in bringing these violations to trial. According to figures compiled by Payne, Lessa, and Pereira (Payne et al. 2015), of all the trials held throughout the world where a guilty verdict was reached, 50 percent were in Latin America. This fact undoubtedly has to do with the events that various Latin American countries faced, such as the transition to democracy, armed conflict, subsequent peace processes, the increasing role of the judicial powers, the strengthening of human rights movements, international defense networks, etc.

In this context, the domestic judicial powers become a privileged arena insofar as the trials were, and are, an important way to establish legal responsibilities for human rights violations. Given the dynamic conditions in which the transitional and post-conflict justice trials occurred, studies in this area have articulated several concerns.

First, we present the particularities of the studies that revealed how the arena was established; we also discuss the studies that focus their analysis on the factors that made it possible for human rights violation trials to be held and persist over time. Second, the analysis focusses on the consequences of the judicialization of human rights violations, the effects of these trials, and the dilemmas faced by the judicial powers in an era of legal responsibility for human rights violations.

Conditions for Establishing the Arena: Why Were Trials Possible?

It is not a simple task to bring serious human violations to trial and obtain a verdict. Powerful actors are involved, so bringing serious human rights violations to trial involves a level of complexity that surpasses ordinary trials (Roht-Arriaza 2006). Yet, in several Latin American countries, during the initial years of the transition process, not only were there trials that penalized the guilty parties (both state and private agents, such as corporations in the latter case), and brought reparations for damages to the victims, such trials have been sustained over decades (Payne and Pereira 2016).

This momentum sustained over time has even been given a name, i.e., "post-transitional justice mechanisms." It confirmed that domestic judicial powers were indeed a key arena for fighting against impunity for human rights violations, especially when judicial powers achieved acceptable levels of independence (see González-Bertomeu's chapter in this volume.) In this context, it is indeed relevant to ask about the conditions that made it possible for these trials to be held and sustained. The case of Argentina is revealing. The judicialization of human rights violations occurred during the military dictatorship has been maintained for over three decades, during which time different stages can be identified in terms of the support given by the executive or legislative branches to these trials. During this period, the judicial arena often worked as an escape valve (Smulovitz 2013). This is similar to what is occurring in Guatemala even when the judicial arena does not enjoy a high degree of independence vis-à-vis the political powers and the country's elites, a situation that contrasts with that of Peru (Benítez Jiménez 2017). Interestingly, as an example, in 2016 the Journal of Genocide Research published several articles that analyze the genocide in Guatemala and its implications (VVAA 2016).

An explanation of what made these trials possible is attributed to several extrajudicial and judicial conditions. The more important among the former are the executive branch's political will (Couso 2005), the possibility of overturning amnesties (Roht-Arriaza 2014), the nature of the transition to democracy (Dutrénit and Varela 2010), and civil society's ability to legally mobilize (Collins 2010; Lessa 2013). Many of these explanations overlap.

In terms of the judicial or legal features, several conditions stand out. These cover a wide range of factors, including the level of judicial independence (Skaar 2011); the possibility for victims to participate in a criminal trial through figures such as private prosecutors; the roll of the public prosecutor's office in investigating crimes against humanity (Michel and Sikkink 2012); the available legal framework, specifically provisions contained in human rights treaties in terms of holding individuals accountable for human rights violations (Dancy and Sikkink 2012); the learning curves of judges regarding the tools necessary to hold these types of trials (González Ocantos 2014); the influence of international pressure on judges, as seen in Chile following the application of universal jurisdiction to Pinochet (Huneeus 2010); and a new generation of judges who bring changes to the legal ideology and favor a proactive attitude in human rights cases (Couso and Hilbink 2011).

As we can see, the multiple political, social, and legal factors are considered requisites for a trial to take place. Nonetheless, given the evidence that these factors are valid but fragmentary, we need to find options that integrate them in order to offer more in-depth responses. This attempt to fashion an integral response arose with studies that refer to the so-called "era of accountability in human rights" and seek to explain the factors that made the era possible. In this regard, two views were articulated: one that attributes accountability to the presence of a "cascade of justice," while the other points to strategies that aim to "encircle" impunity.

The first viewpoint maintains that we are in a period of a "cascade of justice" (in which the trials in Latin America have been key) (Sikkink 2011). Less tolerance for human rights violations is attributed to greater support for a social norm that rejects impunity. The cascade of justice occurs by socializing an external norm opposed to impunity, which is shared by different actors, among them judiciaries. At the other extreme, the viewpoint that stresses encircling impunity holds that the increase in legal responsibility for human rights violations is not related to the socialization of a norm opposed to impunity, given that we can see favorable results from accountability even when amnesty laws are in force or partially in force (Payne et al. 2015). Instead, this view identifies the presence of four factors that "encircle" impunity, in spite of the existence of amnesty decrees: judicial leadership, demands made by civil society, international pressure, and the absence of actors with veto (Payne et al. 2015).

Beyond the interest created by the study of conditions that make it possible for trials of human rights violations that occurred during authoritarian governments or armed conflicts to go forward, less attention has been paid to impunity in the face of multiple types of human rights violations that take place continually in the region. An exception to this is the pioneering work of Daniel Brinks regarding police violence in Brazil, Argentina, and Uruguay (Brinks 2007). Given the increase in violence in the region, the analysis of conditions that help overcome impunity linked to these human rights violations should be a fruitful future research line.

Beyond the concerns regarding the holding of trials, a question surfaces about the consequences that this process entails and the tensions that must be dealt with.

Consequences of the Arena: The Effects of Legal Responsibility Trials in Human Rights Matters

The first question to be addressed has to do with the effects of trials to promote democracy and human rights. The pioneering initiatives in this regard seek to systematize information on a worldwide scale in order to overcome a casuistic approach and identify overall regularities. This is done by compiling databases that document trials, and other mechanisms, and relate them to the level of consolidation of democracy and respect for human rights. Results have been positive and Latin America is often cited. These methods show that in Latin America holding trials is related to lower human rights violations (Sikkink and Walling 2007). Further, they also show that when trials are combined with other mechanisms of transitional justice, there are positive gains in terms of consolidating democracy (Olsen et al. 2010).

The other discussion regarding the effects of the accountability era revolves around the degree of adequate punishment, i.e., there is a tension between seeking the maximum possible punishment or allowing controlled impunity.

This tension arises in domestic courts when punishments for guilty parties need to be reconciled with different standards. For example, the Inter-American Court of Human Rights states that, amnesties are not an obstacle for bringing to trial those accused of human rights violations and crimes against humanity. There is a local standard, however, whereby domestic laws reduce sentences in order to achieve peace or a certain political stability, thus creating conditions of controlled impunity (Roht-Arriaza 2014). The case of the various peace accords in Colombia and their corresponding legal frameworks involve concessions in the event of a maximum sentence; these are examples of strategies that have been developed in this regard and the tensions they involve.

As we have shown here, certain studies have focused on judicial powers that become arenas in which to further the cause of legal responsibility in matters of human rights. In the studies discussed, two things seem clear: First, at different moments multiple factors can bolster the judicial arena to promote legal responsibility, even though this is not exempt from tensions, as we see in recent studies on the "era of accountability." Second, the factors and consequences of daily impunity of human rights violations have not been studied much, nor have the influence of these trials within the judicial branch itself, the dilemmas faced by judges, their pedagogic effects, and other types of effects, etc. These agendas are relevant future research topics.

Lastly, we discuss the third group within the literature that problematizes the legal institutions in human rights, i.e., the group that focuses on the judicial role in social justice.

Legal Institutions as Arenas for Social Justice

Within the third agenda, human rights are conceived as a mechanism that promotes social transformation, specifically social justice for the less fortunate. Human rights, explicitly social rights, have become mechanisms for resisting both the market economy and neoliberalism that have engulfed the region in the past few decades. From this perspective, the judicialization of social, economic, and cultural rights is a path to change.

These studies are grounded in analyzing public policies and examining how a human rights perspective can be incorporated in them. They touch on the relationship between human rights and development, speculating specifically about a development theory that places rights at the forefront (Abramovich and Pautassi 2006; Cornwall and Niuamy-Musembi 2004). They also cover a more classical discussion within the field of law and society about the transformative potential of the courts in particular and legal institutions more generally (Abel 2010).

Next, we discuss studies that examine the creation and functioning of the arena.

Conditions That Make the Arena Possible: The Justiciability of Social Rights

In line with the concern for social justice, within Latin America there has been discussion regarding the justiciability of social rights. This paradigm of justiciability advocated, and advocates, legal enforcement of social, economic, and cultural rights (Courtis 2007; Langford 2008), made patent by what Langford et al. call concern over judicial precedents for social rights (Langford et al. 2017a). In Latin America, where the positivist legal perspective was preeminent during the better part of the twentieth century, we should not be surprised that the mainstream legal perspective considers social rights as programmatic rights that fall under the responsibility of the executive and legislative branches, and thus are outside the judicial branch's purview (Abramovich et al. 2002.) This is why studies have discussed creating conditions to convert the judicial powers into an arena for social justice, i.e., to protect and guarantee social, economic, and cultural rights. It is in this arena that concerned actors can mount resistance to market forces and, together with the changes in legal ideas referred to previously, create a receptive environment for this type of demands in some countries' judicial sphere (Gargarella 2006).

This perspective proved fruitful and the region saw an increase in the judicialization of social rights, as documented in several studies (Langford 2008; Saffon and García-Villegas 2011). Given this new role of the judicial powers in the region, numerous studies expressed an interest in the conditions that made judicialization possible, which is clearly not distributed evenly throughout the area. Several Latin American countries and other countries of the Global South have been examples of this tendency, especially Brazil, Argentina, and Colombia.

Studies on judicialization analyzed it as a process. It began as litigation and ended with compliance of sentences that then had an impact in developing public policies. In this sense, the various components of the process came under scrutiny. Authors examined the characteristics of litigation (Peruzzotti and Smulovitz 2006; Smulovitz 2010; Brinks and Botero 2010), conditions for access to justice (Wilson 2009), the particularities of the tribunal's institutional makeup (Wilson 2011), and the legal and constitutional framework. These were elements unearthed by scholarly research that shed greater light on the characteristics of the courts' decisions, either in favor or against social rights, and specifically regarding the transformative potential of the status quo of the law and legal institutions (Gauri and Brinks 2008; Yamin and Gloppen 2011).

The specter that ran (and runs) through this literature is the law and legal institutions' ability for transformation. Beyond certain literature's pessimism regarding the courts' potential to be an agent of social change (Hirschl 2009; Rosemberg 2008), another perspective arose, if not exactly optimistic, at least it was open to analyzing the impact and consequences of the judicialization of social rights on an empirical basis (Gargarella et al. 2006). This concern is a leitmotif in studies that explore the consequences of the judicialization of social rights.

The Functioning of the Arena: How Much Does it Contribute to the Judicialization of Social Transformation?

As the number of legal decisions regarding social rights increases, measuring their impact becomes a problem.

A topic of inquiry revolves around how to conceptualize and measure the impact of legal decisions. This line of study revisits some of the previous tensions that arose during the law and society movement in the United States. The realist perspective of the law considers that a legal decision's impact can be materially measured. The constitutive perspective that holds that both the material and the symbolic results must be taken into account (Rodríguez-Garavito 2010) opposes the realist view.

It is important to note that this line of inquiry is not limited to Latin America but is rather an overarching concern of law and policy studies (Kapiszewski and Taylor 2013).

More recently, we have seen exercises that involve cases in Latin America. Two of the principal subjects of interest have been the distributive impact of legal decisions on social rights and the level of enforcement of sentences by government agencies (Langford et al. 2017b). Gauri and Brinks undertook an important study to measure the main beneficiaries of judicialization of demands for social rights (Brinks and Gauri 2014). As part of a conversation regarding the transformative potential of the law and legal institutions, these studies mainly discuss whether the judicialization of social rights translates into benefits for the middle and wealth classes (Landau 2012), or has a broader distributive and political effect (Prado 2013; Botero 2015).

A trait of these Latin American studies involves their fundamental focus on four countries (Colombia, Brazil, Costa Rica, and Argentina), leaving many other countries to be analyzed. Furthermore, although it is clear that these studies have different emphases, not all countries are at the same stage, meaning that there is still a wide field of research open for each one of the questions covered herein. Yet undoubtedly, the main research challenge has to do with the analysis of the distributive impact of the judicialization of social rights, the diverse responses in the legal environment, and a maturing process in terms of the courts' activism.

Lessons Derived from the Three Agendas

This review makes it clear that, during the past two decades in Latin America, the legal institutions have become key arenas for developing different human rights agendas. This involvement of the judiciary brought with it the development of specific research agendas as well as a growing intersection among the topics covered by these agendas.

Two agendas are especially relevant in light of our review: First, the consequences of judicialization; and second, the increasing concern around the impact and enforcement of sentences.

What we discern is that judicial powers have overlapping agendas: enforcement of international law; legal responsibility; and social justice. The influence of the Inter-American Court's jurisprudence on amnesties and the tensions within the judicial powers when dealing with peace processes in which special punishment conditions have been legislated, are an example of these overlaps. The same can be said regarding the use of Inter-American jurisprudence regarding the right to life within a domestic litigation on topics such as the property of indigenous groups (in the case of *Comunidad Indígena Yakye Axa* v. *Paraguay*), or the situation of street children (in the case of Villagrán Morales v. El Salvador).

In fact, less attention has been given to the bilateral relation between the concern over legal responsibility for human rights violations and concern for social justice. Although they refer to two matters that arise in different environments, there is a space where both concerns intersect from the standpoint of victims' rights following human rights violations. We note a tendency in several sentences handed down by the Inter-American Court of Human Rights to examine the relationship between human rights violations and the conditions of structural inequality that make these violations possible, such as in the case of Inés Fernández v. Mexico (Corte Interamericana de Derechos Humanos 2010b). It is possible that this tendency will be given attention in future research on its implications.

A question arises from both processes: What type of reparations is adequate when victims belong to disadvantaged groups? A topic of discussion that has been analyzed particularly in the case of Colombia is the need for transformative reparations that not only compensate damages but also modify victims' structural circumstances (Uprimny-Yepes and Guzmán-Rodríguez 2010). These authors discuss the relation between transitional justice and conditions of structural equality in which transitional justice not only considers reparation for victims or punishment for perpetrators of human rights violations, but also the opportunity to change those conditions that made human rights violations possible and thus affected these groups.

Sadly, violence and human rights violations continue to occur and acquire different characteristics than those that were common during the Cold War or South America's military dictatorships or the Central American armed conflicts. Thus, new research is needed on the characteristics and scope of the judicial powers and their possibilities to implement transformative reparations.

In addition, these three agendas have a very small intersecting space. Each agenda implies the evolution of different processes that, as they take hold in the same space, can influence and modify it. How these three processes transform judicial power as an arena and the possibility of undertaking different functions is a pending topic in the study of the influence of judicialization of human rights protection.

As we analyze judicial powers as arenas for developing Latin American human rights agendas, we can clearly see that the judicial powers function as a space that promotes (or fails to promote) human rights. Yet we do not understand how assuming these new functions influenced the operation of the judicial powers themselves. Specifically, we lack analysis on how they modified their organization and what repercussion this had on its members. In short, the studies reviewed herein have investigated the challenges and tensions that the judicial powers face in promoting human rights, but they have overlooked the consequences that this type of involvement has for the judicial powers as organizations, its members as individuals, and the latter's relations with other political and social actors. Therefore, an important field of research awaits scholars of law and society who are interested in both human rights and the functioning of law institutions.

There are another two considerations regarding research agendas: one linked to research methodology and another related to the countries studied.

In terms of the research methodology, there has been progress regarding the panorama suggested by Kapiszewski and Taylor in 2008 (Kapiszewski and Taylor 2008): Although case studies still predominate, comparative research is increasing. An excellent example is Michel and Sikkink's study on the operation of the penal justice system in dealing with transitional justice in Uruguay, Guatemala, and Mexico. Another is the book *Shifting Legal Visions* by Ezequiel González Ocantos (González Ocantos 2016) regarding the judicial response to holding persons accountable for human rights violations in Peru, Argentina, and Mexico. Still another example is Sandra Botero's analysis (Botero 2015) of how courts have developed ways of monitoring fulfillment of sentences or the cases of social rights, minorities, or disadvantaged persons in Argentina and Colombia. Further examples include the conditions that facilitate pro-rights legal activism in the case of the right to health in Colombia and Costa Rica (Wilson 2009), or the differences in judicial stances on the rights of sexual minorities and the right to health, as César Valderrama examines for Colombia and Mexico (Valderrama Gómez 2015). In his 2007 study, Daniel Brinks discussed (Brinks 2007) the operation of the courts vis-à-vis judicial violence in Uruguay, Brazil, and Argentina. Studies have also been published on the courts and the defense of human rights. For example, the volume edited by Ansolabehere, Valdés, and Vázquez (2015) regarding the importance of legal institutions in the enjoyment of human rights, the factors that help improve the defense of human rights (Lessa et al. 2014), and widening victims' rights in the criminal justice system (Michel and Sikkink 2012).

We currently find diversity in research designs and greater rigor in this field of study. Yet, as Julio Ríos-Figueroa (Ríos-Figueroa 2012) mentions in his review of law and society studies in Mexico, a gap needs to be bridged, which requires upgrading research methods, offering more insightful explanations, and integrating the internal and external perspectives on the law in these studies.

Finally, we should mention a characteristic of the geographic scope of these studies: Unsurprisingly, the scope changes in each of the agendas, given the types of processes that are addressed. An analysis of the judicial powers as arenas for enforcing international human rights law combines studies in this field with readings of case studies in which Chile, Argentina, Colombia, Brazil (as a negative example), and (more recently) Mexico received more attention. In terms of the accountability agenda, the group of countries studied has clearly increased. Those on Central America (Guatemala and El Salvador) have complemented previous studies on Chile, Argentina, Uruguay, and Colombia. Regarding the third agenda, three countries have been studied the most: Argentina, Colombia, Brazil, and, to a lesser degree, Costa Rica. These countries have dominated the field because the judicial powers operate as arenas in which social rights cases are heard.

As we can see, the geographic scope of the case studies is limited, suggesting the need to undertake studies based on mixed methods in which the scope of area studies is complemented by the depth of case studies or small *N* studies.

Conclusions

One of the traits of Latin American human rights agenda is judicialization. Acknowledgment of judicialization and the political importance of the judiciaries led to the study of the conditions that made this change possible and its subsequent consequences. These concerns overlap two classical discussions in the field of law and society: the gap between law in the books and law in action and the potential for the law to undertake social transformations.

The main contribution of this chapter was to map the three human rights agendas that have problematized the judicial powers as arenas: the enforceability of international human rights law; legal responsibility for human rights violations; and social justice for disadvantaged groups. These concerns cannot be separated from three events that occurred in Latin American in the past three decades: democratization (and setbacks to democracy); market-friendly economic reforms; and changes in legal ideas summarized as the constitutionalization of law and inter-nationalization of constitutional law.

The following table (Table 19.1) systematizes the tensions and challenges of the judicial powers as arenas for each one of the three agendas.

Table 19.1 Tensions and Challenges of Judicial Powers as Arenas for Human Rights

	Enforcement of International Human Rights Law	*Legal Responsibility for Human Rights Violations*	*Social Justice*
How judicial power is conceived	Arena for enforcement of international human rights law and strengthening institutions	Arena to bring to trial those responsible for human rights violations and reparations for victims	Arena to further social justice through protection for social, economic, and cultural rights
Conditions that made establishing the arena possible	Changes in the structures of legal opportunities and in legal and professional ideas	Legal and extra-legal factors that made it possible for human rights trials to proceed	Justiciability of social, economic, and cultural rights
Consequences of judicialization	Degree to which the judicial branch appropriated the instruments of international human rights law. Relations between the Inter-American Court of Human Rights and domestic courts	Impact and tensions of human rights trials on the political system	Conditions that facilitate the judicialization of social rights and its results

Source: Table created by author.

Although the implications of the judicial arena in these different agendas were considered separately for analytical purposes, we can see that they intersect. The clearest is the enforcement of international human rights law, accountability and social transformation. Yet the intersection between the social justice agenda and accountability has received less treatment, which is also true for the implications of the intersection among the three agendas.

The analysis undertaken herein allows us to conclude that, although the importance of the judicial powers in protecting human rights has been acknowledged, we lack a study of the implications that these new roles have for the judiciaries, their organization, agents, and relationships with other extrajudicial actors. The next phase in researching each of these agendas might be called the results of judicialization on the organization of the judicial branch.

Finally, to implement this pending agenda, we should bear in mind methodological sophistication and the use of mixed methods.

Notes

1 The concept of judicialization has been the subject of the literature on law and politics, a reflection of the increase in the use of the tribunals in order to resolve different political and social conflicts, and, among the latter, human rights cases (Sieder et al. 2005; Ferejohn 2002).
2 An example of this in Latin America is the growing importance of the Inter-American Court of Human Rights, national human rights institutions (see Uggla's chapter in this volume), anti-discriminatory institutions, etc.
3 The diversity of countries in the region prevents us from considering the tendencies outlined herein as uniform.
4 Furthermore, around the first decade of the twenty-first century, Latin America underwent a neo-constituent process, known as New Latin American Constitutionalism, which produced the constitutions of Bolivia, Venezuela, and Ecuador and combined a comprehensive recognition of rights with a clear centralization of power in the executive branch (Gargarella 2015).
5 In 2009, the Inter-American Court of Human Rights issued a guilty verdict against Mexico in the case of Rosendo Radilla Pacheco, disappeared by members of the Mexican Army during the 1970s in the state of Guerrero. This sentence is considered a turning point in the relationship between the Mexican Supreme Court and the Inter-American Court of Human Rights, given that, following the sentence, the former began deliberating on its responsibility in abiding by decisions handed down by the latter.

References

Abel, Richard L. 2010. Law and Society: Project and Practice. *Annual Review of Law and Social Science*, 6: 1–23.

Abramovich, Víctor, Christian Courtis, and Luigi Ferrajoli. 2002. *Los Derechos Sociales Como Derechos Exigibles*. Trotta Madrid.

Ansolabehere Sesti, Karina. 2014. Difusores y Justicieros: Las Instituciones Judiciales en la Política de Derechos Humanos. *Perfiles Latinoamericanos*, 22(44): 143–69.

Basch, Fernando, Leonardo Filippini, Mariano Nino, Felicitas Rossi, and Bárbara Schreiber. 2010. La Efectividad del Sistema Interamericano de Protección de Derechos Humanos: Un Enfoque Cuantitativo Sobre su Funcionamiento y Sobre el Cumplimiento de sus Decisiones. *Sur-Revista Internacional de Derechos Humanos, São Paulo*, 7(12): 9–35.

Benítez Jiménez, Maira. 2017. *Justicia Transicional y Movilización: Implicaciones Socio-Legales de los Juicios en Guatemala y Perú*. Mexico: FLACSO-Mexico.

Botero, Sandra. 2015. *Agents of Neoliberalism? High Courts and Rights in Latin America*. Available at: www.sas.upenn.edu/dcc/sites/www.sas.upenn.edu.dcc/files/uploads/Botero%20-%20Courts%20(Penn%20DCC%20Conference).pdf. Accessed October 19, 2018.

Botero, Sandra. 2015. *Courts that Matter: Judges, Litigants and the Politics of Rights Enforcement in Latin America*. Notre Dame.

Brinks, Daniel M. 2007. *The Judicial Response to Police Killings in Latin America: Inequality and the Rule of Law*. Cambridge University Press.

Brinks, Daniel M. and S. Botero. 2010. Inequality and the Rule of Law: Ineffective Rights in Latin American Democracies. In *American Political Science Association Annual Meeting*. Available at: http://kellogg.nd.edu/odonnell/papers/brinks.pdf. Accessed October 19, 2018.

Brinks, Daniel M. and Varun Gauri. 2014. The Law's Majestic Equality? The Distributive Impact of Judicializing Social and Economic Rights. *Perspectives on Politics*, 12(2): 375–93.

Collins, Cath 2010. *Post-Transitional Justice. Human Rights Trials in Chile and El Salvador*. Pennsylvania, EU: Pennsylvania State University Press.

Contesse, Jorge. 2013. *¿La Última Palabra? Control de Convencionalidad y Posibilidades de Diálogo con la Corte Interamericana de Derechos Humanos*. Sela, Yale Law School. Available at: https://law.yale.edu/system/files/documents/pdf/sela/SELA13_Contesse_CV_Sp_20130401.pdf. Accessed October 19, 2018.

Corte Interamericana de Derechos Humanos. 2010a. "Caso Radilla Pachecho vs. Estados Unidos Mexicanos." Available at: www.corteidh.or.cr/docs/casos/articulos/seriec_209_esp.doc. Accessed October 19, 2018.

Corte Interamericana de Derechos Humanos. "Fernández Ortega y Otros vs. México" (Corte Interamericana de Derechos Humanos de Agosto de 2010). Available at: www.ordenjuridico.gob.mx/JurInt/STCIDHM2.pdf. Accessed October 19, 2018.

Couso, Javier A. 2005. "The Judicialization of Chilean Politics. The Rights Revolution that Never Was." In *The Judicialization of Politics in Latin America*, edited by Rachel Sieder, Line Schjolden, and Alan Angell, 105–29. New York: Palgrave Macmillan.

Couso, Javier A. 2013. "The Implementation of the Inter-American Human Rights System's Decisions in Chile." (Unpublished Material). Retrieved from The Implementation of the Inter-American Human Rights System's Decisions in Chile.

Couso, Javier A. and Lisa Hilbink. 2011. "From Quietism to Incipient Activism." In *Courts in Latin America*, edited by Gretchen Helmke and Julio Ríos-Figueroa, 99. Cambridge, New York: Cambridge University Press.

Dancy, Geoff, and Kathryn Sikkink. 2012. "Ratification and Human Rights Prosecutions: Toward a Transitional Theory O Treaty Compliance." *Journal of International Law and Politics*, 44 (Spring): 751–90.

Dutrénit Bielous, Silvia and Gonzalo Varela Petito. 2010. *Tramitando el Pasado. Violaciones de los Derechos Humanos y Agendas Gubernamentales en Casos Latinoamericanos*. Mexico: FLACSO-Mexico/CLACSO.

Engstrom, Par, and Andrew Hurrell. 2013. "Why the Human Rights Regime in the Americas Matters." *Human Rights Regimes in the Americas*, 29–55.

Gargarella, Roberto. 2006. ¿Democracia deliberativa y judicialización de los derechos sociales? *Perfiles Latinoamericanos*, 14(28): 9–32.

Gargarella, Roberto. 2015. *La Sala de Máquinas de la Constitución: Dos Siglos de Constitucionalismo en América Latina (1810–2010)*. Buenos Aires: Katz Editores.

Gargarella, Roberto, Pilar Domingo and Theunis Roux. 2006. *Courts and Social Transformation in New Democracies: An Institutional Voice for the Poor?* Ashgate Publishing.

Gauri, Varun and Daniel M. Brinks. 2008. *Courting Social Justice: Judicial Enforcement of Social and Economic Rights in the Developing World*. Cambridge University Press.

González Ocantos, Ezequiel. 2014. Persuade Them or Oust Them: Crafting Judicial Change and Transitional Justice in Argentina. *Comparative Politics,* Forthcoming, 46(4): 279–98.

González Ocantos, Ezequiel. 2016. *Shifting Legal Visions. Judicial Change and Human Rights Trials in Latin America*. New York: Cambridge University Press.

Haire, Susan. 2010. "Relations among courts." In *The Oxford Handbook of Law and Politics (Vol. 3)*, edited by Keith E. Whittington, R. Daniel Kelemen and Gregory A. Caldeira. New York: Oxford University Press.

Helmke, Gretchen and Julio Ríos-Figueroa. 2011. *Courts in Latin America*. Cambridge University Press.

Hilbink, Lisa. 2006. Beyond Manicheanism: Assessing the New Constitutionalism. *Maryland Law Review*, 65: 15.

Hilbink, Lisa. 2012. The Origins of Positive Judicial Independence. *World Politics*, 64(4): 587–621.

Hillebrecht, Courtney. 2014. *Domestic Politics and International Human Rights Tribunals: The Problem of Compliance*. Cambridge University Press.

Hirschl, Ran. 2009. *Towards Juristocracy: The Origins and Consequences of the New Constitutionalism*. Harvard University Press.

Huneeus, Alexandra. 2010. Judging from a Guilty Conscience: The Chilean Judiciary's Human Rights Turn. *Law and Social Inquiry*, 35(1): 99–135. Available at: https://doi.org/10.1111/j.1747-4469.2009.01179.x. Accessed October 19, 2018.

Huneeus, Alexandra. 2011. Courts Resisting Courts: Lessons from the Inter-American Court's Struggle to Enforce Human Rights. *Cornell International Law Journal*, 44(3): 101–42.

Kapiszewski, Diana and M.M. Taylor. 2008. Doing Courts Justice? Studying Judicial Politics in Latin America. *Perspectives on Politics*, 6(4): 741–67.

Kapiszewski, Diana and Matthew M. Taylor. 2013. Compliance: Conceptualizing, Measuring, and Explaining Adherence to Judicial Rulings. *Law and Social Inquiry*, 38(4): 803–35. Available at: https://doi.org/10.1111/j.1747-4469.2012.01320.x. Accessed October 19, 2018.

Kapiszewski, Diana, Gordon Silverstein, and Robert A. Kagan (Eds.). 2013. *Consequential Courts: Judicial Roles in Global Perspective (Comparative Constitutional Law and Policy)*. Cambridge University Press.

Keck, Margaret E. and Kathryn Sikkink. 1998. *Activists Beyond Borders: Advocacy Networks in International Politics*. Cambridge University Press.

Landau, David. 2012. The Reality of Social Rights Enforcement. *Harvard International Law Journal*, 53: 189.

Langford, Malcom. 2008. *Social Rights Jurisprudence: Emerging Trends in International and Comparative Law*. Cambridge University Press.

Langford, Malcom, César Rodríguez-Garavito, and Julieta Rossi (Eds.). 2017a. *Social Rights Judgments and the Politics of Compliance: Making it Stick* (First edition). Cambridge: Cambridge University Press.

Langford, Malcom, César Rodríguez-Garavito, and Julieta Rossi. 2017b. *Social Rights Judgments and the Politics of Compliance: Making It Stick*. Cambridge University Press.

Lessa, Francesca. 2013. *Memory and Transitional Justice in Argentina and Uruguay: Against Impunity*. Springer.

Lessa, Francesca, Tricia D. Olsen, Leigh A. Payne, Gabriel Pereira, and Andrew Reiter. 2014. Overcoming Impunity: Pathways to Accountability in Latin America. *International Journal of Transitional Justice*, 8(1): 75–98.

López Pacheco, Jairo A. 2015. *El Campo de Acción Colectiva de las Organizaciones Defensoras de los Derechos Humanos: Los Casos de Colombia y México*. Doctoral Thesis, FLACSO-Mexico.

Michel, Verónica and Katryn Sikkink. 2012. *Participation Rights of Victims in Criminal Proceedings and Human Rights Prosecutions*. Mimeo.

Nunes, Rodrigo M. 2010. Ideational Origins of Progressive Judicial Activism: The Colombian Constitutional Court and the Right to Health. *Latin American Politics and Society*, 52(3): 67–97.

Oglesby, Elizabeth and Diane Nelson. 2016. Guatemala, the Question of Genocide. *Journal of Genocide Research* 18(2–3).

Olsen, Tricia D., Leigh A. Payne, and Andrew G. Reiter. 2010. *Transitional Justice in Balance: Comparing Processes, Weighing Efficacy*. US Institute of Peace.

Payne, Leigh A., Francesca Lessa, and Gabriel Pereira. 2015. Overcoming Barriers to Justice in the Age of Human Rights Accountability. *Human Rights Quarterly*, 37(3): 728–54. Available at: https://doi.org/10.1353/hrq.2015.0040. Accessed October 19, 2018.

Payne, Leigh A. and Gabriel Pereira. 2016. Corporate Complicity in International Human Rights Violations. *Annual Review of Law and Social Science*, 12: 63–84.

Peruzzotti, Enrique and Catalina Smulovitz. 2006. *Enforcing the Rule of Law: Social Accountability in the New Latin American Democracies*. University of Pittsburgh Press.

Popovski, Vesselin, Nicholas Turner, Thomas Karl Wagner, and Greg Lowden. 2008. *The Human Rights Regime in the Americas*. Report. UNU-ISP Policy Briefs.

Prado, Mariana Mota. 2013. The Debatable Role of Courts in Brazil's Health Care System: Does Litigation Harm or Help? *The Journal of Law, Medicine and Ethics*, 41(1): 124–37. Available at: https://doi.org/10.1111/jlme.12009. Accessed October 19, 2018.

Ríos-Figueroa, Julio. 2012. Sociolegal Studies on Mexico. *Annual Review of Law and Social Science*, 8(1): 307–21. Available at: https://doi.org/10.1146/annurev-lawsocsci-102811-173928. Accessed October 19, 2018.

Rodriguez-Garavito, César. 2010. Beyond the Courtroom: The Impact of Judicial Activism on Socio-economic Rights in Latin America. *Texas Law Review*, 89: 1669.

Roht-Arriaza, Naomi. 2006. "The new landscape of transitional justice." In *Transitional Justice in the Twenty-First Century*, edited by Naomi Roht-Arriaza and Javier Mariezcurrena. Cambridge University Press.

Roht-Arriaza, Naomi. 2014. *After Amnesties are Gone: Latin American National Courts and the New Contours of the Fight Against Impunity*. Scholarly Paper, Social Science Research Network. Rochester, NY. Available at: http://papers.ssrn.com/abstract=2409077. Accessed October 19, 2018.

Rosemberg, Gerald N. 2008. *The Hollow Hope: Can Courts Bring About Social Change?* (Vol. 2). Chicago: University of Chicago Press.

Saffon, María Paula and Mauricio García-Villegas. 2011. Derechos sociales y activismo judicial. La dimensión fáctica del activismo judicial en derechos sociales en Colombia. *Revista Estudios Socio-Jurídicos*, 13(1). Available at: www.redalyc.org/resumen.oa?id=73318918004. Accessed October 19, 2018.

Salazar Ugarte, Pedro. 2012. "Garantismo y neoconstitucionalismo Frente a Frente: algunas claves para su distinción." In *Un Debate Sobre el Constitucionalismo*, edited by Luigi Ferrajoli. Madrid: Marcial Pons.

Saldivia, Laura. 2003. "Derechos Humanos y Derecho de Interés Público en Argentina: ¿Quiebre o Continuidad?" *Documento de Trabajo 2.* Facultad de Derecho, Universidad de Palermo.

Serrano García, Sandra. 2017. *La Recepción de los Criterios Interamericanos en las Corte de Colombia y México: De las Ideas a los Resultados.* Mexico: IIJ UNAM.

Sieder, Rachel, Line Schjolden, and Alan Angell. 2005. *The Judicialization of Politics in Latin America.* Palgrave Macmillan.

Sikkink, Kathryn. 2005. "The Transnational Dimension of the Judicialization of Politics in Latin America." In *The Judicialization of Politics in Latin America*, edited by Rachel Sieder, Line Schjolden and Alan Angell, 263–92. New York: Palgrave Macmillan.

Sikkink, Kathryn. 2008. La dimensión transnacional de la judicialización de la política en América Latina. En Sieder, Rachel; Schjolden, Line; Alan Angell (ed.) (2008) *La Judicialización de La Política En América Latina*, (Journal Article): 315–49.

Sikkink, Kathryn and C.B. Walling. 2007. The Impact of Human Rights Trials in Latin America. *Journal of Peace Research*, 44(4): 427–45.

Skaar, Elin. 2011. *Judicial Independence and Human Rights in Latin America: Violations, Politics, and Prosecution.* Palgrave Macmillan.

Smulovitz, Catalina. 2010. Judicialization in Argentina: Legal Culture, or Opportunities and Support Structures? In *Cultures of Legality: Judicialization and Political Activism in Latin America*, edited by Javier Couso, Alexandra Huneeus and Rachel Sieder. Cambridge: Cambridge University Press.

Smulovitz, Catalina. 2013. "The past is never dead": Accountability and Justice for Past Human Rights Violations in Argentina. *After Oppression,* 64–85.

Staton, Jeffrey K. and Alexia Romero. 2011. *"Clarity and Compliance in the Inter-American Human Rights System."* Presented at the American Political Science Association Meetings.

Valdés-Ugalde, Francisco and Karina Ansolabehere. 2012. "Panorama político. Conflicto constitucional en América Latina: entre la inclusión y el cinismo." In *América Latina en los Albores del Siglo XXI, 2. Aspectos Sociales y Políticos*, edited by Martin Anyul Puchet, Mariano Rojas, Rodrigo Salazar, Giovanna Valenti, and Francisco Valdés Ugalde, 235–58. Mexico: FLACSO, Mexico.

Uprimny-Yepes, Rodrigo and Diana Esther Guzmán-Rodríguez. 2010. In Search of a Transformative and Participatory Concept of Reparations in the Context of Transitional Justice. *International Law*, 17: 232–86.

Valderrama Gómez, César. 2015. *El Papel de las Audiencias en la Protección de Derechos y la Construcción de Legitimidad Judicial los Casos de Colombia y México.* Doctoral Thesis, FLACSO-Mexico.

Von Bogdandy, Armin. 2015. Ius Constitutionale Commune En América Latina: Una Mirada a Un Constitucionalismo Transformador (Ius Constitutionale Commune in Latin America: A Look at a Transformative Constitutionalism). *Revista Derecho del Estado* 34: 3–50.

Wilson, Bruce M. 2009. Rights Revolutions in Unlikely Places: Costa Rica and Colombia. *Journal of Politics in Latin America*, 1(2): 59–85.

Wilson, Bruce M. 2011. "Enforcing rights and excercising an accountability function. Costa Rica Constitutional Chamber of the Supreme Court." In *Courts in Latin America*, edited by Gretchen Helmke and Julio Ríos-Figueroa. Cambridge: Cambridge University Press.

Yamin, Alicia Ely and Siri Gloppen. 2011. *Litigating Health Rights: Can Courts Bring More Justice to Health.* Cambridge, MA: Human Rights Program, Harvard Law School /Harvard University Press.

20
DEGLOBALIZATION AND REGIONAL HUMAN RIGHTS

Alexandra Huneeus

The human rights system of the Americas has flourished since the close of the Cold War. People throughout the region turn to the Organization of American States (OAS) human rights system, commonly known as the Inter-American System (IAS), as a court of last resort when national justice systems fail to protect their rights. But these national justice systems have also internalized the IAS: most litigation that cites the American Convention on Human Rights takes place not in Costa Rica or Washington, DC, where the Inter-American Human Rights Court and Commission sit, respectively, but in domestic courts throughout the region.

Yet current changes in the geopolitical landscape are disrupting this human rights system in new ways. The deep background to the rise in power of the IAS has been the *Pax Americana* established after the Second World War; and, subsequently, the post-Cold War commitment by the United States and Europe and a host of new democracies to free markets and economic integration. Today, however, as liberal ideologies lose ground to conservative or leftist populisms that emphasize nationalist ideology; as Russia and China challenge United States hegemony and the United States turns further inward; and as states pull back on globalization of trade and other forms of legal integration, it is important to reconsider the future of human rights protection in Latin America. It now seems likely that, as suggested by Stephen Hopgood (2014), we are moving not toward a post-Westphalian order with porous borders and weak sovereignty, but toward a neo-Westphalian order of inward looking policies and multi-polarity. In such a scenario, what becomes of human rights protection at the regional level?

To pose this question is not to suggest that the IAS is under existential threat. The world's three main regional rights systems have shown themselves to have a certain degree of stickiness: Britain is for now staying within the jurisdiction of the European Court of Human Rights, Brexit notwithstanding. African states threatening to remove themselves from the jurisdiction of the International Criminal Court are not threatening to leave the African Union's System but rather, in some ways, to strengthen it. In Latin America, democracy is the norm, the Venezuelan crisis notwithstanding. Indeed, the states, such as Ecuador, that at first threatened to follow Venezuela's example of denouncing the American Convention have remained decidedly engaged.

The point, rather, is to consider that human rights systems are shaped and constrained not only by law and domestic politics, but also by the geopolitical context, which originally allowed them to emerge. The regional rights systems began as part of the same post-War impulse – an effort by Europe and the Americas alike to distinguish themselves from the fascist regimes of the past, as well as the Soviet regime. They played a role legitimating a particular international order, and their influence spread apace with free market democracies. In this way, the American-led global order was the shared backdrop against which variation in the spread of human rights law and institutions was studied. Scholars in recent years have explored how differences in domestic legal and political factors enhance or diminish the impact of regional rights regimes. Now, however, the American-led world order is under challenge, and the larger geopolitical trends that served only as a background emerge as a variable of interest. The prospect of neo-Westphalia, in other words requires a new approach. We must (re)turn to the study of geopolitics, and how larger political trends, too, shape the development of human rights systems.

This chapter revisits the body of legal and socio-legal scholarship on the IAS, with reference to scholarship on regional human rights in Europe, both to examine how it can be re-read to inform new questions posed by the changing world order, and to consider what questions it has failed to ask. The chapter unfolds in three main parts after the introduction. It begins by looking to origin stories: the creation and development of human rights systems during the Cold War era. In Latin America, this era shows us how regional institutions emerged and survived in a time in where human rights ideas held less legitimacy, democracies were fragile, and authoritarian government often looming. The early period thus could be re-read as a roadmap for how the regional systems contend with greater instability and democratic backsliding. The second section considers the post-Cold War era, when trade globalization, democratization, and the embrace of human rights combined to foster the growth of the IAS. Socio-legal scholarship on this era focuses on the relationships between the international institutions and various domestic constituencies, including judges and civil society. The challenge emerges of connecting the story of these relationships between particular institutions to macro-level geopolitical trends obscured by the institutionalist focus: what exactly, for example, is the relationship between globalization of rights and globalization of trade?[1] The third section turns to the current era: as the United States further recedes from a human rights inflected foreign policy, will the institutional relations that form the backbone of the IAS nonetheless endure, and for how long? What strategies will the regional rights systems use to survive and will they change fundamentally in their effort to do so? If it is too soon to answer these questions definitively, it is timely to use them as guides for further study.

Human Rights in Cold War and Dictatorship (1948–1990)

Samuel Moyn (2010) has argued that the ascendance of the human rights ideas begins not in the immediate post-War period, but in the 1970s, when the Carter administration in the United States made it a foreign relations priority. Moyn would thus have us focus our historical study of human rights on the time when the political winds were affable, and state institutions became committed to the idea of human rights. But today, as these very factors begin to waver, it seems timely to revisit the earlier period – when human rights institutions existed despite the fact that human rights ideas had less salience, and when competing ideologies, such as nationalism and socialism, had stronger sway. The pre-seventies trajectory might reveal something about how human rights institutions endure when human rights ideas are not ascendant.

The IAS was modeled, in great part, on the Council of Europe System (COE) that predates it (even as the European system borrowed from the Organization of American States [OAS's] prior human rights declaration of 1948), and so the European System's history is also of interest here. The European Convention on Human Rights (ECHR) entered into force in 1953, and the ECHR opened its doors in 1959. Viewed retrospectively from the heights of the post-Cold

War rights revolution, this period does not inspire much admiration. Moyn argues that the COE System was "essentially stillborn" (2010, 80), highlighting how in its first case, *Lawless* v. *Ireland*,[2] the ECHR failed to challenge Britain's use of emergency measures and indefinite detention without trial. At this time the European System was still small and centered in Western Europe. When larger states did join they did so without submitting to the jurisdiction of the ECHR, and by excluding large swaths of colonial territories (Article 56, the European Convention's "colonial clause," gives states the option to include colonial territories, which is also to say that they are otherwise excluded).

On closer inspection, this deferential behavior reveals itself to be not (only) a sign that human rights were not yet ascendant, but also a strategy to balance the difficult challenges facing the ECHR. On the one hand, judges did not want to scare away new states with forceful judgments on sensitive matters of national security. On the other hand, the ECHR could not be seen to be undermining human rights through a restrictive reading of the European Convention. Mikael Rask Madsen argues that the judges chose a strategy of appeasement that he titles legal diplomacy: they were mindful not to alienate the larger, colony-holding states, opting to use their judgments to create a viable future for the ECHR rather than to offer a rich and expansive reading of the convention (2011). This meant ignoring ongoing colonial endeavors and ducking out of polemical rulings that might cause states to recoil. The ECHR focused on more quotidian issues:

> setting up subtle tests of proportionality to examine restrictions aimed at legitimate ends, establishing the tests of, for example, access to personal information contained in medical files, the scope of the duties of authorities to consult trade unions … or the status of "illegitimate children."
>
> *(Wojciech 2009, 406)*

Taken together the early rulings depict a Europe of few and fairly minor legalistic violations to human rights (and not a Europe engaged in violent colonial repression in, for example, Algeria). This is exactly the image Europe wanted to project during the Cold War. Part of the work of the regional human rights system at this time, in other words, was that of forging an identity for Western Europe.

The IAS's institutions took root in a different context. Significantly, the OAS includes within it not just the Latin American states that have been most active in creating the Inter-American Human Rights System, but also the United States. In other words, the hegemon was an outsized member, working from within to advance its Cold War foreign policy. Further, Latin America was a region still characterized by economic underdevelopment and political instability. Its place in the geopolitical order, in other words, was vastly different from that of Western Europe. Another difference is that the IAS began its work at a later date: the Commission opened its doors in 1959, and the ECHR in 1979. Further, the ECHR did not really begin having an active docket until the 1990s. For this earlier Cold War period, the IAS worked with a commission alone, whereas the COE system had both commission and ECHR starting in 1959.

In this context, the IAS forged a working strategy different from that of the COE, focused on diplomacy rather than case-based adjudication (Huneeus and Madsen 2018). The first cases of the IAS were cases of political oppression that were threatening to the peace and security of the region, quite the opposite of the legalistic cases on ECHR docket. Further, the cases on which the commission focused were often a priority for the United States: human rights in Cuba after the 1959 revolution, for example, was an early focus (Dykmann 2004, Medina 1988). Further, as there was no case system yet in place, human rights was a top-down endeavor, in which the CIDH (Comisión Interamericana de los Derechos Humanos) and OAS states, rather than individual litigants and their lawyers, decided on the shape of the IAS agenda. The commission's first in-country visit to Argentina was made possible because a United States diplomat persuaded the Argentine government to allow the commission to visit as a condition for United States aid (Kelly 2018). A skeptical reading of the commission at this time, therefore, might describe it as merely a tool of United States interests. And yet, it was by making itself useful to the United States-dominated OAS that the commission was able to eventually gain relative autonomy. For example, it introduced the practice of issuing country reports in the Cuba case, but then the United States could not balk when the commission used the same technique in other cases.[3]

This review suggests that there are at least two sets of working methods for regional human rights systems from this earlier Cold War period (Huneeus and Rask Madsen 2018): the COE utilized a strategy of legal diplomacy, issuing minimalist and non-controversial rulings that depicted a rule-bound Europe perfecting its democratic practices. The IAS invented a more political human rights diplomacy, harnessing United States foreign policy interests to advance a human rights agenda, but slowly carving out a space of relative autonomy. Both systems were able to persevere until such a time as human rights ideas began to occupy a more important place, and competing ideologies receded, opening the way to different ways of working.

Revisiting this period thus provides indications of what may unfold in our own times: the IAS may revert to a less judicialized approach to human rights issues, or, insofar as it remains focused on case adjudication, it may adopt a more deferential, pragmatic jurisprudence. At the same time, this rough sketch also indicates that there is room for much further study of the pre-nineties era of the IAS, along the lines of some of the historical studies of the early COE. A closer history of the IAS might focus on the great differences between the early period, 1959–1973, and the years spanning 1970 to 1990. Madsen has argued that the 1970s mark a new era for the ECHR as it begins to assert itself in a postcolonial era. At the same time, Patrick Kelly argues that 1973 marks a dramatic turning point in Latin America, as human rights become the discourse through which to describe and oppose the Chilean *coup d'état*. How did this affect the Inter-Ameircan Commission's working strategy? Such a history might also inquire into the role that lawyers and academics and other advocacy groups played during this early era. In the context of the IAS it is interesting to note that the only scholarship about the Inter-American System created during this early period was itself a kind of diplomacy – pro-IAS interventions by activist lawyers in the face of state threats.[4] In other words, this scholarship was written in response to particular political challenges that the IAS would intermittently face, and should itself now be viewed as part of the effort to construct the system in the face of its critics. Finally, it would be important for today's scholars, with current pressures in mind, to uncover the role of social movements in the construction of the IAS: existing accounts tend to emphasize the role of states.[5]

The struggle of the commission to survive during the 1950s through 1970s has only one historically informed book-length work devoted to it.[6] Yet it is this earlier period that is perhaps holds the key to deeper understanding of the present. Further this inquiry must be undertaken free from teleology – free from the knowledge of what the system would become, or at least of the sense that there was something inevitable about the emergence of the IAS and the rise of human rights as the preferred language for making certain political claims.

Globalization, Democratization, Judicialization (1990–2016)

The end of the Cold War marked a new era for the IAS, as it did for the European human rights system. As democratization and new constitutions spread, and as more countries submitted to the jurisdiction of the Inter-American Court and the European Court of Human Rights alike, both courts began to have more influence in their regions.

The IAS moved, not without controversy, to a more adjudicative model of human rights. The commission prioritized the case system, retreating from its practice of diplomatic interventions into political crises of the Cold War era. The ECHR began to decide cases more regularly, and by 2000 had begun creating a significant body of jurisprudence that was influencing how domestic courts articulated human rights. The United States did not ratify the convention or otherwise change its formal relation to the OAS human rights system at this time. But Latin America had by now become less of a foreign policy priority than it had been at the height of the Cold War, and a certain lack of attention to the region allowed the IAS to evolve more autonomously than it had in the past, with its main interlocutors located in Latin America.

For Europe, democratization meant that Eastern European countries began to join the COE. Suddenly, therefore, the European Court found itself grappling with recalcitrant states and issues similar to those that had challenged the IAS in the 1980s. Further, the number of petitions ballooned: not only did the ECHR grow from 24 states in 1990 to 47 states today, but as these states often failed to comply fully with court judgments, more and more petitions claiming the same problem would be filed. To this day, despite several innovative efforts, the ECHR has yet to resolve its docket crisis. Perhaps the worst offender in this sense is Russia. For while the United States never submitted to the jurisdiction of the Inter-American Court, Russia became part of the COE System in 1996, creating an abiding source of tension from within the COE.

An important shift in this era for both the Inter-American and European human rights courts is that they move from being a supranational system that exists outside of states, engaging with states only via the executive branch's foreign affairs institution, to a system that is embedded domestically and is directly engaged by diverse constituencies at the state-level (Helfer 2008). This shift is particularly notable in Latin America starting in the 2000s. New constitutions and courts that interpret them to bring the American Convention directly into domestic law have meant that domestic judiciaries also play a direct role in examining the system, and have a direct interest in it. Local judges and lawyers begin to actively engage with the IAS, and to find that they have a stake in its construction. Further, the commission and ECHR create a system of equitable remedies that often require action not just from the executive, but also from other branches of government, thereby expanding its base of state interlocutors to include not just the executive and the judiciary but also, for example, legislatures, and bureaucracies charged with education, culture, and policing.

The move toward case adjudication meant that victims of human rights violations and nongovernmental organizations (NGOs) began to play an institutionalized role in defining the agenda of the IAS, as they are now the ones who bring cases to the IAS. Domestic and international NGOs grew to have part of their identity grounded in litigation before the system. *Centro de Justicia Internacional* (CEJIL), for example, a Washington, DC-based NGO devoted to Inter-American human rights litigation, has become a defining interlocutor. But other actors, such as *Corporación Colectivo de Abogados José Alvear Restrepo* (CAJAR) in Colombia, Asociación Pro Derechos Humanos (APRODEH) in Peru, and *Centro de Estudios Legales y Sociales* (CELS) in Argentina, have also become important players in shaping the IAS.

Another set of actors with a growing stake in the IAS has been scholars. As the ECHR's body of jurisprudence has grown, and as, in some states, constitutional law has merged with human rights law, and both gained in prestige, more legal scholars have begun to write about the IAS. Law schools began offering human rights courses as part of their curriculum; and law journals began to publish articles focused on Inter-American jurisprudence with more frequency. Through the act of publishing, this set of interlocutors writes the IAS into existence in the scholarly imagination, giving it a higher profile, even as their own professional identity becomes tied to the IAS.

Most of the scholarship on the IAS during this era analyzes its jurisprudence (particularly ECHR judgments and commission reports) in different areas of human rights law. Taken together, this body of work tracks the shift over time in the type of human rights matters that come before the IAS. Earlier, analyzes of the duty of the state to punish atrocity crimes and the right to freedom of expression and access to information predominated. Since the 2010s, the right of indigenous peoples to traditionally held lands and to culture; and the right of access to reproductive technology, have taken on more importance.[7] A search for articles about the system conducted in March 2017 pulled up roughly 40 articles between 2014 and 2017 whose main topic was the IAS.[8] The majority focus on doctrinal developments in indigenous rights; reproductive rights; and women's rights. Some also focused on the reception of Inter-American jurisprudence by national courts, with each article usually focusing on one country.

The scholarship in this period is not only doctrinal, however. Scholars informed by the social sciences also begin to pay attention to the IAS, at times employing empirical methodology – ranging from qualitative interviews with deeply embedded actors (Engstrom 2014) to quant-itative analysis of compliance patterns (Hillebrecht 2014) or citation patterns (Schonsteiner 2016) – to cast light on its development. In particular, scholars begin to look at the evolution of the IAS within particular states, trying to understand its growing influence in national political settings,[9] or else striving to explain variation in the impact of the IAS by comparing its institu-tional relationships and performance across states.[10] The first focus has been domestic courts: as in Europe, scholars began to study the different dialogs the ECHR in particular was having with local courts, viewing it not only as a matter of doctrinal but also institutional development. Some of the scholarship goes beyond courts, examining different interlocutors the IAS may have, such as interactions with civil society and executives and legislatures, and how these rela-tionships shape identities, political movements, and state responses.

This strand of scholarship, in other words, has turned toward the study of the IAS institutions as political actors that interact with other political actors, and in particular other national legal institutions, as well as civil society groups and social movements more generally. The relation-ships they form, it observes, account for the IAS's ability to shape politics and have impact at the domestic level. The focus is not on doctrine, nor is it even solely on compliance (although there are many articles that do emphasize compliance processes) (Par 2018). The focus, rather, is on how relationships with different state and non-state actors evolve and shape the impact of the IAS; the variation is in the different actors, and at times in the differences between states. It is a vein of scholarship in conversation with the emerging study of judicialization at the inter-national level more generally.[11]

And yet, in face of the current shift in geopolitical dynamics, this approach falls short. The institutionalist turn moves our attention away from the executive branch, and away from diplo-macy and the OAS as the political home of the IAS, and toward other actors within the govern-ment, and within civil society, thereby obscuring the role foreign policy might play in the system's evolution. But today we need to understand the geopolitics. The relationships of Mexico, Brazil, and the United States to each other and to the IAS seem especially salient to the evolution of the Inter-American System. Indeed, the earlier, Cold War era studies of the IAS payed more attention to the role of the United States than do the later post-1990s studies. Of the 40 articles written in between 2014 and 2016 on the Inter-American System noted above, only one analyzes the relationship of the IAS to the United States and geopolitical issues.[12]

Further, the institutionalist and doctrinal scholarship alike have had a bias toward success stories. In some ways, the scholarship has been Pollyanna-ish, downplaying opposition to and failures of the IAS, and perhaps unthinkingly caught up in a kind of teleology that views ever stronger human rights institutions as somehow inevitable. In particular, studies have not given us a rich, empirically informed account of the 2012 push in the OAS General Assembly to reform the commission, which was born of a shared opposition to the IAS, or of a similar effort in 1993, as states began to resent the commission's ongoing interventions despite democratization (Gonzalez 2013, 67). This stands in contrast to the European System, where the moments of reform and backlash are the focus of much scholarship.[13] Additionally, the institutionalist scholarship has tended to focus on states that have thicker relations to the IAS, as this is where there was more judicial activity, and where the system's bright future seemingly lay. But it is important to understand those states that are more distant members. What does the IAS look like, for example, in less liberal states, such as Bolivia and Ecuador under President Correa? Such a case may hold important lessons, revealing how such a system fares in a less hospitable context in which competing ideologies of indigeneity and socialism are important.

Some of this is already changing, with IAS scholars showing a new interest in backlash and reform, as the next section shows.

Human Rights, Nationalism, and Deglobalization (2017 and Thereafter)

Until 2016, court-focused studies in particular seemingly presumed a world favorable to ever greater global exchange, viewing growing globalization as in some sense inevitable, rather than as politically contingent. But if we are now facing a time of nationalist sentiment and less porous borders – if we are moving toward neo-Westphalia – how does this affect the direction and study of the regional human rights systems, and one might add, international courts more generally? Recently historians have highlighted the role of the United States, and the pro-rights pivot of the Carter administration in particular, in launching the human rights revolution (Moyn 2010). Does the fact that the United States was important in ushering in the global human rights revolution mean that it will also play a role in its diminution? Or has the genie, having engaged with a whole new group of interlocutors, escaped the grasp of states?

In light of the history revisited in the prior two sections, three possible scenarios suggest themselves. The first is the end-times scenario (Hopgood 2014). It imagines that without the support of the United States executive branch, and with many states adopting more nationalist and populist policies, the project of international human rights through international organizations comes crashing down or, alternatively, will quietly fade into irrelevance. As the United States further turns away from human rights in its foreign policy, it is likely that the language of international human rights will lose some of its power, and that the institutions will follow. Venezuelan President Hugo Chavez's denunciation of the American Convention and withdrawal from the Inter-American Court in 2012 took place swiftly and with relatively few repercussions, reminding us how fragile international commitments can be, and how vulnerable to nationalistic politics. As a result, the Inter-American Rights System has been sidelined as the region tries to address the political crisis unfolding in Venezuela under President Maduro. The scuttling of the Southern African Development Community tribunal for a rights-based judgment, also in 2012, further underlines the lesson (Alter, Gatthi, and Helfer 2016).

Insofar as it is a predictive rather than normative endeavor, however, the end-times scenario has two blinds pots. It can be faulted for overemphasizing the role of the state, as opposed to non-state actors, and for overemphasizing in particular the role of the United States in the realm of human rights activity across the globe. Recent scholarship has shown that the states of the Global South, and particularly non-state actors from the Global South, have played an often overlooked role in constructing human rights systems, and in making human rights ideas prominent (Kelly 2018, Sikkink 2017). Social movements and NGOs have been a driving force in defending and shaping the IAS; redefining its docket (for example, broadening its docket to include indigenous rights and reproductive rights in recent years); defending it against attacks; and guiding specific legal interpretations of the American Convention and other legal commitments (Lessard 2011; Brewer and Cavallaro 2008; Santos 2015). Without these actors, the IAS would not have evolved as it has, and might have already been scuttled, or dramatically curtailed, by the OAS.

Second, the end-times scenario overlooks the stickiness and adaptability of institutions. Part of what distinguishes the new Westphalia from the old is that it is inhabited by transnational human rights regimes. These institutions have been around long enough to become embedded in at least some domestic legal systems, "making possible their continuity despite the realignment of global power relations" (Sikkink 2017, 11). Even if it is true that the emergence of the human rights movement was ushered in by Carter's foreign policy and other contingent events in the 1970s, states are not the only significant players on the international plane: international institutions themselves are strategic actors who will seek to survive beyond the particular configuration of ideas and circumstance that led to their creation (Dimaggio and Powell 1983; March and Olson 1989; Keohane and Martin 1995).

One way they can do this is by making themselves useful to those constituencies who will support them. In particular, human rights institutions can create strategic alliances, wherein their interlocutors are not just nation-states that demand deference, but include other actors, and in particular groups of transnational, national, and networked NGOs that themselves create alliances to push particular rights agendas. In this way, we can imagine a fervid defense of a stronger and more autonomous regional system than that experienced in the Venezuela and South American Development Community (SADC) examples. César Rodríguez makes a Trump-era call for these actors to civil society organizations to pursue what he calls "multiple boomerang" strategies, or "actions coordinated by several organizations in different countries, in order to exert simultaneous pressure on the governments to which each of them has access."[14] Indeed, he claims that it was just such an NGO alliance "that blocked the attacks of Latin American states against the Inter-American Human Rights System."[15] Whether this was the only effective force against the "attacks" is arguable, but Rodríguez is right to highlight such alliances as an effective mode of action facilitated by social media and communications.

If the IAS does survive, then, what strategies will it pursue to survive in this new geopolitical context? Perhaps its past holds an answer. A second possible scenario for the IAS's future is that of *strategic deference*: it will re-fashion itself to accommodate more populist politics, or at least to stay more under the radar until a more auspicious time. Politically inflected decision-making occurs in even the most liberal democratic times, but it could become more pronounced, in much the same way that the European Court of Human Rights adopted a strategy of legal diplomacy in the 1950s and 1960 (Madsen 2011). Indeed, some maintain that the IAS has already moved in this direction. If military coups and dictatorships are no longer characteristic of political life, the region has experienced a rise in the more subtle and legalistic forms of democratic backsliding of recent years (Huq and Ginsburg 2017). Executives have pushed back against the IAS with threats of reform, and the Inter-American Commission has been plunged into a financial crisis. Meanwhile, high courts around the region have also pushed back, refusing to comply with the Inter-American Court's orders, or curtailing its legal influence in the domestic sphere (Contesse 2019; Solely and Steininger 2018). Meanwhile, scholars have argued that the ECHR should be more prudent and legalistic in its jurisprudence, both as a survival strategy and a commitment to the rule of law (Contesse 2018; Dulitzky 2015; Malarino 2012). At times, these reproaches seem to have effect. A 2015 judgment in favor of Venezuela, only a few years after it had denounced the American Convention, was decried by long-time observers and participants as a capitulation to the IAS's critics, and as an effort to pander to politics. Recent judgments seem to retreat on expansive readings of freedom of expression and the duty to prosecute atrocity crimes.

Note that strategic deference is not the same as complete dependence. The term suggests that the judicial actor will only yield if it calculates it has no other choice. But the flipside of strategic deference is relative autonomy. Sometimes it is the state that will yield, foregoing its preference in the short-term in order to nurture the appearance of judicial independence. For even in oppressive times, "the forms and rhetoric of law acquire a distinct identity which may, on occasion, inhibit power and afford some protection to the powerless."[16] In this sense, the Venezuela example is misleading. Chavez's Venezuela had sequestered itself from the IAS. There were many judgments against Venezuela, it is true. But there was little local litigation that referred to the IAS (despite the best efforts of local lawyers). The Venezuela case, while important, thus does not bear out how an attempt to ignore or withdraw from the IAS might play out in those states where the IAS is deeply embedded. In Colombia, the American Convention is woven into the constitution, and the constitutional court regularly reviews local matters through the lens of the Inter-American Court's jurisprudence. Denunciation in such a scenario is arguably tantamount to a constitutional amendment. These legal footholds make it more cumbersome and costly, in terms of reputation, for governments to simply ignore or withdraw from the IAS. Further, the regional human rights systems can make themselves useful to states by providing an imprimatur of legitimacy in the human rights realm. It is not that the human rights movement or IAS could continue indefinitely in face of hostility from the United States and OAS: it is a creature of the OAS and ever vulnerable to its politics. Rather, it is that a strategic IAS would be able to withstand some pushback. Once human rights have been institutionalized, they acquire a force of their own, and the scope of autonomy from raw politics may be reduced but not entirely erased by a turn toward nationalist populism. The strategic deference scenario thus seems more sophisticated in its understanding of institutions, and pays attention to the pre-1970s trajectories of the regional rights systems. Alternatively, the third scenario is that the IAS may take an entirely different tack, moving away from case adjudication and from judicial forms. As noted in section one, the IAS has a political as well as a judicial modality. Indeed, the adjudicative model only became central after the 1990s, with the spread of democracy, constitutional courts, and the rise of the human rights movement. Were the IAS resolution of individual petitions to become too constrained, the commission could turn its energy to the diplomatic intervention style of acting that characterized it in the Cold War era. The IAS first established itself not by staying out of the way so much as by seeking human rights common ground with the United States, and exploiting those areas in order to take a stand. The focus was the commission, not the ECHR, and direct lobbying and political agreement with the executive, rather than individual complaints. We can thus imagine an IAS that, like European rights system in the 1960s, engages in legal diplomacy, and, like the CIDH of the 1960s and 1970s, is politically engaged. Some argue that human rights advocates have been wrong to focus so much on the law and legal systems in their advocacy, to the detriment of both the human rights movement, and of international law itself (Wuerth 2017). Perhaps this will be a time of less judicial engagement.

Even if the IAS reverts to a more political modality, this would not be a simple return to the past. We live in a world that is politically fragmented, and Washington, DC does not hold the same position it once did, so other strategies and alliances would play a bigger role. The commission could reemerge as an actor conducting political diplomacy for human rights, partnering at one moment with the United States State Department, at another with other OAS governments but also with transnational NGO networks, to advance distinct human rights issues in the multiple boomerangs Rodriguez has described. Further, we live in a world with a potent infrastructure in place that facilitates transnational exchange. Strategic alliances would be more fluid, easier to make and unmake than in the past.

Finally, to circle back to the beginning, nationalist populism is on the rise. This trend is fueled in part by discontent with the political order that facilitated free trade, deregulation of the market, and reducing the role of the state. One of the arguments made by the end-times scholars is that human rights have been invented and claimed principally by the world's elites. This means not only that it is liable to misperceive the actual lived experience of those it seeks to help in the Global South, but also that it has paid little heed to the concerns of the working class. A critique of the current human rights regime, in other words, is that it simply fails to address the problem of middle class dislocation and job stagnation due to economic globalization, and of rising inequality within states (Moyn 2017). Perhaps, in this third scenario, and no longer constrained by individual focused case-based adjudication, human rights institutions and actors will forge new alliances and make themselves useful to a new set of interlocutors and norm entrepreneurs.

So far, the two main organs of the IAS seem to be following a mix of the second and third scenarios. While it has seemingly retreated on some doctrines, the ECHR in particular issued a series of judgments in 2017 that were anything but legalist and deferential: one announced a progressive doctrine on gay marriage, one focused on transversal environmental claims, and one elaborated a new doctrine for Economic, Social and Cultural Rights claims. The ECHR was once again boldly, progressively developing human rights doctrine, defying those calling for a more incremental approach. Interestingly, two of the judgments were issued not in case-based claims but rather as advisory opinions. Perhaps the ECHR will use advisory opinions to issue progressive jurisprudence and inspire civil society and human rights lawyers, while developing a different strategy for individual cases and constitutional court judges. In other words, even as we seek to understand the past anew as a way of exploring the present, it is important that we also keep attune to the possibility of innovation. The IAS may yet forge a new survival strategy that mixes law and utopia – the uneasy tension at the core of international human rights law – in an innovative way.

The agenda for IAS scholarship, then, should include inquiry into the strategies it is using in this changed time. In particular, empirical scholarship should focus more on the foreign diplomacy of states, and on civil society, to explain the directions the IAS is taking. These are two areas that have been studied less in recent years, but which will likely become important moving forward. More deeply, the alliance between human rights ideas and movements, on the one hand, and law and litigation, on the other, has been at the core of the post-nineties rise of human rights. It now deserves more critical inquiry.

Conclusions

This chapter began by arguing that we must reconsider the role of geopolitics in shaping regional human rights systems if we are to understand and analyze the present and imagine the future. The analyzes conducted suggest several new directions for scholarship on the IAS, and human rights more generally in the region. First, the pre-1970s past now becomes more important, recast no longer as a stillborn or quiet period, but a period of active endurance in a time of ideological contestation. The experience of IAS states that are not active players is also important. Second, however, what we learn from that deep past cannot be imported wholesale. We must be careful to consider the politics of institutions once they have become more entrenched.

A difference with that past is that the IAS is embedded in many national legal systems, and has compliance constituencies within and beyond the state. Finally, drawing upon these ideas, the chapters considered distinct possible future scenarios for the IAS in a less globalizing world. These scenarios could also be viewed as hypotheses or theories that provide guidance for further study of the IAS.

Even as the chapter predicts that the IAS will continue on, adapting to the new geopolitical context, it has not engaged in the normative debate over whether human rights *should* reinvent themselves for the future, or whether they should be cast aside to make room for new ideologies, and eventually institutions, more able to address growing inequality and middle class discontent. One consideration for this normative debate is that the IAS and its allies have shown a surprising level of resilience. The IAS may yet forge a new survival strategy that engages law and utopia – the uneasy tension at the core of international human rights – in an innovative way that speaks to these concerns.

Notes

1 Sam Moyn's exploration of this question sidelines the role Latin American states and NGOs (Kelly [2018] and Sikkink [2017]. See also Garth Bryant and Dezalay, Yves, *The Internationalization of Palace Wars* [Chicago, 2002]).
2 *Lawless* v. *Ireland* Appl no 332/57 (ECtHR, 1 July 1961).
3 The commission's first two country reports both focused on Cuba. See www.oas.org/en/iachr/reports/country.asp. Accessed December 5, 2018.
4 See, for example, Juan Méndez and Francisco Cox (eds.), *El Futuro del Sistema Interamericano de Protección de los Derechos Humanos* (San José: IIDH, 1998).
5 J.A. López Pacheco, S. Hincapié Jiménez, "Derechos humanos y activismo legal transnacional. Estrategias de las ONG en México y Colombia," 25(49) 7–34 *Perfiles Latinoamericanos* (2017).
6 Klass Dykmann, *Philanthropic endeavors or the exploitation of an ideal?: the human rights policy of the Organization of American States in Latin America (1970–1991)*, (Madrid: Vervuert, 2004).
7 The literature on indigenous rights issues in the IAS continues to grow. A few examples include James Anaya and Robert Williams, "The Protection of Indigenous Peoples' Rights over Lands and Natural Resources under the Inter-American Human Rights System," *Harvard Human Rights Journal* 14(3) (2001); Jo M. Pasqualucci, "The Evolution of International Indigenous Rights in the Inter-American Human Rights System," *Human Rights Law Review 6(2) (2006)* 281–322; Thomas Antkowiak, Rights, Resources and Rhetoric: Indigenous Peoples and the Inter-American Court, *University of Pennsylvannia Journal of International Law* 35(1) 113–187. For examples of scholarship on gender in the IAS, see Medina Quiroga, Cecilia, "Human Rights of Women: Where are we now in the Americas?" in Manganas, A. (ed.), *Essays in Honour of Alice Yotopoulos- Marangopoulos*, Vol. B. Nomiki Bibliothiki Group, (Panteion University, Atenas, 2003); Badilla, Ana Elena, e Isabel Torres García, "La protección de los derechos de las mujeres en el Sistema Interamericano de Derechos Humanos" in IIDH, *El Sistema Interamericano de Protección de los Derechos Humanos y los derechos de poblaciones migrantes, las mujeres, los pueblos indígenas y los niños, niñas y adolescentes*, Vol. I. (IIDH, San José, Costa Rica, 2004); Enzamaria Tramontana, "Hacia la consolidación de la perspectiva de género en el Sistema Interamericano: avances y desafíos a la luz de la reciente jurisprudencia de la Corte de San José," Revista IIDH 53 (2011) 141–181; Vinodh Jaichand and Ciara O'Connell, "Bringing It Home: The IAS and State Obligations – Using a gender approach regionally to address women's rights violations domestically," *Inter-American and European Human Rights Journal*, 3 (2010), pp. 58–67.
8 The search was conducted in English and Spanish, in Lexis and Pathfinder, seeking within the 2014 to March 2017 period. Only articles that had at least one-third of their content related to the Inter-American Court/Commission/Human Rights were included. The databases used were West Law, EBSCOhost (all), JSTOR, Human Rights Quarterly, Heins Online, Google Scholar Search. The terms used were "inter-american court/commission," "sistema/comisión interamericana."
9 An example of this kind of work focused on Argentina is Par Engstrom, "A special relationship gone normal? Argentina and the Inter-American Human Rights System, 1979–2013," *Pensamiento Propio* 38(18) (2013) 115–147. An example focused on Brazil is Cecelia MacDowell Santos, "Transnational

Legal Activism and the State: Reflections on Cases against Brazil in the Inter-American Commission on Human Rights," *Sur – Revista Internacional de Direitos Humanos* (August 1, 2008).

10 Examples include F. Basch et al., 'The Effectiveness of the IAS of Human Rights Protection: A Quantitative Approach to its Functioning and Compliance With its Decisions,' (2010) 7 *Sur – International Journal of Human Rights* 9; Courtney Hillebrecht, *Domestic Politics and International Human Rights Tribunals: The Problem of Compliance* (2014); Oscar Parra-Vera "'Empoderamiento institucional' e iniciativas progresistas: Impacto del Sistema Interamericano de Derechos Humanos en tensiones y choques entre órganos del Estado," *Revista Pensamiento Jurídico* 43 (Universidad Nacional de Colombia, 2016) 405–442.

11 See Karen Alter, *The New Terrain of International Law: Courts, Politics, Rights* (Princeton 2014).

12 Par Engstrom, "El Sistema Interamericano de Derechos Humanos y Las Relaciones Estados Unidos-America Latina," *Foro Internacional* 55(2) (2015) 454–502.

13 One difference between the two systems is that COE states explicitly reform the institutions through protocols, whereas the American States have never done so. The COE reforms are thus become open and transparent, and the resulting protocols and declarations receive much scholarly commentary. By contrast, reform to the IAS seems mostly to be driven by the ECHR and commission themselves. See Gerald L. Neuman "Import, Export, and Regional Consent in the Inter-American Court of Human Rights," *The European Journal of International* Law Vol. 19 no. 1 (2008) 101–123.

14 César Rodríguez-Garavito, "Trump's victory could push the human rights movement to transform," December 10, 2016 www.opendemocracy.net/c-sar-rodr-guez-garavito/trump-s-victory-could-push-human-rights-movement-to-transform

15 Ibid.

16 E.P. Thompson, *Whigs and Hunters: The Origin of the Black Act*, (New York: Pantheon 1976) at 266.

References

Alter, Karen, James Thuo Gathii, and Larry Helfer. 2016. "Backlash against International Courts in West, East and Southern Africa: Causes and consequences." *European Journal of International Law*, 27(2): 293–328.

Basch, Fernando, Leonardo Filippini, Ana Laya, Mariano Nino, Felicitas Rossi, and Bárbara Schreiber. 2010. "The Effectiveness of the Inter-American System of Human Rights Protection: A Quantitative Approach to its Functioning and Compliance with its Decisions." *Sur – International Journal of Human Rights*, 7(12).

Brysk, Alison. 1993. "From Above and Below: Social Movements, the International System, and Human Rights in Argentina." *Comparative Political Studies*, 26(3): 259–85.

Cavallaro, James L. and Stephanie Erin Brewer. 2008. "The Virtue of Following: The Role of Inter-American Litigation in Campaigns for Social Justice." *Sur – Revista Internacional de Direitos Humanos*, 5(8).

Contesse, Jorge. 2019. *Resisting the Inter-American Human Rights System*, 44 Yale J. Int'l L.

Dykmann, Klass. 2004. *Philanthropic Endeavors or the Exploitation of an Ideal? The Human Rights Policy of the Organization of American States in Latin America (1970–1991)*. Madrid: Vervuert.

Engstrom, Par. 2013. "A Special Relationship Gone Normal? Argentina and the Inter-American Human Rights System, 1979–2013." *Pensamiento Propio*, 38, (June-December 2013) 115–50.

Gonzales, Felipe. 2013. *El Sistema Interamericano de Derechos Humanos: Transoformaciones y Desafios*. Tirant lo Blanc: Valencia.

Hawkins, Darren and Wade Jacoby. 2010. "Partial Compliance: A Comparison of the European and Inter-American Courts for Human Rights." *Journal of International Law and International Relations*, 6(1): 35–85.

Helfer, Laurence R. 2008. "Redesigning the European Court of Human Rights: Embeddedness as a Deep Structural Principle of the European Human Rights Regime." *European Journal of International Law*, 19: 125–59.

Hillebrecht, Courtney. 2014. *Domestic Politics and International Human Rights Tribunals: The Problem of Compliance*. Cambridge.

Hopgood, Stephen. 2013. *The Endtimes of Human Rights*. Cornell.

Huneeus, Alexandra. 2011. "Courts Resisting Courts: Lessons from the Inter-American Court's Struggle to Enforce Human Rights." *Cornell International Law Journal*, 44(3): 494–533.

Huneeus, Alexandra. 2015. "Human Rights between Jurisprudence and Social Science." *Leiden Journal of International Law*, 28(2): 255–66.

Huneeus, Alexandra, and Mikael Rask Madsen. 2018. "Between Universalism and Regional Law and Politics: A Comparative History of the American, European, and African Human Rights Systems." *International Journal of Constitutional Law,* 16(1): 136–60.

Huq, Aziz Z. and Tom Ginsburg. Forthcoming. "How to Lose a Constitutional Democracy." (January 18, 2017), *UCLA Law Review,* 65. Available at: http://dx.doi.org/10.2139/ssrn.2901776. Accessed February 2, 2017.

Kelly, Patrick William. 2018a. *Sovereign Emergencies: Latin America and the Making of Global Human Rights Politics.* Cambridge.

Kelly, Patrick William. 2018b. "What Is Hope For?" *Los Angeles Review of Books.* Available at: https://lareviewofbooks.org/article/what-is-hope-for/. Accessed July 13, 2018.

Keohane, Robert O. and Lisa L. Martin. 1995. "The Promise of Institutionalist Theory." *International Security,* (Summer, 1995) 20(1): 39–51.

Krsticevic, Viviana. 2007. "Reflexiones sobre la ejecución de sentencias de las decisiones del sistema interamericano de protección de derechos humanos." En Viviana Krsticevic and Lilliana Tojo (eds.), *Implementación de las Decisiones del Sistema Interamericano de Derechos Humanos: Jurisprudencia, Normativa y Experiencias Nacionales.* Available at: www.corteidh.or.cr/tablas/23679.pdf Consulted March 28, 2019.

Madsen, Mikael Rask. 2011. "Legal Diplomacy – Law, Politics and the Genesis of Postwar European Human Rights." In Hoffman, S.L. (ed.), *Human Rights in the Twentieth Century: A Critical History,* Cambridge University Press.

March, James G. and James P. Olsen. 1989. *Rediscovering Institutions: The Organizational Basis of Politics.* New York: The Free Press.

Medina Quiroga, Cecilia. 1988. *The Battle of Human Rights.* Springer.

Moyn, Samuel. 2014. *The Last Utopia: Human Rights in History.* Harvard University Press.

Moyn, Samuel. 2018. *Not Enough: Human Rights in an Unequal World.* Harvard.

Santos, Cecelia MacDowell. 2015. "Transitional Justice from the Margins: Legal Mobilization and Memory Politics in Brazil." In Nina Schneider and Marcia Esparza (eds.), *Legacies of State Violence and Transitional Justice in Latin America: A Janus-Faced Paradigm?* New York: Lexington Books: 37–72.

Schönsteiner, Judith. 2016. "El Derecho Internacional de los Derechos Humanos en el Tribunal Constitucional Chileno: El Mínimo Común Denominador." *Revista de Derecho de la Universidad Austral de Chile* (Valdivia), Año 29, Vol. 1, 2016, 197–226 (Scielo/Scopus).

Sikkink, Kathryn. 2017. *Evidence for Hope: Making Human Rights Work in the 21st Century.* Princeton.

Wojciech Sadurski. 2009. *Partnering with Strasbourg: Constitutionalisation of the European Court of Human Rights, the Accession of Central and East European States to the Council of Europe, and the Idea of Pilot Judgments.* 9 HUM. RTS. L. REV. 397: 406.

Wuerth, Ingrid B. 2017. "International Law in the Post-Human Rights Era." 96 *Texas Law Review* 279.

PART III

Law and Social Movements

21

THE JUDICIALIZATION OF POLITICS IN LATIN AMERICA

Bruce M. Wilson and Camila Gianella

Introduction

Three decades ago Latin American judiciaries, especially superior courts, attracted little interest from academics because they tended to act as political ciphers exercising little independence from their executive branch, or as supine institutions with no discernible political function. However, Latin America has witnessed the rise of newly assertive courts that are willing and able to act as independent accountability agents regulating executive and legislative power and adjudicating the constitutionality of laws, decrees, and regulations. Moreover, some superior courts have breathed new life into previously non-justiciable constitutional rights and now routinely protect the rights of even the most vulnerable, politically, and socially-marginalized citizens. Those changes were the perfect spur for socio-legal scholars to analyze courts and to understand the origins of the new role as well as the impact of courts' intervention on social and political life. This chapter reviews the existing literature highlighting the different approaches used to understand the increasingly important role of courts over the last 30 years.

The first part of this chapter traces the rapid transformation of Latin American courts that began in the 1980s, identifies the motivation for those judicial reforms, and the approaches used to understand the metamorphosis of many Latin American superior courts. We sample the rapidly growing comparative judicial politics literature that has made strides to remedy the "paucity of research on the role courts actually play or may play in different nations" identified by Irwin Stotzky as recently as 2004 (2004, 198–9). That literature has employed different approaches and methodologies to understand judicial behavior and the rise, and in some cases, fall of judicial independence. Early literature frequently concentrated on international agencies' central role in the judicialization of politics and were followed by studies that focused on domestic factors and detailed country case studies. These case studies in turn facilitated paired, cross-country comparisons on specific issues, and aided in the creation of databases that generate large-*n* multi-country statistical analyzes; institutionally-strategically focused approaches complement social movement approaches leading to broader perspectives on the phenomenon of judicialization emphasizing the wider opportunity structures and the role played by social movements.

The second part of the chapter addresses some of these literatures (particularly the rational choice, historical institutional, and social movements approaches) that analyze the more assertive behavior of Latin American superior courts and the extent and impact of their interventions in politics and policy making. The chapter also examines some of the many ways courts have affected the political lives of countries, including through judicial review, upholding the rule of law, equilibrating the political balance of powers, and generating and enforcing citizens' rights. Here we touch on the increased accountability function exercised by superior courts and then employ brief case studies of LGBTI (lesbian, gay, bisexual, transgender, and intersex) and health rights to reveal the process through which the constitutional rights of some of the most vulnerable sectors of society have been advanced in some countries. The final sections highlight attempts by elected executives to recapture and retake control of superior courts, and explore the rise of nascent backlashes against unpopular judicial victories.

Judicialization of Politics

Gretchen Helmke and Julio Rios-Figueroa open their 2011 book, *Courts in Latin America*, with the emphatic statement that: "Courts are central players in Latin American politics." To most scholars of contemporary Latin American politics, this is an uncontroversial and widely-accepted statement of fact. Yet, surprisingly, just three decades ago the opposite was generally true for nearly all Latin American superior courts: Mecham (1959) states, nowhere were "constitutions more elaborate and less observed" than in Latin America; 20 years later, Karst and Rosenn (1975:79) observe that in no country did the "judiciary wield significant political power"; and Rodríguez et al. (2003, 157) conclude that constitutions were viewed largely as "aspirational" documents "routinely accompanied ... by provisions for their suspension in times of political crisis" (Loveman 1993, 5). That is, superior courts, and the constitutions from which they draw their power and legitimacy, were largely irrelevant to the quotidian lives of Latin Americans.[1] Early research on Latin American superior courts tended to be skeptical or pessimistic about superior courts' capacity to affect social change or exercise a meaningful accountability function to check the behavior of the other branches of government (e.g., Hammergren 1998; Larkins 1998; Garcia 1998; Jarquín and Carrillo 1998).

As Sieder, Schjolden, and Angell (2005) note, however, not all Latin American superior courts were completely dormant. There are notable cases where superior courts' actions were politically significant precisely because of their judicial inaction that allowed executives to routinely exceed their constitutional remits; or where courts acted as political ciphers for the political and/or economic elites to thwart the policies of governments elected reformist platforms (Chile in the early 1970s, for example).[2] This means that the judicialization of politics is more than just the exercise of judicial review by superior courts (Sieder et al. 2005, 3). Rather, the "judicialization of politics" should be treated as a broader phenomenon encompassing the "increased presence of judicial processes and court rulings in political and social life, and the increasing resolution of political, social or state-society conflicts in the court." Although, the judicialization of politics in Latin America developed unevenly across the region and within countries over time and was driven by different motivations and outcomes, as Daniel Brinks (2012, 61) concludes, in Latin America "the days when authoritarian and democratic leaders alike could safely ignore their apex courts, trampling on rights and transgressing the constitutional separation of powers" have long gone.

Explanations for the Waking of Latin American Superior Courts

Smulovitz (2008) and Domingo (2010), among others, have stressed a variety of institutional and political conditions that influenced the timing and direction of the recent wave of judicialization of politics in Latin America.[3] In some countries, institutional reforms took the form of constitutional processes and the adoption of new constitutions, which in the late 1980s and early 1990s created and/or strengthened superior courts' ability to act independently of the other branches of government. Some of these new apex courts were deliberately created to be easily accessible to ordinary citizens. In Colombia, for example, the promulgation of the 1991 Constitution marked a new era in politics through a process of judicializing key aspects of Colombian politics. The 1991 Constitution was written as an inclusive document as part of an attempt to end years of political violence that had plagued the country and included major conceptual and structural innovations that helped contribute to a subsequent rise in judicial interventions on social and economic rights. The new constitution included a mechanism for the protection of fundamental constitutional rights, *acción de tutela*, that allows any citizen to demand immediate protection of his or her constitutional rights (González and Durán 2011, 54),[4] and it established "a specialized tribunal overseeing a new 'constitutional jurisdiction,' which extended to all Colombian judges" (Yamin and Parra-Vera 2010, 109).

By way of contrast, the start of the judicialization of politics process in Costa Rica, the hemisphere's oldest democracy, took place in a well-functioning democratic state that was not experiencing any major political crises or political turmoil. Instead a little discussed, minor constitutional amendment in 1989 created a constitutional chamber of the supreme court, which quickly became one of the most powerful and assertive courts in the Americas (Navia and Ríos-Figueroa 2005). As in Colombia, and in contrast to the pre-reform situation in Costa Rica, access to the new constitutional chamber of the supreme court is very open: it requires no lawyers, no fees, few legal formalities, and a very broad definition of legal standing. In both countries, the pre-reformed superior courts were politically insignificant institutions with little interest or experience in holding the executive and legislative branches of government to account or in recognizing and protecting citizens' constitutional rights. The reformed courts, as asserted by Rios-Figueroa and Helmke (2011), quickly became central actors in the political lives of their respective countries.

Institutional reforms also took place at the judicial system level across the region where a broad acceptance of the need to promote the rule of law was viewed as a necessary, integral step of democratization; judicial system reforms were perceived as central to the overall democratic reforms and to protect human rights, enhance social justice, and promote democracy, law and order, also sponsored judicial reforms in many transitional democracies in the Global South, particularly in Latin America (Carothers 2001).[5] Strengthening the rule of law was also seen as essential for the adoption of free market economic policies aimed to strengthen private investment, which led to important international support for judicial reforms in the region (McAuslan 1997). Funding and planning for the reforms was provided by international development agencies, international financial institutions (IFIs), and nongovernmental organizations (NGOs). Starting in the 1980s, these agencies pushed judicial reform as a central part of their democratization and economic development aid plans across the Global South, including in Latin America and the Caribbean. It was argued that strengthening domestic judicial systems and courts would limit governments' capacity to interfere in free markets and would protect property rights and thus foster investment and economic development (Domingo and Sieder 2001; Faundez, 1997; Messick 1999; Wilson, Rodríguez, and Handberg 2004). The United States Agency for International Development (USAID), a major sponsor of judicial reform, for example, states that "an effective judicial system is integral to the economic growth and well-being of a society" (Vaky 1998, 137). Luis Salas argues, "At the core of this new law reform movement is a belief in the inevitability of global economic integration and the evolution of legal systems to meet the challenges of the new neo-liberal market economies" (Salas 2001, 17). This interest in judicial reform was reflected in major investments by international agencies including the World Bank, the Inter-American Development Bank (IDB), the United Nations Development Program (UNDP), governmental agencies, and nongovernmental institutions, which together invested nearly US$1 billion in the decade starting in the mid-1990s (DeShazo and Vargas 2006).

Institutional reform was not limited to the level of the judiciary, but also transformed state apparatus with the "gradual expansion of quasi-judicial agencies, such as specialized boards or tribunals, ombudsmen, or arbitrating panels" (Domingo 2010) that can also check the actions of political and state agencies. However, the early judicialization of politics in Latin America was closely tied to judicial reforms and the democratization process that swept across much of the region starting in the late 1970s and spanning the next two decades. Within that process, O'Donnell (1999) identified the need for a major horizontal accountability role for politically independent, well-functioning superior courts to force power holders to govern within the limits of their constitutional remits.

Socio-legal scholars, thus, began to examine the conditions under which superior courts were able and/or willing to exercise their constitutionally-mandated accountability function. Case studies from Latin America and Africa demonstrate that even formally independent courts might hesitate to exercise an accountability function to limit the actions of a popularly elected executive or legislature when other institutional rules (appointments, funding, etc.,) undercut that *de jure* independence Gloppen (2004, 2010). In that research, Gloppen et al. (2010) identify three sets of factors and demonstrate how their interaction can explain different levels of judicial accountability across countries and across time: each country's socio-political tradition and context, individual motivations of judges, and the institutional structures.

In the context of Latin America, where many citizens feel politicians do not represent their interests, this new judicial venue to press their demands was crucial.[6] Democratization processes and the search for justice for human rights abuses perpetrated by the authoritarian governments of the mid-1970s to the 1990s helped civil society organizations become sophisticated users of courts to challenge the actions and inactions of even the most powerful groups. Regardless, the denunciations of human rights abuses that resulted in positive outcomes for the victims, the combination of new institutional structures and the context, indubitably advanced civil society organizations' capacity to strategically litigate in court and to publically claim rights that were previously ignored by the popularly elected branches. NGOs operating in Latin America employed the principles of international human rights law to engage indifferent domestic judges and prosecutors to address and pursue human rights abuses perpetrated by authoritarian regimes (González-Ocanto 2016).

A third variable identified by Gloppen et al. (2010) concerns the role of judges. A considerable literature examines the significance of United States Supreme Court justices' political, economic, religious, social, and educational backgrounds on their voting decisions (see for example, Epstein and Knight 1998). In the Latin American context, a growing literature similarly examines the role of individual apex court magistrate decision-making processes, particularly as it applies to the judicial independence of the court. Helmke (2005), for example, shows how Argentine justices, even in times of military dictatorship, still have the capacity to make decisions that reflected their own preference and their understanding of the political context within which they operated. Similarly, Rodriguez-Raga (2011) examines the factors that allow Colombian Constitutional Court magistrates to vote against the executive's preferences.

The arena provided by the courts to such "non-partisan" causes has been central to the process of the judicialization of politics; it has allowed weakly-organized groups, powerless minorities, and individuals with urgent matters to present their claims in front of a receptive, powerful public institution. Therefore, the growing use of courts in Latin America should be understood as a search for spaces for political participation within a context of diminishing trust in traditional paths of political participation, such as political parties rather than a reflection of growing confidence in the judiciary itself.[7] This is not to suggest universal support for litigation as a strategy to overcome politically and socially-marginalized groups caught up in a democratic deficit. Indeed, a great deal of literature, primarily from the United States, views litigation strategies as undemocratic (Scalia 2015), ineffective (Rosenberg 1991), or harmful (Klarman 2005; Rosenberg 2008).

Increased autonomy and accountability of superior courts via institutional reforms, though, has not all been unidirectional or without political contestation. There have been some recent successful efforts by elected politicians to limit superior court autonomy through "court stuffing" to reassert executive control over the court and thus diminish courts' capacity to exercise their accountability function; in these cases superior courts began to resemble the pre-reformed captured superior courts. For example, the 2009 dismissal of the Bolivian Constitutional Court and the 2013 political reshuffling of the Venezuelan Supreme Court are two examples of naked political takeovers of previously independent superior courts. These "alteration of institutional arrangements," identified and analyzed by Pérez-Liñán and Castagnola (2016, 396), harm judicial stability as "constitutional amendments and replacements offer a window of opportunity to reorganize the composition of the judiciary." The impact of the Venezuelan "court stuffing" can be seen in the supplicant actions of the court during the Chavez and Maduro administrations when its assertive actions on behalf of President Maduro after the 2015 elections undermined the democratic election results and thwarted the agenda of the anti-Maduro majority in congress; or when it stripped the national congress of its powers in early 2017.

Nicaragua provides an illustrative example of how elected executives can undermine strong, independent judiciaries: the *Frente Sandinista de Liberación Nacional* (FSLN) captured the country's supreme court as part of a larger ongoing project to control all major governmental institutions and effectively blur the lines between the political party and state institutions. The Nicaraguan Constitution's prohibition on consecutive reelection (with a maximum of two non-consecutive terms) was a major roadblock to sitting President Daniel Ortega's desire to seek immediate reelection. Lacking the required supermajority in the national legislature to amend the constitution, Ortega and 100 FSLN mayors instead flooded the constitutional chamber of the supreme court with claims challenging the constitutionality of the reelection prohibition arguing it was a violation of their political participation rights. In 2009, a court majority found in Ortega's favor (Constitutional Chamber of the Supreme Court of Nicaragua 2009) allowing him and other elected officials to seek reelection. Vilma Nuñez, head of a leading Nicaraguan Human Rights group, points to the absurdity of the decision claiming: "This is the only country in the world where the court has declared the constitution unconstitutional" (Johnson 2010). The court's decision led to non-FSLN appointed justices to boycott the proceedings, which in turn permitted Ortega to stuff the court with *suplentes* (supplemental magistrates) to replace the boycotting *magistrados propetarios* (tenured magistrates). Consequently, President Ortega and his party effectively exercise control over all branches of government and have reduced the superior court to its traditional supine position vis-à-vis the popularly elected branches. In the 2016 election, the Nicaraguan Supreme Court removed the leader of the main opposition party, *Partido Liberación Independiente* (PLI), effectively clearing the road for Ortega to win a third consecutive term as president (Lakhani 2016). The alterations to the institutional arrangements that made judicialization viable, reflect how politics still can take over the courts.

Bringing Politics to the Court: Checks and Balances of Judicialization

Superior courts have inserted themselves or been inserted into a wide range of policy fights that necessarily make enacting economic and/or social policies slower and more difficult. In the Brazilian case, Taylor (2008, 3) notes that the federal courts frequently are

> called upon to evaluate the decisions of congress or the president, and on a fair number of such occasions, courts effectively halted policy implementation and sent policy makers back to the drawing board, with effects that reverberated across the entire body politic.

Courts in Brazil, and elsewhere in Latin America, "have helped to define the alternative available to policymaker, legitimating or de-legitimating certain policy choices" (Taylor 2008, 3).

While reinvigorated courts did not necessarily produce the pro-free market, pro-business decisions that many of the international funding agencies had anticipated (Wilson Rodríguez and Handberg 2004), they did become central to many public policy debates. Reformed courts were increasingly willing and able to challenge presidential control over public policy and to hand defeats to major government policy initiatives. In some cases, newly assertive superior courts re-equilibrated the balance of power between government branches. For example, a decision by the Sala IV in Costa Rica ended the Legislative Assembly's presumption that its "power to legislate was absolute" (Urcuyo 1995) by ruling a 35-year-old constitutional amendment barring presidential reelection as unconstitutional. This decision sent a very clear message to the congress concerning its policymaking limitations.[8] Because the Sala IV has the power to review bills and laws for constitutionality, it has become a tool of the opposition parties to send bills to the court for a ruling on their constitutionality as a delaying and/or blocking tactic against government bills. This effectively grants more political bargaining power to smaller, nongovernment parties in congress, which has had a significant impact on policy outcomes and the types of policies that can be successfully debated in congress (Wilson 1998, 2011).

Health Rights Litigation

Health rights litigation is an example of recent research on the role and impact of superior courts in Latin America. The research builds on the earlier country case studies to examine a single important issue in a cross-national (and regional) context (see Yamin and Gloppen 2011, for example). It also builds on the research on policymaking and the increasingly important political tactic of challenging policy on procedural grounds or the constitutionality of a bill's content at the superior court. Frequently, the judicial review actions of the superior courts impact legislators' and executive lawmaking capacities as well as citizens' specific constitutional rights. An illustrative example can be seen in the litigation of health rights in Latin America, which brings together policymaking, individual rights, and the domestic application of international legal instruments. Litigation for health rights also illustrates a perceptible shift in the action of courts and the attention of scholarly research on courts in Latin America, from a concern with judicial independence and accountability, to a more sophisticated focus on explaining the role of judges in deciding cases, the role of courts in policy design, and the implementation of their decisions on healthcare systems as well as their distributional effects.

Many Latin American constitutions do not contain an explicit constitutional right to health and even some of those with explicit constitutional right to health, such as Colombia, the right was not intended to be a justiciable right that could be litigated in the courts. This is, in part, why the rise of health rights litigation in superior courts has been very controversial. It is also controversial because superior court responses to litigation impact issues of medical ethics, government health policy, health priority setting, and the central role medical experts in deciding healthcare decisions. Medical decisions involve highly technical, complicated, and complex areas historically not addressed in courts where magistrates are experts in the law not medicine. The rapid growth in litigation involving the right to health is diverse as are court responses to the litigated claims. In some countries, superior courts have created a justiciable right to health based on other constitutional rights including the right to dignity, social security, life, a clean environment, minorities' rights, as well as on the content of international legal instruments.

Courts' experience with health cases has led to a more profound understanding of other rights, for example, the Colombian Constitutional Court (CCC) has protected the right to health in three ways. First, it found the right to health enforceable when it is connected to questions of the right to life, personal integrity, and human dignity; thus allowing Colombians to request procedures not included in the healthcare system (POS) in a broader range of situations than just imminent death (Yamin, Parra-Vera, and Gianella-Malca 2011; Corte Constitucional de Colombia 2008). Second, the court recognized the fundamental nature of the right to health where claimants are subject to special protection, such as children, indigenous populations, or people with mental or physical disabilities. In these cases, the court has called for the effective guarantee of certain health services. Third, the court has gradually left the doctrine of connection (between health and life with dignity) to justify the enforceability of the right to health and recognized the right to health as a fundamental right. Yet, for the court, constitutional rights are not absolute; they may be legitimately limited in accordance with criteria of reasonableness and proportionality. As with other constitutional rights, the court recognizes that while the right to health has a programmatic character, it carries obligations that can require immediate fulfillment, either because they do not necessitate additional resources or because the severity and urgency of the case requires immediate action.

The intervention of courts in health rights cases, especially those involving access to prescription drugs, treatments, and supplies, have attracted a great deal of attention because of its presumed negative impact on health systems' financial sustainability and the fear that litigation could increase inequality by favoring those able to litigate (usually wealthier citizens) against those who cannot (the poorest). There is, though, little evidence to support the inequality effect of health rights litigation (Yamin and Gloppen 2011), and without acknowledging the gravity of the system financial sustainability concerns, and the need to recognize the very real budget limitations of health systems. It is true that in some cases court interventions have forced governments to fund the court-mandated health rights decisions, improve health spending, and to prevent public resources misuse (Yamin and Gloppen 2011; Norheim and Wilson 2014).

Latin American superior courts have not been indifferent to the economic health system sustainability concern. It is possible to argue that during the first years of health rights litigation in the region the economic sustainability arguments were not at the core of the decisions. However, it is also true that through the years, countries with the highest number of right to health legal claims (Brazil, Colombia, and Costa Rica) have developed an increasing awareness of the health system's economic sustainability. For example, in the CCC's 2008 decision, T-760, it required major reforms of the Colombian health system, but the court took into consideration the system's economic sustainability and ordered "that whatever reform was adopted for the healthcare system to comply with the decision rendered by the court, it should be financially sustainable" (Cepeda-Espinosa 2011).

Critics of the courts' indifference toward the economic sustainability of the healthcare system tend to be part of the general criticism of the process of judicialization of the politics in Latin

America and court's capacity and/or legitimacy to decide contentious social policy issues. The criticism is in part because judges tend not to have the necessary highly technical understanding of the subject matter. While it is true that many of these issues are complex, when judges intervene in ESCR (economic, social, and cultural rights) cases, they are basing their decisions on existing rules within a system and expert evidence that limits their discretion (Courtis 2008). However, it is also true that regulating frameworks are not always in place and it is common for judges to have remind the state to meet its systematically neglected obligations (Sabel and Simon 2004), which presents judges with the challenge of also having to monitor the implementation of a policy that lacks a monitoring framework.

Latin American courts have found different ways to deal with these challenges. As in civil and political rights cases, such as those concerning torture, extrajudicial killings, or gender violence, courts require opinions and reports from relevant authorities and experts (Staveland 2010; Rodríguez-Garavito 2010; Gianella-Malca 2012). Expert opinions, though, can be wrong and lead to inadequate judgments, for example, a doctor might recommend a treatment for a patient that is not the most appropriate for the patient's condition. Courts must therefore have access to trustworthy sources that provide alternative opinions. In the case of Costa Rica, after years of significant growth in the number of health rights claims, the court agreed to accept evaluations on medication claims from the independent Cochrane Collaboration and also to implement specialized training for court employees to help the court make more informed decisions on health rights cases (Norheim and Wilson 2014).

A different set of lessons brought by the right to health litigation (and other highly technical issues) in Latin America are related to the outcomes of the judicialization, and about the capacity of court decisions to significantly improve policy outcomes (Rosenberg 1991, 2008), as health policies, which are a target of different interest groups including users, health professionals' organizations, the state, insurance companies, and pharmaceutical industry. On this issue, the experience from Latin America shows mixed results. While acknowledging court interventions have allowed preservation of the quality of life of many people, it is also true that when courts have been used to challenge the power of major economic groups, which are also linked with political power, judicialization has perhaps had a more modest impact. In these cases, the political will of the government tends to have been central to design measures truly targeted to improve the health system. Perhaps one of the more outstanding examples of this is the efforts deployed by the Colombian Government to control the public expenses on high cost drugs with a process control policy introduced in 2012 that includes a price reference system, which according to the Colombian Ministry of Health saved the government approximately 230 million US dollars by May 2015. The implementation of this policy, which was heavily criticized, especially by the pharmaceutical industry, was possible with government support. Another side of this issue is the petition handled by Peruvian civil society organizations, including organizations of HIV (human immunodeficiency virus) patients, for a compulsory license on the patents that cover atazanavir, an HIV drug. This one drug accounts for 50 percent of the Peruvian government's HIV/AIDS (acquired immunodeficiency syndrome) treatment budget and because the patent is held Bristol-Myers Squibb, it is significantly more expensive in Peru than other Andean countries. In response to legal action, the Ministry of Health was able to negotiate a major price reduction from an international company. The judicialization of the right to health in Latin America is a clear example of the role courts can play when they are accessible and allows quick responses to urgent claims that in many cases are life or death situations. However, the impact on health systems and on its ability to prevent new violations of the right to health, are somewhat limited, even in cases with assertive courts and complex monitoring systems for decisions.

Social, Economic, and Cultural Rights Litigation

For many political actors and scholars of Latin American politics, courts were viewed not just as institutions unable or unwilling to defend constitutional rights, but agents inclined to act in the interests of the elite; agents much more likely to harm to rights of marginalized groups than help them. According to Ran Hirschl (2004), courts are designed by political elites to fortify the status quo and to block any real socio-political change through a democratic process. Thus, newly strengthened superior courts were believed to have effectively cemented their role as barriers to the pursuit of constitutional rights enforcement. Javier Couso, in a study of Chilean courts, concludes that progressive groups "regarded law and the courts not as an instrument, but as an obstacle to social change" (2006, 62). That is, these groups saw courts as an oppressive arm of the state rather than an available legal opportunity (Hilson 2002; Wilson and Rodríguez 2006) structure that might facilitate enforcement of their rights. As Brinks and Gauri (2012) conclude, even if courts are "friendly," it would be "unreasonable to expect that the courts will consistently produce outcomes that are significantly more pro-poor than the results achievable through conventional politics." Just because assertive superior courts produce strong jurisprudence protecting and expanding some constitutional rights, does not mean that all rights will be protected equally or at all (Langford et al. 2016). Brinks (2008, 142) in a study of police killings in Latin America, concludes that, "political rights are alive and vibrant in São Paulo, and yet the police routinely violate fundamental civil rights and, in practical terms, [the police] remain above the law." The inability of victims of police violence to harness the power of even an assertive court to protect their constitutional right to life, among other rights, is outside of the scope of this chapter, but it should be noted that the mere existence of an assertive, rights-friendly superior court and a rights-rich constitution is insufficient to mobilize the protective power of the court to defend all rights.

And yet, in many Latin American countries, reinvigorated courts have stepped in to fill a democratic void and protect the interests and rights of even the most vulnerable members of society. It should be noted that the judicialization of politics through litigation can be employed as part of a broader strategy to increase visibility of an issue, increase popular support, or as a recruitment tool (McCann 1994), none of which requires courts to decide in favor of the litigants (NeJaime 2012) or "increase pressure on policymakers or forcing an authority to meet and negotiate" (Langford 2013). There was, then, no automatic opening of a favorable legal opportunity structure that socially and politically vulnerable groups and individuals might harness to protect their constitutional rights. Charles Epp (1998), in an examination of four common law legal systems (United States, India, Britain, and Canada), concludes that for organizations to harness the power of courts to advance their rights interests requires more than just rights-rich constitutions and rights-friendly judges; rather, it also requires deep-pocketed support structures to fund and push the cases through the relevant legal channels and large, diverse law firms with the willingness and capacity to make the legal arguments to claim the rights at the different court levels. Others have argued that courts cannot bring about social change (Rosenberg 1991) or will, through their jurisprudence, generate a backlash that will actually harm the interests of the litigants (Klarman 2005; Rosenberg 2008).

Litigating LGBTI Rights

While some Latin American countries have benefited from these conditions that allow even the most marginalized people to have their day in court, in other countries, social mobilization and support structures have been either occasionally or completely absent. Brief examples of LGBTI equality struggles in different countries can illustrate this point: In Costa Rica although homosexual behavior was legalized in the late nineteenth century, their rights were routinely trampled and LGBTI citizens were pushed to the margins of society, suffering the opprobrium of an overwhelming majority of citizens and no political party championed even their most basic rights. The state and private actors routinely and legally discriminated against LGBTI people in employment, housing, and education. Until a pro-LGBTI rights decision in the mid-1990s by the Sala IV, for example, the police routinely harassed people they believed to be gay; now police harassment is no longer a significant issue and rarely results in litigation.[9] Similarly, the state even used vaguely worded regulations to prevent any pro-LGBTI organization from becoming a legally registered organization until the newly created ombudsman's office threatened to litigate in 1995. The civil registry had previously argued that LGBTI groups did not comply with Article 3 of the Law of Association, as their behavior undermined "good customs and morality."[10] Yet, within the Sala IV's first decade, its rulings in response to LGBTI individuals' *amparo* claims, effectively ended most discrimination by state agencies. But in 2006 the court decided against Same-Sex Marriage (SSM) and pushed the small LGBTI organizations into a political maelstrom that their nascent organizations were ill-equipped to contain the political backlash, let alone successfully advocate and advance their rights within a hostile Legislative Assembly.

The Mexican LGBTI case illustrates a different story of political arenas, the judicialization of politics, and the advancement of SSM rights and reveals a clear connection between the role of more inclusive political parties and the advancement of LGBTI rights. When the PRD (Partido de la Revolución Democrática) government of Federal District of Mexico (DF) in Mexico City passed a law recognizing SSM in the DF, groups hostile to the law filed a case with the Mexican Supreme Court. The court, though, ruled in favor of the DF's SSM law and set the stage for a series of legal cases at state and national courts to require recognition of SSM in states that were hostile to the DF's SSM law. These legal cases ultimately resulted in the expansion of marriage equality to other states and the recognition of SSM performed in the DF in all other Mexican states. This litigation strategy to nationalize SSM concluded with the Mexican Supreme Court's issuance of a jurisprudential thesis declaring unconstitutional the definition of marriage as "between a man and a woman" (Khan 2015). Because the dominant parties at the national level remained hostile to LGBTI people, the courts were the only remaining option to expand recognition of Mexico City's same-sex law and to press for the right to SSM in the rest of the country.

Backlash

The creation of strengthened superior courts that permitted the use of litigation strategies by marginalized groups and individuals to secure constitutionally-protected rights, though, is not without potential pitfalls (Klarman 2005; Rosenberg 2008). Unpopular judicial victories can spawn significant backlashes mobilizing voters against the successful litigant's interests and/or new laws or regulations that reverse or undermine their previous judicial victories. In the case of LGBTI people in Latin America, in spite of some significant legal victories, there remain few political parties that act as unconditional allies (Araujo Herrera 2015) and in spite of all the progress by LGBTI citizens, there are only 15 openly lesbian or gay national legislators in the whole region (Corrales 2015).[11] Furthermore, popular support for LGBTI rights remains low, especially on the issue of SSM (Alcántara and Rivas 2013), which amplifies the potential for political backlash against LGBTI interests in response to their litigation victories.

This type of backlash is particularly well-documented in the case of SSM rights in the United States. Rosenberg (2008) notes that early SSM legal victories in some states in the United States led to a major political backlash resulting in the adoption of a national level law defining marriage as between one man and one woman. At the state-level, numerous state constitutions were amended to explicitly prohibit SSM and/or deny recognition of SSM performed in other states. It is also argued that ultimately the backlash against SSM helped reelect President George W. Bush by energizing "moral-issues" voters to turn up at the polls in unusually large numbers. Rosenberg (2008) concludes that LGBTI rights were set back by a generation as a result of the early positive court decisions. Rosenberg's conclusions are disputed by Keck (2009) and by developments that resulted in legalization of SSM across the whole of USA due to the United States Supreme Court's *Obergefell* v. *Hodges* decision in 2014. Further challenges to Rosenberg's conclusions is the rapid change in public support for SSM, which increased from 27 percent in 1996 to 64 percent in 2017 suggesting a significant positive impact of litigation for SSM (Gallup 2017).

Examples of litigation for SSM in Costa Rica illustrate the backlash and the possible limitations of how far courts are willing or able to go when popular opinion is massively against the claimant. In Costa Rica after many years of Sala IV decisions affirming the rights of LGBTI people, a 2003 case claiming that the prohibition of SSM was unconstitutional was rejected by the court in a split (five to two) decision. The court pushed the issue to the legislative assembly and requested that the Assembly clarify the legal inequality faced by same-sex couples. In response, the LGBTI organizations had to demand SMM a political arena where they had few allies and no support from any major political party to advance the SSM bill through congress. Instead, groups with animus toward LGBTI people demanded a referendum to vote to include a constitutional ban on SSM in the constitution. While the Sala IV halted a move to hold the referendum that would have allowed people to vote on the rights of a minority group, the issue has remained log-jammed in congress for more than a decade with very little hope of legislation in the manner suggested by the court being passed.

The case of Colombia, though, shows that when courts are willing to protect minority rights, such as SSM, courts can take risks and make unpopular rulings that legislators might be more reluctant to make due to their pressing need to seek reelection. An illustrative example of this is the bill presented to the Colombian Senate in 2003 to legalize same-sex civil unions and recognize the rights of same-sex couples, but it was rejected in June 2007. This rejection reflects both the lack of popular support for LGBTI rights and the superior organization of conservative groups that mobilized large numbers of congress people to oppose LGBTI rights in the popularly elected chamber. The bill's failure forced LGBTI organizations to reevaluate their strategies and to use their litigation experience to return to the friendlier arena of the constitutional court, which allows more focus on legal constitutional issues and is less concerned with the beliefs of the super majority of Colombians, over 60 percent in 2015, opposed to legalizing SSM. The court required the legislature to remedy the lack of legal protection faced by same-sex couples through "comprehensive, systematic, and orderly legislation" before a June 20, 2013 deadline. The court informed congress that if it failed to pass the required legislation within the two-year window, same-sex couples could request a notary or a court to recognize their partnership.

When the congress failed to meet the 2013 deadline, notaries and judges began to register SSM. In response well-organized conservative forces pushed back against SSM and initiated a two-and-a-half-year period of legal uncertainty for SSM. LGBTI rights groups, for their part, continued a legal battle for SSM through the court, which culminated in April 2016 when the CCC issued a decision legalizing SSM. The intervention of the CCC has been a milestone in the fight for SSM, and more broadly LGBTI rights recognition in Colombia. Organizations supporting SSM found in the court an arena to dispute and advance in the protection of LGBTI people rights, including property rights, inheritance, and adoption showing that even in a hostile political context with high levels of public animus and little political support, courts can play a key role in advancing rights through reforming legislation and policies.

Conclusions

The start of the judicialization of politics in Latin America can be understood in its temporal context of redemocratization, the accompanying political and judicial reforms, and the adoption of neoliberal economic policies. While much of the international aid that fostered and financed judicial reforms was motivated by a desire to spur economic growth by strengthening independent judiciaries and protecting private investment, an unanticipated consequence of the reforms was the creation of legal opportunity structures across the region and the facilitating of courts' newly assertive role holding other branches to account. Research on judicial reforms tends to focus on international agencies' role and motivations and the factors that underpinned and supported judicial independence and the rule of law.

The newly created legal opportunity structures enabled the rise of rights revolutions in some Latin American countries, which allowed social movements to bypass hostile or indifferent popularly elected branches of government and, instead, to harness the power of the courts to protect their interests. The rights revolutions and the rise of assertive courts posited new questions for researchers concerning the judicialization of politics in Latin America. Scholars of Latin American courts were redirected to examine why courts behaved as they did, how were vulnerable citizens able to harness the power of the courts, and what was the impact of court decisions? A variety of methodological approaches ranging from institutional-structural to game theoretic approaches have been used to examine how judges, individuals, and groups have used courts and to better understand how court magistrates make decisions and the extent to which those decisions are complied with (see Table 21.1). The increased volume of research published information on Latin American courts allowed more sophisticated methodologies to build on detailed country studies to explain the role of courts in the policymaking process and on policy implementation, especially with respect to rights. But as Helmke and Rios-Figueroa (2011, 22) book on Latin American courts notes, "there is no one best way to study courts" and that methodological "pluralism is particularly important."

In conclusion, superior courts have become increasingly important in the political lives of most Latin American citizens over the last three decades and have become strong defenders and enforces of constitutional and human rights. The extent to which each court is able to remain independent of the executive and/or legislative branch depends to differing extents on the formal institutional rules and the courts' internal operation and appointment rules. That is, in some cases, Colombia, for example, the new constitutional court coupled with the rights-rich constitution, and broad standing and lack of formality has led to a large number of cases being filed with the court and that court becoming part of an accessible legal opportunity structure for rights claims as well as becoming a strong accountability agent. But these developments in judicial assertiveness are not unidirectional; in Nicaragua and Venezuela, for example, appointing party-loyalists as magistrates undermined the formal independence of superior courts rendering their significant accountability powers mute; these two courts have effectively returned to being ciphers for the ruling political parties, which is forcing scholars and activists to return to their earlier concern with questions of judicial independence and accountability.

Table 21.1 Examples of Studies Analyzing Judicialization of Politics in Latin America

Area	Authors	Type of Data Analyzed
Use of courts, factors that allow the use of courts	Jaramillo and Alfonso (2008)	Analysis of legal mobilization toward decriminalization of abortion in Colombia
	Bergallo (2011)	Original database of judicial case trends. Analysis of jurisprudence
	Albarracín (2011)	Analysis of legal mobilization toward recognition of same sex couples rights in Colombia
	González and Bergallo (2017)	Analysis of the history of the development of health exception legal arguments in Latin America
How courts make decisions, what affects courts' rulings	Perez-Liñan and Castagnola (2016)	Original database of constitutional changes and judges from 18 Latin American countries (Argentina, Bolivia, Brazil, Chile, Colombia, Costa Rica, the Dominican Republic, Ecuador, El Salvador, Guatemala, Honduras, Mexico, Nicaragua, Panama, Paraguay, Peru, Uruguay, and Venezuela) between 1904–2010
	González-Ocanto, 2016	Case studies: two cases with observable sustained waves of prosecutions against human rights violations (Argentina and Peru) and one case with not (Mexico)
Effects	Rodríguez Garavito and Rodríguez (2010)	Analysis of implementation process of the constitutional court ruling, including policy reforms, and impact on public opinion
	Ferraz (2011)	Analysis of trends of claimants' profiles, service claimed, in cases regarding the right to health against the Ministry of Health in Brazil
	Sepúlveda y Rodríguez Garavito (2011)	Analysis of implementation process of two Colombian Constitutional Court rulings, including policy reforms, and impact on public opinion
	Gianella (2013)	Analysis of implementation process of Colombian Constitutional Court ruling, including policy reforms, framing of the right to health
	Bergallo (2016)	Analysis of jurisprudence, legal strategies, and legal developments toward decriminalization of abortion in Latin America

Source: Table created by author.

Notes

1 This previous insignificance of Latin American superior courts is reflected in Tate and Vallinder's (1995) seminal work, *The Global Expansion of Judicial Power*, which contains no chapter on any Latin American court.
2 It should be noted that many superior courts, including the Bolivian Supreme Court, already had judicial review powers, but elected not to animate them or exercise their role as the protector of constitutional rights.

3 It is beyond the scope of this chapter to provide a detailed explanation of each of these conditions; however, here we provide a brief general description.

4 *"Tutela"* or *"amparo,"* is a uniquely Latin American legal invention with origins in Mexico's 1857 Constitution. Currently, these writs are used across nearly all Latin America judicial systems and permitting individuals to challenge in court the unconstitutional actions of popularly elected governments and private entities.

5 Popkin (2000), though, warned that democracy building efforts without the establishment of the rule of law are necessarily incomplete.

6 See, for example, Corral (2010); Corporación Latinobarómetro (2015).

7 Average levels of trust of Latin American judiciaries is in general very low and has rarely increased above 30 percent since mid-1990s. (Corporación Latinobarómetro 2015).

8 Sala Constitucional, Res. No. 2003–02771, it should be noted that the decision was a reversal of the court's own previous majority decision (Resolución 7818–00) in 2000 that upheld the constitutionality of the reelection prohibition.

9 Police harassment was a particular problem for LGBTI people until the court decision. One gay night club owner noted that in the 1980s "the police would arrive and take you away … all the time, on weekends, during the week, with no respect for people's basic human rights" (Gourgy 2004).

10 Ley de Asociaciones, No. 218 Art. 3 (Costa Rica) (translation by authors).

11 Some political parties, including the Frente Amplio (Uruguay), the Workers Party (Brazil), Frente Amplio (Peru) and the Party of the Democratic Revolution (Mexico) are supportive of many LGBTI issues, but in many countries no major political party is supportive of LGBTI rights.

References

Albarracín, Mauricio. 2011. Social Movements and the Constitutional Court: Legal Recognition of the Rights of Same-Sex Couples in Colombia. *Sur. International Journal*, 8(14): 7–31.

Alcántara, Manuel and Cristina Rivas. 2013. *El Matrimonio de Personas del Mismo Sexo y los Legisladores Latinoamericanos*. Salamanca: Proyecto Élites Latinoamericanas (PELA), Universidad de Salamanca (1994–2015).

Araujo Herrera, Mariana. 2015. LGBT Rights in Latin America: Do Progressive Laws Equal Progressive Societies?. *Council on Hemispheric Affairs*, October 21.

Bergallo, Paola. 2016. "Interpretando derechos: La otra legalización del aborto en América Latina." In *Debates y Reflexiones en Torno a la Despenalización del Aborto en Chile*, edited by Lidia Casas and Delfina Lawson. Santiago de Chile: Ediciones Loñ.

Bergallo, Paola. 2011. Aborto y Justicia Reproductiva: Una Mirada Sobre el Derecho Comparado. *Cuestión de Derechos*, 1, 1–20.

Brinks, Daniel. 2008. *Inequality and the Rule of Law: The Judicial Response to Police Violence in South America*. Cambridge: Cambridge University Press.

Brinks, Daniel. 2012. "A Tale of Two Cities: The Judiciary and the Rule of Law in Latin America." In *Routledge Handbook of Latin American Politics*, edited by Peter Kingstone and Deborah Yasher. New York and London: Routledge.

Brinks, Daniel and Varun Gauri. 2012. The Law's Majestic Equality? The Distributive Impact of Litigating Social and Economic Rights. *Policy Research Working Paper*. Washington, DC: The World Bank.

Carothers, Thomas. 2001. "The Many Agendas of Rule of Law Reform in Latin America." In *Rule of Law in Latin America: The International Promotion of Judicial Reform*, edited by Rachel Sieder and Pilar Domingo. London: Institute of Latin American Studies.

Cepeda-Espinosa, Manuel José. 2011. Transcript: Social and Economic Rights and The Colombian Constitutional Court. *Texas Law Review*, 89: 1699–705.

Constitutional Chamber of the Supreme Court of Nicaragua. 2009. "Case No. 602–09, in the Amparo Writ Ortega et al. v. the Supreme Electoral Council of the Republic of Nicaragua." October 19.

Corporación Latinobarómetro. 2013. *Informe 2013*. Santiago de Chile: Corporación Latinobarómetro.

Corporación Latinobarómetro. 2015. *Informe 1995–2015*. Santiago de Chile: Corporación Latinobarómetro.

Corral, Margarita. 2010. Partidos Políticos y Representación en América Latina. *Perspectivas desde el Barómetro de las Américas: 2010* (36).

Corrales, Javier. 2015. *LGBT Rights and Representation in Latin America and the Caribbean: The influence of Structure, Movements, Institutions, and Culture*. LGBT Representation and Rights Initiative/University of North Carolina at Chapel Hill.

Corte Constitucional de Colombia. 2008. "Sentencia T-760 de 2008." Bogotá: Magistrado Manuel José Cepeda-Espinosa.

Courtis, Christian. 2008. *Courts and the Legal Enforcement of Economic, Social and Cultural Rights*. Geneva: International Commission of Jurists.

Couso, Javier A. 2006. "The Changing Role of Law and Courts in Latin America: From an Obstacle to Social Change to a Tool of Social Equity." In *Courts and Social Transformation in New Democracies: An Institutional Voice for the Poor?*, edited by Roberto Gargarella, Pilar Domingo, and Theunis Roux. Aldershot: Ashgate: 61–82.

DeShazo, Peter and Juan Enrique Vargas. 2006. *Judicial Reform in Latin America. An Assessment*. Washington, DC: Center for Strategic and International Studies.

Domingo, Pilar. 2010. Judicialization of Politics or Politicization of the Judiciary? Recent Trends in Latin America. *Democratization* 11(1): 104–26.

Domingo, Pilar and Rachel Sieder. 2001. *Rule of Law in Latin America: The International Promotion of Judicial Reform*. London: Institute of Latin American Studies.

Epp, Charles. 1998. *The Rights Revolution: Lawyers, Activists, and Supreme Courts in Comparative Perspective*. Chicago: The University of Chicago Press.

Faundez, Julio (Ed.). 1997. *Good Government and Law: Legal and Institutional Reform in Developing Countries*. London: MacMillan Press.

Ferraz, Octavio L.M. 2011. "Brazil. Health Inequalities, Rights, and Courts: The Social Impact of the Judicialization of the Health." In *Litigating Health Rights. Can Courts Bring More Justice to Health?*, edited by Alicia Yamin and Siri Gloppen. Cambridge, MA: Harvard University Press: 76–102.

Gallup. 2017. *US Support for Gay Marriage Edges to New High*. Available at: www.gallup.com/poll/210566/support-gay-marriage-edges-new-high.aspx. Accessed May 7, 2018.

Gianella-Malca, Camila. 2012. "Ready to respect the court ruling?" Paper presented at *European Network on Latin American Politics VI Annual Meeting*. Bergen: University of Bergen.

Gloppen, Siri, Bruce Wilson, Roberto Gargarella, Elin Skaar, and Morten Kinnader. 2010. *Courts and Power in Latin America and Africa*. New York: Palgrave Macmillan.

González Ocantos, Ezequiel. 2016. *Shifting Legal Visions. Judicial Change and Human Rights Trails in Latin America*. New York: Cambridge University Press.

González, Ana Cristina and Paula Bergallo. 2017. "The Health Exception in Latin America: An Autochthonous Experience of Transnational Advocacy." Paper presented at the Latin American Studies Association Annual Congress. Lima.

González, Ana Cristina and Juanita Durán. 2011. Impact of Court Rulings on Health Care Coverage: The Case of HIV/AIDS in Colombia. *MEDICC Review* 13(3): 54–7.

Gourgy, Andrea. 2004. Tolerance for Gays Improving, Not Perfect. *Tico Times*. Available at: www.ticotimes.net/2004/06/25/tolerance-for-gays-improving-not-perfect. Accessed May 7, 2018.

Hammergren, Linn. 1998. Fifteen Years of Judicial Reform in Latin America: Where We Are and Why We Haven't Made More Progress, USAID Global Center for Democracy and Governance. Available at: www.pogar.org/publications/judiciary/linn2/latin.pdf. Accessed May 7, 2018.

Helmke, Gretchen and Julio Ríos-Figueroa. 2011. *Courts in Latin America*. New York: Cambridge University Press.

Hilson, Christopher. 2002. New Social Movements: The Role of Legal Opportunity. *Journal of European Public Policy*, 9(2): 238–55.

Hirschl, Ran. 2004. *Towards Juristocracy: The Origins and Consequences of the New Constitutionalism*. Cambridge, MA: Harvard University Press.

Jaramillo Sierra, Isabel C. and Tatiana Alfonso Sierra. 2008. *Mujeres, Cortes y Medios: La Reforma Judicial del Aborto*. Bogotá: Siglo del Hombre Editores/Universidad de Los Andes.

Jarquín, Edmundo and Fernando Carrillo (Eds.) 1998. *Justice Delayed: Judicial Reform in Latin America*. Washington, DC: Inter-American Development Bank.

Johnson, Tim. 2010. Despite Constitution, Nicaragua's Ortega Plans to Stay in Power. *McClatchy*, August 5. Available at: www.mcclatchydc.com/news/nation-world/world/article24589570.html. Accessed May 7, 2018.

Kahn, Carrie. 2015. How Mexico Quietly Legalized Same-Sex Marriage. *All Things Considered*, June 16. National Public Radio.

Karst, Kenneth L. and Keith S. Rosenn. 1975. *Law and Development in Latin America: A Case Book*. California: University of California Press.

Keck, Thomas. 2009. Beyond Backlash: Assessing the Impact of Judicial Decisions on LGBT Rights. *Law and Society Review*, 43(1): 151–85.

Klarman, Michael J. 2005. Brown and Lawrence (and Goodridge). *Michigan Law Review*, 104(3): 431–89.

Lakhani, Nina. 2016. Nicaragua suppresses opposition to ensure one-party election, critics say. *Guardian*. Available at: www.theguardian.com/world/2016/jun/26/nicaragua-opposition-daniel-ortega-presidential-election. Accessed May 7, 2018.

Langford, Malcolm. 2013. "Housing Rights Litigation: Grootboom and Beyond." In *Socio-Economic Rights in South Africa: Symbols or Substance?*, edited by Malcom Langford, Ben Cousins, Jackie Dugard and Tshepo Madlingozi. Cambridge: Cambridge University Press.

Langford, Malcolm et al. 2016. *Making it Stick: Compliance with Socio-Economic Rights Judgments in Comparative Perspective*. Cambridge: Cambridge University Press.

Larkins, Christopher M. 1998. The Judiciary and Delegative Democracy in Argentina. *Comparative Politics*, 30: 423–43.

Loveman, Brian. 1993. *The Constitution of Tyranny: Regimes of Exception in Spanish America*. Pittsburgh: University of Pittsburgh Press.

McAuslan, Patrick. 1997. "Law, Governance and the Development of the Market: Practical Problems and Possible Solutions." In *Good Government and Law: Legal and Institutional Reform in Developing Countries*, edited by Julio Faundez. Macmillan Press: 25–50.

McCann, Michael. 1994. *Rights at Work: Pay Equity Reform and the Politics of Legal Mobilization*. Chicago: The University of Chicago Press.

Mecham, J. Lloyd. 1959. Latin American Constitutions: Nominal and Real. *The Journal of Politics*, 21: 258–75.

Messick, Richard E. 1999. Judicial Reform and Economic Development: A Survey of the Issues. *The World Bank Research Observer*, 14(1): 117–36.

Navia, Patricio, and Julio Ríos-Figueroa. 2005. The Constitutional Adjudication Mosaic of Latin America. *Comparative Political Studies*, 38(2): 189–271.

NeJaime, Douglas. 2012. Cause Lawyers Inside the State, *Fordham Law Review*, 81: 649–704.

Norheim, Ole Frithjof and Bruce Wilson. 2014. Health Rights Litigation and Access to Medicines: Priority Classification of Successful Cases from Costa Rica's Constitutional Chamber of the Supreme Court. *Health and Human Rights*, 16(2).

Pérez-Liñán, Aníbal, and Andrea Castagnola. 2016. Judicial Instability and Endogenous Constitutional Change: Lessons from Latin America. *British Journal of Political Science*, 46(2): 395–416.

Popkin, Margaret. 2000. *Peace Without Justice Obstacles to Building the Rule of Law in El Salvador*. University Park: Pennsylvania State University Press.

Rodríguez-Garavito, César (Ed.). 2010. *Más Allá del Desplazamiento: Políticas Derechos y Superación del Desplazamiento en Colombia, Colección Estudios CIJUS*. Bogotá: Universidad de Los Andes, Facultad de Derecho, Centro de Investigaciones Sociojurídicas-CIJUS.

Rodríguez-Garavito, César, Rodrigo Uprimny and Mauricio García-Villegas. 2003. "Justice and Society in Colombia: A Sociolegal Analysis of Colombian Courts." In *Legal Culture in the Age of Globalization: Latin America and Latin Europe*, edited by Lawrence Friedman and Rogelio Pérez-Perdomo. Stanford: Stanford University Press: 134–83.

Rodríguez-Garavito, César and Diana Rodríguez. 2010. *Corte y Cambio Social: Cómo la Corte Constitucional Tranformó el Desplazamiento Forzado en Colombia*. Bogotá: Dejusticia.

Rosenberg, Gerald. 1991. *The Hollow Hope: Can Courts Bring About Social Change?* Chicago: The University of Chicago Press.

Rosenberg, Gerald. 2008. *The Hollow Hope: Can Courts Bring About Social Change?* Second edition. Chicago: The University of Chicago Press.

Sabel, Charles and William Simon. 2004. Destabilization Rights: How Public Law Litigation Succeeds. *Harvard Law Review*, 117(2004): 1015–101.

Salas, Luis. 2001. "From Law and Development to Rule of Law: New and Old Issues." In *Source Rule of Law in Latin America: The International Promotion of Judicial Reform*, edited by Pilar Domingo and Rachel Sieder. London: Institute of Latin American Studies.

Scalia, Antonin. 2015. Obergefell v. Hodges 2015. Available at: www.supremecourt.gov/opinions/14pdf/14-556_3204.pdf. Accessed May 7, 2018.

Sepúlveda, Magdalena and César Rodríguez. 2011. Colombia: la Corte Constitucional y su Contribución a la Justicia Social. *Teoría y jurisprudencia de los derechos sociales. Tendencias incipientes en el derecho internacional comparado*. Bogotá: Universidad de Los Andes y Siglo del Hombre Editores.

Sieder, Rachel, Line Schjolden, and Alan Angell. 2005. "Introduction." In *The Judicialization of Politics in Latin America*, edited by Rachel Sieder, Line Schjolden and Alan Angell. Basingstoke and New York: Palgrave Macmillan.

Smulovitz, Catalina. 2008. La política por otros medios. Judicialización y movilización legal en la Argentina. *Desarrollo Económico*, 48(190/191): 287–305.

Staveland, Kristi. 2010. *Litigating the Right to a Healthy Environment. Assessing the Policy Impact of 'The Mendoza Case.'* Bergen: Department of Comparative Politics, Bergen University.

Stotzky, Irwin P. 2004. "Lessons Learned and the Way Forward." In *Democratization and the Judiciary*, edited by Siri Gloppen, Roberto Gargarella, and Elin Skaar. London: Frank Cass, 198–202.

Tate, C. Neal and Torbjörn Vallinder. 1995. *The Global Expansion of Judicial Power*. New York: NYU Press.

Taylor, Matthew M. 2008. *Judging Policy: Courts and Policy Reform in Democratic Brazil*. Stanford: Stanford University Press.

Urcuyo, Constantino. 1995. La Sala IV: Necesarios Límites al Poder [The Sala IV: Necessary Limits on Power]. *Revista Parlamentaria*, 3(3): 17–50.

Vaky, Paul. 1998. "U.S. Agency for International Development." In *Justice Delayed: Judicial Reform In Latin America*, edited by Edmundo Jarquín and Fernando Carrillo. Washington, DC: Inter-American Development Bank.

Wilson, Bruce. 1998. *Costa Rica: Politics, Economics, and Democracy*. Boulder, CO: Lynne Rienner Publishers Inc.

Wilson, Bruce. 2011. "Enforcing Rights and Exercising an Accountability Function: Costa Rica's Constitutional Court." In *Courts in Latin America*, edited by Gretchen Helmke and Julio Ríos-Figueroa. Cambridge: Cambridge University Press.

Wilson, Bruce and Juan Carlos Rodríguez. 2006. Legal Opportunity Structures and Social Movements: The Effects of Institutional Change on Costa Rican Politics. *Comparative Political Studies*, 39(3): 325–51.

Wilson, Bruce, Juan Rodríguez and Roger Handberg. 2004. The Best Laid Schemes … Gang Aft A-Gley: Judicial Reform in Latin America-Evidence from Costa Rica. *Journal of Latin American Studies*, 36: 507–31.

Yamin, Alicia Ely and Siri Gloppen (Eds.). 2011. *Litigating Health Rights: Can Courts Bring More Justice to Health?, Human Rights Program Series*. Cambridge, MA: Harvard Universtiy Press.

Yamin, Alicia Ely and Oscar Parra-Vera. 2010. Judicial Protection of the Right to Health in Colombia: From Social Demands to Individual Claims to Public Debates. *Hastings International and Comparative Law Review*, 33(2): 101–29.

Yamin, Alicia Ely, Oscar Parra-Vera, and Camila Gianella-Malca. 2011. "Judicial Protection of the Right to Health in Colombia: An Elusive Promise?" In *Litigating Health Rights, Can Courts Bring More Justice to Health?*, edited by Alicia E. Yamin and Siri Gloppen. Cambridge, MA: Harvard University Press.

22

SOCIETY, THE STATE, AND RECOGNITION OF THE RIGHT TO A SELF-PERCEIVED GENDER IDENTITY

Laura Saldivia Menajovsky

Introduction

In recent years formal and informal initiatives aimed at recognizing the rights of people with diverse sexual orientations and gender identities have carved out an important place on the global geopolitical stage, advanced through dissection, debate, and reformulation of diverse national and international experiences. These initiatives have been combined creatively and effectively both to facilitate their inclusion in a common body of law and their dissemination throughout the international human rights system.

Argentina has played a central role in this regard. In 2010 it was among the first countries in the world to recognize marriage equality for homosexuals[1] and in 2012 was the first to recognize the right to a self-perceived gender identity, after unanimous approval of the Law of Gender Identity Number 26.743[2] (henceforth, the "Law") by the national Congress. Notably, Argentina's importance in terms of recognizing the rights of lesbians, gays, bisexuals, and transgender people (LGBT)[3] is largely due to the struggles of the country's LGBT movement.[4]

The model implemented by the "Law" holds that only the person can decide about his/her/they gender identity, this decision is the only valid criterion for establishing the person's gender. This ruling overturns the model that prevailed before the "Law," still valid in many parts of the world, which holds that only experts (doctors, judges, administrative authorities) are authorized – following psychological and medical expert opinions – to decide a person's "true" gender, which is limited to either female or male. The previous framework stipulated that people who cannot be included, or choose not be included, in the mainstream sex/gender binarism, are deemed to be ill. Thus, following prescription of treatment and strict control over "ambiguous" sexuality/gender, medical, administrative, and legal authorities define the "illness," curing and disciplining the body according to strict a male/female binarism. By contrast, the "Law" depathologizes people by recognizing their ability to decide their gender identity.

In the following section, I first highlight characteristics of the Argentine "Law" and then briefly review the struggle for recognition of the rights of transgender persons that led to the approval of this legislation. I then emphasize the democratic nature of the struggle for LGBT rights. I subsequently explore the general context in Latin America regarding acceptance of the gender depathologization paradigm, and conclude with some brief final reflections.

On the "Law" and Some of its Insubordinations

Approval of a law that bestows the right to a self-percieved gender identity is a sign of extraordinary progress in recognizing the human rights of transgender people. It recasts the traditional relationship between gender, the material nature of the body, and body modification, thus toppling the power of judges, administrative personnel, experts, and doctors to decide on a person's gender identity. Now that the "Law" is in force, processing a name change in public registries and identification (ID) cards or undergoing sex-modification surgeries or treatments depends solely on those who wish to undertake these modifications. Thus, Argentina has established a viable depathologization model that is opening public space for personal determination of one's gender identity. Four years after the passage of the "Law," more than 10,000 people had signed up to have their national identity document reflect their choice of name and gender.[5]

The main reason for this normative recognition is the structural inequality in which transgender people find themselves (Berkins 2007), which is made worse by the absence of basic rights, such as those now recognized by the "Law."

The "Law" stipulates that a personal gender determination is the sole valid indicator of a person's gender. Thus, it prevents judges and administrative authorities from deciding whether or not to implement gender changes on identity documents (birth certificate, passport, etc.,) and in one's body.[6] Furthermore, it gives preference to a person's informed consent on decisions regarding medical treatments or surgeries,[7] and, in what may be its most progressive feature, it recognizes the right of minors to a gender identity.[8] In keeping with these directives, there is no obligation to obtain genital surgery or hormone or psychological treatments in order to change one's gender identity on public registries or documents,[9] since the biological aspect is subordinated to self-perception of one's gender. Although contained in a positive normative framework, the "Law" works to counteract some of the essentialist debate regarding traditional notions of sex and gender that equate genitals with gender. It thus favors a system in which the autonomy of trans corporalities is taken into account in interactions between persons and institutions.

Another paradigmatic aspect of the "Law" requires public or private healthcare providers, to respect the rights established therein. In other words, if so requested, it requires providers to carry out pertinent treatments and surgeries at no cost, thus acknowledging that the right to health is crucial for making a gender identity viable. To this end, the "Law" mandates that treatments and surgeries be included in the Mandatory Medical Program (PMO in Spanish), consisting of a basic basket of benefits that guarantees medical aid to recipients. Healthcare providers must offer PMO benefits and other compulsory coverage, without waiting periods, limitations due to pre-existing conditions, or admission requirements. In other words, the main objective of this provision in the "Law" is to facilitate access to treatments deemed indispensable for substantive implementation of the right to a gender identity, without which effective exercise of this right would be impossible.[10]

This legislation also involves state recognition that transgender persons were denied their humanity, having suffered systematic violations of their human rights by governments and individuals. For this reason, the "Law" represents historical reparation of different types of violence, i.e., pathologization, discrimination, and/or criminalization. Furthermore, one of the "Law's" merits is that it dismantles, or at least creates the conceptual construct that endeavors to dismantle, certain subordinations that are inherent to oppositional pairs, which open the door to hierarchical and oppressive relationships and cause immeasurable personal suffering. One of the subordinations under critical scrutiny is biology versus a person's gender perception, affording the latter the power it previously lacked. The "Law" upends some of the essentialist and restrictive effects of the traditional sex/gender coupling that establishes one's genitality and intergender sexual relations as the only possible gender identity, and instead favors the autonomy of trans corporalities. This in turn leads to reassessment of another subordination: that of the individual patient to medical science. The former's decision is now the only one that matters, this being a new aspect diametrically opposed to the supposed pathologizing *truth* of science. In this new formulation, the law also ceases to be a lackey of medical science by subordinating the latter to the depathologizing language of the "Law."

Another original feature of the "Law" is its subversion of the mainstream framework of knowledge. The legal tools that are currently upending knowledge regarding the right to a gender identity belong to a set of principles and regulations created in various peripheries. One periphery raised the question of who produces gender identity. In the depathologizing model of the right to a gender identity, LGBT activists from various countries prepared the "Principles of Yogyakarta" (hereinafter "Principles"), which were transplanted into the "Law" in Argentina.[11] This legal transplant was not an initiative on the part of the country's authorities and lawmakers, but rather was conceived and promoted by the same people to whom the "Law" applies. The Argentine state did indeed approve the statute, but non-state actors discussed, developed, drafted, and promoted it, without help from state institutions; the latter participated only in the final phase of legislative debate and approval. This sequence of events only came after an intense lobbying effort by the LGBT movement to convince lawmakers and state officials that their demands had to be included in legislative bills.[12] The second periphery refers to the fact that the regulation that makes gender identity a human right (i.e., the "Principles"), is not included in any kind of formal law (local or international). It is, rather, an outcome of soft law, a quasi-legal instrument that has no binding legal force, or whose legally binding force is weaker than that of traditional law.[13] The third periphery alludes to the fact that the first jurisdiction to acknowledge and apply the model of self-perceived gender identity, is a country, Argentina, that is on the periphery with respect to the traditional core countries where normative knowledge is produced.[14] In turn, Argentina exports and disseminates the model to other countries. This process disrupts and subverts traditional ways that knowledge is colonialized, whereby knowledge is predominantly produced in the Global *North*, i.e., in prestigious and core jurisdictions, while its consumption or reception generally occurs in the Global *South*.[15]

Many innovative ideas regarding the right to a gender identity that originated in different kinds of peripheries are spreading to various other core or periphery countries. They are also spreading to the regional and international human rights' systems, that are beginning to use, transplant, and disseminate these innovations. By so doing, countries and international bodies are challenging traditional notions of who the producers and receptors of knowledge are.[16] Currently many core countries and international bodies are beginning to incorporate a depathologized gender model, a model created on the margins of international law by persons whose gender identity or sexual orientation is considered to be on the fringes of what is socially acceptable. The model's first concrete application occurred in a peripheral country. Thus, peripheral academia, activism, and jurisprudence are quickly consolidating as the norm throughout the world, and upending their subordinate role in the global production and dissemination of legal perspectives. This mobility of the right to a gender identity is but one of the many legal "migrations" that are occurring globally. A growing number of these legal movements and complex cross-fertilizations characterize the current legal environment, in which the authority behind decisions in some jurisdictions is increasingly influencing rulings in others.[17] Many national and/ or international decision-making bodies seek legal sources that are non-binding to them, since rulings originate outside of their legal boundaries, yet they end up influencing national law. These non-binding legal sources include, among others, comparative law, international law, and transnational law.[18]

In addition to these characteristics, the "Law" enjoys a special mantle of legitimacy since it is the outcome of struggles waged by LGBT organizations that drafted and promoted the law. In a circumstance that should be celebrated, the same people to whom the "Law" is aimed at were its authors. In what follows, I outline the steps taken by these actors.

The Road to the Recognition of the Right to Gender Identity[19]

A starting point in discussing the journey toward the recognition of the right to gender identity involves the return to democracy in 1983 in Argentina, after seven years of a bloody military dictatorship. Military repression had devastating consequences for enforcement of human rights and respect for democratic institutions. The period following the dictatorship was characterized by strong social expectations, especially among sectors that sought to broaden citizens' agency through the recognition of rights that until then had been denied.

In the initial period of the restauration of democracy, the constitutional government paid special attention to reinstating democratic institutions. This was an urgent and unavoidable task, especially since the new government of Argentina inherited a repressive security apparatus that had tortured and disappeared citizens in an atmosphere of repression of civil liberties. In such a context, the government emphasized strengthening respect for personal freedom.[20] The democratic opening that followed included an overall liberalization of sexual practices and discourses. A growing legitimacy of human rights discourse helped in this regard and encouraged positive attitudes about sexual diversity to be more widely disseminated. One author pointed out that:

> the possibilities were broadened for raising questions in the political arena concerning intimacy, the body, gender, and sexuality. In other words, some of the conditions that affect the social processes of visibility and invisibility of sexual diversity and those who comprise it were modified.
>
> *(Moreno 2008, 227)*

This new scenario presented an opportunity to expand and diversify LGBT organizations' demands and their ways of communicating. Paradoxically, in spite of the liberalization of discourses and sexual practices, LGBT persons continued to experience stigma, discrimination, lack of access to basic services (marriage, adoption, name changes on registry and personal ID records, sex-reassignment surgeries, etc.,). Gender diverse persons were also criminalized, insofar as they were detained by security forces to assess their identity and charged with supposed misdemeanors or offenses. This type of repression reflected the persistence, even under a democratic administration, of the dictatorship's repressive apparatus. In Argentina, regulations such as police edicts and criminal codes were used to legitimize state violence against homosexuals and transvestites in an effort to "cleanse" society of the "social pathologies" that the sexually diverse "embodied."

In an environment in which rights were restricted or denied, LGBT organizations understood early on that they needed to join with other social groups and pool their demands. Consequently, political, theoretical, and experiential coordination appeared on various fronts: feminists, groups of women, gays, lesbians, transvestites and transsexuals, human rights activists, professionals, political party members, trade union members, artists, journalists, intellectuals, university students, and victims of police repression (Bellucci 2010, 2014; Bellucci and Palmeiro

2013). LGBT and feminist activists formed coalitions and alliances that transcended very dissimilar historical traditions and experiences. They identified a common adversary, heteronormativity and its patriarchy, and worked together to topple the pillars of prevailing sexual policy based on equating sexuality and reproduction. Their common objectives included sexual freedom, free sexual choice, the right to decide about one's body, and the right to abortion. Here, feminism provided a framework of support and an enabling common voice. In the end, these social groups helped to articulate the demands of diverse sexual minorities as an inseparable part of the move to democratize Argentine society, in which human rights would play a leading role.

During the 1990s, all manner of resources were mobilized (economic, emotional, legal, medical, etc.,) during a grassroots response to the HIV (human immunodeficiency virus) epidemic that focused public attention on a subject directly connected with human sexuality (Sívori 2008). The need to control the epidemic was widely accepted, both socially and politically, and so facilitated public visibility of homosexuality. Transvestites and transsexuals mobilized and made their demands heard.[21] The trans movement collectivized their concerns, transformed them into a struggle, and merged the notion of "gender identity" into the language of their demands. Initially, relationships among transvestite, transsexual, and gay organizations were hardly pacific, even though the latter contributed in bringing the former some visibility,[22] but the fact that they faced two mutual adversaries (the police and the Catholic Church), helped LGBT groups find common ground. Along the road to social acceptance of the fact that sexual minorities have rights, several milestones stand out as agreements were forged and common ground was found among the many sexual diversity groups, both among themselves and with other actors (the three branches of government, the media, etc.,). These alliances serve to explain the success of the LGBT groups.

The first milestone was the 1994 reform of Argentina's constitution giving constitutional rank to the main international human rights instruments and recognizing the rights of minority groups, which consolidated arguments justifying the protection for groups in a situation of disadvantage.[23] This reform was followed two years later by the enactment of the first Constitution of the City of Buenos Aires, which opened public discussion of the rights of sexual minorities by banning discrimination based on sexual orientation. A third moment came when parades of pride slowly began including first lesbians and later transvestites, transsexuals, and transgender people. Parades of pride became one of the prevailing events where the LGBT movement gained public visibility.[24] Parade organizers were able to combine a space for the celebration of diversity with an act to protest and denounce the violence and discrimination faced by LGBT people.[25] Another key moment that catalyzed the organization and mobilization of transvestites and transsexuals was the discussion and struggle against Buenos Aires police edicts that criminalized prostitution, homosexuality, and dressing as a gender different from the one shown on ID documents (Sabsay 2011; Fernández 2004; Berkins 2003).

A fifth milestone in the struggle for visibility and social and legal recognition involved conflicts brought before the Supreme Court in the cases of the Argentine Homosexual Community "CHA," and the Association for the Struggle for Transvestite and Transsexual Identity "ALITT." These cases entailed petitions of legal status for nongovernmental organizations (NGOs) working to defend the rights of LGBT minorities.[26] Fifteen years passed between the judgments handed down in each case: the first in 1991 and the second in 2006. The administrative authority in charge of granting legal status to civil associations, the *Inspección General de Justicia* (Inspector General for Justice, or IGJ), had rejected requests by both organizations alleging that they failed to fulfill the requirement of supporting the common good established under Article 33 of the Argentine Civil Code. Both plaintiffs appealed the decisions to the National Chamber of Civil

Appeals, which issued an opinion upholding the IGJ's decision. In the end, both cases reached the Supreme Court but were resolved differently.

In the former, the Supreme Court confirmed the decisions of the IGJ and the National Chamber of Civil Appeals. In the latter, the Supreme Court modified its jurisprudence by ruling that denial of state recognition of an association whose principal objective is to struggle against discrimination of sexual minorities is unconstitutional and violates international human rights instruments signed and ratified by Argentina. The Supreme Court considered that the denial of legal status for the ALITT constituted unjustifiable discrimination and its right to association should be recognized in the name of respect for human dignity.[27] Further, the Supreme Court expressly recognized the tribulations faced daily by LGBT persons.[28] For the first time, the Supreme Court referred to the exclusion, marginality, and oppression that sexual minorities encounter every day, in terms that underscore the genocidal consequences of the prejudices that exist against them.[29]

Undoubtedly, the Supreme Court's decision regarding "ALITT" was fundamental in sorting out and promoting the demands for protection of LGBT people. The favorable climate created by this ruling led to another significant achievement: pension benefit was granted to the surviving partner of a homosexual couple upon the death of one of them. Two years after the "ALITT" ruling, a decision about gay pension rights that was denied in the lower courts and, previously, in the administrative office remained pending before the Supreme Court. The executive branch became involved and ordered the National Social Security Administration (ANSES) to reverse its previous position and recognize pension rights following the death of a domestic partner of a homosexual couple.[30] Simultaneously, LGBT organizations took measures to eliminate stereotypes and promote positive responses to sexual diversity. These actions were framed in the so-called "policy of visibility," i.e., "a set of strategies to critique [traditional perspectives] and create new social patterns of 'representation, interpretation, and communication'" (Moreno 2008, 232). It was in this environment that trans persons would gradually make their name and presence felt both within and outside the sexual diversity movement.

Before its approval in 2010, the LGBT movement's struggle to win approval of the Marriage Equality Law centered on lobbying legislators and filing legal protection demands, given the refusal of civil registries to marry homosexual couples.[31] This strategy eventually bore fruit when the law was approved, which led to the recognition of the right to gender identity. As with marriage equality, the struggle for the right to gender identity was waged within the court system, specifically through the "CHA" and "ALITT" cases, and others that petitioned for the right to change one's name and submit to gender-affirmation surgery. Other cases were aired in congress by lobbying legislators. With a clear strategic objective, LGBT organizations based their demands on a discourse that focused on and emphasized the value of the right to equality and non-discrimination. This particular focus highlighted the structural dynamics behind subjugation of groups of disadvantaged people. Previously, the center of attention had been mainly on the limits placed on personal autonomy that translated into restrictions on the right to marry, to adopt, and to submit to gender-reassignment procedures. With this change of strategy on framing and presenting demands, the LGBT movement confirmed that the principal reason for disallowing same-sex marriages was based on notions that the sexually diverse were considered inferior, second class, compared to heterosexuals, thus violating the right to equality and non-discrimination.

Movement demands also helped reveal the extreme degree of marginalization that the transgender community faced and the extent to which heteronormativity and gender binarism furthered discrimination. The movement argued that the imposition of heterosexuality and gender binarism as the only valid life option has been the principal cause of the subordination and violence against those that differ from them. The use of this broad strategy based on the structural underpinnings of the law on non-discrimination allowed the LGBT movement to expand what both the state and society considered legitimate and normal.

On a more symbolic plane, it is also important to emphasize that the road that led to approval of the right to a gender identity is interwoven with the efforts to develop and strengthen a human rights rhetoric as a way of confronting torture, forced disappearances, and the abduction of children during the civic-military dictatorship.[32] Given the seriousness of abuses, relatives of the disappeared, or abducted, and victims forced into exile discovered and learned to use the precarious international human rights protection mechanisms as the only available resource to demand human rights for victims of repression (Saldivia 2015a; Mattarollo 1999). This discovery accompanied a theoretical-practical construction of a formal human rights system and a human rights discourse to investigate violations committed by the dictatorship and bring responsible parties to justice. This effort sought to embed a degree of institutionality and respect for the rule of law. The human rights discourse, envisioned and practiced mainly by the human rights social movement made up of relatives and victims of the dictatorship, became ingrained and grew to be widely practiced in Argentina, a characteristic that currently many Argentines consider to be a matter of national pride.[33]

During their struggle, human rights organizations focused on recovering the children who were born during their mothers' imprisonment and later abducted by members of the military.[34] These children's personal identity was completely suppressed through alteration of infants' names, dates of birth, and essential information on public documents such as birth certificates. Indeed, the phenomenon of infant abduction brought to the public's attention the gravity of suppressing one's identity based on biological and historical information. For this reason, obliterating this type of information is considered a violation of human rights and, in parallel, having a personal identity is acknowledged as a fundamental human right.[35] This recognition highlighted the relevance that people confer on the respect for personal identity. The movement for the rights of transgender persons used this respect as a platform from which to base the right to gender identity. Thus, from the beginning of the struggle, transgender persons understood the strategic and substantive importance of defining gender identity based on human rights protection, in a manner similar to what occurred with the identity of the abducted children. This link allowed them to eschew gender identity definitions based on a psychiatric discourse that ignores trans persons' decisions regarding their perception of their gender. While the plight of kidnapped babies deals with personal identity in terms of one's origins, whose biological truth can be ascertained with DNA tests, trans persons base their personal identity on an aspect that deals with gender, whose truth can only be proved or determined based on one's own perception.

The transgender movement discerned how to link their lived experiences to this understanding regarding the scope and consequences that the denial of personal identity has for human beings. The right to gender identity grew from this conceptual framework by incorporating its language in the demands for the recognition of trans person's rights, being the right to identity the core right from which the possibility of fulfilling and exercising other rights emanates (housing, health, education, access to justice, etc.,). By strategically adapting the discourse of human rights to its demands, the LGBT movement made it easier for the wider public to deal with its vindications, given that the discourse was widely circulated and internalized by legislators, judges, public officials, academics, and human rights activists. In addition, a late unconditional support from the Plaza de Mayo mothers and grandmothers helped to ratify a tightly knit, strategic alliance of cooperation and mutual recognition.[36]

Another pertinent reason behind the movement's decision to imbibe from human rights discourse has to do with the extreme vulnerability of trans people, who urgently need access to the material conditions necessary in order to fully enjoy basic human rights. Thus, the right to equality, in its most robust definition, was given preference over the previous emphasis on personal autonomy. Adoption of human right's discourse was largely responsible for the success in obtaining laws recognizing marriage equality and the right to gender identity. During the discussion and lobbying of both laws, diverse currents of activists with the Argentine LGBT movement put aside, or refrained from making public, internal political differences in favor of promoting and supporting passage of both laws to protect sexual-minority rights. Their success largely hinged on this approach.[37]

Human rights discourse has taken hold in Argentina together with an important consolidation of a general global system of human rights protection. Argentine activists, academics, experts, legal practitioners, legislators, and public authorities have leveraged the international human rights system to argue in favor of protecting rights and, in so doing, they have helped to define the system and provide interpretations involving the particular development of human rights discourse in Argentina. In addition, the 1994 constitutional reform that granted constitutional status to the main international human rights instruments also provided legal arguments that justified extending human rights protections to groups at a disadvantage, among them sexual minorities. The struggle outlined here unveils the close ties that exist between the state (its diverse parts and actors) and society. Undoubtedly, the activism encouraged by the LGBT movement not only had an impact in achieving rights that were previously denied, it also influenced how the state itself was rebuilt; for example, the state is currently shedding its traditional aversion to sexual and gender diversity. Thus, the state can be seen as a construct shaped by specific historical events and subjective interactions that cross-cut diverse dimensions and registries (Sieder 2011, 169–70). Clearly, this transformation of the state does not occur everywhere simultaneously or to the same degree. On the contrary, in its multifaceted internal practices, homophobic and transphobic discourses continue to exist alongside the formal legitimacy granted to LGBT demands. Nonetheless, the transformational shift is already occurring and, thanks to the tenacity of the LGBT movement, seems unstoppable.

In the following section, I explore the role of Latin American countries in the ongoing movement toward recognizing the right to a depathologized gender identity.

Latin America and Gender Identity

Argentina's history in recognizing the rights of LGBT persons is part of a social process of shaping constitutional meanings that informs and includes the formal and informal international spheres, consisting of interactions between civil society and national and international structures. Since 2012 when the "Law" took effect, throughout the world important jurisprudence is rapidly disseminating that defends gender identity based on self-perception. This phenomenon is being replicated in countries seeking to promote regulations and decisions that, as in Argentina, depathologize gender identity (Saldivia 2017). Latin America merits special attention given its prompt and increasingly wider acceptance of the right to gender identity.

In 2015, the Colombian government emitted Decree 1227 requiring notaries and the registry office to process requests from transgender persons wishing to change the sex designated in their identity documents to the one acquired or desired.[38] The regulation eliminates the need for medical exams before changing one's sexual identity in official documents. The decree comes after sustained meetings between government officials and civil society organizations that defend the rights of trans people, particularly the Aquelarre Trans Coalition (made up of organizations such as PAIIS, Colombia Diversa, Fundación Procrear, Fundación Santa María, PARCES Ong, GATT, and Colectivo Entre-tránsitos).[39] Several Argentine activists who had prepared the bill in the lead-up to the passage of the Argentine "Law" worked with Aquelarre Trans and Colombia Diversa to discuss and draft initial versions of the regulation.[40]

Several months previously, the Legislative Assembly of Mexico City approved (with 42 votes in favor, none against, and six abstentions) a law that eliminated legal proceedings for people wanting a gender identity change. The legal requirement was replaced with a simple administrative procedure at the office of the civil registrar. The law implemented reforms and amendments to numerous sections of the Mexico City Civil Code and Civil Procedures aimed at ensuring "recognition of the right of all persons to a gender identity through an administrative procedure before the Mexico City Civil Registry."[41] Several state offices (including the Mexico City Council to Prevent and Eliminate Discrimination [CONAPRED]) and civil society organizations that defend the rights of trans persons, particularly Coalición T47, worked jointly to have the law approved.

Exactly one year after the enactment of the Argentine Law on the Right to Gender Identity (DIG), the Chilean bill that recognizes and protects the right to gender identity[42] entered into legislative procedure (May 2013). Since then the treatment of the bill has been delayed in various ways (see www.iguales.cl/incidencia-politica/ley-de-identidad-de-genero/). During these five years of discussion, modifications took place that were limiting the original aspirations of the project. Finally, the Congress of Chile in the month of September of the year 2018 approved the project of "Law of gender identity" proposed by the Government. This initiative allows the registration of sex change for people over 14 years. A trans person over the age of 18 can make the change of name and sex in a Civil Registry office under his own will and with two witnesses. Young people between 14 and 18 years must have the permission of their parents or guardians and make the request before a family judge, who will define whether the petition proceeds or not. Additionally, they will have to present background information about both their psychosocial and family contexts. Despite the questionable limits of this norm (judicializes, does not recognize transgender children, establishes excessive administrative procedures, married persons must divorce in order to change gender since in Chile there is not egalitarian marriage),[43] the LGBTI community from that country received the law positively. Despite this setback, Chile is breaking ground in terms of prohibiting gender-assignment surgeries to intersex babies.[44] Notice 18 published on December 18, 2015, and titled: "Instructions on Certain Aspects of Health Care for Intersex Boys and Girls," issued by the subsecretary of public health, ordered medical centers throughout Chile to halt all surgeries of intersex boys and girls, thus ending unnecessary treatments to "normalize" infants' sex, such as irreversible genital operations. The notice states that a waiting period will be in effect until underage children "are old enough to decide about their bodies." It also instructs health services to create working groups of experts and to follow current guidelines to select a sex for civil registry purposes, but without surgeries.

In 2016, Bolivia joined the tendency throughout Latin America in favor of recognizing the right to a gender identity. The Bolivian legislature passed Law Number 807 on Gender Identity that allows transsexual and transgender persons, 18 years or older, to change their name and gender on personal documents (May 21, 2016). Several years before these experiences, the latest constitutional reforms of Ecuador and Bolivia have recognized the right to non-discrimination based on gender identity, even though, it must be said, the first country is far from recognizing a self-perceived gender model.[45]

The Democratic Nature of Recognizing LGBT Rights

In Argentina, recognition of the rights of sexual minorities was the result of a democratic process involving intense and complex deliberations. A diverse set of actors availed themselves of the opportunity to express their feelings, both backers and detractors, the Catholic Church among the latter. The social process that created pertinent constitutional language began when the LGBT movement waged a dogged struggle for recognition of their civil and social rights. The ensuing dialog continues to bear fruit among diverse government institutions, elites, communications media, social movements, clergy, and other mobilized sectors of civil society, such as student organizations and trade unions. The participation of such a broad spectrum of society widens the scope of protection afforded by the constitution's language on equality, including formal protection for those neglected until recently. The constitution also addresses the structural reasons behind the vulnerability of the LGBT minority and widens appropriate protections.

The process of giving real meaning to the constitution in the case of rights recognition for LGBT individuals was an especially vibrant process, given the many diverse interactions between civil society and state agencies. Seyla Benhabib calls these types of processes "democratic iterations," which are:

> Complex processes of public argument, deliberation, and exchange through which universalist rights claims and principles are contested and contextualized, invoked and revoked, posited and positioned, throughout legal and political institutions, as well as in the associations of civil society. These can take place in the "strong" public bodies of legislatures, the judiciary, and the executive, as well as in the informal and "weak" publics of civil society associations and the media.
>
> *(2005, 130)*[46]

This democratic deliberation consists of multiple interactions and an ongoing public process of understanding, creative appropriation, re-appropriation, and transformation of ideas and meanings through reasoning, responding, revising, and rejecting. These processes are complex and essentially cultural.

Special mention should be made of the LGBT social movement's participation. This key actor moved the process forward by exposing and visibilizing their history of lack of access to their rights, thus questioning the legal and social status quo based on regulations of a universal nature that subordinate them. They took up the gauntlet by proposing rights that are more contextualized and open to the demands of sexual minorities. As I mentioned previously, over two decades in Argentina there were many and varied discussions and contributions that fashioned this narrative about a nascent democracy. Perhaps the most relevant factor in this deliberative narrative, since they constituted the first step in the movement toward "getting laws passed," were the marches, the organization of the movement, i.e., a true struggle for visibility on the streets. Another major debate arose due to differences of opinion between the executive branch and the Supreme Court. This give-and-take arose repeatedly: when legal status to LGBT associations was denied by the inspector general for justice; the shift in judgments by two supreme courts, with different sitting members in the "CHA" and "ALITT" cases; public interest litigation encouraged by LGBT organizations in favor of the right to health and protection for HIV/AIDS (acquired immune deficiency syndrome) patients; passage of Article 11 of the Constitution of the City of Buenos Aires that explicitly forbade discrimination based on sexual orientation (1996); repeal of police edicts in Buenos Aires (1998); recognition by the City of Buenos Aires of civil unions (2006); further intervention by the executive branch through the National Administration of Social Security (ANSES in Spanish) to recognize the right of the surviving member of a homosexual couple to a pension; requests for protection presented to the Argentina justice system following denial of marriage opportunities for same-sex couples, ultimately resolved by the Supreme Court; the perhaps delayed involvement of the legislative branch in this process of democratic iteration, lobbying, and activism by the LGBT movement; applications presented to the justice system requesting authorization to change one's name and sex; resistance by the clergy and conservative sectors of society; opinions of professors and experts in the field aimed at the mass media and congressional public hearings; in the *amicus curiae* presented to the Supreme Court; among many other discussions and confrontations of ideas regarding the scope of protection of LGBT rights.

The international sphere was and is highly influential in the democratic iteration process, particularly in relation to its interaction with events at a national level. Declarations, resolutions, and decisions taken by the international and regional human rights system were crucial in shaping a multinational dialog that played a central role in recognizing LGBT rights.[47] The 1994 reform of Argentina's Constitution created enabling conditions for these international inputs by incorporating the principal international human rights instruments into the constitution and including new rights in its text. In addition, as mentioned earlier in this review of the situation in Latin America, once the Argentine law on the right to a gender identity was passed, another layer of exchange and dialog ensued as other nations began to emulate the Argentine model.

The content of these iterations has been quite varied, including all manner of narratives or social signifiers from those in favor of (or opposed to) recognizing LGBT persons as full citizens. A main characteristic of democratic iterations is that they can transform ideas that were mainstream up to that point, by altering viewpoints that were considered valid and opening public scrutiny of ideas that were once excluded and scorned. This process can be enriching if it brings about social change through transformation of certain aspects of the dominant ideology in an effort to halt the oppression of disadvantaged groups (Crenshaw 2006). In spite of reflecting the prevailing ideology, rights could be treated as political action resources, that is to say, they can be reinterpreted and adjusted to include subordinate groups.

Final Reflections

The experience of Argentina reviewed in this chapter demonstrates that it is possible to conceive of a gender identity model that is respectful of transgender people's rights. Indeed, beyond the optimism created by growing legal recognition of a model of sexuality based on personal perception, we should recall that such acknowledgment is still a step ahead of society's comprehension of gender identity (which remains largely binary and static). Therefore, the approval of legal measures, such as the "Law" and similar measures in Latin America, are undoubtedly a symbolic sea change, since they help promote and demand effective recognition of the legal and political visibility won by trans people during the past two decades. Furthermore, these types of measures generate conditions that enable social acceptance and provide tools to address and transform the violence and discrimination against LGBT minorities. Their mere existence, however, will not promptly banish the violence and social exclusion that gender non-conformist persons continue to experience; on the contrary, violence and exclusion persist. For this reason, the efforts of concerned people and institutions should not aim solely at expanding the boundaries to incorporate a depathologized paradigm of gender and sexuality; they must also seek to challenge the reality of exclusion in line with the inclusive temperament of this paradigm.

Notes

1 Argentina was the twelfth country in the world to pass a law on marriage equality (Law Number 26.618).
2 In 2012, Decree 1007/2012 expanded the law to include persons in situations of migration. Further, in 2015, Decree Number 903/2015 defined Article 11 of the "Law" to include free provision of all necessary partial and/or total surgeries to achieve desired gender changes.

3 Since the 1990s, the term transgender or *trans* is used to designate persons whose identities, practices, or beliefs regarding sex/gender do not conform to traditional social expectations regarding the sex assigned or designated at birth. In a broad and inclusive sense, the movement to promote transgender people's rights uses these terms strategically, since they are also employed to name the oppression and exclusion experienced by many people who are marginalized by binary constructs of sex/gender. See Currah (2006, 3–7).

4 In accordance with the characteristics identified by Charles Tilly, the LGBT community qualifies as a social movement. Tilly maintains:

> As it developed in the West after 1750, the social movement emerged from an innovative, consequential synthesis of three elements: 1) a sustained, organized public effort making collective claims on target authorities (let us call it a *campaign*); 2) employment of combinations from among the following forms of political action: creation of special-purpose associations and coalitions, public meetings, solemn processions, vigils, rallies, demonstrations, petition drives, statements to and in public media, and pamphleteering (we can call the variable ensemble of performances the *social movement repertoire*); and 3) participants' concerted public representations of WUNC: worthiness, unity, numbers, and commitment on the part of themselves and/or their constituencies (call them *WUNC displays*).
>
> *(2004, 3–4)*

Some of the organizations that comprise the movement are the Argentina Homosexual Community (CHA), the Argentina Federation of Lesbians, Gays, Bisexuals and Trans (FALGBT), Futuro Transgenérico, Movimiento Andidiscriminatorio de Liberación (MAL), Asociación Lucha por la Identidad Travesti-Transexual (ALITT), and Asociación Travestis, Transexuales y Trans Argentina (ATTTA).

5 More than 10,000 trans people changed their name on their identity document with the gender-identity law, Telam, May 9, 2016, www.telam.com.ar/notas/201605/146664-ley-identidad-genero-aniversario-dni-trans.html. Consulted August 7, 2017.

6 Articles 1, 2, 3, and 11.

7 Article 11.

8 Article 5. For an analysis regarding the first application of this clause regarding the experience of a six-year-old trans girl, see Saldivia (2016).

9 Article 11.

10 Article 11 of the RGI statute has been regulated by Executive Decree 903/2015. This regulation understands total and partial surgical interventions to be those surgeries needed to adjust the body to the self-perceived gender identity, and indicates that these include: enhancement mastoplasty; mastectomy; augmentation gluteoplasty; orchiectomy; penectomy; vaginoplasty; clitoroplasty; vulvoplasty; hysterectomy and oophorectomy; vaginectomy; metoidioplasty; scrotoplasty; phalloplasty; and penile prosthesis. The regulation clarifies that this list is not exhaustive. It adds that integral hormone treatments are understood to be those that aim to change the secondary characteristics that result from sex glands, so that an individual's appearance corresponds to the self-perceived gender.

11 Specifically, Article 2 of the "Law" adopts the definition of gender identity verbatim from the preamble of the "Principles."

12 Various authors emphasize the important role played by activists from international and/or local social movements, as well as directors and staff of NGOs regarding their conceptualization of LGBT human rights, their institutionalization and vernacularization, i.e., taking ideas from one context to another, adopting, and shaping them. See Thoreson 2014; Levitt and Merry 2009.

13 According to Klabbers (1996: 167), *soft law* refers to a "wide grey area filled with those documents and instruments that are not clearly law, but about which it cannot be said that they are juridically insignificant."

14 I take this distinction between locations of normative production and reception from Lopez Medina 2009, see also Lopez Medina 2005.

15 References to North and South are not necessarily geographic but rather designate the unequal distribution of political, economic, military, and cultural power among countries of the world. For a critique of the center-periphery dynamics regarding academic law and legal clinics, see Bonilla (2013).

16 See Saldivia 2017, Chapter 6.

17 Outstanding studies on these legal migrations and cross-fertilizations include: Merry (2006); Dezalay and Garth (2012); and Ansolabehere (2014).

18 In terms of the tensions that are inherent to the notion of constitutional self-governance and claims of authority by international law, see Choudhry (2011).

19 This section is a summarized version of Saldivia, Laura (2017) "Chapter 2".

20 In various cases decided by the Supreme Court during the first years of the democratic era, the judges grounded their decisions within the special political and historical context surrounding the transition to democracy. Accordingly, they found the principle of autonomy to be a fundamental foundation on which to base the re/construction of a democracy that respects human rights. Exemplary cases include "Fiorentino" (Fallos 306, 1752 [1984]), regarding the unconstitutionality of forced entry into a home by the police with no protection of privacy and of limits to freedom of expression; "Sejean" (Fallos 1986, 308, 2268), regarding the unconstitutionality of prohibiting absolute divorce; "Portillo" (Fallos 1989, 312, 496) regarding acceptance of conscientious-objector status as a legitimate basis to refuse obligatory military service; and "Bazterrica" (Fallos 1986, 308, 1392), regarding the unconstitutionality of criminalizing drug possession for personal consumption.

21 The first transvestite group to organize was the Association of Argentine Transvestites (ATA) in 1991. Shortly afterwards, due to internal differences over acceptance or rejection of the practice of prostitution, the ATA split into two organizations: Organization of Transvestites and Transsexuals of the Argentine Republic (OTTRA) and the Association in Struggle for Transvestite and Transsexual Identity (ALITT).

22 See Berkins (2003); Fernández (2004). It took time for gays and lesbofeminists to acknowledge the transvestite and transsexual movement fully, a period during which they should overcame their repudiation of transvestism.

23 The scope of this reform can be appreciated by the fact that currently judges render verdicts after considering both international human rights instruments included in the constitution and the decision of international bodies charged with interpreting and applying these instruments. See, among others, the following Supreme Court cases: "Giroldi" (Fallos 1995, 319, 514) and "Espósito" (Fallos 2004, 327, 5668). This jurisprudence was confirmed by the Supreme Court following reports by the Inter-American Commission on Human Rights in the cases of "Bramajo" (Fallos 1996, 319, 1840) and "Romero Cacharane" (Fallos 2004, 327, 388). Similarly, the Supreme Court recognized that the jurisprudence of the European Court of Human Right constitutes a valid hermeneutic model of interest for interpreting the Inter-American Convention on Human Rights in the following cases: "Viaña" (Fallos 1995, 318, 2348), "Nardelli" (Fallos 1995, 319, 2557), and "Llerena" (Fallos 2005, 328, 1491). In a recent case, a majority of judges of the Supreme Court ruled that states are obligated under all circumstances to implement the Inter-American Commission's "Article 51" reports, and that Argentina is required to spare no effort in implementing the commission's recommendations (Fallo CSJN, "Carranza Latrubesse, Gustavo v. the National State," August 6, 2013).

24 The eighth GLTT and B March of Pride in 1999 is emblematic in this regard.

25 For a detailed description of its content and dynamic, see the surveys conducted by Carlos Fígari, Daniel Jones, Micaela Libson, Hernán Manzelli, Flavio Rapisardi, and Horacio Sívori, "Sociabilidad, Política, Violencia y Derechos. La Marcha del Orgullo GLTTB de Buenos Aires 2004. Primera Encuesta," supported by the Instituto de Investigaciones Gino Germani (IIGG) Área Queer – Laboratorio de Políticas Públicas (LPP) and the Centro Latinoamericano de Sexualidad y Derechos Humanos (CLAM), and Tomás Iosa, Hugo H. Rabbia, Ma. Candelaria Sgró Ruata, José Manuel Morán Faúndes, and Juan Marco Vaggione, "Política, sexualidades y derechos. Primera Encuesta Marcha del Orgullo y la Diversidad" Córdoba, Argentina 2010.

26 *Comunidad Homosexual Argentina* "CHA," (CSJN Fallos 314:1531 [1991]) and *Asociación Lucha por la Identidad Travesti-Transexual* "ALITT," (CSJN Fallos 329:5266 [2006]).

27 "ALITT," paragraph 11.

28 The Supreme Court recognized that sexual minorities:

> not only suffer social discrimination but are also seriously victimized through ill treatment, pressure, rape, aggression, and even murder. As a result of the prejudice and discrimination that deny them job opportunities, sexual minorities are practically condemned to marginalization that is often aggravated by belonging to the more underprivileged sectors of society, with disastrous consequences for their quality of life and health, given their high mortality rates, all of which has been verified by field investigations.
>
> *(Ibid., paragraph 17)*

29 "ALITT," paragraph 16.

30 Resolution 671/2008 indicates that same-sex cohabitants have a right to a pension upon death of the retiree, or upon retirement due to a disability, or if affiliated to the public social security regime or a pension plan.

31 For a reconstructon of the steps that led to approval of the equal marriage law, see Hiller (2010).

32 For further information on the relationship between the military and other sectors of Argentine society, see Verbitsky and Bohoslavsky (2013).

33 The practices of the National Commission on Disappeared Persons (CONADEP) and the trials and sentences handed down to the dictatorship's military junta are examples of this.

34 An estimate of 500 children disappeared in this fashion. To date (8/10/2017), 122 persons have recovered their identity. See www.abuelas.org.ar/noticia/bienvenido-a-la-verdad-nieto-799 Consulted September 22, 2017.

35 The Inter-American Court of Human Rights has emphasized the importance of this right. First "as a set of attributes and characteristics that allows for the individualization of a person in society." Second, as "one of the ways to facilitate the exercise of the right to legal standing, a name, a nationality, registration in the civil registry, family relations, among other rights recognized by international instruments." Third, lack of recognition "may mean that a person cannot obtain access to legal acknowledgement of his/her existence, making it more difficult to fully enjoy civil, political, economic, social, and cultural rights," according to the decision handed down in "Gelman v. Uruguay," February 24, 2011, paragraphs 122 and 123.

36 See Cristian Alarcón, "Un Jueves Diferente en la Plaza," *Página 12*, December 6, 1998. Available at: www.pagina12.com.ar/1998/98-06/98-06-12/pag15.htm. Consulted August 7, 2017.

37 Needless to say, inside the Argentine LGBT movement there are deep dissagreements on instrumental normative and expressive claims. According to Mario Pecheny:

> Regardless of ideological and strategic conflicts, within social movements for sexual minorities lie substantial disagreements in the domains of ethical-normative and expressive validity claims. It is these disagreements that often explain the conflictive interactions that occur under the guise of dissent in the strategic domain.
>
> *(Pecheny 2010, 288)*

38 Decree 1227, June 2015.

39 Conservative sectors in Colombia with strong ties to the Catholic Church opposed the new regulation. In the months following approval of the Attorney General's decree, these sectors requested that all declarations in favor of LGBTI rights be ruled invalid. Examples are the decree referred to above, relating to Sentence T-478 of 2015 from the constitutional court in the case of Sergio Urrego regarding discrimination at school based on sexual orientation and gender identity, and the sentence of the Colombian Constitutional Court recognizing equal adoption rights. See "Mi sexo, mi cédula, yo decido," Diario El Espectador, Octubre 30, 2015. Available at: www.elespectador.com/noticias/bogota/mi-sexo-mi-cedula-yo-decido-articulo-596196 Consulted August 7, 2017.

40 According to AboSex: https://abosex.wordpress.com/2015/06/30/colombia-despatologiza-y-desjudicializa-el-reconocimiento-de-la-identidad-de-genero/. Consulted August 7, 2017.

41 Judgment approved by the Mexico City Legislative Assembly, November 2014.

42 Bulletin number 8.924-07.

43 For a critical analysis of the chielan Law view Laura Saldivia Menajovsky "Columna sobre la Ley de género: Y nos siguen tratando como enfermos", The Clinic, 9/9/2018, www.theclinic.cl/2018/09/09/columna-sobre-la-ley-de-genero-y-nos-siguen-tratando-como-enfermos/

44 See, Morgan, "Chilean Ministry of Health issues instructions stopping 'normalizing' interventions on intersex children," Organization Intersex International Australia, 11/1/2016 Available at: https://oii.org.au/30250/chilean-ministry-stops-normalising/ Consulted August 7, 2017.

45 Constitution of Ecuador, Article 14. II and Constitution of Bolivia, Article 11.

46 Benhabib revisits Robert Cover's notion of "jurisgenerative" policy, which:

> makes reference to iterative actions through which a democratic people who consider themselves subject to certain guiding regulations and principles re-appropriate and reinterpret these, proving that they are not just the subjects of laws but also the authors behind laws.
>
> *(Cover, 1983, 131)*

47 See Saldivia Menajovsky 2017, Chapter 6. Levitt and Merry (2009) have called the process of local appropriation and adoption of ideas and strategies created abroad "vernacularization," analyzing how global ideas on women's rights are introduced in local contexts and what response is produced locally.

References

Ansolabehere, Karina. 2014. Difusores y justicieros. Las instituciones judiciales en la política de derechos humanos. *Perfiles Latinoamericanos* 22(44): 143–69.

Bellucci, Mabel, 2010. *Orgullo. Carlos Jáuregui, una biografía política*. Buenos Aires: Emecé.

Bellucci, Mabel. 2014. *Historia de una Desobediencia. Aborto y Feminismo*, Buenos Aires: Capital Intelectual.

Bellucci, Mabel and Cecilia Palmeiro, 2013. "Lo queer en las pampas criollas, argentinas y vernáculas." In Ana María Fernandez and Wiliam Siqueira Peres (Eds.), *La Diferencia Desquiciada. Géneros y Diversidades Sexuales*, Buenos Aires: Editorial Biblios: 43–74.

Benhabib, Seyla. 2005. *El Derecho de los Otros*, Barcelona: Editorial Gedisa.

Berkins, Lohana. (Coord.). 2007. *Cumbia, Copeteo y Lágrimas. Informe Nacional sobre la Situación de las Travestis, Transexuales y Transgénero*, Buenos Aires: ALITT.

Berkins, Lohana 2003. "Un itinerario político del travestismo." In Diana Maffia (Ed.), *Sexualidades Migrantes. Género y Transgénero*, Buenos Aires: Feminaria Editora: 127–37.

Bonilla, Daniel. 2013. "Legal Clinics in the Global North and South: Between Equality and Subordination. An Essay." In *Violencia, legitimidad y orden público, Seminario en Latinoamérica de Teoría Constitucional y Política, SELA 2012*, Buenos Aires: Libraria: 310–46.

Choudhry Sujit (ed.) 2011. *The Migration of Constitutional Ideas*. Cambridge and New York: Cambridge University Press.

Cover, Robert. (1983). "The Supreme Court, 1982 Term – Foreword: Nomos and Narrative." Faculty Scholarship Series. Paper 2705. Available at: http://digitalcommons.law.yale.edu/fss_papers/2705. Accessed August 7, 2017.

Crenshaw Kimberlé. 2006. "Raza, reforma y retroceso: transformación y legitimación en el derecho contra la discriminación." In García-Villegas, M. Jaramillo Sierra, I.C. and Restrepo Saldarriaga, E. (Eds.), *Crítica Jurídica*, Bogotá: Uniandes: 97–123.

Currah, Paisley. 2006. "Gender Pluralisms under the Transgender Umbrella." In Paisley Currah, Richard M. Juang, and Shannon Price Minter (Eds.), *Transgendered Rights*. Minneapolis: University of Minnesota Press: 3–7.

Dezalay Yves and Bryant Garth (Eds.). 2012. *Lawyers and the Construction of Transnational Justice Law, Development and Globalization*. London and New York: Routledge.

Fernández, Josefina. 2004. *Cuerpos Desobedientes. Travestismo e identidad de género*, Buenos Aires: Edhasa.

Hiller, Renata. 2010. "Matrimonio Igualitario y Espacio Público en Argentina." In Martin Aldao and Laura Clérico (Coords.). *Matrimonio Igualitario. Perspectivas Sociales, Políticas y Jurídicas*. Buenos Aires: Eudeba: 85–130.

Klabbers, Jan. 1996. "The Redundancy of Soft Law." *Nordic Journal of International Law* 65: 167–82.

Levitt, Peggy and Sally Merry. 2009. "Vernacularization on the ground: local uses of global women's rights in Peru, China, India, and the United States." *Global Networks* 9(4): 441–61.

Lopez, Diego. 2009. "¿Por qué hablar de una 'teoría impura del derecho' para América Latina?" In Daniel Bonilla Maldonado, *Teoría del Derecho y Trasplantes Jurídicos*. Bogotá: Siglo del Hombre Editores, Universidad de Los Andes, Pontificia Universidad Javeriana-Instituto Pensar: 37–90.

Lopez, Diego. 2005. *Teoría Impura del Derecho. La Transformación de la Cultura Jurídica Latinoamericana*, Bogotá: Legis, 3rd edition.

Mattarollo, Rodolfo. 1999. "Aportes de la lucha contra el terrorismo de Estado al Derecho" written for the international seminar "CELS. 20 años de historia," p. 25. Available at: www.cels.org.ar/web/wp-content/uploads/1999/12/MVJ-Las-estrategias-durante-la-dictadura-y-los-desafios-desde-la-transicion-hasta-el-presente.pdf. Accessed September 16, 2017.

Merry, Sally. 2006. *Human Rights and Gender Violence: Translating International Law into Local Justice* (Chicago Series in Law and Society), Chicago: The University of Chicago Press.

Moreno, Aluminé. 2008. "La Invisibilidad Como Injusticia. Estrategias del Movimiento de la Diversidad Sexual." In Mario Pecheny, Carlos Figari, and Daniel Jones, (Eds.), *Todo Sexo es Político. Estudios Sobre Sexualidades en Argentina*, Buenos Aires: Libros del Zorzal: 217–40.

Pecheny, Mario. 2010. "The Rationale of Collective Action within Sexual-Rights Movements: An Abstract Analysis of very concrete experiences." In Javier Corrales and Mario Pecheny (Eds.), *The Politics of Sexuality in Latin America: A Reader on Lesbian, Gay, Bisexual, and Transgender Rights*, Pittsburgh: University of Pittsburgh Press: 283–89.

Sabsay, Leticia. 2011. *Fronteras Sexuales. Espacio Urbano, Cuerpos y Ciudadanía*, Buenos Aires: Editorial Paidós.

Saldivia, Laura. 2015a. "Abogados/as que Resistieron: Una Forma Transformadora de Ejercer el Derecho." En Juan Pablo Bohovslavsky (ed.) *¿Usted también doctor? Complicidad de Funcionarios Judiciales y Abogados Durante la Dictadura*, Buenos Aires: Siglo Veintiuno Editores: 269–88.

Saldivia, Laura, 2015b. "Contexto y Originalidad del Derecho a la Identidad de Género en Argentina." In *SELA 2014: 20 años del SELA*. Seminario en Latinoamérica de Teoría Constitucional y Política, Buenos Aires: Libraria: 253–87.

Saldivia, Laura. 2016. "El Reconocimiento del Derecho a la Identidad de Luana." In Valeria Pavan (Ed.), *Niñez Trans. Experiencia de Reconocimiento y Derecho a la Identidad*, Editorial Universidad Nacional de General Sarmiento: 77–87.

Saldivia, Laura. 2017. *Subordinaciones Invertidas: Sobre el Derecho a la Identidad de Género*, Mexico: Editorial Universidad Nacional Autónoma de México UNAM, and Buenos Aires: Editorial Universidad Nacional de General Sarmiento.

Sieder, Rachel. 2011. "Contested Sovereignties: Indigenous Law, Violence and State Effects in Postwar Guatemala." *Critique of Anthropology* 31(3): 161–84.

Sívori, Horacio. 2008. "GLTTB y otros HSH. Ciencia y Política de la Identidad Sexual en la Prevención del SIDA." In *Todo Sexo es Político. Estudios Sobre Sexualidades en Argentina*: 245–75.

Tilly, Charles. 2004. *Social Movements, 1768–2008*. Paradigm Publishers.

Thoreson. 2014. *Transnational LGBT Activism: Working for Sexual Rights Worldwide*, Minneapolis: University Of Minnesota Press.

Verbitsky Horacio and Juan Pablo Bohoslavsky. 2013. *Cuentas Pendientes. Los Cómplices Económicos de la Dictadura*, Buenos Aires: Ediciones Siglo Veinte.

Constitutions

Bolivia. 2009. Constitución Política del Estado de Bolivia. Artículo 11. Available at: www.oas.org/dil/esp/Constitucion_Bolivia.pdf. Accessed August 9, 2017.

Ecuador. 2008. *Constitución de la República del Ecuador. Artículo 14. II.* Available at: www.inocar.mil.ec/web/images/lotaip/2015/literal_a/base_legal/A._Constitucion_republica_ecuador_2008constitucion.pdf. Accessed August 9, 2017.

Websites

ABOSEX. 2015. [Blog]. Colombia despatologiza y desjudicializa el reconocimiento de la identidad de género. AboSex: Abogadxs por los derechos sexuales. Available at: https://abosex.wordpress.com/2015/06/30/colombia-despatologiza-y-desjudicializa-el-reconocimiento-de-la-identidad-de-genero/. Accessed August 9, 2017.

Abuelas de Plaza de Mayo. 2017. [online] An estimate of 500 children disappeared in this fashion. To date (8/10/2017), 122 persons have recovered their identity. Conferencia de prensa por la restitución del nieto 122. Available at: www.abuelas.org.ar/noticia/bienvenido-a-la-verdad-nieto-799. Accessed September 23, 2017.

Alarcón, Cristian. 1998. [online] "Un Jueves Diferente en la Plaza," *Página12*, December 6. Available at: www.pagina12.com.ar/1998/98-06/98-06-12/pag15.htm. Accessed August 9, 2017.

Cámara de Diputados de Chile. 2013. [online] *Proyectos de Ley. Segundo Trámite Constitucional*. Número de boletín: 8924–07 Available at: www.camara.cl/pley/pley_detalle.aspx?prmID=9331&prmBL=8924-07. Accessed August 9, 2017.

Erazo, Catalina. 2015. [online] Mi Sexo, Mi Cédula, yo Decido. *Diario El Espectador*, October 30. Available at: www.elespectador.com/noticias/bogota/mi-sexo-mi-cedula-yo-decido-articulo-596196. Accessed August 9, 2017.

IGUALES. 2017. [Blog] *Ley de Identidad de Género*. Available at: www.iguales.cl/incidencia-politica/ley-de-identidad-de-genero/ (Accessed August 9, 2017).

Morgan. 2016. [online] *Chilean Ministry of Health issues instructions stopping "normalizing" interventions on intersex children*. Organization Intersex International Australia Limited. Available at: https://oii.org.au/30250/chilean-ministry-stops-normalising/. Accessed August 9, 2017.

TÉLAM. 2016. [online]. *More than 10,000 trans people changed their name on their identity document with the gender-identity law*. May 9. Available at: www.telam.com.ar/notas/201605/146664-ley-identidad-genero-aniversario-dni-trans.html. Accessed August 9, 2017.

23

LAW, GENDER, AND SOCIAL MOVEMENTS IN LATIN AMERICA

Moral Negotiations and Uneven Victories in Feminist Legal Mobilization

Marta Rodriguez de Assis Machado,
Ana Luiza Villela de Viana Bandeira and Fernanda Emy Matsuda

The organized women's movement in Latin America emerged in the late 1970s in the context of democratization and the transition from dictatorship. As women increasingly entered universities and the labor market, the ideology of family, church, and motherhood, heavily exploited by authoritarian governments, was gradually challenged. At the same time, as social inequalities sharpened, poor women organized within their communities to improve their life conditions. Although they were capable of mobilizing a considerable female contingent, these movements were not exactly feminist in nature. Women in marginal urban settlements affirmed their rights to better living conditions primarily as mothers and wives. The Catholic Church, despite its social agenda,[1] was not willing to abandon its traditional discourse on the role of women. Although it advocated increased participation by women in the public sphere and community, the church remained steadfastly opposed to sexual equality, divorce, contraception policies, decriminalization of abortion, and homosexuality. The politicization of living conditions only intersected with the politicization of motherhood and gender when working class women came into contact with white, highly-educated, middle class activists from leftist organizations and feminist groups, many newly arrived back from exile. These women shifted the debate to topics such as equality at work and sexual freedom. But their links with poor women meant their feminist activism was also sensitive to social inequalities and the problems most affecting working class women. This union of middle class feminists focused on the social reproduction of gender roles and poor women committed to improving their living conditions constituted the field of women's mobilization in many Latin American countries – an active, diverse, complex, and often contradictory field, where women were gradually entering into gender politics but feminism did not become homogeneous. One of the inherent contradictions at the root of Latin America feminisms is linked precisely to the presence of both feminist and feminine demands (Alvarez 1990).[2] Against this background, the different worldviews, discourses, gender categories, rights, and public policies of diverse collective actors interact and compete. This constitutive diversity is key to understanding how the Latin American feminist movement is able to negotiate with more conservative sectors and accommodate some of their more traditional conceptions of gender.

Since the transition to democracy and the approval of new constitutions, feminist movements in the region have adopted strategies to fight for rights in different institutional spaces of the state, at federal, state, and municipal level, in all three branches, as well as within international bodies (Santos 2007). During the 1990s the field became professionalized and internationalized (Alvarez 1998). Some "historical" feminists took on roles in state institutions, either as elected representatives or as advisors and members of governmental teams; others joined non-governmental organizations (NGOs) engaged in lobbying, advocacy, and national and international litigation strategies.[3] Advances were uneven: some demands were recognized in constitutions or specific laws, others were translated into public policies, and others have not advanced or have even receded.

The comparison between the *fields of strategic mobilization*[4] around domestic violence and abortion is paradigmatic because it demonstrates this uneven advancement of feminist demands. These two issues, both fundamentally important in the fight for control over women's bodies, illustrate the very different dynamics at play with regard to acceptance of discourses, the presence (or absence) of positive synergies with state institutions, formations of allies and enemies, as well as successes, threats, and setbacks for women's rights. In the following sections we briefly reconstruct the processes of legal mobilization that have occurred in these fields in Brazil; rather than attempting to account for all the complexitites in each case, we focus on the moments where moral negotiations proved crucial. Two cases that reached the supreme court are more closely analyzed, although again for reasons of space we do not cover all contextual issues in this narrative. In our analysis, we draw on the results of two different empirical research projects: the first, on legal mobilization concerning the adoption of Maria da Penha Law and Femicide Act and their acceptance by courts; the second, still in progress, on legal mobilization on abortion rights in Brazil.[5] In both cases we reconstruct processes of legal mobilization through a review of secondary documention and bibliographical resources, and the following primary sources: (i) the minutes of the Brazilian Constituent Assembly; (ii) the records concerning the legislative process of the Maria da Penha Law and the Femicide Act; (iii) decisions of the courts of appeal from nine states regarding the implementation of Maria da Penha Law (from September 2006 to December 2010); (iv) bills presented in favor of and opposing abortion from 1989 to 2015; (v) two cases that reached the supreme court on the constitutionality of Maria da Penha Law (ADC 19 and ADI 4.424); and (vi) the anencephalic fetus case that reached the supreme court (including the initial petition, interim decisions, speeches in the public hearing, and the final decision).

In this chapter we argue that moral disputes and processes of discursive negotiation are key to explaining the differences between the two fields of legal mobilization. To date, Latin American feminist movements have tended to choose the state as their main arena of collective action and confrontation (Safa 1990; Jelin 1987). As we demonstrate in subsequent sections, the ability to circumvent, negotiate or resignify dominant cultural representations of women, gender, and family were crucial to feminist victories at key moments in the struggle for institutional change. We focus here on the Brazilian feminist movement, but comparable dynamics are in evidence in other Latin American countries.

Brazil is an important example of the development of a highly professionalized feminist activism that conquered important spaces within the state bureaucracy – this process started early in 1985 with the advent of the State Women's Councils and gained momentum in 2003 with the creation of the Special Secretariat for Women's Affairs during the first government of Luiz Inácio Lula da Silva (2003–2006). Feminists deployed national and international strategies of mobilization and occupied strategic posts in the executive branch, yet they only managed to advance some of their demands in the realm of public policy. As in other countries in the region, socio-legal mobilization on these two key issues resulted in, on the one hand, a broadening of protection against domestic violence through the passing of criminal laws and, on the other hand, threats and backlashes in the sphere of sexual and reproductive rights (Ruibal 2014).

The first decade of the twenty-first century was marked by efforts across the region to draft laws to combat violence against women, with an emphasis on domestic violence.[6] By contrast, the issue of abortion not only faced difficulties in advancing as part of a rights agenda, but also suffered setbacks in many countries.[7] Numerous Latin American constitutions protect life "since conception," including those of El Salvador, the Dominican Republic and Ecuador (Jurkewicz 2011). In most countries abortion is still a crime, with very few exceptions, and some governments have recently passed legislation that totally bans abortion, even in cases of pregnancy as a result of sexual violence or medical risks to the life of the pregnant woman. Pro-choice and anti-abortion transnational networks operate across the region, with these actors moving within governments, legislatures, and courts. In Brazil, in common with neighboring countries, there is enormous resistance in the public sphere to discussion of women's sexual and reproductive rights, emanating particularly from religious groups.[8] In Brazil and other countries, battles were fought through different state arenas to modify legislation and increase the possibilities for legal abortion. The weight of conservative forces in the legislature in particular, encouraged feminist agendas to move to the courts (García Pereanez 2010).[9] In what follows, we examine features common to both fields of socio-legal mobilization with the aim of generating hypotheses for comparative studies.

Legal Mobilization, Framings, and Cultural Politics

Studies of mobilization and political confrontation have highlighted factors that explain the success or failure of collective action in achieving social and institutional change. These include resources, organizational structures (McCarthy and Zald 1977), and performances and repertoires of action (Tilly 1995). The prevailing political opportunity structure, (including opportunities, restrictions, and threats) explains an important part of collective action processes, pointing to institutional spaces more or less open to civil society participation, as well as the willingness and sensitivity of public officials to incorporate, negotiate, or suppress demands (Tarrow 1988). The ability to gain allies within and outside the political system or to mobilize countermovements has also demonstrated itself to be crucial. This is because "opposing movements influence each other both directly and by altering the environment in which each side operates. The opposing movement is a critical component in the structure of political opportunity the other side faces" (Meyer and Staggenborg 1996, 1633). All these factors expand or limit forms of organization and action, and are capable of influencing movements' legal strategies, although analysis of the use of law by countermovements is relatively new to socio-legal studies in Latin America (Teles 2010).

Symbolic and cultural disputes over processes of definition and interpretation of reality have gained greater ground in studies on social movements in recent decades, based on the concept of framing processes (Snow et al. 1986, 2000). Social movements not only act on the world – through protest and demands for change – but also form frameworks, interpreting and disputing meanings. Framing processes are continuous and contextual, involving attempts by opposing social movements to gain public legitimacy for their demands. Analytically, the concept of "frame" means that political disputes are inseparable from their cultural dimensions; meanings are constitutive of processes that, either implicitly or explicitly, seek to redefine social power. This occurs, for example, when social movements seek alternative meanings for such concepts or constructs as democracy, race, gender, family, etc. (Alvarez, Dagnino, and Escobar 1998, 7).

While the concept of framing has gained importance in studies of social movement strategies, the use of frameworks and the cultural dimensions of disputes are much less in evidence in studies on legal mobilization. Analysis of the effects of accommodations or interpretive battles and their specific features in the field of law is even less frequent (Vanhala 2009; Pedriana 2006). We argue here that the moral and cultural dimensions of confrontations between opposing social movements are crucial to fully understand processes of legal mobilization. Studies on the behavior of courts, by contrast, do focus on the argumentative structure of decisions (Dworkin 1988; Alexy 1989; Günther 1993) and their consistency (Puschel 2010; Mendes 2011), However, these studies do not always capture the flows between institutions and civil society, which in turn highlight the moral dimension at stake in every winning argument in the field of law. Nor can processes of institutional maintenance or changes achieved through action before the courts be observed in their entirety merely by analyzing decisions and precedents. The stability of a decision, for example, cannot always be explained by previous decisions and supporting legal arguments. In some cases, it is the scope and strength of dominant cultural and moral categories that supports the legal positions.

The category of framing focuses our analytical attention on an intermediate space straddling law, morals, and culture, and serves as a useful category for observation of the interaction between formal and informal spheres. Demands for rights, legal solutions, and public policies are supported by arguments that articulate or assume moral and cultural conceptions, going beyond legal language. In the field of law, frameworks reflect disputes over models of regulation (forms of legal treatment of a problem and its configuration in the legal system), supported simultaneously by arguments rooted in other types of legitimation: moral, scientific, cultural, political, and so forth. Legal frameworks have both an institutional and systemic component – as illustrated for example, by the framing of an issue within legal norms – allied with symbolic representations pertaining to cultural and moral spheres.

Political confrontation within the feminist field (in both formal and informal arenas) has its specificity in an intense mobilization of symbolic representations of gender, the role of women, and family. Feminist demands and discourses can be more or less de-stabilizing to dominant representations. And this dimension is important in order to understand the scenario of opportunities and challenges in feminist legal mobilization. Some agendas have been more palatable than others, and this difference is related to the ability of feminist discourses to accommodate, negotiate, or reframe existing moral and cultural categories. By proposing an analysis that is more contextual, relational, and dynamic, in this chapter we use the concept of framing in order to understand the disputes at stake in processes of judicialization of gender relations.

Comparing Two Subfields of Feminist Mobilization: Domestic Violence and Abortion

Domestic violence and abortion are issues that were present from the outset of the Latin American feminist movement. Since then, however, they have experienced very different patterns of acceptance and rejection. While curbing domestic violence proved relatively uncontroversial, the agenda of abortion was rejected by the Catholic Church and by some left-wing activists who viewed it as part of a liberal agenda for invoking women's autonomy and freedom of choice. It was never a priority among other women's demands that enjoyed more consensus, such as combating domestic violence, building kindergartens, or ensuring maternity leave and women's access to the labor market (Moraes and Sorj 2009, 11–2).

The conflict between feminists and the Catholic Church over the issue of abortion was strongly evident around the drafting of Brazil's 1988 Constitution. At that time, feminists presented the Women's Rights Charter, a document addressed to assembly members containing a series of demands, among them the right to abortion. The Catholic Church, in turn, pressured the Constituent Assembly to include a clause protecting the right to life "starting at conception" (Rocha 2006). Feminists managed to block this regressive proposition, but it was never possible to advance the decriminalization of abortion. By contrast, domestic violence gained institutional recognition at the beginning of Brazil's democratic transition. The creation of the first women's police station in São Paulo in 1985 was a milestone in terms of public recognition of the seriousness of the problem (Santos 2005). Complaints about how the justice system dealt with issues of violence[10] and the demand for approval of specific laws to deal with gender violence were the subject of mobilization by the women's movement during the 1990s and 2000s. During this period, these demands were echoed in international documents, thereby gaining significant leverage.[11] Cases in the international arena fueled the fight for approval of specific laws against domestic violence in several countries in Latin America. In Brazil, a series of piecemeal laws were passed during this period,[12] but none met movement demands for a comprehensive legal framework to develop innovative public policies.

In the case of abortion, law proved to be a resource for the opposition. Since 1940, Brazil's criminal code has stated that abortion is a crime and only provides exceptions to this rule when the pregnancy endangers the mother's life and/or when pregnancy results from rape.[13] Despite this, access to legal abortion services in public hospitals is extremely limited. Brazilian feminists were divided between those who advocated complete decriminalization of abortion and others who wanted first to guarantee the implementation of what was already a right (the regime of exceptions). Over time the latter, less radical demand gained more traction within the agenda of feminist social movements. In terms of frameworks, from the initial stages of mobilization over abortion the strategy of the women's movement was not to focus on moral confrontation and women's autonomy. In the "Carta das Mulheres" (Women's Letter), the issue was addressed in the double register of gender and health. The framework of autonomy progressively disappeared from the discourse of the feminist movement and in the 1990s and 2000s it opted entirely for a framework of public health, focusing on the issue of unsafe abortions (Barsted 1992, 124).

From the mid-1980s feminists worked to establish alliances in the state and federal governments, making progress with regard to regulation and implementation of legal abortion via executive action. In 1989, the first public hospital that performs legal abortion in the country was inaugurated in São Paulo and almost ten years later, the first technical standards regulating legal abortion were drawn up.[14] With the increased presence of the women's movement in the executive branch during the first Lula government (2002–2006),[15] the most advanced technical standards to date for legal abortion were issued by the Ministry of Health. Notable feminist victories included an end to the requirement for a formal complaint before the police in order to access abortion in cases of rape[16] and the stipulation that the national healthcare system provide legal abortion services. Efforts aimed at implementing legal abortion increased during this period. The intensified mobilization culminated in organized participation in the First National Conference on Policies for Women,[17] convened by the federal government, which produced a National Policy Plan for Women that included the commitment to "revise the legislation on voluntary termination of pregnancy."

The legislature was an important arena for mobilizing pro and against abortion in the 1990s and a privileged space to seek greater resonance for social movement frames. An analysis of the bills presented to the Brazilian congress shows that public health frames predominated after the promulgation of the 1988 Federal Constitution. The 1990s were marked by two important international conferences: the UN Conference on Population and Development held in Cairo in 1994 and the Fourth World Conference on Women in Beijing in 1995. The international interpretative framework strengthened national processes of mobilization and signaled abortion as a question of public health and as a human right. Only a minority of pro-abortion projects advanced gender frames such as autonomy ("abortion as a right of women to decide over their own body") and arguments critiquing patriarchal culture. After the year 2000, no pro-abortion bill advocated action based on the empowerment of women; the proposals from this period are justified entirely through the frame of public health. This framework signals the consequences of illegal abortion – high rates of mortality and injury of women – and emphasizes their unequal distribution according to race and class. One of the bills connected unsafe abortion practices to violence, constructing women as the victims of prohibition. The frame of public health allowed a pro-abortion position to be elaborated through a discourse of protection, as opposed to one emphasizing autonomy.

Although the Brazilian legislature has been a key space of dispute for movement and countermovement allies, changes in abortion regulation didn't occur through this path, with pro-abortion bills frequently eliciting anti-abortion bills and so on – yet it was progressively occupied by the countermovement.

The demand for a law on domestic violence was also strongly justified both by the National Policy Plan for Women and by the international sphere, given the need to bring Brazil's legal system in line with international conventions and agreements ratified by the state. Mobilization intensified and reached its peak with input from the Inter-American Human Rights System, which in the Maria da Penha case found the Brazilian State responsible for omission and negligence in the fight against domestic violence. In 2002, the campaign for the Maria da Penha Law was launched, with the formation of a consortium of NGOs working in the area of violence against women and human rights (Maciel 2011, 102; Alvarez 1998). Joint efforts by this group and the Federal Secretariat for Women's Policies resulted in a bill submitted to congress. After difficult negotiations and lobbying, this was approved in 2006 and led to the creation of Law 11.340/2006 – known as the "Maria da Penha Law" in reference to the origins of the campaign that resulted in its adoption. The law was considered an important victory for feminist mobilization. In the following years the law would face enforcement challenges. Although only a handful of judges and courts questioned its constitutionality, their opposition reached the public sphere. The Secretary for Women's Policy and the executive resorted to the supreme court as a strategy to strengthen the law's implementation.[18] On February 9, 2012, the supreme court confirmed the constitutionality of the Maria da Penha Law.

A similar attempt to link mobilization and the executive with the goal of changing the law was tried with regard to abortion. Based on the National Plan for Women, the federal government sought to advance the abortion agenda in the legislature and within a tripartite commission with representatives from the executive, civil society, and the legislature itself. A bill was sent to congress proposing the decriminalization of abortion up to the twelfth week of pregnancy (Rocha 2006, 373). After an offensive by religious groups, the project lost the support of the executive and was blocked in the legislature. The countermovement mobilized in both institutional and informal spheres with the specific goal of halting any advances on the issue of abortion. In 2006, the *Parliamentary Front in Defense of Life* and the *Brazil without Abortion Movement* were formed, which began lobbying for revision of the technical measures and proposed a series of conservative bills. In addition to working within state institutions, pro-life groups launched the *National Campaign for Life* and held marches throughout the country. They also exercised considerable influence over congressional and presidential elections. Lula, the incumbent candidate for president, faced strong condemnation for adopting pro-abortion measures during his first term. The ideological policing of parliamentary candidates was carried out via the campaign "For a Parliament in Defense of Life," with the slogan "Vote for Life: Vote for Candidates against Abortion."

Cornered for suspicion of involvement in corruption scandals, the second Lula government (2006–2010) backtracked on abortion rights.[19] The government was weakened and less popular, so the executive refrained from confrontations over unpopular causes such as abortion, given its need for support from conservative sectors in order to maintain its ability to govern. In the 2010 election campaign, with a female candidate running for the first time, abortion became a central theme. Dilma Rousseff was strongly censured when she supported the first draft of the Third National Human Rights Plan. The media coverage of the abortion agenda was intense and all major presidential candidates in the 2010 elections were questioned about their positions on abortion (Machado 2012, 30–2). In the face of strong public pressure, the then-candidate Rousseff was forced to recant and sign the "Open Letter to the People of God," pledging not to take measures in favor of legalizing abortion if she were to be elected, a promise she kept to during her two terms in office.

Between 2000 and 2010 the conservative movement increased their allies in parliament. The number of anti-abortion projects in this period exceeded the number of those advocating an expansion of abortion rights. There was also a significant change in the frameworks and types of bills proposed by conservatives. In addition to continuing to criminalize women who abort, conservative bills came to adopt a protective framework, championing rights for the fetus and advocating the provision of social assistance to women who do not resort to abortion, especially those who chose not to make use of the limited provisions for legal abortion. Most striking is the way in which the frame of protection of women, an important strategy of the feminist movement, came to be disputed and appropriated by the countermovement.

The principle feminist victory on sexual and reproductive rights in this decade was obtained in the supreme court in 2012.[20] After sustained civil society mobilization, which involved pro- and anti-abortion organizations speaking at a public hearing as *amici curiae*, the Brazilian Supreme Court recognized another cause for legal abortion – when the fetus is proved to be anencephalic. It was the first time since the twentieth century that a legal ruling expanded the grounds for legal abortion. The declaration of the constitutionality of the Maria da Penha Law by the supreme court occurred in the same year, but the issue of domestic violence was accorded much higher priority within the government's agenda. Following the enactment of the law, the federal government launched its campaign on the Maria da Penha Law under the slogan "the Law is Stronger" and promoted its implementation via the restructuring of public agencies, the installation of new services and campaigns to disseminate the law in the public sphere and among agents of law enforcement. The increased presence of religious and conservative congressmen did not hinder a further legislative victory for feminists in this field: the adoption of a law on femicide in 2015. As was the case with the Maria da Penha Law, the approval of a law on femicide was the product of intense discussion and negotiation involving NGOs and institutions, and international factors.[21] The bill was sponsored by the "female caucus" in congress and enjoyed support from various parties, including the more conservative sectors. The proposal mentions the importance of recognizing that women are killed *because* they are women, "exposing the fracture of gender inequality that persists in our society." However, during the vote on the floor, the original bill underwent a change of paramount importance: the term homicide "against women for reasons of gender" was replaced with the phrase "against women on the grounds of the condition of the female sex." This change was a request made by the then-president of the house of representatives – the same representative who announced that a vote to legalize abortion would only occur over his dead body. The episode illustrated both the opposition to gender issues in the parliament, but also the ways in which action on domestic violence was able to circumvent gender trouble. Conservatives are fine with the idea of protecting women, but they want to prevent the application of the law to groups other than women, such as transvestites and transgender people.

The preceding analysis reveals the circulation and intense flow of mobilization within informal and institutional spheres in the definition of gender policies, where institutional responses and public legitimacy are built simultaneously and feed each other. Either public mobilization is triggered in order to strengthen an institutional initiative, or institutional flows provide impetus to moral disputes within society. Legal framings – comprising both the language of law and moralizing conceptions – proved to be important not only in the instrumentalization of institutional strategies such as the introduction of a proposal or the filing of a legal action before the supreme court, but also activated public debate. The following section analyzes two important victories of the Brazilian feminist movement before the supreme court in order to trace more closely how negotiations over interpretations relate to the concrete achievements of the feminist social movement.

A Slippery Slope: From Protection of Women to Protection of the Family

Although the Maria da Penha Law expressly recognizes "gender-based" violence, acknowledging gender hierarchies and women's human rights, it makes two ambivalent movements. First, gender violence is confined to the domestic and family space. In the architecture of the Brazilian legal system, it is aligned with Article 226, 8, of the Federal Constitution, which requires the state to "ensure assistance to everyone in the family, creating mechanisms to suppress violence within its relations." Second, the policy mechanisms proposed, which provide for prevention, social assistance to women suffering domestic violence, and interim measures of protection and tougher penalties, have a primarily protective bias. The decision to opt for these frameworks – protection and family – was quite successful in breaking ground in the legal system and within the public policy agenda. Violence exercised against wives and companions mobilizes indignation. Calls for the "human dignity" of women (even recognized in the Catholic encyclical) and a "life without violence" are claims that are capable of penetrating the most conservative of contexts. The figure of the woman-victim (wife and mother) generates sympathy and can attract allies to the cause without generating opposition. At the same time, protection against aggression still allows for the framing of human rights arguments and the expansion of possibilities of accessing the justice system; this line of argument allowed the Maria da Penha case to be brought to the Inter-American System. It was also decisive in defending the law against charges of unconstitutionality. In the protective frame, however, women are constructed as similar to other vulnerable figures within the family, such as children and the elderly, who need to be protected (Debert and Gregori 2008, 170). In the debate around enforcement of the law, the framework of protection ended up colliding with autonomy. The circumscription of gender violence to the domestic sphere and the family paved the way for the law to come under a broader framework of family protection. Space does not permit analsyis of the counterproductive consequences of the use of these frameworks, but critics have highlighted the negative consequences for women when the justice system decides to act in the name of family protection. These range from women who cannot file complaints at police stations to those who find themselves pressured by public officials to forgive or be reconciled with their aggressor in order to preserve the family (Alvarez 2010; Macaulay 2006). The dilution of gender violence within the politics of family protection also entails the risk of avoiding discussion of the asymmetries of power between genders within the family environment (Debert and Gregori 2008). In addition, once framed within the family, other forms of gender violence end up being excluded from the protection system, such as racist violence, and violence against prostitutes and transvestites. The selection of legitimate victims demanding protection – the non-self-sufficient heterosexual woman; the dependent spouse with no agency – and the definition of accepted forms of violence (by which violence on the grounds of gender is minimized) creates what Santos has called "paradoxical citizenship" (Santos 1999).

Regarding the questioning of the Maria da Penha Law by the judiciary, the most frequent argument used against the constitutionality of the law was based on the equality principle, as the law is applied only in cases of domestic violence against *women*. Many decisions defended the law by criticizing views of formal equality and reaffirming the protection frame. The law has also been defended by some legal experts and judges as a law that protects the family rather than women on the basis of their gender condition per se. Affirmative action in favor of minorities entered the debate in many judicial rulings in different state courts, but the protection frame defined women as vulnerable individuals, similar to the elderly and children.[22] When the case arrived at the supreme court, these reasons were also used to sustain decisions in favor of the law. Judge Marco Aurélio de Mello, the case rapporteur, posited that differentiation based on the gender of the victim is not a disproportionate or illegitimate measure, as women are vulnerable when it comes to violence occurring within the family. He also compared the Maria da Penha Law to other normative acts passed in order to protect groups in need, such as the Statute of Children and Adolescents and the Statute of the Elderly. The framework of protection collided directly with autonomy when it addressed women's possibilities of deciding whether or not to continue with criminal proceedings against their aggressor. The majority of supreme court justices favored the pressing of charges regardless of the victim's preferences; their argument was based on the need for women's protection from pressure by their aggressor. Judge Marco Aurélio observed that in the vast majority of cases, victims tended to withdraw their complaints in order to try and guarantee their own safety. He stated that enabling victims to decide whether or when to initiate prosecution would mean disregarding fear, threats, psychologica,l and economic pressure, and historically and culturally determined power inequalities, further reducing the protection of the victim and perpetuating violence, discrimination and assaults on human dignity. Judge Peluso was the only dissenting opinion on this point, his ambivalent position appealed to the grounds of both autonomy and protection of the family. He explicitly refuted the argument of other justices about female victims' unwillingness to pursue prosection, emphasizing the importance of "the exercise of the substantial core of human dignity which is to be responsible for one's own destiny." According to Peluso, overruling the woman's unwillingness to press charges entails two risks: first, the possibility that women would be inhibited from seeking help, as they would not be able to influence the course of the criminal action or halt it; and second, the possibility that the offender is sentenced, leading to unpredictable consequences within the family in cases where peaceful coexistence between a woman and her partner has been reached. On the one hand, Justice Peluso underlined the importance of recognizing women's autonomy and the risks of defining them solely as victims. But on the other hand, he also affirmed the importance of protecting the family, reinforcing the reconciliation of the couple as a value the judiciary should protect. Peluso thus articulated an ambivalent discourse whereby woman's autonomy is recognized as a means of protecting the family. This reading of the goals of the law was not isolated nor new. Other supreme court judges defended the constitutionality of the Maria da Penha Law by referring to the protection of the family provided for in the Federal Constitution (Judges Luiz Fux and Lewandowski). In other instances, the protection of the family has proved to be an important moral frame used by judges to defend the constitutionality of the domestic violence legislation.[23]

Abortion: Competing Uses of Protection and Family Frames

We have to consider that this control [of women over their bodies] can create very serious problems in the family structure and marriage, if there is conception and the husband wants this [...] I think that a woman who is happy and a woman who has a stable marriage, a woman who has the love of her husband and who loves her children after they've grown [...] a woman of such conditions, she will never belong [...] to these positions favorable to abortion, positions that are conducive to divorce, positions that favor the breakdown of family and marriage.

Congressman João de Deus of the Workers' Party[24]

This comment was made by a congressman during the National Constituent Assembly, in opposition to feminists' proposals to revise the criminalization of abortion. In his speech, he argued that the right to abortion and women's control over their own bodies would signify a breakdown of the family. The pro-life and pro-family framework has always been associated with countermovement discourses. For the anti-abortion movement, the agenda of abortion defies the reproductive-normative model, the sacredness of motherhood and the traditional family system in which women lack decision-making autonomy over their own destiny. The first anti-abortion documents released by the National Confederation of the Bishops of Brazil (Conferencia Nacional dos Obispos do Brasil – CNBB) – "The Exhortation of the Apostolic Family Consortium" (1981) and the "Charter of Family Rights" (1983) emphasized the dangers of homosexual relationships and abortion to Christian moral and family values. One of the stated goals of the first national meeting of the anti-abortion movement in 1994 was to align anti-abortion actions, and monitor feminist mobilization in congress and the bills in progress "that defied family values and life according to Catholic dictates." In the 2006 elections, the theme of the defense of life and family was intensively deployed in the public sphere. The Catholic Church launched the document: "Declaration on Ethical Requirements in Defense of Life," which aimed to "mobilize families and communities to encourage city councilmen, congressmen, and senators from their electoral base to uphold and promote life and the family." In the same year, the National Association of Women for Life of Rio de Janeiro launched the "Manifesto in Defense of Life" that speaks of "the vocation [of women] of motherhood" and woman's "sublime mission to transmit and preserve life." Although the most radical and countercultural arguments of sexual liberalization and freedom of choice and the body have been residual in the Brazilian feminist movement, which preferred instead to use a framework of public health, the anti-abortion discourse emphasized abortion as something inherently detrimental to the family.

It is difficult to measure the importance and impact of opposition to abortion based on the family frame. But it is notable that one of the only and most significant pro-abortion victories – the anencephalic fetus case in the supreme court – emerged within this framework and managed to assume ownership of the issue on this point. The legal strategy pursued by feminists was to differentiate the case of the anencephalic fetus from abortion in general, therefore circumnavigating the moral and legal difficulties and obstacles posed by the general debate on abortion.[25] The termination of pregnancy involving a viable fetus would involve weighing up the pros and cons allegedly at play: on the one hand, the unborn child's potential for life and on the other, the freedom and individual autonomy of the pregnant woman. Yet in the case of an anencephalic fetus, it was argued, this conflict was absent as there was no fetal life to protect. Neither was this a case of women who do not choose motherhood, but rather women who want to be mothers, but cannot, due to unviability of the fetus. During the public hearing, feminist organizations sought to bring stories to the court (presented either in person, or through reports or films) of women who requested permission to terminate such pregnancies. These always involved women who wanted to be mothers, most within a marital relationship. In the case of anencephaly, a child desired and "loved even before being created" was depicted as fatally affected by an irreversible diagnosis. A married couple that had experienced an anencephalic pregnancy and was able to terminate the pregnancy appeared at the public hearing with their two daughters – symbolizing that the termination of a pregnancy in the past did not go against the family. One key feminist activist at the public hearing that took place on August 28, 2008, stated that women who have abortions are not "future mothers, but women who do not desire a pregnancy at a certain point in their lives," arguing that, by contrast, women who terminated an anencephalic fetus had an identity as a mother and a desire for motherhood.[26] Moving away from abortion in general was a key strategy ensuring success of the demand. In their decisions, the judges voting for approval made it clear that they were not ruling for abortion in general, nor could their decisions be used as precedent for abortion. Indeed the sanctity of motherhood was recalled and defended by the judges who voted in favor of the procedure: for example, Judge Carlos Britto stated, "pregnancy is a process aimed at the spectacle of the world, the spectacle of life," and "the most sublime and strongest content of all love [is] maternal love," while Judge Carmen Lucia argued that "the mother's dignity goes beyond herself, beyond her body." We do not analyze all the reasons for the decisions here, but note that among the judges who decided in favor of "anticipated delivery" (termination) in the case of anencephalic fetuses, there was no incompatibility between this position and the defense of family, repro-normativity and the sacredness of motherhood. The framework of autonomy, little explored by pro-choice activists during the public hearing, was referred to by some of the judges, yet they did not recognize choice in all circumstances, but only when autonomy was balanced against the non-viable life: "the right of a woman to self-determination is at stake, to choose, to act according to her will in a case of absolute impossibility of extrauterine life."[27]

Organizations defending the measure emphasized the suffering of women and employed a bridging-framing with torture, arguing that being obliged to carry an anencephalic pregnancy to term and then bury the child after birth constituted a form of torture. Women's suffering was recognized in several of the votes in favor of approval and was treated in most cases under the framework of dignity. However, some judges who recognized suffering as a reason to authorize the procedure pointed out that not only women suffered, but also the father and the family. The compulsory maintenance of pregnancy, according to Judge Marco Aurélio, "results in imposing on a woman, on her respective family, damage to their moral and psychological integrity" (ADPF 54). Judge Carmen Lucia said that:

> we must remember that the father also suffers terribly; the family can suffer and can unravel – and this is not unusual; the father's rights must also be taken into account in this discussion; [...] When we talk about dignity, we are speaking about the dignity of all concerned: the fetus, the woman, the father, the siblings.
>
> *(ADPF 54, 175 Justice Carmen Lucia's vote)*

The use of the image of the female victim of suffering and torture not only had more appeal than the woman who exercises her desires in relation to her own body, but also benefited from advances achieved in recent years within the master frame of violence, particularly in terms of campaigns focused on domestic violence and the approval and implementation of the Maria da Penha Law. The gains, as well as the dangers of this approach, are evident.

The anencephalic pregnancy case demonstrates how movement and countermovement can compete for the same frame. The family frame, which always formed the cornerstone of the anti-abortion movement position, was used by the pro-abortion movement in order to neutralize opposition to the measure. The protection frame was also employed to address the protection of women, but as we have shown, this can quickly be appropriated as a means to justify protection of the family.

Conclusions: Framings, Strategic Negotiations, and Ambivalences

The dual constitution of the Brazilian (and Latin American) feminist movement, containing *feminine* and *feminist* demands and activists, reveals different dynamics between social movement demands and institutional arenas. Although both violence and abortion were important issues for the movement, they show markedly different outcomes in terms of institutional victories. When it comes to garnering allies, not generating opposition, and securing greater acceptance within both the public sphere and formal institutions, the less controversial issues in relation to traditional gender arrangements tend to be the more successful. This chapter has offered a brief comparison of the fields of violence and abortion in Brazil, based on analysis of events and observation of the political, cultural, and moral environment, which facilitated or hindered change. The movement to secure legislation on domestic violence was favored by a number of elements, including: the role of the executive in policy formation, its openness to social movement actors and discourses, the lack of opposition forces, and greater receptivity to the issue in the public sphere. By contrast, the abortion movement's stagnation and risks of setbacks for women occurred within a context that included the loss of institutional allies, colonization of parliament by opposition groups, and the organization of a strong countermovement mobilizing society on moral grounds. We have argued here that the ability of both issues to permeate institutional contexts is affected by their discursive frames and the socio-moral contexts within which they are mobilized. Opportunities either narrow or widen according to processes of frame negotiation with traditional values and concepts regarding gender and family. In the two cases analyzed, political confrontation involved a strategic game in the utilization of frames by institutional actors, movement, and countermovement. While defense of traditional conceptions of the family and women's roles was central to the anti-abortion movement, the feminist movement shifted toward more negotiated frames, thereby avoiding direct confrontation. Gender violence acquired a more palatable framework, such as domestic, marital, or family violence, reinforcing a protection frame as opposed to one of autonomy. In all cases the protection of women was quite important to justify public policy, including within the legal sphere. The passing of the femicide law – which excluded gender from its wording – reveals a striking aspect of the contention over feminist agendas in Brazil: namely that the gender framework itself can present an obstacle to the institutionalization of certain feminist demands.

As for the abortion field, the initial discourse of female autonomy among feminists of the 1970s segued into a language of reproductive rights and public health by the 1990s, influenced by the international conferences of Cairo and Beijing. The high female mortality rates due to unsafe abortions strengthened the argument based on public health. Protection frames that emphasize the victimhood of women were also considered: women as victims of sexual violence; women suffering from carrying an anencephalic fetus to term; or women as victims of unsafe abortion practices. Abortion has advanced only through stealth occupation of institutional spaces, far removed from public visibility. The technical measure regulating legal abortion emerged from the umbrella of procedures to be adopted in cases of sexual violence. Camouflaging it as "pregnancy prophylaxis" or "therapeutic anticipation of delivery" was a resource for making headway within institutional spheres. Even then it was difficult to overcome the confrontation posed by the countermovement's emphasis of the role of woman as mother and protection of family. The feminist movement's most important victory in the supreme court was reached only through a process of argumentative negotiation. In both cases analyzed, the supreme court decisions favorable to women affirmed the frameworks of protection and family.

Legal frames are not only used to instrumentalize institutional actions; they also travel between formal and informal public spheres. In observing legal mobilization, it is important to observe not only institutions but also the flow and displacements that occur, whether in disputes over institutional strategies or within the public sphere. The language of the law is used in campaigns and speeches within the public sphere and moral discourses are articulated within formal institutional spheres. By allowing for observation of the connection between systemic aspects of law and moral, religious, cultural, and scientific arguments, the category of framing provides a privileged perspective to observe these dynamics. Within this flow of mobile frames, symbolic and institutional disputes are mutually reinforced. For example, in the case of domestic violence, the victory in the Inter-American Court that fueled the mobilization of NGOs at national level was used to strengthen the campaign for the law, a demand that had existed for quite some time. The victory of the law's adoption, in turn, served as symbolic capital for dissemination – "the law is stronger" was the motto of one of the principle campaigns aimed at raising awareness and strengthening criminal prosecutions of domestic violence. In addition, the supreme court was used for the purposes of symbolically strengthening the law.

On the other hand, frames also embody the relationship between institutional responses, movement, and countermovement. The presence of the opponent on the battlefield unleashes a proactive process of contrary arguments and modulation of frameworks in order to avoid or reduce confrontation. In the case of abortion, the moral conflict triggered by conservatives in the public sphere can explain the setbacks abortion suffered institutionally, as well as the strategy of feminists to use less radical frameworks and invest in occupying less visible spaces. There is an additional dimension of the use of frames in disputes within formal institutions – particularly courts – as a stage for projecting the confrontation into other spheres (Kirchheimer 1961; Barkan 2007). In this sense, going beyond the outcome of the court case itself, the function of any dispute is to expand the scope of confrontation and the frameworks mobilized therein. Frameworks that are more advantageous for winning a case may not in fact be those that most impact the dominant moral discourse. The discursive strategies of movements within state institutions are the result of a permanent tension between two dimensions in any dispute; negotiating frameworks to advance the achievement of rights and those deployed to amplify confrontational frameworks.

In response to the strong countermovement presence in the case of abortion, the strategy of the Brazilian feminist movement focused on institutional mobilization signified the use of more negotiated frameworks. It was only when the movement left the institutions and went to the streets and the Internet that the agenda became more radicalized. Recent trends signal a radicalization of politics in the fields of both violence and abortion. In terms of violence, semantic accommodation through family and domesticity are being questioned and the regulatory frame is increasingly being used to take on other forms of gender violence. The increased attention to sexual violence and violence against the LGBTI (lesbian, gay, bisexual, transgender, and intersex) community has broadened the scope of the debate and highlighted conflicts that extend beyond the family environment. In terms of abortion, to the extent that institutionalized forms of activism are perceived as unpromising, the movement has become more radical both in repertoire and framing. Young feminism, less institutionalized and more willing to explore issues of sexuality and the body, has advanced and returned to the streets in 2015, in what came to be known as the "feminist spring."[28] Under the banners of "Cunha Out" (opposing conservative Evangelical Congressman Eduardo Cunha) and "My Body, My Rules," the fight for abortion rights and against conservative setbacks took on a more disruptive form. The politicization of gender in the future of the Brazilian women's movement seems inevitable.

Notes

1 The Catholic Church played an important role in the formation of these popular movements in many Latin American countries, including Brazil, especially through the ecclesiastical base communities, guided by liberation theology (Sader 1988).

2 In this chapter we use *women's movement* and *feminist movement* interchangeably. We understand this as a politically and socially heterogeneous field of mobilization that encompasses both forms of politicization: women's mobilization to improve their living conditions (frequently accepting a traditional division of gender roles and not necessarily identifying themselves as feminists) and mobilizations based on questioning gender roles. Sonia Alvarez names these as *feminine* and *feminist* mobilization. The first has *practical* demands and "grows out of and accepts prevailing feminine roles and asserts rights on the basis of those roles." The second entails *strategic* goals, such as women's emancipation or gender equality (Alvarez 1990, 24–5). Molyneux (1986) also refers to the combination of practical and strategic demands as a feature of Latin American women's mobilization.

3 The case of Maria da Penha Maia Fernandes, presented by the Center for Justice and International Law (CEJIL) and the Latin American and Caribbean Committee for the Defense of Women (CLADEM) to the Inter-American Commission on Human Rights in 1998 (marking the first time the Convention of Belém do Pará was applied), and the *Campo Algodonero* case on femicide in Mexico, presented in 2002, are successful examples of organized feminist actions within the Inter-American System for the Protection of Human Rights.

4 We refer here to the idea of *field* inspired by Flingstein and MacAdam (2011), who define strategic action fields as a constructed mesolevel social order in which individual and/or collective actors are attuned to and interact with one another on the basis of shared (which is not to say consensual) understandings about the purposes of the field, relationships to others in the field (including who has power and why), and the rules governing legitimate action. In this chapter we understand the *women's mobilization field* as concerning womens life conditions or gender equality issues. Gender violence and abortion rights constitute subfields within this broader field.

5 The narrative on the mobilization of the Maria da Penha Law is partially rooted in the research project *The Law Seen From the Inside (and From the Outside): Disputing the Interpretation of Maria da Penha Law in the Brazilian Courts*, funded by CNPq (the Brazilian National Council for Scientific and Technological Development) and coordinated by Marta Machado and José Rodrigo Rodriguez. On abortion lawfare we present here a brief and partial narrative of the data generated by the research project *Abortion Rights Lawfare in Latin America*, coordinated by Rachel Sieder (Chr. Michelsen Institute, Norway).

6 Some 16 countries in Latin America have approved specific laws to prohibit violence against women, some addressing "domestic" and "intrafamily" violence (Brazil, Bolivia, El Salvador, Colombia, Panama, Chile, Paraguay, Honduras, Puerto Rico, and Uruguay) or specifically addressing "violence against women" (Argentina, Peru, Costa Rica, Guatemala, Mexico, and Venezuela). See "Respostas à violência baseada em gênero no Cone Sul: avanços, desafios e experiências regionais," Regional Report from United Nations Office for Drugs and Crime, June of 2011, available at: www.unodc.org/documents/lpo-brazil/Topics_crime/Publicacoes/Respostas_Violencia_Genero_Cone_Sul_Port.pdf. Accessed September 24, 2017. By March 2015, 16 Latin American countries had criminalized femicide (Argentina, Bolivia, Brazil, Chile, Colombia, Costa Rica, El Salvador, Ecuador, Guatemala, Honduras, Mexico, Nicaragua, Panama, Peru, Dominican Republic, and Venezuela).

7 In Latin America, countries are divided between those that allow abortion in cases of sexual violence and risks to women's health (Colombia, Peru, Ecuador, Bolivia, and Argentina), and those that absolutely prohibit abortion (Chile, Nicaragua, and El Salvador). In Uruguay and French Guiana, abortion is not a crime (Jurkewicz 2011). Mexico's abortion legislation varies across the states of the federation; it is decriminalized in the first trimester of pregnancy in the Federal District but still a crime in most states of the federation, with different regimes of exception in place (Ruibal 2014).

8 IBOPE, Católicas pelo Direito de Decidir. Pesquisa IBOPE JOB2105. 2010. [Internet]. Available at: http://catolicas.org.br/wp-content/uploads/2011/01/publicacao-Ibope-Catolicas-Aborto-2011. compressed.pdf. Accessed September 24, 2017; C. Dides et al., *Estudio de opinión pública* sobre aborto y derechos sexuales y reproductivos en Brasil, Chile, México y Nicaragua (Santiago: FLACSO, 2011); and A. Faundes et al. "Brazilians have different views on when abortion should be legal, but most do not agree with imprisoning women for abortion." *Reproductive Health Matters* 21/42, November 2013, pp. 165–73.

9 For example, Colombia expanded the legal grounds for abortion through the C-325 Constitutional Court ruling in 2005, which deemed abortion legal when the pregnancy posed a risk to the mother's life or was a result of rape. A feminist victory also happened in Brazil, in 2012, when the supreme court authorized interruption of pregnancy in case of anencephalic fetus.

10 Research on women's police stations points to precarious facilities and lack of employee training (Debert and Gregori 2002; Santos 1999).

11 Convention on the Elimination of All Forms of Discrimination Against Women (CEDAW), 1979, and the Inter-American Convention on the Prevention, Punishment and Eradication of Violence against Women (Convention of Belem do Para), 1994.

12 For example Law 10.778/2003 (compulsory notification of health authorities, charged with caring for women victims of violence in public and private services) and Law 10.886/2004 (which created the crime of domestic violence as part of the penal code).

13 Article 128 in the Brazilian Penal Code.

14 Published in 1998, the *Technical Measure for the Prevention and Treatment of Injuries Resulting from Sexual Violence against Women and Adolescents* was of the outcome of feminist dialog within the Ministry of Health.

15 In addition to the creation of the Special Secretariat for Women's Policy, Lula named a militant feminist to lead the area of Women's Health at the Ministry of Health.

16 This was the result of the *Technical Measure for Prevention and Treatment of Injuries Resulting from Sexual Violence against Women and Adolescents*, available at: http://bvsms.saude.gov.br/bvs/publicacoes/ prevencao_agravo_violencia_sexual_mulheres_3ed.pdf. Accessed June 25, 2016.

17 National conferences about public policies were held during the first Lula administration as a means of increasing civil society participation in public policy formulation (Faria et al. 2012).

18 In 2007, the Office of the Presidency proposed the Direct Action of Constitutionality (known as an ADC) number 19 to request confirmation of the constitutionality of the most controversial articles of the law: Article 1 (restricting the application of the law to women would be an affront to the principle of equality); Article 33 (creation of Domestic Violence Courts, that would hinder jurisdiction conferred to the states to determine local judicial organization); and Article 41 (excluding the application of Law 9.099/95 to crimes involving domestic and family violence against women). In 2010, another case involving the law arrived at the supreme court, the Direct Action of Constitutionality (known as an ADI) number 4.424, proposed by the Attorney General, which questioned the need for women's authorization in order to prosecute for bodily injury.

19 The "Mensalão" scandal marked the start of the crisis of Lula government (Cesarino 2006, 44–5).

20 Supreme court, action for noncompliance with fundamental concept (ADPF 54). Available at: http:// redir.stf.jus.br/paginadorpub/paginador.jsp?docTP=TP&docID=3707334. Accessed September 24, 2017.

21 The bill was the result of work by the Joint Parliamentary Inquiry Commission (CPMI) on domestic violence against women, composed of federal congressmen and senators who traveled to 18 states, conducting public meetings and hearings and gathering documents and testimonies. The CPMI's final report diagnosed an "upswing of femicide in the country, continued high levels of violence against women and tolerance by the state" (CPMI 2013, 8) and proposed changes in legislation to better fight violence against women. The bill's explanatory memo cited international instruments such as the United Nation's protocol for investigations of murder and commission on the status of women, the condemnation of Mexico for the Campo Algodonero case and legislative changes in Latin America aimed at the adoption of femicide as a crime.

22 In 2009, the State Appellate Court in Rio Grande do Sul ruled that the state would have the power to "establish laws to protect groups of vulnerable individuals" (Criminal Appeal 70030827380, Judge rapporteur Elba Aparecida Nicolli Bastos). In another case that year before the same court, judges cited the protection of the elderly and of children and adolescents as constitutional examples of the "legislating power of the state to create laws establishing special treatment for minority groups of citizens" (Habeas Corpus 70031748676, Judge rapporteur Elba Aparecida Nicolli Bastos).

23 Several decisions issued by state courts defend the law as a mechanism for protecting the family – "the value of the law is protecting the family and of each individual within the family, a provision also contained in the Constitution" (Brazil, Mato Grosso do Sul State Appellate Court 2009. Criminal Appeal 2009.025378–7, Judge Dorival Moreira dos Santos). In protecting women, the state would address their "gender condition" and also assist the family by creating mechanisms to prevent violence in its relationships, as provided for in the constitution; the law should be defended as "the practice of domestic violence entails, as a rule, damaging consequences throughout the family institution" (Criminal Appeal 2009.025378–7, 2009d).

24 Congressman João de Deus of the Workers' Party before the "Commission on family, education, culture and sports, science and technology and communication – Subcommittee on the family, the minor and the elderly" during the Constitutional Commitee's debate in 1988's, page 207 of the Minute of the Constituent Assembly. Available at: www.senado.leg.br/publicacoes/anais/constituinte/sistema.pdf. Accessed May 5, 2017.

25 According to Débora Diniz, representative of ANIS – Institute for Bioethics, Human Rights and Gender, the main proponents of this strategy, the concept of therapeutic anticipation of delivery would provide a "legal, ethical, medical and moral shift" to the terms of the debate on abortion.

26 Intervention made by Debora Diniz, representative of ANIS – Institute for Bioethics, Human Rights and Gender at the public hearing at the supreme court. Available at: www.stf.jus.br/arquivo/cms/processoAudienciaPublicaAdpf54/anexo/ADPF54__notas_dia_28808.pdf. Accessed May 5, 2017.

27 Supreme court decision referenced at footnote 28, p. 67.

28 The so-called "feminist spring" was a peak of feminist mobilization in 2015, which started with campaigns on social networks and then took to the streets. The campaign #primeiroassédio where women recounted the first time they were harassed, has been reproduced more than 100,000 times on Twitter. In the #meuamigosecreto campaign, women denounced everyday situations of machismo on social networks. The hashtag was mentioned 170,000 times on Twitter. On November 2015, the Black Women's March took place, and there were several protests against the Statute of the Unborn and specifically against congressman Eduardo Cunha (a former senator and evangelical who promotes projects supported by the evangelical caucus in congress). See http://thinkolga.com/2015/12/18/uma-primavera-sem-fim/. Accessed June 25, 2016.

References

ADPF 54 (Supreme Court, Action for Noncompliance with Fundamental Concept). Justice Marco Aurélio's Preliminary Decision, dated July 1, 2004, p. 86. Available at: http://redir.stf.jus.br/paginadorpub/paginador.jsp?docTP=TP&docID=3707334. Consulted April 1, 2019.

Alexy, Robert. 1989. *A Theory of Legal Argumentation*. Oxford: Clarendon Press.

Alvarez, Marcos C., Alessandra Teixeira, Maria Gorete Marques de Jesus, Fernanda E. Matsuda, Caio Santiago, and Veridiana Domingos Cordeiro. 2010. *O Papel da Vítima no Processo Penal*. Brasilia: Ministério da Justiça, Série Pensando o Direito, 24.

Alvarez, Sonia E. 1990. *Engendering Democracy in Brazil: Women's Movements in Transition Politics*. Princeton: Princeton University Press.

Alvarez, Sonia E. 1998. "Latin American feminisms 'go global': trends of the 1990s and challenges for the new millennium." In *Cultures of Politics, Politics of Cultures: Re-visioning Latin American Social Movements*, edited by Sonia E. Alvarez, Evelyn Dagnino and Arturo Escobar, 293–324. Boulder: Westview Press.

Alvarez, Sonia E., Evelyn Dagnino, and Arturo Escobar. 1998. "Introduction: the cultural and the political in Latin American social movements." In *Cultures of Politics, Politics of Cultures: Re-visioning Latin American Social Movements*, edited by Sonia E. Alvarez, Evelyn Dagnino and Arturo Escobar. Boulder: Westview Press.

Barkan, Steven E. 2007. Criminal Persecution and the Legal Control of Protest. *Mobilization International Journal*, 11(1): 181–95.

Barsted, Leila Linhares. 1992. Legalização e Descriminalização do Aborto no Brasil: 10 anos de Luta Feminista. *Revista Estudos Feministas*, Florianópolis, 0: 104–30.

Cesarino, Leticia Maria C. N. 2006. *Acendendo as Luzes da Ciência para Iluminar o Caminho do Progresso: Ensaio de Antropologia Simétrica da Lei de Biossegurança Brasileira*. Dissertação de mestrado em Antropologia, Universidade de Brasília.

Debert, Guita Grin and Maria Filomena Gregori. 2008. Violência e Gênero: Novas Propostas, Velhos Dilemas. *Revista Brasileira de Ciências Sociais*, 23(66): 165–85.

Debert, Guita Grin and Maria Filomena Gregori. 2002. "As delegacias especiais de polícia e o projeto gênero e cidadania." In *Gênero e Cidadania*, edited by Mariza Corrêa. Campinas: Núcleo de Estudos de Gênero-Pagu/Unicamp.

Dworkin, Ronald. 1988. *Law's Empire*, Cambridge, MA: Harvard University Press.

Günther, Klaus. 1993. *The Sense of Appropriateness: Application Discourse in Morality and Law*. New York: State University of New York.

Faria, Claudia Feres, Viviane Petinelli Silva and Isabella Lourenço Lins. 2012. Conferências de Políticas Públicas: Um Sistema Integrado de Participação e Deliberação? *Revista Brasileira de Ciência Política*, 7: 249–84. Available at: https://dx.doi.org/10.1590/S0103-33522012000100011. Accessed May 5, 2017.

Flingstein, Neil and Douglas McAdam. 2011. Toward a General Theory of Strategic Action Fields. *Sociological Theory*, 29(1): 1–26.

García Pereanez, José Antonio. 2010. Consideraciones Sobre la Despenalización del Aborto en Colombia. *Iatreia*, 23(3): 294–301. Available at: www.scielo.org.co/scielo.php?script=sci_arttext&pid=S0121-07932010000300012&lng=en&tlng=. Accessed May 5, 2017.

Jelin, Elizabeth. 1987. "Introduction." In: *Ciudadania e Identidad: Las Mujeres en los Movimientos Sociales Latino-Americanos*, edited by Elizabeth Jelin. Geneva: United Nations Research Institute for Social Development.

Jurkewicz, Regina Soares. 2011. *Quem Controla as Mulheres? Direitos Reprodutivos e Fundamentalismos Religiosos na América Latina*. São Paulo: Católicas pelo Direito de Decidir.

Kirchheimer, Otto. 1961. *Political Justice. The Use of Legal Procedure for Political Ends*. Princeton: Princeton University Press.

Macaulay, Fiona. 2006. Judicialising and (de)Criminalising Domestic Violence in Latin America. *Social Policy and Society*, 5(1): 103–14.

Machado, Maria das Dores Campos. 2012. Aborto e Ativismo Religioso nas Eleições de 2010. *Revista Brasileira de Ciência Política*, 7: 25–54.

Maciel, Débora Alves. 2011. Ação Coletiva, Mobilização do Direito e Instituições Políticas: O Caso da Campanha da Lei Maria da Penha. *Revista Brasileira de Ciências Sociais*, 26(77): 97–111.

McCarthy, John D. and Mayer N. Zald. 1977. Resource Mobiliation and Social Movements: A Partial Theory. *American Journal of Sociology* 82(6): 1212–41.

Meyer, David S. and Suzanne Staggenborg. 1996 Movements, Countermovements, and the Structure of Political Opportunity. *American Journal of Sociology*, 101(6): 1628–60.

Mendes, Conrado Hübner. 2011. Neither Dialogue nor Last Word. *Legisprudence*, 5: 1–40.

Moraes, Aparecida F. and Bila Sorj (Eds.). 2009. *Gênero, Violência e Direitos na Sociedade Brasileira*. Rio de Janeiro: 7 Letras.

Molyneux, Maxine. 1986. "Mobilization without emancipation? Women's interests, state, and revolution." In *Transition and Development: Problems of Third World Socialism*, Edited by Richard R. Fagen, Carmen Diana Deere and José Luis Coraggio. Berkeley: Center for the Study of the Americas.

Pedriana, Nicholas. 2006. From Protective to Equal Treatment: Legal Framing Processes and Transformation of the Women's Movement in the 1960s. *American Journal of Sociology*, 111(6): 1718–61.

Ruibal, Alba. 2014. *Reform and Backlash in México Abortion's Law: Political and Legal Opportunities for Mobilization and Counter-Mobilization*. Paper presentred to the Annual Meeting of the American Political Science Association, Washington, DC: 28–31 de agosto.

Rocha, Maria Isabel Baltar da. 2006. A Discussão Política Sobre Aborto no Brasil: Uma Síntese. *Revista Brasileira de Estudos de População*, 23(2): 369–74.

Sader, Eder 1988. *Quando Novos Personagens Entraram em Cena. Experiências, Falas e Lutas de Trabalhadores da Grande São Paulo (1970–1980)*. Rio de Janeiro: Paz e Terra.

Safa, Helen Icken. 1990. Women's Social Movements in Latin America. *Gender and Society*, 4(3), Special Issue Women and Development in the Third World: 354–69.

Santos, Cecília MacDowell. 1999. "Cidadania de gênero contraditória: queixas, crimes e direitos na delegacia da mulher em São Paulo." In: *O cinquentenário da Declaração Universal dos Direitos do Homem*, 315–52. Edited by Amaral Junior and Cláudia Perrone-Moisés. São Paulo: Edusp.

Santos, Cecília MacDowell. 2005. *Women's Police Stations: Gender, Violence and Justice in São Paulo, Brazil*. New York: Palgrave Macmillan.

Santos, Cecília MacDowell. 2007. Ativismo Jurídico Transnacional e O Estado: Reflexões Cobre casos Apresentados Contra O Brasil na Comissão Interamericana de Direitos Humanos. *Sur-Revista Internacional de Direitos Humanos*, 7: 27–57.

Snow, David A., E. Burke Rochford Jr., Steven K. Worden, and Robert D. Benford. 1986. Frame Align-
ment Processes, Micromobilization, and Movement Participation. *American Sociological Review*, 51(4):
464–81.

Snow, David A., Robert Benford, Holly McCammon, Lyndi Hewitt, and Scott Fitzgerald. 2014. The
Emergence, Development, and Future of the Framing Perspective: 25+ Years Since 'Frame Align-
ment.' *Mobilization*, 19(1): 23–46.

Tarrow, Sidney. 1988. *Power in Movement: Social Movements, Collective Action and Politics*. Nova York: Cambridge University Press.

Vanhala, L. 2009. Anti-discrimination Policy Actors and their use of Litigation Strategies: The Influence
of Identity Politics. *Journal of European Public Policy*, 16: 738–54.

24

TRANSITIONAL JUSTICE AND THE POLITICS OF PROSECUTING GROSS HUMAN RIGHTS VIOLATIONS IN LATIN AMERICA

Elena Martínez Barahona and Martha Gutiérrez

Introduction

Societies in transition face the challenge of addressing past violations of human rights. Enormously different measures have been adopted, including mechanisms aimed at finding out the truth about what happened, establishing some measure of justice, or trying in some way to repair the damage caused. Some societies have preferred to do nothing in this regard and instead to institutionalize policies of forgetting through amnesties. All these mechanisms (truth-seeking, justice, reparations, and amnesty) are termed *transitional justice*.[1] This concept emerged in the 1990s to refer to political and legal responses to the crimes of repressive regimes (Teitel 2003), and is centered primarily on the complex notions of "transition" and "justice."

Latin America is the region in the world that has made most progress in dealing with violations committed during military rule or internal armed conflict through transitional justice mechanisms. Transitional justice studies is a field where academic research, practice, and politics are intertwined. Indeed, many of the earliest studies were written by practitioners. Briefly, this chapter aims to map the state-of-the-art of transitional justice studies in Latin America, distinguishing between countries and transition type. We describe the development and evolution of the field in the region, considering how it is linked to specific measures and advances in different countries. Finally, we signal some emerging questions that derive from our review.

Transition Types and Justice Mechanisms

The literature on transitional justice mechanisms in different Latin American countries has tended to reflect the distinct nature of those mechanisms, as well as their timing (see Table 24.1). The variation in transitional justice mechanisms is linked in turn to the diverse ways in which the transitions occurred across the region. And the diversity and richness of these lived experiences has directly influenced the ways in which analysts have approached the field. Table 24.1 signals the different transitions and transitional justice measures applied across Latin America. Although most countries have shifted from authoritarian to elected democratic government (Argentina, Uruguay, Brazil, Chile, Paraguay, Bolivia, Haiti, Honduras, Panama, and Venezuela), facilitating diverse transitional justice measures, others had to confront an internal armed conflict, with the challenges this poses not only for peace but also for transitional justice (Guatemala and El Salvador).[2] In other cases the moment of the transition is not so evident, with violations of human rights occurring during civilian authoritarian governments when political repression was used as important mechanism of social control, especially against the left, workers unions, and other dissident groups, for example, Peru during the Fujimori regime (1990–2000), the 12 years of the Balaguer government in the Dominican Republic (1966–1978), Ecuador, mainly under the government of Febres Cordero (1979–1988), Mexico (1969–1990), or Colombia.

One classification refers to the *type* of transitional justice mechanism adopted, and here two groups can be identified:

a   Those countries in which several transitional justice measures have been adopted (even if the results and effectiveness of such measures have differed between them). This group includes Argentina, Uruguay, Chile, El Salvador, Guatemala, Bolivia, Haiti, Honduras, and Peru. In almost all cases truth commissions, trials, and reparations have been implemented, with the most significant justice achievements registered in Argentina and Chile and uneven results across the other countries. This variation is reflected in the larger number of studies existing on Argentina and Chile

b   Those countries where the truth commission has been the main transitional justice mechanism adopted (although in some cases there have also been some isolated trials and reparations). This group includes Brazil, Panama, and Paraguay.

In the literature, this diversity is reflected in works that focus on one kind of mechanism (truth commissions, trials, or reparations) and others that observe the interaction between the different aspects. Regarding truth commissions, Hayner's classic work (2001) in its second edition (2011) includes the truth commissions of Guatemala, Peru, Bolivia, Argentina, Chile, El Salvador, Haiti, Paraguay, Uruguay, Panama, and Ecuador and aims to evaluate their impact in terms of their self-proclaimed goals, which included the establishment of truth about past human rights violations, assistance to victims, the pursuit of justice, and support for institutional reforms. Popkin and Roht-Arriaza (1995) examined the achievements and limitations of Chile and El Salvador's truth commissions, and Popkin and Bhuta (1999) offered a comparative analysis of the targeted efforts to face the abuses of the past through truth commissions in Argentina, El Salvador, Chile, Honduras, Guatemala, and South Africa.

Regarding *trials*, Collins, Balardini, and Burt (2013) map trials on human rights violations related to oppressive regimes in Argentina, Chile, and Peru. They gathered and standardized information, while also suggesting a theoretical frame to analyze strategic decision-making for the judicialization of the cases, examining the results of collaboration between different civil society and state actors in terms of judicial outcomes. Martínez, Gutiérrez, and Rincón (2012) compare truth, justice, and reparation measures in Guatemala and El Salvador, including a map of the few trials that have taken place. Ansolabehere (2014) analyzes the role of institutions in transitional, post-transitional and post-conflict justice, referencing a range of studies that focus on domestic judicial accountability over time: Argentina (Smulovitz 2013); Chile (Collins 2009; Huneeus 2010); Guatemala (Gutiérrez 2015b); Uruguay (Skaar 2011); and Peru (Laplante 2009; Burt 2012).

With regard to *amnesties*, the book edited by Payne, Abrão and Torelly (2011) offers a comprehensive analysis, and includes the work of authors such as Sikkink and Engstrom, who focus on amnesty and international law, as well as comparative works by Mallinder, Olsen, Payne, and Reiter, and specific chapters on Uruguay and Brazil. Concerning *reparations*, Correa (2011) analyzes the programs implemented in Argentina, Chile, and Peru, while Abrão and

Torelly (2011) consider the reparations program as a central pillar of Brazil's efforts to confront the past. Lastly, the recent book edited by Skaar, García-Godos and Collins (2016) presents an ambitious and systematic attempt to provide in-depth comparative analysis of transitional justice processes in the region, describing transitional justice mechanisms and their evolution over time in nine Latin American transitional justice cases (Argentina, Uruguay, Brazil, Chile, Paraguay, El Salvador, Guatemala, Peru, and Colombia).

A second classification refers the moment (*sequencing*) in which transitional justice mechanisms have been applied. According to this frame, three different groups of countries can be identified:

a   Those where transitional justice mechanisms were applied immediately after transition, including Argentina, Uruguay, Chile, El Salvador, Guatemala, Bolivia, Haiti, and Honduras. In many of these countries transitional justice measures overlap with post-transitional justice, as indicated in Table 24.1
b   Those cases where transitional justice mechanisms have mainly been applied in post-transitional contexts, many years after the transition to democratic rule. Here we find cases of truth commissions so late in relation to the facts they investigate that, according to Freeman´s definition (2006, 32), they are in danger of not being considered truth commissions at all, but rather historical investigations. These include Brazil´s Truth Commission (which investigated – between May 2012 and December 2014 – violations that occurred between 1946 and 1988), Paraguay (which investigated –between June 2004 and August 2008 – human rights violations that occurred between 1945 and 1989) or Panama (which – between January 2001 and April 2002 – investigated the murders and disappearances which occurred during the military dictatorship through the years 1968 to 1989).
c   Countries where it is very difficult to identify the moment of the transition or where the conflict is still ongoing – the Peruvian and Colombian cases.[3] In Peru, the truth commission (2003) elaborated a report on internal armed violence between 1980 and 2000, including that perpetrated by the insurgent groups *Sendero Luminoso* and the Movimiento Revolucionario *Túpac Amaru* (MRTA), and that attributable to the military's counterinsurgent operations. One of the main consequences of this process of transitional justice was the 25-year prison sentence imposed on former President Alberto Fujimori for grave and serious violations of human rights committed during his government (1990–2000).

In Colombia the Justice and Peace Law (Law 975), approved in 2005 during the government of Alvaro Uribe and centered mainly on paramilitary actors, established a legal framework for the demobilization of armed actors who contributed to truth-finding. During the government of Juan Manuel Santos, a frame of transitional justice was established dealing with reparations and land restitution, via Law 1448–2011. In 2012, peace negotiations between the government and the FARC (Revolutionary Armed Forces of Colombia) guerrilla produced a constitutional amendment, which aimed to provide a legal framework for peace involving amnesty, which sparked a heated national debate about peace and justice dilemmas. Polarization and division on these transitional justice issues came into sharp relief when ratification of the peace settlement was narrowly rejected in a plebiscite held in October 2016. Although the Colombian congress eventually ratified the Havana peace agreements, the challenge of guaranteeing victims' rights in the post-peace dispensation continues.

Scholars have reflected on these differences of transitional justice sequencing. The first contributions date from the end of the 1990s, for example, the compilation by Kritz (1995), which focused on Argentina, Uruguay, Brazil, and Chile, all countries that adopted transitional justice mechanisms at the moment of transition.[4] These initial studies were mainly concerned with the risks transitional justice mechanisms might imply for democratic consolidation. Yet other authors posited that transitional justice would become a normalized part of politics, at the same time expanding the meaning of transition itself (Teitel 2003).

As many transitional justice mechanisms began to be implemented in post-transitional contexts, the term *post-transitional justice* started to be adopted. Collins (2012) defined this as challenges to the agreements made at the time of the transition regarding truth, justice, and reparations, or to the extent of such initial agreements. Skaar's work (2010) focuses on judicial proceedings, whether criminal or civil trials, held at least one electoral cycle after the transition to democracy (concretely in Argentina, Chile, and Uruguay). These authors stand apart from the so-called *classic school of transitional justice*, which tended to concentrate on elite choices about the adoption of transitional justice mechanisms at the moment of transition. In one sense this differentiation between transitional and post-transitional justice seems self-evident for Latin America, yet it is not unproblematic, as the division between transition and post-transition is not always analytically clear.

In addition to the cases mentioned on p. 378, there are others where transitional justice measures have barely been applied, or those where their application has been deemed unsuccessful or ideologically driven, including the Dominican Republic, Ecuador, Venezuela, and Mexico. For this reason, they are not included in Table 24.1. In the Dominican Republic, some minimal measures on transitional justice have been implemented, although not in relation to Trujillo's 31-year dictatorship (1930–1961), which was responsible for the deaths of more than 50,000 people, or the 12 years of the Balaguer period (1966–1978), characterized by widespread political repression.[5] The *Memorial Museum of Dominican Resistance*, inaugurated in 2011, was a private initiative providing a record of the victims, a measure with strong symbolical value in a country characterized by official amnesia. Ecuador had two truth commissions, the first in 1996, established by former President Abdalá Bucaram to investigate 176 unresolved cases of human rights violations committed since 1979; and the second in 2007 by President Rafael Correa to investigate multiple human rights violations registered mostly under the government of Febres Cordero (1984–1988), a period in which the politics of state terrorism were used to combat not only subversive organizations (Alfaro Vive Carajo and Montoneras Patria Libre) but all the legal left and popular movements. However, the Ecuadorian case has been widely criticized for the political use of truth commissions, the last formed by people close to the government, former employees, and open defenders of the ruling coalition. Something similar occurred with Venezuela's Commission for Justice and Truth (2013), created with the objective of sanctioning the torture, disappearances, and other human rights violations that occurred during the fourth republic (1958–1998). This was strongly criticized for its political character and in the event no transitional justice measures were applied. Mexico's "Special Commission of 1968," in 1998, tried unsuccessfully to clarify the events surrounding the deaths that occurred in the Plaza of the Three Cultures, on October 2, 1968, in Tlatelolco.[6] In 2001, President Vicente Fox created a special prosecutor's office for Political and Social Movements in the Past (FEMOSPP), with the objective of investigating the "dirty war" in the 1970s and 1980s, as well as the student massacres that occurred in 1968 and 1971. The FEMOSPP was dissolved in 2007. One of its outcomes was the unprecedented indictment in November 2006 of a former president (Luis Echevarría, 1970–1976), for genocide relating to the Tlatelolco massacre. Echevarría was absolved in 2009. Subsequently, a commission to investigate crimes during the dirty war of the 1960s and 1970s in the Mexican state of Guerrero was set up in 2012. While this body confirmed that the state practiced a policy of extermination against political opponents in Guerrero during that period, it had minimal impact outside of certain academic circles and human rights organizations.[7]

Table 24.1 Variation of Transitional Justice Measures

Country	Conflict Duration/ Human Rights Violations Period	Year of Formal Transition	Violence (All Figures are Contested Estimates)	Type and Sequencing of Official Transitional Justice Measures	
				Under Transitional Government	Later (Post-Transitional)
Transition to Democracy Countries					
Argentina	1976–1983	1983	10,000–30,000 dead and detained-disappeared (dd) extensive torture	Truth commission (1983), trials, amnesty, reparations	Large-scale trials from 2000
Uruguay	1973–1985	1984	190 dead and dd, 200,000 tortured	Truth commission (1985), amnesty	Trials second truth commission (2000) reparations
Brazil	1946–1988	1985	420 dead and dd, extensive torture	Amnesty	Truth commission (2012)
Chile	1973–1990	1991	3,200 dead and dd, 40,000 tortured	Truth commission (1990), amnesty, reparations	Second truth commission (2003), large-scale trials from 1998
Paraguay	1954–1989	2003*	400 dead and dd, 20,000 tortured	No amnesty Truth commission later	Reparations Truth commission (2003)
Bolivia	1964–1982	1982	200 dead and dd	Truth commission (1982) Trials (García Meza conviction)	Reparations
Haiti	1957–1994	1994	60,000 dead	Truth commission (1996) Trials (*Tonton Macoute*)	
Honduras	1963–1982	1982	184 dd (majority between 1980–1984)	Truth commission (1994) Amnesty	

Panama	1968–1989	1989	100 dead and dd		Truth commission (2001)
Transition to Peace					
El Salvador	1980–1992	1991	50,000 killed and dd	Truth commission (1992), amnesty	
Guatemala	1958–1994	1996	200,000 killed, some in acts of genocide	Truth commission (1994), limited amnesty	Trials (Rios Montt trial 2013) and some others
Hybrid Cases					
Peru	1980–2000	2000**	69,000 dead and dd, 600,000 internally displaced	Truth commission (2001), trials, reparations	Fujimori conviction 2009, other high level trials ongoing
Ongoing Conflict					
Colombia	Since 1958	Ongoing	Large-scale killings, four million internally displaced	Conditional amnesties, trials, reparations, truth-seeking	

Source: Based on Skaar, García-Godos, and Collins (2016).

Notes

* Dictator Alfredo Stroessner was ousted in a palace coup in 1989, but his Colorado Party continued in power until 2008. The Paraguayan Truth Commission investigated human rights violations from 1954 up to the time of its establishment in 2003.

** The year 2000 marks the end of the authoritarian civilian Fujimori presidency (1990–2000) and the beginning of discussion of transitional justice mechanisms.

The Development of the Transitional Justice Field in Latin America

Having signaled the evolution and sequencing of the adoption of transitional justice mechanisms in Latin America, we now turn to the evolution of transitional justice studies. We focus on works of comparative political science that seek to explain the emergence and nature of transitional justice and to measure its effects over time. For reasons of space we do not cover individual case studies nor the extensive anthropological literature on transitional justice experiences in the region.[8]

Five issues characterize the development of the field of transitional justice studies in Latin America: (a) works linked to transition; (b) research focusing on the relationship between transitional justice, democracy, and human rights; (c) causal studies, which seek to explain the emergence and timing of transitional justice mechanisms; (d) research which considers the contribution of the Inter-American Human Rights System to transitional justice; and (e) the emerging body of studies considering the issue of the gender in transitional justice.

The Dilemmas of Transition

Initial research on transitional justice, at least since the term was coined in the Salzburg conference in 1992 (Arthur 2011), were related to the dilemmas arising from the need to confront past human right violations and achieve democratic stability, within the frame of the third wave of democratization (Huntington 1994). Teitel (1995), for example, explores the relation between punishment and democracy, referring to the lack of legitimacy that could affect Southern Cone regimes in the absence of accountability for past human rights violations committed under military rule. In a similar sense, by addressing the dilemma of how to face the past without endangering the transition to democracy, O'Donnell and Schmitter (1986) signaled that in Latin America the close association between the armed forces and acts of repression would make it more difficult for military officers to disassociate themselves from past atrocities. The more serious and egregious the repression, the higher the resolve to not revisit the past. O'Donnell and Schmitter signaled that the passage of time would facilitate policies of clemency, but that the fact that repression was so extensive would make such options more difficult to pursue.

Studies centered on the *peace-versus-justice* debate deserve a separate mention. A central argument has been that pursuing prosecutions during an active conflict can delay or otherwise interfere with the negotiation of peace (Snyder and Vinjamuri 2003; Kim and Sikkink 2010; Uprimny, Sánchez, and Sánchez 2014). This dilemma has led to the adoption of amnesties to guarantee *ex post facto* immunity from criminal prosecution.

Transitional Justice, Democracy, and Human Rights

With the passing of the years and the adoption of different transitional justice mechanisms in each country where there were transitions to democracy or peace in Latin America, studies began to emerge which paid particular attention to transitional justice choices over time and their implications for democracy and human rights.

From a historic and normative perspective, Fletcher, Weinstein, and Rowen (2009) reflect on the dynamics and timing of transitional justice. Retrospectively analyzing seven case studies, including two from Latin America (Argentina and Guatemala), they uncovered a general rule that after a period between six years and eight years changes tended to occur and transitional justice mechanisms subsequently adopted – in contrast to those adopted at the start of transition – paid more attention to victims, frequently through financial reparations.

Sikkink and Booth Walling´s work (2007) explores the permanence and evolution of the transitional justice measures adopted in Latin America. Their study concludes that in most of the countries in the region, the agreements made during the transitions suffered modifications with the passing of time, and that while the initial option that prevailed was the establishing of truth commissions, trials subsequently occurred. Through their empirical analysis of judicial processes in the region, Sikkink and Booth Walling (2007) went beyond the normative discussions on truth/justice that had initially tended to prevail in the transitional justice field, and echoed earlier analysis by Lutz and Sikkink (2001), who referred to a *justice cascade* (signaling the tendency of democratizing states to bring those responsible for past violations of human rights to trial). Sikkink and Booth Walling (2007) evaluated the impact of human rights trials and truth commissions on the consolidation of democracy and state practices regarding human rights. Their conclusions indicate that trials did not undermine democracy, nor did they imply an increase in conflict or human rights violations. They also showed that in Latin America, transitional justice mechanisms were frequently combined, and that trials also took place in countries where truth commissions had initially been the main transitional justice mechanism, even challenging amnesties put in place at the time of transition.[9]

Olsen, Payne, and Reiter (2010) analyze changes in human rights and democracy indicators against transitional justice measures on a database from 161 countries. Their findings emphasize that legal convictions in cases of human rights violations do not necessarily imply a significant statistical improvement in rights observance. On the contrary, they found that the adoption of truth commissions in the absence of any other complementary transitional justice measures tends to be associated with a deterioration of human rights. The combination of trials and amnesties correlates with improvements, as does the combination of trials, amnesties, and truth commissions. The study also provided evidence on the sequencing of transitional justice measures: new democracies initially adopt amnesties, then trials and then many years after the transition, opt for restorative justice measures.

In 2011, Sikkink presented the conclusions of an investigation published in 2010 – along with Hunjoon Kim – on the impact of trials and their role in preventing future repression, after some academics questioned the results of the study published by Sikkink and Booth Walling (2007). Kim and Sikkink (2010) contrast the impact of truth commissions and trials in 100 countries, which have undergone transitions, finding that those countries, which held trials over more years tended to have better human rights practices. They also found – contrary to the conclusion of Olsen et al. (2010) – that truth commissions also contribute to improving rights protection, and that the dissuasive effect of trials also operates across borders, reaching neighboring countries.

The Search for Explanations

In addition to analyzing the adoption of different mechanisms of transitional justice over time, and their impact on democracy and human rights, research on transitional justice has enquired into those factors that determine policies toward the past. Yet while numerous cases studies exist, there are few systematic comparisons explaining the adoption of different transitional justice mechanisms or accounting for their different outcomes. Within more causal studies there are competing perspectives, such as those emphasizing international factors in contrast to those who focus on domestic factors (although most consider both).

In the 1990s, Linz and Stepan (1996) explored how decisions are made during transitions and how these can be affected by variables related to actors, previous regime type and leadership during the transition, as well as variables of context, such as international influences and decision-making environments. Olsen, Payne, and Reiter (2010) examine transitional justice mechanisms deployed between 1970 and 2007, and which factors (political, financial, international, and social) facilitate or impede their adoption. They warn that, despite the extensive literature on transitional justice, the numerous hypothesis that have been generated have not been rigorously tested, meaning that a robust universal theory of transitional justice has yet to be constructed. Their empirical analysis suggests that fears of endangering transition processes appear not to limit justice options (as the literature previously assumed), that authoritarian legacies persist long into the future, and that new democracies tend to be cautious. All this makes it difficult to test the hypothesis that adopting decisive justice measures risks democratic stability. Olsen, Payne, and Reiter (2010) also emphasize the need to theorize more about combinations of transitional justice mechanisms, given that countries tend to use various measures rather than opt for one or another.

These authors also consider the role of the international community in influencing decisions on transitional justice. Among such factors, they mention the spread of international norms or the "justice cascade," international defense networks, and the contagion effect, according to which trials in one country tend to encourage trials in neighboring countries. The results of their statistical analysis goes against the hypothesis sustaining the contagion effect. Concerning the justice cascade (whereby adoption by states of international human rights norms is assumed to lead to more accountability trials), they find this effect is concentrated in Europe and Latin America.

Lessa et al. (2014) offer a study that combines both international and domestic factors, exploring four factors associated with *accountability* for past crimes in the new democracies about which there is broad agreement within the literature. These are: (1) lawsuits pursued by civil society actors; (2) judicial leadership in the domestic sphere; (3) the absence of veto players; and (4) international pressure. Their analysis shows that none of these factors alone is sufficient to overcome impunity; however, a dynamic interaction between them explains a higher tendency toward accountability. When accountability predominates along the accountability versus impunity continuum, amnesty laws cease to be an obstacle for trials and convictions. In this manner studies such as that by Lessa and her colleagues place amnesty laws at the center of analyses seeking to explain shifts toward greater accountability

Other studies center on the factors, which might explain greater accountability through criminal trials. Gonzales-Ocantos (2014) asks how the diffusion of international human rights norms to domestic judicial actors (a diffusion promoted by domestic and international human rights nongovernmental organizations [NGOs]) leads those actors to adopt daring decisions against impunity. He finds that, contrary to what some studies suggest, higher levels of criminal accountability do not depend on higher judicial independence, but rather on the "politicization" of the judiciary via pedagogical interventions by NGOs, as well as strategies to renew or replace judges. Collins (2006) questions the practical effects of action by global civil society to promote transitional justice trials. In her analysis of post-transitional justice in Chile she highlights the importance of domestic factors, among them pressures from internal actors and processes of judicial change. Jelin (2007), in her analysis of the ways in which social demands for public memorialization in the Southern Cone have changed over time, similarly underlines the importance of domestic actors.

This brief review reveals great variance among causal studies on transitional justice mechanisms; some, such of that of Olsen et al. (2010) focus on factors explaining their adoption, while others, such as Lessa et al. (2014) are more concerned with the factors explaining moves to greater accountability. A number of comparative studies on transitional justice mechanisms in Latin America deserve mention here: the volume edited by Barahona de Brito, González-Enríquez, and Aguilar (2001) contains chapters on the role of international actors in national accountability processes (by Roht-Arriaza); on the Southern Cone experiences (by Barahona de Brito), and on Central America (by Sieder), all of which address questions of truth, justice, and memory. More recently, the book edited by Skaar, García-Godos, and Collins (2016) systematically explores the impact of transitional justice mechanisms in Argentina, Brazil, Chile, Colombia, El Salvador, Guatemala, Paraguay, Peru, and Uruguay. It focuses on the historical context of the conflicts and the timing and sequencing of the transitional justice mechanisms applied in each country. Its overall aim is to analyze the different strategies and their contribution to peace and democratization, combining deep contextual analysis of each country with a systemic comparison.

These regional studies agree that besides it being common for several mechanisms to be adopted simultaneously, their sole existence is no guarantee of advances on impunity or accountability. Think, for example, of the cases in which amnesties are not able to halt advances in justice or, on the contrary, those where limited amnesties do not guarantee more judicial accountability. This conclusion ratifies the observations of Thoms, Ron, and Paris (2010) that we still lack conclusive evidence about the negative and positive impacts of transitional justice mechanisms.

Contribution of the Regional Human Rights System to Transitional Justice

International factors are often cited as one of the central explanations for changes in the adoption of transitional justice mechanisms over time, and their influence is particularly marked in Latin America. The regional human rights system has long provided victims with a forum when national justice systems have been inaccessible or actively hostile. Despite the limits of the Inter-American System's influence on domestic transitional justice processes,[10] Inter-American Court rulings have contributed to developing doctrine on disappearance, amnesties, the victim's rights to the truth, the obligation of states to prosecute, and judicial guarantees.

Key rulings of the Inter-American Court can be considered pioneers in struggles for justice, truth, and reparations (*Velasquez Rodríguez* v. *Honduras* 1988); reinterpreting domestic amnesty laws (*Barrios Altos* v. *Peru* 2001; *Almonacid* v. *Chile* 2006) or forced disappearance (*Goiburú* v. *Paraguay* 2006; *Contreras* et al. v. *El Salvador* 2011); defining the right of truth as a social right and a form of reparation (*Gomes Lund–Guerrilha do Araguaia* v. *Brazil* 2010; *Gelman* v. *Uruguay* 2011) or denouncing the ongoing denial of truth or justice (*Serrano-Cruz Sisters* v. *El Salvador* 2005; *García Lucero* v. *Chile* 2013), among others.

A number of studies analyze relations between the Inter-American Human Rights System and advances in transitional justice in the region (Salazar and Antkowiak 2007; Huneeus 2011). Concerning individual countries, we can highlight studies in Brazil (Torelly and Abrao 2012); Colombia (Bernardi 2013); El Salvador (Martínez Barahona and Gutiérrez forthcoming); Guatemala (Davis and Warner 2007; Martínez and Gutiérrez forthcoming); Mexico (Dutrénit 2012; Bernardi 2015b); Peru (Sandoval 2008; Burt 2009; Bernardi 2015a); and Uruguay (Dutrénit 2012). In general, these studies find that the Inter-American System has a positive effect on the domestic sphere, or, at the very least, it constitutes the only way to pursue justice on behalf of the victims in those countries where transitional justice measures fail to move forward.

Transitional Justice and Gender

Most of the limited number of studies on transitional justice and gender center on women as victims of sexual violence (Hastings 2002; Boesten 2010). Despite sexual crimes in armed conflicts being a longstanding practice of warfare, only recently have they been typified as international human rights crimes. The creation of the International Criminal Tribunals for the former-Yugoslavia and Rwanda facilitated the development of jurisprudence determining sexual crimes as serious international crimes. Although the connections between transitional justice and gender are evident, these lines of research have not been developed in-depth in Latin America. Some studies exist for the cases of Guatemala (Crosby and Lykes 2011; Duggan, Paz y Paz Bailey, Guillerot 2008; Rosser 2007; Paz y Paz Bailey 2006), Peru (Laplante 2007; Guillerot 2006), or Colombia (Chappell, Grey, and Waller 2013; Meertens and Zambrano 2010).

In these three countries, sexual violence has been a habitual practice and part of military strategy within their respective armed conflicts. In Peru, hundreds of Quechua speaking women were raped during two decades of internal war (1980–2000) in farming communities and military bases as part of a planned strategy of repression against subversion.[11] Something similar happened during Guatemala's civil war and in 2016 the first trial for sexual crimes during the armed conflict resulted in the conviction of military officers.[12] In Colombia, the country's Constitutional Court has deemed sexual violence a systemic, habitual, and generalized practice used by all the actors in the Colombian conflict. Some authors have also analyzed the approaches of truth commissions to issues of gendered harm (Rosser 2007; Valji 2006), while others have pointed to the low participation of women in negotiations and peace agreements, as well as the subsequent search for justice and democratization (Buckley-Zistel and Zolkos 2012; Fitzsimmons 2000).

From an anthropological perspective, Theidon (2006) examines lethal violence against women in communities affected by the conflict in Peru during the 1980s and 1990s, on many occasions perpetrated by relatives or close members of their communities, as well as practices of communal justice around these crimes and their impact on reconciliation processes. Subsequently (2007) Theidon analyzed testimonies given by women in the context of the Peruvian Truth and Reconciliation Commission, calling attention to how the accounts of harm narrated by women were, in many cases, limited to the narrating of the sexual aggression they had endured, ignoring the fact that gender crimes are not only sexual in nature. In her work on processes of Disarmament, Demobilization and Reintegration (DDR) carried out in Colombia under the government of Álvaro Uribe, Theidon insists that these programs and transitional justice processes more generally require a gendered analysis if they are to transform the violent masculinities, which characterize former combatants (Theidon 2009).

Challenges in the Study Field of Transitional Justice

Although throughout the different sections of this chapter we have pointed to some of the deficiencies that exist in transitional justice studies in Latin America, there are also a number of other areas of research that merit future development. Here we signal three: greater methodological-theoretical innovation; transitional justice and social and economic rights; and the links between public opinion and transitional justice.

As Gómez Isa (2010, 189) has stated, transitional justice has experienced a kind of "epistemic success," placing it at the center of discussions about processes of political transition and conflict resolution. However, paradoxically, this relative success has been accompanied by highly limited advances in the development of theory (De Greiff 2009, 22), which might explain the versatility of transitional justice. The generalized conviction about the usefulness of existing concepts and mechanisms has also led to conceptual stretching and their application to contexts, which in a strict sense, are not transitional (Gómez Isa 2010, 190). This pressure to widen the spectrum of the application of transitional justice may affect questions of conceptual definition and the operability of the mechanisms themselves. Transitional justice has been expanded to contexts where conflict remains ongoing or in its final stages (Colombia); cases which failed to confront past abuses at the moment of transition (Dominican Republic); contexts where it is deployed as an instrument to confront abuses in the present (Mexico); to resolve human rights violations in specific political situations (Honduras); or is used in highly partisan and ideological ways (Ecuador or Venezuela).

The need for conceptual precision, and to guard against conceptual stretching, which may empty the term of content, are challenges that the field of transitional justice studies continues to face. The most promising line of enquiry is to focus on the mechanisms themselves – truth, justice, and reparations – distinguishing their particularities. Truth therefore, extends beyond truth commissions (with their different characteristics and achievements), to include efforts undertaken in the search for disappeared people. In justice, we should look not just to the presence or absence of trials, but to their content, timing, and who the defendants are (issues of chain of command, and so forth). Finally, when it comes to mechanisms for reparations, we should analyze their content and nature, and the extent to which they benefit not just victims but also other socially vulnerable or historically underprivileged actors.

Together with greater conceptual precision, there exists a need for theoretical frameworks, which can facilitate detailed and systematic comparison of the different transitional justice mechanisms and account for their contrasting trajectories. Such frameworks would contribute to the development not only of studies that investigate decisions adopted in transitional moments, but also to analysis of their evolution and implementation, whether that be because the initial agreements have been overcome or deepened with time, or because social change has occurred, which allows for transitional justice mechanisms to be revisited (Gutiérrez 2015a). Recent studies have tried to overcome these challenges by resorting to a methodology that allows for the comparison of countries with different trajectories (Skaar, García-Godos, and Collins 2016). However, more systematic comparative studies are still needed in the field of transitional justice within Latin America and beyond the region.

A second issue is that while transitional justice studies have prioritized consideration of civil and political rights violations, they have paid less attention to financial crimes and corruption and their connection to the violation of civil and political rights, or to social and cultural rights. Despite much theorization, there is little empirical research exploring the relationship between transitional justice and economic structures. One recent example by Dancy and Wiebelhaus-Brahm (2015) tests a model seeking to evaluate how transitional justice has affected financial structures in Argentina.

Third, while many studies exist of victims and their experiences, not many have been carried out via representative samples, nor do many studies exist which differentiate attitudes between victims and non-victims toward transitional justice. Survey data remains scant. Nussio, Rettberg, and Ugarriza (2015) found no statistical differences in the attitudes of victims and non-victims to transitional justice mechanisms, contradicting previous findings suggesting that victims favor punitive justice over the politics of forgetting (see Aguilar, Balcells, and Cebolla on the Spanish case 2011). More studies of public opinion could test traditional arguments or hypotheses about the social and political impacts of violence and transitional justice.

Conclusions

This chapter has signaled the principle and most recent debates on transitional justice mechanisms in Latin America, prioritizing comparative social science studies. We have emphasized that although scholars initially feared that transitional justice would endanger democratic transitions, the passage of time has shown that the risks were less than initially imagined. At present it is argued that transitional justice mechanisms can improve human rights indicators and democracy, although there is still no consensus about their impact on peace or democratic consolidation.

We have also argued that comparative studies on transitional justice mechanisms need to be strengthened, paying more attention to their consequences and the implications for the region's democracies. Comparative work should include not only the successful cases, but also those least analyzed, which are invariably those where transitional justice measures have barely been implemented or have been unsuccessful. "Failures" may prove to be temporary over time, as demands for justice do not disappear with transition. In this sense, we have underlined the ongoing and dynamic nature of transitional justice mechanisms.

Ultimately, a dialog between academics and practitioners is required, which builds on the findings of previous studies, no small challenge in a field characterized by different disciplines and perspectives.

Notes

1 Transitional justice refers to those mechanisms, formal or informal, adopted to confront violations in the past, which include trials, truth commissions, amnesties, and reparation programs, among others.
2 Although we might also mention here those cases where revolutions ended the dictatorships of Batista and the Somoza (Cuba and Nicaragua), in the global discourse on transitional justice, Nicaragua is treated as a divergent case since in none of its two transitions (1979 and 1990) have transitional justice measures been applied. In 1979, special tribunals were established to punish the thousands of Somocistas without any judicial guarantees. The same can be said of the measures pursued by the Castro regime against the pro-Batista elite after 1959 (Barahona de Brito et al. 2002, 34).
3 Peru offer a case of multiple transitions, from both authoritarian rule in 1980 and armed conflict in the 1990s, plus an authoritarian democracy in 2000.
4 Kritz compiled three volumes on the results of the project of "Transitional Justice" from the United States' Institute for Peace, which looked to answer questions about how to deal with the past. Volume One gathers general considerations and extracts of publications by Zalaquett, O'Donnell, and Schmitter, Huntington, Huyse, Linz, Teitel, among others; Volume Two looks at studies by country – from Europe and Latin America – and Volume Three gathers laws, resolutions, reports, and other primary documents of the transitions analyzed.
5 After the fall of Trujillo's dictatorship in 1961, the Dominican Republic did not experience another military dictatorship, despite the political instability that characterized the first half of the 1960s, including a short civil war and an occupation by the United States. The 12-year Balaguer government, which started in 1966, combined clearly authoritarian elements with other facilitators of a future democratic transition, and it was not until 1978 that the Dominican Republic was able to hold competitive elections. The Dominican transition, originating in an authoritarian civil government and not dictatorship, was not included in the initial transitional justice studies (Espinal 1987).
6 Dozens of students and civilians died in crossfire in which the army and police participated: estimates of deaths range between 25 and 350.
7 Calls have been made for a truth commission to clarify human rights violations that have occurred in the context of the Mexican state's "war on drugs" from 2006 onwards.
8 Transitional justice has moved from concerns about how to confront the past to exploring how to ensure a better future, particularly for victims, whose subjective experiences are increasingly explored in a range of anthropological publications: Theidon (2012) on Peru; Viaene (2013) or Nelson (2009) on Guatemala; Vera Lugo (2015) on Colombia; and Robben (2000) on Argentina. Theidon and Betancourt (2006) analyze regional and local realities in the paramilitary demobilization process implemented in Colombia. Vera Lugo (2015) also examines the demobilization process that occurred after 2005, particularly the unanticipated effects of the law, which regulated it. Following a tendency, which questions transitional justice as a top-down construction, Viaene (2013, 108) shows how for the indigenous Q'eqchi Community in Guatemala, taking those responsible for massive human rights violations to trial is not desirable, thereby questioning dominant paradigms of transitional justice.

9 This study does not consider the number of trials or sentences but rather the existence of judicial activity, in such way that the higher the number of years with trials, the more continuity of judicial proceedings or judicial activity.

10 Limits refers to the temporal restrictions on jurisdictio, levels of noncompliance, and the dissatisfaction of some states with the entire system.

11 The truth and reconciliation commission registered 538 cases of collective and individual sexual violations; 449 of these were perpetrated by Sendero Luminoso and the Movimiento Revolucionario Túpac Amaru (MRTA) and the rest by members of the armed forces. However, only 14 cases have been investigated, and only three have reached the courts. There are also thousands of cases of almost 2,000 women who were forcibly sterilized during the government of Alberto Fujimori in Peru (1990–2000) awaiting justice.

12 On February 2016, retired Lieutenant Colonel Steelmer Reyes Girón and former military commissioner (civilian at the service of the army) Heriberto Valdez Azij were convicted of kidnapping 11 Maya-Q'eqchi' women and forcing them into sexual slavery on a military base.

References

Abrão, Paulo and Torelly, Marcelo. 2011. "The reparations program as the lynchpin of transitional justice in Brazil." In *Transitional Justice: Handbook for Latin America*, edited by Félix Reátegui, 407–40. Brasilia: Brazilian Amnesty Commission, Ministry of Justice.

Abrão, Pablo and Torelly, Marcelo. 2012. "Resistance to Change: Brazil's persistent amnesty and its alternatives for Truth and Justice." In *Amnesty in the Age of Human Rights Accountability*, edited by Francesca Lessa, and Leigh Payne, 152–81. New York: Cambridge University Press.

Aguilar, Paloma, Balcells, Laia, and Cebolla-Boado, Hector. 2011. "Determinants of Attitudes toward Transitional Justice: An Empirical Analysis of the Spanish Case." *Comparative Political Studies* 44(10): 1397–430.

Ansolabehere, Karina. 2014. "Difusores y justicieros. Las instituciones judiciales en la política de derechos humanos." *Perfiles Latinoamericanos* 44: 143–69.

Arthur, Paige. 2011. "How transitions reshape human rights: a conceptual history of transitional justice." In *Transitional Justice: Handbook for Latin America*, edited by Félix Reátegui, 73–134. Brasilia: Brazilian Amnesty Commission, Ministry of Justice.

Barahona de Brito, Alexandra, Aguilar Fernández, Paloma, and González-Enríquez, Carmen, eds. 2001. *The Politics of Memory: Transitional Justice in Democratizing Societies*. New York: Oxford University Press.

Beristaín, Carlos Martín, comp. 2011. *Contribución de las políticas de verdad, justicia y reparación a las democracias en América Latina*. San José de Costa Rica, Instituto interamericano de Derechos Humanos (IIDH).

Bernardi, Bruno. 2013. "O sistema interamericano de direitos humanos e a lei de justiça e Paz na Colômbia: política doméstica e influência de normas internacionais." *Contexto Internacional* 35: 139–72.

Bernardi, Bruno. 2015a. "O sistema interamericano de direitos humanos e a justiça de transição no Peru." *Revista de Sociologia e Política* 23(54): 43–68.

Bernardi, Bruno. 2015b. "O sistema interamericano e a justiça de transição no México." *Lua Nova* 94: 143–81.

Boesten, Jelke. 2010. "Analysing rape regimes at the interface of war and peace in Peru." *International Journal of Transitional Justice* 4(1): 110–29.

Buckley-Zistel, Susanne and Zolkos, Magdalena. 2012. "Introduction." In *Gender in Transitional Justice*, edited by Susanne Buckley-Zistel and Ruth Stanley, 1–33. New York, NY: Palgrave Macmillan.

Burt, Jo-Marie. 2009. "Guilty as charged: the trial of former President Alberto Fujimori for human rights violations." *International Journal of Transitional Justice* 3(3): 384–405.

Burt, Jo-Marie. 2012. "Accountability after atrocity in Peru: the trial of former President Alberto Fujimori in comparative perspective." In *Critical Perspectives in Transitional Justice*, edited by Nicola Palmer, Phil Clark and Danielle Granville, 119–46. Cambridge: Intersentia Publishing Ltd.

Chappell, Louise, Grey, Rosemary, and Waller, Emily. 2013. "The Gender Justice Shadow of Complementarity: Lessons from the International Criminal Court's Preliminary Examinations in Guinea and Colombia." *International Journal of Transitional Justice* 7(3): 455–75.

Crosby, Alison and Brinton Lykes, M. 2011. "Mayan women survivors speak: the gendered relations of truth telling in post-war Guatemala." *International Journal of Transitional Justice* 5(3): 456–76.

Collins, Cath. 2006. "Grounding global justice: international networks and domestic human rights accountability in Chile and El Salvador." *Journal of Latin American Studies* 38(4): 711–38.

Collins, Cath. 2009. "Human rights trials in Chile during and after the Pinochet years." *International Journal of Transitional Justice* 4(1): 67–86.

Collins, Cath. 2012. "The end of impunity? Late justice and post-transitional prosecutions in Latin America." In *Critical Perspectives in Transitional Justice*, edited by Nicola Palmer, Phil Clark and Danielle Granville, 399–423. Cambridge: Intersentia Publishing Ltd.

Collins, Cath; Balardini, Lorena, and Burt, Jo-Marie. 2013. "Mapping perpetrator prosecutions in Latin America." *International Journal of Transitional Justice* 7(1): 8–28.

Correa, Cristián. 2011. "Reparation programs for mass violations of human rights: lessons from experiences in Argentina, Chile and Peru." In *Transitional Justice: Handbook for Latin America*, edited by Félix Reátegui, 441–76. Brasilia: Brazilian Amnesty Commission, Ministry of Justice.

Dancy, Geoff and Wiebelhaus-Brah, Eric. 2015. "Bridge to human development or vehicle of inequality? Transitional justice and economic structures." *International Journal of Transitional Justice* 9(1): 51–69.

Davis, Jeffrey and Warner, Edward. 2007. "Reaching beyond the state: judicial independence, the Inter-American Court of Human Rights, and accountability in Guatemala." *Journal of Human Rights* 6: 233–55.

Duggan, Colleen, Paz y Paz Bailey, Claudia, and Guillerot, Julie. 2008. "Reparations for sexual and reproductive violence: prospects for achieving gender justice in Guatemala and Peru." *International Journal of Transitional Justice* 2(2): 192–213.

Dutrénit, Silvia. 2012. "Sentencias de la corte interamericana de derechos humanos y reacciones estatales. (México y Uruguay ante los delitos del pasado)." *América Latina Hoy* 61: 79–99.

De Greiff, Pablo. 2009. "Una concepción normativa de la justicia transicional." In *Justicia y Paz. ¿Cuál es el precio que debemos pagar?* Edited by Alfredo Rangel, 17–74, Bogotá , Intermedio Editores.

Espinal, Rosario. 1987. *Autoritarismo y democracia en la política dominicana.* San José, Costa Rica: Instituto Interamericano de Derechos Humanos (IIDH).

Fitzsimmons, Tracy. 2000. *Beyond the Barricades: Women, Civil Society, and Participation after Democratization in Latin America.* New York and London: Garland Publishing.

Fletcher, Laurel E.; Weinstein, Harvey M., and Rowen, Jamie. 2009. "Context, timing and the dynamics of transitional justice: a historical perspective." *Human Rights Quarterly* 31: 163–220.

Freeman, Mark. 2006. *Truth Commissions and Procedural Fairness.* Cambridge: Cambridge University Press.

Gómez Isa, Felipe. 2010. "Retos de la justicia transicional en contextos no transicionales: el caso de Colombia." In *Transiciones en Contienda. Disyuntivas de la justicia transicional en Colombia desde la experiencia comparada*, edited by Michael Reed y María Cristina Rivera, 188–211. Bogotá: Centro Internacional para la Justicia Transicional.

González Ocantos, Ezequiel. 2014. "Persuade them or oust them: crafting judicial change and transitional justice in Argentina." *Comparative Politics* 46(4): 479–98.

Guillerot, Julie. 2006. "Linking gender and reparations in Peru: a failed opportunity." In *What Happened to the Women? Gender and Reparations for Human Rights Violations*, edited by Ruth Rubio-Marín, 136–93. New York, NY: Social Science Research Council.

Gutiérrez Salazar, Martha Liliana. 2015a. *From the Conflict to the Injustice: Impunity in El Salvador and Guatemala. Measuring justice pathways and seeking explications.* PhD diss, University of Salamanca.

Gutiérrez Salazar, Martha Liliana. 2015b. "Justicia postransicional en Guatemala: el rol de los jueces en la protección de derechos humanos." *Revista de Ciencia Política* 35(2): 347–70.

Hayner, Priscilla. 2001. *Unspeakable Truths. Confronting State Terror and Atrocity.* New York: Routledge.

Hayner, Priscilla. 2011. *Unspeakable Truths. Transitional Justice and the Challenge of Truth Commissions.* New York: Routledge.

Huneeus, Alexandra. 2011. "Courts resisting courts: lessons from the Inter-American Court's Struggle to Enforce Human Rights." *Cornell International Law Journal* 44(493): 493–533.

Huntington, Samuel. 1994. *The Third Wave. Democratization in the late twentieth century.* Barcelona: Paidós Editions.

Jelin, Elizabeth. 2007. "Public memorialization in perspective: truth, justice and memory of past repression in the Southern Cone of South America." *International Journal of Transitional Justice* 1 (1): 138–56.

Kim, Hunjoon and Sikkink, Kathryn. 2010. "Explaining the deterrence effect of human rights prosecutions." *International Studies Quarterly* 54(4): 939–63.

Kritz, Neil, ed. 1995. *Transitional Justice: How Emerging Democracies Reckon with Former Regimes.* Washington, DC: United States Institute of Peace.

Laplante, Lisa J. 2007. "Women as political participants: Peru's approach to psychosocial post-conflict recovery." *Peace and Conflict: Journal of Peace Psychology* 13, 313.

Laplante, Lisa. 2009. "Outlawing amnesty: the return of criminal justice in transitional justice schemes." *Virginia Journal of International Law* 49: 8–26.

Lessa, Francesca, Olsen, Tricia, Payne, Leigh, Pereira, Gabriel, and Reiter, Andrew. 2014. "Overcoming impunity: pathways to accountability in Latin America." *The International Journal of Transitional Justice* 8(1): 75–98.

Linz, Juan and Stepan, Alfred. 1996. *Problems of Democratic Transition and Consolidation: Southern Europe, South America, and Post-Communist Europe.* Baltimore: Johns Hopkins University Press.

Lutz, Ellen and Sikkink, Kathryn. 2001. "The justice cascade: the evolution and impact of foreign human rights trials in Latin America." *Chicago Journal of International Law* 2 (1): 1–34.

Martínez Barahona, Elena, Gutiérrez Salazar, Martha, Liliana y Rincón Fonseca, Liliana. 2012. "De la locura a la esperanza: ¿Nunca más? Impunity in El Salvador and Guatemala." *América Latina Hoy* 61: 101–36.

Martínez Barahona y Gutiérrez (forthcoming). "Impact of the IAHRS in the fight against impunity for past crimes in El Salvador and Guatemala." In *Beyond Compliance: Assessing the Impact of the Inter-American Human Rights System,* edited by Par Engstrom.

Meertens, Donny and Zambrano, Margarita. 2010. "Citizenship deferred: the politics of victimhood, land restitution and gender justice in the Colombian (post?) conflict." *International Journal of Transitional Justice,* 4(2): 189–206.

Nussio, Enzo, Rettberg, Angelika, and Ugarriza, Juan E. 2015. "Victims, nonvictims and their opinions on transitional justice: findings from the Colombian case." *International Journal of Transitional Justice* 9(2): 336–54.

Mutua, Makau. 2015. "What is the future of transitional justice?" *International Journal of Transitional Justice* 9: 1–9.

Nelson, Diane. 2009. *Reckoning: The Ends of War in Guatemala.* Duke University Press.

O'Donnell, Guillermo and Schmitter, Phillipe. 1986. *Transitions from Authoritarian Rule. Tentative Conclusions about Uncertain Democracies.* Buenos Aires: Paidós.

Olsen, Tricia, Payne, Leigh, and Reiter, Andrew. 2010. *Transitional Justice in Balance: Comparing Processes, Weighing Efficacy.* Washington, DC: United States Institute of Peace Press.

O'Rourke, Catherine. 2012. "Transitioning to what? Transitional justice and gendered citizenship in Chile and Colombia." In *Gender in Transitional Justice,* edited by S. Buckley-Zistel and R. Stanley, 136–60. New York and London: Palgrave Macmillan.

Payne, Leigh, Abrão, Paulo, and Torelly, Marcelo, eds. 2011. *A Anistia na Era da Responsabilização: O Brasil em Perspectiva Internacional e Comparada.* Oxford: Oxford University, Latin American Centre.

Paz y Paz Bailey, Claudia. 2006. "Guatemala: gender and reparations for human rights violations." In *What Happened to the Women? Gender and Reparations for Human Rights Violations,* edited by R. Rubio-Marin, 101–03. New York, NY: Social Science Research Council.

Popkin, Margaret and Roht-Arriaza, Naomi. 1995. "Truth as justice: investigatory commissions in Latin America." *Law and Social Inquiry* 20(1): 79–116.

Popkin, Margaret and Bhuta, Nehal. 1999. "Latin American amnesties in comparative perspective: can the past be buried?" *Ethics and International Affairs* 13: 99–122.

Robben, Antonius. 2000. "The assault on basic trust: disappearance, protest, and reburial in Argentina." In *Cultures under Siege, Collective Violence and Trauma,* edited by Antonius Robben and Marcelo M. Suárez-Orozco, 70–101. Cambridge: Cambridge University Press.

Rosser, Emily. 2007. "Depoliticised speech and sexed visibility: women, gender and sexual violence in the 1999 Guatemalan Comisión para el Esclarecimiento Histórico Report." *International Journal of Transitional Justice* 1(3): 391–410.

Salazar, Katya, and Antkowiak, Thomas. 2007. *Victims Unsilenced: The Inter-American Human Rights System and Transitional Justice in Latin America.* Washington, DC: Due Process of Law Foundation.

Sandoval, Clara. 2008. "The challenge of impunity in Peru: the significance of the Inter-American Court of Human Rights." *University of Essex Research Repository* 5 (1): 1–20.

Sikkink, Kathryn. 2011. "El efecto disuasivo de los juicios por derechos humanos." *Anuario de Derechos Humanos* 7: 41–61.

Sikkink, Kathryn y Booth Walling, Carrie. 2007. "The justice cascade and the impact of human rights trials in Latin America." *Journal of Peace Research* 44(4): 427–45.

Skaar, Elin. 2011. *Judicial Independence and Human Rights in Latin America: Violations, Politics, and Prosecution.* New York: Palgrave Macmillan.

Skaar, Elin; García-Godos, Jemima, and Collins, Cath, eds. 2016. *Transitional Justice in Latin America. The Uneven Road from Impunity towards Accountability.* New York: Routledge.

Smulovitz, Catalina. 2013. "The past is never dead: accountability and justice for past human rights violations in Argentina." In *After Oppression. Transitional Justice in Latin America and Eastern Europe*, 64–85. UN.

Snyder, Jack and Vinjamuri, Leslie. 2003. "Trials and errors: principle and pragmatism in strategies of international justice." *International Security,* 28(3): 5–44.

Teitel, Ruti. 1995. "How are the new democracies of the Southern Cone dealing with the legacy of past human rights abuses?" In *Transitional Justice: How Emerging Democracies Reckon with Former Regimes: General Considerations*, edited by Neil Kritz, 146–53. Washington, DC: United States Institute of Peace Press.

Teitel, Ruti. G. 2003. "Transitional justice genealogy." *Harvard Human Rights Journal* 16: 69–94.

Theidon, Kimberly. 2006. "Justice in transition: the micropolitics of reconciliation in post-war Peru." *Journal of Conflict Resolution,* 50(3): 433–57.

Theidon, Kimberly. 2007. "Género en transición: sentido común, mujeres y guerra." *Análisis Político* 60: 3–30.

Theidon, Kimberly. 2009. "Reconstructing masculinities: the disarmament, demobilization, and reintegration of former combatants in Colombia." *Human Rights Quarterly* 31: 1–34.

Theidon, Kimberly. 2012. *Intimate Enemies: Violence and Reconciliation in Peru*. Philadelphia: University of Pennsylvania Press.

Theidon, Kimberly, and Betancourt, Paola. 2006. "Transiciones conflictivas: combatientes desmovilizados en Colombia." *Análisis Político* 58: 92–111.

Thoms, Oskar; Ron, James and Paris, Ronald. 2010. "State-level effects of transitional justice: What do we know?" *International Journal of Transitional Justice* 4(3): 329–54.

Uprimny, Rodrigo; Sánchez Duque, Luz Maria, and Sánchez León, Nelson Camilo. 2014. *Justicia Para la Paz. Crímenes Atroces, Derecho a la Justicia y Paz Negoaciada*. Bogotá: Centro de Estudios de Derecho, Justicia y Sociedad, DeJusticia.

Valji, Nahala. 2006. *Truth Commissions and Gender: Principles, Policies and Procedures*, New York: ICTJ.

Vera Lugo, Juan Pablo. 2015. "Memorias emergentes: las consecuencias inesperadas de la Ley de Justicia y Paz en Colombia (2005–2011)." *Estudios Socio-Jurídicos* 17(2): 13–33.

Viaene, Lieselotte. 2013. "La relevancia local de procesos de justicia transicional. Voces de sobrevivientes indígenas sobre justicia y reconciliación en Guatemala posconflicto." *Antípoda: Revista de Antropología y Arqueología* 16: 85–112.

PART IV

Emergent Topics

25

URBAN REGULATION AND THE LATIN AMERICAN CITY

Rodrigo Meneses Reyes

Urban regulation represents a complex set of rules, institutions, and procedures under which two different and often contradictory processes, planning, and change, may take place. Yet, in many Latin American countries where seven of every ten inhabitants work in the informal economy and one-third of urban residences are irregular in different levels (Davis 2012; Fernandes 2011) one question any socio-legal scholar should ask herself is: What is and has been the role of law in naming, ruling, and processing such diversity of social relations? This chapter aims to offer a preliminary and tentative answer to that question by illustrating how both, social and legal scholars, have understood the role of law in the configuration of the urban space in Latin America.

As Azuela stated more than 20 years ago (1991), for most of the scholars analyzing the relationship between law and the cities in Latin America, "the legal" has represented a normative standard through which it is possible to illustrate the gap between the plans to regulate the conformation and development of the urban landscape, and the everyday life of the cities. In other words, it seems that the legal/illegal dimensions of the social life have been used as a qualitative marker applied to indiscriminately characterize different forms of using, living, and lodging the urban space that, although popular, may not be concordant with what a series of legal actors have considered as necessary to constitute an ideal city.

As a consequence, a characteristic of this debate is the deep interest generated by the role of law in regulating a set of social practices deployed by the urban poor, like the irregular occupation of land or the use of the public space for survival purposes. The analysis of those practices is "often accompanied by moral outrage denouncing the terrible living conditions and uncontrolled [illegality] in giant 'megacities' that are said to be 'out of control'" (Angotti 2013).

However, when seen closely, it seems that these practices have not only constituted highly regulated contexts of interaction between the state and the urban poor, thereby challenging their presumed illegal character, but have also demonstrated that the law is more than a simple instrument of class oppression, or a social means, which may be mobilized by a particular social group in order to achieve a particular interest, as some political scientists have suggested. Indeed, most of these practices have constituted specific conflictive relations, which have contributed to develop comprehensive regulatory regimes as well as an extensive reflection on how to accommodate different interests, needs, and rights within the urban realm.

Taking these considerations as a point of departure, this contribution is divided in two main sections. In the first section, I review the existent research about the regulation of the urban residential spaces, in which I highlight the changing and often indeterminate nature of urban property regimes in Latin America. In the second section, I present the works that address the regulation of the streets and I discuss how urban regulation has also assigned specific functions to the public space and particular ways of being there.

Both sections present a similar structure. Each section starts by illustrating the way in which some legal and urban scholars have characterized Latin American cities, their practices and ways of development, as spatial representations of the allegedly weak or inexistent culture of legality experienced in the region. Then, I illustrate how this representation of the urban space has contributed to neglect the fluid, diverse, and sometimes instrumental role played by legal institutions in the configuration of the everyday urban life.

To do so, I have summarized contemporary research on law, space, and urban practices in the region. In particular, I describe how the deplorable housing and living conditions experienced in most Latin American cities have contributed to develop a more nuanced, yet dynamic, representation of the law and the legal system as a particular social field where the legal status of certain urban practices should not be taken for granted.

The Regulation of Urban Residential Spaces

In most Latin American countries, a principal way of accessing housing for the urban poor has been through the occupation of land without having a legal authorization to do so. To illustrate the relevance of this process of urbanization in the constitution of Latin American cities, it suffices to note that in Venezuela, almost 61 percent of the population lives in informal settlements, in Lima, Perú 35 percent, in Rio de Janeiro, Brazil 19 percent, while in Mexico City this type of human settlements has been responsible for at least 65 percent of the urban growth (Connolly 2003; Meneses and Pellissery 2015).

In terms of urban regulation, a primary implication running through this particular way of accessing housing is that a considerable amount of the urban environment has been constructed and developed outside the official rules, institutions, and procedures created by one set of imaginative legal actors in order to organize and distribute the urban space (Azuela 2005). Yet, this way of informal urban developing has also contributed to the unfolding of more imaginative and sometimes controversial legal forms for planning and adapting the legal order to the urban reality. This process has been called "regularization" (Ward 2003) and captures the adaptive capacity of both urban regulation and planning systems to name and simplify social reality. Regularization entails the reconfiguration of the legal status of a particular way of occupying or constructing the urban space, which tended to be out of the legal order, given its lack of legal regulation or its illegal character.

However, despite the diversity of legal and social relations that may be involved in this debate, when analyzing this particular social practice "the default view implicit in government policies, development initiatives and theoretical accounts is premised on a dualistic logic that assumes tenure to reside either entirely inside or completely outside the law" (Van Gelder 2010, 239). In other words, although Latin American cities have been characterized as places located inside or outside the legal order, socio-legal literature has demonstrated that such a characterization is neither adequate nor sufficient to capture the flux and often ambiguous relation that exists between the law and the social practices that have contributed to develop the urban space in the region.

As a matter of fact, irregular human settlements have been defined as a set of places where economic exclusion, territorial stigmas, small misbehaviors, and crime are concentrated, thereby generating a circle of violence and delinquency (Lemaitre 2014; Meneses and Pellissery 2015).

Thus, for instance, some criminological studies have characterized these spatial formations as places where weak informal controls are linked with the presence of crime, since "residents [of these areas] have less access to jobs and less exposure to conventional role model, and relatively few working class and middle class households to serve as buffers against the effects of uneven and poor economic conditions" (Ceccato and Kahn 2007, 1636). Examples of these kinds of places are Brazilian favelas as well as some *barrios pirata* in Colombia, where the everyday interactions between police forces and some criminals who reside in those informal human settlements have served to create a particular social order (Penglase 2008).

Of course, it is difficult to demonstrate that the absence or presence of weak, informal controls may be enough to explain the levels of violence and crime experienced within these irregular settlements. However, what seems important to stress is that in some cases the reaction of the state to "recover" and bring a legal order within these territories have generated more violence (Valenzuela 2013). To a certain extent, this spatial concentration of crime, social disorder, and state intervention has reinforced the illegal character of these human settlements (Azuela 1991).

Despite this, it is important to stress that, formally speaking, not all the residents of these places live there illegally and not all crime in the city occurs within the limits of these human settlements (Meneses and Pellissery 2015). To be sure, while from a legal positivist perspective illegal human settlements are those, which are not legally developed, socio-legal literature has demonstrated that the legal status of these places may vary from illegal or irregular to regularized settlements (Azuela 1989; Van Gelder 2010).

The causes of this illegality may vary from unauthorized land developments to the occupation of land with an alternative or different legal status, such as settlements developed over land originally reserved for agrarian uses or the occupation of environmental reserves – i.e., The Mexican *Ejido* (Assies and Duhau 2009). At the same time, it is important to note that the "illegal" character of these human settlements depends on legislation, which is constantly changing. Thus, for instance, through Latin American cities it is possible to find different moments and initiatives through which the state has tried to regularize these pieces of urban land. In this regard, Bogotá, Caracas, Lima, and Mexico City have been widely explored as specific case studies to show how the legal status of a human development may vary according to the political will and the people's capacity to trade their political support for the legal recognition, or tolerance of their settlements (Castells 1983).

As some authors suggested, in Latin American countries regularization programs follow two main paradigms (Fernandes 2011). The first, involves the narrow legalization of tenure through titling. The second combine legal titling with the upgrading of public services, job creation, and community support structures. Whatever the outcomes and effects these initiatives have had, what is important to note is that it is precisely in this "transformative" aspect of the law that some illegal settlements may be regularized, which is, transformed to some degree in legal pieces of property, thereby challenging the preexistent illegal label some scholars have ascribed to these places.

Moreover, in many cities this transformative character of the law has contributed to constitute another set of social interactions between the state and the urban poor, normally defined as clientelism or patronage, and which broadly speaking consist in the interchange of certain benefits, such as the regularization of a piece of land, in exchange for political support (Azuela and Cruz 1989; Pérez-Perdomo and Nikken 1979).

In other cases, legal transformations in urban property regimes have been also the product of a series of conflict through which the urban poor have mobilized the legal system in their favor. Indeed, there is a growing field of socio-legal studies that seeks to study the process through which the urban poor have been able to invoke and defend their right to have a place to live in the Latin American city, thereby generating particular forms of citizenship (Holston 2008; Fischer 2008; Houtzager 2007; Azuela and Meneses 2014).

This particular form of informal urban development performed by the urban poor has also been labeled as one of the main causes of the environmental degradation experienced in some Latin American cities. However, as Satterthwaite demonstrated (2003) up until now, there is little evidence of urban poverty being a significant contributor to environmental degradation. In fact, irregular human settlements constitute a specific, but not unique, form of informal urban development widely present in Latin American cities. Other forms include the development of exclusive elite districts in natural or environmental reserves (Evans 2002; Azuela and Cosacov 2013) and the existence of gated-communities where the non-residents' access and transportation is illegally restricted (Caldeira 2000). In the first case, this way of urbanizing the space poses several questions about the social aspirations and capacity to access wealthy housing conditions within a green environment on one hand, and the common needs to live in an ecological sustainable city. In the second case, gated-communities have been considered as a material representation of the crisis of public space and urban order in a stratified society, where people isolate themselves in order to avoid crime, secure class reproduction, and gain control over their immediate environment (Álvarez-Rivadulla 2007; Duhau and Giglia 2008).

The gap between these different forms of informal urban development, however, has also contributed to reinforce the character of certain Latin American cities as territories of socio-spatial segregation, where some forms of informal urban development may be tolerated and regularized, while others are in constant risks of being criminalized and punished (Sabatini 2006; Lungo and Baires 2001; Peters and Skop 2007). In other words, what socio-legal literature has demonstrated through these years is that in most Latin American cities:

> there is a continuum of tenure categories ranging in levels of security from pavement dwellers to freehold owners and that policies which involve dramatic transformations from one category to another may distort land markets and expose vulnerable social groups, such as tenants, to eviction.
>
> *(Payne 2001, 415)*

Following this line, different authors have established that legal systems also have contributed to the informal development of Latin American cities in two main ways (Fernandes and Maldonado 2009). First, through the exclusionary land, property rights, and registration legal provisions. It refers, essentially, to the lack of land regulation or high regulatory standards that have supposedly characterized the development of Latin American cities. However, some other scholars have empirically demonstrated that in certain Latin American cities "higher levels of regulation have lower rates of compliance with property laws" (Monkkonen and Ronconi 2013, 1951) thus, suggesting that sometimes the problem is not the absence of rules for governing the city but their lax enforcement.

Second, through flawed planning systems adopted in many large cities (Fernandes and Maldonado 2009). This way refers to the challenges faced by collaborative planning. Here the literature also shows that despite the potential that collaborative planning has had in Latin America as a progressive praxis of social movements and local governance, this form of urban planning has been also mobilized by certain social groups to approve elitists planning laws (Fernandes and Maldonado 2009), thereby suggesting that "better plans, planning processes and redistributive land-market instruments [may also] fail to produce better cities" (Klink and Denaldi 2016, 402).

Finally, although relevant in international discussions on urban regulation and urban planning, the socio-legal study of land use conflicts and neighborhood disputes in the everyday constitution of Latin American cities remain scarce, although some interesting works are available (see Meyer and Bähr 2004; Duhau and Giglia 2008; Levy et al. 2011; Matta 2016).

The Regulation of the Streets

If the development and organization of residential spaces have represented an important regulatory issue in many Latin American cities, the organization and distribution of public spaces does represent another important feature of this process. To be sure, public spaces represent important spaces of socialization in Latin American countries (Low 2000). It is over the streets that many Latin American citizens earn a living, express their commitment with different political causes and spend a considerable amount of time in traveling from their homes to their workplaces.

Indeed, street working represents one of the most visible and documented practices in the Latin American urban realm. From Ciudad Juárez, Mexico (Staudt 1996) to São Paulo Brazil (Cuvi 2016), the default view implicit in governance policies, public opinion, police activities, and theoretical accounts, often conceptualize people using the sidewalk in order to survive as a matter of "micro political" variables for measuring the "health" of the urban environment and its rule of law (Meneses 2011).

This conceptualization of street working activities may be intimately related to its character of urban problem, where the act of surviving on and through the streets, appears as a systemic occupation of the public space that bothers the rest of the users of the streets, presents an obstacle for transit, and promotes the reproduction of other illegal activities, such as crime (Cross 1998; Bromley 2000; Barbosa 2008; Meneses 2011). As such, street working has been conceived as a difficult and normatively puzzling challenge to the state's capacity to manage the public space.

On one hand, it has taken the form of a public problem largely determined by the urban elites who frequently identify street livelihoods as a primary urban issue having implications on traffic and sanitation. Since street workers are not evenly spread across the city, but concentrated in specific locations typically characterized as "hot spots" of pedestrian and vehicular congestion, the argument is that both the number of street workers and levels of congestion are expected to further increase. This type of concentration would then cause traffic accidents, increase the levels of vehicle-generated air pollution and impede police efficiency (Bromley 2000).

On the other hand, street working activities have been considered as those engaged in a more highly disreputable and often illegal set of social practices, where the massive and (il)licit occupation of the public space is seen as the "tip of the iceberg" of a more extensive pattern of illegal behaviors that include tax evasion and the sale of counterfeit goods. This complex set of behavior also contemplates the bribes street workers are often required to pay to police and other law enforcers, as well as the opportunities they provide for pick-pocketing, snatched thefts, or armed assaults (Meneses 2014; Cuvi 2016).

In sum they represent:

> a set of less visible but more common practices [than crime] that citizens participate in is the daily noncompliance with the law […] practices that, in a much more extended manner, promote distrust and, further, promote their own acceptance, generating better conditions for illegality.
>
> *(Pérez 2008)*

399

Yet, again, a closer observation to this urban practice suggests that this conceptualization of street working activities appears as an oversimplification of the role of law in addressing these urban issues.

Indeed, through Latin American cities urban authorities have been publicly encouraged to design and enforce different regulatory strategies in order to govern the streets. In some cases, these strategies include the massive mobilization of police authorities against street workers, an attitude that has been analyzed by some scholars as an example of how neoliberal politics have increasingly criminalized and punished urban poverty (Müller 2013).

In other cases, these initiatives have included the relocation of street workers, provision of closed public spaces (plazas and public markets), the recognition of street working as a legal and legitimate activity and even the introduction of a highly specific set of rules for organizing the times and places in which street working may take place (Donovan 2008; Bromley and Mackie 2009; Meneses 2011; Cuvi 2016).

These actions are founded on the conviction that street level economic activities can be effectively controlled by deterring its most visible forms and keeping them out of certain locations, such as historic places or business districts. However, in other cases, such as in Mexico, Colombia, or Brazil, the regulation of street working activities has been also the product of the way in which street workers themselves have invoked and mobilized their right to work in judicial scenarios, thereby contributing to develop a regulatory regime that administrates this right in the urban environment (Donovan 2008; Meneses 2011; Meneses 2014; Cuvi 2016).

Consequently, urban authorities have designed and deployed several laws, ordinances, and legal enforcement strategies to regulate the commercial and labor uses of the streets in order to publicly show their power or disposition to enforce the law and improve the urban order (Cross 1998; Barbosa 2008). Yet, in some other cases, these legal initiatives have had more general targets, such as changing entirely the way in which the urban population uses the public space.

Thus, for instance, it has been recently documented how some Latin American urban authorities have observed the regulation of the public spaces a totalizing solution to the problems experienced in their cities. Such has been the case of Mexico City, regarding insecurity issues (Davis 2007; Meneses 2013a) as well as the case of Bogotá, where authorities have introduced a new mode of planning focused on education and reform in order "to produce new social and cultural norms leading to the (re)formation of civil society" (Berney 2011) and, which has been denominated pedagogical urbanism.

In both cases, however, these initiatives have been based on restricting the uses of the streets and an intense scrutiny of public behavior, which have resulted in the construction of a particular version of the public space that "at once depoliticizes the claims to public space of subjects such as street vendors and the homeless and claims a new role for the middle class in the city" (Galvis 2014).

Examples of this process of reconfiguration of the Latin American public space include the introduction of legal stipulations based on the "broken-windows" model (Campesi 2010; Davis 2007; Meneses 2013b), the introduction of new technologies to govern the city (such as parking meters) (Leal 2016) and the enactment of highly differentiated public spaces where buses and bicycles move around the city through segregated transport facilities (Cervero et al. 2009; Torres et al. 2013; Meneses 2015). Yet, it is perhaps in the regulation of social protest that has become more evident how the capacity of the state to differentiate the uses of the public space can affect the way in which people express and travel through the city.

As some authors have established, for several decades the streets of Latin American cities have served as a means to express and manifest people's dissatisfaction with governments' policies and decisions (Eckstein 2001). In most cases, this form of protest has been protected under the people's constitutional freedoms of expression and association. However, in recent years, urban authorities have enacted different rules in the region in order to establish "protest permit systems," which have tried to shape the places and times in which protests may take place. Yet, despite this regulatory shift, empirical research on the effects and targets of this process in the region remain unexplored.

Conclusions

This contribution aimed to answer what is and has been the role of law in naming, ruling, and processing such diversity of social relations. This chapter offered a preliminary and tentative answer to that question by illustrating how both social and legal scholars, have understood the role of law in the configuration of the urban space in Latin America. In particular, it has been shown that the allegedly informal character of cities in the region could not be explained, at least in part, without taking law seriously. Within this promising present, however, future research is still needed on the importance of urban conflict in shaping Latin American legal systems as well as on the effects that new regulatory shifts and practices are generating over the peoples' right to the city.

An important socio-legal consequence of this regulatory distribution of the urban space has been the constitution of the Latin American urban space as neither an inherently stable nor static environment "since it represents the regularities of past interactions, which are modified by new ones: it is a continually evolving, adaptive process [where] norms are taken into account, but do not necessarily determine behavior in the relationships" that take place on the city (Hill 1974, 231). In sum, the narrative before exposed shows that, through urban regulation, both the population and the authorities, have constantly (re)imagined the actual and legal environment of the city and its physical elements in several different ways. Throughout its enactment and enforcement, it has transformed some of the designated functions of the urban realm into new ones, thereby shaping and reshaping the legal limits of Latin American urban space.

References

Angotti, Tom. 2013. Urban Latin America: violence, enclaves, and struggles for land. *Latin America Perspectives*, 40: 5–20.

Álvarez-Rivadulla, María José. 2007. Golden ghettos: gated communities and class residential segregation in Montevideo, Uruguay. *Environment and Planning A*, 39(1), 47–63.

Assies, Willem and Emilio Duhau. 2009. "Land tenure and tenure regimes in Mexico: an overview." In J. Ubink, A. Hoekema, and W. Assies. Amsterdam (Coords.). *Legalising Land Rights. Local Practices, State Responses and Tenure Security in Africa, Asia and Latin America*. 355–85. Leiden: Leiden University Press.

Azuela, Antonio. 1989. *La ciudad, la propiedad privada y el derecho/por Antonio Azuela de la Cueva* (No. 341.5 A9).

Azuela, Antonio. 1991. "La sociología Jurídica frente a la urbanización en América Latina: Agenda y estrategias para la investigación." In *Sociología Jurídica en América Latina*, 147–74. Instituto Internacional de Sociología Jurídica de Oñati: The Oñati International Institute for the Sociology of Law.

Azuela, Antonio. 2005. "Mexico City: the city and its law in eight episodes." In Andreas Philippopoulos-Mihalopoulos (Ed.) *Law and the City*. New York and London: Routledge.

Azuela, Antonio and María Soledad Cruz. 1989. "La institucionalización de las colonias populares y la política urbana en la Ciudad de México (1940–1946)." *Sociológica*, 4: 111–34.

Azuela, Antonio and Natalia Cosacov. 2013. "Transformaciones urbanas y reivindicaciones ambientales. En torno a la productividad social del conflicto por la construcción de edificios en la Ciudad de Buenos Aires." *EURE* 39: 149–72.

Azuela, Antonio and Rodrigo Meneses. 2014. "The everyday formation of the urban space." In I. Braverman, N. Blomley, D. Delaney, and A. Kedar (Eds.). *The expanding spaces of law: A timely legal geography.* Stanford: Stanford University Press.

Barbosa, Mario. 2008. *El Trabajo en las Calles: Subsistencia y Negociación Política en la Ciudad de México a Comienzos del Siglo XX.* Colegio De Mexico AC.

Berney, Rachel. 2011. Pedagogical urbanism: creating citizen space in Bogotá, Colombia. *Planning theory,* 10(1): 16–34.

Bromley, Ray. 2000. Street vending and public policy: a global review. *International Journal of Sociology and Social Policy,* 20(1/2): 1–28.

Bromley, Rosemary and Peter Mackie. 2009. Displacement and the new spaces for informal trade in the Latin American city centre. *Urban Studies,* 46(7): 1485–1506.

Caldeira, Teresa. 2000. *City of Walls: Crime, Segregation, and Citizenship in São Paulo.* California: University of California Press.

Campesi, Giuseppe. 2010. Policing, urban poverty and insecurity in Latin America: the case of Mexico City and Buenos Aires. *Theoretical Criminology,* 14(4): 447–71.

Ceccato, Vânia, Robert Haining, and Tulio Kahn. 2007. The geography of homicide in São Paulo. *Brazil Environment and Planning A,* July 2007 39: 1632–53, doi:10.1068/a38283

Cervero, Robert, Olga Sarmiento, Enrique Jacoby, Luis Fernando Gómez, and Andrea Neiman. 2009. Influences of built environments on walking and cycling: lessons from Bogotá. *International Journal of Sustainable Transportation,* 3(4): 203–26.

Connolly, Priscilla. 2003. *Urban Slums Reports: The Case of Mexico City.* Mexico, Universidad Autónoma Metropolitana-Azcapotzalco: Mexico City. 30.

Cross, John. 1998. *Informal Politics: Street Vendors and the State in Mexico City.* Stanford: Stanford University Press.

Cuvi, Jacinto. 2016. The politics of field destruction and the survival of São Paulo's street vendors. *Social Problems,* 63(3): 395–412.

Davis, Diane. 2007. El factor Giuliani: delincuenda, la "cero tolerancia" en el trabajo policiaco y la transformación de la esfera pública en el centro de la ciudad de México. *Estudios sociológicos,* 639–81.

Davis, Diane. 2012. "Analytical foundations for the study of informality: a short introduction." In Felipe de Alba and Frederic Lesemann (Eds.) *Informalidad, Incertidumbre, Metrópolis y Estado: Como Gobernar la Informalización?* Coedition PUEC-UNAM, INRS and Collegium de Lyon (EURIAS).

Donovan, Michael. 2008. Informal cities and the contestation of public space: the case of Bogotá's street vendors, 1988–2003. *Urban Studies,* 45(1): 29–51.

Duhau, Emilio and Ángela Giglia. 2008. *Las Reglas del Desorden: Habitar la Metrópoli.* Siglo XXI.

Eckstein, S. (Ed.). (2001). *Poder y Protesta Popular: Movimientos Sociales Latinoamericanos.* Siglo XXI.

Evans, Peter. 2002. *Livable cities? Urban Struggles for Livelihood and Sustainability.* California: University of California Press.

Fernandes, Edesio and María Mercedes Maldonado. 2009. Law and land policy in shifting paradigms and possibilities for action. *Land Lines,* 19(4): 14–19.

Fernandes, Edesio. 2011. *Regularization of Informal Settlements in Latin America.* USA: Lincoln Institute of Land Policy.

Fischer, Brodwyn. 2008. *A Poverty of Rights: Citizenship and Inequality in Twentieth-Century Rio de Janeiro.* Standford: Stanford University Press.

Galvis, Juan Pablo. 2014. Remaking equality: community governance and the politics of exclusion in Bogotá's public spaces. *International Journal of Urban and Regional Research,* 38(4): 1458–75.

Hill, S. 1974. Norms, groups and power: the sociology of workplace industrial relations. *British Journal of Industrial Relations,* 12(2), 213–35.

Holston, James. 2008. *Insurgent Citizenship: Disjunctions of Democracy and Modernity in Brazil.* Princeton: Princeton University Press.

Houtzager, Peter. 2005. The movement of the landless (MST), juridical field, and legal change in Brazil. *Law and Globalization from Below: Towards a Cosmopolitan Legality,* 218–40.

Klink, Jeroen and Rosana Denaldi. 2016. On urban reform, rights and planning challenges in the Brazilian metropolis. *Planning and Development,* 15(4): 402–17.

Leal, Alejandra. 2016. "You cannot be here": the urban poor and the specter of the Indian in neoliberal Mexico City. *The Journal of Latin American and Caribbean Anthropology,* 539–59.

Lemaitre, Julieta. 2014. "Constitution or barbarism? How to rethink law in 'lawless' spaces." In César Rodríguez (ed.) *Law and Society in Latin America: A New Map.* New York and London: Routledge.

Levy, Lidia, Eva Gertrudes Jonathan, Luis Gustavo Grandinetti Castanho de Carvalho, and Humberto Dalla. 2011. Mal-estar contemporâneo e conflitos entre vizinhos. *Revista Mal-estar E Subjetividade,* XI(3): 1125–42.

Low, Setha. 2000. *On the Plaza.* Austin: University of Texas.

Lungo, Mario and Sonia Baires. 2001. "Socio-spatial segregation and urban land regulation in Latin American cities." In *International Seminar on Segregation in the City,* Cambridge, MA, USA.

Matta, Juan. 2016. Entre vecinos eso no se hace. Sentidos de justicia y de vecindad en el marco de un dispositivo institucional de administración de conflictos. *Antípoda. Revista de Antropología y Arqueología,* 24: 55–71.

Meneses, Rodrigo. 2011. *Legalidades Públicas: El Derecho, el Ambulantaje y las Calles en el Centro de la Ciudad de México (1930–2010).* Universidad Nacional Autónoma de México, Instituto de Investigaciones Jurídicas.

Meneses, Rodrigo. 2013a. Crime, street vendors and the historical Downtown in post-Giuliani Mexico City. *International Journal of Criminology and Sociology,* 2: 186.

Meneses, Rodrigo. 2013b. Out of place, still in motion shaping (im) mobility through urban regulation. *Social and Legal Studies,* 22(3): 335–56.

Meneses, Rodrigo. 2014. Ambulantaje en la ciudad de México y la justicia federal. *Estudios Sociológicos de El Colegio de México,* 32(94): 73–102.

Meneses, Rodrigo. 2015. Law and mobility: ethnographical accounts of the regulation of the segregated cycle facilities in Mexico City. *Mobilities* 10(2): 230–48.

Meneses, Rodrigo and Sony Pellissery. 2015 "Slums." In Mehmet Odekon (Ed.) *The SAGE Encyclopedia of World Poverty.* SAGE.

Meyer, Kerstin and Jürgen Bähr. 2014. La difusión de condominios en las metrópolis latinoamericanas. *Revista de Geografía Norte Grande,* 32: 39–53.

Monkkonen, Pavo and Lucas Ronconi. 2013. Land use regulations, compliance and land markets in Argentina. *Urban Studies,* 50(10): 1951–69.

Müller, Markus. 2013. Penal statecraft in the Latin American City assessing Mexico City's punitive urban democracy. *Social and Legal Studies* 22(4): 441–63.

Payne, Geoffrey. 2001. Urban land tenure policy options: Titles or rights? *Habitat International,* 25(3): 415–29.

Penglase, B. 2008. The bastard child of the dictatorship: the Comando Vermelho and the birth of "narco-culture" in Rio de Janeiro. *Luso-Brazilian Review,* 45(1), 118–45.

Pérez, Catalina. 2008. Distrust and disobedience: discourse and practice of law in Mexico. *Rev. Jur. UPR,* 77:345.

Pérez-Perdomo, Rogelio and Pedro Nikken. 1979. *Derecho y Propiedad de la Vivienda en los Barrios de Caracas.* Fondo de Cultura Económica y Universidad Central de Venezuela Caracas.

Peters, Paul and Emily Skop. 2007. Socio-spatial segregation in metropolitan Lima, Peru. *Journal of Latin American Geography,* 6(1): 149–71.

Sabatini, Francisco. 2006. *The Social Spatial Segregation in the Cities of Latin America.* Washington, DC: Inter-American Development Bank.

Satterthwaite, David. 2003. The links between poverty and the environment in urban areas of Africa, Asia, and Latin America. *The ANNALS of the American Academy of Political and Social Science,* 590(1): 73–92.

Staudt, Kathleen. 1996. Struggles in urban space street vendors in El Paso and Ciudad Juárez. *Urban Affairs Review,* 31(4): 435–54.

Torres, A. et al., 2013. The Ciclovia and Cicloruta programs: promising interventions to promote physical activity and social capital in Bogotá, Colombia. *American Journal of Public Health,* 103(2): e23–30.

Valenzuela, Alfonso. 2013. Urban surges power, territory, and the social control of space in Latin America. *Latin American Perspectives,* 40(2): 21–34.

Van Gelder, Jean-Louis. 2010. Tales of deviance and control: on space, rules, and law in squatter settlements. *Law and Society Review,* 44(2): 239–68.

Ward, P. 2003. "Regularization in Latin America: lessons in the social construction of public policy." In G. Jones (Ed.) *Urban Land Markets in Transition,* Cambridge, MA: Lincoln Institute of Land Policy (CDRom).

26

LANDSCAPES OF PROPERTY

Socio-Legal Perspectives from Latin America

Tatiana Alfonso

Property is a crucial institution to understand the distribution of goods in society and even though most socio-legal scholars would agree on such a statement, the law and society field in Latin America has approached the analysis of property on a fragmented manner. Despite this tendency, property is one of those classic legal institutions in which Latin American scholars have responded to specific social phenomena with novel and important theoretical and methodological contributions. Categories such as informality or plurality in property rights are clear contributions from the region that, consistent with the ides of law in action, have enhanced our theoretical understanding of how legal institutions work on the ground, shaping and responding to different social orders.[1] The term and frame "property rights" have been associated for a long time with the liberal idea of the law and the state that privileges Western conceptions of ownership within a free market logic and low levels of state intervention. Latin American socio-legal scholarship has been instrumental in expanding such framework of property rights to more inclusive and alternative forms of ownership and possession of resources, drawing the lines for a promising and productive research area in the field.

This chapter maps the socio-legal literature on property, approaching the legal institution as a mean and as an end. The latter aims to understand how the institution itself has been treated in the field and what theoretical and methodological contributions to the understanding of property have come from Latin America. The perspective of property as means aims to map the trajectory of the interaction between typical legal doctrine with works grounded in a "law in action" perspective. This type of analysis goes beyond the normative features of an institution and seeks to explain the relation between law and society, through a classic site of interest in the legal field. The study of particular institutions that are central to many Western societies turn to be good sites to map the shifts within an academic field; in this case, the analysis of how property has been studied in socio-legal scholarship elucidates a historical trajectory of debates about how law and society are related and how we should study such relation.[2]

The study of property in Latin America came out of the traditional law school room toward the social laboratory of law and society scholars a long time ago, and the region has contributed with at least four lines of research and theory about how property works in society. This chapter classifies the socio-legal literature on property in the region in four landscapes: the discussions about property and development; the binary formal versus informal property rights; legal pluralism on property rights; and the liminality of property in a globalized age. The first question, originally devised as a law and development question have led to a conversation about institutional reforms for economic – and more recently – social development. The second set of questions addressed the urbanization process of Latin American cities that – in a classic framing of law and society in the region – was disorganized and marked by a significant gap between property rights in the books and property on the ground. This line of research has established a solid conversation with urban studies, urban planning, and more recently with discussions about the "right to the city." The third type of question that was – at least in part – a reaction to the explanation of urbanization in binary terms, argues that the Latin American context should not be explained from the formality/informality duo but from the idea of plurality of legal forms that results from the interaction between legal and social conditions. This line of works has built up their arguments on the idea of property as legal knowledge and it is a critical perspective of the law as an instrument for social change. The fourth set of questions – still scarce in the Latin American context – tackle the issue of property rights over intellectual goods in a globalized age. The chapter also includes a fifth line in which property is barely mentioned and does not stand alone, but it is in the margins of all the debates: territorial rights of indigenous and tribal peoples in Latin America.

The chapter adopts this organization in order to show that, the debates around a traditional legal institution departed from basic "law and society" ideas – such as law in action and rights as tools for change – but as time has passed by, every line of research has developed new theoretical and conceptual frameworks, paving the road to new dialogs and consequently, landing in very diverse theoretical arenas. As the chapter shows the fragmented character of the discussion about property in society, it proposes future and promising research lines that integrate some of the debates of the literature for understanding what I call configurations of property in the region. In doing so, the chapter also advocates for an integrated socio-legal understanding of property rights and their constitutive role in social relations.

I organize the literature in sets of research questions for two reasons. The first one is that the study of property or any legal institution as lenses for society or social problems is particularly complex in terms of disciplines. Many disciplines have paid attention to property, as an object of study and as a variable for their own questions; for example, in politics and political science, property has been treated as a variable to understand political processes as rural mobilization or democratic consolidation (Albertus 2015a, 2015b; Gutiérrez Sanín 2010; Saffon 2015); in sociology, property has been understood as a set of relations (Benda-Beckman Von, Benda-Beckman Von, and Eckert 2009), and the result of social struggles (Reyes 2009), in institutional economics as a group of formal and informal norms that shape behavior (North 1990; Ostrom 2005; Cárdenas 2010), and in anthropology as a type of language and knowledge (Riles 2004). Such diversity requires addressing common concerns rather than disciplinary debates.

Second, the organization of the literature in research questions allowed me to highlight the contributions in the field that have come from the study of Latin American contexts. That is the case for example, of the existence of the social clause in national constitutions in Latin America, the binary between formality and informality as one of the main explanations of property rights, the idea of plurality of property relations, and all the contributions on territorial rights. The weakness of this organization is of course, that it is not possible to draw an integrated chronological narrative of different types of research on the topic. This shortfall, however, seems to be a feature of any field of study, which never responds to organized and linear patterns in time.

Introduction

Very often when legal scholars and social scientists talk about property, the audience – regardless of the political and ideological position – tend to think of private property of individuals, the classic liberal idea of full ownership that imposes restrictions for the state to intervene, and market transactions that produce economic gains for some and dispossession for others. The liberal idea of property in law, politics, and economics was built upon Locke's basic definition of property as a basic and fundamental individual liberty, which purpose is to satisfy individual preferences and serve as a commodity for a market exchange.[3]

Legal scholars, however, have debated for decades what are and should be the contours of property and whether it should be understood as a right, as a relation (Singer 2000), or more recently as constellations of relations (Benda-Beckman Von, Benda-Beckman Von, and Eckert 2009). Most of the legal approaches, though, do not support their arguments on systematic empirical data of how property rights work on the ground. Socio-legal scholarship on the other hand, has contributed with this perspective and has come to fill the empirical lagoon that normative approaches have left and through that approach, has contributed to expand the liberal conception of property.

The First Landscape: Law, Development, and Property Rights

The relation between property and development has a long and multifaceted history. Economists and political scientists have agreed that individual property is a necessary condition for economic development because property rights matter for wealth distribution in a society (Cole 2014; Cole and Grossman 2002). According to the economists, effective and clear property rights matter for development and for the stability of transactions (De Soto 2000). Development economics has devoted special attention to formalization of property rights in developing countries as a tool for improving economic conditions (Galiani and Schargrodsky 2010; Peña et al. 2016).[4] All these approaches, while empirically grounded, rarely unpack what property means in terms of rights and tend to operate under the assumption that most of the times, the legal aspect of property – except for legal title – is not definitive to understand paths for development (Easterly 2013).

On the contrary, in the socio-legal field this question was first tackled by the law and development movement that believed in the centrality of the law for promoting economic development (Trubek and Galanter 1974; Mota Prado 2016; Tamanaha 2011). The law and development movement emerged in the 1960s and aimed not only to answer the question about how legal institutions influence economic development, but pursued a policy agenda in which law was the basic tool to engineer the social and economic change that was necessary to achieve the goals of development in poor countries (Trubek et al. 2013). As the founders of the law and development movement have widely recognized, the movement's ideals and goals were based on a liberal legalism that failed because it was ethnocentric and overstated the role of law in society (Trubek 1990; Trubek and Galanter 1974).

For the first wave of law and development, the state should be the actor pushing for legal reforms and economic transformation. Following that idea and echoing the peak of agrarian reforms in Latin America, some scholars worked on research and policy proposals on land and agrarian reforms as tools for economic change (Karst 1968; Thomas 1972).[5] The first wave of the law and development movement believed on legal reform for achieving equality in society but as their basic assumptions were embedded in Western conceptions of the law, property rights – in the context of agrarian reforms in Latin America – were understood as the allocation and redistribution of land on an individual basis and formalization of private property rights. This interest and effort, though, lost its importance as several of the agrarian reforms in the region encountered political obstacles that showed the limits of the law as a tool to promote social change. Conversely, and just as Davis and Trebilcock (2008) have argued for the entire movement, the attempts of understanding social change as the result of legal reform, overlooked the interaction between informal methods of social control and the political obstacles for an effective reform.

The law and development movement faded out rapidly as an academic movement but its agenda remained alive in development agencies and in research on law and economics. These new actors working on the relation between law and development endorsed another type of conception of property rights. For the law and economics scholarship, property rights are central to economic analysis because they provide the basis for market exchanges (Cole and Grossman 2002; Allen 1998) and for development agencies, property rights are part of the package of tools for stabilizing market transactions and securing the transmission of capital and investment (Davis and Trebilcock 2008). Both approaches shared the assumption that effective private property rights facilitate the exchange of goods and create economic growth and that, the allocation of property rights has an impact on efficiency of resources (Cole and Grossman 2002).[6] Also, as development agencies started their work along the lines of the Washington Consensus (Babb 2009), redistribution and inequality were left out of the goals for development and therefore, individual private property became the prototypical institution that had to be enforced and strengthened.

However, Latin American legal scholars have contributed to the expansion of the conception of property, both in socio-legal research and in policy agendas. The first salient contribution has come from legal doctrine and has contended that from a normative point of view, property should be understood from a non-individual perspective and should have a social function that is, to create social good. The *social function of property* is one of the focal points of debate in the Latin American legal academy and politics. The idea of a social function of property emerged in the European doctrine (Duguit 1975, 1969) and exists in the doctrinal discussion in the United States as the social obligation norm (Alexander 2009; Alexander and Peñalver 2012; Alexander 2010). In Latin America, most of the countries included a social clause in their constitutions starting in the 1960s with the peak of agrarian reforms.[7] As a result, Latin American legal scholars have written extensively on the history of when and how the social clause entered the domestic constitutional scenarios in Latin America (Villegas Del Castillo 2012), the meaning of such func-tion in the context of state obligations to ensure rights for all the citizens (Bonilla 2013), the extent to which the clause affects the exercise of property, under what circumstances the duty of owners to comply with the social clause is fulfilled, and the conditions that allow the state to enforce the social clause to impose restrictions to property such as taxation or expropriation (Alviar 2012; Varón et al. 2017). More recently, the content of the social clause has also been revised to incorporate the environmental function (Foster and Bonilla 2013), which is the idea that owners cannot use their property without taking environmental norms into account.

The literature on the social clause has been highly relevant to rethink issues of access to the land for peasants and ethnic groups amid economic and democratic transitions and land struggles across the region (Ondetti 2016). While the academic dialog seems to be confined to the legal field, we can see explicit uses of these ideas on courts' decisions (Antkowiak 2014, 2008)[8] and state policies fueled by development goals. In fact, the revival of the law and development movement in the past 20 years (Trubek and Santos 2013) has created new communication channels between the literature on property rights and development in a new fashion.

New agendas of the contemporary wave of law and development are less centered in liberal conceptions of property and pay more attention to alternative forms of property in rural and urban settings (De Schutter 2011; Grossi 1986), differential paths for granting access to groups traditionally excluded (i.e., women or indigenous peoples' right to land) (Escobar 2008, 1995; Rittich 2005), and a human rights language (Alston and Robinson 2005). This shift in the current line of research goes beyond the linear idea of transplants of Western legal institutions into developing countries that plagued the first generation of law and development and leaves room for considering non-Western conceptions of property rights, in particular, cultural conceptions related to property that stem from the study of Latin American and African contexts. It is also an expression of one of the features of the revival of the law and development movement that has addressed the critique of ethnocentrism of the first law and development wave by paying more attention to the local context (Mota Prado 2016). However, they still respond to the classic assumption of the first law and development movement wave according to which legal institutions are well-suited tools for creating the necessary conditions to achieve the goals of development (Friedman 1986).

The scholarship in this landscape assumes – both explicitly and implicitly – an instrumental role of the law for triggering economic change and development and include elements as gender or traditional forms of property only to the extent that those are "good for development" (World Bank 2001; De Schutter 2011) and creates some links with literature on institutional economics and sociological institutionalism in order to assess the effect of diverse institutional arrangements on development outcomes (Cárdenas 2010; North 1990; Ostrom 1990). The underlying interest on development is probably one of the reasons why the dialog between this type of research and development agencies is so fluid. In fact, most of the people that conduct this type of research are simultaneously academics and consultants for development agencies[9] and they usually include policy recommendations that may stem from rigorous consideration of the legal institution on the ground and its effects in equality, dignity, and development, expanding the conceptual frontier of property.

After several decades of reflection on the relationship between property and development, however, there is not a definitive or conclusive answer. As shown on p. 407, there is a clear expansion of the liberal paradigm of property that grew from the consideration of property rights on the ground in rural areas of developing countries and Latin American social clause. As a result, there are new ways to think about property and redistribution, inequality, and development.

Second Landscape: The Formality – Informality Urban Binary

Socio-legal scholars in Latin America in the 1990s started to call the attention of traditional legal scholars about how property did not properly exist in Latin American realities and the region was in fact, the kingdom of informality. In this line of research, property rights are defined along the binary: formality versus informality (De Soto 2000).

Several scholars in law and society studies have developed this version of Latin American property rights especially in urban settings pointing that the realities of Latin American cities are way too far from the regulation issued by the state for private and public spaces (Azuela 2013, 1991; Azuela and Meneses 2014). This point of departure fueled many studies on how informality in property rights is related to informal urban land markets (Rico 2009), processes of massive and unplanned growth of the cities (Davis 2016, 2006), surplus value, taxation and valuation of city-land with the correspondent social inequality (Azuela 2013) urban poverty and lack of basic goods and services. Some socio-legal works have also looked at the formality and informality of property rights in rural areas, based on the same idea of the distance between what public and private law establishes, and what people actually do in practice with the land (Glenn 2008; Assies 2008).

Although informality in rural settings is one of the big issues in the first landscape described here, there is a professional divide between scholars and literature working on urban settings and rural programs. As a result, the language of property rights change dramatically between the two landscapes as well as the tools that each community use to do research and policy proposals. Whereas in rural settings the question about formality and security of tenure is in the middle of the research questions, in urban studies we find that questions about land use, public goods and services, taxation, and urban marginality, are the most salient ones. A brief description of each of the groups might clarify this point.

The attention in urban settings went from explanations of informal property rights to the use of public spaces and more specifically to the regulation of the streets and housing as versions of public and private property in the city,[10] while research in rural settings started to assess the shifts from public to private tenure and vice versa, as well as the social and historical determinants (Assies 2008). In the first set of works, we find constant reflections on how property, use and occupation of the city space relate to safety, poverty, and exclusion. This literature, although also inspired in the "law on the books versus law in action idea" – or precisely because of that reason – has established a more solid dialog with urban planners and urban policymakers. The community of socio-legal scholars that analyze property-related problems in the city gather around conferences of the right to the city, meetings of planners that aim to organize the growth of the urban areas, and centers that design policies for urban development (for example, the Lincoln Institute for Land Policy). This line of research has a weaker presence in doctrinal academic debates about property, in part, because the technical knowledge and language that urban planning uses, created a new framework in charge of developing new concepts to understand and manage the increasing urbanization of Latin American cities. On the other hand, the great contribution of this dialog between scholars of urban studies and policymakers and planners, is the extraordinary development of tools to understand the difference between property, land-use, and land-value and surplus, as dimensions of how the state may deal with informality and formal rights. In this regard, urban studies of property in Latin America have contributed enormously to unpack what property means normatively and empirically.

Only recently, law and society studies on the right to the city started to engage seriously with a long tradition of urban studies in social science (Azuela and Meneses 2014). Geography and sociology have analyzed for a long time, diverse processes of construction of the space of the city with special attention to segregation patterns (Caldeira 2000); mechanisms and actors that create new spaces in the city – formal and informal – through mobilization and the causal relation between neoliberal policies and the creation of slums (Álvarez Rivadulla 2017; Evans 1995), and the relationship between urbanization and democratization that creates productive contexts for social mobilization and citizenship recognition (Murphy 2015; Holston 2008).This engagement has a great potential as urban planning and the right to the city appropriates knowledge of social processes and effects of the organization of the city as inputs for policies.

In the second group of research – formality and informality in rural contexts – we find the development of concepts as new enclosures, dispossession, privatization, and alternative uses of barren lands. In this area, scholars tend to analyze whether informality is a risk factor for poverty (Fergusson 2013), forced displacement due to extractive projects (Harvey and Varela Mateos 2007), violence or industrialization of economies (Reyes 2009; Gutiérrez Sanín 2010), or state failure. The concepts in this string of research are not even remotely connected to the tools of urban planners but closer to general ideas of rural development, determinants of land tenure, and economic implications of each of the extremes of the binary. This set of works tend to engage in a more productive dialog with actors thinking about development and in those situations, the binary is reframed as a development question.

The debate on formality and informality has always had a clear policy dimension since De Soto published its (in)famous book on the impact of informality on economic growth.

De Soto's advocacy for formalization and titling process in the cities expanded to rural settings and even to collective forms of property (Albright and De Soto 2008), and became extremely popular as a recipe for economic growth and development from a neoliberal perspective. As De Soto's became more famous, critiques to this approach raised at the international level as well as at the domestic one. Under the umbrella of those critiques, fell the general explanation of the opposition between formality and informality of property rights. Socio-legal scholars, in particular, articulated a critique that called for a new understanding of property in developing contexts, which constitutes what I present here as the third landscape, which is the idea of plurality of legal forms.

Third Landscape: It is Not Informality but Different Meanings of Property

Legal scholars working on legal pluralism have contributed to the discussions on property arguing that the Latin American context is not adequately explained from the idea of informality. First, because it reproduces a colonial way of thinking about developing countries in which other social forms of organization are judged with a Western standard of law as the main criteria for social organization. Second, the binary of formality and informality leads to the idea of the informal as illegal and the formal as legal when, in fact, those categories are not equivalent. Third, the continuum between the formal and the informal ignores alternative forms of relation between the individuals and the law. As a response, scholars in this landscape contend that contexts outside of the North are best described and explained if we understand different forms and meanings of property (Rico 2009; Latorre 2015b; Riles 2004).[11]

One of the main contributions of this theoretical framework is the idea that legal institutions, and property are forms of knowledge that individuals acquire and use in their everyday lives to make sense of their experience, to navigate state procedures, and to acquire recognition (Riles 2004; Latorre 2015a). As Sieder explains,[12] this approach requires engaging with anthropological debates on sovereignty and recognition of social forms of organization of indigenous peoples and other subaltern groups. For the specificities of property, that idea would entail to understand better and deeper, alternative forms of land tenure and the cultural spectrum of property.

On the other hand, this research agenda calls for ethnographic accounts of how people construct ideas of property and how they construct property through the interaction and navigation with the state, beyond the idea of property as an asset for market transactions (Latorre 2015b). This landscape ends up establishing a solid dialog with other subfields that assume that law is a constitutive element of social reality and has been very prominent in Latin America as a contendor of linear and liberal accounts and programs to recognize and allocate property rights.

Fourth Landscape: Liminal Space and Institution in the Middle of Economic Globalization

Finally, a short mention to a global trend that has a very specific connotation in Latin America: the movement from typical property rights over material things toward intellectual property rights in a globalized economy. As intellectual property gained relevance in the global legal community, the movement toward a liberal and individual idea of property seemed to start involving communities in Latin America. The increasing importance of intellectual property rights, however, showed the traditional emphasis on market transactions in which, all the contributions and debates about property and development for poor countries seemed irrelevant. Moreover, poor and middle-income countries and communities seemed to be sentenced to lose access to basic and traditional forms of knowledge such as traditional uses of crops, traditional handcraft techniques, and traditional forms of naming products and goods. The global struggle against the so-called privatization of intellectual creations resulted in ideas of free license (as the creative commons platform) and shared knowledge-production systems. The research on this area in Latin America exhibits a rapid growth at analyzing the effects of intellectual property rights on domestic systems of innovation (Villamizar, Castro, and Cano 2008) and the impact of allocation of such type of property over traditional knowledge of indigenous peoples and peasantries (Ibarra 2011). It is the advocates, though, who seem to be engaging the most with these debates from a perspective of plurality of legal forms by overturning the system of intellectual property rights in favor of indigenous communities: in 2016, the Guatemalan National Movement of Maya Weavers proposed a national bill in congress to obtain the collective intellectual property over Maya textile creations – the huipiles. According to the indigenous organization, the cotton dress contains traditional knowledge and without the protection of their right to property, foreigners and outsiders would continue the long theft of their ancestral knowledge. This type of strategy is not only novel because of the argument of traditional knowledge applied to one specific material good but especially because the bill seeks the recognition of property rights for a collective subject. The proposal seeks to fulfill two objectives: recognition of collective intellectual property; and access to the benefits of traditional property law, without resigning to their own forms of knowledge and organization.[13] This type of strategy is becoming more common across the region – for example, the emergent struggle of the *voladores de papantla* in Mexico that are seeking to obtain recognition of their traditional knowledge on a sacred ritual that has become popular and is used by people who do not belong to the community.

This emergent line of activism is bringing back the strongest element of property – the right to exclude others – for the protection of cultural forms and values that liberal conceptions of property never considered.

Collective Territorial Rights as Means for Redistribution Amid Legal Violence Over Property Rights

In sociology, anthropology, and political science there is a shared belief that property is an indicator or proxy for citizenship and state recognition. Research on Latin America, especially after the so-called "multicultural turn," has shown that the legal recognition of property rights for ethnic groups created new forms of citizenship that enhanced political participation and rhetorical inclusion of disadvantaged groups (Yashar 2005; Sieder 2011). During the last two decades of the twentieth century, Latin American countries went through a wave of multicultural reforms that aimed to include indigenous peoples and Afrodescendants in the discourse of the nation and to promote their economic and social inclusion.[14] One of the key elements of the multicultural constitutional wave was the recognition of the right to the land granted in a particular institutional form: *collective property rights*.

As we have seen in the first landscape of socio-legal scholarship, property is usually regarded as a necessary asset to enter into market economies and to overcome poverty; however, since ethnic groups and peasants are still at the bottom of the distribution of every Latin American country, after almost 30 years of the existence of collective property institutions in Latin America, they do not seem to be producing better economic and social results for rural communities. Most collective arrangements over land in Latin America were granted as non-market assets in order to ensure that the traditional disadvantaged groups did not lose the land through a market in which they probably could not compete. As a result, the institutional arrangement for those lands impede people to sell, lease, rent, trade, or parcel out, any portion of the land. Yet, ethnic communities and social organizations in rural areas across the region have suffered several forms of dispossession – via illegal violence as well as dispossession through legal mechanisms.

Despite the dominance of private property as a fundamental right in most of the domestic legal orders in Latin America, this type of land allocation is grounded in a non-liberal conception of property in many ways: it is collective, it is not disposable for market transactions, assume that social organization underlies the material and formal existence of collective property, but also, communities do not have an absolute right to exclude others or the state – as liberal individual private property does. This combination of elements creates a very particular configuration of property rights that constitutes one of the institutional contributions of Latin America to the study of property. At the same time, and as shown in the four landscapes of socio-legal research depicted in this chapter, private property rights are still prevalent in socio-legal thinking and doctrinal debates. Unlike the research on property and development, in this line of research, land is not a commodity and it is not meant to become one. There is no room for informality in this type of collective rights recognition because the states granted land titles and created the administrative procedures to ensure access to it; there is a question of enforcement of the procedures due to the resistance of political and economic elites but it is not an informality issue (Saffon 2010). It is certainly an institutional arrangement that recognizes cultural conceptions and appropriation of property and plural legal forms as it includes traditional legal systems of organization in colonial settings (Mosquera Rosero-Labbé, Laó-Montes, and Rodríguez-Garavito 2010; Sieder 2010). However, the framing that has been used to understand, explain, and advocate for collective land tenure is not property, but territorial rights and ethnic politics. Consequently, the idea of territory has been distant from the idea and debates on property rights – as an academic framework.

In this line of research, we find extensive works on the field of ethnic politics that analyzes the emergence of new political identities and ethnic social movements in Latin America (Álvarez, Dagnino, and Escobar 1998; Asher 2009; Paschel 2010), and the wave of multicultural reforms and ways of inclusion that came along with them (Yashar 2005; Van Cott 2000). Of special interest in the field of identity politics are the works that analyze ethnic-based claims in relationship with processes of state formation, which highlight that political identities are socially constructed, historically contingent, open to change, and institutionally bounded (Yashar 2005; French 2009; Richards 2004). All the discussions of identity politics and the state have contributed to our understanding of why indigenous identities became politically salient and how the articulation of them was particularly important in relation to land rights and claims of collective property (French 2009; Escobar 2008). This trend of research, however, has not explored sufficiently how those processes have resulted – or not – in development outcomes and welfare for ethnic communities. In fact, some scholars have pointed out that the multicultural perspective has often displaced the claim about structural inequalities (Engle 2010; Sieder 2011), and have showed that while multicultural reforms have worked in terms of recognition, they have been accompanied by neoliberal economic policies that have prevented ethnic groups from achieving any sort of redistributive outcome (Hale 2002, 2006; Sieder 2011). Thus, although there has been abundant theoretical work on the emergence of collective property institutions and on the ways in which such institutions are supposed to work, there is not enough empirical research that explores the extent to which those collective property institutional arrangements are working to make rural communities better off. More importantly, all the assertions about collective property rights in this line of research fall short analyzing the variation between institutional designs of collective property regimes and even less research on the diversity of economic and political outcomes of the collective arrangements.

As I argue here, while all the research on territorial rights as forms of recognition is already a Latin American contribution, it might benefit from integrated dialogs with all the landscapes of property that I have described in this chapter. There are some recent attempts to integrate concepts and debates on property rights to the conversation on territorial rights and autonomy of rural communities. In order to present the existent literature and the attempts of bringing together the conceptual frameworks, I use the case of Colombia as a paradigmatic case in which land struggles have been fierce for social organizations and also deeply explored in socio-legal research.[15] As the Colombian case shows, framing of land rights in the rural context has moved closer to the debates on property in the middle of a democratic transition. I close the chapter, showing how this movement between conceptual frames, has important implications for conducting socio-legal research, open important theoretical and empirical questions, and signal promising lines for future research.

Colombia has one of the strongest protections against market dispossession for collective lands in Latin America. Unlike other countries that have dismantled the legal features that protect collective territories from being sold, parceled out, or leased on an individual basis,[16] collective arrangements over land in Colombia are legally excluded from any commercial transaction. However, as law and society research has shown, illegal armed groups and legal commercial actors (Marín Correa 2012; Rodríguez-Garavito, Alfonso Sierra, and Cavelier-Adarve 2008, 2009; Alfonso et al. 2011) have targeted collective lands creating the largest material dispossession in the long-dated armed conflict (Rodríguez-Garavito, Alfonso Sierra, and Cavelier-Adarve 2009). The combination of economic interests (Ojeda 2011) with the increase of extractive projects that came with the new extractive boom in the country (Toro Pérez et al. 2012, Garay Salamanca 2014) and the interests of territorial control of illegal armed actors, have eroded the security of tenure for collective subjects as well as for peasants. In the middle of several transitions, peasants have come to claim territorial rights and ethnic groups have demanded basic protections of private property such as the right to exclusion.

As Colombia started to ride the path of democratic transitions with the demobilization process of paramilitaries in 2005 and the process of reparation of victims in 2011, land struggles jumped to the middle of the stage in public policies. Peasants – with right to individual property and possession of land as well as ethnic groups acquired the possibility to claim the material possession and legal right to property over the land that they have lost during the conflict. The institutional counterpart of those claims, new institutions for land restitution and reparation were created and started to work. For land struggles, the agency for land restitution (Unidad de Restitución de Tierras – URT) took the burden of recovering the land to be restituted to peasants and ethnic groups. In doing so, the URT had to design and pursue judicial actions for the processes of restitution. The general task of restitution implied to consider individual property arrangements as well as collective. For the first ones – mostly peasants that had been officially recognized as victims and demonstrated land losses due to the conflict – the URT had to use the special law on victims and land restitution with a general underlying framework of civil law. For the collective subjects –indigenous and Afrodescendants – the agency had to use the special decrees on victims and land restitution for each ethnic group. Both types of instruments required different legal and social information and such necessity, I argue, was one of the first encounters between property debates and territorial rights. While peasants are usually under the umbrella of civil law in which they have to prove legal possession or individual title – with all the bureaucracy described by Barrera and Latorre in this volume – most ethnic communities have to demonstrate ancestral occupation and use of the land, the limits of their collective title, and the losses in material tenure. That is equivalent to say that peasants must deal with traditional frameworks of property rights that include their right to be formalized and restituted and, once they have access to property, at least in the books they can exclude third parties and organize their economic activities. Ethnic communities, on the other hand, must demonstrate cultural, economic, and material dispossession of their territory without engaging with other formal aspects of property and at the end, even if they recover the land, they do not have the right to exclude third parties from their territory.[17]

The second big encounter between property and territory came with the peace process between the Colombian government and the FARC (Revolutionary Armed Forces of Colombia). The first point of the agreement is the agrarian reform – that Colombia never went through – and it is one of the most important steps for a successful transition regarding the conflict between these two actors. Once the agreement was approved, the Colombian government created new institutions to carry out the rural policies that former agencies never did. The National Land Agency (Agencia Nacional de Tierras – ANT) oversees and executes the distribution of land for landless peasants and ethnic communities, the formalization of legal and legitimate possession for peasants, the expropriation of land to individuals that do not fulfill the social clause of property, and the organization of the information system about land in the country. In order to comply with the legal mandate, the ANT needs to conduct a national cadastral exercise and identify who owns what, who has material possession of land, and who should have legal property rights over land. The procedures for peasants – under a property rights framework – and for ethnic groups – under a territorial perspective – need to be differentiated. However, the language of formalization does not include a comprehensive perspective of the cultural and economic dimension of ethnic territories. Moreover, both types of communities need to construct their territorial organization in harmony with municipal plans that define land use and economic activities. As a result, the state agency needs to start integrating both frameworks to fulfill the promise of land tenure security and rural development. Even if the state agency reconciles the procedures and conceptions for both types of land tenure, the question about rural development needs to be addressed, because different types of property locate subjects in different positions to start working for development outcomes. Those two goals are huge stakes to prevent the repetition of the conflict and they might need to integrate the protection of property rights with the traditional forms of tenure and property.

Scholars conducting law and society research have been useful and instrumental to the policy changes in Colombia by highlighting the problems of defending territorial rights without the respect of basic features of property such as self-determination and the right to exclusion of third parties in the name of the collective. For peasants, scholars have also shown the importance of the right to self-determination when it comes to extractive projects using popular consults (Rodríguez Franco 2016) – as parallel of prior consultation for ethnic groups.

The Colombian context illustrates a shifting conceptual framing from land and territorial rights to debates on property as a response to the involvement of academics and policymakers, with pressing social issues. Land struggles for ethnic communities are getting closer to the defense of a collective private property because of the certainty and the attack on one of the main dimensions of it: the right to exclusion. On the other hand, peasants might find useful the framework of territorial rights as a dimension for their autonomy and own forms of development.

This move, however, poses serious challenges. The defense of territorial rights with a property framing, faces the risk of falling under the liberal impulse to conflate autonomy with market transactions. The neglect of the property framing, though, might expose peasants and ethnic groups to legal entitlements that exist only in the books.

Finally, the Colombian context also illustrates how law and their correspondent conceptual frameworks, mediate between social and economic processes of social outcomes and struggles in society.

Fragmented Landscapes and Empirical Lagoons: Markers for Future Agendas

As I showed in this chapter, debates on property in law and society studies departed from a shared idea of law on the books versus law in action but landed in different types of research, theoretical and policy debates. So many times, it is a matter of framing: while sociologists and other social scientists working on urban problems or rural movements frame the questions in terms of social mobilization, territory, or the right to the city, legal scholars have framed the problem as one of right to private property. This disconnection seems to suggest that the legal lenses are quite narrow to understand why and how property becomes an institution that mediates between social grievances, waves of liberal economic reforms, and access to goods and services that both, disadvantaged and privilege people, demand.

I propose here that the integration of the conversation is useful for theoretical and pragmatic reasons. Besides the brief case that I presented as an example, the dialog between urbanism, zoning and planning, development questions, and strategies to protect those who fight for their survival in urban and rural settings, is a productive encounter for domestic and international research on property. An example of this line of research is the exploration of a regional dimension of property and territorial rights through the lenses of the judgments of the Inter-American Court of Human Rights on indigenous peoples and their right to the land. There is a pending analysis of how the judgments of the regional court may be implemented at the domestic level, depending on the type of property regimes that each country recognizes. As in the Colombian case, configurations of property – understood as different combinations of dimensions of property allow for deeper understandings of how property is shaping identities, distribution, and development.

Notes

1 As we explain in the introduction of this volume, one of the features of law and society scholarship in Latin America is the combination of academic production with activism and advocacy of a significant number of socio-legal scholars. Property rights, especially in the urban context and territorial rights – that are now in the process of integration in the discussions about property, are clear examples of the interaction between those spheres.

2 This is also a methodological proposal to approach legal institutions as lenses to map the evolution of conceptual and theoretical debates within a field or subfield of study.

3 For a detailed overview of the liberal conception of property in legal doctrine, see Diamond (2009).

4 Most of the current literature on development economics agrees that formal property rights are necessary but not sufficient conditions for economic development.

5 Several academic institutions in the United States created specialized centers on land issues and agrarian reforms, to support agrarian reforms across Latin America. See for example, the history of the Land Tenure Center at the University of Wisconsin-Madison that was created in 1962 to promote equitable and sustainable land stewardship and prepared countless working papers on land reforms in Chile, Perú, and Colombia during the 1960s and 1970s. See: www.nelson.wisc.edu/ltc/. Accessed July 2, 2017.

6 Research on law and economics is not conclusive about what type of property rights are the right ones for efficiency. The definition of property rights in the economic literature is usually vague. For a long discussion on disciplinary bias and misunderstandings between law and economics on this issue, see Cole and Grossman (2002).

7 For a detailed inventory of Latin American constitutions that have included the social clause, see Saffon, Maria Paula, "Property and Land," in Conrado Hübner Mendes and Roberto Gargarella (eds.), *The Oxford Handbook of Constitutional Law in Latin America,* forthcoming.

8 See for example, the decisions of the Inter-American Court of Human Rights against Paraguay regarding land rights for indigenous peoples, in which the court not only protects the ancestral right to indigenous peoples but decide that Paraguay has to expropriate the land in order to satisfy the rights of the indigenous community over the interest of the private owners.

9 See for example, the guidelines of the United States aid agency regarding property rights and land rights in developing countries: www.usaid.gov/news-information/fact-sheets/red-land-and-rural-development-program. Accessed July 2, 2017.

10 For a detailed explanation of how law and society studies have approached the cities, see the chapter of Meneses in this volume.

11 See a detailed exposition of this approach in Chapter 7 on *Ethnography, Bureaucracy, and Legal Knowledge in Latin American State Institutions* by Barrera and Latorre in this volume.

12 See Chapter 4 by Rachel Sieder in this volume.

13 For a commentary on this type of claim, see www.cbc.ca/news/canada/north/cultural-appropriation-make-it-illegal-worldwide-indigenous-advocates-say-1.4157943. Accessed July 2, 2017.

14 The following countries included multicultural provisions in their constitutions: Argentina (1944); Bolivia (1994); Brazil (1988, 1994, 1997); Chile (1989, 1994, 1997); Colombia (1991); Costa Rica (1996,1997); Dominican Republic (1996); Ecuador (1996, 1998); Mexico (1992, 1994); Nicaragua (1987, 1995); Panama (1994); Paraguay (1992); Peru (1993); and Uruguay (1997).

15 The presentation of the Colombian case is limited exclusively to the issues of land conflicts and within those debates. I limit the information to the facts and research that became points of encounter between the framing of territorial rights and property.

16 Mexico is probably the most extreme case in the opposite side because of the constitutional reform of constitutional Article 27 in 1992, allowed the fragmentation of *ejidos* – the paradigmatic institution for collective organization of peasants that triumphed with the Mexican revolution and was established in the 1917 Constitution.

17 The analysis of how the URT has performed its duties is beyond the scope of this chapter. However, as an illustration, it is worth mentioning that the first ethnic case that the URT took to the judiciary was rejected because the lawsuit was trying to exhibit formal proves under the civil law, that does not apply to ethnic groups in the country.

References

Albertus, Michael. 2015a. *Autocracy and Redistribution: The Politics of Land Reform.* New York: Cambridge University Press.

Albertus, Michael. 2015b. "The Role of Subnational Politicians in Distributive Politics: Political Bias in Venezuela's Land Reform under Chávez." *Comparative Political Studies.*

Albright, Madeleine K. and Hernando de Soto. 2008. Empowering the Poor Through Property Rights. In *Making the Law Work for Everyone.* New York, NY: Commission on Legal Empowerment of the Poor and the United Nations Development Programme.

Alexander, Gregory. 2009. "The Social Obligation Norm in American Property Law." *Cornell Law Review* 94:745.

Alexander, Gregory and Eduardo Peñalver. 2012. *An Introduction to Property Theory.* Cambridge: Cambridge University Press.

Alexander, Gregory S. and Eduardo M Peòalver. 2010. *Property and Community.* Oxford; New York: Oxford University Press.

Alfonso, Tatiana, Libia Grueso, Magnolia Prada, and Yamile Salinas. 2011. *Derechos Enterrados. Comunidades Etnicas y Campesinas en Colombia.* Bogotá: Ediciones Uniandes.

Allen, Douglas W. 1998. "Property Rights, Transaction Costs, and Coase: One More Time." In *Coasian Economics: Law and Economics and the New Institutional Economics,* edited by S.G. Medema. Boston: Kluwer.

Alston, Philip and Mary Robinson, eds. 2005. *Human Rights and Development. Towards Mutual Reinforcement.* Oxford: Oxford University Press.

Álvarez Rivadulla, María José. 2017. *Squatters and the Politics of Marginality in Uruguay.* Cham: Palgrave Macmillan.

Álvarez, Sonia E., Evelina Dagnino, and Arturo Escobar. 1998. "Introduction: The Cultural and the Political in Latin American Social Movements." In *Cultures of Politics and Politics of Cultures: Revisioning Latin American Social Movements,* edited by Sonia E. Álvarez, Evelina Dagnino and Arturo Escobar. Oxford: Westview Press.

Alviar, Helena. 2012. "Más allá de la Constitución: Obstáculos a la Función Social de la Propiedad." In *La Función Social de la Propiedad en las Constituciones Colombianas,* edited by Helena Alviar García. Bogotá: Universidad de Los Andes.

Antkowiak, Thomas M. 2008. "Remedial Approaches to Human Rights Violations: The Inter-American Court of Human Rights and Beyond." *Columbia Journal of Transnational Law* 46 (2).

Antkowiak, Thomas M. 2014. "Rights, Resources, and Rethoric: Indigenous Peoples and The Inter-American Court." *University of Pennsylvania Journal of International Law* 35 (1).

Asher, Kiran. 2009. *Black and Green. Afro-Colombians, Development, and Nature in the Pacific Lowlands.* Durham: Duke University Press.

Assies, Willem. 2008. "Land Tenure and Tenure Regimes in Mexico: An Overview." *Journal of Agrarian Change* 8(1): 33–63.

Azuela, Antonio. 1991. "La sociología jurídica frente a la urbanización en América Latina: agenda y estrategias para la investigación." In *Sociología Jurídica en América Latina.* Oñati: Instituto Internacional de Sociología Jurídica de Oñati.

Azuela, Antonio, ed. 2013. *Expropiación y Conflicto Social en Cinco Metrópolis Latinoamericanas.* México: UNAM, Instituto de Investigaciones Sociales.

Azuela, Antonio, and Rodrigo Meneses. 2014. "The Everyday Formation of the Urban Space." In *The Expanding Spaces of Law: A Timely Legal Geography*, edited by I. Braverman, N. Blomley, D. Delaney and A. Kedar. Palo Alto: Stanford University Presss.

Babb, Sarah. 2009. *Behind the Development Banks. Washington Politics, Poverty, and the Wealth of Nations.* Chicago, IL: The University of Chicago Press.

Benda-Beckman Von, Franz, Keebet Benda-Beckman Von, and Julia Eckert. 2009. *The Power of Law in a Transnational World, Anthropological Enquiries.* New York and Oxford: Berghan Books.

Bonilla, Daniel, ed. 2013. *La Función Social de la Propiedad.* Buenos Aires: Eudeba.

Caldeira, Teresa. 2000. *City of Walls: Crime, Segregation, and Citizenship in São Paulo.* Berkeley: University of California Press.

Cárdenas, Juan Camilo. 2010. *Dilemas de lo Colectivo. Insituciones, Pobreza y Cooperación en el Manejo Local de los Recursos de Uso Común.* Bogotá: Ediciones Uniandes.

Cole, Daniel. 2014. "The Law and Economics Approach to Property." *Indiana Legal Studies Research Paper* 277.

Cole, Daniel H., and Peter Z. Grossman. 2002. "The Meaning of Property Rights: Law versus Economics?" *Land Economics* 78(3): 317–30.

Davis, Diane. 2006. "Undermining the Rule of Law: Democratization and the Dark Side of Police Reform in Mexico." *Latin American Politics and Society* 48(1): 55–86.

Davis, Diane. 2016. "La Producción del Espacio y la Violencia en las Ciudades del sur Global: Evidencia de América Latina." *Nóesis. Revista de Ciencias Sociales y Humanidades* 26 (52).

Davis, Kevin E., and Michael Trebilcock. 2008. "The Relationship between Law and Development: Optimists Versus Skeptics." *New York University Public Law and Legal Theory Working Papers* Paper 72.

De Schutter, Olivier. 2011. "The Green Rush: The Global Race for Farmland and the Rights of Land Users." *Harvard International Law Journal* 52(2):503–59.

De Soto, Hernando. 2000. *The Mystery of Capital: Why Capitalism Triumphs in the West and Fails Everywhere Else.* New York, NY: Basic Books.

Diamond, Michael R. 2009. "The Meaning and Nature of Property: Homeownership and Shared Equity in the Context of Poverty." *Saint Louis University Public Law Review* 29: 85–112.

Duguit, León. 1969. "Changes of Principle in the Field of Liberty, Contract, Liability and Property." In *The Progress of Continental Law in the Nineteenth Century*, edited by Layton Bartol and Ernst Bruncken. New York: August M Kelly Publishers.

Duguit, León. 1975. *La Transformación del Derecho Público y Privado.* Buenos Aires: Editorial Heliasta.

Easterly, William. 2013. *The Tyranny of Experts. Economists, Dictators and the Forgotten Rights of the Poor.* New York, NY: Basic Books.

Engle, Karen. 2010. *The Elusive Promise of Indigenous Development. Rights, Culture, Strategy.* Durham: Duke University Press.

Escobar, Arturo. 1995. *Encountering Development. The Making and Unmaking of the Third World.* Princeton, NJ: Princeton University Press.

Escobar, Arturo. 2008. *Territories of Difference: Place, Movements, Life, Redes.* Durham: Duke University Press.

Evans, Peter. 1995. *Embedded Autonomy. States and Industrial Transformation.* Princeton, NJ: Princeton University Press.

Fergusson, Leopoldo. 2013. "The Political Economy of Rural Property Rights and the Persistence of the Dual Economy." *Journal of Development Economics* 103: 167–81.

Foster, Sheila and Daniel Bonilla. 2013. "La función social de la propiedad en perspectiva comparada." In *La función social de la propiedad*, edited by Daniel Bonilla. Buenos Aires: Eudeba.

French, Jan Hoffman. 2009. *Legalizing Identities. Becoming Black or Indian in Brazil's Northeast*. Chappel Hill: The University of North Carolina Press.

Friedman, Lawrence M. 1986. "The Law and Society Movement." *Stanford Law Review* 38: 763.

Galiani, Sebastian and Ernesto Schargrodsky. 2010. "Property Rights for the Poor: Effects of Land Titling." *Journal of Public Economics* 94: 700–29.

Garay Salamanca, Luis Jorge, ed. 2014. *Minería en Colombia. Fundamentos para superar el modelo extractivista*. 4 vols. Vol. 1, *Minería en Colombia*. Bogotá, Colombia: Contraloría General de la República.

Glenn, Jane Matthews. 2008. "Informal formality: tenantries, ejidos and family land." *International Journal of Law in Context* 4(2): 135–48.

Grossi, Paolo. 1986. *Historia del Derecho de Propiedad: La Irrupción del Colectivismo en la Conciencia Europea*. Barcelona: Ariel.

Gutiérrez Sanín, Francisco. 2010. "Land and Property Rights in Colombia -Change and Continuity." *Nordic Journal of Human Rights* 28(2): 230–61.

Hale, Charles. 2002. "Does Multiculturalism Menace? Governance, Cultural Rights and the Politics of Identity in Guatemala." *Journal of Latin American Studies* 34 (3): 485–524.

Hale, Charles. 2006. "Activist Research v. Cultural Critique: Indigenous Land Rights and the Contradictions of Politically Engaged Anthropology." *Cultural Anthropology* 21(1): 96–120.

Harvey, David and Ana Varela Mateos. 2007. *Breve Historia del Neoliberalismo*. Tres Cantos, Madrid: Akal.

Holston, James. 2008. *Insurgent Citizenship. Disjunctions of Democracy and Modernity in Brazil*. Princeton: Princeton University Press.

Ibarra Rojas, Lucero. 2011. "The Interaction between Law, Economics and Indigenous Cultures: The Ocumicho Devils." *Oñati Socio-Legal Series* 1(1).

Latorre, Sergio. 2015a. "El papel de los Aspectos Formales y Técnicos en el Debate Sobre el Acceso a la Tierra en Zonas de Conflicto en Colombia." *Pensando lo Rural, Observatorio de Problemas Rurales Contemporáneos (CERES)*.

Latorre, Sergio. 2015b. "The Making of Land Ownership: land titling in rural Colombia. A replay to Hernando de Soto." *Third World Quarterly* 36 (8):1546–1569.

Marín Correa, Alexánder. 2012. "Caso tipo Macondo en Mapiripán." *El Espectador*, August 20, 2012, Tema del día. Available at: www.elespectador.com/impreso/temadeldia/articulo-368868-caso-tipo-macondo-mapiripan. Accessed August 20, 2012.

Mosquera Rosero-Labbé, Claudia, Agustín Laó-Montes, and César Rodríguez-Garavito, eds. 2010. *Debates Sobre Ciudadanía y Políticas Raciales en las Américas Negras*. Bogotá, Colombia: Universidad del Valle Universidad Nacional de Colombia.

Mota Prado, Mariana. 2016. "The Past and Future of Law and Development." *University of Toronto Law Journal* 66(3): 297–300.

Murphy, E. 2015. *For a Proper Home: Housing Rights in the Margins of Urban Chile, 1960–2010 University of Pittsburgh Press*. Pittsburgh, PA: University of Pittsburgh Press.

North, Douglas. 1990. *Institutions, Institutional Change and Economic Performance*. Cambridge: Cambridge University Press.

Ondetti, Gabriel. 2016. "The Social Function of Property, Land Rights and Social Welfare in Brazil." *Land Use Policy* 50: 29–37.

Ostrom, Elinor. 1990. *Governing the Commons: The Evolution of Institutions for Collective Action*. Cambridge: Cambridge University Press.

Ostrom, Elinor. 2005. *Understanding Institutional Diversity*. Princeton, NJ: Princeton University Press.

Paschel, Tianna S. 2010. "The Right to Difference: Explaining Colombia's Shift from Color-Blindness to the Law of Black Communities." *American Journal of Sociology* 116(3): 729–69.

Peña, Ximena, María Alejandra Vélez, Juan Camilo Cárdenas, and Natalia Perdomo. 2016. "Collective Property Leads to Private Investments: Lessons from Land Titling in Afro Colombian Communities." 2016 World Bank Conference on Land and Poverty, Washington, DC, March 14–18, 2016.

Reyes, Alejandro. 2009. *Guerreros y Campesinos: El Despojo de la Tierra en Colombia*. Bogotá: Grupo Editorial Norma.

Richards, Patricia. 2004. *Pobladoras, Indígenas and the State. Conflicts Over Women's Rights in Chile*. New Jersey: Rutgers University Press.

Rico, Laura. 2009. *Ciudad Informal. La Historia de un Barrio Ilegal*. Bogotá: Universidad de Los Andes.

Riles, Annelise. 2004. "Property as Legal Knowledge: Means and Ends." *Journal of the Royal Anthropological Institute* 10(4).

Rittich, Kerry. 2005. "The Properties of Gender Equality." In *Human Rights and Development. Towards Mutual Reinforcement*, edited by Philip Alston and Mary Robinson. Oxford: Oxford University Press.

Rodríguez-Garavito, César, Tatiana Alfonso Sierra, and Isabel Cavelier-Adarve. 2008. "Racial Discrimination and Human Rights in Colombia." In *Global Justice Series*. Bogotá: Observatory on Racial Discrimination.

Rodríguez-Garavito, César, Tatiana Alfonso Sierra, and Isabel Cavelier-Adarve. 2009. *El Desplazamiento Afro. Tierra, Violencia y Derechos de las Comunidades Negras*. Bogotá: Universidad de Los Andes.

Saffon, Maria Paula. 2010. "The Project of Land Restitution in Colombia: An Illustration of the Civilizing Force of Hypocrisy?" *Revista de Estudios Socio-Jurídicos* 12(2): 109–94.

Saffon, Maria Paula. 2015. "When Theft Becomes Grievance: Dispossessions as a Cause of Redistributive Land Claims in 20th Century Latin America." Doctor of Philosophy, Political Science, Columbia University.

Sieder, Rachel. 2010. "Legal Cultures in the (Un)Rule of Law: Indigenous Rights and Juridification in Guatemala." In *Cultures of Legality: Judicialization and Political Activism in Latin America*, edited by Javier A. Couso, Rachel Sieder and Alexandra Huneeus, 161–81. Cambridge: Cambridge University Press.

Sieder, Rachel. 2011. "Pueblos Indígenas y Derecho(s) en América Latina." In *El Derecho en América Latina: Un Mapa Para el Pensamiento Jurídico del Siglo XXI*, edited by César Rodríguez-Garavito. Argentina: Siglo Veintiuno Editores S.A.

Singer, Joseph William. 2000. *Entitlement: The Paradoxes of Property*. New Haven: Yale University Press.

Tamanaha, Brian Z. 2011. "The Primacy of Society and the Failures of Law and Development." *Cornell International Law Journal* 44: 209–47.

Toro Pérez, Catalina, Julio Fierro Morales, Sergio Coronado Delgado, and Tatiana Roa Avendaño. 2012. *Minería, Territorio y Conflicto en Colombia*. Bogota: Censat Plataforma Colombiana de Derechos Humanos, Democracia y Desarrollo Universidad Nacional de Colombia.

Trubek, David M. 1990. "Back to the Future: The Short, Happy Life of The Law and Society Movement." *Florida State University Law Review* 18(1): 1–55.

Trubek, David M., Helena Alviar García, Diego Coutinho, and Alvaro Santos, eds. 2013. *Law and the New Developmental State*. New York: Cambridge University Press.

Trubek, David M., and Marc Galanter. 1974. "Scholars in Self-Strangement: Some Reflections on the Crisis in Law and Development Studies in the United States." *Wisconsin Law Review*.

Van Cott, Dona Lee. 2000. *The Friendly Liquidation of the Past: The Politics of Diversity in Latin America*. Pittsburgh: University of Pittsburgh Press.

Varón, Margarita, Tatiana Alfonso Sierra, Nataly Buitrago, and Javier Caropresse. 2017. *Follow-up on the Colombian Peace Agreements and Land Tenure Issues: Transitions, Property Rights and Tenure Security*. World Bank Conference on Land and Poverty, Washington, DC.

Villegas Del Castillo, Catalina. 2012. "¿Es la función social de la propiedad una cláusula de papel?" In *La Función Social de la Propiedad en las Constituciones Colombianas*, edited by Helena Alviar García. Bogotá: Universidad de Los Andes.

World Bank. 2001. *Engendering Development: Through Gender Equality in Rights, Resources and Voice*. Washington, DC: World Bank.

Yashar, Debora J. 2005. *Contesting Citizenship in Latin America*. First edition. Cambridge: Cambridge University Press.

27

NEW INFLUENCES ON LEGALITY AND JUSTICE IN LATIN AMERICA

Corruption and Organized Crime

Linn Hammergren

Corruption and organized crime are no strangers to Latin America, but their forms, dimensions, and likely impacts are undergoing significant changes. This chapter explores these themes in three parts: a review of what is known about regional trends; an overview of relevant research; and some final observations regarding impacts on legality and justice. The discussion focuses on four countries: Brazil; Colombia; Guatemala; and Mexico. They are chosen neither as extreme nor necessarily typical cases, but rather as countries where interest in both topics has generated significant amounts of information.

What We Know About Changing Patterns of Crime and Corruption

For the most part our knowledge of recent developments originates with government sources (investigations, and crime statistics), subsequent media reports and independently conducted surveys. This information is briefly summarized here before proceeding to a discussion of how researchers have dealt with and added to it.

On corruption: Although always considered a significant problem, attention to and thus the growth of knowledge about corruption had been displaced until recently by the preoccupation with crime. On corruption, our most systematic information still comes from survey organizations like Transparency International, Latinobarómetro, and LAPOP (Latin American Public Opinion Project). Regionally, they record consistently high levels over the past two decades. There are significant differences among countries with Chile and Uruguay constantly rated as least corrupt, and others experiencing occasional shifts in relative rankings. There is, nonetheless, considerable uniformity across time and countries as to the agencies and agents most often involved – police, teachers, health workers, court staff, and other government employees who deal directly with the public. However, surveys capture petty corruption (bribes paid by service users) rather than incidents involving higher-level officials. Participants in "grand corruption" are unlikely to volunteer information even in anonymous polls. Moreover, the one-man-one-vote survey logic would make their "votes" relatively less important.

For grand corruption, the principal sources of information are government investigations, eventual media reports, and occasionally, investigative journalism. Brazil's most significant ongoing investigation is Lava Jatos ("carwash," bribes and kickbacks linked to PETROBAS, the state-run oil company), but it has important cases from the late-1980s onwards (Olinger 2013,

115–16; Powers and Taylor 2011, 2–3). Colombia's Fiscalia and police uncovered cases of high-level corruption over the same period, as did Mexico's federal agencies. In all three, however, accused defendants frequently avoid convictions by manipulating legal procedures (or the judges). Guatemala saw less action until cooperation between CICIG (International Commission against Impunity in Guatemala) and Guatemala's Public Ministry and investigative police-initiated cases against over 200 government officials (including the nation's president and vice-president) and private entrepreneurs. A second round appears to target local authorities.

Such well-publicized examples make it hard to identify trends. They do indicate a greater willingness to investigate powerful actors and for media to report findings (and occasionally do independent investigations). Moreover, although possibly a consequence of investigators' current focus, it appears that grand corruption increasingly involves networks of actors, thus constituting a form of organized crime. The occasional backhander to secure a contract is being replaced by sophisticated structures, especially at the national level and in larger municipalities.

On organized crime: Since the mid-1990s, organized criminal groups (OCGs) have drawn more attention as a consequence of their violent actions and international pressures. Usual targets are drug trafficking organizations (DTOs or cartels), youth gangs (called maras or pandillas), and lesser OCGs with drug trafficking ties (in Colombia, bancrims, in Brazil, the Comandos). There is also growing concern with the (further) criminalization of paramilitary and self-defense groups and police and military involvement through coercion, collusion, or on their own initiative. Mexico's Zetas are one example, a particularly violent cartel formed by ex-military officials. In Brazil, police-initiated social cleansing operations evolved into milicias specializing in extortion and control of the informal economy (Olinger 2013, 121–2).

Like corruption, organized crime has a lengthy history in the region. Earlier manifestations had a limited territorial base, engaging in non-drug contraband; gambling (Brazil's *jogo de bicho*); illegal mining; trafficking in timber, wildlife and persons; cattle rustling; robberies especially of vehicles; and piratería (illegal reproduction largely of CDs, DVDs, and books). A few moved into drug trafficking. Those that did not, receive less media and public attention because of their locations (often in rural, frontier areas), size, and for some, their nearly traditional status within the informal economy (contraband, jogo de bicho, and piratería). As information on their operations is limited, they are not discussed here.

Once drug trafficking emerged on a large scale (from the 1970s in Colombia, somewhat later in the other countries), conditions changed dramatically. At the risk of overgeneralizing, the following appear to be recent trends:

Compared to older OCGs, DTOs are larger, with broader national coverage, and more frequent international links. Their initial hierarchical structure is gradually evolving into flatter organizations and networks as they adapt to internal and external pressures.

Established DTOs increasingly outsource tasks (drug distribution, collection of protection money, and assassinations) or delegate some territorial operations to smaller organizations in return for a share of their earnings – what Wainwright (2016) calls "franchising."

DTOs also adapt by diversifying into other criminal and some legal activities (as a way of laundering and using earnings).

Crime is also evolving. Thus, kidnapping is being superseded by extortion because it is less risky and more effective. The shift affects a variety of OCGs, including maras, pandillas, and the Colombian bancrim. Cross-border operations have increased to capture new opportunities and escape law enforcement pressures. Mexican cartels have moved into Central America, competing and cooperating with "homegrown" DTOs. While crime often involves violence, contemporary OCGs use violence strategically, to claim territory (often against other gangs), cow victims into compliance, or, somewhat perversely and often counterproductively, to dissuade law enforcement agencies from pursuing them. Communication technology allows OCGs to operate from prisons. In Mexico and Guatemala many run extortion rings this way. Brazil's Comandos originated as alliances formed in prisons (Denyer Willis 2015; Silvestre 2014) and are still managed by incarcerated leaders.

Arrests/elimination of their leaders and inter- and intra-organizational conflicts have fragmented first-generation DTOs. Dudley (2014) citing official sources estimates that Mexico's seven major cartels have generated 60 to 80 offshoots and that Colombia's four paramilitary factions are now "dozens." Fragmented organizations are less capable of infiltrating national governments, but still capture local authorities or communities without governance structures.

Even in these four countries, there are significant differences in OGC organization and methods. These include: the relative importance accorded youth gangs versus OCG/DTOs; impacts on crime levels; and links to government authorities.

Of the four nations, only in Guatemala (and the other Northern Triangle countries, Honduras and El Salvador) do youth gangs (maras or pandillas) receive the bulk of public, government, and media attention. Despite involvement in drug trafficking, Guatemala's family-controlled OCGs operated without much government interference until the incursion of the more violent Mexican cartels. Although youth gangs exist in Brazil and Colombia, neither treats them as a distinct problem, at most, concerned about their use by DTOs and smaller OCGs. Mexican authorities paid attention only to those with drug trafficking links working in border areas – either migrants from the Northern Triangle in the South or in the North, a mix of United States-linked (Mara Salvatrucha and Barrio 18) and "generational" gangs (traditional to the region; USAID 2006).

Official statistics on the number and membership of Central American youth gangs are widely regarded as unreliable. There is also disagreement on the influence of United States-based gangs. Some observers credit United States deportation policies with a major role (UNODC 2012, 28). Most argue that the gangs first emerged independently, but that United States contacts "modernized" their operations and drew them further into the drug economy. El Salvador may be the exception given the massive deportations early in its gangs' history.

Among the four countries, DTOs receive most attention in Colombia and Mexico. In Colombia, guerrilla and paramilitary groups complicate the picture, increasingly controlling cultivation and feeding the formation of more localized bacrims. In both countries, arrests of cartel heads led to internal warfare among the survivors and displacement of some factions into other urban and rural areas (as well as other nations). Medellín, once a success story for reducing crime is seeing levels rise again (Giraldo Ramírez 2012), but Colombian criminal groups also remain active in isolated rural districts, what the government calls the "consolidation zones." In Mexico, the states of Guerrero and Michoacán now register the highest violence levels, produced by a mix of fragmented DTOs, other OCGs, and paramilitary or self-defense groups, often with links to state and local authorities.

Brazil's situation is unique owing to the organization of its principal OCGs into regional groups (the Comandos) with drug trafficking as only part of their criminal repertoire. The Comandos are also distinguished by their collective (and often imprisoned) leadership and their territorial base within urban slums (favelas) and peri-urban areas, using local youth as their "soldiers." In these locations, they aim at controlling all criminal activities, constituting an alternative form of governance (Garzón 2008; Denyer Willis 2015). Recent state occupation of Rio's most problematic favelas forced displacement of some groups to other communities and regions. As Brazil is not a drug-producing country, its OCGs obtain supplies from external sources (principally Bolivia), control local distribution and function as intermediaries for international transit.

In contrast with corruption, there is little doubt that crime has risen throughout the region over the past 20 years. There is less agreement on the impact of OGCs independently of factors like unemployment, erosion of traditional social controls, and demographics (a more youthful population). Except for Mexico during Calderon's war on DTOs (2006–2012), police usually credit gangs and OCGs with less than half of homicides. It is evident nonetheless that the number and possibly membership of OCGs have increased as has the criminal activity (drug trafficking, new crimes, and those they appropriated from earlier groups) they control.

International experts often argue that while drug trafficking has exacerbated violence, crime levels and security problems are largely dependent on "weak governance and powerful sub-state actors" (UNODC 2012, 5). The imperfect relationship between countries' drug-related activity and violence levels and the fact that OCGs operate most freely in areas with less state presence support that conclusion. On the other side of the coin, OCG and especially DTO infiltration of national- and local-level governments has received most attention in Mexico (where many believe it is ongoing; see Curzio [2000] on campaign financing) and Colombia (where except in the consolidation zones it seemingly peaked in the 1990s; see Camacho Guizado [1996] and Reina [1996]). Brazil's Comandos and Guatemala's maras lack capacity to infiltrate national institutions. However, Guatemala has a long history of military and ex-military involvement in organized crime and grand corruption (Lopez 2011), OCG ties with local authorities, and more recent DTO financing of political parties (CICIG 2015). Within the countries' justice sectors, lower-level police are the most vulnerable to bribes, threats, or outright collusion with OGCs. Interference with higher-level police, judges, and prosecutors is less common, with Mexico having the most reported cases.

How Research on Latin America Has Dealt with the Themes

This discussion uses a broad definition of research, extending beyond work done by full-time academics, published in scholarly journals, and/or emphasizing hypothesis testing and theory building. As applied to Latin America, more classical scholarship has not ignored corruption and organized crime, but gives neither topic systematic attention. Its focus is rarely OCGs, instead tracing variations in crime levels within and across countries, documenting impacts on the economy and government policies, and identifying causal factors. Some of this literature is referenced below, but most is extraneous to present purposes.

The reasons for the relative lack of attention are obvious. Neither theme easily lends itself to the quantitative approach increasingly privileged by academic disciplines. Data on corruption are largely limited to surveys, most done by specialized institutes and used by external researchers for cross-national analysis. The development of alternative measures and especially indices (e.g., the World Justice Project, and World Governance Indicators) has become a project on its own, but produces little additional research.

Surveys also capture respondents' experience with crime. LAPOP for example, has expanded these sections of its questionnaires, probably because they interest funders like the United States Agency for International Development (USAID). Aside from surveys (including smaller independent efforts; e.g., Schedler [2015], and Aguirre and Herrera [2012]) the principal quantitative data on crime are government statistics. In Latin America their quality is often poor and publicly accessible data are highly aggregated, geographically and substantively (by type of crime), thus limiting analysis. A more qualitative, ethnographic understanding of crime or corruption requires spending time, if not with the criminals than with those responsible for investigating them. For foreigners that can be difficult, but such in-depth investigation involves personal risks even for local researchers (Maldonado 2013; Estrada-Iguíniz 2015). Journalists doing investigative research may not live to publish it or if they do, often enter voluntary exile.

Research on corruption is relatively less dangerous, but beyond survey data, the issue is what information to collect, how to collect it, and its value for further analysis. Brazilian researchers' (Ferraz and Finan 2008; Pereira and Melo 2015) use of municipal audits to measure corruption requires public accessibility and comparably disaggregated data for comparison – so far limited to electoral outcomes. One further impediment is a dearth of interesting research questions. Except for Klitgaard's (1998) increasingly criticized equation C = M + D – A (corruption results from monopoly plus discretion minus accountability), macroeconomic analyses (see works cited in Stephenson [2015]) linking corruption to economic or political development or some high-level theorizing about incentives (Rose-Ackerman and Truex 2012; Khan 2006), students of corruption have produced little to orient quantitative or qualitative research. Themes of interest might include patterns in incidence and type, shifts between petty and grand corruption, impacts and extent of institutional "capture" as well as facilitating conditions, and the relationship to organized crime. The recent high-level cases in Brazil, Guatemala, and Mexico, may spur researchers' attention, although as with Colombia's earlier revelations (here linked to DTOs), this may not last long.

Lack of attention does not mean denial of existence or broader impacts. Those writing on Latin American justice and politics commonly mention corruption, but their comments have varied little over the past two decades. As with much work on OCGs, more focused treatments typically provide details on specific cases or practices with little further analysis (e.g., Due Process of Law 2007; Transparency International 2007). Also noteworthy is the absence of attention to corruption (or organized crime) in the quantitative analyzes of high court decisions affecting government policies and basic rights. Once cases of corruption and official complicity in criminal acts reach the high courts this may change, but the "strategic decision–making" literature (Helmke 2005; Helmke and Rios 2011; Kapiszewski 2012) never mentions corruption or threats (beyond losing one's job) as factors shaping justices' decisions. This is not surprising for Brazil, whose constitutional court (Supremo Tribunal Federal) largely escapes suspicion, but it is for Argentina and many countries not yet studied where judicial corruption, politicization, and vulnerability to coercion are common complaints.

For organized crime, there is a rapidly accumulating literature on Latin America, of which only a sample is referenced here. Most of it is highly descriptive, based on press reports, interviews with government officials, and whatever statistics are publically available. It is notably short on theory building, except for retrospective explanations of changes in organization, criminal specializations, and national and international links. It also rarely references the much larger body of work developed outside the region (For extra-regional examples, see Paoli [2014], and Benson and Zimmerman [2010]). The authors are less frequently academics than journalists and staff of private foundations, government agencies, and international organizations. Many are Latin Americans or long-term residents, using their advantages of permanent presence and easier access to media and government sources. Their work is increasingly available or at least referenced in edited volumes and working papers published by United States and European non-governmental organizations (NGOs), foundations, and universities. Specialized websites (e.g. Security Sector Reform [SSR] Resource Center, InSight Crime) republish media and some research reports.

Whatever the researchers' nationality or professional profile, work on organized crime typically takes one of two focuses – DTOs or youth gangs. The distinction made sense ten years ago, but is less tenable today considering the proliferation of offshoots of larger OCGs, the "graduation" of youth gangs into organizations of older members wholly focused on crime, and the shifting relationships and roles among all of them. Several overview studies (UNODC 2012; Dudley 2012, 2014; Bagley 2012) in fact propose more complex structural and functional typologies, especially for DTOs.

Although no less descriptive, an earlier set of works on maras/pandillas drew on surveys (financed by donors, international organizations, and occasionally governments) and fieldwork directly with gangs. Seemingly fieldwork has become too dangerous even for local researchers. The absence of more recent surveys with actual or potential gang members suggests they have also become risky. One alternative (Vilalta and Fondevila 2014) is to interview detainees, but in countries with high impunity, this is a non-representative group (the least successful who were apprehended). When work on youth gangs attempts to identify causes, it often takes a sympathetic view, stressing poverty, lack of alternative opportunities, reactions to hardline government policies, stigmatization, and pressures from the OGCs (e.g., Fontes 2014; Jones 2014). Mauricio Rubio (2011) is a dissenter in identifying elite members in many gangs (contradicting the poverty, lack of opportunity these as well as the notion that addressing both would discourage gang membership).

Much of the content of these descriptive studies differs from the initial summary only in the level of details included. Additional research distinguished by its more innovative approaches and findings follows four lines of investigation: studies of communities infiltrated by OCGs; work, often interview-based, on migrants and other victims of OCGs; statistical analyses linking crime levels with socioeconomic characteristics, and some tentative theory building.

The community-focused studies have produced provocative insights into how OCGs operate in isolated areas where they formed or relocated. Some research stresses the infiltration of local institutions (mayors, police, and others), what might be called the Iguala effect. However, the majority (Bulla and Guarín 2015 [and other Fundación Ideas para la Paz documents]; Estrada-Iguíniz 2015; Kyle 2015; Garcíia Villegas 2008) emphasize that criminal presence induces local (and locally-situated national) officials to look the other way, even letting OCGs exercise real community control. A further finding from those working in rural areas (Kennedy 2014; Kyle 2015; Witte 2015) is that much of the local economy and many families may depend, directly or indirectly, on crime-linked activities – ranging from drug cultivation or other "subcontracted" work to providing meals and other legitimate services to the invading bands. Because it is still more risky, work in urban communities is infrequent, but some researchers (Denyer Willis 2015) have found criminal bands resolving minor disputes and imposing some kind of order.

Work with victims is growing because of concerns with child migrants. Here fieldwork can be done by interviewing detained migrants or in centers (largely in Mexico) providing assistance to those in transit. In addition to research by independent scholars (Kennedy 2014; Voght 2013), several national and international human rights organizations have funded more extensive projects (Musalo et al. 2015; Mexico, Comisión Nacional de los Derechos Humanos 2011). Again the findings are largely descriptive, focusing on reported reasons for migration, the difficulties experienced by migrants, and an inventory of the criminal groups who assist and abuse them. However, while exploiters may belong to larger organizations, the migrants can rarely identify them definitively (Zetas, a local organization, a mara, or something more indeterminable). As with the community studies, some research reveals a host of informal, but legitimate businesses profiting from the migrants – exchanging money or selling them food, clothing, and other supplies.

While less relevant (because they do not differentiate organized from common crime) there are studies using an epidemiological approach to identify factors influencing crime levels within and across communities (Ingram 2014; Ingram and Curtis 2015; CAF 2014, comparing Buenos

Aires and Bogotá, 97–104). Most attempt to link crime to socioeconomic variables, but the dependence on relatively disaggregated government statistics, which also rely on what citizens report (or police encounter), poses limitations. Through victims' surveys we know that much crime goes unreported and that this varies by crime type. While facing some of these constraints, Ingram's work in Mexico (2014) and Central America (2015) is noteworthy, first for his access to more disaggregated government statistics and second for his findings on the impact of employment and education on crime levels among neighboring municipalities. However, his work does not identify the role of OCGs or gangs.

Finally, there is tentative theory building. This includes attempts to trace the relationships among different "levels" of criminal activity and criminal networks (Dudley 2014; Garzón Vergara 2008, 2012; Sánchez Valdés 2014; UNODC 2012) and speculative work on the trajectories of individual members (Bailey and Ortega 2010; Mahaedevan 2011). The latter focuses on youth-at-risk, starting with the observation that passage "up" the criminal justice pyramid is not automatic. The interest in individuals is understandable given efforts to discourage gang membership, but it may be less useful than work, mostly from developed countries, on the evolution of organizations. Svetlana Stephenson's research on Russia (2015) and the articles in Hazen and Rogers (2014) are important in emphasizing that youth gangs are a universal phenomenon across history. It is their passage from neighborhood packs, involved in minor malfeasance and territorial defense to something more dangerous that requires explanation. More generally, theory building and all research on Latin American crime and corruption still suffer from neglecting (and being neglected by) work arising in other regions.

Impacts of Corruption and Organized Crime on Legality, Governance, and Justice: Implications for Research

This topic is saved to the end as it is where both knowledge and research are most limited, in Latin America and elsewhere. Research on organized crime and corruption focuses largely on "supply" and "demand," or the push-pull factors explaining emergence, forms, locations, and dimensions. Its authors largely agree that both are harmful not only for their immediate effects but also for their impacts on governance. As specifically regard the justice sector, infiltration, and other interference by criminal/corrupt actors damage service quality, while augmenting the perception that state institutions are neither effective nor trustworthy. In Latin America, surveys, popular protests, and other direct action indicate that citizens feel less secure, are unsatisfied with government responses, seek protection in measures ranging from vigilantism to migration, and are losing faith in justice institutions if not the entire democratic process.

These downstream consequences have inspired little further research. What exists is largely limited to analysis of survey results. While not distinguishing OCGs, LAPOP's exploration of links between citizens' attitudes toward government and their experience with crime and perceived security (or with corruption) support the conventional understandings with a few notable exceptions. These include the inverse relationship between support for government performance and tolerance of political diversity (Azpuru and Zechmeister 2015, 120–5), interpreted as undermining democratic values.

Peripheral findings from other work offer further insights. That they are peripheral is indicative of one problem: those studying governance, legality, and justice treat crime, corruption, and violence as negative but undifferentiated influences, while those exploring the latter are more interested in their forms and incidence than political repercussions. Falling between the stools are the variations in citizen responses and how they affect governance variables and their further institutionalization.

Here organized crime and corruption are best treated separately. Although neither survey nor statistical databases separate organized from common crime, some inferences can be drawn from work tracing relationships among violence, criminality, and perceptions of (in)security. First, as research on DTOs now recognizes (Lajous 2016; articles in Journal of Conflict Resolution 2015), it is not crime writ large but crime affecting citizens directly that increases their insecurity and alters engagement with and demands on governance institutions. When DTOs branch out to extortion and kidnapping or engage in violent conflicts, citizens react. When they stick to their business (drugs) they are less threatening. DTOs have not disappeared from Colombia (which remains a principal cocaine producer), but they have curbed their visible violence. México's Ciudad Juárez is considered a success because of the precipitous declines in its homicide rates. DTOs remain active there and possibly continue to infiltrate state institutions, but not in manners the public notices (Fundación MEPI 2015). The fixation on youth gangs in Guatemala (and the entire Northern Triangle) is related. DTOs operate in these countries, but it is the maras/pandillas (via extortion, assassinations, and other crime) that bring demands for government action.

Second, is research linking violence, OCG strategies and government responses? In parts of Mexico, Colombia, and Brazil, "visible" violence has declined because of diminished conflicts among OCGs and between them and government (sometimes aided by informal pacts with local or national authorities). São Paulo's declining homicide rates post-2000 are believed to have less to do with "better policing" than with the Primer Comando Conjunto's domination of criminal groups operating there (Denyer 2015). Moreover, throughout Latin America, a good proportion of homicides are police killings, which also decline with non-aggression pacts or OCGs' adoption of less violent tactics.

Finally, are findings on citizen responses to perceived insecurity. In both Guatemala and Mexico citizens have resorted to "protective" measures that are either intrinsically criminal (lynching) or easily criminalized (self-defense organizations). Studies of OCG-infiltrated rural and peri-urban communities suggest other reactions. In Colombia and Mexico, inhabitants may maintain a largely indirect involvement in the drug economy while benefiting from OCG-provided dispute resolution, social control, and occasional financing of local projects. OCGs in Brazil's favelas provide less employment but do offer social control. However, urban communities infiltrated by youth gangs (Guatemala and other Northern Triangle countries), receive none of these "benefits" and lacking conditions permitting self-help (because of the gangs' proximity), direct their frustrations toward the state.

Collectively, these observations suggest room for work on how OCG operations affect citizens' attitudes toward state justice and legality/lawfulness. They indicate varying reactions even among those living alongside OCGs. On the basis of Central American experience, observers first argued that heightened insecurity encouraged a "mano dura" outlook. However, a desire for security can encourage other responses. The three typical reactions – formation of self-defense groups, acceptance of OCG social control, and efforts to enlist state agencies – merit exploration of the conditions under which they occur and their downstream effects. The first two might alter definitions of legality, based less in state law than in community norms or preferences for predictability, while increasing distrust in state institutions. The third may privilege the mano dura, an extremely punitive enforcement of existing law.

Those who have risked entering these communities rarely ask those questions (see however, Aguirre and Herrera [2012]). It may be time to do so or to find other approaches, including different survey questions and sampling techniques, to explore how differences in OCG operations affect citizen attitudes and behavior. Except for survey evidence, cross-national research would be difficult, but it may be more useful to compare different populations in the same country. Equally important and equally unattended is the question of how governments respond and with what effects. Does the new push for community mobilization (promoted by donors and some national programs) enhance security, and if so where? How does this compare to the "send-in-the-troops" strategy in Brazil's favelas or to the various pacts with OCGs and gangs? And what do these responses portend for future governance development?

Turning to corruption, surveys, the principal data source, pose two problems – respondents' inaccurate reporting of petty corruption and limited experience with grand corruption. Interestingly, analyses linking citizens' experience to their attitudes run somewhat counter to conventional wisdom. Specifically, LAPOP has identified mismatches between citizen experience and perceptions of overall government corruption. Haiti with many bribes reported but relatively low citizen perceptions of overall corruption is an extreme example, but in countries with limited self-reported experience, citizens may still rate their governments as very corrupt (Azpuru and Zechmeister 2015, 56–61). LAPOP's explanation, resting on the influence of media coverage of grand corruption, has implications for recent investigations and for Pereria and Melo's (2015) "paradox of … popular corrupt politicians," which they attribute to expenditures on public goods. While not explored by the Brazilians, it has been suggested that citizens' limited exposure to media reports also explains their failure to oust corrupt mayors.

Along these lines, the publicity afforded recent national investigations had immediate effects on public images of state institutions. Except in Mexico where no agency benefited, it improved perceptions of prosecution and police, while worsening opinions about legislators and executive officials and potentially judges, depending on how they deal with the cases. In Guatemala and Brazil, it brought down or threatens to bring down governments; complaints about violent crime were eclipsed by mass anti-corruption demonstrations. Moreover, the Guatemalan experience inspired investigations elsewhere in Central America and beyond, the arrest of police authorities in El Salvador and Honduras, and the proposed formation of CICIG-like entities in both countries. The obvious questions raised by these events are first whether public outrage will last long enough to provoke more than a few arrests and if it does, whether it will produce changes in the behavior of public officials, the performance of justice institutions, public attitudes toward all forms of corruption, and the concerns with crime and insecurity.

Although their work on corruption and organized crime constantly provides new details on operations, it is unlikely that researchers are finding anything not already known by the region's police and prosecutorial authorities. Theory building is limited and at best retrospective (i.e., *ex post* explanations). Useful as this may be for outside observers, researchers inevitably seem to be one step behind a dynamically changing situation. Given the futility of competing with government investigators or journalists specializing in these themes (e.g., Martínez), researchers working on these topics might devote more effort to exploring the governance implications – a theme outside the purview of both of these primary sources. Three issues merit attention:

Effects on attitudes toward governance and justice – declining trust in state and especially justice institutions, is a near universal phenomenon, hardly limited to Latin America. However, the region is starting from a low base, so the issue is whether citizen attitudes (and the attitudes of which citizens) have been still more adversely affected and what this portends for their future demands on and willingness to engage with the state.

Effects on attitudes toward legality/lawfulness – LAPOP analyses, the visible impact as well as research on electoral results, and the community studies indicate that tolerance for corruption and OCGs varies among portions of the population. Some differences stem from relative exposure to information, but others are founded in experience. Is the tolerance stable, is it affecting more or fewer citizens, what further problems could it bring and how is the justice sector performance affecting these developments?

Effects on justice reforms – Mexico and Guatemala have been implementing reforms for two decades with limited success in combating OCGs or corruption. Brazil and Colombia started from a higher base, but their progress has also been slow. Except in Brazil, reforms emphasized new procedures with more attention to grand principles than to efficacy on the ground. The mano dura backlash was one consequence. Some obvious needs (e.g., real police reform – higher budgets for better policing; performance monitoring; modern, results-based management) have long been resisted. Anti-corruption drives could further postpone adoption, but to deal with organized and common crime, they will have to occur.

The common thread linking these areas is the question of how short-term changes in citizen experience can obstruct or promote institutional development. Knowing more about the changes would help; tracking influences on existing institutions is vital. Research has provided anecdotal evidence; the challenge is to use it to develop new approaches to investigating the answers. Since insufficient attention to these themes is universal, perhaps because the problems are less extreme elsewhere, this is an area where researchers could take the lead with Latin American examples.

References

Aguirre, Ochoa, Jerjes Izcoatl, and Hugo Amador Herrera Torres. 2012. "Societal Attitudes and Organized Crime in Mexico: The Case of Michoacan, Mexico." *Journal of Humanities and Social Science,* 2(16): 79–85.

Astorga, Luis. 2000. "Organized Crime and the Organization of Crime." In John Bailey and Roy Godson (Eds.). Organized Crime and Democratic Governability: Mexico and the U.S.–Mexican Borderlands. University of Pittsburgh Press; 58–82.

Azpuru, Dinorah and Elizabeth J. Zechmeister. 2015. "Political Culture of Democracy in Guatemala and in the Americas, 2014: Democratic Governance across 10 years of the Americas Barmometer." USAID, March.

Bagley, Bruce. 2012. "Drug Trafficking and Organized Crime in the Americas: Major Trends in the Twenty-First Century." Washington, DC. The Wilson Center.

Bailey, John and Daniel Ortega. 2010. "Interactive Dynamics of 'Common' and 'Organized' Crime in Latin America: Concepts and Hypotheses." Available at www.wilsoncenter.org/index.cfm?topic_id=1425&categoryid=34F61C49-AF18-8F3B-9CD0E09642AB4BF1&fuseaction=topics.events_item_topics&event_id=607885. Accessed August 19, 2017.

Benson, Bruce L. and Paul R. Zimmerman (Eds.). 2010. *Handbook on the Economics of Crime.* Northampton, MA: Edward Elgar.

Berk-Seligson, Susan, Diana Orcés, Georgina Pizzzolitto, Mitchell Seligson, and Carole J. Wilson. 2014. *Impact Evaluation of USAID's Community-Based Crime and Violence Approach in Central America: Regional Report for El Salvador, Guatemala, Honduras and Panama.* Available at www.vanderbilt.edu/lapop/carsi/Regional_Report_v12d_final_W_120814.pdf. Accessed August 19, 2017.

Bulla, Patricia and Sergio Guarín. 2015. "Seguridad Rural en Colombia." Bogotá: Fundación Ideas para la Paz. Available at: http://cdn.ideaspaz.org/media/website/document/55e0c4e3e93c2.pdf. Accessed August 19, 2017.

Camacho Guizado, Alvaro. 1996. "Narcotráfico, coyuntura y crisis: Sugerencias para un debate." In Francisco Leal Buitrago (Ed.). *Tras las Huellas de la Crisis Política,* Bogota: TM Editores; 129–51.

Clausen, Bianca, Aart Kraay, and Peter Murrell. 2010. "Does Respondent Reticence Affect the Results of Corruption Surveys? Evidence from the World Bank Enterprise Survey for Nigeria." Washington, DC: The World Bank, Policy Research Working Paper 5415.

Corporación Andino de Fomento (CAF). 2014. *Por Una América Latina Más Segura: Una Nueva Perspectiva Para Prevenir y Controlar el Delito.* Bogotá: CAF.

CICIG (International Commission Against Impunity in Guatemala). 2015. "El financiamiento de la política en Guatemala." Available at www.cicig.org/uploads/documents/2015/informe_financiamiento_politicagt.pdf. Accessed August 19, 2017.

Curzio, Leonardo. 2000. "Organized Crime and Political Campaign Finance in Mexico." In John Bailey and Roy Godson (Eeds.). *Organized Crime and Democratic Governability: Mexico and the U.S.-Mexican Borderlands,* University of Pittsburgh Press; 83–102.

Denyer Willis, Graham. 2015. *The Killing Consensus: Police, Organized Crime, and the Regulation of Life and Death in Urban Brazil.* University of California Press.

Dudley, Steven. 2011. "Drug Trafficking Organizations in Central America: Transportistias, Mexican Cartels, and Maras," In Cynthia Aronson and Eric Olson, *Organized Crime in Central America: The Northern Triangle,* Washington, DC: Woodrow Wilson Center; 18–61.

Dudley, Steven. 2014. "Criminal Evolution and Violence in Latin America and the Caribbean." Available at www.insightcrime.org/news-analysis/evolution-crime-violence-latin-america-caribbean. Accessed August 19, 2017.

Due Process of Law Foundation. 2007. *Controles y Descontroles de la Corrupción Judicial: Evaluación de la Corrupción Judicial y de los Mecanismos Para Combatirla en Centro América y Panamá.* Washington, DC: DPLF.

Estrada-Iguíniz, Margarita. 2015. "A la deriva: Vida cotidiana y violencia en Huitzilac, Morelos, México." *Latin American Research Review,* 50(1): 76–94.

Ferraz, Claudio and Frederico Finan. 2008. "Exposing Corrupt Politicians: The Effects of Brazil's Publicly Revealed Audits on Electoral Outcomes." Available at http://eml.berkeley.edu/~ffinan/Finan_Audit.pdf. Accessed August 19, 2017.

Fontes, Anthony W. 2014. "Beyond the Maras: Violence and Survival in Urban Central America." Available at: www.wilsoncenter.org/sites/default/files/Fontes_2014_FINAL.pdf. Accessed August 19, 2017.

Fundación MEPI. 2015. "El milagro falso de Ciudad Juárez." Available at: www.fundacionmepi.org/notas/el-milagro-falso-de-ciudad-juarez/. Accessed August 19, 2017.

García-Villegas, Mauricio (Ed) 2008. *Jueces sin Estado: La Justicia Colombiana en Zonas de Conflicto Armado.* Bogotá: Siglo de Hombres.

Garzón Vergara, Juan Carlos. 2012. *The Rebellion of Criminal Networks: Organized Crime in Latin America and the Dynamics of Change.* Washington, DC: Woodrow Wilson Center, March.

Garzón Vergara, Juan Carlos. 2008. *Mafia and Company: The Criminal Networks in Mexico, Brazil and Colombia.* Washington, DC. The Wilson Center.

Giraldo, Jorge. 2012. *Seguridad en Medellín: El Éxito, sus Explicaciones, Limitaciones y Fragilidades.* Washington, DC: The Wilson Center. Available at: www.wilsoncenter.org/sites/default/files/Presentacion%20 Giraldo.pdf. Accessed August 19, 2017.

Hazen, Jennifer M. and Dennis Rogers. 2014. *Global Gangs: Street Violence across the World.* Minneapolis: University of Minnesota Press.

Helmke, Gretchen. 2005. *Courts Under Constraints: Judges Generals, and Presidents in Argentina.* Cambridge: Cambridge University Press.

Helmke, Gretchen and Julio Rios-Figueroa (Eds.). 2011. *Courts in Latin America.* Cambridge: Cambridge University Press.

Ingram, Matt. 2014. "Community Resilience to Violence: Local Schools, Regional Economies, and Homicide in Mexico's Municipalities." In Shirk, David A. Shirk, Duncan Wood and Eric L. Olson (Eds.). 2014. *Building Resilient Communities in Mexico: Civil Responses to Crime and Violence*, Washington, DC: Woodrow Wilson Center; 25–64.

Ingram, Matt and Karise M. Curtis. 2015. "Violence in Central America: A Spatial View of Homicide in the Region, Norther Triangle and El Salvador." In Eric Olson (Ed.), *Crime and Violence in Central America's Norther Triangle: How U.S. Policy Responses are Helping, Hurting, and Can be Improved.* Washington, DC: Wilson Center.

Jones, Nathan P. 2014. "Understanding and Addressing Youth in 'Gangs' in Mexico." In David A. Shirk, Duncan Wood and Eric L. Olson (Eds.), *Building Resilient Communities in Mexico: Civil Responses to Crime and Violence.* Washington, DC: Woodrow Wilson Center: 89–118.

Journal of Conflict Resolution (JCR): *Special Issue on Drug Violence in Mexico,* December 2015.

Kapiszewski, Diana. 2012. *High Courts and Economic Governance in Argentina and Brazil.* Cambridge: Cambridge University Press.

Kennedy, Elizabeth. 2014. "No Childhood Here: Why Central American Children are Fleeing Their Homes." Washington: American Immigration Council. Available at: www.immigrationpolicy.org/perspectives/no-childhood-here-why-central-american-children-are-fleeing-their-homes. Accessed August 19, 2017.

Khan, M. 2006. *Governance and Anti-Corruption Reforms in Developing Countries: Policies, Evidence and Ways Forward*. United Nations Conference on Trade and Development, G-24 Discussion Paper No. 42. Available at: www.g24.org/Publications/Dpseries/42.pdf. Accessed August 19, 2017.

Klitgaard, Robert. 1998. *Controlling Corruption*. University of California Press.

Kyle, Chris. 2015. *Violence and Insecurity in Guerrero*. Washington, DC. Wilson Center. Available at: www.wilsoncenter.org/sites/default/files/Violence%20and%20Insecurity%20in%20Guerrero.pdf. Accessed August 19, 2017.

Lajous, Andres. 2016. Como dejó de ser Ciudad Juárez una de las ciudades más violentos del mundo. Available at: http://andreslajous.nexos.com.mx/?p=2137. Accessed August 19, 2017.

Lopez, Julie. 2011. "Guatemala's Crossroads: The Democratization of Violence and Second Changes." In Cynthia Aronson and Eric Olson, *Organized Crime in Central America: The Northern Triangle,* Washington, DC: Woodrow Wilson Center; 140–242.

Mahadevan, Prem. 2011. *A War Without 'Principals;' Narco-Violence in Mexico*. Athens: Reach Institute for European and American Studies (RIEAS).

Maldonado Aranda, Salvador M. 2013. "Desafios etnográficos en el estudio de la violencia: experiencias de una investigación." Available at: www.scielo.org.ar/scielo.php?script=sci_arttext&pid=S1851-169420 13000100006. Accessed August 19, 2017.

Martinez, Oscar. 2016. *A History of Violence: Living and Dying in Central America*. (Translated by John Washington and Daniela Ugaz) Brooklyn: Verso.

Medel, Monica and Francisco Thoumi. 2014. "The Mexican Drug Cartels." In Letizia Paoli (Ed.), *Oxford Handbook of Organized Crime*. Oxford University Press; 196–218.

Mexico, Comisión Nacional de los Derechos Humanos. 2011. Informe Especial sobre Secuestro de Migrantes en Mexico. Available at: www.cndh.org.mx/sites/all/doc/Informes/Especiales/2011_sec-migrantes.pdf. Accessed August 19, 2017.

México Evalúa. 2015. Prevención del delito en México: ¿Cuáles son las prioridades? Available at http://mexicoevalua.org/2015/06/prevencion-del-delito-en-mexico-cuales-son-las-prioridades/. Accessed August 19, 2017.

Mingardi, Guaracy. 1992. *Tiras, Gansos e Trutas: Segurança Pública e Policia Civil em São Paulo (1983–1990)*. São Paulo: Corag.

Musalo, Karen, Lisa Frydman, and Pablo Ceriani Cernadas. 2015. Niñez y migración en Centro y Norte América: causas, políticas, prácticas y desafios. Center for Gender and Refuge Studies. Available at: www.acnur.org/t3/fileadmin/Documentos/Publicaciones/2015/9927.pdf?view=1. Accessed August 19, 2017.

National Strategy Information Center, Culture of Lawfulness Project. 2012. *Building a Culture of Lawfulness: A Guide to Getting Started*. Washington DC: NSIC.

Olinger, Marianna. 2013. "La propagación del crimen organizado en Brasil: una mirada a partir de lo ocurrido en la última década." In Juan Carlos Garzón and Eric L. Olson (Eds.), *La Diáspora Criminal: La difusión transnacional del crimen Organizado y cómo contener su Expansión*. Washington, DC: Wilson Center; 101–42.

Paoli, Letizia (Ed.). 2014. *The Oxford Handbook of Organized Crime*. Oxford: Oxford University Press.

Pereira, Carlos and Marcus André Melo. 20156. "Reelecting Corrupt Incumbents in Exchange for Public Goods: Rouba mas faz in Brazil." *Latin American Research Review,* 50(4): 88–115.

Pérez, Ana Lilia. 2012. *El Cartel Negro: Como el Crimen Organizado se ha Apoderado de Pemex*. Mexico: Grijalbo.

Power, Timothy J. and Matthew M. Tayor. 2011. "Accountability Institutions and Political Corruption in Brazil." In Power and Taylor (Eds.), *Corruption and Democracy in Brazil: The Struggle for Accountability*. Note Dame: University of Notre Dame Press; 1–28.

Ramírez, Jorge Giraldo. 2012. *Seguridad en Medellín: El Éxito, sus Explicaciones, Limitaciones y Fragilidades*. Washington, DC: The Wilson Center. Available at: www.wilsoncenter.org/sites/default/files/Presentacion%20Giraldo.pdf. Accessed August 19, 2017.

Reina, Mauricio. 1996. "La mano invisible: Narcotráfico, economía y crisis." In Francisco Leal Buitrago (Ed.), *Tras las Huellas de la Crisis Política*, Bogotá: TM Editores; 153–180.

Rose-Ackerman, Susan and Rory Truex. 2012. *Corruption and Policy Reform*. Working paper prepared for the Copenhagen Consensus Project, April 27.

Rubio, Mauricio. 2011. "Elite membership and Sexualized Violence Among Central American Gangs." In Thomas Bruneau, Lucía Dammert, and Elizabeth Skinner (Eds.), *Maras: Gang Violence and Security in Central America,* Austin. University of Texas Press; 159–80.

Sánchez, Victor Manuel. 2014. Criminal Networks and Policies. Available at: www.wilsoncenter.org/sites/default/files/criminal_networks_sanchez.pdf. Accessed August 19, 2017.

Schedler, Andreas. 2015. *En la Niebla de la Guerra. Los Ciudadanos Ante la Violencia Criminal Organizada.* Mexico: CIDE.

Silvestre, Giane. 2014. Polícias e Ministério Público: Tensões no campo da investigação do crime em São Paulo. *Confluências Revista Interdisciplinar de Sociologia e Direito,* 16(3): 106–24.

Stephenson, Matthew. 2014. "Klitgaard's Misleading 'Corruption Formula'." Available at: http://global anticorruptionblog.com/2014/05/27/klitgaards-misleading-corruption-formula/. Accessed August 19, 2017.

Stephenson, Matthew. 2015. "Corruption and democratic institutions: a review and synthesis." In Susan Rose-Ackerman and Paul Lagunes (Eds.) *Greed, Corruption and the Modern State: Essays in Political Economy,* North Hampton, MA: Edward Elgar; 92–133.

Stephenson, Svetlana. 2015. *Gangs of Russia: From the Streets to the Corridors of Power.* Cornell University Press.

Transparency International. 2007. *Global Corruption Report: Corruption in Judicial Systems.* Cambridge: Cambridge University Press.

UNODC (United Nations Office on Drugs and Crime). 2012. *Transnational Organized Crime in Central America and the Caribbean: A Threat Assessment.* Available at: www.unodc.org/toc/en/reports/TOCTACentralAmerica-Caribbean.html. Accessed August 19, 2017.

USAID. 2006. *Central America and Mexico Gang Assessment.* Washington, DC: USAID, April.

Vilalta, Carlos and Gustavo Fondevila. 2014. *Perfiles Criminales II: Teorías, Correlativos y Políticas Preventivas.* Mexico: CIDE.

Vogt, Wendy A. 2013. "Crossing Mexico: Structural Violence and the Commodification of Undocumented Central American Migrants." *American Ethnologist,* 40(4): 764–80.

Wainwright, Tom. 2016. *Narco-Economics: How to Run a Drug Cartel.* New York: Public Affairs.

Witte, Eric. A. 2015. *Broken Justice in Mexico's Guerrero State.* New York: Open Society Foundation.

World Bank. 2013. *Making Brazilians Safer: Analyzing the Dynamics of Violent Crime.* Washington, DC: World Bank, Report number 70764.

Zepeda, Guillermo Lecuona. 2012. *Seguimiento del Proceso de Implementación de la Reforma Penal en México Estados de Chihuahua, Estado de México, Morelos, Oaxaca y Zacatecas, 2007–2011.* Washington DC: USAID.

Websites and Online Databases

Fundación Ideas para la Paz. Bogotá, Colombia. Available at: www.ideaspaz.org/. Accessed December 8, 2017.

InSight Crime. Available at: www.insightcrime.org/. Accessed December 8, 2017.

Latin American Public Opinion Project (LAPOP). Nashville, TN. Available at: www.vanderbilt.edu/lapop/. Accessed December 8, 2017.

Latinobarómetro. Opinión Pública Latinoaméricana. Santiago, Chile. Available at: www.latinobarometro.org/lat.jsp. Accessed December 8, 2017.

Security Sector Reform (SSR) Resource Centre. Available at: www.ssrresourcecentre.org/. Accessed December 8, 2017.

Transparency International. Available at: www.transparency.org/. Accessed December 8, 2017.

Oficina de las Naciones Unidas Contra la Droga y el Delito (UNODC). Available at: www.unodc.org/. Accessed December 8, 2017.

World Justice Project. Available at: http://worldjusticeproject.org/. Accessed December 8, 2017.

Worldwide Governance Indicators. Available at: http://info.worldbank.org/governance/wgi/index.aspx#home. Accessed December 8, 2017.

28

THE "NEW MILITARISM" AND THE RULE OF LAW IN LATIN AMERICAN DEMOCRACIES

Julio Ríos-Figueroa

Two paradoxes characterize the role of the armed forces in an already large (and increasing) number of contemporary Latin American democracies. Whereas the traditional war between states is nowadays rare, it is not true that most states are at peace. On the other hand, whereas military coups are not frequent phenomena,[1] it is not true that the armed forces have been successfully subordinated to civilian rule. In the last 20 years, a "new militarism" (Diamint 2015) has been emerging across many countries that involves on the one hand the participation of armed forces in internal security affairs including fighting against insurgency, counterinsurgency, organized criminal violence, paramilitarism, terrorism, and even violent or massive protests (Pion-Berlin 2012, 76). But the "new militarism" also involves some overt military alliances between the armed forces and specific governments as in the ALBA countries: Bolivia; Cuba; Ecuador; Nicaragua; and Venezuela (Diamint 2015, 156). This chapter discusses a series of novel challenges that this "new militarism" poses for the democratic rule of law.

Due to a legacy of military interventions, authoritarianism, and instability across the region the armed forces got used to be unaccountable and to a large extent to impunity for acts that surpassed the bounds of the permissible under a specific military service. Under democracy, this is no longer admissible. Countries in the region require an appropriate accommodation of the armed forces to the democratic rule of law, even if they are actively involved in internal security matters: their performance and use of lethal force should be different from that under authoritarianism. In this chapter, I review three issues where there new militarism is clashing with the rule of law and democracy: (i) the definition and mission of the armed forces in the constitution and the presence of military officers in the government; (ii) the scope of the military justice and the characteristics of its internal processes; and (iii) the role of national constitutional courts and the Inter-American Court of Human Rights (IACHR) in regulating the military jurisdiction and the use of force.

The socio-legal scholarship on the armed forces in Latin America is scarce. There is a rich historical literature on the role of the armed forces in the region (e.g., Loveman 1993, 1999), and also a body of literature on civil-military relations specially since the wave of democratization in the 1980s (Agüero 1995; Pion-Berlin 2001), but not as many analysis using a social science framework to analyze the legal impact of the armed forces' involvement in the politics and society of Latin American countries. I am thinking, for instance, on Robert Barros's analysis of Chilean dictatorship and the Military Junta rule using the framework of constitutionalism (Barros 2002), Anthony

Pereira's analysis of the role of military courts and political trials during under the latest military regimes in Argentina, Brazil, and Chile (Pereira 2005), or Julio Faúndez's book using a democratization framework to analyze the pervasive and corrosive role of the armed forces in Chilean democratic legality and practice from the 1920s and until the coup of 1973 (Faúndez 2011). The point of this chapter is that the impact of the armed forces on the legal and constitutional quality of the region's third-wave democracies has been high and is likely to be higher, thus reinforcing the need for more socio-legal analysis of this phenomenon.

The Armed Forces in the Constitution and in the Government

The focus of this chapter is on the challenges inherent in building a "democratic army," an army that unconditionally supports democratic governance and performs its key missions abiding to the rule of law. This enterprise is inherently conflictive among other reasons because it is not clear what belongs to the "civil" or to the "military" spheres, and it essentially involves striking a delicate balance between ensuring the loyalty of the military to the popularly elected politicians while simultaneously granting to the military sufficient autonomy and strength to successfully discharge its functions and execute its missions (Barany 2012). It is of the essence not only to consider on one side of the question, i.e., assessing the degree of civilian control over the armed forces, but also to pay attention to the military side of things, such as its requirements to perform efficiently and its capacity to carry out its security missions (Brunneau 2013, 143; Pion-Berlin 2012, 76).

The first task is to clearly establish in the constitution the definition and the general mission of the armed forces. Regarding their definition, Latin American constitutions generally provide a list of the three institutions that are part of the armed forces: the army, the navy, and the air force (e.g., Article 73 of the Mexican Constitution of 1917, or Article 165 of the Peruvian Constitution of 1993). The most sensitive issue regarding this list is the inclusion of other forces that are generally in charge of internal security. For instance, Article 328 of the Constitution of Venezuela of 1999 states: "The National Armed Force is comprised of the Army, the Navy, the Air Force and the National Guard." Another example is the 1982 Constitution of Honduras that in Article 273 states: "The Armed Forces include the High Command, the Army, the Navy, the Air Force, the Force of Public Security, plus the institutions that are recognized in its organic law."[2] This is a sensitive issue because, as we will discuss shortly, the main goal of the armed forces is generally to protect the sovereignty and territorial integrity of the country from external threats whereas the main goal of the police forces is to protect it from internal threats as well as the maintenance of order and stability. When police and armed forces are included in the same definition jurisdictional and practical confusion is more likely.

The mission of the armed forces as it is established in the constitution is key and reflects, to a good extent, the ideal role of the armed forces in each country. The traditional role of the armed forces is the defense of the sovereignty of the state and the integrity of its territory from external threats. However, some Latin American constitutions also include in the mission of the armed forces their participation in fighting internal threats. The most recent example is the 2008 Constitution of Ecuador that in an amendment to Article 158 (passed on December 2015) stated: "The mission of the Armed Forces is to defend the sovereignty of the state, the national integrity, and complementarily to provide support in the integral security of the state."[3] This inclusion may be consequential: in Mexico, for instance, complaints against the armed forces for human rights violations before the National Commission of Human Rights have been steadily increasing since the Armed Forces were deployed to fight the "war against drugs" (see for example, Díez 2012; Fondevila and Quintana 2015).[4]

The 1993 Constitution of Peru correctly distinguishes that the mission of the armed forces is to "guarantee the independence, sovereignty, and territorial integrity of the republic" (Article 165), that that of the National Police is to "guarantee, maintain, and reestablish the internal order" (Article 166). Other constitutions make explicit the conditions under which the armed forces can be called upon to face internal threats. For instance, in the Brazilian Constitution of 1988, Article 142 states that the armed forces can contribute to internal "law and order" when requested by the "constitutional powers." Finally, other constitutions explicitly state that the armed forces can participate in policing functions and in fighting internal threats under conditions of emergency or state-of-siege, such as Article 137 of the Peruvian Constitution of 1993 (see for example, García and Uprimny 2005).

It is noteworthy that some Latin American constitutions used to include as part of the Armed Forces' mission something as subjective and vague as the defense of "la patria" (the fatherland) or even the "national pride and honor." As Loveman has pointed out, this was more common in nineteenth century constitutions and according to him at least partly explains the frequency of military interventions (Loveman 1999). Despite its vagueness and anachronism, today we can read in Article 244 of the Constitution of Guatemala of 1985 that: "the mission of the Armed Forces is to maintain the independence, sovereignty and honor of Guatemala." Similarly, in Article 101 of the 1980 Chilean Constitution, one reads that: "to defend the fatherland" is part of the mission of the armed forces. Even the 2008 Constitution of Bolivia, one of the most *avant-garde* constitutions according to many scholars (e.g., Wolff 2012), states in Article 244:

> The mission of the Armed Forces is to defend and to preserve the independence, security, and stability of the State as well as the national honor and sovereignty; the Armed Forces also have to defend the rule of the Political Constitution, guarantee the stability of the legitimately constituted government, and to participate in the integral development of the State.
>
> *(Wolff 2012)*

Notice the inclusion, in Bolivia's Constitutional Article 244, of the defense of both the "national honor" and "the political constitution," which of course can conflict under some circumstances. The most appropriate general mission for the Armed Forces under democracy arguably is the "defense of democracy" (as in Article 150 of the 2008 Constitution of Ecuador), the "defense of the institutions of the republic" (as in Article 252 of the 2010 Constitution of the Dominican Republic), or maybe even the "defense of the alternation in the Executive Power" (Article 272 of the 1982 Constitution of Honduras; though it is uncertain how exactly the armed forces should obey this mandate). In a constitutionalist perspective, perhaps the main goal of the armed forces should be (in addition to the defense of national sovereignty and territorial integrity) the defense of the constitution itself because the armed forces owe its existence to it. For instance, in Article 217 of the 1991 Constitution of Colombia one can read that one of the missions of the armed forces is to "defend the constitutional order." This has been consequential: the Constitutional Court argued that from that mission it follows that crimes committed by members of the armed forces under service that violate human rights should be tried in ordinary (not military) courts because they go against the main mission of the armed forces (cf. C-358 1997 MP Eduardo Cifuentez Muñoz, see Ríos-Figueroa 2016, ch. 3).[5]

Of course, there may be important differences regarding the actual functions performed by the armed forces and what the constitution establishes. Differences between what is constitutionally stated and what actually happens tend to be greater in countries that face external and internal threats because under them the people may pressure the government to call the army, and this can be accompanied with granting them more autonomy in exchange for its participation. However, the active participation of the army in security threats, in particular of the internal kind, increases the likelihood of accidents, tragedies, or plain human rights violations, which in turn impulses the citizens to demand more government control of the armed forces eventually also generating civil–military tensions. As Narcís Serra puts it: "internal armed conflict that has necessitated army intervention, whether ongoing or recent, places the military in a position of strength in relation to a civil government that, precisely because such conflict exists, cannot have firm foundations" (Serra 2010, 67). Kohn also argues, "peacetime military policy excites the most friction between civilian and military officials, and offers the greatest opportunities for the military to exercise its influence" (Kohn 1997, 145).

As mentioned at the outset, the number of Latin American countries facing internal threats (such as fighting against guerrilla organizations, organized crime, and drug traffickers) with the Armed Forces is increasing. The list currently (2016) includes Brazil, Colombia, El Salvador, Guatemala, Honduras, Mexico, and Peru. Interestingly, in many of these countries despite formal military reform they retain significant control over the investigation of charges, and actively work to obstruct the transfer of cases to civilian courts or refuse to release evidence when requested by civilian authorities (Kyle and Reiter 2012, 382). The downside of this direct involvement, as Rut Diamint (2015, 157) explicitly puts it, is that "in no case—not one—has a Latin American military's involvement in civil policing improved public security. If anything, as a string of disturbing Human Rights Watch reports attests, military policing has raised concerns over human-rights abuses." Respecting human rights and the rule of law are not luxuries that Latin American countries can ill afford. A military acting like a police force "threatens not only the rights of civilians and military officers but also its own proper institutional identity" (Diamint 2015, 157).

Consider now the participation of military officers in the government. There can be one or more government ministries devoted to defense and security issues. When there is one ministry for each branch of the armed forces (army, navy, and the air force) it is more likely that military officials exert influence on areas that are arguably more "civilian" such as maritime transport and ports as well as air travel and airports (Serra 2010, 182). In addition, a single defense ministry facilitates coordination between armed forces, the civil government, and the public at large. As the former defense minister in Spain puts it, "the connecting link between government and the armed forces and, to a large extent, between them and society, is the defense minister" (Serra 2010, 242). Thus, the creation of a single ministry of defense is key in the process of establishing proper democratic bounds between the "civil" and the "military." Now, the minister can be a civilian or a military officer. Whereas in the first stages of a transition to democracy from an authoritarian regime a military defense minister can make key contributions, eventually "the minister has to be a civilian if the government wishes to make it crystal clear that it decides and leads defense policy, that is, if it wants to stabilize a situation of democratic consolidation" (Serra 2010, 242). Moreover, a single ministry led by a civilian helps reframing the ideals and goals of the military-as-institution under the democratic framework (Agüero 1995, 214).

Latin American democracies display interesting variation regarding the number of ministries devoted to the armed forces and the identity of the holders of their top positions (i.e., civilian or military). Figure 28.1 (left panel) shows average values on the index of military participation in government over the period 1978–2012 for the 18 largest Latin American countries (except Cuba). The index takes values from 0 to 9 depending on the number of government ministries devoted to the Armed Forces (e.g., different ministries for the army, navy, and air force instead of a single ministry of defense) and on whether the head of the ministry is a military officer or a civilian (and on whether the civilian is a male or female).[6] Higher values correspond to higher

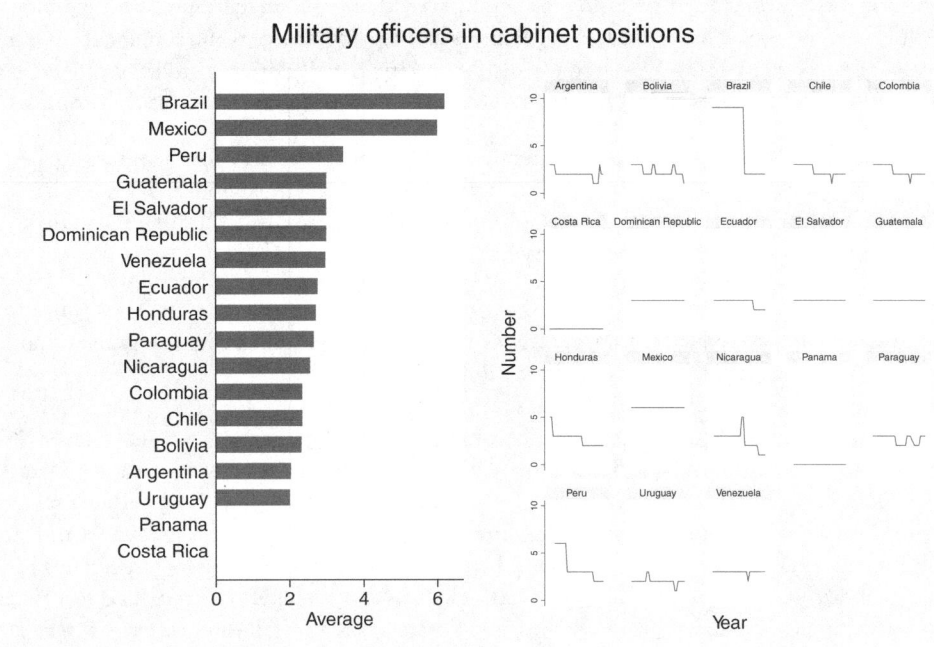

Figure 28.1   Military Participation in Government, 1978–2013

levels of military participation in government, and thus arguably to higher probabilities of military officers getting involved in properly civilian affairs.[7] Figure 28.1 shows that Brazil is the country with the highest average and Costa Rica and Panama, where there are no armed forces, have the lowest average. Of course, there are changes across time (Figure 28.1, right panel). In Brazil, for instance, since 1999 there is a single ministry of defense headed by a civilian politician. In Peru, a single ministry of defense was created in 1985, but it was usually headed by military officers until 2003 (Brunneau 2013, 152; Hunter 1997).

In sum, Latin American democracies still have much to do in terms of the constitutional role of the armed forces and their incorporation into and participation in the government. Of course there are countries where the accommodation of the armed forces within a constitutional democratic framework is more advanced (notably Argentina). But there are others where the armed forces fit with this framework is far from ideal, and when this is compounded by an active involvement of the armed forces in security crises (internal or external) the prospects for a proper accommodation are not bright. This lack of fit shows more clearly in specific dimensions of the armed forces, such as the military justice and the more general military jurisdiction to which we now turn.

Military Justice and the Military Jurisdiction

The military jurisdiction reinforces the armed forces as an institution as it serves them to uphold distinct values and criteria. This is fine, but it also explains why the armed forces are tempted to use their justice system as a source of privilege, even in consolidated democracies, promoting values or criteria that in some occasions may be in tension, or even opposed, to those of the democratic society. The question is how autonomous and how broad the military justice should be: If it is very autonomous, procedural guarantees and legal standards that are obligatory in the ordinary justice system could be overlooked. If it is very broad, not only military officers but also civilians could be investigated and tried in the military jurisdiction. In transition contexts,

> the military try to maintain an independent system of justice in order to guarantee immunity for their previous behavior, as a way of camouflaging actions that represent an abuse of human rights, or simply as a means to grant themselves a different status and privileges in respect of civil society.
>
> *(Serra 2010, 73)*

Therefore, attempts to reduce the autonomy or the scope of the military justice system tend to create tensions between civilians and the armed forces.[8]

How broad is the military jurisdiction in Latin American democracies? Figure 28.2 shows the average of an index on the *de jure* scope of military jurisdiction that allows us to assess this element both across countries and across time within countries.[9] The index covers the 18 largest Latin American countries from 1978 to 2013, and it takes values from 0 to 7 depending on what the constitution of each country says regarding the question: who can be judged in military courts, and when? Higher values correspond to a broader scope of military jurisdiction, for instance where the constitution allows that both civilians and members of the armed forces can be judges in military courts in times of peace.[10] Figure 28.2 shows that in average the *de jure* scope of military jurisdiction is broadest in Paraguay and narrowest in the Dominican Republic. Across time within the same country, however, there is little variation in the *de jure* scope of military jurisdiction (Figure 28.2, right panel).

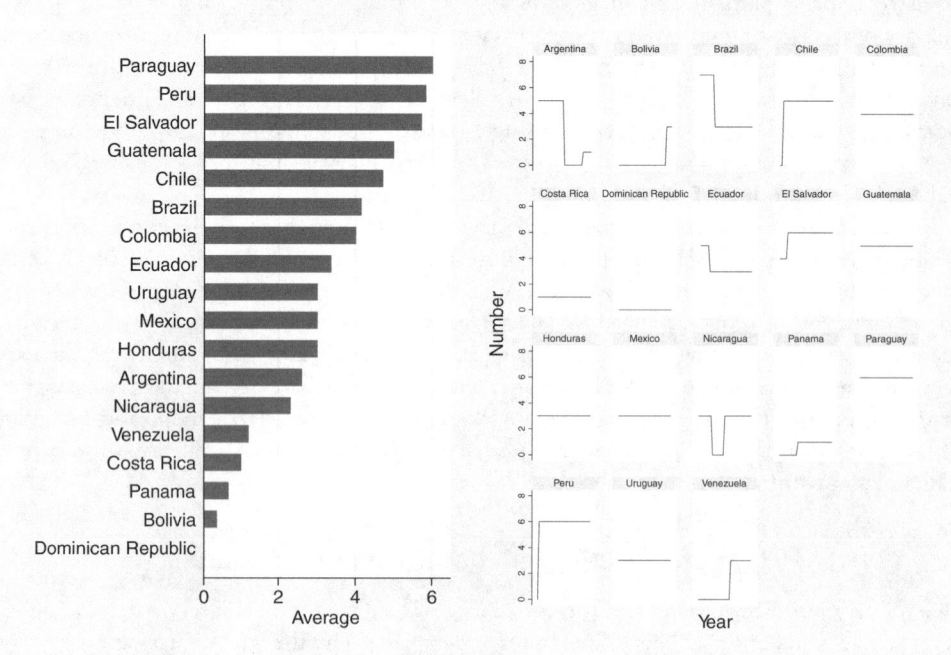

Figure 28.2 De Jure Scope of Military Jurisdiction, 1978–2013

Whereas the index in Figure 28.2 shows the *de jure* scope of military jurisdiction, recent scholarly assessments of military reform, that include reforms to the scope of the military jurisdiction, are overall consistent with it. For instance, Anthony Pereira notes that:

> whereas in Argentina democratization resulted in the exclusion of civilians from the jurisdiction of peacetime military justice, the rigorous subjection of military courts to civilian review, and the sending of cases involving nonmilitary crimes of military and police personnel to civilian courts. In Mexico, in contrast, crimes of a nonmilitary nature are tried in military courts, which are not fully subject to civilian review. Brazil and Chile have the broadest military court jurisdiction. There civilians are subject to military justice, civilian courts have limited review powers over military courts, and nonmilitary crimes by both police and armed forces personnel are tried in military courts.
>
> *(Pereira 2001, 559)*

Similarly, a recent article by Kyle and Reiter (2012, 36–9) classifying Latin American countries regarding their progress in reforming the military justice system, locates Costa Rica, Panama, Nicaragua, and Argentina as countries that have experienced significant reform; Ecuador and Paraguay in the category of incomplete reform; Bolivia and Peru as having experienced a minor reform; and Chile and Mexico with no reform. Kyle and Reiter add that in seven countries (Dominican Republic, El Salvador, Guatemala, Honduras, Colombia, Uruguay, and Brazil) reforms efforts have produced contentious responses from the armed forces. It is possible to establish the following connection (but a systematic analysis would be appropriate): countries that are experiencing internal security crisis faced with the armed forces tend to be the ones where military justice reform is less developed.

Another relevant dimension of the military jurisdiction is the autonomy of the military justice system, or the extent to which its procedures can deviate from those followed by courts in the ordinary justice system. In other words, this dimension touches upon issues such as the duration of military investigations and trials, the composition of military tribunals, and the procedural rights of both plaintiffs and defendants in military trials. In this dimension one also finds, in one extreme, a military justice system that follows the exact same procedures that are found in the ordinary system and, in the other, a military justice that is highly autonomous and can follow or not such procedures and whose decisions are not appealable before ordinary courts (including the supreme court). Again, these extremes are analytically useful to locate specific cases within the continuum even if they are mere theoretical and no real examples can be found of them.

Take, for instance, the case of Peru. Eto Cruz and Landa posit that the 1993 Constitution of that country "explicitly prohibits that the decisions of the Supreme Council of the Military Jurisdiction can be reviewed by the ordinary courts, including any sentence even of life imprisonment." These authors add that "this is dangerous not only for those civilians who challenge the state in a violent fashion but also, and fundamentally, to the military itself" (Eto, Landa, and Palomino 1997, 390). At the other extreme, we find the case of Argentina where two justices argued (in a dissenting opinion) that the military justice system is altogether unconstitutional in a case that challenged the lack of due process guarantees in the military justice that reached the supreme court in 2007. Justices Zaffaroni and Lorenzetti argued that the military justice itself violates key constitutional principles such as judicial independence and the neutrality of the judge (see *Caso López* Fallos 54:577; 310:1797, March 2007). Interestingly, one year later (in 2008) the Argentinean Congress following that reasoning derogated the military justice.

Note, finally, that the two dimensions of the military jurisdiction (its scope and its degree of autonomy) are related but also clearly distinguishable. For instance, think about a hypothetical case of a strictly military crime (such as insubordination or desertion) committed by an active member of the armed forces during a specific mission. This case satisfies all the requirements to be investigated and tried in the military justice system. However, there is still the question of how autonomous is that system, that is how exactly that case will be investigated and tried. In some countries military judges can be active members of the armed forces, whereas in other countries this has been prohibited on grounds that being an active member (and usually a superior vis-à-vis the defendant) violates the principle of neutrality (see Lovatón Palacios 2007 for an interesting analysis of this issue in the case of Peru). Moreover, in some countries the composition of the military court could be challenged before an ordinary tribunal, as well as other procedures and decisions based on the due process rights of both the victim and the defendant (as was the case in Argentina). The two dimensions, therefore, provide a framework for analyzing the fit of the military jurisdiction and the military justice with a broader rule of law, constitutionalism framework, and to explore both the causes and consequences of the fit or lack thereof.

Judicial Oversight of the Armed Forces

Third-wave Latin American democracies display variation in another aspect is closely related to the accommodation of the armed forces to the democratic rule of law: the role of national constitutional courts and the IACHR. Although judicial review or constitutional adjudication has been present in at least some countries in the region since the second half of the nineteenth century, it was not until the last three decades that there is a clear regional shift (though not in all countries at the same time) to delegate this authority to judges who were also made independent, at least in paper (Ríos-Figueroa 2011). Autonomous constitutional courts have been created in countries such as Brazil or Colombia. Supreme courts, or one of its chambers, have been invested with greater constitutional review powers in Costa Rica or Mexico. Access to constitutional justice has been broadened considerably in countries like Colombia or Costa Rica. The list of justiciable rights has been expanded in virtually all constitutions of the region. In general, the gist of this institutional change is the incorporation of a new actor, the constitutional judges, with power to breathe new life into new or reformed constitutions across the region. But variations in the timing and content of judicial reforms are expressed in diverse levels of independence, access, and judicial review powers.

To the extent that constitutional courts are independent, accessible, and that have ample judicial review powers they are more to contribute to striking a democratically accepted balance between the exercise of civilian authority and the legitimate needs of the military in its pursuit of national security (Ríos-Figueroa 2016). Civilian control over the military is not a fact but a process that needs to recognize the specifics of the military organization. As Kohn puts it: "[The] Military cannot perform its duty, nor can civilians exercise their authority, unless the machinery of government allows military and civilian perspectives to mix in the formulation of policy" (Kohn 1997). Constitutional courts can be forums where Kohn´s concern is addressed, where military and civilian perspectives in the pursuit of order and security that constitutional justice can be mixed, under the principles and values of the constitution.

The intervention of constitutional courts in military-related issues is not always positive. In Bolivia in 2003, after months of massive demonstrations, the government called the military to combat protesters. By the end of the year, after a series of confrontations, the death toll reached 80 people and the wounded were in the hundreds (Kyle and Reiter 2012, 389). Some military officials were accused of having used force disproportionately and of having violated human rights. For years, in Bolivia cases like these were sent to military courts.[11] But on May 6, 2004 the Bolivian Constitutional Tribunal ruled that military personnel allegedly responsible for human rights violations had to be tried in civilian courts (Sentencia Constitucional 0664/2004-R). In reaction to this ruling, the leaders of the military confined their troops to barracks and held an all-day meeting to decide on a response. In an open letter, the military threatened the court with "grave consequences," and in the ensuing political standoff, the Bolivian president and the high courts dropped their efforts to hold the military accountable (Pion-Berlin 2010, 537–9).

Interestingly, the Bolivian Constitutional Tribunal cited a decision by the Colombian Constitutional Court in support of its ruling, in which the latter argued that the link between a crime and military service, a requisite to be tried in military courts, is severed in cases of grave violations of human rights (C-358 1997 MP Eduardo Cifuentes Muñoz). But in contrast to the Bolivian decision that came suddenly, without a warning, the Colombian one built on a jurisprudential trend of gradual but progressive limitation of the scope of military jurisdiction.[12] Again in contrast to what happened in Bolivia, the Colombian armed forces accepted a ruling that they knew was coming and they have come to adopt the criteria that military courts should never investigate or try grave human rights violations.

The IACHR also has been an important actor regarding the accommodation of the armed forces to the region's third-wave democracies and rule of law standards. The IACHR's jurisprudence on this issue has arguably reached a normative consensus around three points: civilians do not belong in military courts under any circumstance; only members of the armed forces for strictly military crimes committed under service can be investigated and tried in this special jurisdiction; but, when grave human rights violations are involved military officials should go to ordinary courts. However, individual countries fall below/on/above the standard and the timing, velocity, and historical patterns greatly differ among countries. In Brazil, for instance, civilians constituted 13.5 percent of defendants in military court cases in the period 2002–2012 (some 2,555 cases).[13] In contrast, as mentioned above, the Argentinean Congress in 2008 derogated the Code of Military Justice and the whole military jurisdiction considering it unconstitutional.

Since its creation and until 2015, the IACHR has decided 140 cases related to criminal law and, out of these, approximately 12 percent deal directly with the military jurisdiction (Ferrer 2016, 59).[14] In what effectively is a noteworthy jurisprudential development, the IACHR has consistently argued:

> In a state that upholds the democratic rule of law the military jurisdictional should be an exceptional jurisdiction with a limited scope with the main goal of protecting the persons and interests strictly linked to the functions and missions of the armed forces. Therefore, the military jurisdiction should only investigate and try active members of the armed forces for crimes strictly related to their performance under a specific service or mission.
>
> *(Case Radilla Pacheco v. Estados Unidos Mexicanos, paragraph 272)*[15]

Similarly, the IACHR has established that "the military jurisdiction is not the appropriate jurisdiction to investigate and try cases of grave human rights violations, those belong to the ordinary justice system."[16] In sum, through a rich and thorough jurisprudence the IACHR has established the three clear criteria mentioned above to determine the proper scope of the military jurisdiction: (i) only members of the armed forces, and never civilians, belong to the military jurisdiction; (ii) only for crimes strictly related to the exercise of the military function and that take place during a specific mission; and (iii) cases of grave human rights violations never belong to the military jurisdiction (cf. Ferrer 2016, 65–6).

The IACHR has also established clear criteria regarding the internal procedures of the military jurisdiction, or its autonomy from the ordinary justice system. Specifically, it has touched upon the question of who should (or should not) be judges in military tribunals in order to guarantee the principles of independence and neutrality. The IACHR has argued that when the military prosecutors or judges are active members of the armed forces their impartiality is compromised because "it is likely that they have a direct interest in the case, a position taken, a preference for one of the parts in the case, and in general that they are directly involved in the specific controversy,"[17] due to the fact that the armed forces have simultaneously to combat certain groups and to investigate and try members of those same groups (that may be civilians or military officers involved in those cases).[18]

The potential lack of impartiality when active members of the armed forces serve as military judges and prosecutors also stems from the hierarchical nature of the institution, and the likelihood that superiors may oftentimes be investigating or judging the performance of their subordinates. This insert in the processes elements that are alien to the specifics of the case such as the expectation of getting a promotion or other kind of professional incentives, as well as discipline and loyalty issues.[19] According to former Inter-American Judge Diego García Sayán, an additional problem is that the military judges and prosecutors generally do not enjoy the minimum guarantees of tenure and do not possess an adequate legal education to deal with the complex juridical issues that reached the door of military tribunals (cited in Ferrer 2016, 68). A recent case decided by the IACHR, *Argüelles y Otros* v. *Argentina* (2014) has expanded the controls over the military jurisdiction to those involving economic matters and due process. In this case, the IACHR sided with the military officers who filed a complaint arguing that their right to counsel and their right to an expedited trial had been violated in the military justice system.

The regulation of the use of force has not directly addressed by the IACHR as part of the military jurisdiction. However, this court has established some relevant precedents in this relevant topic. For instance, the IACHR has argued "in times of peace the agents of the State should distinguish between persons that due to their actions pose an imminent threat of death or serious injury and those that don't, and use lethal force only against the former."[20] Similarly, it has argued "the use of lethal force and fire arms should be banned in general and strictly regulated in laws that should be interpreted restrictively, leaving it only to situations in which it is absolutely necessary."[21]

When members of the armed forces participate in internal security missions, it is imperative that they observe strictly these (and others) principles regarding the use of lethal force. Moreover, they have to be trained in them because generally the military officers are prepared to attack, as a proactive force, whereas involvement in internal security oftentimes requires prevention, a reactive attitude. The criteria and standards on the use of lethal force are highly consequential for the members of the armed forces because they help to eventually determine whether a crime was committed and whether it should be tried in a military or an ordinary court.

Conclusions

The "new militarism" in the region raises novel and relevant challenges to the democratic rule of law. The general idea developed in this chapter is that Latin American countries in the last 30 years have been developing, at different rates and in different forms, ways to transform their armed forces from the challenge to stability and democracy that they often were in the past into relevant actors that are key for the sustainability and strength of democracy and the rule of law. The chapter reviews three areas where the "new militarism" and the democratic rule of law are in direct contact: (i) the definition and mission of the armed forces in the constitution and the presence of military officers in the government; (ii) the scope of the military justice and the characteristics of its internal processes; and (iii) the role of national constitutional courts and the IACHR in regulating the military jurisdiction and the use of force. The region displays interesting variation across these three areas, something that calls for explain both its causes and perhaps more importantly its consequences.

Other topics that have been relatively unexplored but are both interesting and relevant for Latin American democracies are the relationship between the IACHR, the national courts, and the national governments in cases that have to do with the armed forces, the military jurisdiction, and the use of force. What explains variation in compliance with IACHR decisions across national courts governments? Have successful national experiences, such as Colombia's, influence the Inter-American institutions and how? What are the connections between these processes and the amnesties, and different transitional justice measures and processes that have been implemented across many countries in the region?[22] The "new militarism" should not be taken lightly. Though it does not involve overt international wars and coups d'état, if the challenges it poses are not dealt with appropriately, it has the potential to hollow out and destabilize Latin American democracies.

Socio-legal perspectives on the "new militarism" across Latin America are likely to be particularly fruitful. Employing social science theory to analyze a legal phenomenon, usually located in the borders of the constitutional and the political spheres, may help take these topics out of the "high politics" and "military specialists'" realm and link them to the experiences of the increasing number of people that are suffering the consequences of militarized security. This is a topic that cuts across courts and judges, of different types, human rights, and the legal and constitutional quality of Latin American current democracies.

Notes

1 In fact, most coup attempts have failed. The successful cases include Haiti in 1991 and 2004 when President Aristide was deposed by the military in both occasions, and arguably the cases of Honduras in 2009 and of Ecuador in 2000 when Presidents Zelaya and Mahuad, respectively, were deposed with the help of the military but a military regime was not established afterwards. In turn, the failed coup attempts include Venezuela in 1992 and in 2002 (Hugo Chávez was the plotter the first time, and the victim the second); Paraguay in 1996, when General Lino Oviedo tried to depose President Wasmosy. Somewhat different are the so-called self-coups with military help, a successful one in Peru in 1992 led by President Fujimori, and a failed one in Guatemala in 1993 lead by President Serrano (see for example, Marsteinderet and Berntzen 2008; Pérez-Liñán 2010).
2 In countries with no armed forces, such as Panama or Costa Rica, their constitution establishes that (as in Article 12 of the Costa Rica Constitution of 1949): "The Army is proscribed as a permanent institution. For the vigilance and security of the public order there will be the necessary police forces."
3 The Mexican Supreme Court in its decision AI 1/1996 argued that it is constitutional that the armed forces partake in internal security affairs as long as it they do so by invitation from the civilian authorities (see Ríos-Figueroa 2016, ch. 5).
4 The number of complaints was 398 in 2007 and jumped to 2,190 in 2011. See Comisión Mexicana de Defensa y Promoción de los Derechos Humanos. 2013. *Jurisdicción militar: impunidad y violaciones a los derechos humanos. Análisis enero.*
5 MP stands for "Magistrado Ponente," the judge who writes the draft of a decision that is discussed by the court.
6 Data was obtained from webpages of the ministries of defense, the ATLAS RESDAL (2012), the Cross National Time Series Data Archive (Data Banks International).

7 Though my interpretation of what the measure captures is slightly different, I coded the variable based on Pion-Berlin who argued that:

> where civilians control a single defense military ministry, military autonomy is at its lowest. Where military-supervised defense ministry or separate branch ministries under civilian control exists, then military autonomy is higher. And it is higher still where cabinet-ranking military ministers run their own bureaucracies.
>
> *(Pion-Berlin 1992, 88)*

8 The armed forces during and after regime transitions may also want to block the reform of military justice in order to cloak the previous arbitrary use of military courts in the mantle of legality and juridical tradition, creating a positive legal project around repression that is at least partly credible (Pereira 2001, 560).

9 Data was collected from national constitutions.

10 The variable takes the value of 0 when the constitution of the country does not mention the military jurisdiction; value of 1 when it says there is no military jurisdiction; value of 2 when nobody can be tried in military courts for human rights violations; value of 3 when only military officials for strictly military crimes belong to the military jurisdiction; value of 4 when military officials under service belong to the military jurisdiction; value of 5 when military officials always belong to the military jurisdiction; value of 6 when even civilians under emergency can be tried in military courts; and value of 7 when even civilians in no emergency situations can be tried in military courts.

11 In Bolivia, since the transition to democracy in 1982, human rights cases involving members of the military were handled by military tribunals that protected its members and failed to advance cases ... Despite hundreds of deaths at the hands of security forces, there were no convictions from 1985 to 2003.

> *(Human Rights Watch World Report 2013)*

12 Details on the jurisprudential line can be found in Ríos-Figueroa (2016) in Chapter 3.

13 "Julgamento Militar é posto em debate," *O Globo*, August 3, 2014.

14 The list of the IACHR's most notorious cases on the topic includes the following: (1) *Caso Loayza Tamayo* v. *Perú. Fondo.* Sentencia del 17 de Septiembre de 1997, Serie C, núm. 33; (2) *Caso Loayza Tamayo* v. *Perú. Reparaciones y Costas.* Sentencia del 27 de Noviembre de 1998, Serie C, núm. 42; (3) *Caso Castillo Petruzzi y otros* v. *Perú. Fondo, Reparaciones y Costas.* Sentencia del 30 de Mayo de 1999, Serie C, núm. 52; (4) *Caso Cesti Hurtado* v. *Perú. Fondo.* Sentencia del 29 de Septiembre de 1999, Serie C, núm. 56; (5) *Caso Durand y Ugarte* v. *Perú. Fondo.* Sentencia del 16 de Agosto de 2000, Serie C, núm. 68; (6) *Caso Cantoral Benavides* v. *Perú. Fondo.* Sentencia de 18 de Agosto de 2000, Serie C, núm. 69; (7) *Caso Bámaca Velásquez* v. *Guatemala. Fondo.* Sentencia del 25 de Noviembre de 2000, Serie C, núm. 70; (8) *Caso Las Palmeras* v. *Colombia. Fondo.* Sentencia del 6 de Diciembre de 2001, Serie C, núm. 90; (9) *Caso Myrna Mack Chang* v. *Guatemala. Fondo, Reparaciones y Costas.* Sentencia del 25 de Noviembre de 2003, Serie C, núm. 101; (10) *Caso 19 Comerciantes* v. *Colombia. Fondo, Reparaciones y Costas.* Sentencia del 5 de Julio de 2004, Serie C, núm. 109; (11) *Caso Lori Berenson Mejía* v. *Perú. Fondo, Reparaciones y Costas.* Sentencia del 25 de Noviembre de 2004, Serie C, núm. 119; (12) *Caso de la Masacre de Mapiripán* v. *Colombia. Fondo, Reparaciones y Costas.* Sentencia del 15 de Septiembre de 2005, Serie C, núm. 134; (13) *Caso Palamara Iribarne* v. *Chile. Fondo, Reparaciones y Costas.* Sentencia del 22 de Noviembre de 2005, Serie C, núm. 135; (14) *Caso de la Masacre de Pueblo Bello* v. *Colombia. Fondo, Reparaciones y Costas.* Sentencia del 31 de Enero de 2006, Serie C, núm. 140; (15) *Caso Almeonacid Arellano y Otros* v. *Chile. Excepciones Preliminares, Fondo, Reparaciones y Costas.* Sentencia del 26 de Septiembre de 2006, Serie C, núm. 154; (16) *Caso La Cantuta* v. *Perú. Fondo, Reparaciones y Costas.* Sentencia del 29 de Noviembre de 2006, Serie C, núm. 162; (17) *Caso de la Masacre de la Rochela* v. *Colombia. Fondo, Reparaciones y Costas.* Sentencia del 11 de Mayo de 2007, Serie C, núm. 163; (18) *Caso Escué Zapata* v. *Colombia. Fondo, Reparaciones y Costas.* Sentencia del 4 de Julio de 2007, Serie C, núm. 165; (19) *Caso Zambrano Vélez y Otros* v. *Ecuador. Fondo, Reparaciones y Costas.* Sentencia del 4 de Julio de 2007, Serie C, núm. 166; (20) *Caso Tiu Tojín* v. *Guatemala. Fondo, Reparaciones y Costas.* Sentencia del 26 de Noviembre de 2008, Serie C, núm. 190; (21) *Caso Usón Ramírez* v. *Venezuela. Excepción Preliminar, Fondo, Reparaciones y Costas.* Sentencia del 20 de Noviembre de 2009, Serie C, núm. 207; (22) *Caso Radilla Pacheco* v. *México. Excepciones Preliminares, Fondo, Reparaciones y Costas.* Sentencia del 23 de Noviembre de 2009, Serie C, núm. 209; (23) *Caso Fernández Ortega y Otros.* v. *México. Excepción Preliminar, Fondo, Reparaciones y Costas.* Sentencia del 30 de Agosto de 2010, Serie C, núm. 215; and (24) *Caso Rosendo Cantú y Otra* v. *México. Excepción Preliminar, Fondo, Reparaciones y Costas.* Sentencia del 31 de Agosto de 2010 Serie C, núm. 216.

15 Case *Radilla Pacheco* v. *Estados Unidos Mexicanos*, paragraph 272, p. 78. Available at: www.corteidh. or.cr/docs/casos/articulos/seriec_209_ing.pdf. Consulted March 31, 2019.
16 Case *Nadege Drozema* v. *República Dominicana*, paragraph 187.
17 Case *Palamara Iribarne* v. *Chile*, paragraph 146.
18 Case *Durand y Ugarte* v. *Perú*, paragraph 125.
19 Case *Castillo Petruzzi y Otros* v. *Perú*, paragraph 130.
20 Case *Zambrano Vélez y Otros* v. *Ecuador*, paragraph 85.
21 Case Familia Barros v. Venezuela, paragraph 49.
22 Between the 1980s and 1990s 16 Latin American countries passed amnesty laws to prevent potentially destabilizing criminal investigations (Sikkink and Walling 2007). Some of these amnesties were blanket amnesties, like the one passed by the Peruvian Congress in 1995. Others like for example, the Argentine and Guatemalan amnesties, contemplated exceptions.

References

Agüero, Felipe. 1995. *Militares, Civiles y Democracia. La España Postfranquista en Perspectiva Comparada*. Madrid: Alianza Editorial.

Barany, Zoltan. 2012. *The Soldier and the Chaning State. Building Democratic Armies in Africa, Asia, Europe and the Americas*. Princeton, NJ: Princeton University Press.

Barros, Robert. 2002. *Constitutionalism and Dictatorship: Pinochet, the Junta, and the 1980 Constitution*. New York, NY: Cambridge University Press.

Brunneau, Thomas. 2013. Civilians and the military in Latin America: The absence of ancentives. *Latin American Politics and Society* 55(4): 143–60.

Diamint, Rut. 2015. A new militarism in Latin America. *Journal of Democracy* 26(4): 155–68.

Díez, Jordi. 2012. "Civic–military relations in Mexico: The unfinished transition." In Rodric Ai Camp (Ed.). *The Oxford Handbook of Mexican Politics*. New York: Oxford University Press, 265–85.

Eto, Gerardo, Cesar Landa Arroyo, and José Palomino Manchego. 1997. "La justicia militar en el Perú." In Germán Bidart and José Palomino (Eds.). *Jurisdicción Militar y Constitución en Iberoamérica*. Lima: Grijley, 353–463.

Faúndez, Julio. 2011. *Democratización, Desarrollo y Legalidad. Chile, 1831–1973*. Santiago, Chile: Universidad Diego Portales.

Ferrer Mac-Gregor, Eduardo. 2016. Las siete principales líneas jurisprudenciales de La Corte Interamericana de Derechos Humanos aplicable a la justicia penal. *Revista IIDH* 59(1): 29–118.

Fondevila, Gustavo and Miguel Quintana-Navarrete. 2015. War hypothesis: drug trafficking, sovereignty, and the armed forces in Mexico. *Bulletin of Latin American Research*: 1–17.

García, Mauricio and Rodrigo Uprimny. 2005. "La normalization de L'exceptionnel. sur le contrôl jurisdictionnel des États d'urgence en Colombie." In Marie Julie Bernard and Michel Carraud (Eds.). *Justice et Démocratie En Amérique Latine*. Grenoble: PUG, 117–43.

Human Rights Watch. 2013. *Human Rights Watch World Report*. 2013. New York, NY: Human Rights Watch.

Hunter, Wendy. 1997. Continuity or change? Civil–military relations in democratic Argentina, Chile, and Peru. *Political Science Quarterly* 112(3): 453–75.

Kohn, Richard. 1997. "How democracies control the military." *Journal of Democracy* 8(4): 140–53.

Kyle, Brett and Andrew Reiter. 2012. Dictating justice: Human rights and military courts in Latin America. *Armed Forces & Society* 38(1): 27–48.

Kyle, Brett. 2013. Militarized justice in new democracies: Explaining the process of military court reform in Latin America. *Law and Society Review* 47(2): 375–407.

Lovatón, David. 2007. *Tribunal Constitucional y Reforma de la Justicia Militar*. Lima: Palestra.

Loveman, Brian. 1993. *The Constitution of Tyranny. Regimes of Exception in Spanish America*. Pittsburgh, PA: University of Pittsburgh Press.

Loveman, Brian. 1999. *For la Patria: Politics and the Armed Forces in Latin America*. Willmington: Scholarly Resources.

Marsteinderet, Leiv and Einar Berntzen. 2008. Reducing the perils of presidentialism in Latin America through presidential interruptions. *Comparative Politics* 41(1): 83–119.

Pereira, Anthony. 2005. *Political (In)Justice. Authoritarianism and the Rule of Law in Argentina, Brazil, and Chile*. Pittsburgh, PA: University of Pittsburgh Press.

Pereira, Anthony. 2001. Virtual legality authoritarian legacies and the reform of military justice in Brazil, the Southern Cone, and Mexico. *Comparative Political Studies* 34(5): 555–74.

Pérez-Liñán, Aníbal. 2010. *Presidential Impeachment and the New Politics of Instability in Latin America.* New York, NY: Cambridge University Press.

Pion-Berlin, David. 1992. Military autonomy and emerging democracies in South America. *The Journal of Comparative Politics* 25(1): 83–102. Available at: www.jstor.org/stable/422098?origin=crossref. Accessed January 16, 2016.

Pion-Berlin, (Ed.) 2001. *Civil-Military Relations in Latin America. New Analytical Perspectives.* Chapell Hill, NC: The University of North Carolina Press.

Pion-Berlin. 2010. Informal civil-military relations in Latin America: Why politicians and soldiers choose unofficial venues. *Armed Forces and Society* 36(3): 526–44.

Pion-Berlin. 2012. "The Latin American military." In Peter Kingstone and Deborah J. Yashar (Eds.). *Routledge Handbook of Latin American Politics.* New York, NY: Routledge, 76–87.

RESDAL. 2012. *Atlas Comparativo de la Defensa en América Latina y el Caribe.* Buenos Aires.

Ríos-Figueroa, Julio. 2011. "Institutions for constitutional justice in Latin America." In *Courts in Latin America*, eds. Gretchen Helmke and Julio Ríos-Figueroa. New York, NY: Cambridge University Press, 27–54.

Ríos-Figueroa, Julio. 2016. *Constitutional Courts as Mediators. Armed Conflict, Civil-Military Relations, and the Rule of Law in Latin America.* New York, NY: Cambridge University Press.

Serra, Narcís. 2010. *The Military Transition. Democratic Reform of the Armed Forces.* New York, NY: Cambridge University Press.

Sikkink, Kathryn and Carrie Booth Walling. 2007. The impact of Human Rights trials in Latin America. *Journal of Peace Research* 44(4): 427–45.

Wolff, Jonas. 2012. "New Constitutions and the Transformation of Democracy in Bolivia and Ecuador." In Detlef Nolte and Almut Schilling-Vacaflor (Eds.). *New Constitutionalism in Latin America. Promises and Practices.* New York, NY: Ashgate, 183–202.

Constitutions

Bolivia. 2008. Constitución Política de Bolivia. Article, 244.

Costa Rica. 1949. Constitución Política de la República de Costa Rica.

Ecuador. 2008. Constitución de la República del Ecuador. Articles, 150 and 158.

Honduras. 1982. Constitución Política de Honduras. Article, 272.

México. 1917. *Constitución Política de los Estados Unidos Mexicanos.* Articles, 73 and 165.

Panamá. (año?). Constitución Política de la República de Panamá.

Perú. 1993. *Constitución Política del Perú.* Articles, 165 and 166.

República Dominicana. 2010. Constitución de la República Dominicana. Article, 252.

Legal Documents

Comisión Mexicana de Defensa y Promoción de los Derechos Humanos. 2013. *Jurisdicción militar: impunidad y violaciones a los derechos humanos. Análisis enero.* Available at: www.cmdpdh.org/publicaciones-pdf/cmcpdh-briefing-enero-2013-justicia-militar-sk.pdf. Accessed January 16, 2016.

México. Suprema Corte de Justicia de la Nación. 1996. *Acuerdo del Pleno de la Suprema Corte de Justicia de la Nación, Decision AI 1/1996.* México.

(cf. C-358 1997 MP Eduardo Cifuentez Muñoz)

Caso López Fallos 54:577; 310:1797, March 2007).

Sentencia Constitucional 0664/2004-R).

C-358 1997 MP Eduardo Cifuentes Muñoz).

Case *Argüelles y otros* v. *Argentina.*

Case *Radilla Pacheco* v. *Estados Unidos Mexicanos*, paragraph 272.

Case *Nadege Drozema* v. *República Dominicana*, paragraph 187.

Case *Palamara Iribarne* v. *Chile*, paragraph 146.

Case *Durand y Ugarte* v. *Perú*, paragraph 125.

Case *Castillo Petruzzi y otros* v. *Perú*, paragraph 130.

Case *Zambrano Vélez y Otros* v. *Ecuador*, paragraph 85.

Case Familia Barros v. Venezuela, paragraph 49.

29

DRUGS AND THE LAW IN LATIN AMERICA

The Legal, Institutional, and Social Costs of Drug Policy

Alejandro Madrazo Lajous and Catalina Pérez Correa

Introduction

Drug laws and drug policy is one of the topics where law and society methodologies have more interestingly and abundantly been used in Latin America. This is not to say that law and society literature regarding drug laws is abundant in absolute terms; but it is so in relative terms, when compared to other areas of legal studies in Latin America, where law and society approaches are far from mainstream. Drug laws tend to be primarily criminal laws or intimately linked to criminal law. For many academics that study criminal laws in books – from a formal or merely procedural perspective – drug laws and drug policy have been of little interest. However, for those who study criminal law in action and have come face to face with the effects drug laws have on the criminal justice system, they have sparked more interest. In discourse, Latin American drug policy primarily focuses on reducing the supply side of illicit drugs by targeting organized crime; yet, in practice, legal institutions continue to target consumers and use supply-reduction oriented laws to extort and criminalize users. How does this happen? We will explain how the increasingly punitive enforcement of drug laws has implied the militarization of public safety in the region, the increase of sanctions for drug crimes, the frequent violation of due process right and the increase of illegal practices by authorities, including torture and illegal use of lethal force. This has happened on occasion in spite of liberalizing reforms to regulation, yes; but as we shall argue, it also happens because of the way these "liberalizing" reforms are designed and embedded in a mostly punitive system.

This chapter is divided into three sections. The first section explains how drug laws and policy are overwhelmingly a matter of criminal law and the key aspects of how criminal law regulates drug policy. The second section explores how this translates in practice and the impact that making drugs a criminal matter has had on both drug phenomena and criminal institutions, and points out some of the deviations and innovations in drug laws in recent years. The final section of conclusions will return to the question of how it is that new trends to have a more consumer-tolerant drug policy fail to counter the overwhelmingly punitive nature of the system and lay out two potential agendas for further research. There is much complexity to drug policies across the continent and even more so in the way they actually play out in practice. Much of this chapter generalizes trends in the region and exceptions often escape its scope.

447

We primarily use examples from Colombia and México to explain trends, as the effects of drug policy in these countries have been widely documented, but will also include information from other Latin American countries when available. As this text shows, the criminalization of consumers is the overarching common thread for the continent, as are the criminal responses in general, in spite of the increasingly common discursive shift calling for the prioritization of health approaches.

Drug Laws in Latin America: Criminalization of Users, Centralization and Regimes of Exception

The standard state response to drugs in Latin America, as in most of the world, is punitive and repressive.[1] This emphasis on repression and punishment has warranted the Organization of American States to endorse and encourage a shift toward a health perspective and health interventions on drug policy and regulation.[2] But, as this chapter will show, this shift is a pending task in the region. Latin America deals with drug control predominantly through criminal law institutions – and not through service-oriented health laws and institutions. Governments throughout the region have favored centralization of drug control and military participation in supply-reduction efforts over local government or police participation. Drug control efforts have also led many countries in the region to adopt criminal justice regimes of exception for drug crimes that limit defendant's procedural rights and expand police and prosecutorial discretion. In the region, drug policy has become a key vehicle enabling for human rights violations and the collapse of stout democratic and constitutional regimes.[3] Understanding the main aspects of regional drug laws provides an opportunity for understanding the problems of drug law practice.

With differences in language and technical definitions, all or most production, cultivation, processing, transportation, distribution, publicity, sale, promotion, and prescription of illicit drugs – marihuana, cocaine, heroin, other psychoactive plants and their derivatives, and synthetic psychoactive substances – are banned by criminal laws in the region. At the same time, use of illicit drugs is often not a crime or, if formally a crime, one that is not punishable. Yet, even though discursively or on the books, repression and punishment are directed toward drug trafficking and associated activities (that is, toward supply), consumers (that is, demand) are, in practice, the main target of repression. Several factors, including corruption and the existence of ineffective and efficient justice systems, explain this outcome. The formal underpinnings of drug laws are, however, a key factor that partakes in explaining the criminalization of consumers. We will therefore first focus on this aspect of drug prohibition in Latin America.

Drug users are criminalized, to begin with, because the commodity they consume is produced and distributed through an industry that is banned. That is, there is no legal access to these drugs. Thus, users participate in – more precisely, they are provided illicit substances by – a market that is clandestine and criminal. The legal mechanism through which consumers are usually brought into the criminal justice system is by making possession of drugs a crime.[4] In order to consume an illicit drug, one must first possess it, so although the actions of use or consuming are not formally criminal offenses, drug users need to incur in a criminal activity.[5] Table 29.1 shows how, although drug use is not a crime in most countries, possession is.

In order to avoid consumers being sanctioned as drug dealers, some countries in Latin America (like Colombia, Mexico, Peru, and Uruguay) have established a system of tolerated thresholds; that is, amounts formally deemed to correspond to a dose for personal and immediate use, which establish a ceiling under which the possession of the drug is not punished, so as to not criminalize users for using. Above those amounts, however, possession is punished without

Table 29.1 Is Consumption and/or Possession of Illicit Substances a Crime?

Country	Consumption	Possession	Regulation (Synthesis)
Argentina	No	Yes	Drug possession for personal use is considered a crime (Article 14 of Law 23.737). However, in 2009, the supreme court declared that the part of the article that criminalized possession for use is unconstitutional
Bolivia	No	Yes	Possession for use is a crime, punishable with forced treatment, according to Article 49 of Law 1008. However, in practice this law is not applied.
			If a medical examination determines that a person carries more than is needed for his or her personal use, he or she is prosecuted for trafficking (Article 49 of Act 1008)
Brazil	No	Yes	Possession for personal use and possession without intent are considered crimes. Article 28 of Law 11.343/06, states that the judge must determine if the substance is for personal use through taking into account, among other things, the nature of the substance, the amount carried, and the criminal record of the person. Possession for personal use is criminally punished, although not with prison time
Colombia	No	Yes	Consumption is constitutionally prohibited, but the constitutional court declared that the article from the criminal code that penalized possession for personal use is unconstitutional. The supreme court has ruled that possession for personal consumption should not be criminalized even if it surpasses the established dose for personal use★
			Possession without intent is considered a crime★★
Costa Rica	No	No	Possession for personal consumption is not a crime. Possession is only a crime if it is determined that the person's intent is to "distribute, trade, supply, manufacture, develop, refine, transform, extract, prepare, cultivate, produce, transport, store or sell drugs, substances, or products referred to in this Act, or to cultivate the plants from which such substances or products are obtained" (Article 58 of Act 8204).
			Possession of seeds with the capacity to germinate or of other natural products that produced the referred drugs is a crime and is criminally sanctioned (Article 58 of Law 8204). However, in practice and as a result of the general attorney's guidelines, this law is not applied and consumers are rarely detained by police
Ecuador	No	Yes	Possession without intent is illegal, but when it is for consumption it is not punished (Article 220 of the Organic Comprehensive Criminal Code). Possession without intent is established by threshold amounts

continued

Table 29.1 Continued

Country	Consumption	Possession	Regulation (Synthesis)
Mexico	No	Yes	Possession for personal consumption is illegal, but it is not criminally prosecuted if it is for consumption, provided it does not exceed the maximum thresholds established by the General Health Act, and as long as it is not done in places such as schools or prisons and is one of the substances covered by the General Health Law. Possession without intent above the established thresholds is a criminal offense
Peru	No	Yes	Possession for use is not criminally sanctioned as long as it is below the established thresholds allowed and the person is not in possession of two or more illicit substances
Uruguay	No	Yes	Possession is a crime but it is exempt from punishment if the amount is "intended for personal consumption." In the case of cannabis, the possession of up to 40 grams or six psychoactive cannabis plants is legal for personal consumption (Article 7, Law 19.172)
			Possession is a crime if the person does not have the corresponding legal authorization (Article 5, Law 19.172)

Source: Catalina Pérez-Correa, Alejandro Corda, and Luciana Boiteux. 2015. *Drug Consumption and Consumers in Latin America*. Mexico: CEDD, p. 3.

Notes

★ Criminal Appeals Chamber, Supreme Court of Colombia. *Sentence No. 29183*, M.P. José Leonidas Bustos Martínez, 2008.

★★ However, according to the supreme court, when possession is above dose for personal use, additional criteria can be used to demonstrate that possession is for personal use and should not be criminalized. See Criminal Appeals Chamber, Supreme Court of Colombia. *Sentence No. 42617,* M.P. Gustavo Enrique Malo Fernández, 2014. In 2016, the supreme court also stated that a literal interpretation of the thresholds is unconstitutional and that other evidence should be taken into account. See Criminal Appeals Chamber, Supreme Court Colombia. *Sentence No. 41760 SP2940*, M.P. Eugenio Fernández Carlier, 2016.

need for further evidence to prove intent to distribute or sell.[6] Dosages however, tend to be low especially when taking into account that, consumers have incentives to acquire more than one dose of the substance, so as to minimize the number of times they come into contact with the clandestine market. In the case of some drugs, such as cocaine, "personal use" amounts are so low that they sometimes fall below the usual dose for a single use.[7] As will be shown in the next section, threshold systems have not prevented criminalization of users in the region and have had the opposite effect, since users are not only detained – by police or military – to ascertain quantities, but often punished as drug dealers for possessing more the rigid, tolerated amounts.[8]

Another formal legal aspect that plays a central role in understanding how drug laws play out in action is jurisdiction: who, in government, is in charge of establishing drug laws and/or their application? Most countries in Latin America have centralist regimes and thus criminal prosecution is usually jurisdiction of the national government (i.e., federal or central). The quintessential example is Colombia where criminal prosecution is competence of the central government. Repression of drug markets and prosecutions involve, importantly, Colombia's national police and, more notoriously, its army.[9] Drug crimes were, until the 1987 jurisdiction of military courts.[10] A court ruling in 1987 banned military trials for drug crimes, but allowed for military authorities to govern large portions of territory deemed "theater of operations" of the drug war. After the ruling, a judicial system of exception was established for drug crimes, formally ascribed to civil judicial authorities, but substantively similar to military courts that until then had processed them. We will further detail the Colombian regime of exception below.

Other countries have mixed regimes. Argentina, a federal republic, concentrates criminal prosecution of drug laws in a single national jurisdiction, which has become increasingly punitive since the 1970s.[11] Recent reforms, however, allowed the possibility of local authorities to prosecute certain drug crimes (simple possession, use and micro dealing) under federal law (Law 23.737) if they adhere to specific conditions.[12] Mexico is a particularly complex case. Historically, criminal laws and criminal prosecution under federal law and state law were strictly separated: state governments had default jurisdiction in criminal matters; but the federal government exercised that jurisdiction in territories under its direct authority or else in matters of federal jurisdiction, such as health (and, thus, "crimes against health" or drug crimes). States had full autonomy regarding their criminal policy since the consolidation of federalism in the mid-nineteenth century. The launch of the drug war at the beginning of the twenty-first century altered that equilibrium. Up until 2009, Mexico's drug laws were strictly federal.[13] That year, for the first time in history, Mexico's Congress enacted criminal legislation establishing that some crimes (micro-trafficking and other small-scale crimes) were to be pursued through "concurrent" federal and state jurisdictions.[14] Importantly, even though persecution and punishment falls within state jurisdiction, only the federal government can determine the content of drug laws, including definitions of crimes.[15] The question of jurisdiction is relevant to understand how resources are allocated in countries with overburdened criminal justice systems and where local resources are scarce. It is also relevant to understand the nature of abuses committed by the different security forces, whether military or civil.

Some Latin American countries have adopted a fully separate, exceptional criminal justice regime for drug trafficking and/or organized crime. These regimes pivot on reduced due process rights for people suspected or accused of drug crimes, and enhance the discretional sphere of decision-making to criminal authorities such as prosecutors or detectives. Examples from Mexico and Colombia help understand this trend. In Colombia – as in most democracies committed to the rule of law – the general procedural rule is that people can only be detained either because they are caught in the act of committing a crime or else because of an existing judicial order. For people accused of drug crimes, however, people can be detained through the figure of "arraigo," for up to seven days by executive authorities without the intervention of the judiciary (without a judicial order).[16]

Mexico's states and federal government incorporated their own versions of *arraigo* to their ordinary criminal procedures, beginning in the early 80s. It was, however, deemed unconstitutional by the supreme court in 2005; in response, congress passed a constitutional amendment in 2008 explicitly providing *arraigo* with constitutional grounding and broadening the possibility of detention at an undisclosed location, without charge, for up to 80 days, if it is deemed that such a detention will advance an investigation.[17] In other words, after the 2008 constitutional amendment, it is not even necessary for the person detained to be suspected of having committed a crime or for there to actually be a specific crime, which is being investigated. The 2008 constitutional amendment went further than that: it set up – at the constitutional level – a parallel criminal justice system where restricted procedural rights for the accused and amplified discretionary powers to authorities are the driving logic.[18] Such restrictions include longer detention periods for pretrial investigations, detention without charge (*arraigo*, described on p. 451), isolation during detention, mandatory pretrial detention, the presumptive validity of proof registered in the criminal investigation without the possibility of judicial evaluation, seizure of assets (in Spanish, *extinción de dominio*) presumed to be the result of criminal activities without the need of a guilty verdict,[19] among others.[20] In most, if not all, Latin American countries, the general trend is for increased penalties, new crimes, and limited rights for people accused or convicted of drug crimes.[21]

There have been, however, important revisions to the punitive trends. These have come, mostly, from the judiciary: Colombia's, Argentina's, Mexico's, and Chile's judiciaries have in recent years introduced alterations. In 2009, Argentina's Supreme Court declared the unconstitutionality of Article 14 (second paragraph of Act 23.737), which punishes possession for personal consumption.[22] The court's ruling stated that punishing possession was unconstitutional when that it does not result in a specific hazard or harm to the rights or goods of third parties.[23] However, the revoked article (and thus the crime of possession remains as law and continues to justify detentions).[24]

In 1994, Colombia's Constitutional Court also ruled that possessing drugs for personal consumption could not, under the constitution, be a crime and thus established a "ceiling" system. In 2008, Colombia's Constitutional Court introduced the concept of "supply dose":[25] an amount adequate for a consumer to possess in order to have continued access for a reasonable period of time, in contrast to the dose for "immediate" consumption, which was on the books beforehand. A constitutional amendment of 2009[26] attempted to revert the court's ruling by elevating prohibition to a constitutional rank and was followed by a legal amendment in 2011 eliminating tolerance for possession of "personal dose." The court's response was swift. In a case stemming that same year, the court reaffirmed that, under the constitution possession and consumption could not be criminal offenses.[27] In March of 2016, the Constitutional Court further ruled that criminalizing merely based on thresholds is unconstitutional and stated that other evidence should be taken into account.[28]

Mexico's Supreme Court's historic ruling of November 2015[29] held that the administrative ban on marihuana consumption for recreational purposes was unconstitutional, because it disproportionately restricted the fundamental right to freely develop one's personality.[30] The ruling has stemmed a national debate and a long list of legislative initiatives to regulate cannabis and its different uses, but has had no immediate impact except for the four plaintiffs, as Mexico's judicial system allows for broad striking of laws only under exceptional circumstances. In Chile, a 2016 ruling by its highest court rendered the prosecution of home cultivation of cannabis for personal use constitutionally protected, establishing that even if the plants are visible from the street, that is not sufficient cause for the police to enter a house.[31]

The biggest outlier regarding prohibition is Uruguay, which has a legislative, not a judicial source. In 2013, Uruguay adopted a fully-fledged legalization of cannabis – only cannabis – that not only included self-production and "cannabis clubs" (cooperatives for producing marihuana without profit), but also a system of production, preparation, distribution, and sale of cannabis and its products. In practice, it consists of parallel systems in which possession for personal use of up to 40 grams, or else cultivation, production, storage, etc. of cannabis of up to 480 grams annually are allowed, while the choice between membership to a cannabis club or acquisition from an authorized point of sale are exclusionary: one can find supply in a club or in the commercial system, but not both.[32] However, for other drugs, the country has maintained a discretionary system that often leads to the processing of illicit drug users.

Another trend that competes with regulation is the establishment or adaptation of the American model of "drug courts." Even though "consumption" of illicit drugs is not usually a crime in Latin America and drug courts were established in the United States as a mechanism to divert people charged with consumption from prison, this has been a quickly growing model throughout Latin America, with unclear results. By 2014, 14 counties in the region had adopted this model.[33] Drug courts function through the suspension of criminal procedure for a crime committed *under the influence of a substance*, when the accused agrees to subject herself to treatment under judicial guidance. During treatment, the case remains suspended, conditional on continued and successful treatment.[34] If the participant fails to complete treatment, her criminal case is reopened and tried through ordinary procedure.

Drug courts present several problems but interesting opportunities to study drug laws. Perhaps the most obvious one is that it continues to respond to a health issue from a criminal law perspective, judicializing treatments and relying on criminal law judges to treat users. In practice, the model has most often reverted to the end-result of the American model that inspired it: to divert users from prison sentences forcing them to undertake treatment under judicial authority. By 2015, 92.3 percent of all participants of drug court programs in Mexico were in the program for simple possession of marihuana.[35]

The Practice of Drug Laws and Drug Policy Institutions

In this section, we address some of the main issues studied when looking at the practical implications of drug law enforcement. These are: supply-reduction efforts; criminalization of drug users; the use of prisons as a deterrent for drug crimes; drug laws and women; and due process violations resulting from the enforcement of drug laws. Given the length of this text other important issues, such as policing, sentencing biases, political use of drug law enforcement,[36] forced migration,[37] and the impact on health of drug law enforcement,[38] have been left out but present important opportunities to further study regional drug laws and their effects.

Supply-Reduction Efforts

Supply reduction has, for years, been the central objective of drug policies in the region, under the influence of the United States.[39] Although drug use seldom represents a major health problem for Latin American communities,[40] much of the substantive efforts and financial resources invested in supply reduction justify the investment as a way protecting potential users from access to drugs.

The resources invested in supply reduction, however, confirm these efforts have been highly inefficient, often leading to the arrest and criminalization of small-scale dealers or users. Mexico's federal government, for instance, spent an estimated 814 billion pesos in drug policy during the Calderón administration of which 2.91 percent were allocated by the federal government to drug policy in the aggregate areas of prevention, treatment, and human rights – that is, in demand reduction. In contrast, the areas of "law and order" – supply reduction – represent 97.09 percent of those resources.[41] Under Plan Colombia, the United States and Colombian governments spent approximately 812 million US dollars annually, which amounts to 1 percent of Colombia's gross domestic product (GDP).[42] A cost-efficiency analysis of the investment in supply-reduction efforts concludes that keeping 1 kilogram of cocaine from reaching the United States by attacking production in Colombia costs about 163,000 US dollars; and by attacking trafficking (that is, transportation) costs about 3,600 US dollars.[43]

An analysis of cost-effectiveness of Mexico's drug war under the Calderón administration documents growing inefficiency as more resources were poured into Mexico's drug war.[44] Between 2004 and 2006 Mexico spent an estimated 0.13 percent of its GDP on enforcing prohibition – that is, supply-reduction activities; every peso invested represented between 3 to 5 pesos in the earnings lost by drug trafficking organizations (DTO's). By 2009, Mexico was spending 0.35 percent of its GDP on its drug war, but for the period 2007–2009, the estimate was that every peso invested in supply reduction by the government translated into DTOs lost earnings for merely 1.5 pesos. Tellingly, during the 2007–2009 periods, the Mexican government reduced its budget allocation for demand reduction efforts from six million US dollars per year, to 2.6 million US dollars.

In a context of such disproportionate investment in a punitive drug policy, it seems unsurprising that people involved with illicit drug markets – that is, consumers – end up criminalized. Security institutions in the region are often corrupt or inefficient and operate so as to make easy arrests that require less effort. Analyzing drug policy from the supply-demand dichotomy obscures the fact that supply-reduction efforts, when channeled through the state's punitive apparatuses – police, criminal justice, and military intervention – seem to be linked with criminalization of users. As the next section shows, different studies show repression has mostly focused on the weak (users, petty dealers, and poor women) and not against organized criminals who supply drugs.

Criminalization of Drug Users: Criminal Law as a First Response

If one had to oversimplify what the dominant trend of drug policy in Latin America is, it would be: harsh criminal punishment for all involved in drug markets with a sphere of tolerance and protection for consumers; with little investment in prevention; and treatment or in the promotion of sustainable economic development in areas that participate in cultivation of illicit crops.

In Colombia, for example, budget allocated in 2010 to drug policy was distributed 5.5 percent to alternatives to development, such as crop substitution; 4.1 percent to reducing demand, 25.7 percent to "legal and institutional reinforcement" (i.e., mostly investing in the repressive apparatus of the state) and 64.2 percent to reducing supply.[45] In Argentina, also, between 2002 and 2010, the proportion of spending was approximately 82 percent for reducing supply and 18 percent for reducing demand.[46] In Peru, between 2002 and 2010, only 8.5 percent of government drug-related budget allocations went to prevention and treatment while the bulk of resources was spent on interdiction.[47]

In terms of the tolerance established for consumers, data shows that laws have been insufficient in protecting users from arrest and extortion; most resources are actually aimed at detaining, processing, and often sanctioning users. In other words, far from creating a protection for the user, the state seems to focalize repression against them. According to a study by Research Consortium on Drugs and the Law (CEDD), the criminalization of consumers cuts across the region. Most of the detentions made by police are related to use or simple possession, that is, possession above the tolerated thresholds. In Argentina, for example, the Attorney for Drug Crimes (Procuraduría de Narcocriminalidad) reported in 2012 alone, 9,414 criminal investigations opened for possession for personal consumption. In Mexico, between 2009 and May of 2013, 140,860 people were detained by federal authorities for illicit drug use and 52,074 criminal investigations for "use" (consumo) were initiated (even though, as explained on p. 454, use itself is not a criminal offense).[48]

Users are often brought into the system through the crime of simple possession, for carrying any amount over the established thresholds or, in systems that are discretionary, because the judge deemed the amount to be for something other than personal and immediate use. In Mexico, for example, just at the federal level, 175,993 people were detained for possession, between 2006 and 2014. In addition, 87,746 criminal investigations were initiated for possession of drugs without intent to sell or distribute (simple possession).[49] In Ecuador, between 2007 and

2014, the public defender's office aided 15,532 people detained for possession and in 2014, 5,103 people were found guilty for possession out of a total of 6,467 detainees for drug crimes. This means 79 percent of people detained for drug crimes were convicted for possession, showing the law is primarily focused on punishing consumers and not on the supply side, as it is stated.[50]

An outlier in the criminalization of users is Costa Rica, where there are no thresholds for personal use, but rather a discretionary model based on evidence and mitigating factors found in the commission of a crime.[51] In that country, the attorney general's office has disseminated guidelines mandating for arrests made for consumption to be dismissed. This has prevented the arrest of users by the police, with the result that neither use nor possession is criminalized.[52]

Drug Laws and the Use of Prisons

One of the issues that has most frequently been studied in the area of drug policy is the use of prisons as a deterrent (or incapacitation) mechanism for drug crimes[53]. Even where drug courts appear as an alternative to the use of prisons, as described in the previous section, incarceration is still a possibility for people who fail to complete the program successfully.

Although the information is not always uniform and/or available, the statistics of people in prison for drug crimes shows a steady increase in incarceration for such crimes. Today one out of every five people in prison in Latin America are accused of drug crimes.[54] Also, in many countries, drug crimes are the main reason why women are incarcerated. In Argentina, Brazil, and Costa Rica, over 60 percent of women are in prison for drug crimes.[55] Although the region has seen a general increase in prison population, prison population for drug crimes has grown at a faster rate. Table 29.2, shows the number of people imprisoned for drug crimes, the percentage this number represents of the total prison population, the increase in imprisonment for drug crimes, and the increase in overall prison population. As Table 29.2 shows, in Brazil, Colombia, Uruguay, Argentina, and Mexico, the prison population for drug crimes has increased at a faster level than the overall prison population; while Ecuador, Bolivia, Peru, and Costa Rica show a faster increase in the general prison population than the prison population for drugs. This means

Table 29.2 People Imprisoned for Drug Crime, Percentage Drug Crimes Represent the Total Prison Population, Increase in Drug Population in Prison and Increase in Overall Prison Population

	Population in Prison for Drugs	Drug Crimes (%)	Increase in Prison Population for Drugs (%)	< >	Increase in Overall Prison Population (%)
Ecuador	6,467 (2014)	24 (2014)	63 (2010–2014)	<	98 (2010–2014)
Bolivia	3,939 (2013)	27 (2013)	32 (2001–2013)	<	158 (2001–2013)
Peru	16,526 (2013)	24 (2013)	46 (2008–2013)	<	56 (2008–2013)
Costa Rica	4,745 (2011)	26 (2011)	126 (2006–2011)	<	131 (2006–2011)
Brazil	138,198 (2012)	25 (2012)	320 (2005–2012)	>	51 (2005–2012)
Colombia	23,141 (2014)	20 (2014)	269 (2000–2014)	>	136 (2000–2014)
Uruguay	1,265 (2013)	13 (2013)	39 (2009–2013)	>	15 (2009–2013)
Argentina	6,979 (2013)	11 (2013)	113 (2002–2013)	>	39 (2002–2013)
Mexico	26,098 (2013)	10 (2013)	19 (2011–2013)	>	7 (2011–2013)

Source: Alejandro Corda. 2015. *Drug Policy Reform in Latin America: Discourse and Reality.* Mexico: CEDD, p. 5. Data shows latest information available.

that in five of the nine countries studied, the prison population for drugs is growing faster than the general prison population.

Prisons in Latin America have often been linked to health risks and human rights violations. It is thus paradigmatic that they are used as the principal instrument to protect health (drug laws purportedly seek to protect either individuals or the public health). Many prisons in Latin America present serious overcrowding,[56] corruption,[57] lack of medical services and drinkable water, have poor hygiene, deficient sanitary facilities,[58] and high numbers of unprotected sexual encounters – including many incidents of sexual abuse. Some of these factors partially explain the higher prevalence (when compared to the general population) of certain diseases within prisons such as HIV/AIDS (human immunodeficiency virus/acquired immunodeficiency syndrome), hepatitis C, scabies, lice, etc.[59] Apart from being dangerous for the individuals placed in prison, these conditions mean higher health risks for their families who visit them there.[60]

Given high levels of prison violence, the use of prisons implies a higher risk of death, meaning they can be considered a risk to human life. In Mexico, for example, in 2008, the risk of dying inside a prison was five times higher than for people outside prisons. In 2009, the homicide rate was 2.4 times higher within prisons than outside.[61] The principle reason given by the press to explain riots and homicides within prisons is the control of the illicit markets, including illicit drug markets within the prisons. According to the Centro de Investigación y Docencia Económica (CIDE) prison survey (2009), 15 percent of inmates in Mexico City prisons accepted consuming alcohol or drugs within the prison during the past month.[62] And, as the survey notes, this percentage probably does not represent the real incidence of drug and alcohol use, as inmates tend to underreport their participation in illicit activities.

Plugge et al. (2009) also showed that inmates had an increased risk of cardiovascular disease.[63] This may be explained by the higher prevalence of tobacco smoking and the lack of physical activity among inmates, which lead to obesity. It could also be related to the stress that criminal procedure, trials, and imprisonment produce on people who are subjected to them. Another study showed that 63.6 percent of visiting family members of inmates reported having health problems, many of them stress-related, as a consequence of their family member's imprisonment.[64] This data strongly suggests that using prison, in the name of protecting health through drug laws, actually generate more harm to public health than the protection it achieves (by inhibiting drug use).

In addition to the poor conditions that prevail in Latin American countries, studies have shown, that the criminal justice system in the region often disproportionately tries and punishes populations that are economically and socially excluded.[65] Others have shown how the use of prisons, the punishment preferred by today's criminal justice systems, not only affect those who are in prison, but also contribute to the impoverishment of families and communities that were already marginalized.[66] In other words, the diverse studies question the neutrality of the criminal justice system, pointing to a disproportionate use of drug laws to punish minority groups and previously marginalized sectors.

Drug Laws and Women

There is an interesting gender component in the application of drug laws both worldwide, which is also present in Latin America. Even when more men are, in absolute numbers, imprisoned for drug offenses, the rate of women imprisoned has grown more rapidly. According to Malinowska-Sempruch and Rychkova, in Latin America, between 2006 and 2011, the female prison population increased from 40,000 to more than 74,000, with some women facing sentences as high as 30 years.[67] In several Latin American countries, drug crimes are the main reason why women are imprisoned, especially in the federal justice systems, where the most serious crimes should be prosecuted and sanctioned. In Argentina, for example, 65 percent of women were in prison at the federal level for drug crimes. In Brazil, also 60 percent of women were in prison in 2013 for the same reason. In Costa Rica, 75 percent of women were in prison in 2011 accused of drug crimes.[68]

Other studies show women usually share a similar socio-demographic profile. They are young, poor, single mothers. In Brazil, for example, almost 55 percent of women incarcerated are of African descent.[69] Many of the women imprisoned for drug crime are often heads of household that care for young children or other family members.[70] Because of this, their imprisonment has extremely negative effects on their families, communities, and society in general.

Most of these women are involved in the low-level rungs of drug trafficking but face extremely long sentences.[71] In Mexico, for example, the CIDE inmate survey of federal prisons showed that 98.9 percent of women sentenced for drug crimes had no prior convictions, 88 percent of them had only been accused of a drug crime (that is, they were not accused of other crimes and so their offense was strictly non-violent), and 91.6 percent had not been carrying a weapon.[72] It also showed that while only 2 percent of male inmates had their partners in prison, 22 percent of women had their partners in prison, suggesting some of them were accused of bringing drugs into prisons for their partners to sell (a relatively common practice in a prison system in which inmates are not provided basic necessities such as toiletry, water, food, or bed by authorities).[73] As stated by the Guide for Policy Reform in Latin America, as minor actors in drug trafficking, these women are easily replaced, and their arrest has no impact on reducing drug trafficking or improving citizen security, tackling violence, or reducing the corruption generated by the illegal business.[74]

Due Process Violations and the Selective Enforcement of Drug Laws

In this last section, we look at examples from two countries (Colombia and Mexico) where drug policies have had deep negative impact and that help illustrate the punitive focus in the region. We will use Colombia as a case study for continued criminalization of drug users through police practices and administrative regulations, and Mexico as an example of how police practices, in the context of a drug war, deteriorate to the point of representing a serious threat to human rights and even limited government. Although other countries, especially in Central America have suffered negative consequences, Mexico and Colombia have widely documented the human and institutional cost of the current prohibition model. Both countries have been largely militarized and have created regimes of constitutional exceptions to handle illicit drug organizations. The extent of this chapter only allows us to tackle these examples, although others exist throughout Latin America.

In Colombia, use of illicit drugs is not a crime and the infractions on restrictions to use (such as consuming in public places) are not crimes. Nevertheless, users are systematically criminalized by policy through the application of administrative regulations, as Lemaitre and Albarracín (2011) show.[75] Through ethnographic field research these authors detail how consumers are often detained and taken to detention centers; most often when profiled by police officers as people who are deemed, by them, likely to be involved in public disturbances, theft, etc. This profiling allows police to sort between consequences of public use of drugs: in higher-end neighborhoods the police limit themselves to registering the incident, asking the person to leave the public space and, occasionally seizing the substance. In contrast, in marginalized communities, detention for a period of 12 to 24 hours – which is the harshest administrative sanction available to police and in theory to be used exceptionally – is used, most often on young poor men gathering in groups on the street.

According to Lemaitre and Albarracín's work (2011), police perceive that using harsher sanctions on wealthier individuals can result in problems with their superiors.[76] In contrast, poor young men are "perceived by the community and by the police itself as real or potential aggressors: usually unemployed, profiled as petty pickpockets, thieves, gang members, petty drug dealers and the like" (Lemaitre 2011, 257).[77] Existing criminal law can explain why police target drug users. Crimes such, as theft, require witnesses, and these are hard to come by in a context of distrust by the community of the judicial system. With pressure from communities to deal with risky young men, but without collaboration of witnesses, police use administrative sanctions for public use of drugs as a way to remove these young men from the street.[78] The study shows how police deal with petty crime through the administrative regulation of drug use. As in other countries, it is possible to witness a conflation between drug use, marginalization, and petty crime in police practices.[79]

Studies of Mexico's application of drug laws also portray a harsh reality. A study by Ana Laura Magaloni shows how torture and mistreatment grew in 2006 – when incoming President Calderón launched the war on drugs.[80] According to the study, two phenomena could explain this increment: militarization and an increased focus on drug crimes. Starting in late 2006 an important portion of detentions has been carried out by the military. During the bulk of the Calderón Administration, the army was responsible for 25 percent of all federal detainees, a massive number second only to the (increasingly militarized) federal police, which was responsible for 37.1 percent of detentions.[81] Drug crimes account for 34.3 percent of sentenced prisoners detained *before* Calderón took office, but nearly doubled to account for 65.7 percent of those detained during the Calderón Administration.[82] Using information from the only existing federal prison population survey, Magaloni classified cases so as to identify the presence of torture and mistreatment according to different criteria: gravity and institutional involvement in mistreatment;[83] type of crime; and institution responsible for the detention. Magaloni then created two cohorts: people detained before the Calderón administration (that is, before the militarized "war on drugs") and during that administration. The study shows that mistreatment and violence perpetrated against detainees increased importantly during the Calderón administration. Interestingly, when observing specific types of mistreatment, institutional involvement, and disaggregating by type of crime, the data shows a general increase in alleged torture and mistreatment during detention; with an even more notorious increase (and gravity of the alleged mistreatments reported for people detained for drug crimes) (see Table 29.3). Another study by the Johns Hopkins-Lancet Commission on Drug Policy confirmed the focalization of mistreatment or torture: in Mexico, it became 1.57 times more probable to experiment torture or abuse

Table 29.3 Mistreatment by Type of Crime

Action/Crime	Kidnaping		Homicide		Drug Crimes	
	Before Calderón (%)	*During Calderón (%)*	*Before Calderón (%)*	*During Calderón (%)*	*Before Calderón (%)*	*During Calderón (%)*
Kicking	5.58	2.79	7.11	1.27	10.66	37.31
Asphyxia	6.95	3.09	8.49	1.54	9.27	37.45
Electric shocks	6.06	1.82	6.67	1.21	7.88	44.85

Source: Ana Laura Magaloni. 2015. "La arbitrariedad como método de trabajo: la persecución criminal durante la administración de Felipe Calderón," En *De la Detención a la Prisión. La Justicia Penal a Examen*, edited by Catalina Pérez-Correa. México: CIDE, p. 43. Translation by authors.

during detention for a drug crime after the onset of the war on drugs than prior to December 2006.[84]

Magaloni's study (2015) shows that use of the military not only means that the army does *more* of what is done, but also that, in doing more police and security work, it relied more heavily on abuse and torture.[85]

Although these are only examples from two countries, they help see the problems drug laws create when applied. This is especially the case when policy makers ignore the limitations and/ or realities of the institutions charged with implementing them. The examples also help see that drug policy affects criminal policy and criminal justice institutions in ways that are not apparent by only looking at laws in paper.

Conclusions

Framing an analysis of drug policy in the Americas as one that can separate between supply reduction and demand reduction fails to make visible the most important and common thread for the region: the criminalization of consumers. When we analyze drug policy starting from the supply-demand dichotomy, we fail to see that supply-reduction efforts, when channeled through the state's punitive apparatuses – police, criminal justice, and military intervention – most often translate in action against the very people drug policy is supposed to protect: users. Different studies show that repression has been privileged over prevention of problematic drug use and treatment. Repression, however, is not usually deployed against organized criminals who supply drugs. Rather, it is aimed at users, who come to be criminalized and victimized by both the state and criminals, toward poor women who are used by criminal organizations, or toward petty dealers who are easily replaced and seen as expendable both by authorities and organized crime.

The study of drug laws and drug policy opens several research agendas. First, further research needs to delve deeper in the study of the mechanics of how users come to be criminalized. The design of formal law certainly plays a part – and we've attempted to briefly explain how – but important questions still need to be answered through fieldwork. For instance, ethnographic studies could bring forth information regarding police practices, as Lemaitre and Albarracín (????) did.[86] Another area of research is the impact that politics and policies of drug prohibition have on the shape of the broader legal system, specifically but not limited to the criminal justice system. The many exceptions are due to process rights and the increased centralization and militarization of supply-reduction efforts have warranted major surgery of legal systems and even constitutional regimes. How do these changes play out in practice? What changes do they mean for due process rights or even institutional arrangements? Drug policy, specifically drug prohibition, is an important driving force for (negative) change in the region. Much more attention should be paid to it, lest we find ourselves at a loss when prohibition is gone, but the punitive regimes set in place to enforce it remain.[87]

Notes

1 Catalina Pérez Correa, Alejandro Corda, and Luciana Boiteux, *La Regulación de la Posesión y la Criminalización de los Consumidores de Drogas en América Latina* (México: CEDD, 2015), 1. Available at: www. drogasyderecho.org/publicaciones/pub-priv/Catalina_v09.pdf. Accessed December 4, 2017.

2 Organización de los Estados Americanos (OEA), *El Informe de Drogas de la OEA: 16 Meses de Debates y Consensos* (Guatemala: OEA, 2014), 14. Available at: www.oas.org/docs/publications/LayoutPubg AGDrogas-ESP-29-9.pdf. Accessed December 4, 2017.

3 Antonio Barreto and Alejandro Madrazo, "Los costos constitucionales de la guerra contra las drogas: dos estudios de caso de las transformaciones de las comunidades políticas de las Américas," *Isonomía*, No. 43 (October 2015): passim.

4 With the exception of Costa Rica, see Table 29.1.

5 Catalina Pérez Correa, Alejandro Corda and Luciana Boiteux, *Drug consumption and consumers in Latin America* (Mexico: CEDD, 2015), 8. Available at: www.drogasyderecho.org/publicaciones/pub-priv/catalina_i.pdf. Accessed December 4, 2017.

6 As noted in the synthesis of Colombia in Table 29.1, the supreme court has declared this use of thresholds as incompatible with the constitution.

7 Thus for example, the tolerated threshold for cocaine in Mexico is 0.5 grams but the minimum market dosage is 1 gram. See Catalina Pérez Correa, Karen Silva and Carlos de la Rosa, "(Des)proporcionalidad y delitos contra la salud en México," *Documento de Trabajo de la División de Estudios Jurídicos (CIDE)*, No. 59 (August, 2012): 7. Available at: www.libreriacide.com/?P=docs_trabajo&PRODfamily=dt&PRODclassification=202. Accessed December 4, 2017.

8 The recommendation is to use thresholds as floors below which no users can be punished but not as ceiling above which users are automatically punished without proof of intent. See Pérez Correa, *Drug Consumption and Consumers in Latin America*, 7.

9 The National Drug Council and the National Drug Office are charged with coordinating drug policy, which involve both security forces and the ministries of health, education and communications. Rodrigo Uprimny and Diana Esther Guzmán, "Políticas de drogas y situación carcelaria en Colombia," in *Sistemas Sobrecargados. Leyes de Drogas y Cárceles en América Latina*, edited by Pien Metaal and Coletta Youngers (Amsterdam-Washington: TNI-WOLA, 2010), 41–2.

10 For more details on Colombia's militarization of drug policy, see Antonio Barreto and Alejandro Madrazo, "Los costos constitucionales de la guerra contra las drogas: dos estudios de caso de las transformaciones de las comunidades políticas de las Américas," *Isonomía*, No. 43 (October 2015): 151–93.

11 Alejandro Corda, "Encarcelamientos por delitos relacionados con estupefacientes en Argentina," in *Sistemas Sobrecargados. Leyes de Drogas y Cárceles en América Latina*, edited by Pien Metaal and Coletta Youngers (Amsterdam-Washington: TNI-WOLA, 2010), 11.

12 Alejandro Corda, Araceli Galante and Diana Rossi, *Personas que Usan Estupefacientes en Argentina: de "Delincuentes-Enfermos" a Sujetos de Derechos* (Buenos Aires: Intercambios Asociación Civil-Universidad de Buenos Aires, 2014). Available at: www.drogasyderecho.org/publicaciones/prop_del/argentina-usuarios.pdf. Accessed December 4, 2017. Also see Código Penal Argentino, Ley N° 23.737, Article 34. Available at: http://infoleg.mecon.gov.ar/infolegInternet/anexos/0–4999/138/texact.htm. Accessed December 4, 2017.

13 That is, they were both pronounced and executed by federal authorities. The dating deserves some caveats. The possibility of having crimes of "concurrent" jurisdiction was constitutionally introduced in 2005, when congress passed a bill proposed by President Fox, very similar to the one approved in 2009. The bill included the introduction of the "personal dosage" system – the *roof* version of this system. Because the introduction of tolerance to possession was met with skepticism by the United States authorities, President Fox vetoed his own bill, so only the constitutional amendment authorizing congress to establish crimes of "concurrent" jurisdiction stood. It would take four years, and the launching of a militarized drug war, to have the bill passed in 2009 with no qualms from the United States government.

14 The crimes labeled "narcomenudeo," which consist of three different actions: (i) sale or distribution of the most common illicit drugs; (ii) possession with the intent of sale or distribution; and (iii) possession without the intent of sale or distribution. See Ley General de Salud (Mexico), Title XVIII, Chapter VII, articles 473–82. Henceforth, the crimes of distribution and possession with or without the intent to distribute were to be prosecuted by state authorities when these crimes were committed under specific amounts (the result of multiplying the personal dosage thresholds by 1,000). Exceptionally, at least in theory, the attorney general's office can prosecute any drug crimes that correspond to state jurisdiction when they are committed by organized crime, when they are first to initiate an investigation or when the attorney general's office simply decides to request that state attorney general's offices relinquish a case.

15 Suprema Corte de Justicia de la Nación (Mexico). *Controversia Constitucional 20/2010.* Available at: www2.scjn.gob.mx/ConsultaTematica/PaginasPub/DetallePub.aspx?AsuntoID=117071. Accessed December 4, 2017.

16 Barreto, *Los Costos Constitucionales de la Guerra Contra las Drogas*, 177.

17 See Alejandro Madrazo, "El impacto de la política de drogas 2006–2012 en la legislación federal," *Cuadernos de Trabajo del Seminario del Programa de Política de Drogas (CIDE)*, No. 7 (June 2014). Available at: http://ppd.cide.edu/documents/302668/0/Libro%207.pdf. Accessed December 4, 2017.

18 Alejandro Madrazo, "Marco normativo nacional de la política de drogas," en *El mal Menor en la Gestión de las Drogas. De la Prohibición a la Regulación*, edited by Bernardo González-Aréchiga, David Pérez, Alejandro Madrazo and José Antonio Caballero (Mexico: Mc Graw Hill, 2014), 65.

19 For a description of the formal regime of the "extinción de dominio" at the federal level, see infra note 20. For a more detailed description of the regime in Mexico City, see Asamblea Legislativa del Distrito Federal (ALDF), *Para la Libertad ... Siete Leyes Históticas de la IV Legislatura* (México: ALDF-Porrúa, 2009), 163–190. For an analysis of the implementation of similar "extincción de dominio" regulation in Colombia, see Manuel Iturralde and Libardo José Ariza, "El tratamiento penal del narcotráfico y delitos conexos," in *Políticas Antidroga en Colombia: Éxitos, Fracasos y Extravíos*, compiled by Alejandro Gaviria and Daniel Mejía (Bogotá: Universidad de Los Andes, 2011), 289–93.

20 See Madrazo, *El Impacto de la Política de Drogas 2006–2012 en la Legislación Federal*.

21 See Barreto, *Los Costos Constitucionales de la Guerra Contra las Drogas*, 178. In general, also see Catalina Pérez Correa (coordinator), *Justicia Desmedida: Proporcionalidad y Delitos de Drogas en América Latina* (Mexico: Fontamara, 2012).

22 Intercambios Asociación Civil, "Fallo 'Arriola' de la Corte Suprema sobre tenencia de estupefacientes para consumo personal," Proyecto de TNI sobre Reformas a las Leyes de Drogas. Available at: http://druglawreform.info/es/informacion-por-pais/america-latina/argentina/item/386-fallo-arriola-de-la-corte-suprema. Accessed December 4, 2017.

23 See Alejandro Corda, *La Estrategia Fallida: Encarcelamientos por Delitos Relacionados con Estupefacientes en la Argentina* (Buenos Aires: Intercambios Asociación Civil-Universidad de Buenos Aires, 2016). Available at: http://intercambios.org.ar/wp-content/uploads/2016/09/2016.-Corda.-La-estrategia-fallida.pdf. Accessed December 4, 2017. See also Corte Suprema de Justicia de la Nación Argentina. A. 891, XLIV (Arriola Ruling). Available at: http://druglawreform.info/images/stories/documents/fallo-arriola.pdf. Accessed December 4, 2017.

24 Catalina Pérez Correa and Coletta Youngers (editors), *En Busca de los Derechos: Usuarios de Drogas y las Respuestas Estatales en América Latina* (México: CEDD-CIDE, 2014), 170.

25 Pérez Correa, *En Busca de los Derechos*, 82.

26 Colombian Congress. *Acto Legislativo 02 de 2009*. Available at: www.alcaldiabogota.gov.co/sisjur/normas/Norma1.jsp?i=38289. Accessed December 4, 2017.

27 Pérez Correa, *En Busca de los Derechos*, 82.

28 See Criminal Appeals Chamber, Supreme Court Colombia. *Sentence N° 41760 SP2940*, M.P. Eugenio Fernandez Carlier, 2016.

29 Suprema Corte de Justicia de la Nación (Mexico). *Amparo en Revisión 237/2014*. Available at: www.smartclub.mx/uploads/8/7/2/7/8727772/doc.pdf. Accessed December 4, 2017.

30 Mexico's criminal prohibition on drugs is a function of their administrative ban. That is, crimes are defined as the carrying out of activities in relation to substances that are administratively banned. See Mexico's Federal Criminal Code, Articles 193–198. The court pronounced itself on the administrative ban on consumption and ruled that connected activities fell under constitutional protection too, including cultivation.

31 See Suprema Corte de Justicia de Chile, "Sentencia de la Corte Suprema de Chile sobre autocultivo de cannabis," *Revista Pensamiento Penal*. Available at: www.pensamientopenal.com.ar/fallos/43105-sentencia-corte-suprema-chile-sobre-autocultivo-cannabis. Accessed December 4, 2017.

32 Pérez Correa, *En Busca de los Derechos*, 141.

33 Pérez Correa, *En Busca de los Derechos*, 161.

34 Tania Tlacaelet Ramírez, "La expansión de los tribunales de drogas en México," *Cuadernos de Trabajo del Monitor del Programa de Política de Drogas (CIDE)*, No. 21 (2016). Available at: http://politicadedrogas.org/PPD/documentos/20160824_141453_21_cide3.pdf. Accessed December 4, 2017.

35 Ibid.

36 Guillermo Trejo and Sandra Ley, "Federalism, drugs, and violence. Why intergovernmental partisan conflict stimulated inter-cartel violence in Mexico," *Política y gobierno*, Vol. 23, No. 1 (2016): 9–52.

37 Laura H. Atuesta, "Addressing the Costs of Prohibition: Internally Displaced Populations in Colombia and Mexico," in *Ending the Drug Wars. Report of the LSE Expert Group on the Economics of Drug Policy*, (London: LSE, 2014).

38 Adriana Camacho and Daniel Mejia, "Consecuencias de la aspersión aérea en la salud: evidencia desde el caso colombiano," in *Costos Económicos y Sociales del Conflicto en Colombia: ¿Cómo Construir un Posconflicto Sostenible?*, compiled by María Alejandra Arias, Adriana Camacho, Ana María Ibáñez, Daniel Mejía and Catherine Rodríguez (Bogotá, Universidad de Los Andes, 2012), 117–38.

39 For ample documentation of the United States foreign policy in Latin America and the war on drugs, see Coletta Youngers and Eileen Rosin (editors), *Drugs and Democracy in Latin America. The Impact of U.S. Policy* (Boulder: Lynne Rienner Publishers, 2005). The United States influence in regional drug policy is not limited to foreign policy, however. For instance, Daniel Mejía reports that between 2000 and 2006, the United States directly financed 42 percent of the Colombian government's efforts to reduce production, mostly through aerial spraying of coca fields, and 67 percent of the Colombian government's efforts to cut off trafficking. Daniel Mejía, "Políticas antidroga en el Plan Colombia: costos, efectividad y eficiencia" in *Políticas Antidroga en Colombia: Éxitos, Fracasos y Extravíos*, compiled by Alejandro Gaviria and Daniel Mejía (Bogotá: Universidad de Los Andes, 2011), 76–7.

40 See, for instance, Alejandro Madrazo and Angela Guerrero, "Más caro el caldo que las albóndigas," *Nexos*, December of 2012. Table 29.2 compares deaths caused by overdose with deaths stemming from violence associated with drug trafficking and other causes of death. See also Joanne Csete et al., "Public health and international drug policy," *The Lancet Commissions*, Vol. 387, No. 10026 (April 2016): 1427–1480. Available at: www.thelancet.com/journals/lancet/article/PIIS0140-6736(16)00619-X/abstract. Accessed December 4, 2017. For a critique on the instruments for assessing drug use in Mexico, see Beatriz Caiuby Labate and Pamela Ruiz Flores, "Midiendo el uso de drogas ilegales en México: reflexiones sobre las Encuestas Nacionales de Adicciones y una encuesta independiente," *Cuadernos de Trabajo del Seminario del Programa de Política de Drogas (CIDE)* No. 13 (2015). Also see Gregorio Martínez, Jorge Valdez and Federico Ramos, "Drogas y salud pública" in *El mal Menor en la Gestión de las Drogas. De la Prohibición a la Regulación*, edited by Bernardo González-Aréchiga, David Pérez, Alejandro Madrazo and José Antonio Caballero (Mexico: McGraw-Hill, 2014), 197–233. For the case of Colombia, see Adriana Camacho, Alejandro Gaviria and Catherine Rodríguez, "El consumo de droga en Colombia" in *Políticas Antidroga en Colombia: Éxitos, Fracasos y Extravíos*, compiled by Alejandro Gaviria and Daniel Mejía (Bogotá: Universidad de Los Andes, 2011), 41–65.

41 Laura H. Atuesta, "La política de drogas en México 2006–2012: análisis y resultados de una política prohibicionista," *Cuadernos de Trabajo del Seminario del Programa de Política de Drogas (CIDE)*, No. 1 (December 2014).

42 Mejía, *Políticas Antidroga en el Plan Colombia*, 70.

43 Mejía, *Políticas Antidroga en el Plan Colombia*, 77.

44 The following lines summarize the central findings of Héctor Mauricio Núñez and Rafael Garduño, "Un análisis económico de la oferta de drogas ilícitas y la política contra el narcotráfico en México 2004–2009," *Cuadernos de Trabajo del Seminario del Programa de Política de Drogas (CIDE)*, No. 2 (June 2014).

45 Comisión Asesora para la Política de Drogas en Colombia (CAPDC), *Lineamientos Para un Nuevo Enfoque de Política de Drogas en Colombia* (Bogotá: CAPDC, 2015), 26. Available at: www.odc.gov.co/Portals/1/comision_asesora/docs/informe_final_comision_asesora_politica_drogas_colombia.pdf. Accessed December 4, 2017.

46 Coletta Youngers and Catalina Pérez Correa (editors), *In Search of Rights: Drug Users and State Responses in Latin America* (Mexico: CEDD-CIDE, 2014), 146. Available at: www.drogasyderecho.org/publicaciones/prop_del/full-report-english.pdf. Accessed December 4, 2017.

47 Coletta Youngers, *In Search of Rights*, 146.

48 Pérez Correa, *La Regulación de la Posesión y la Criminalización de los Consumidores de Drogas en América Latina*.

49 Catalina Pérez Correa, Rodrigo Uprimny and Sergio Chaparro, "Regulation of Possession and the Criminalization of Drug Users in Latin America," in *After the Drug Wars. Report of the LSE Expert Group on the Economics of Drug Policy* (London: LSE, 2016). Available at: www.lse.ac.uk/IDEAS/publications/reports/pdf/LSE-IDEAS-After-the-Drug-Wars.pdf. Accessed December 4, 2017.

50 Pérez Correa, *La Regulación de la Posesión y la Criminalización de los Consumidores de Drogas en América Latina*, 1.

51 Pérez Correa, Regulation of Possession and the Criminalization of Drug Users in Latin America, 36.

52 Some legal references for this have been established in several appeals issued by the Third Chamber of the Supreme Court, where custodial sentences for people who had in their possession up to 200 grams of marijuana or cocaine were revoked for lack of evidence to prove the intent of distribution or sale of

the seized drugs. See Ernesto Cortés Amador, "Control social del consumo de drogas en Costa Rica. Para orientar las políticas nacionales de drogas hacia el enfoque de derechos humanos" (Master's dissertation, Universidad para la Cooperación Internacional, 2013). Available at: www.uci.ac.cr/Biblioteca/Tesis/PFGMCSH45.pdf. Accessed December 4, 2017.

53 Rodrigo Uprimny, Diana Guzman and Jorge Parra, *Addicted to Punishment: The disproportionality of Drug Laws in Latin America* (Bogotá: Dejusticia-CEDD, 2013). Available at: www.opensocietyfoundations. org/sites/default/files/addicted-punishment-20130530.pdf. Accessed December 4, 2017.

54 Alejandro Corda, *Drug Policy Reform in Latin America: Discourse and Reality* (Mexico: CEDD, 2015). Available at: www.drogasyderecho.org/publicaciones/pub-priv/alejandro_i.pdf. Accessed December 4, 2017.

55 Alejandro Corda, *Drug Policy Reform in Latin America.*

56 Elias Carranza, "Situación penitenciaria en América Latina y el Caribe. ¿Qué hacer?," *Anuario de Derechos Humanos,* No. 8 (2012): 31–66. Available at: www.anuariocdh.uchile.cl/index.php/ADH/article/viewFile/20551/21723. Accessed December 4, 2017.

57 Comisión Interamericana de Derechos Humanos, *Informe Sobre los Derechos Humanos de las Personas Privadas de Libertad en las Américas* (Washington: OEA, 2011). Available at: www.oas.org/es/cidh/ppl/docs/pdf/ppl2011esp.pdf. Accessed December 4, 2017.

58 Comisión Interamericana de Derechos Humanos, *Informe Sobre los Derechos Humanos de las Personas Privadas de Libertad en las Américas.*

59 See Organización Mundial de la Salud and Programa Conjunto de las Naciones Unidas sobre el VIH/SIDA, *VIH/SIDA: Prevención, Atención, Tratamiento y Apoyo en el Medio Carcelario* (Nueva York: ONU, 2007); Elena Izazola, Antonio Labastida and Ruth Villanueva, "La situación actual del VIH/SIDA en prisiones en México. Identificación de prácticas institucionales útiles," in *Estudios de Caso de Prácticas Adecuadas Sobre VIH/sida en Prisiones de América Latina,* edited by José Antonio Izazola and Elena Izazola (Mexico: Fundación Mexicana para la Salud-Instituto Mexicano de Prevención del Delito e Investigación Penitenciaria, 1998); Marcela Briseño, *Garantizando los Derechos Humanos de las Mujeres en Reclusión* (México: INMUJERES, 2006); Mercedes Peláez, *Derechos de los Internos del Sistema Penitenciario mexicano* (Mexico: Cámara de Diputados-UNAM, 2000).

60 See Catalina Perez-Correa, De la Constitución a la prisión. Derechos fundamentales y sistema penitenciario," in *La Reforma Constitucional de Derechos Humanos: Un Nuevo Paradigma,* coordinated by Miguel Carbonell and Pedro Salazar (Mexico: UNAM, 2011).

61 México Evalúa, *Índice de Desempeño del Sistema Penal* (Mexico: México Evalúa, 2010), 22.

62 Elena Azaola and Marcelo Bergman, *Delincuencia, Marginalidad y Desempeño Institucional. Resultados de la Tercera Encuesta a Población en Reclusión en el Distrito Federal y el Estado de México* (Mexico: CIDE, 2009), 55.

63 Emma H. Plugge, Charles E. Foster, Patricia L. Yudkin and Nicola Douglas, "Cardiovascular disease risk factors and women prisoners in the UK: the impact of imprisonment," *Health Promotion International,* Vol. 24, No. 4 (October 2009): 334–43.

64 Catalina Pérez Correa, *Las Mujeres Invisibles: Los Costos de la Prisión y los Efectos Indirectos en las Mujeres* (México: Banco Interamericano de Desarrollo, 2015). Available at https://publications.iadb.org/handle/11319/7235. Accessed December 4, 2017.

65 See Catalina Pérez Correa, "Marcando al delincuente: estigmatización, castigo y cumplimiento del derecho," *Revista Mexicana de Sociología,* Año 72, No. 2 (Spring 2013): 287–311; Libardo José Ariza and Manuel Iturralde, *Los Muros de la Infamia: Prisiones en Colombia y América Latina,* (Bogotá: Universidad de Los Andes, 2011); Gabriel Bouzat, "Desigualdad, delito y seguridad en la Argentina," in *Inseguridad, Democracia y Derecho: Seminario en Latinoamérica de Teoría Constitucional y Política 2010* (Buenos Aires: Libraria, 2011), 120–135; Lourdes Peroni, "Seguridad y Desigualdad. ¿Desprotegidos y Perseguidos?," in *Inseguridad, Democracia y Derecho: Seminario en Latinoamérica de Teoría Constitucional y Política 2010* (Buenos Aires: Libraria, 2011), 136–57.

66 Pérez Correa, *Las Mujeres Invisibles.*

67 Kasia Malinowska-Sempruch and Olga Rychkova, "Measuring the Impacts of Repressive Drug Policies on Women" in *After the Drug Wars: Report of the LSE Expert Group on the Economics of Drug Policy* (London: LSE, 2016), 109. Available at: www.lse.ac.uk/IDEAS/publications/reports/pdf/LSE-IDEAS-After-the-Drug-Wars.pdf. Accessed December 4, 2017.

68 WOLA, IDPC, DeJusticia, CIM-OAS, *Women, Drug Policies, and Incarceration A Guide for Policy Reform in Latin America and the Caribbean,* 2016, 9. Available at: www.wola.org/sites/default/files/WOLA%20 WOMEN%20FINAL%20ver%2025%2002%201016.pdf. Accessed December 4, 2017.

69 Luciana Boiteux, *The Incarceration of Women for Drug Offenses* (Mexico: CEDD, 2015), 1. Available at: www.drogasyderecho.org/publicaciones/pub-priv/luciana_i.pdf. Accessed December 4, 2017.

70 WOLA, *Women, Drug Policies, and Incarceration*, 10.

71 WOLA, *Women, Drug Policies, and Incarceration*, 10.

72 Catalina Pérez Correa, Elena Azaola, Juan Salgado Ibarra and others, *Primera Encuesta a Población Interna en Centros Federales de Readaptación Social* (Mexico: CIDE, 2012). Available at: http://biiacs-dspace.cide.edu/handle/10089/16531. Accessed December 4, 2017.

73 For more information on this see Pérez Correa, *Las mujeres invisibles*.

74 WOLA, *Women, Drug Policies, and Incarceration*, 10.

75 Julieta Lemaitre and Mauricio Albarracín, "Patrullando la dosis personal: la represión cotidiana y los debates de las políticas públicas sobre el consumo de drogas ilícitas en Colombia," in *Políticas Antidroga en Colombia: Éxitos, Fracasos y Extravíos*, compiled by Alejandro Gaviria and Daniel Mejía (Bogotá: Universidad de Los Andes, 2011), 237–69. The following two paragraphs summarize some of the key findings in this research.

76 Lemaitre, *Patrullando la Dosis Personal*, 255.

77 Lemaitre, *Patrullando la Dosis Personal*, 257. Author's translation.

78 Lemaitre, *Patrullando la Dosis Personal*, 252.

79 For empirical studies, form a different disciplinary perspective, on the use of administrative regulations by police to work with drug users in Mexico see for instance, Leo Beletsky et al., "Implementing Mexico's "Narcomenudeo" drug Law Reform. A Mixed Methods Assessment of Early Experiences Among People Who Inject Drugs," *Journal of Mixed Methods Research*, Vol. 10, No. 4 (October 2016): 384–401.

80 Ana Laura Magaloni, "La arbitrariedad como método de trabajo: la persecución criminal durante la administración de Felipe Calderón," in *De la Detención a la Prisión. La Justicia Penal a Examen*, edited by Catalina Pérez Correa (Mexico: CIDE, 2015), 31.

81 Magaloni, *La Arbitrariedad Como Método de Trabajo*, 36.

82 Magaloni, *La Arbitrariedad Como Método de Trabajo*, 43.

83 Of the more than 16 different reported types of mistreatment upon being detained, she chose three as proxy to represent increasing gravity and, also, increasing probability of institutional involvement or tolerance: kicking, asphyxia, and electric shocks.

84 Csete, *Public Health and International Drug Policy*, 8.

85 Magaloni tells us that under Calderón administration "the army [took up] police duties in a general mater, and they replicated the arbitrary practices of the police at the moment of detention." Magaloni, *La Arbitrariedad Como Método de Trabajo*, 37.

86 Lemaitre, *Patrullando la Dosis Personal*, 251–2.

87 See Antonio Barreto and Alejandro Madrazo, "Los costos constitucionales de la guerra contra las drogas: dos estudios de caso de las transformaciones de las comunidades políticas de las Américas," *Isonomía*, No. 43 (October 2015) passim:

References

Ariza, Libardo José and Manuel Iturralde. 2011. *Los Muros de la Infamia: Prisiones en Colombia y América Latina*. Bogotá: Universidad de Los Andes.

Asamblea Legislativa del Distrito Federal (ALDF). 2009. *Para la Libertad … Siete Leyes Históricas de la IV Legislatura*. México: ALDF/Porrúa.

Atuesta, Laura H. 2014. "Addressing the Costs of Prohibition: Internally Displaced Populations in Colombia and Mexico." In *Ending the Drug Wars. Report of the LSE Expert Group on the Economics of Drug Policy*. London: LSE.

Atuesta, Laura H. 2014. La política de drogas en México 2006–2012: análisis y resultados de una política prohibicionista. *Cuadernos de Trabajo del Seminario del Programa de Política de Drogas (CIDE)*, 1.

Azaola, Elena and Marcelo Bergman. 2009. *Delincuencia, Marginalidad y Desempeño Institucional. Resultados de la Tercera Encuesta a Población en Reclusión en el Distrito Federal y el Estado de México*. Mexico: CIDE.

Barreto, Antonio and Alejandro Madrazo. 2015. Los costos constitucionales de la guerra contra las drogas: dos estudios de caso de las transformaciones de las comunidades políticas de las Américas. *Isonomía*, 43: 151–93.

Beletsky, Leo, Karla D. Wagner, Jaime Arredondo, Lawrence Palinkas, Carlos Magis Rodriguez, Nicolette Kalic, Natasha-Ludwig-Barron, and Steffanie A. Strathdee 2016. Implementing Mexico's "Narcomenudeo" Drug Law Reform. A Mixed Methods Assessment of Early Experiences Among People Who Inject Drugs. *Journal of Mixed Methods Research*, 10(4): 384–401.

Boiteux, Luciana. 2015. *The Incarceration of Women for Drug Offenses*. Mexico: CEDD. Available at: www.drogasyderecho.org/publicaciones/pub-priv/luciana_i.pdf. Accessed December 4, 2017.

Bouzat, Gabriel. 2011. "Desigualdad, delito y seguridad en la Argentina". In *Inseguridad, Democracia y Derecho: Seminario en Latinoamérica de Teoría Constitucional y Política 2010*, 120–25. Buenos Aires: Libraria.

Briseño, Marcela. 2006. *Garantizando los Derechos Humanos de las Mujeres en Reclusion*. México: INMUJERES.

Camacho, Adriana and Daniel Mejia. 2012. Consecuencias de la aspersión aérea en la salud: evidencia desde el caso colombiano. In *Costos Económicos y Sociales del Conflicto en Colombia: ¿Cómo Construir un Posconflicto Sostenible?*, compiled by María Alejandra Arias, Adriana Camacho, Ana María Ibáñez, Daniel Mejía and Catherine Rodríguez, 117–38. Bogotá: Universidad de Los Andes.

Carranza, Elias. 2012. Situación penitenciaria en América Latina y el Caribe. ¿Qué hacer? *Anuario de Derechos Humanos*, 8: 31–66. Available at: www.anuariocdh.uchile.cl/index.php/ADH/article/viewFile/20551/21723. Accessed December 4, 2017.

Código Penal Argentino, Ley N° 23.737, Article 34. Available at: http://infoleg.mecon.gov.ar/infolegInternet/anexos/0-4999/138/texact.htm. Accessed December 4, 2017.

Colombian Congress. *Acto Legislativo 02 de 2009*. Available at: www.alcaldiabogota.gov.co/sisjur/normas/Norma1.jsp?i=38289. Accessed December 4, 2017.

Comisión Asesora para la Política de Drogas en Colombia (CAPDC). 2015. *Lineamientos Para un Nuevo Enfoque de Política de Drogas en Colombia* Bogotá: CAPDC. Available at: www.odc.gov.co/Portals/1/comision_asesora/docs/informe_final_comision_asesora_politica_drogas_colombia.pdf. Accessed December 4, 2017.

Comisión Interamericana de Derechos Humanos. 2011. *Informe Sobre los Derechos Humanos de las Personas Privadas de Libertad en las Américas*. Washington: OEA. Available at: www.oas.org/es/cidh/ppl/docs/pdf/ppl2011esp.pdf. Accessed December 4, 2017.

Corda, Alejandro, Araceli Galante, and Diana Rossi. 2014. *Personas que Usan Estupefacientes en Argentina: de "Delincuentes-Enfermos" a Sujetos de Derechos*. Buenos Aires: Intercambios Asociación Civil-Universidad de Buenos Aires. Available at: www.drogasyderecho.org/publicaciones/prop_del/argentina-usuarios.pdf. Accessed December 4, 2017.

Corda, Alejandro. 2015. *Drug Policy Reform in Latin America: Discourse and Reality*. Mexico: CEDD. Available at: www.drogasyderecho.org/publicaciones/pub-priv/alejandro_i.pdf. Accessed December 4, 2017.

Corda, Alejandro. 2016. *La Estrategia Fallida: Encarcerlamientos por Delitos Relacionados con Estupefacientes en la Argentina*. Buenos Aires: Intercambios Asociación Civil-Universidad de Buenos Aires. Available at: http://intercambios.org.ar/wp-content/uploads/2016/09/2016.-Corda.-La-estrategia-fallida.pdf. Accessed December 4, 2017.

Corte Suprema de Justicia de la Nación Argentina. *A. 891, XLIV* (Arriola Ruling). Available at: http://druglawreform.info/images/stories/documents/fallo-arriola.pdf. Accessed December 4, 2017.

Cortés Amador, Ernesto. 2013. *Control Social del Consumo de Drogas en Costa Rica. Para Orientar las Políticas Nacionales de Drogas Hacia el Enfoque de Derechos Humanos*. Master's dissertation, Universidad para la Cooperación Internacional. Available at: www.uci.ac.cr/Biblioteca/Tesis/PFGMCSH45.pdf. Accessed December 4, 2017.

Criminal Appeals Chamber, Supreme Court Colombia. *Sentence N° 41760 SP2940*, M.P. Eugenio Fernandez Carlier, 2016.

Csete, Joanne, Adeeba Kamarulzaman, Michel Kazatchkine, Frederick Altice, Marek Balicki, Julia Buxton, Javier Cepeda, Megan Comfort, Eric Goosby, João Goulão, Carl Hart, Thomas Kerr, Alejandro Madrazo Lajous, Stephen Lewis, Natasha Martin, Daniel Mejía, Adriana Camacho, David Mathieson, Isidore Obot, Aedolu Ogunrombi, Susan Sherman, Jack Stone, Nandini Vallath, Peter Vickerman, Tomáš Zábranský T., and Chris Beyrer. 2016. Public health and international drug policy. *The Lancet Commissions*, 387(10026): 1427–80. Available at: www.thelancet.com/journals/lancet/article/PIIS0140-6736(16)00619-X/abstract. Accessed December 4, 2017.

Gaviria, Alejandro and Daniel Mejía (Eds.). 2011. *Políticas Antidroga en Colombia: Éxitos, Fracasos y Extravíos*. Bogotá: Universidad de Los Andes.

González-Aréchiga, Bernardo, David Pérez, Alejandro Madrazo and José Antonio Caballero (Eds.). 2014. *El mal Menor en la Gestión de las Drogas. De la Prohibición a la Regulación*. Mexico: McGraw Hill.

Intercambios Asociación Civil. *Fallo 'Arriola' de la Corte Suprema Sobre Tenencia de Estupefacientes para Consumo Personal. Proyecto de TNI Sobre Reformas a las Leyes de Drogas.* Available at: http://druglaw reform.info/es/informacion-por-pais/america-latina/argentina/item/386-fallo-arriola-de-la-corte-suprema. Accessed December 4, 2017.

Izazola, Elena, Antonio Labastida, and Ruth Villanueva. 1998. "La situación actual del VIH/SIDA en prisiones en México. Identificación de prácticas institucionales útiles." En *Estudios de Caso de Prácticas Adecuadas Sobre VIH/sida en Prisiones de América Latina*, edited by José Antonio Izazola and Elena Izazola. Mexico: Fundación Mexicana para la Salud/Instituto Mexicano de Prevención del Delito e Investigación Penitenciaria.

Labate, Beatriz and Pamela Ruiz Flores. 2015. Midiendo el uso de drogas ilegales en México: reflexiones sobre las Encuestas Nacionales de Adicciones y una encuesta independiente. *Cuadernos de Trabajo del Seminario del Programa de Política de Drogas (CIDE)* 13.

London School of Economics (LSE). 2016. *After the Drug Wars. Report of the LSE Expert Group on the Economics of Drug Policy.* London: LSE. Available at: www.lse.ac.uk/IDEAS/publications/reports/pdf/LSE-IDEAS-After-the-Drug-Wars.pdf. Accessed December 4, 2017.

Madrazo, Alejandro. 2014. El impacto de la política de drogas 2006–2012 en la legislación federal. *Cuadernos de Trabajo del Seminario del Programa de Política de Drogas (CIDE)*, 7 (June). Available at: http://ppd.cide.edu/documents/302668/0/Libro%207.pdf. Accessed December 4, 2017.

Madrazo, Alejandro and Angela Guerrero. 2012. Más caro el caldo que las albóndigas. *Nexos*, December.

Magaloni, Ana Laura. 2015. "La arbitrariedad como método de trabajo: la persecución criminal durante la administración de Felipe Calderón." En *De la Detención a la Prisión. La Justicia Penal a Examen*, edited by Catalina Pérez Correa, 29–54. Mexico: CIDE.

Metaal, Pien and Coletta Youngers (editors). 2010. *Sistemas Sobrecargados. Leyes de Drogas y Cárceles en América Latina.* Amsterdam-Washington: TNI-WOLA.

México Evalúa. 2010. *Índice de Desempeño del Sistema Penal.* Mexico: México Evalúa.

Núñez, Héctor Mauricio and Rafael Garduño. 2014. Un análisis económico de la oferta de drogas ilícitas y la política contra el narcotráfico en México 2004–2009. *Cuadernos de Trabajo del Seminario del Programa de Política de Drogas (CIDE)*, 2 (June).

Organización de los Estados Americanos (OEA). 2014. *El Informe de Drogas de la OEA: 16 Meses de Debates y Consensos.* Guatemala. Available at: www.oas.org/docs/publications/LayoutPubgAGDrogas-ESP-29-9.pdf. Accessed December 4, 2017.

Organización Mundial de la Salud and Programa Conjunto de las Naciones Unidas sobre el VIH/SIDA. 2007. *VIH/SIDA: Prevención, Atención, Tratamiento y Apoyo en el Medio Carcelario.* Nueva York: ONU.

Peláez, Mercedes. 2000. *Derechos de los Internos del Sistema Penitenciario Mexicano.* Mexico: Cámara de Diputados/UNAM.

Pérez Correa, Catalina. 2011. "De la Constitución a la prisión. Derechos fundamentales y sistema penitenciario." En *La Reforma Constitucional de Derechos Humanos: Un Nuevo Paradigma*, coordinated by Miguel Carbonell and Pedro Salazar. Mexico: UNAM.

Pérez Correa, Catalina (Ed.). 2012a. *Justicia Desmedida: Proporcionalidad y Delitos de Drogas en América Latina.* Mexico: Fontamara.

Pérez Correa, Catalina, Elena Azaola, Juan Salgado Ibarra et al. 2012b. *Primera Encuesta a Población Interna en Centros Federales de Readaptación Social.* Mexico: CIDE. Available at: http://biiacs-dspace.cide.edu/handle/10089/16531. Accessed December 4, 2017.

Pérez Correa, Catalina, Karen Silva, and Carlos de la Rosa. 2012c. (Des)proporcionalidad y delitos contra la salud en México. *Documento de Trabajo de la División de Estudios Jurídicos (CIDE).* 59 (August). Available at: www.libreriacide.com/?P=docs_trabajo&PRODfamily=dt&PRODclassification=202. Accessed December 4, 2017.

Pérez Correa, Catalina. 2013. Marcando al delincuente: estigmatización, castigo y cumplimiento del derecho. *Revista Mexicana de Sociología*, 72(2): 287–311.

Pérez Correa, Catalina and Coletta Youngers (editors). 2014. *En Busca de los Derechos: Usuarios de Drogas y las Respuestas Estatales en América Latina.* México: CEDD-CIDE.

Pérez Correa, Catalina, Alejandro Corda, and Luciana Boiteux. 2015a. *Drug Consumption and Consumers in Latin America.* Mexico: CEDD. Available at: www.drogasyderecho.org/publicaciones/pub-priv/catalina_i.pdf.. Accessed December 4, 2017.

Pérez Correa, Catalina, Alejandro Corda, and Luciana Boiteux. 2015b. *La Regulación de la Posesión y la Criminalización de los Consumidores de Drogas en América Latina.* México: CEDD. Available at: www.drogasyderecho.org/publicaciones/pub-priv/Catalina_v09.pdf. Accessed December 4, 2017.

Pérez Correa, Catalina. 2015c. *Las Mujeres Invisibles: Los Costos de la Prisión y los Efectos Indirectos en las Mujeres*. México: Banco Interamericano de Desarrollo. Available at: https://publications.iadb.org/handle/11319/7235. Accessed December 4, 2017.

Peroni, Lourdes. 2011. "Seguridad y Desigualdad. ¿Desprotegidos y Perseguidos?" In *Inseguridad, democracia y derecho: Seminario en Latinoamérica de Teoría Constitucional y Política 2010*, 136–57. Buenos Aires: Libraria.

Plugge, Emma H., Charles E. Foster, Patricia L. Yudkin, and Nicola Douglas. 2009. Cardiovascular disease risk factors and women prisoners in the UK: the impact of imprisonment. *Health Promotion International*, 24(4): 334–43.

Suprema Corte de Justicia de Chile. Sentencia de la Corte Suprema de Chile sobre autocultivo de cannabis. *Revista Pensamiento Penal*. Available at: www.pensamientopenal.com.ar/fallos/43105-sentencia-corte-suprema-chile-sobre-autocultivo-cannabis. Accessed December 4, 2017.

Suprema Corte de Justicia de la Nación (Mexico). *Amparo en Revisión 237/2014*. Available at: www.smartclub.mx/uploads/8/7/2/7/8727772/doc.pdf. Accessed December 4, 2017.

Suprema Corte de Justicia de la Nación (Mexico). *Controversia Constitucional 20/2010*. Available at: www2.scjn.gob.mx/ConsultaTematica/PaginasPub/DetallePub.aspx?AsuntoID=117071. Accessed December 4, 2017.

Tlacaelet, Tania. 2016. La expansión de los tribunales de drogas en México. *Cuadernos de Trabajo del Monitor del Programa de Política de Drogas (CIDE)*, 21. Available at: http://politicadedrogas.org/PPD/documentos/20160824_141453_21_cide3.pdf. Accessed December 4, 2017.

Trejo, Guillermo and Sandra Ley. 2016. Federalism, drugs, and violence. Why intergovernmental partisan conflict stimulated inter-cartel violence in Mexico. *Política y Gobierno*, 23(1): 9–52.

Uprimny, Rodrigo, Diana Guzman, and Jorge Parra. 2013. *Addicted to Punishment: The Disproportionality of Drug Laws in Latin America*. Bogotá: Dejusticia-CEDD. Available at: www.opensocietyfoundations.org/sites/default/files/addicted-punishment-20130530.pdf. Accessed December 4, 2017.

WOLA, IDPC, DeJusticia, CIM-OAS. 2016. *Women, Drug Policies, and Incarceration. A Guide for Policy Reform in Latin America and the Caribbean*, 9. Available at: www.wola.org/sites/default/files/WOLA%20WOMEN%20FINAL%20ver%2025%2002%201016.pdf. Accessed December 4, 2017.

Youngers, Coletta and Catalina Pérez Correa (Eds.). 2014. *In Search of Rights: Drug Users and State Responses in Latin America*. Mexico: CEDD/CIDE. Available at: www.drogasyderecho.org/publicaciones/prop_del/full-report-english.pdf. Accessed December 4, 2017.

Youngers, Coletta and Eileen Rosin (Eds.). 2005. *Drugs and Democracy in Latin America. The Impact of U.S. Policy*. Boulder: Lynne Rienner Publishers.

INDEX